Conversing by Signs

Robert Blair St. George

POETICS OF

IMPLICATION

IN COLONIAL

NEW ENGLAND

CULTURE

Conversing by Signs

THE

UNIVERSITY

OF NORTH

CAROLINA

PRESS

CHAPEL HILL

& LONDON

Manufactured in the United States of America

This book was set in Minion by Eric M. Brooks

Book design by April Leidig-Higgins

The paper in this book meets the guidelines for
permanence and durability of the Committee on
Production Guidelines for Book Longevity of the
Council on Library Resources.

Library of Congress Cataloging-in-Publication Data
St. George, Robert Blair. Conversing by signs:
poetics of implication in colonial New England
culture / Robert Blair St. George. p. cm. Includes
bibliographical references (p.) and index.
ISBN 0-8078-2382-1 (cloth: alk. paper).—
ISBN 0-8078-4688-0 (pbk.: alk. paper)
1. Material culture—New England—History—
18th century. 2. Material culture—New England—
History—17th century. 3. New England—
Civilization—18th century. 4. New England—
Civilization—17th century. 5. Landscape—Social
aspects—New England—History—18th century.
6. Landscape—Social aspects—New England—
History—17th century. 7. Architecture and
society—New England—History—18th century.
8. Architecture and society—New England—
History—17th century. I. Title.
F7.S8   1998   97-18537
974'.02—dc21   CIP

02 01 00 99 98   5 4 3 2 1

Chapter 1 is a substantially revised and expanded version of "Bawns and Beliefs: Architecture, Commerce,
and Conversion in Early New England," originally
published in *Winterthur Portfolio* 25, no. 4 (Winter
1990): 241–87. Reprinted by permission of Winterthur
Museum and the University of Chicago Press.

For Caroline

The visible brings the world to
us. But at the same time it reminds us ceaselessly that it is a
world in which we risk to be lost.
The visible with its space also
takes the world away from us.
Nothing is more two-faced. . . .

To this human ambiguity of the
visible one then has to add the
visual experience of absence,
whereby we no longer see what
we saw. We face a *dis*-appearance.
And a struggle ensues to prevent
what has disappeared falling
into the negation of the unseen,
defying our existence.

Thus the visible produces faith
in the reality of the invisible, and
provokes the development of
an inner eye which retains, and
assembles and arranges as if an
interior, as if what has been seen
will be forever partly protected
against the ambush of space,
which is absence.
—John Berger,
  "The Place of Painting"

CONTENTS

TABLES

ACKNOWLEDGMENTS

I have been the recipient of good counsel, stimulating conversation and argument, and useful references from many kind people in different fields. For their assistance with research, I am indebted to the following institutions and individuals: American Antiquarian Society (Nancy Burkett); Connecticut Historical Society (Ruth Blair); Danvers Historical Society (Richard Trask); Dedham Historical Society (Electa Kane Tritsch); Essex Institute (Irene Norton, retired); Henry Whitfield State Historical Museum (Michael McBride); Historical Society of Pennsylvania (Dan Rolph); Ipswich Historical Society (the late Elizabeth Newton); Library Company of Philadelphia (Phil Lapsansky); Massachusetts Historical Society (Peter Drummey); National Museum of American History (Anne Golovin, Paula Myers, and Rodris Roth); Society for the Preservation of New England Antiquities (Lorna Condon, Richard Nylander, and Ellie Reichlin, retired); Watkinson Library, Trinity College (Jeffrey Kaimowitz); and Winterthur Museum (Eleanor N. Thompson). I am also grateful to these public repositories for their assistance: Connecticut State Library, Division of Archives and History (Hartford); Guilford Town Hall (Guilford, Connecticut); Massachusetts Archives (Boston); New York Public Library, Division of Manuscripts (New York); Suffolk County Probate Records (Boston); Town Clerk's Office of Windsor, Connecticut. I am also pleased to acknowledge the generous support of a Henry F. du Pont Research Fellowship from Winterthur Museum in spring 1987 and an NEH Fellowship at the Newberry Library in spring 1988. These two institutions gave me the space and warm sense of belonging to a scholarly community that I needed in order to map the terrain covered in this book.

Portions of the present work were presented at various institutions and conferences and in lectures, and my ideas profited from the discussion and comments of colleagues on these occasions. Sections of chapter 1 were presented at meetings of the American Folklore Society, at the "Agrarian Reform and the Built Environment in Nineteenth-Century New England" conference in Bethel, Maine, at the "Peoples in Contact" conference held at the Haffenreffer Museum of Anthropology of Brown University, at the 1986 World Archaeological Congress (Southampton and London), and in lectures at the Connecticut Historical Society, the Newberry Library, and the Society for the Preservation of New England Antiquities. Fragments of chapter 2, on architecture, the human body, and medical beliefs, were tested at meetings of the College Art Association, Michael Zuckerman's group of early Americanists in Philadelphia, the Society for the Study of Architecture in Canada, and the Vernacular Architecture Group (UK) and in lectures at the Department of Anthropology, University of Massachusetts, the Maison des Sciences de l'Homme at the University of Paris, and the V&A/Royal College of Art Graduate Program. The materials on artisan politics and ritual house assaults in chapter 3 found critical audiences at meetings of the Boston Area Early American History seminar, the Chicago Area Labor History Group, and the Institute of Early American History and Culture and in lectures given at the Department of Folklore and Folklife at the University of Pennsylvania and the Yale University American Studies colloquium. Earlier versions of chapter 4 were tested at lectures at the Wadsworth Atheneum and the National Portrait Gallery. At these various institutions, presentations, and colloquiums, I appreciated the comments of Richard L. Bushman, Abbott Lowell Cummings, Russell Handsman, Susan E. Hirsch, Fred Hoxie, Elizabeth M. Kornhauser, George Kubler, Irving Lavin, Mary Beth Rose, Steve Rossworm, Viola Sachs, Neal Salisbury, Susan Prendergast Schoelwer, William S. Simmons, Charles Suamarez Smith, John Styles, John Tyler, and Alfred F. Young.

I have had several fine teachers whose example and continued collegiality have strengthened my work. I am grateful to Henry Glassie for his gift of supportive critique, the passion and precision of his own published works, and his patience in waiting for this book. It is a long-overdue expression of gratitude for his example and friendship. I have also benefited from the work and collegiality of Kenneth L. Ames, Dan Ben-Amos, the late Kenneth S. Goldstein, Dell Hymes, John F. Szwed, and Don Yoder, each of whom helped me out in the classroom and later in correspondence or conversation.

Other folklorists shared their own work with me and listened to my arguments as they developed. I am especially indebted to Roger Abrahams, Thomas Carter, Sunie Davis, Elaine Eff, Susie Fair, Deborah Kapchan, Margaret Mills, Jerry Pocius, Jack Santino, and John Michael Vlach. I am indebted to several fine colleagues at the University of Pennsylvania for sharing their ideas and discussing my work with me, including Elizabeth Johns, Webb Keane, Dan Rose, Carroll Smith-Rosenberg (now at the University of Michigan), and Peter Stallybrass. I also thank Richard Beeman, Richard S. Dunn, and Michael Zuckerman, for the active community of historians they bring together at the Philadelphia Center for Early American Studies, and members and affiliates of the center for friendship and discussions. I wish especially to thank Robert Cantwell, whose many critical comments on the manuscript were very helpful.

As a folklorist interested in bringing ethnographic methods of investigating local poetics to the practice of early American history, I have been struck by one difference (among many) between the two disciplines. Having written about the experiences and *mentalité* of early Americans, I cannot do what folklorists normally do—begin by thanking their "informants," their co-conspirators in fieldwork and interpretation. Instead, I can thank my tutors in early American history who have patiently helped me imagine past peoples into reality—"to start them into life," as someone in the 1790s once said of Ralph Earl's portraits. I am indebted to Jean-Christophe Agnew, Elizabeth Blackmar, Timothy H. Breen, David Cressy, Nina Dayton, John P. Demos, J. Ritchie Garrison, David D. Hall, James Henretta, Rhys Isaac, Kevin M. Sweeney, Laurel Thatcher Ulrich, Shane White, and Stephanie G. Wolf. For help with art and material culture, I am grateful for the collegial guidance of Maurice Barley, Richard Candee, Abbott Lowell Cummings, Frank and Jeannie Demers, Jonathan L. Fairbanks, Alan Gailey, Anne Grady, Paul Groth, Bernard L. Herman, Patricia Hills, Carl Lounsbury, Jules D. Prown, Alice Gray Read, Philip Robinson, James Sexton, John Smith, Peter Smith, Robert F. Trent, Dell Upton, Barbara MacLean Ward, and Camille Wells.

During the 1993–94 academic year I was fortunate to spend a visiting year teaching in the American Studies Program and Department of Anthropology at the College of William and Mary, and it was during this year that I formulated the shape and content of this book. For stimulating conversations and encouragement, I am indebted to James Axtell, Kathleen Bragdon, Chandos Brown, Marley Brown, Robert A. Gross, Grey Gundaker, Tomoko Hamada, Arthur Knight, Steve

People in colonial New England lived in a densely metaphoric world. The sermons they heard, the Bible verses they read aloud, and the cries of the afflicted suggest the dense layering of meanings they shaped on a daily basis. Ordinary houses may have modeled the perfect geometry of heaven or may have shown how easily that ordained perfection could be toppled. Familiars invaded bodies without warning, witches passed with ease through locked doors, houses blew down in a gust of angry, providential wind. Farms, fields, and town plans may have been less dramatic but were no less burdened with hidden significance. Wealth could be a sign of the merchant's overweening worldly inclination or a token that God's grace had touched a humble yeoman. These mundane sites referenced and played with the many bodies that colonists inhabited, and through pragmatic evocation raised to conscious speculation their similarity to other places, other bodies. The density of apprehension, memory, and imagination in colonial New England culture lies at the core of this book. I call this density the poetics of implication.

This book examines expressive culture in one corner of colonial America. My concern is to discover an approach to poetics that spans a wide variety of symbolic forms and communicative processes: language, objects, movement, faith. I struggle against divisions in interpretive approach that allow convenient boxes to be drawn around humanistic thought. I have inhabited some of these tiny apartments: "material culture," "folklore," "museum person," "early American studies," "residual culture." I have grown claustrophobic. Let me shake these labels. Like other containers of academic convenience, these categories are inadequate to approaching lived experience in either past or present.

2

In fact, as I researched this book, I felt almost envious of seventeenth-century English people, those individuals whom I had otherwise trained myself to regard with consummate suspicion, since their culture was one in which the visual vied with the verbal for semiotic authority, even as it labored to hold the mythic weight of text and image in perfect equipoise. Poets, painters, and philosophers engaged in what sounds to me like great sports; they performed "verbal limning" and shaped "topiary poems," playful examples of imaging text or textualizing space. The visual was as significant as the verbal in early modern English culture because the former was believed to be the "outer" sense that led most directly to the verbal "inner" realm where common sense, fantasy, and memory joined external perceptions in understanding. According to Paolo Lomazzo, bodily motions were on an even par with words. By means of "the severall passions and gestures which mans bodie is able to performe," or his "outward and bodily Demonstrations," he maintained, "mens inward motions and affections may be said as well (or rather better) signified, as by their speech."[1] In seventeenth-century New England, if not among today's practicing historians, word and thing were inextricably linked, referentially interdependent, constantly implicated in each other's ways of making meaning.

Implication. From the Latin *im* + *plicare*, meaning "to fold together." According to the *Oxford English Dictionary*, it is the "art of implying," a poetic technique for conveying thoughts that are "implied though not formally expressed by natural reference." Implication is "the action of involving, entwining, or entangling." It describes a state of referential "intertwisting" when an intimate connection between or combination of artifacts or utterances is the norm. These definitions were attached to the word in seventeenth-century England. Robert Boyle equated *implicate* with *intangle* in 1666, while others found synonyms in *wrapped up, knit, insinuate, infer, associate, incriminate, involve*, and in "implicated Involutions and fetterings."[2] Implication opens to view much of what we normally term the symbolic; however, it exposes it not by reifying "meaning" in isolated events but by suggesting an open-ended skein of entangled, involved descriptive passages that loop back continually and bring normally latent tissues that tie one referent to another, and another, and another, and . . . into public view. In any colonial situation, attention to the poetics of implication can discover the nervous, unsteady assumptions that often underlie the appearance of stability and authority.

A poetics of implication might include feelings, evanescent moods, the unmapped circuitry of intimation and insinuation, and the coding of fragmentary utterances to suggest underlying coherence. This circuitry makes apparent different qualities of implication. Metaphor is central because, like symbolic practices generally, it works through indirection. For me techniques of indirect reference, and not an ideal of bourgeois transparency, lie at the center of claims to public culture. Things and words that carry more than one meaning simultaneously often do the essential political work of addressing several "levels" of cultural "reality" in terms with which different social groups or interests can imaginatively and readily identify. Implicative techniques are essential to what one Boston town committee in 1769 called "the art even of political appearance."[3]

Implication appears as a political art as one considers its possible sources. A body of research that helped to suggest ways I might think about indirect reference in material culture explores the doctrine of "associationism" in early modern architectural theory. While much of this work concentrates on the ambiguous meanings of decorative vocabulary, the same lesson can be read into architectural form. The associations or evocations of places implicated by other places emerge as the hair trigger of human imagination shoots from place to place; Hobbes thought the "train of imagination" was what linked images and experiences in the coherent motions of memory.[4]

The subtle traces of previous lexical change or social use in everyday speech provided another suggestive alternative. Reported speech varies across cultures and works in different ways but recognizes the way that any utterance indirectly implicates previous exchanges in the style and substance of what is being said. Language, Mikhail Bakhtin argued in his classic definition, "becomes 'one's own' only when the speaker populates it with his own intention, his own accent, when he appropriates the word, adapting it to his own semantic and expressive intention. Prior to this moment of appropriation, the word does not exist in a neutral and impersonal language," he continued, "but rather it exists in other people's mouths, in other people's contexts, serving other people's intentions: it is from there that one must take the word, and make it one's own." The resulting stratigraphy of accumulated associations and quotation pushes language toward symbolic compression. "Language," Bakhtin admitted, "is populated—overpopulated—with the intentions of others." And the same process of languages indirectly borrowing and referencing one another was already recognized during the seventeenth century. One linguist warned how long any study of the English language would take, "which you may easily beleeve, considering the great store of strange words, our speech borrows, not only from the Latine and Greeke, (and som from the ancient Hebrew) but also from forraine vulgar Languages round about us."[5]

Finally I have drawn from students of popular culture aware of the slippage of traditions across boundaries of class or caste into new repertoires, and how these traditions may be recontextualized in new ways. Concerning the mixture of hybrid fragments in seventeenth-century New England, historian David D. Hall has argued that "we may speak of a lore of wonders that descended to the colonists from Scripture, antiquity, the early Church and the Middle Ages. . . . Whenever the colonists spoke or wrote of wonders, they drew freely on this lore; theirs was a borrowed language." "All of this borrowing," he explains, "enriched the lore of wonders with the debris of much older systems of ideas." The literature of wonders was "a strange mixture of ideas and themes" and "was charged with several meanings." What keeps popular culture a consistent source of novelty, however, is the motion and politics of the appropriative act itself. The constancy of theft makes culture a hotbed of dynamic change. As one critic has suggested, the territory of appropriation is also "the ground on which the transformations are worked. In the study of popular culture we should always start here: with the double stake in popular culture, the double movement of containment and resistance, which is always inevitably inside it."[6]

By claiming indirection—reporting and appropriating, containing and resisting aboard the train of imagination—as its domain, implication extends to include such referential strategies as metaphoric compression, symbolic condensation, and symbolic diffusion. Each of these plays a role in the transformative work that implication accomplishes in culture. The first treats the hypersaturation of specific tropes or places with so many meanings that they almost seize up with the semantic burden they must carry; in seventeenth-century Holland, for example, whales assumed so many iconic and practical roles that the cry of "Whale!" could mean any one (or all) of a dozen things simultaneously, depending on the contextual position of the crier and listeners. The condensation of symbols, which Mary Douglas used to explain the remarkable authority invested in the sacrament of communion, instead deals with invocations of spirit so intense that the bread and wine are phenomenologically transformed, as affecting presences, into body and blood; the name is the thing named. Symbolic diffusion, by contrast, occurs when the symbolic force or charisma of a sacred or iconic center becomes entangled with the world beyond its edges. In this book I specifically discuss the diffusion into ordinary houses of the "living" architecture of the Puritan meetinghouse, itself suffused with the anthropomorphic task given it by Saint Paul, and the diffusion of an aesthetics of communion into consumption, labor actions, and the horrors of colonized peoples and monstrous births.[7]

Implication also sheds light on intertextuality. Many texts work by drawing within their pale of artifice and reference other texts; the process is central to poetry and to the cannibalization of speech genres, popular theater, and plot play that have defined novelization as a semiotic force since the Renaissance. Such moves are, however, often suggested by the ways in which a word, a gesture, a costume, or a genre implicates the related logic of another form. Implication provides a trace of connection between disparate phenomena. In this book, for example, I develop in detail the metaphoric connections between buildings and bodies and, with such indirect connections outlined, suggest the intertextual play that informed ritual attacks on houses in eighteenth-century New England. As a genre, the house attack relied upon intertextual debts to skimmingtons, funeral processions, and executions.

Indirect expression and intertextual reference: many historians will wonder why such concerns should even be included in our chronology of America's colonial past. One reason is that they make a productive mess of chronology itself. One narrative twist I encountered made me aware of growing inconsistencies in the accepted explanation of cultural change in New England. An impressive body of scholarship I had read in graduate school suggested that people in colonial New England somehow grew more "enlightened" beginning, say, in the 1730s or 1740s. The limiting and ascetic quality of seventeenth-century covenant theology yielded, however uneasily, to more individualistic anticipations of wealth and salvation. The self-denying strain of Puritan piety gave way (did it ever exist?) beneath the self-affirming pressures of trade and material ambition. Hit with the full force of liberation and guilt during the Great Awakening, people in Connecticut and Massachusetts became unhappy entrepreneurs, aware somehow that success in the marketplace came only at the expense of the metaphysical. Domestic landscapes changed. The eighteenth century brought an expanded traffic in ready-made consumables, and new "Georgian" houses grew larger, brighter, warmer, and more comfortable with each passing decade. It brought also the universalizing promise of an empirical science grounded in proof and skepticism. New explanations came for earthquakes, quicksand, and drought.

But the old culture simply would not disappear. Intense seventeenth-century fears over "unworthiness" or inadequate "preparation" for communion and public declaration of conversion persisted in some parishes into the 1790s. Many material objects remained unchanged as well. Saltbox houses built in the 1780s were identical in form to those constructed in the 1680s. And old forms remained adaptable. English barns were refitted for new kinds of husbandry. New consumer goods were put to old uses, thus compromising any "gentility" indexed by patterns of consumption alone. Even the so-called new science, despite having had its brief argued in almanacs as early as the 1670s, failed to displace established theories of divine causation and heavenly analogy; instead, the new science actually may have strengthened religious culture. By the time of the Revolution, God's providence still worked through conflagration, disease, hailstorms, thunder, and lightning. An electric simultaneity of implied cultural connections survived in the colonial shadows of imperial enlightenment.[8]

Another reason why implication matters concerns the recognition that colonial cultures contained mixtures at different levels of conservative and innovative practices. Here, implicative techniques—intimation, entanglement, compression, condensation, diffusion, intensification, distraction, and temporal shifts—served to rescue the contingency of different parts of colonial culture from invisibility.

Through such indirect strategies as reported speech, implicated placement, implicature in spoken conversation, and bodily mimesis, critical encounters in contact zones were typified by dialogism, borrowed expressions, autoethnographic writing, architectural hybridity, cultural play in general. To consider the poetics of implication within the broader rubric of play—that is, ludic acts in which possibilities for political alterity are held up for intense evaluation, reflection, and reflexivity—is for me a productive way of thinking about symbolic communication in colonial cultures. Focus on one cultural form, and intertextual neighbors drag into view, kept uncomfortably visible by the kind of emergency pressure that colonial situations often engender. Society is vulnerable. Recognitions of the Other in the sentient Self are unnerving. Indirect statements are vital to both the cant of conquest and the double-talk of colonial relations.

Poetics of implication introduces a loose, open-ended structure of feeling that works through indirection and intertextuality to create a dynamic center for political play. Implicative techniques are immanent, however, only in particular performances and places, two concepts that had changing meanings in early modern English culture. *Performance* was shifting during the seventeenth century from a word that designated a ceremonial activity to one that suggested illusion and the masking of motive through artificial misrepresentation. It has remained in the realm of theatrics ever since. But by *performance* I do not mean only dramaturgical interactions of powerful individuals ("historical actors") and their audiences ("witnesses"). While these dyadic events may qualify as performative, the intended quality of communication and experience that performances entail interests me more. Cultural performances are intensified expressions of high affect and indirect, implicative reference that stand out from routine communicative passages because of their self-referencing style. Performances vary enormously. Some can be momentary, interspersed in quotidian movements, environments, conversation or natural discourse. Others, like epic narrative, can last hours, even days. In performance people call attention to poetic registers and, in so doing, highlight the multiple roles an individual plays in shifting configurations of community. As the buildings, bodies, crowd actions, and portraits I explore in this book demonstrate, performances help keep social, psychological, and epistemic systems open-ended and transformative in potential.[9]

No exploration of cultural performances should focus so exclusively on implication that it divorces it from everyday life, that realm of invisible politics and commonsense routine. Performances draw force from the places where they happen. The power of place in everyday life suggests that local geography, conceived as a matrix of memory sites fusing conflict and accord, loss and renewal, may be a more powerful principle in the lives of ordinary people than mere chronology. Historians of early New England, however, inevitably see the Puritans as concerned more with narratives of temporal deliverance than with places of action and memory. They stress a lineal concept of time—whether of providential time, eschatology, millennial zeal for the "end times," or the opening of the seven seals when the New Israel descends to earth—as the existential axis of New England culture. But the people who actually lived there had their own understanding of place.

New England Puritans managed memory and searched for revelation through the material world. The shaping of memory was controversial during the seventeenth century, as the dialectical divisions and classifications of Petrus Ramus had for many orthodox Puritans replaced any emphasis on the memory theater popularized during the fifteenth and sixteenth centuries and taken to its greatest complexity in Italy. In New England the Ramist logic of memory confirmation seems to have been followed (so the writings of ministers suggest), and local places were dismissed as too variable, too untrustworthy. "God has declared himself to be . . . no respecter of places," Cotton Mather observed. "Our meeting-places are no more sacred than the ancient synagogues," he added, noticing even that "some excellent men of the episcopal way itself, have been above the conceit of 'any difference in places.'"[10]

As they followed the Ramist renunciation of the memory theater, however, individuals in colonial New England still attended closely to "common places." Some of their closet logopietism may even have come from contradictions within Ramus himself, since his writings at times used familiar locations to drive home specific arguments. Even such canonical Puritan texts as John Winthrop's *Journal* and Samuel Sewall's *Diary* are filled with site-specific jottings; close observation of space as well as time was crucial to their conception of history. But perhaps the best indication that the English never completely abandoned the familiar logic of the memory theater came when Edward Winslow in 1623 discovered one of the techniques used by the Pokanoket to recall past events, a technique that resonated well with the pre-Ramist confirmation of memory in his own culture. "Instead of records and chronicles, they take this course," he observed.

> Where any remarkable act is done, in memory of it, either in the place, or by some pathway near adjoining, they make a round hole in the ground, about a foot deep, and as much over; which when others passing by behold, they inquire the cause and occasion of the same, which once being known, they are careful to acquaint all men, as occasion serveth, therewith; and lest such holes should be filled or grown up by any accident, as men pass by, they will oft renew the same; by which means many things of great antiquity are fresh in mind. So that as a man travelleth, if he can understand his guide, his journey will be the less tedious, by reason of the many historical discourses [which] will be related to him.[11]

The connection of place and memory in early New England culture gained additional support from a belief that two planes of material reality coexisted, one in this world and one in the next. Wherever the sacred plane between these realms was pierced or broken—by the appearance of a witch, or a house shattered by sudden lightning—the place where this cosmic opening of one world into the next occurred was carefully recorded. According to William Hubbard, in 1643, "on the 18th of January, there were strange sights seen about Castle Island, and the Governor's Island over against it, in form like a man, that would sometimes cast flames and sparkles of fire." That same night, Hubbard continues, "a voice was heard between Boston and Dorchester upon the water in a dreadful manner, crying out 'boy, boy, come away, come away,'" and then, according to Hubbard, "it shifted suddenly from one place to another a great distance, about twenty miles." Many such stories attested to the power associated with places pierced and fixed by revelation, places that became sites of local legend production for the next century.[12]

With a theory of place articulated that tied revelation and remembrance to specific occurrences and locations, people used pilgrimage and ritual processions to sacralize the graves of ministers and exploited the power of key places—for example, Boston's town house, customs house, and Old South meetinghouse—to make public statements of dissatisfaction over trade or imperial policy. As geographer Allan R. Pred has suggested, such places are known through the appropriation and transformation of authority they represent. "The assemblage of buildings, land-use patterns and arteries of communication that constitute place as a visible scene," Pred maintains, "cannot emerge fully formed out of nothingness and stop, grow rigid, indelibly sketched in the once-natural landscape. Whether place refers to a rural village or a metropolis, an agricultural area or urban-industrial complex or some other observational entity, it always represents a human product. Place, in other words, always involves an appropriation and transformation of space and nature that is inseparable from the reproduction and transformation of society in time and space."[13]

This book consist of four chapters, each of which explores the relationship of performance and place to shed light on techniques of implication. Each chapter breaks down into numerous shorter sections, each of which examines a fragmentary topic that relates to the discussion in the entire chapter. In different ways, the development of fragmentary sections mimes the way my research proceeded. I have long dwelled in the territory of fragments. There is little romance in residual culture. I pieced together patches and spots of evidence that, while symbolically whole in their own right (a house, for example, or a riot, or a portrait), normally lack language sufficient to secure them easily to accepted documentary techniques. To be sure, my interest in approaching politics and religion as material phenomena is related to various initiatives in ethnographically based cultural studies, broadly speaking. But to engage this approach and extend it backward in time obliges me to work judiciously across different bodies of evidence. And the poetics of implication risks methodological dangers common to lyric possession: a hankering after coincidence, an undisciplined notion of influence, and a failure to confront the complexities of intention.[14]

Chapter 1 introduces the reader to one place: a farmstead built in Guilford, Connecticut, during the 1640s. Built by the town's wealthiest landowner, Samuel Desborough, this domestic site anchored Guilford's local geography by indirectly fusing it to the defensive "bawn" enclosure remembered from England's expansion into the Ulster Plantations, the fortified enclosed complexes built along England's northern border country, merchants' premises and the qualities of virtue and citizenship they borrowed from classical Roman villas, and finally, the tradition of agricultural reform that swept through England just as New England was being colonized. Its meaning was thus metaphorically compressed—not as much as a Dutch whale, perhaps, but on its way.

Chapter 2 focuses on an additional layer of significance in which ordinary houses—Desborough's included—were deeply implicated: the human body. I am aware that in diverse cultures and historical periods "the body" never exists in any singular "naturalized" state. Rather, different practices of embodiment, defined through gender, class, religion, labor, or medicine, exist alongside one another in any culture.[15] This chapter argues the metaphoric reality of an anthropomorphic house that Puritans built from assorted imagined timber in the Bible, poetry, building manuals, and diaries. As we have seen with ideas about performance and place, general medical understanding of the body was shifting in the seventeenth and eighteenth centuries; at the same time, embodiment was at the heart of Puritan prescriptive aesthetics, which I argue was rooted in the complex politics of communion and covenant theology. Analogies of buildings and bodies come as no surprise, since cultures from ancient Rome to contemporary West Africa and Indonesia have indexed space using the human body. What it more significant is the political modeling it performed for colonial society; in images of unity versus "multiplicitie," beauty versus deformity, and Self versus exoticized Other, implication lies at the heart of embodiment.

With implied connections of individual structures and metaphors of embodiment accomplished, chapter 3 looks at one place where buildings and bodies collided: the ritual "mobbing" or attacking of a house. Reaching a zenith during the 1760s, house attacks had a history extending back though the English Civil War to the mid-sixteenth century. Their logic was clear. If a house could be analogically identified with the body of its owner, then the attack constituted a symbolic murder, a high order of shaming that had close cousins in skimmingtons and rough music. Like these events, house attacks targeted individuals who had overstepped local rules for moral action.

As immersed as the house assault was in the republican critique of imperial cosmopolitan culture, linkages between social rank and material trappings survived the 1770s completely intact. Chapter 4 shows how vital objects and political discourse were to Connecticut Federalists searching for ways to allegorize themselves in the present. I suggest that the challenge facing Connecticut's new gentry lay in transforming themselves into something they had never been. Born neither to wealth nor inherited property, they had risen through the muscle of new industries and shipping ventures. When they came to assert their gentry status in the mid-1780s, they needed to have a portrait hanging in the parlor. They needed appearances of themselves that symbolically marked their disappearance from the hard work of daily conflicts over politics, religion, and an increasingly restive laboring population. Ralph Earl's portraits of people and their houses reveal the tensions between the difficult reality of actually living in the new republic and a continuing attempt to construct it as an Arcadia in which Connecticut's new Federalist aristocracy could imagine itself as a social class occupying, unchallenged, the new "head" of the postrevolutionary social body. The anchoring of postrevolutionary commodity culture in seventeenth-century metaphysical thought emerges in the paintings themselves, as Earl's patrons sit poised between the polite trappings of commercial success and the powerful ongoing image of the house as embodiment of heaven, lineage, family, and self.

The continuities are many. One is the remarkable vitality of seventeenth-century popular culture and its periodic later recurrence as a basis for labor actions, evident in attacks on the distorted bodies of moral transgressors during the 1760s and in the soul effigies on gravestones that I argue stood behind the stiff gestures and glaring eyes on "likenesses" painted in the 1790s. Different elements in this culture remained particularly effective: the central identity drawn between house and body; discourses of affliction, captivity, and deliverance; the radical edge of covenant theology, especially when the Antinomian implications of free grace were split from civic obedience and the work of deference. There are also remarkable continuities in how colonized Others destabilized their colonizers; as I point out in chapters 1, 2, and 4, the figure of the Other—in Africa, Ireland, Native America—called forth the dangerous instabilities within English culture.

Amid the continuities of my argument lies a paradox. Despite their more humble social origins, Ralph Earl's Connecticut sitters came through the Revolution reproducing a system of power relationships and social prerogative that the Revolution had in part been staged to call into question. This was but one jagged edge of the revolutionary settlement. But Federalist arguments defending a fixed and "natural" hierarchy, the dangers of "mixed" democracy, and the construction of a neo-Augustan country landscape that echoed with the gentle estate Isaac Royall built outside Boston in the 1730s provide clear indications that assumptions concerning what was "colonial" in New England culture persisted despite the overlain invention of the early Republic. The persistent attitude of a colonial gentry similarly circumscribed its impatient treatment of organized labor, the poverty yet surprising "Englishness" of Native Americans living in "early national" Connecticut, the poverty yet quasi Indianness of white dirt farmers living in log houses, and outbreaks of popular violence that deflated any confident assertion of virtue and discipline.

Because of these (and other) continuities in social discipline, I regard New England culture as still "colonial" in the 1790s (and later), even though the periodicity of the "early Republic" had already begun. It may be possible, however, to approach the uncomfortable reality of overlapping political structures from an opposite position. A rhetoric of national affiliation extends back to seventeenth-century England and mingles with the providential mythology of the founding generation. The colonists, of course, considered themselves part of the English nation, but they also used their common religious history to argue they were a nation apart, an "English Israel." Cotton Mather admitted outright that his congregation might blur the distinction between the two nations, claiming, "My hearers all this while know not whether I am giving an Account of Old Israel or of New England so Surprising has been the parallel." Thus the inhabitants of New England actually belonged simultaneously to two imagined nations and saw their position in each as predestined and privileged. In another sermon Mather pinpointed the birth of this doubled nationalist sentiment more precisely: "God brought a Nation out of the Midst of a Nation."[16]

The particular circumstances that gave rise to this doubled sense of nationalism among the New England Puritans may have been atypical. But if the work of national fiction cut a doubled figure, the formation of colonial subjectivity was likely even more complex, given that the various colonized peoples within New England—including various Native American societies as well as the enforced labor of Irish, Scots, and Welsh prisoners captured during Cromwell's conquest of the Celtic fringe—needed to mold their mimetic strategies in relation to two orders of imperial authority, as well as nurture and protect their own cultural terrain.[17] The imagined space of the New England colonies was thus always calibrated in terms of the English nation's psychic demand for cheap labor, guaranteed markets, slaves, and exotic peoples, those polluted but desired, low Others. Writing to John Winthrop in 1645, Emanuel Downing advised that if war with the Narraganset seemed inevitable, at least they might wrest some profit from captives. "If upon a Just warre the Lord should deliver them into our hands, wee might easily have men women and children enough to exchange for Moores, which wilbe more gaynefull pilladge for us then wee conceive," Downing wrote, adding, "for I doe not see how wee can thrive untill wee get into a stock of slaves sufficient to doe all our buisines. . . . And I suppose you know verie well how wee shall maynteyne 20 Moores cheaper than one English servant."[18] Such exacting calculations of bodily exchange and value suggest a need to control not only the economics of colonization but also the destabilizing and unsettling encounters of English civility with native peoples.

Performances and places in colonial New England implicated an energetic cultural inheritance that worked as a buttress against precisely these problems. Desborough's enclosed Connecticut farmstead, the metaphoric compression and diffusion of the human house, and the house attacks I explore here were all in this sense strategically overdetermined. They were saturated with values, some redundant and others marking a challenge, that evoked and enclosed the particular histories needed for colonization to take hold and flourish. Buildings and bodies in colonial New England may have changed between the construction of Desborough's manor house in the 1640s and the 1796 completion of Elijah Boardman's mannered house in New Milford. But much remained strangely the same. Farms, bodies, "mobbings," and portraits: these performances and places are our zones of contact with the poetics of implication.

1 Implicated Places

THE REFORMER'S ZEAL

In 1760 Jared Eliot published *Essays upon Field Husbandry in New England.* An anthology of six essays written between 1748 and 1759, it offered a set of systematic principles to convince farmers that "experimental" husbandry would bring self-sufficiency, profit, and pride to their lives. For Eliot, a minister in Killingworth, Connecticut, the work appeared at an auspicious time. Halfway through the Seven Years' War, at an economic and political low point in New England's history, he mapped the problems of ordinary citizens onto those faced by the colonies. Family order cracked. Competition for arable land proved overwhelming as inheritance strategies failed to safeguard economic stability through time. Civil law and religious congregations also felt the strains of faction, declension, and schism as new social bodies formed and reformed. If New England's yeoman farmers would change their ways, Eliot argued, husbandry would use less land and be more profitable, family structure would cohere, and the colonies would find themselves less dependent on mercantile economic policy and Crown prerogative.

Change occurred neither quickly nor easily. Eliot brought an avowed skepticism to the task of reform. His first essay claimed, "What hath been inserted in this Essay only upon hear-say, is not offered as certainly to be depended upon; but only as probably and worthy to be tryed." Cultivation and ploughing techniques learned by rote from one's elders, for example, might prove less helpful to family farms and to New England's wracked economy than new ideas drawn from careful observation. "Tradition is a very slippery Tenure," Eliot cautioned, "and a slender Pin to bear any great Weight for a long Time." He spoke with authority, since he knew Connecticut's fields and farmers well. Born in Guilford in November 1685, he had taken the time when young to talk with local elders. "I remember when I was a boy," he recalled late in 1747, "I heard a very ancient Woman of good Credit say, that she had seen Twenty broad Pieces paid down for a Two Year old Heifer, which is now Equal to *Two Hundred and Fifty Pounds* Old Tenor." Another "Man of *Guilford*" told him that common sea salt fattened fields as well as dung and that "he had tried it upon his Wheat-Land" and "it assisted and increased his Crop very well." Although Eliot's life soon took him to Yale, to a long tenure in the pulpit in nearby Killingworth, and to frequent travels throughout southern New England, he remained a lifelong student of Guilford's agrarian landscape. He chose it for his own "experiments." A committed advocate of reclaiming arable land from flooded terrain, in 1748 he "began last March, to Drein another Meadow of Forty Acres, up in Guilford Woods."[1] Guilford was the place and local society Eliot knew best.

Along the Connecticut shore Eliot viewed the draining of salt marshes and wet meadows as essential in confronting problems of land shortage and declining agrarian profits. Although he saw agriculture through a political lens, his faith in "experimental" agricultural knowledge came not only from walking the fields with local farmers but also from extensive reading. He grounded his attempt to reshape New England's society through agricultural "improvement" in the previous arguments of seventeenth-century English reform writers, including Walter Blith and Samuel Hartlib. "I had often met with it," Hartlib had explained, "that our Nation being much exhausted and Ruined by the Civil War, retrieved their great Losses by some new Husbandry, and in a little time, Recovered themselves and got to a better State than ever." The question Eliot pondered was precisely *how* they made such a recovery. He found the answer, he admitted, "by Reading *Mr. Hartlib's Book of Husbandry*." The solution for Connecticut was the introduction of clover grass.

A FAMILIAR FARMSTEAD

Eliot's choice of Hartlib was ironic. In seizing on *Samuel Hartlib His Legacie: Or, An Enlargement of the Discourse of Husbandry*, Eliot was relying on a book actually penned by Robert Child, who had visited Boston in the 1640s. Curiously, Child drew into his discussion many positive aspects of New England agriculture that he had discovered through empirical observation. Eliot paradoxically advocated as emblematic of English agricultural "improvement" the one work at that time penned by someone who had already actually been to New England, "experi-

enced" local agricultural practices, and then packed his book with recommenda-
tions from New England concerning draining land and schedules for successful
cultivation. In fact, tangible evidence that an earlier (i.e., pre–English Civil War)
and very complex tradition of farm management and farmstead design had made
the Atlantic crossing lay literally next door the entire time he was growing up in
Guilford. The property was then owned by Josiah Rossiter (1646–1716), a magistrate and leading landowner in the town. Josiah had inherited the estate intact
from his father, Bray Rossiter (1610–72), a gentleman farmer known more for his
role as a leading physician in early Connecticut than for any remarkable skill in
husbandry. Fortunately the elder Rossiter drew a plan of the complex, probably
when he acquired the property in October 1651 (fig. 1).[2]

Three enclosed courtyards defined the property: a "greate Court," an inner
"Court" to the immediate rear of the house, and a fenced-in "greene Corte" or
formal area of lawn set off in front. A gatehouse at the plan's lower right corner
guarded access to the "greate Court," a large yard through which cattle and oxen
passed on their way to their respective stalls. This courtyard also positioned the
rear of the house and the inner "Court" in relation to the "brewhouse & bakehouse" and "wood house," in which fuel necessary for these and other domestic
functions lay ready for use. In between the "greate Court" and "greene Corte" lay
a hedge of rosemary, which contemporary herbalists maintained would purify the
air, guard domestic spaces against polluting odors, and promote the generative
and regenerative meanings of weddings and funerals. The rear dooryard, or inner
"Court," organized activities involving household members on a daily basis. At
the upper left corner of the plan a second gatehouse marked the entrance from
"Desborough Lane" and proclaimed the power and authority of the householder
to visitors. An adjacent area designated for "the horses" allowed riding mounts a
place to be watered and tied up overnight. Between the gatehouse and a set of
"stayres" attached to the rear of the main dwelling house, an open pen for milk
cows, identified by Bray Rossiter's preferred West Country dialect term, "biere
hag" (byre + hag[gard], or pen), permitted women in the household ready access
to their daily round of dairying chores. While servants in the house's kitchen or
kitchen chamber—rooms at what they would have termed the "lower" end of the
house—looked out over mud and manure in the "greate Court," the family at the
"upper" end enjoyed a privileged view of their "greene Court," fruit orchard, garden, and small pond. A small stream flowing from the pond probably supplied
spring water to the "waterhouse," before winding into nearby salt marshes.[3]

This "ancient" building form, its peripheral walls rising like protective barriers
against the outside world, cast a dark shadow over Jared Eliot's experimental epis-
teme and conflicted openly with his vision of liberal economic reform and market
agriculture (fig. 2). Conflicting ideas of domestic order shaped the landscape of

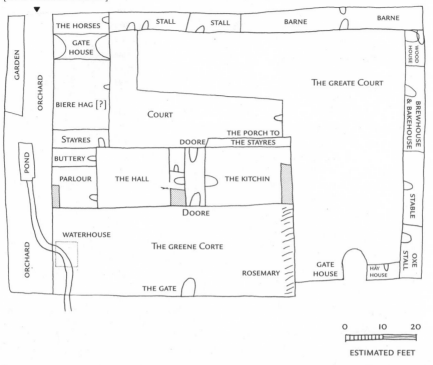

GARDEN

ORCHARD

THE HORSES

GATE HOUSE

STALL   STALL   BARNE   BARNE

WOOD HOUSE

THE GREATE COURT

BIERE HAG [?]

COURT

BREWHOUSE & BAKEHOUSE

POND

STAYRES   DOORE   THE PORCH TO THE STAYRES

BUTTERY

PARLOUR   THE HALL   THE KITCHIN

STABLE

DOORE

ORCHARD

WATERHOUSE

THE GREENE CORTE

ROSEMARY   GATE HOUSE   HAY HOUSE   OXE STALL

THE GATE

0   10   20

ESTIMATED FEET

Figure 1. Bray Rossiter, plan of farmstead in Guilford, Connecticut, ca. 1651. Shaded areas denote hearth locations. Ink on vellum, H. of drawing 9½" (24.1 cm), W. 6½" (16.5 cm). (Drawing by the author)

early Guilford during Eliot's lifetime no less than they had during the period of the town's initial establishment in the late 1630s. But how? The precise social origins of and formal antecedents to enclosed domestic complexes in British North America have never been correctly charted, their interconnections revealed, nor their cultural logic as specifically colonial places thoroughly investigated. As I explore the felt tensions of Guilford's early social geography, tensions that are typically erased by studies of "regional continuity" from Old England to New, I want to expand the poetics of implication that suffused the enclosed farmstead that Jared Eliot knew from his youth.

Without minimizing the complex's protective purposes, I see it as part of a larger cultural process of molding beliefs to the contours of colonization and commerce to the discipline of imperial expansion. This project drove God's Englishmen to defend the church militant against infidels while also attempting their wholesale conversion to the Protestant faith and the currencies of nascent capitalism. Part of the calculated expansion of England's economy thus was rooted,

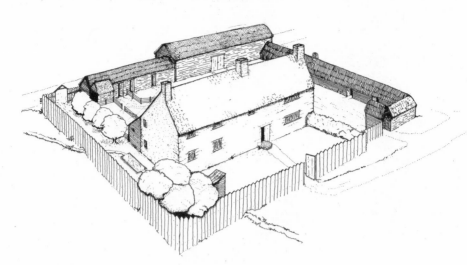

Figure 2. Conjectural view of Guilford farmstead from the southwest, ca. 1641. (Drawing by the author)

paradoxically, in the retention of enclosed and protective settlement forms that looked back toward the fixed security of feudal social relations at the same time that commodity relations were loosening the parameters of social place. The case was little different outside Guilford. Elsewhere in New England other leading citizens sought to contain mercantile activity within a neofeudal social order. John Endicott, a successful English merchant, member of the Massachusetts Bay Company, and that colony's first governor, moved to his large estate north of Salem in 1632, where "he lived in a sort of feudal style, surrounded by his servants."[4]

An overemphasis on defense and the sad politics of colonization can obscure other lines of inquiry. In this case, it threatens to erase the cultural work done by protective merchant premises and classical agricultural theory—which both similarly championed the enclosed homestead as a means of efficiently organizing aristocratic concepts of fixed social rank while protecting the commodities and interests of individual landowners—in the programs of English social and economic reform supporting colonial initiatives. I argue that an English mythology of protected people and protected markets was transferred to and reproduced in New England, and that the meaning of the domestic complex shown in Rossiter's sketch derived from various English and Continental antecedents that extended beyond mere defense to encompass a series of architectural exchanges between sacred reference and secular action dating from the late fourteenth century. The Guilford farmstead may represent only a single complex of buildings on the property of a single individual, but it was a place that implicated other places. I suggest that each implicated place brought its metaphoric power to bear on how living individuals experienced this one Guilford farmstead. The compound was essentially an overdetermined place, a record of previous structures that established its apprehended trajectory in the social, sensate world.

The farmstead plan was first attributed to Rossiter in 1897, when town historian Bernard Christian Steiner suggested that it represented Rossiter's own Guilford estate. In 1855 Charles J. Hoadly, librarian of Trinity College in Hartford, may have realized the historical significance of the drawing, penned by Rossiter on a piece of vellum he had used to rebind a late-sixteenth-century medical treatise. At some point before he returned to England in 1652, Edward Hopkins, a wealthy London merchant and the colony of Connecticut's first governor, gave the medical text to physician Rossiter, who proudly inscribed "Ex dono dom[inu]m Hopkins—Bray Rosseter his booke" on the front cover. That explained Hoadly's discovery of a manuscript note pasted inside, a letter Rossiter had written in 1668 to protect himself in the event one of his Guilford patients died. In December 1855, Hoadly recorded that he had sent a copy of the 1668 letter to Ralph D. Smith, Guilford's celebrated historian, genealogist, and Steiner's grandfather.[5]

If Hoadly notified Smith about the sketch at that time, no mention of it appears in Smith's *History of Guilford, Connecticut, from Its First Settlement in 1639* (1877) or in his detailed article on the Rossiter family's genealogy (1901). Hoadly apparently thought the plan represented Hopkins's large estate in Hartford, despite the fact that the handwriting plainly matches that in Rossiter's 1668 letter. Yet Steiner, who had edited both of his grandfather's works for publication, knew of the drawing while preparing his own history of Guilford in 1897. Referring to Rossiter's inscription upon receiving the text from Hopkins, Steiner stated that the book contained "a plan, thought to be that of his house in Guilford." Presumably, if he had known of the drawing while editing his grandfather's book in the mid-1870s, he would have noted its existence at that point. We can assume that between 1877 and 1897 Steiner first recognized the plan as a representation of Rossiter's Guilford estate as purchased in 1651. It was perhaps Steiner (or someone he knew) who made the "Tracing of diagram on Bray Rossiter's Valesius" that was donated to Guilford's Whitfield house museum in early July 1904.[6]

Two weeks later, architect Norman M. Isham donated a sketch he had made, based on the tracing, of what the "possible superstructure" of the complex might have looked like (fig. 3). Isham actually had drawn the view in October 1903, shortly after he completed a major restoration of the Henry Whitfield house, also in Guilford, suggesting that he may have been in direct contact with Steiner during that project. It is not surprising that Isham would have been consulted during the restoration. He was already a recognized expert on the earliest houses in Guilford and nearby New Haven. In *Early Connecticut Houses* Isham demonstrates that he had looked in detail at the actual fabric of the Whitfield house and made an effort to square what he observed with earlier accounts of the building by historian Smith and others. Isham had also made an effort to reconstruct the interior plan and furnishing scheme of Theophilus Eaton's house in New Haven. All three of these efforts—the reconstructed view based on the Rossiter sketch, the Whitfield house analysis, and the Eaton house furnishing plan—reveal Isham's careful and imaginative use of evidence but also his investment in the colonial revival movement at the turn of the twentieth century. His view of Rossiter's farmstead is a case in point. The overall configuration is faithful to the plan, but specific details—the generically "colonial" cupolas on the barn and the distant pavilion at the far corner of the garden, his decision to give the house three large facade gables and additional ones to the near gatehouse and outbuildings, the large number of windows in the house and the outbuildings, and the fences and their quaintly arched openings—all reveal Isham's skill in transforming the substance of colonial reality into the style of colonial revivalism.[7]

PEOPLE AND PROPERTY

Rossiter's plan could show a house he fondly recalled from his English upbringing or one that he had encountered elsewhere in New England before settling in Guilford. But did he actually build the complex shown in the drawing? If not, who did? Guilford's early land records reveal that Rossiter purchased his estate from Samuel Desborough, the town's first magistrate and its wealthiest planter. According to the deed, the property Desborough sold to Rossiter included "one p[ar]cell of upland *adioyneing to his house,* containeing & allowed for thirteene acres—more or lesse." In its meeting at Guilford on June 9, 1651, the General Court announced: "Mr. Rossiter admitted & approved a planter here in the purchase of Mr. Disborough's accomodations." So a house was already standing on the Desborough property when Rossiter both drew and acquired it, a point that was soon absorbed into local tradition. According to Thomas Ruggles, who became Guilford's minister in 1729 and composed a town history of Guilford in 1769, when oral history was still accurate for the previous century, "Dr. Rosseter purchased Mr. Desborow's house and lands of him when he left town with Mr. Whitfield, and returned to England" in 1651.[8] Rossiter may have drawn the complex in 1651, but what he drew was a farmstead and house built by Samuel Desborough soon after his arrival in Guilford in 1641.

Who was Samuel Desborough? Born in 1619, he was the second son of the lord of the manor of Eltisley in West Cambridgeshire. Far from being a calm village, Eltisley was a Puritan stronghold by the time Desborough left in 1639. Continuing lay unrest climaxed in a 1640 petition protesting the "Tyrannicall courses and Ad-

Figure 3. Norman M. Isham, conjectural view of the Guilford complex from the southeast, October 1903. Pencil on paper. (Photo by the author, courtesy of the Henry Whitfield Historical Museum of the State of Connecticut)

ministrations of Dr Wrenn Bishop of Ely," a local supporter of Archbishop William Laud's persecution policies. In his tenure at Ely between 1638 and 1640, Wren had helped to polarize religious debates in the area. In the late 1630s Desborough had fallen in stride with local Puritans and met William Leete in nearby Keyston, Huntingdonshire. Leete likely introduced him to George Fenwick, a landowner from Brinkburn, Northumberland, who controlled the patents to lands in Connecticut. And while reading law in London, Desborough established ties with the congregation gathering around Rev. Henry Whitfield in nearby Ockley, Surrey. Whitfield, the son of a prominent court attorney under Elizabeth I, had also studied law at the Inns of Court and may have met Desborough there. Whether through legal or religious channels or both, Desborough ended up, at age twenty, with Leete, Whitfield, and Fenwick on a ship that arrived in New Haven in 1639.[9]

By 1641 Desborough was in Guilford, recognized as a man of position and responsibility. In that year he was pivotal in drafting the town covenant and the system of landholding based on wealth that defined early Guilford's townscape. He was clear on the qualifications needed for specific land allotments: "all planters desiring accomodation here shall put in the valuation of their estates according to one or other of these four sumes appointed for the rule or proportion, (viz.) either five hundred pounds, Two Hundred and fifty pounds, one hundred pounds, or fifty pounds, according to which last and lowest summe the poorest plantere may put in for and have accomodation suitable of hee desire."[10] His own position in the wealthiest cohort is apparent in the size of his original thirteen-acre grant, which was by far the largest single house lot in town, its nearest rivals being the nine acres owned on South Lane (now Whitfield Street) by Henry Whitfield and by his brother-in-law Jacob Sheafe. Unlike the deep, narrow lots owned by most townsmen, Desborough's had a long frontage along the road.

Through his marriage to Whitfield's daughter Dorothy, Desborough was related to the leading families in town. A connection with the Whitfield clan was a connection to power and an impressive network of subordinate kin relations. Whitfield's wife, Dorothy (now Desborough's mother-in-law), was a sister of merchant Jacob Sheafe. Another Sheafe sister, Margaret, had married Robert Ketchel, and another, Joanna, was the wife of William Chittenden. Through strategic intermarriages of women, the Sheafe clan formed an armature of alliances in early Guilford. Desborough, of the manor born and a member of the lesser gentry in West Cambridgeshire, advanced rapidly in Guilford because family ties linked him on one side to the church and on the other to mercantile and legal interests. Along with Leete he was an organizing "pillar" of the Guilford church and made a freeman of the town in 1643. In 1646 "Mr. Samuell Desbrow [was] chosen magistrat for Guilford for the yeare ensuweinge," a position he filled until he, along with Whitfield, departed for Cromwell's England in late 1651. He seems to have played well the role of magistrate and local notable. Only thirty-one years old when he left, he rested confidently atop the town's pyramid of prestige and power.

The first document to actually describe the property is the inventory made of Bray Rossiter's estate in 1672, which values "The House & Land in Guilford together with severall things appertaineing to ye house" at £80, along with "two Cowes" and "Cattle & horses, sheepe & swine" at more than £43. According to the terms of his will, his son Josiah was "to have his house & land at Guilford," which in fact he had already been given prior to September 30, 1672. Josiah assumed legal ownership when his father's estate was finally settled in March 1673, and he lived there until his own death in 1716. His inventory of that year valued this "dwelling house and barne not finished with 3 acres Homelott" at £99, suggesting that he had continued to develop and maintain the property.[11] That the barn was then "not finished" may suggest that the original barn, constructed by Desborough in the early 1640s and recorded in his father's 1651 survey, stood in need of replacement. Josiah's inventory also clearly states his ownership of "one p[ar]cell of upland adioyneing to his house contayneing & allowed thirteen acres more or lesse," land that corresponded directly to the original, undivided Desborough homestead. His will divided this home lot between his younger two sons, Jonathan and Timothy.[12]

He left the easternmost three acres of the property to Jonathan, including "the dwelling house I now dwell in and the frame of the barne as it may be found at my

Decease with all the originall homestead beside what Timothy hath." Jonathan's share included the old Desborough farmstead that had served his father and grandfather as home; it was this easternmost segment of the ancestral home lot that abutted the minister's lot where Jared Eliot had been raised between 1685 and 1706. Timothy received the other "10 Acres of upland Adjoyning [valued] at £10 [per] Acre with the house where Timothy Dwells at £75 & the barne £15" for a total value of £190. This bequest suggests that Josiah had built a second house for Timothy, "the house that he now dwells in as he found itt and the barne by itt," somewhere to the west of the ancestral homestead. He also granted Timothy a small piece along the western edge of Jonathan's three-acre tract, a piece "about the middle of my homeland where ye house Stands[,] Running the South Line from the north west Corner of his house A Cross the Spring[,] Running the East Line So far as to take in two Roes of apple Trees[,] Running the north Line to the Tobacco pound, and to the South East Corner of the Yard and from thence to the high way."[13]

Although these boundary lines are finally impossible to chart, they suggest that Josiah reserved a small piece on the site of his father's old orchard and garden for Timothy's use; by 1716 Josiah was cultivating tobacco and apples on that ground. Timothy Rossiter died in 1724, after which Jonathan bought out his ten-acre share and gained control of his father's original thirteen-acre estate. In February 1733, when Jonathan sold the property to Josiah Stone, it included at its easternmost end "the messuage or Tenement where I now Dwell With a Dwelling House Barn fences fruit Trees & appurtenances thereon." The language becomes even more precise the next year, when Stone sold just the easternmost plot of land with the old farmstead on it to Andrew Ward, a local justice of the peace, for £255. This tract was identical to the piece that Jonathan had received in his father's bequest. The deed specifies the "house Barn Cowhouse Stables, privey house out houses fences Closes Gardens fruit trees Stoned well & furniture thereto belonging and all & every Tree plant and herb on the Same, the Land Contains About four acres be it more or Less, and was formerly the Estate of Mr Josiah Rossiter Deceased."[14] When compared with the features Rossiter labeled on his plan in 1651, this passage argues that the complex was originally built by Desborough, improved and probably rebuilt by three generations of Rossiters, and stood until the early 1760s. At that point Increase Pendleton acquired the tract with the ancient farmstead and must have razed it to make way for the large dwelling he erected on the site by 1767.

Land records allow an exact determination of where Desborough's farmstead stood along present-day Water Street. Field visits and documentary research suggest a position immediately east of present-day Fair Street. The original homelot was located in the easternmost three-acre parcel of the estate, now the site of the

Guilford post office and the Pendleton house; these buildings sit atop a small knoll of upland with excellent drainage and a fine view of the salt marshes to the south. The former structure was built in the 1960s on land that seems always to have been vacant prior to its construction. The Pendleton house, however, was definitely built on the site of the farmstead complex, and its construction in the late 1760s provides a date by which the Desborough complex must have been razed. According to town engineering reports, an underground spring still exists in this area that may be tentatively identified with the one that watered Desborough's garden pond and ran through his waterhouse to the marshes beyond.[15]

The precise orientation of the farmstead on the Desborough house lot remains unclear. Although the first terrier records Desborough's pre-1648 holdings as "one p[ar]cell of upland adioyneinge to his house, containeing & allowed for thirteene acres—more or lesse, abutting w[i]th the ffront to the lane," this may not mean that the actual front of the house faced the lane; it may merely imply that the property had frontage along it. And consider: if the house faced the lane, as Isham's 1903 view suggested, with the "greene Corte" providing access directly from the street, the house would have faced due north, with the kitchen and adjacent rosemary hedge to the northwest. Yet first-generation New England houses suggest that climatic concerns led owners to place the hall or kitchen of the house to the south or east, even if the house then turned its back on the public way. I suggest that Desborough placed his farm complex so that its rear range of buildings backed onto the lane and its formal "greene Corte" facade looked south across the fields and salt marshes toward the Long Island Sound beyond (fig. 4). Such a position placed the larger of the two gatehouses and the horse stalls close to the town street and, more important, would have allowed Desborough to bring loaded wagons directly into the outside door of his barn. The appearance at street level of a wall of buildings that effectively hid the house from public view undoubtedly struck Jared Eliot as inhospitable, perhaps even hostile, to local townspeople.

DEFENSIVE POSTURES

Having established the social history of the Rossiter plan and that Samuel Desborough actually built the farmstead between 1641 and 1651, we can now explore with equal depth the specific historical origins, associations, and purposes of such elaborate farm complexes in New England's nascent market economy. I have already stressed that Desborough's enclosed complex gained particularly dense metaphoric significance as it referenced architectural strategies for containing people and property—and people *as* property—in early modern European cul-

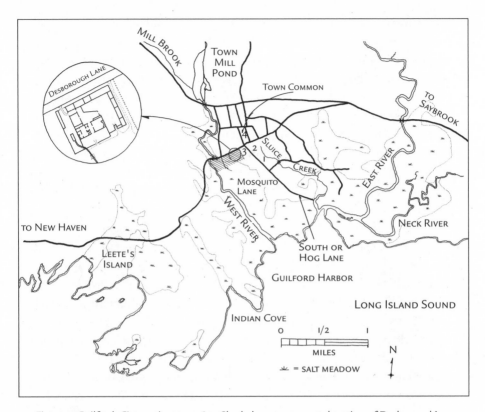

Figure 4. Guilford, Connecticut, ca. 1672. Shaded area represents location of Desborough's original thirteen-acre house lot, owned in 1672 by Bray Rossiter. Inset shows probable orientation of farm structures; numbers refer to four other early stone structures: (1) Henry Whitfield, ca. 1639–40; (2) Jasper Stillwell, ca. 1645; (3) John Higginson, ca. 1641; (4) first meetinghouse, ca. 1639–40. (Map by the author)

ture. The first place it implicated, through its surrounding walls and protective gatehouses, was the fortified domestic compound built by English landlords in zones of imperial expansion where their grasp on local populations was insecure, their dominance in need of symbolic reinforcement.

In 1951 Anthony N. B. Garvan initiated work on the politics of place in early America. He stressed the significance of the "bawn," an enclosed defensive structure built by the English in their Irish colonies to fortify plantations against possible local insurgency, in providing a model for early colonial settlements at Guilford, nearby Saybrook, and Jamestown in Virginia. What, precisely, was a bawn? The Irish word *badhún* meant a small, enclosed compound for cattle. As colonization progressed from the 1560s through the late 1630s, the bawn as constructed by the English planters in Ireland became a fortified homestead with surrounding walls—usually built of stone but also of brick, clay, earthfast and silled timber frame, wattle and daub, and sod—that protected the house, family, and personal property of the plantation's principal landlord from the imagined treachery of the Irish natives they made their tenants. The dwelling house per se could be freestanding in the center of the bawn or, as was the case at the residence built by the Vintners' Company at Bellaghy (fig. 5), connected to its perimeter walls. These walls usually met at small corner towers or flankers, from which entries to the complex could be defended against the "wild Irish," who, according to the English soldier-turned-author Barnaby Rich, preferred to "live like beastes, voide of lawe and all good order," being "more uncivill, more uncleanly, more barbarious and more brutish in their customs and demeanures, then in any other part of the world that is known."[16]

Since Garvan suggested the bawn's relevance to early Guilford, historians John Reps and Nicholas P. Canny and archaeologist Ivor Noël Hume have also argued that English experience in Ireland, particularly in Ulster, provided a template for "reducing" the New World and its native inhabitants to English civility. These scholars are indebted to the pioneering work of Howard Mumford Jones and David Beers Quinn, who first pointed out the interdependency of Ireland and the New World in emergent theories of colonization forwarded by scholars and political leaders attached to late Elizabethan and early Stuart courts. The writings of these individuals, including Thomas Smith, Humphrey Gilbert, and George Carew, constitute the first specifically "colonial" American literature in English.[17]

The bawn connection in colonial Guilford, in fact, has seemed plausible ever since historian Steiner claimed in 1897 that "several of the first houses were built of stone," including the dwellings of Henry Whitfield, John Higginson, Jasper Stillwell, and Desborough. References to lime for building projects in New Haven and Hartford as early as 1639 suggest that masonry construction was employed elsewhere in Connecticut for defensive structures and because stone houses in English culture generally suggested permanence of wealth and authority. The mere presence of these individuals in Guilford—each of whom had close ties to English Puritans with direct commercial interests in the Ulster Plantations and their London backers—suggests that plantation forms already tested in Ireland may have been influential. But Guilford, established in 1639, was actually laid out like the towns built by the London trade companies in Ulster. For example, Desborough's complex stood at the southeast end of Guilford's town common and, like the stone houses of Whitfield, Higginson, and Stillwell, was sited so as to protect the town center from any seaborne enemies—perhaps the Dutch in nearby New York, who were then competing with the English for control of the Indian fur trade in Connecticut—and from Indian attack by land.[18]

Of the four Guilford structures believed to have been built of stone, only Whitfield's surviving house definitely was (fig. 6). It was constructed about 1639–40,

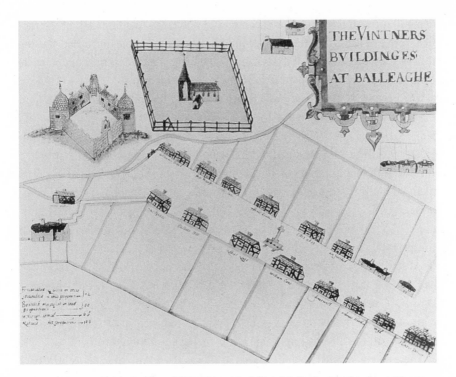

Figure 5. Thomas Raven, "A Plat of the Vintners' Buildings," Bellaghy, Londonderry, 1622. From Thomas Phillips, *Londonderry and the London Companies, 1609–1629* (Belfast: His Majesty's Stationery Office, 1928), facing p. 145.

altered once in 1868 and again in 1902–3, and heavily restored by architect J. Frederick Kelly in the 1930s. The present stairs, although rebuilt, now occupy their proper location. With some renewal of materials, the early rear kitchen survived Kelly's presence unscathed. During restoration Kelly followed the suggestion of Guilford historian Ralph Smith in reconstructing an embrasure for a cannon in the front corner of the house's small south chamber. Smith, who had studied the building with his father, Walter, in the 1850s, interpreted this break in the original masonry fabric as a window when he published an engraving of the structure in 1859. Measured drawings completed by Walter Smith in 1857 before any alterations took place also show that windows originally pierced the south facade and that only the surviving chimney and hearth on the north wall are original. I therefore assume that a framed, internal partition would have separated the main block into a small parlor and a large hall entered directly from the outside through the off-axis front door (fig. 7a). Documentary and archaeological work on several bawns in Ireland and Virginia confirms a similar plan type in those locations (fig. 7c, d), and an excavation at the Whitfield house suggests the structure once may have formed one side of a larger, enclosed complex. Building a stone house as part

of a wall surrounding an enclosed compound was a well-established English practice, dating at least from the plantation of Munster during the mid-1580s. During
the early seventeenth century, especially in the bawns erected by the London trade
companies in their Ulster Plantations, the pattern was codified.[19]

The bawn may have served as a rough prototype for the Whitfield house (and
for defensive structures in the Virginia settlements at Jamestown and Martin's
Hundred), but Desborough's domestic compound followed the concept with
greater precision. Desborough built his house within a peripheral wall, arranged
various outbuildings at perpendicular angles to frame courtyards, and enclosed
them all within a surrounding fence pierced by gates. The plans of bawn complexes built concurrently by the Salters' and Skinners' Companies in county Londonderry, and another at Castlederg in county Tyrone, provide useful formal
comparisons, as do two earlier complexes at the center of Sir Henry Docwra's fortified settlement at Londonderry in 1600. Perhaps not surprisingly, Desborough
had taken a lease for fifteen hundred acres of land in county Meath from the
Drapers' Company in London, an estate he later rented to John Preston, an alder-
man of Dublin. Desborough, like other well-placed men in Massachusetts and
Connecticut, was already implicated in the Irish colonization scheme.[20]

These bawns shared two basic spatial strategies. They employed concentric barriers: gate, enclosed yard (sometimes divided into outer and inner courtyards),
entrance porch of house, sequence of domestic spaces or rooms. Designed to dra-
matize the centripetal movement inward from gate and yard to porch, hall, and
parlor—a social pilgrimage from marginal to central, from partially to fully incorporated in household structure—these compounds also ensured that in case
of enemy attack all points of possible entrance would fall in the sights of gunners
positioned in outer flankers, inner courtyard, and turrets of the house. Doe Castle in county Donegal was described in 1623 as "an ancient strong castle, three stories high, and a bawn of lime and stone . . . with good flankers," and in it the concept of concentric defense is highly developed. Set into a hill, the bawn and its
entry flanker command a view to the northeast; its peripheral wall surrounds the
L-shaped house with corner towers. The end gable of the dwelling is part of the
masonry enclosure, and its core consists of a fortified tower house dating from at
least 1544 (fig. 8).[21]

These bawns also lie at one end of a linear plantation layout. At Bellaghy the
landlord's bawn, adjacent to the established church, secured one end of the town,
while the stone or "cagework" (i.e., timber-framed) houses of the English planters
and then the mud or cob cottages of their "wild" Irish tenants were arrayed along
house lots ranging down the street. Such a location placed the landlord's house a
safe distance from those of his tenants and proffered a garrison for the nearby English planters and their cattle in case of an Irish rebellion. Fear of the Irish was

Figure 6. Henry Whitfield's house, Whitfield Street, Guilford, Connecticut, ca. 1639–40; photograph ca. 1860, prior to any restoration. (Photo courtesy of the Henry Whitfield Historical Museum of the State of Connecticut)

compounded by the English perception that the Irish were either pagans or lapsed Roman Catholics; according to one commentator in the 1570s, the "outwarde behavyor" of the native population made it seem that "they neyther love nor dredd God nor yet hate the Devell, [and] they are superstycyous and worshippers of images and open idolaters." As a result of such distrust, a perceived need to keep the bawn and the church in close proximity sometimes led to their incorporation into a single structure. Nicholas Pynnar, reporting in 1619 on the progress of Thomas Blenerhassett's estate at Coolemackernan in county Fermanagh, revealed that in addition to his bawn, his house, and his "small Village consisting of six Houses built of Cagework, inhabited with *English* . . . He hath begun a Church." The bawn of the Skinners' Company at Dungiven incorporated a twelfth-century Augustinian priory that had been reconsecrated as a Church of England shortly after 1603, mimicking a practice many aristocratic houses had followed since the late fourteenth century.[22]

OTHERING ULSTER

Defense was a concern to English merchants and planters eager to secure ready access to Ireland's iron ore, minerals, fish, wool, and land, all needed in England's

Figure 7. Henry Whitfield's house and its Anglo-Irish relatives (dotted lines represent conjectural locations of original partitions): (a) conjectural plan of Whitfield's house, Guilford, Connecticut, ca. 1639–40, based on measured drawings made by Walter and Ralph Smith of Guilford in 1857; (b) plan of Arthur Allen's house (Bacon's Castle), Surry County, Virginia, 1665 (after Dell Upton, "Vernacular Domestic Architecture in Eighteenth-Century Virginia," *Winterthur Portfolio* 17, nos. 2–3 [Summer–Autumn 1972]: fig. 10); (c) reconstructed plan of Castle Baldwin, near Lough Arrow, county Sligo (after D. M. Waterman, "Some Seventeenth-Century Irish Houses and Their Architectural Ancestry," in *Studies in Building History: Essays in Recognition of the Work of B. H. St. John O'Neil*, ed. E. M. Jope [London: Odhams Press, 1961], fig. 14.8); (d) house at Cregg, near Rosses Point, county Sligo, ca. 1600–1630 (after Waterman, "Some Seventeenth-Century Irish Houses," fig. 14.9). (Drawing by the author)

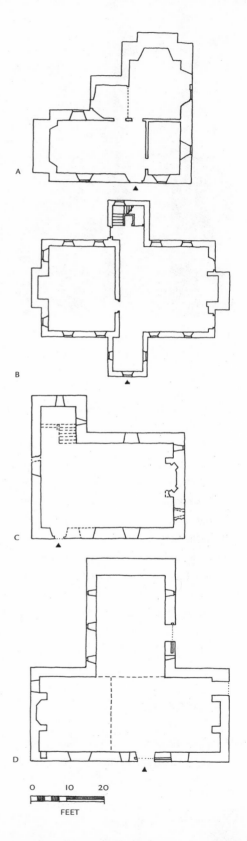

A

B

C

D

0   10   20

FEET

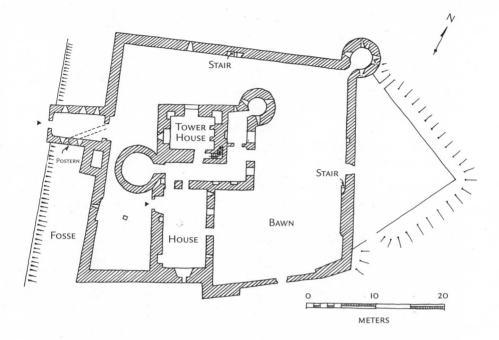

Figure 8. Plan of Doe Castle, Castledoe, county Donegal, ca. 1540 with later additions (after Brian Lacy, ed., *Archaeological Survey of County Donegal: A Description of the Field Antiquities of the County from the Mesolithic Period to the Seventeenth Century A.D.* [Lifford: Donegal County Council, 1983], 357). (Drawing by the author)

resource-starved manufacturing trades and overcrowded agrarian economy. They sought sources for timber badly demanded in shipbuilding, charcoal production, and ironworks, wasting the oak woods at Glenconkeyne and Killetra in south county Londonderry. When combined with the rapid emergence of landless Irish tenants, these pursuits could (and by 1641 did) make the English position precarious. Writing from Ulster to James I in 1614 to criticize what he viewed as the unfulfilled promises of the London trade companies—namely, their decision to settle in areas where Irish were already living in violation of their plan to develop vacant areas first, their slowness in supplying adequate capital for the construction of buildings, their inability to attract skilled artisans to such a shaky project—Thomas Phillips advised, "As now they are, these few British amongst such multitudes of Irish may easily be surprized, their throats cut and their arms taken by the natives who may therewith arm themselves against your Majesty's Loyal Subjects to the utter overthrow of that hopeful Plantation and to the great Danger and Disturbance of the public peace and tranquillity of the whole Kingdom."[23]

For the English, a strategy of concentric household and linear town defense was useful because the Irish were seen as "uncivilized" savages in league with similarly "superstycyous" Spanish papists and bent on dethroning the Stuart king. Distrust emerged from aristocratic and royal paranoia, perhaps, but also from misreadings of divergent cultural practices. As early as 1577 English readers received reports of the exotic primitivism of Irish people, a primitivism that both inverted and threatened the "civilized" logic of accepted English customs. In his popular book on the topic, chronicler Raphael Holinshed revealed in a section devoted to "the disposition and maners of the meere Irish, commonly called the wyld Irishe," that unlike the sober mourning customs of pious Englishmen, upon the death of a loved one the Irish "follow the dead corpes to the grave w[ith] howling and barbarous outcries, pitiful in appearaunce." Their care of newborn children seemed just as strange: "Their infantes of the meaner sort are neither swadled nor lapped in lynnen, but folded uppe starke naked in a blanket till they can go." Or consider, Holinshed suggested, their posture during ceremonial feasts: "In their coshering they sit on straw, they are served on straw and lie upon mattresses and pallets of straw."[24]

Thomas Gainsford, an English soldier who served in the bloody defeat of the Irish at Kinsale in 1601, offered additional details of Irish society: "Here are no towns," he wrote, "or at least very few, but divers castles dispersed, and the inhabitants remove their cabins as their cattle change pasture, somewhat like the Tartarians." From Gainsford's perspective, the lack of permanent land tenure and sedentary agriculture was a sure sign that the Irish were uncivilized barbarians. In addition to seasonal migration patterns, he found Irish family life unusual: "Their marriages are strange, for they are made sometimes so conditionally that upon a slight occasion the man taketh another wife, the wife another husband."[25]

Cultural practices like these were taken by the English as visible signs of Irish depravity: revealing one's inner frailties in confronting death with less than exemplary self-control; failing to discipline and protect properly the weak and newborn; sleeping and eating on straw like an animal; resisting a sedentary agrarian life in a stationary dwelling surrounded by adequate fencing (the English planters in Ulster were uniformly in favor of enclosure); and treating the matrimonial union of property with casual indifference. From an English viewpoint these people lacked the sense of order and self-denial that proper Christian discipline promised. The initial charge laid down in James I's "Preamble of the Londoners' Charter" to plant in Ulster in 1614 was "[t]hat the true Religion of Christ should be there established where few or none were then residing but such as by superstition were departed and almost past hope of recovery."[26]

Rooted in an inability to leap a cultural divide, the tension between British planter and Gael tenant thus began as an effort by the former to "convert" the latter. Convert him to a Protestant Christ. Convert him to the wisdom of sedentary existence as a farm tenant. Convert him into a reliable labor source for market production. Convert him to a loyal defender of Crown interests. Concluding his blistering critique of the London backers of the Ulster scheme, Thomas Phillips expressed the relationship of coercive conversion and commercial capitalism with a vengeance: "The committees of London which solicited and undertook the Plantation of Ulster brought Religion, Honour and Safety in their Tongues to procure the same, as Religion towards God, Honour towards their Prince and Safety to that Kingdom. But in the establishing, execution, and performance thereof they have wholly abandoned and forsaken them all, as if thereby they had a full primary intent and premeditated purpose to fill up their own Purses."[27] In New England as in Ulster, the enclosed bawn was a sign of the contradictory presence in colonization of both material optimism and intercultural fear. But whereas Phillips meant the heathen Irish when he wrote of "AVOIDING OF NATIVES," in New England the "natives" who greeted the English were the various Algonkian peoples of the southern New England coast—the Massachuset, Pokanoket, Narranganset, Nihantic, Mohegan, Pequot, and, in the vicinity of Guilford, the Quiripi—and they presented a variety of new intercultural challenges for which the English were ill prepared.

PERSECUTION AND PROTECTION

English settlers effected a smooth transferal of imagery from the subjugated Irish Gaels to the Native Americans who stood in their way in Massachusetts and Connecticut. They did so by drawing on popular reports like those of Raphael Holinshed and Barnaby Rich. They also relied on the experience of such Boston merchants as Joshua Hewes, Thomas Savage, and William Alford in the Ironmongers', Merchant Tailors', and Skinners' Companies of London before emigration and on the firsthand experience of New England Puritan leaders active as "Adventurers for Ireland," including John Winthrop Jr., Hugh Peter, John Humphrey, and William Willoughby. In New England the official motive for plantation pronounced by Charles I was also the conversion of the native peoples to Christianity. The settlers were to "incite the natives of [the] country to the knowledg and obedience of the onlie true God and Savior of mankinde, and the Christian fayth, which, in our royall intencion and the adventurers free profession, is the principall ende of this plantacion." In New England as in Ireland, the rhetoric of conversion scarcely concealed the planters' lust for land. The zeal with which the New England Puritans imposed their ill-formed stereotypes of Irish culture on the Native Americans was intensified by a distrust of the latter either as unchurched "heathens" or as embodiments of a papist Antichrist similar to the Irish. Puritans, after all, had a long memory for the providential meaning of events in which the legions of

Satan sorely smote the visible Saints of the Church militant. As John Saffin meditated in Boston in 1686, "It is a Received truth that upon Record that in ye Irish Rebellion, Crewell and Barberous Massacre which was perpretated [sic] in Ireland Anno 1641 that there were within two years time Murdered 300,000 English Protestants I say Three Hundred Thousand besides what was kill'd in the War."[28]

When the English arrived in New England and encountered the American Indians, they recognized certain cultural "coincidences" as they mapped these natives onto the Gaelic ones they had just conquered. According to William Wood, the anguished cries of pain one heard when Indians mourned combined a "deep groan with Irish-like howlings"; John Josselyn claimed that "their mournings" were "somewhat like the howlings of the Irish, seldom at the grave but in the Wigwam where the party dyed." Native American mothers did not swaddle their infants but instead strapped them to a board they could easily carry while at work. Edward Winslow discovered that the Pokanoket commonly entertained guests while reclining on low platforms in their wigwams. Further, the Native Americans migrated from inland winter hunting grounds to coastal encampments during the late spring and summer and also defined conjugal obligations in ways that allowed men and women to separate with relative ease.[29]

Other details intensified English memory of Irish customs. Roger Williams observed that the swamps used by the Narraganset to evade their enemies were "like the Boggs to the *Irish.*" Wood noted, "In the wintertime the more aged of them wear leather drawers, in form like Irish trousers," and Winslow claimed, "For their apparel, they wear breeches and stockings in one, like some Irish, which is made of deer skins, and have shoes of the same leather." Martin Pring described a Native American woman near Plymouth as wearing "a Beares skinne like an Irish Mantle over one shoulder."[30] The English also drew explicit connections between New England Indian architectural forms and those they had earlier encountered in Ireland. Upon learning that the Massachuset used underground storage pits to conserve corn supplies through harsh winters, poet William Morrell expressed concern because "the Irish long withstood / The English power, whilst they kept their food" in identical underground barns. New England Indian wigwams were likened to either small, thatched "creats" constructed by the town poor in Ulster ports like Carrickfergus (fig. 9) or "booleying houses" erected by migratory Irish cattle herdsmen in upland summer pastures. Thomas Morton observed, "The natives of New England are accustomed to build them houses much like the wild Irish. They gather poles in the woods and put the great end of them in the ground, placing them in form of a circle or circumference and, bending the tops of them in form of an arch, they bind them together with the bark of walnut trees, which is wondrous tough, so that they make the same round on the top for the smoke of their fire to ascend and pass through. These they cover with mats."[31] In addition to house forms, the plans of entire "native" villages were also superimposed in the English imagination. The circular raths or ring forts of Ulster's pre-Plantation leaders, like the fort of O'Hagan of Tullaghoge sketched by Englishman Robert Barthelet in 1600, were essentially identical to those that Native Americans from southern Maine to eastern Long Island had built prior to, and in the early days of, European settlement.[32]

With explicit analogies like these being drawn between the two native peoples, the resort to bawnlike structures in New England can only represent the extension of an established approach to the strategic problems of securing English culture in an environment believed to be essentially hostile. Admit the economic necessity of subduing new territory, the English theory of colonization argued, and adopt the rhetoric of conversion to imbue the venture with an adequately powerful cultural "mission." The resulting ambiguity of intention, blurring the distinctions between economy and religion, linking nascent commercial capitalism to Christian rebirth with a single stroke, informed the design and function of enclosed settlement strategies. Indeed, the walls of the enclosed bawn, if thick enough, might almost keep at bay aspects of English colonists' own lack of "civility" by projecting it onto the native Irish and Indians. As one New Haven town meeting noted, "Thomas Johnson said he went into the woods, intending to cut some crutches for a hovell," or a cheaply built structure not unlike the Irish creats.[33]

Convinced of the universal significance of their divine "errand," New England Puritans intensified the rhetoric of conversion and defense by building enclosures to protect entire village centers. These "pallisadoes," including one in Windsor, where Bray Rossiter had lived prior to moving to Guilford in 1651, articulated at the level of the town the concept of concentric barriers seen in the Ulster bawns (fig. 10). Town enclosures of this type were metaphorically redundant. They surrounded Christ's visible saints, who in Windsor were also the leading citizens whose house lots happened to be adjacent to the meetinghouse at the village center, with two concentric shields against the threat posed by unconverted and therefore treacherous natives. Just as John Davenport's town plan for New Haven linked the gridded efficiency of the ancient Roman *castra* to visions of the heavenly city recorded in Ezekiel and Revelation, enclosed village centers coupled the commonwealthman's craving for civic discipline with the Puritan's progress from grace, through affliction and divine judgment, to heavenly salvation.[34]

The planning of plantations opened sacred and secular meanings to public view. When John Eliot laid out the street plan of the "praying town" at Natick in 1651—a village in which Native Americans were converted to Christianity and introduced to the discipline of enclosed agriculture and nucleated settlement—his choice of a gridded plan at once invoked the economic efficiency of military design used at Londonderry and Coleraine in the late 1610s and the metaphysical

Figure 9. View of Carrickfergus showing "creats" lived in by the town poor.
From Gilbert Camblin, *The Town in Ulster* (Belfast: W. Mullan, 1951), frontispiece.

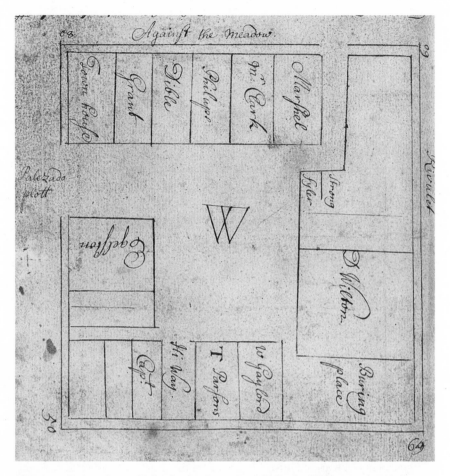

Figure 10. Matthew Grant, "Palizado plott," 1654. From "A Book of Town Ways in Windsor, 1654–1700," showing defensive enclosure constructed at center of Windsor, Connecticut, 1637. (Photo: Robert J. Bitondi, courtesy of Town Clerk's Office of Windsor)

landscape of God's immanent kingdom.[35] It was appropriate that the emblem of the church militant in early New England towns was often a fortified meetinghouse. The first Plymouth meetinghouse (ca. 1622) was outfitted with ramparts for ordnance. In 1654, in New Haven "something was propounded concerning some fortifycation aboute ye meeting house, for securitie of weomen & children"; three years later a listing of that town's ammunition supplies recorded that "the pikes [were] in a chest in the Meeting House." In 1657 the town also voted to set up "the great gunnes in the market place," linking the Christian soldier to commercial capitalism. According to local historian Sidney Perley, the "old Meeting House fort" of Boxford was enclosed in 1673 by a "stone wall five or six feet high and 'three foot brod at the botom.' . . . On the south side the wall was twelve feet, on the other three sides ten feet from the meeting-house. . . . Within this wall, at the south-east corner, a watch-house ten feet square was built." In March 1676, the town of Guilford voted "that there should be two Garrison's one att Mr Eliots house," referring to Jared's father, Joseph Eliot, and "the other at Mr Andrew Lette his house." With such an approach to sacred fortification, it was logical that ministers' houses served as garrisons during Indian attacks and that Whitfield's surviving stone house in Guilford was once part of a larger bawn complex and fitted with a cannon embrasure.[36]

The relationship of Desborough's house to its adjacent outbuildings and courtyards and the date of its construction suggest, as we have seen, a specific debt to the defensive bawn developed in England's Irish colonies. The bawn, however, implicates other defensive strategies used by English landowners during various regional conflicts in the first decades of the seventeenth century. Along the border counties in the north of England, for example, a history of civil unrest between Scottish clans and the administrators of the marchlands in Northumberland and Cumberland extended back into Elizabeth I's reign. Taking advantage of the brief interregnum between Elizabeth's death and the crowning of James I, members of Scottish clans in early 1603 engaged in looting, popular violence, and burning English property. According to the earl of Cumberland, Scots were "even from their cradells bredd and brought up in thefte, spoyle, and bloode." According to Cumberland, their assaults on English life and property warranted severe punishment. But when the pale of English common law enclosed the borders after James I imposed new administrative measures early in 1604, the Scots responded—as had the native Irish and the Welsh when the government forbade them from settling disagreements with armed force—by crowding the courts with grievances. As the bishop of Carlisle noticed, "the vulgar people [were] subtill, violent, litigious, and pursuers of endless suites by appeales, to their utter impoverishment."[37]

With English fear of Scottish incursion at a peak during the first two decades of the seventeenth century, farmers braced themselves for an anticipated influx of "uncivilized" Scots by constructing fortified dwellings termed either "bastles" or what a document of 1715 calls "peel houses," perhaps taking the name from the appeals or, as North Country dialect preferred, the "peels" that agricultural tenants would make to landlords for the renewal of labor contracts. "Inferior landholders" often lived in these houses, one description reveals, and the structures typically had "vaulted apartments to secure their living property in immediate danger, and an out[er] stair leading to upper lodgements for the family." Recent field research on peles and bastles shows these exterior stairs as very similar to the stairs rising along the rear wall of the kitchen shown on Rossiter's plan.[38]

The possible connection of the bastle and pele tradition to Desborough's Guilford house may have been fairly direct, given the close connection between Desborough, his father-in-law, Henry Whitfield, and George Fenwick. Although Whitfield had been minister at Ockley in Surrey, his family's ancestral home was at a place (either "Whitley" or, more likely, "Whitfield") near Hexham in central Northumberland. Fenwick, in charge of land patents in Connecticut, had arrived in New England on the same vessel as both Whitfield and Desborough. Fenwick was born at a bastle called "Butterknowes" at Brinkburn farther to the north along the Scottish marchlands, a landscape torn by sectional conflict since the early seventeenth century (fig. 11). The similarity of the plan of Whitfield's stone house in Guilford to early-seventeenth-century bastles at Upper Denton, Elsdon, Hepple, Otterburn, and Tarset suggests a debt to the Cumberland and Northumberland fortified house. One pele house at Haltwhistle in Northumberland has a single corner cannon opening or watchtower similar to that discovered by Ralph Smith at the Whitfield house.[39]

In the border zone between England and Scotland, designs that have been credited to English origin may actually have been Scottish contributions. Fortified houses in Cumberland and Northumberland probably derived from late medieval pele houses and tower houses in Scotland and Ireland. According to Brian K. Davison, these structures represent a "compromise between comfort and security where the sudden raid is feared more than the prolonged siege." In most cases, tower houses were conceived vertically, as a series of rooms one on top of the other, an arrangement that minimized chances for attack and forcible entry at the ground floor. However, given the traffic patterns present in a tower house, ensuring privacy could be difficult. Privacy could only be protected by additional rooms or wings called "jambs" in Scots dialect. One jamb would result in an L plan and two, as in a tower house at Borthwick in Lothian, in a U configuration (fig. 12). The Desborough and Whitfield houses and the fortified structures of England's border counties have earlier roots in Scotland. The rear kitchen ell at the Whitfield house may be related to the single jamb; as Davison observes, "if the tower is provided with a wing or 'jamb,' the kitchen will be in it." The defensive enclosure surrounding the Desborough house may have its earliest antecedent in late medieval structures in the Scottish marches, for around these houses "there is usually a small walled yard (a 'barmkin' in Scotland, a 'bawn' in Ireland)," which was "intended to house not men-at-arms but sheep and cattle."[40]

These variations in Scottish domestic planning are typically downplayed as likely sources for English architectural ideas. Perhaps this is due to a reluctance on the part of English scholars to admit that their own culture owes a design debt to one of England's colonized peoples. Davison describes the processes of appropriation and subsequent reclamation and revitalization that reveal Scotland as a crucial source for late-sixteenth- and seventeenth-century English fortified houses. "The basic idea—that of a fairly complete house, built room upon room to

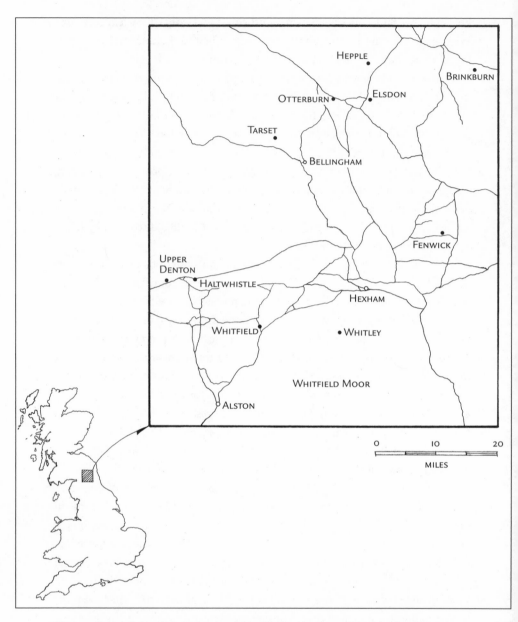

Figure 11. England's Northumberland marchlands, showing sites of surviving bastles and pele houses with connections to Samuel Desborough or early Guilford. Shaded circles represent extant bastle and pele sites; unshaded circles signify large country towns. (Map by the author)

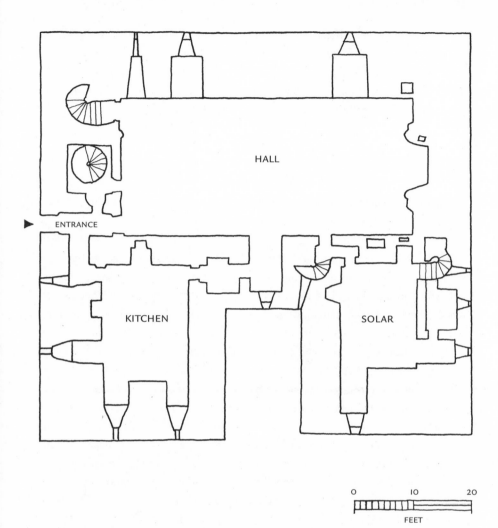

HALL

ENTRANCE

KITCHEN

SOLAR

0   10   20

FEET

Figure 12. Tower house at Borthwick, Lothian, Scotland, fifteenth century (after Brian K. Davison, *The Observer's Book of Castles* [London: Frederick Warne, 1979], 123). (Drawing by the author)

achieve a fair measure of security, but not intended to withstand serious siege— was not confined to Scotland and Ireland," he maintains. In particular, "it was accepted also in England, where it was carried to a considerable degree of sophistication. But it was in Scotland that the idea was continued longest, the later sixteenth and seventeenth centuries seeing an exuberant revival of tower house building for reasons that were social and political rather than military."[41] Elsewhere in England local tensions resulted in defensive structures with surrounding enclosures and cannon placements. Landowners in Westmoreland built pele towers as part of ordinary hall houses. Along the southern coasts of Cornwall, Devon, and Dorset, as well as along the Severn estuary, West Country landowners fortified their farmsteads to protect their estates from periodic raids by coastal pirates plying their shores. Pistol loops were pierced through a defensive platform adjacent to one farmer's house near Hartland in north Devon.[42]

CHANGING PLANS

Each of these fortified compounds, whether in Ireland, Scotland, or England, had a house at its experiential center. The form of the dwelling house Desborough built—located between his "greate Court," inner "Court," and "greene Corte"—deserves special comment. Its center is dominated by a narrow passage that cuts through the house from one side to another. From that cross passage, a visitor moving through the front door could turn right to enter the large kitchen, which had a large working hearth on its gable wall. The "porch to the stayres" was probably an exterior, covered stair connecting the inner court to the second floor or chamber level of the house. This stair allowed servants access from the inner courtyard to lodging chambers over the kitchen without entering the main body of the house, attesting to the role that spatial arrangements often played in segregating the householders from their perceived social inferiors. Across the cross passage lay the hall, a room equal in size to the kitchen and heated only by a small hearth backing onto the passage. To the right as one entered the hall was a small, unlabeled room that may have contained a small stair leading to the hall chamber overhead. Beyond the hall lay a small heated parlor, directly behind which was a small storage room, or "buttery," and another set of stairs that provided the family with a still more private means of reaching their bedchambers. In summary, Desborough's house consisted of a kitchen, cross passage, hall, and parlor. The three principal ground-floor rooms all had their own chimneys. Separate stairs led from each of these rooms to separate chambers in the floor above. A large garret ran the length of the house beneath the roof. Doorways, passages, and stair locations together emphasize the larger role that domestic architecture plays in articulating social rank and providing controlled settings for rituals of status change.

The plan of Desborough's house differs dramatically from surviving post-medieval houses in colonial New England. With the exception of a house built by the Clarke and Lake trading company at Arrowsic, Maine, in 1654, no related examples have been found.[43] The English sources for it warrant attention. It presents a paradox, since most published examples of this house type come from Dorset, east Devon, and especially southern Somerset, emphatically not from the area of

West Cambridgeshire where Desborough had been raised. Instead, the West Country was precisely where Bray Rossiter had been born and lived for twenty years. If anyone could be expected to build a cross-passage house, it might have been Rossiter and not Desborough.[44] Or would it? There is no reason why Desborough could not have built such a structure, although in order to argue he did I need to question the assumption that England's cultural landscape falls conveniently into "lowland" and "highland" zones.

Ever since the publication of Cyril F. Fox's influential *The Personality of Britain* (1932), students of vernacular architecture have followed geographers and agricultural historians in splitting England into a lowland zone in the south and east and a highland zone in the west and north. These respective zones seem distinct in many ways. The lowland zone consists of well-drained, arable acreage, with rich chalk loams and clay supporting a market-oriented mixed economy of cereal cultivation and livestock raising. Common fields surrounded nucleated villages. By contrast, the highland zone is characterized by open, windier landscapes. Its economic mainstays were grazing and dairying. Landholdings were more dispersed and densely settled centers few and far between.[45]

Regional differences in standards of housing were apparent even by the late sixteenth century. In the 1580s Richard Carew observed that the Cornish husbandman "conformithe himselfe with a better supplied civilitie *to the Easterne pattern*," and William Harrison in Essex claimed that domestic technology was "not very much amended as yet in some parts of Bedfordshire and elsewhere further off *from our Southern parts*."[46] While these comments seem clear, Fox owed the idea of "zones" more to earlier scholars than to period documentation. Sydney E. Jones included a "Map of England shewing the principal Geological Divisions," among them soil types and locally available building materials, in his *The Village Homes of England* (1912). The purpose of this map, which Jones argued "forms the key to this volume," was to break the highly varied local landscape of England into five "geological areas" unified by the materials builders had at hand. These areas were (1) the bordering counties of Somerset, Dorset, and Wiltshire; (2) parts of Berkshire and Buckinghamshire; (3) Oxford, Northamptonshire, and Rutland; (4) Hertfordshire, Essex, Cambridge, and Suffolk; and (5) the northern counties of Yorkshire, Lancashire, and Derbyshire. As Jones argued, local carpenters and masons had to accept the geological patterns and built a vernacular architecture in which "harmony with nature" was "all-pervading." "Tradition, or ancient custom, considered as an influence on cottage building, has left its evidence in material form." Following Jones and Fox, local studies approached ordinary houses through a geological approach, as J. Archibald's *Kentish Architecture as Influenced by Geology* (1934) makes apparent. Yet the risk in such an approach was also clear: that vernacular buildings would be viewed through the lens of a geological determinism that would create typologies based on local materials but disregard the connections that plans had to other regions. Jones's 1912 map remained influential enough to be reprinted almost verbatim in Olive Cook and Edwin Smith's *English Cottages and Farmhouses* (1955).[47]

According to defenders of the "zone" approach, preconditions of local social structure merged with economic differences to make postmedieval housing in these two areas in part regionally distinctive as well. Students of vernacular architecture have sketched a complicated picture linking the timing of architectural change to the rhythms of commercial capitalism in the English national economy. Current approaches to exploring how vernacular houses indexed the progress of commercial capitalism began with W. G. Hoskins's assertion in 1953 that a "revolution in housing" swept across the English countryside in the decades from 1570 to 1640. In this "great rebuilding" a rising cohort of bourgeois freeholders or yeomen enlarged existing houses, rebuilt others, or tore down outmoded structures and built entirely new ones in their place. Hoskins argued that as England's commercial economy grew fat with the export of textiles and foodstuffs to the Continent, yeomen involved in market agriculture garnered a surplus that they reinvested in such status objects as "modernized" housing and new interior furnishings.[48]

Economic shifts that put surplus cash in the hands of independent freeholders, including the progress of enclosure and the emergence of an open market in land and speculation in real estate, affected earliest the houses in England's southeastern counties and those belonging to the wealthiest 10 percent of yeomen. Yet as Robert Machin, Barbara Hutton, and N. W. Alcock have demonstrated, market capitalism and architectural change came more slowly and unevenly to England's western and northern counties. In these areas greater variation in domestic improvement was the norm throughout the seventeenth and into the eighteenth century, as people sought both to signal their participation in the national economy and to retain local preferences in room use, household economy, and domestic discipline.[49] One's precise place in the economy and the landscape often meant that Hoskins's architectural "revolution" was less often a dramatic change than a slow, selective process.

No matter where and when change came, the effects were similar. Local preferences modified the pace of housing reform, but the number of function-specific rooms generally increased as parlors, dining rooms, nurseries, studies, galleries, and a host of new spaces drew functions away from the old, multipurpose late medieval hall. Chimneys inserted into old open-hall houses contained the smoke and soot that previously had wafted upward to blacken the timbers of open-hall houses and made houses cleaner and brighter inside. Chimneys also permitted open halls to have ceilings inserted, which in turn allowed the partitioning of additional sleeping chambers. These new spaces granted more bodily privacy to individuals and a greater sense of social segregation between the landowner's family and the mixed company of tenants, hired day laborers, and unemployed vagrants in spaces on the ground floor.[50]

The exact placement of chimneys in either remodeled or new houses, however, varied from region to region. Beginning in the mid-sixteenth century and lasting through the end of migration to New England a century later, chimney stacks appeared in smaller houses with increasing frequency across England. The aged Essex villagers William Harrison talked to in the 1580s noticed "the multitude of chimneys lately erected, whereas in our young days there were not above two or three, if so many, in most uplandish towns of the realm (the religious houses and manor places of their lords always excepted, and peradventure some great personages)."[51] The basic difference between highland and lowland plan types followed from a single social decision: the location of chimneys and the interior placement of hearths shaped how the household would deal with the newest arena of bourgeois social exclusion — the parlor.

Faced with the challenge of modernizing an outdated house or constructing an entirely new one, builders in England's "uplandish" zone usually located a chimney on the partition that backed onto the cross passage; in this position the chimney could have only one hearth that warmed the hall. By locating the hearth at the lower end of the hall near the passage door, the highland-zone family opted not to heat the parlor; it often remained a sleeping chamber or a storage room.[52] They instead placed the chimney where members of the household economy — including laborers and servants — could gain easy access both to the kitchen hearth for meals and to the hall, still the center of family social life. The popularity of this chimney placement may be due to less vertically stratified social structures in isolated highland-zone communities. However, the vision of an "organic" society it inscribed was blurred. It also enabled the head of household to maintain more effective surveillance over his dependents and build an ideology of community that would enhance his own prestige.

Lowland-zone builders put the chimney in a different place. They located the stack on the partition (or in timber houses, in the structural bay) between the hall and the parlor. Both rooms thus had hearths. Unlike their highland counterparts, lowland householders often left the lower service room unheated. The resulting plan arranged an unheated service room, a cross passage, a heated hall that sometimes now functioned as a working kitchen, and a heated parlor whose use was restricted to members of the immediate family and their invited social peers. Here the hall hearth lay on the wall opposite the cross passage. In the more densely populated villages of the lowland zone, householders needed to demarcate differences in social status by creating an atmosphere of social distance in the hall and even more so in the distant parlor. Laborers, renters, and servants, if they gathered to take a meal in the hall or sit with the householder at the fire, had to collect at the upper end of the room. Acutely aware that every step taken toward his family's more private parlor was a sign of preference, the householder could establish minute increments of rank through the careful admission of neighbors and servants to his hall hearth, his heated parlor, and, finally, the most exclusive room of all—the heated parlor chamber.

What made these two ways of rebuilding postmedieval houses different? As Eric Mercer maintains, lowland- and highland-zone house forms addressed the maintenance of both community and social segregation in precise terms. "Where there was a heated parlour," Mercer explains,

> that room was intended as a place for some of the occupants and users of the house to retire to; the third room was not intended as a kitchen; and the main room for both these reasons had much less of the nature of the hall and more the nature of a kitchen. In the house with an unheated parlour the main room was occupied by everyone and remained more of a hall, and because there was another kitchen fireplace in the third room it became less of a kitchen. The differing forms of the through-passage correspond with the presence or absence of a heated parlour and the nature of the parlour reflects the needs of the owner. The variations in these needs from region to region may be supposed to reflect differences in social relationship and in particular the gulf between the "family" and the "hands."[53]

The parlor-hall hearths of the lowland house marked it as a specialized adaptation to the more status-conscious social structures of communities in southern and eastern England, villages whose residents had by 1630 already seen decades of migrants arriving from the depressed local economies of the highland zone looking for work. Early New England households only rarely had to contend with migrant laborers. But the common practice of taking local children as apprentices made distinguishing between members of the household and members of the householder's immediate family especially problematic. In New England the arrangement of rooms and the protected status of the parlor helped to make social positions apparent.[54]

Common lowland houses continued to transform as the social needs of householders changed. Three-room houses that retained a cross passage but had a chimney located between the hall and the parlor—including a dated 1581 example in Whitfield's pastoral town of Ockley, Surrey—were perhaps most common in the late sixteenth and early seventeenth centuries (fig. 13a, b). Some people so desired the exclusivity of their heated parlors that they punched an exterior door directly into it so they could directly receive polite guests without attracting attention from others at home. The original section of Manor Farm at Pulham and a house at Winfarthing in Norfolk retain their exterior parlor doors (fig. 13c, d). Others located a new "lobby entry" into the chimney bay, providing a private family entrance into the upper end of the house apart from the mixed company of farm laborers and servants. This new door could coexist with the old cross passage, resulting in a house with two entrances built in old and New England (fig. 14). The facade announced the segregation of household members within.[55]

Based on surviving evidence, most lowland householders opted only for the lobby entry between the hall and parlor. With a heated parlor they could withdraw socially from other family members. From that point forward, the days of the common cross-passage entry were numbered, and the ancient feature finally was sacrificed in the name of increased privacy for the bourgeois nuclear family. Eliminating the cross passage demoted the social status of the service rooms and occasional working kitchen in the house's lower end, since it lost the front and rear doors that had publicly marked its location and made handling supplies, animals, and fuel much easier. With the disappearance of the old cross passage, the only social membrane remaining between the service rooms, including in some houses the working hearth, and hall was a light partition.

One step remained in demoting service rooms to a completely secondary status. As early as the 1590s homeowners relocated the service and kitchen functions from the lower end of the building to its rear elevation. A pivotal change resulted. Whether they configured it in a projecting "T" or "L" or in a lean-to, people moved their service space(s) to the house's rear. The house now consisted of a hall and parlor entered through a small lobby in front of a central chimney. Across the entire rear of the house ran a lean-to or "outshot" containing various domestic functions—a dairy, chamber, or cheese room—and sometimes the working kitchen hearth opening off the back of the central chimney (fig. 15). Tucked neatly behind a newly balanced facade, the realm of women's work was both hidden from public view and convenient to patriarchal surveillance.

The continuous outshot plan appeared in southeastern England during the last decades of the sixteenth century and so was fully evolved in England before emigration to New England began. Extant room-by-room inventories suggest that it was already common in Massachusetts and Connecticut by the mid-1640s, although rear kitchen hearths remained a statistical rarity until the turn of the eighteenth century. Most of Guilford's early settlers had come from the Wealden areas of Surrey, Sussex, and especially Kent in southeastern England, where internal chimney houses popular since the last quarter of the sixteenth century provided a ready model for domestic arrangements in early Connecticut. Guilford's Comfort Starr house was continuous with their English experience (fig. 16).[56]

In England and New England alike, the removal of service spaces to the rear of

Figure 13. English three-room houses with chimneys inserted between halls and parlors, but which retain cross passages as primary entry and exit: (a) Trout's farm, Ockley, Sussex, late fifteenth century, with dated modifications of 1581 (chimney inserted and hall range rebuilt; after Eric Mercer, *English Vernacular Houses* [London: Royal Commission on Historical Monuments, 1975], 207, fig. 176); (b) house at Kidlington, Oxfordshire, late seventeenth century (after Mercer, *English Vernacular Houses*, 52, fig. 34); (c) original section of Manor Farm, Pulham, Norfolk, early seventeenth century, with secondary parlor entrance; (d) house at Short Green, Winfarthing, Norfolk, early seventeenth century, with secondary parlor entrance (after Mercer, *English Vernacular Houses*, 55, fig. 40). (Drawing by the author)

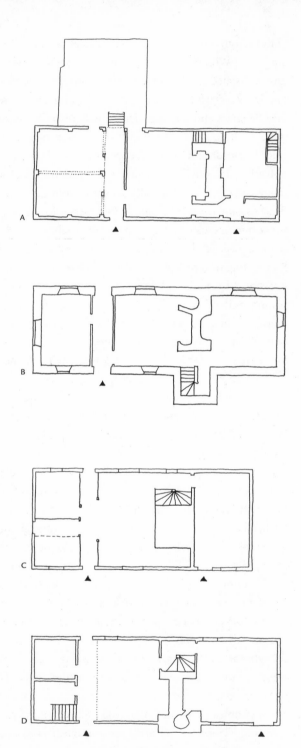

0   10   20

FEET

Figure 14. Detail of map of John Winthrop's "Ten Hills" farm, Massachusetts, 1637. Ink on paper, H. 29½" (74.9 cm), W. 11⅝" (29 cm). (Photo: Massachusetts Historical Society)

the house normally called for a back door that opened directly into the lean-to. Yet in New England, especially in the Connecticut River valley and western New England, the removal of the service rooms sometimes did not preclude leaving the old door in the lower end of the hall—the door that would have opened onto the old cross passage—as the secondary entrance; this door appears most often on the lower (or hall) end gable of the house, near the front corner (fig. 17). Evidence of the earliest end-gable door appears in surviving framing at the Austin-Lord house

Figure 15. English houses with central chimneys and continuous outshots or lean-tos: (a) Glebe Cottage, Hampshire (after R. H. Cake and Elizabeth Lewis, "Paulsgrove House and Seventeenth-Century House Plans in Hampshire and West Sussex," *Post-Medieval Archaeology* 6 [1972]: 169, fig. 77); (b) Yew Tree Cottage, Harbledown, Kent, mid-seventeenth century (after Mercer, *English Vernacular Houses*, 71, fig. 58); (c) Holme Green, Yorkshire, early seventeenth century (after Barbara Hutton, "Timber-Framed Houses in the Vale of York," *Medieval Archaeology* 17 [1973]: 89, fig. 39b); (d) LeBreton Farm, Hampshire, ca. 1630–60 (after Cake and Lewis, "Paulsgrove House," 169, fig. 77). (Drawing by the author)

A
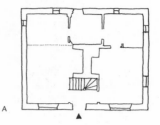

B
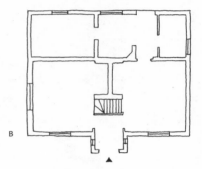

C
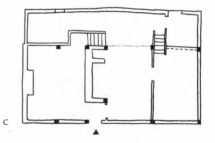

D
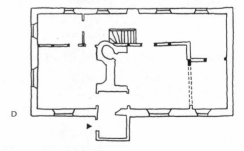

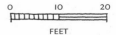

0   10   20

FEET

Figure 16. Comfort Starr's house, Guilford, Connecticut, ca. 1700–1710, showing wall framing and infill of structure. (Photo: Society for the Preservation of New England Antiquities)

in Ipswich, Massachusetts (ca. 1637), and suggests that not all social features of the old cross passage had been effectively eliminated from lowland houses during the early seventeenth century. In western New England the remnant entrance from the old cross passage appeared on end gables as early as the late 1660s and persisted as the preferred informal or direct entry into the 1830s. Traveling from Plymouth, Massachusetts, to Wethersfield in 1789, Samuel Davis remarked disdainfully that the houses he saw as he arrived in the Connecticut River valley had "a door on the end near the front door, which look[ed] awkward." Even though the cross passage had been eliminated, the end-gable door, wherever it appears, signals the persistence of a subtle hegemony of householders mixing informally and "identifying" with their social inferiors. It appears most commonly in the Connecticut River valley, where leading "River God" families exercised precisely such influence on patterns of local deference. A descendant of these deities recalled how her father, "born too soon to relish the freedoms of democracy," insisted on segregating his acquaintances according to the door they were permitted to use. "I have seen his brow lower when a free-and-easy mechanic came to the front door," Catherine Sedgwick recalled, "and upon one occasion I remember his turning off the 'east steps' (I am sure not kicking, but the demonstration was unequivocal) a grown-up lad who kept his hat on after being told to take it off." These houses, which announced a front door that restricts and controls access but provided an end-gable (or back) door for informal, easy entrance by neighbors and servants, were socially ambivalent, their formal type and actual use in conflict.[57]

DEMOGRAPHY AND APPROPRIATION

The intensification of demographic pressures on the southeastern counties suggests that long-distance migration from the north and west to London was common by the beginning of the seventeenth century. Owing to the London metropolitan area's primacy in foreign and domestic trade, in craft production, and as a port of embarkation for colonial departures, a constant stream of people, some landless and poor seeking only subsistence but others economically stable searching for better business connections, a payoff in heightened status and property, or a chance for a merchant to marry well and move into landed society, traveled from provincial towns and rural hamlets to the city. Letters to colonists in New England contain estimates of the number of emigrants leaving London. Pausing at the height of the New England migration, Edward Howes wrote John Winthrop Jr. in June 1636, "'Tis reported that about 57,000 people have left this citty & suburbs within this 3 moneths."[58] Others took to the road when pressures in their rural villages proved too much; putting children out to service was resisted by some husbandmen, while the adverse impact of inheritance customs such as primogeniture on luckless second and third sons meant that staying put would ensure only grating poverty. One resident of Newcastle remarked in 1597, "Sundry [people are] starving and dying in our streets and in the fields for want of bread"; local records confirm that in September and October of that year twenty-five "poore folkes . . . died for want in the streets."[59]

Because of a higher rate of mortality than of birth, crises due to epidemic diseases, and out-migration rates, London and larger country towns actually came to depend on long-distant migrants to fill empty places in their urban economies. This movement of people across England to its "lowland" capital was a definitive sign of its expanding commercial and social significance, but even more dramatic explosions in population often occurred in smaller market towns in Essex, Suffolk, Surrey, Kent, and Norfolk close enough to London to feel its towering influence. When trade was strong, they received a jolt of demographic energy as profits in second-level gathering and distribution attracted outsiders. Migrants to Kent, for example, included some poor artisans who had tramped hundreds of miles in search of work. Indeed, London and Coventry had by the early sixteenth

Figure 17. House, West Granville, Massachusetts, ca. 1770–80, with end-gable door leading to original hall. (Photo by the author)

century already been so overburdened by tramping vagrants, attracted by em-ployment and by poor relief, that they passed ordinances against them.[60]

What seems remarkable is that architectural historians can continue to nurture a mythology of lowland- and highland-zone house types—as if the regions were distinct—while social historians have demonstrated a level of demographic change and population mobility that was unprecedented in early-seventeenth-century English society. The imagined purity of highland and lowland house forms is complicated by an obvious problem: houses supposedly specific to each zone simply do not appear only where they should. Three-room highland houses with a heated kitchen and hall and an unheated parlor—which English scholars term a "type F" plan—can be found in Dorset, Somerset, Oxfordshire, North-amptonshire, Leicestershire, Lincolnshire, and as far east as Buckinghamshire and Hertfordshire (fig. 18); smaller relatives of one- and two-room plans also appear from Cornwall to Oxfordshire to northern Northamptonshire (fig. 19). Arguing that many house forms now often associated with the highland zone once ap-peared more widely to the south and east, Peter Eden has even predicted that an early-seventeenth-century "type F" house would turn up in West Cambridgeshire and adjacent areas of Huntingdonshire.[61]

Lowland houses also appeared in unpredictable places. The earliest lobby-entry house was built not in Essex or Kent but at Kneeshall in Nottinghamshire, be-tween 1522 and 1539. A recent discovery in northeast Wales suggests the lobby-

Figure 18. English three-room ("type F") houses with heated halls but unheated parlors and (probably) external kitchens: (a) house at 20 High Street, Corby, Northamptonshire, 1609 (after Peter Eden, "Post-Medieval Houses in Eastern England," in *East Anglian Studies*, ed. Lionel M. Munby [Cambridge: W. Heffer & Sons, 1968], fig. 4); (b) Beach Tree House, Lower Middleton Cheney, Oxfordshire, ca. 1640 (after Raymond Wood-Jones, *Traditional Domestic Architecture of the Banbury Region* [Manchester: Manchester University Press, 1963], 89, fig. 18); (c) house at South Dalton, Yorkshire, early seventeenth century (after Hutton, "Timber-Framed Houses in the Vale of York," 89, fig. 39c). Heated halls and kitchens, but unheated parlors: (d) manor house, Hornton, Oxfordshire, dated 1607 (after Wood-Jones, *Traditional Domestic Architecture of the Banbury Region*, 83, fig. 17); (e) house at Stalbridge, Dorset, ca. 1600–1620 (after *An Inventory of Historic Monuments in the County of Dorset*, vol. 5, *East Dorset* [London: Her Majesty's Stationery Office, 1975], xlvi); (f) house at King's Cliff, Northamptonshire, seventeenth century (after M. V. J. Seaborne, "Small Stone Houses in Northamptonshire," *Northamptonshire Past and Present* 3, no. 4 [1963]: 150); (g) house at Thenford, Northamptonshire, dated 1638 (after Wood-Jones, *Traditional Domestic Architecture of the Banbury Region*, 143, fig. 38). (Drawing by the author)

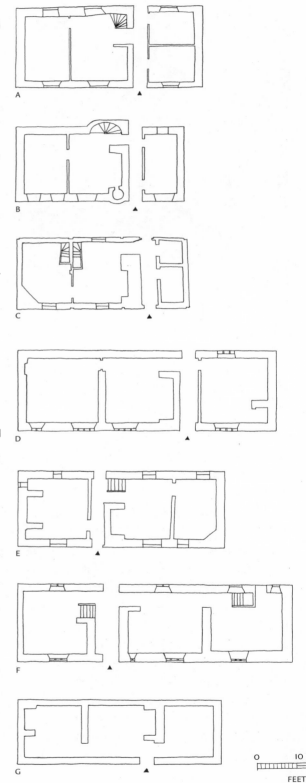

A

B

C

D

E

F

G

0   10

FEET

entry type may have been built there as early a s1580–1600. The suitability of the form to situations where neighbors might be strangers may have underlain its use to house Irish tenants at Moneymore in county Londonderry in 1615. A house at Sulgrave, Northamptonshire, dated 1636 demonstrates that the form won converts in the north and west among bourgeois yeomen whose lives were growing increasingly calibrated to the commercial economy and was an available option even there by the time emigration to New England was in full stride. Jonathan Fairbanks, a wheelwright from Sowerby, Yorkshire, built a house in the late 1630s in Dedham, Massachusetts, that began as a three-room plan with an internal chimney, lobby entry, parlor, hall, and an unheated lower service chamber. By 1668, however, this service room had been sacrificed for a rear lean-to that, though never functioning as a rear kitchen, still allowed Fairbanks to project an image of order out front that masked the "lumber" and disorder that rear storage spaces contained.[62]

However analytical the "regional zone" argument initially appears, it identifies social groups in terms of the cultural texts they share. It makes apparent two theories central to the work of English scholars. By embracing an essentially geological view of houses made of organic, local materials in harmony with nature, early-twentieth-century English scholars like Jones, Archibald, and Cook and Smith effectively removed their subject from the realm of social agency. By interpreting differences in lowland and highland zones as signs of shifting regional economies (mixed cultivation versus dairying, differing access to migrant labor supply, the relative spread and local acceptance of commercial capitalism, and so on), more recent English scholars working in Fox's long shadow—including Hoskins, Barley, Machin, Hutton, and Alcock—somehow leave houses suspended above culture as lived, especially when interpreting the crucial intermingling of Celtic and Anglo-Saxon traditions. Fox, for example, carefully avoided any equation of the highland zone with Celtic and the lowland zone with Anglo-Saxon cultural forces. For him the highland zone was economically more backward and conservative, while the lowland zone was dynamic, the engine of all capitalist progress in land tenure and marketing. Hoskins acknowledged that highland-zone patterns originated in the pastoral economy of "Celtic" culture, and those of the lowland zone bore the imprint of "Anglo-Saxon" clustered settlement and arable farming. But he never brought the two into sustained contact and so was able to imagine certain index architectural features—the highland zone's "long-house" or byre dwelling, for example—as inhabiting a neatly segregated and pure cultural world, even though it emerged precisely where the two historical cultures converged (fig. 20). Such a view grants dangerous priority to a nostalgia for ethnically pure highland (Celtic) and lowland (Anglo-Saxon) cultures and not their constant interaction. The "zone" argument is thus continuous with an antimod-

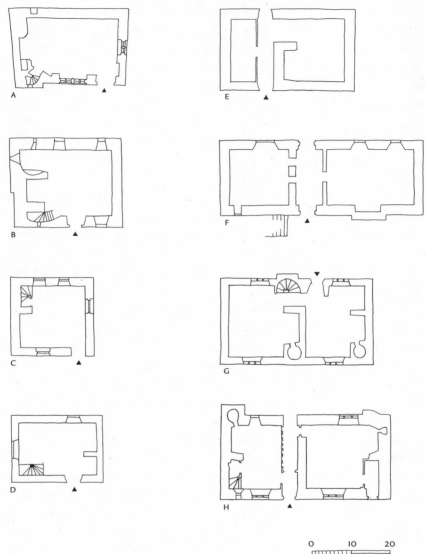

A

E

B

F

C

G

D

H

O   IO   20

FEET

ernism that has informed the study of vernacular architecture from its inception in the mid-nineteenth century, to the country-life, antiurban social milieu that surrounded the young Hoskins, to the enthusiasm many contemporary scholars feel more for rural building traditions than urban ones.[63] This bias should not be surprising, however, given the postimperial reluctance of the English to grant interpretive weight to the presence of Celtic culture within their own borders. I wonder about its impact on architectural study. Are England's ambivalent views on Northern Ireland, Welsh and Scottish nationalist movements, and the revival

Figure 19. Smaller English houses ("type F" subgroups) of single-cell plan with heated hall: (a) Priest's house, Easton-on-the-Hill, Northamptonshire, early sixteenth century (after *An Inventory of the Historical Monuments in the County of Northampton*, vol. 6, *Architectural Monuments in North Northamptonshire* [London: Royal Commission on Historical Monuments, 1984], 59, fig. 80); (b) house (now outbuilding) at Yeo Farm, Chagford, Devon, late sixteenth century (after Mercer, *English Vernacular Houses*, 29, fig. 22); (c) house at Harringworth, Northamptonshire, seventeenth century (after *An Inventory of the Historical Monuments in the County of Northampton*, vol. 6, *Architectural Monuments in North Northamptonshire*, 87, fig. 108); (d) house at Upper Benefield, Northamptonshire, seventeenth century (after M. V. J. Seaborne, "Small Stone Houses in Northamptonshire," *Northamptonshire Past and Present* 3, no. 4 [1963]: 148). Double-cell plan with heated hall: (e) house at King's Sutton, Northamptonshire, ca. 1550 (after Wood-Jones, *Traditional Domestic Architecture of the Banbury Region*, 56, fig. 11); (f) house at Truthall near Helston, Cornwall, late fifteenth century (after E. M. Jope, "Cornish Houses, 1400–1700," in Jope, *Studies in Building History*, 199, fig. 10.3). Double cell with heated hall and parlor: (g) house at Sycamore Terrace, Bloxham, Oxfordshire, ca. 1625 (after Wood-Jones, *Traditional Domestic Architecture of the Banbury Region*, 108, fig. 24); (h) house at King's Sutton, Northamptonshire, early seventeenth century (after Wood-Jones, *Traditional Domestic Architecture of the Banbury Region*, 56, fig. 11). (Drawing by the author)

of the Manx language strangely linked to the denials implicit in the study of folk housing?

What struck with equal force, once I changed my perspective, was how frequent exceptions to the either-or logic of the zones actually are. The extreme heterogeneity of the seventeenth-century English landscape becomes apparent. People in one place appropriated plans and room designations they found worked well someplace else. Strategies of appropriation and borrowing seem as significant as images of regional integrity, and, given the extent and intensity of migration throughout England—but especially from the north and west to the south and east (and London)—between 1570 and 1640, houses that violate the highland-lowland divide come as no surprise. Modernizing his medieval house at North Cray, a Kentish yeoman in the late sixteenth century inserted a chimney that backed onto the cross passage in highland-zone fashion. So did another farmer at White Roding in Essex. Still another house modernized in the late sixteenth century at Barton in West Cambridgeshire resulted, according to one architectural historian, in a design that simply "does not conform to the typologies of late medieval houses in the area."[64]

New England merchants and ministers from the London area built mansions in Boston and Guilford with direct entries to shape an image of hospitality that would enhance their public stature. The plan of Guilford's Whitfield house, for example, falls within an English West Country or highland-zone tradition marked by end-gable chimneys and a "direct entry" or socially open principal ground-floor room; the extreme legibility of its asymmetrical facade allowed visitors to penetrate its interior order with ease. Because of its relative transparency,

Figure 20. Higher Uppacott Farm, Poundsgate, Widecombe-in-the-Moor, Devon, ca. 1570. (Photo by the author)

this West Country plan was soon appropriated by ambitious, would-be elites in both England and its colonies eager to adapt the open plan to their own neofeudal strategies of household hospitality. This seems to have been the case for Henry Whitfield, who came from Surrey. Other early "manor" houses in early America that drew on this concept include the brick mansions of merchant Arthur Allen in Surry County, Virginia (see fig. 7b), and merchant Peter Sargent in Boston. The plans of alms houses, slave houses, and workers' housing were appropriated across regional boundaries because they allowed greater surveillance over people. East Anglian merchants seem to have had oversight in mind when they built highland-zone, direct-entry houses in the "Rows" at Great Yarmouth for their fishery workers in the 1630s.[65]

COMMERCIAL CONNECTIONS

Spatial strategies of New England merchants, whether to protect property or maintain close watch on other people, introduce a second kind of place implicated in the Rossiter plan: early-seventeenth-century quadrangular residences like those designed by Inigo Jones and his followers. The wealthy London backers of the Ulster Plantations and the New England colonies were familiar with Jones's arcaded domestic facades and his enclosures for the duke of Bedford's property at Covent Garden. As merchants, they were familiar with the stylish arcades that lined the interior court of the Royal Exchange. As investors in plantations in Antrim, Tyrone, and Londonderry, they probably also knew the similar arcades lining the piazzas of Coleraine's stylish High Street and the exterior of a fortification built in Londonderry's central market square.[66]

Other early architects also adapted Renaissance forms to the needs of English householders. In designing a small London house for a "Mr. Diball" in 1622, John Smythson employed an urban courtyarded plan (fig. 21). He placed the hall and parlor along the street facade, and a passage pierced through a central chimney offers access to an "Inner Courte," around which cluster the principal service rooms, including milk house, bake house, brew house, kitchen, and larder. A pair of large staircases directly behind the front rooms allowed family members to reach chambers above, and secondary stairs at the rear corners of the courtyard were for servants. Along the rear range of the courtyard a pair of rooms, whose function remains unspecified, probably offered additional apartments from which family and guests could view gardens laid out directly behind the structure.[67]

The designs of architects such as Jones and Smythson are striking for their enthusiastic appropriation of Continental antecedents. The generation of English architects that flourished in London between 1600 and 1640, as had Italian and

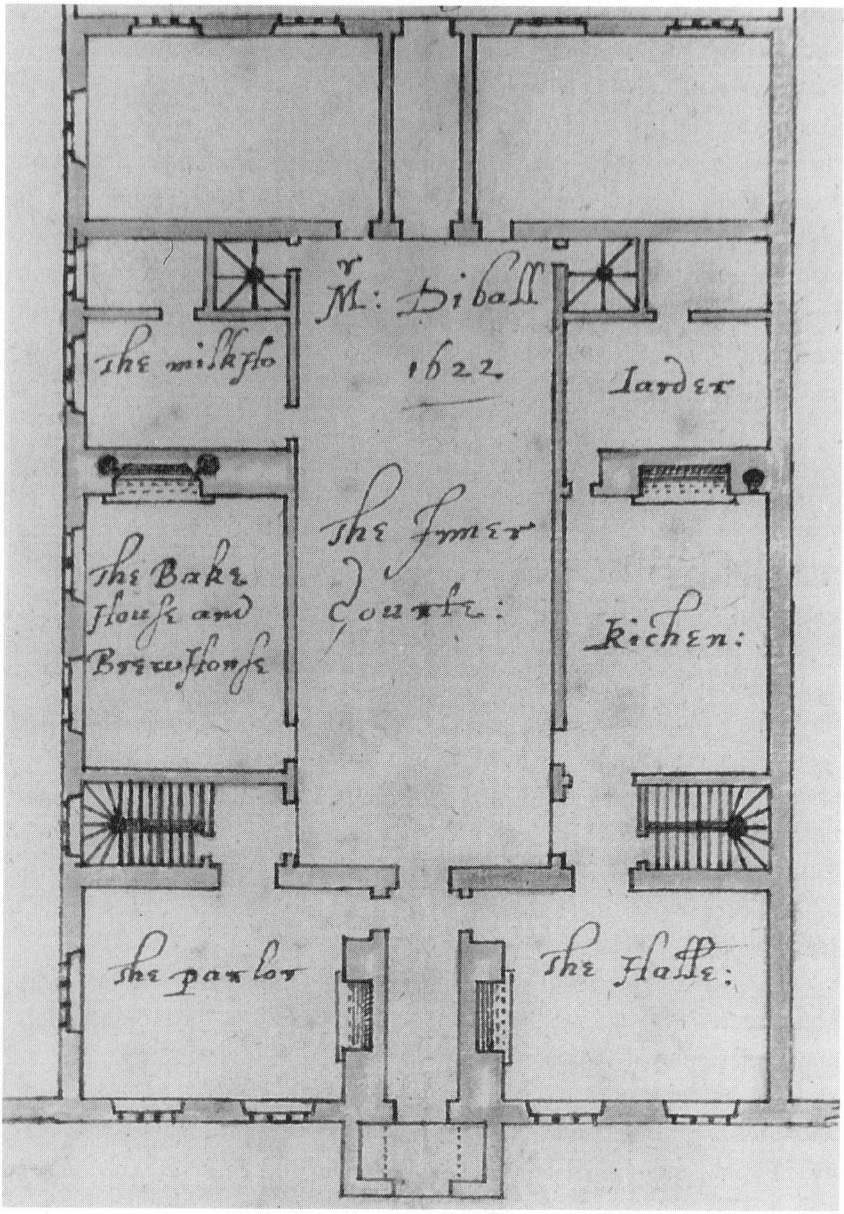

Figure 21. John Smythson, plan of London town house for "Mr. Diball 1622." (Photo: British Architectural Library, Royal Institute of British Architects, London)

French architects decades earlier, saw in the designs of classical antiquity a lost perfection, a "natural" fusion of Vitruvian rationalism and nostalgic virtue linked to classical Roman republicanism. They saw in architectural reform a promise of civic humanist social reform. The house for Diball, for example, derives directly from the mid-sixteenth-century designs of Sebastiano Serlio—whose *Five Books of Architecture* (written during Serlio's 1528–40 sojourn in Venice) Jones also relied on heavily—and from designs of French town houses that were being copied by London merchants from examples they had seen in Paris and in the textile trading centers of Rouen and St. Malo. French urban prototypes became more widely available to modish consumers with the publication of Pierre Le Muet's *Maniere de bastir pour touttes sortes de personnes* in 1623.[68]

The Francophile architectural preferences of English merchants ensured that Continental courtyarded designs arrived in England before the pattern books by Serlio or Le Muet circulated among the landed gentry. Built in London, Oxford, Exeter, Totnes, and perhaps Southampton as early as the 1550s by cloth drapers in the French trade, these fashionable structures were quickly copied by England's hereditary aristocracy in both town and country (fig. 22a–c). These builders were worried about having their public display of power and social legitimacy eclipsed by a group of ostentatious, cosmopolitan merchants intent on blurring social distinctions. By the mid-1560s, for example, Sir William Petre, Elizabeth I's secretary of state, had chosen a courtyarded plan to lend formal coherence to his London town house on Aldersgate Street and his rural retreat at Ingatestone Hall in Essex. Likewise, Sir Thomas Hewett drew upon the small courtyard design for his house at Sawbridgeworth in Hertfordshire, constructed between 1567 and 1590. The early acceptance of the design among the English gentry also may have played a role in the eventual definition of the colonial Irish bawn; Thomas Butler, earl of Ormonde, opted for a courtyarded plan when he built his house at Carrich-on-Suir in county Tiperary in 1565.[69]

When sixteenth- and early-seventeenth-century merchants appropriated these Continental forms to their occupational and social needs, they did so in the context of an established practice of building enclosed structures to protect valued commodities. In such English trading centers as London, Chelmsford, Exeter, Norwich, and King's Lynn, courtyarded mercantile complexes existed by the middle of the fifteenth century, suggesting that these traders, through a skilled combination of diverse traditions, had mastered a "doubling" of architectural strategies long before professional playwrights took advantage of their ludic possibilities. By linking their private home to their counting house, warehouse, and shop stalls, merchants protected commodities and money and simultaneously evoked a series of still older spaces, including benevolent images of the aristocratic courtyarded medieval house dispensing charity, the pre-Henrican monastic

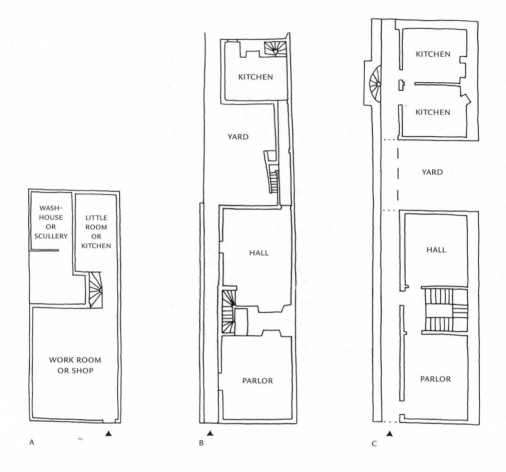

WASH-HOUSE OR SCULLERY

LITTLE ROOM OR KITCHEN

WORK ROOM OR SHOP

A

KITCHEN

YARD

HALL

PARLOR

B

KITCHEN

KITCHEN

YARD

HALL

PARLOR

C

0   10   20

FEET

Figure 22. French and English houses with detached rear kitchens, or "Maison bloc" structures: (a) house at the St. Nicaise cemetery, ca. 1620–50, Rouen (after Raymond Alexandre Quenedey, *L'habitacion rouennaise: Etude d'histoire, de geographie, et d'archaeologie urbaines* [Rouen: Lestrigant, 1926], 340, fig. 71); (b) 47 Broad Street, Oxford, early seventeenth century (after W. A. Pantin, "The Development of Domestic Architecture in Oxford," *Antiquaries Journal* 27 [1947]: fig. 7); (c) house at Totnes, Devon, late seventeenth century (after Michael Laithwaite, "Totnes Houses, 1500–1800," in *The Transformation of English Provincial Towns, 1600–1800*, ed. Peter Clark [London: Hutchinson, 1984], 90, fig. 5a). (Drawing by the author)

courtyard, and the hospitable courtyarded medieval inn, the latter of which frequently doubled as a theater. Deploying the illusions of ecclesiastical and civic stagecraft to mask commercial self-interest may have mimicked an Italian mercantile behavior such as that of the powerful Alberti family of Florence, who had controlled England's wool trade with the Continent and maintained a presence in London between about 1390 and 1450.[70]

The use of built metaphor to mask private interest, the same construction of an "intimate" political and theatrical landscape, made the English merchant's precise ideological stance in the Atlantic republican tradition sometimes difficult to determine. The detection of the merchant's "real" or "true" motives was difficult, and whether one was in London or Boston, the issue remained the same: Did the merchant work for the common good—however the concept might be rationalized—or did he cleverly borrow the *language* and *imagery* of commonwealth in order to diffuse any hostility that might arise as he pursued his own self-interest?

Theoretically, consumers and magistrates in a Puritan society shared a concern about self-interest. In Boston in 1639 the suspicion of "oppression" brought the town's leading trader, a merchant tailor from London named Robert Keayne, to his knees in a successful ritual of public humiliation. But at the same time, other local merchants were building courtyarded complexes that efficiently evoked the doubled, theatrical nature of commerce. In 1638, for example, Boston innholder Samuel Cole sold to Charlestown merchant Robert Sedgwick his tavern complex, including "the old house adjoyning with the shedds, court yeard, garden and appurtenances," for two hundred pounds. In 1639 Boston merchants William and Samuel Hutchinson sold their brother Richard (a "citizen & ironmonger of London") a merchant's premise that included a dwelling house surrounded by "the garden thereunto adjoyning and all courte yardes[,] stables[,] stalles[,] outhouses[, and] commons." Enclosed compounds newly built in the 1630s and early 1640s remained a common feature of Boston's urban landscape throughout the seventeenth century. Merchant William Paddy had, for example, a "Mansion house[,] ground and garden with a small Tenement at the Western end thereof with wells, fences, and whatever else" when he died in Boston in 1680; three years later, merchant Thomas Brattle died possessed of "Dwelling house[,] warehouse and stable with the Stone house . . . with the land[,] pasture[,] gardens therto belonging." And although Henry Whitfield, Guilford's first minister, had emigrated from Canterbury in Kent, his uncle Nathaniel was a "merchant of London," which suggests that urban courtyarded prototypes may have directly informed colonial projects in Guilford.[71]

Just as merchants were busy appropriating "plain speech" from the clergy and using it to mask their own motives, their houses borrowed the classical language of ethical aristocracy to shape efficient outposts of production, processing, and profit. In New England, while "protecting" people from Indian attack, they extended the imperial boundaries of the English market economy. Enclosed domestic complexes such as Desborough's were thus split visible signs. They tethered the cold logic of the expanding commercial world to the rhetoric of the protected, neofeudal economic enclave. They provided a pattern of rational order intended to convert available resources and labor power into marketable commodities, and other peoples to the Puritan faith.

HYBRID HOUSES

Bawn, bastle, premise, theater. As they fused these implicated places in particular forms, ordinary houses reveal the constant transformations of the early modern English landscape. The consequences of this process are nowhere more visible and relevant to Desborough's Guilford house than in houses built where the imagined terrains of the highland and lowland zones overlapped. Peter Eden in 1968 termed "hybrid" those house plans that fused the heated kitchen, cross passage, and hall hearth against the passage (the highland postmedieval chimney configuration) with a heated, socially exclusive parlor (the lowland contribution). Eden was building in part on the earlier field research of Raymond Wood-Jones, who by 1956 had studied houses in the Banbury region that straddles the border of Oxfordshire and Northamptonshire. He interpreted this area as a boundary region between zones that represented a selective fusion of lowland and highland forms. In retrospect, the timing of Wood-Jones's work was pivotal. Just three years after Hoskins published his "Rebuilding of Rural England" essay, Wood-Jones was quietly interrogating the lowland-highland dichotomy upon which its central argument rested. The result, Wood-Jones and then Eden argued, was houses whose plans exactly match that of Desborough's house in Guilford: three heated rooms and a cross passage.[72] Desborough's house is a hybrid design, and were it not for the implicit challenge that such hybrid forms put to the bipartite logic of zones, we would fail to see its synthetic quality.

Hybrid houses exactly like Desborough's were widespread in England. They are still so common in parts of Devon, Dorset, and Somerset that one might conclude they were a peculiarly West Country form. But they appear in northwest Oxfordshire and in both southern and northern Northamptonshire (fig. 23). The scattered distribution pattern suggests that many structures that now have high survival rates in the highland zone in fact may have been more common in the south and east. Given that two of Guilford's earliest carpenters, John Hill and Edward Jones, were from Northamptonshire, surviving structures like the stone house built in 1654 by mason Arthur Grumbold at Weldon (fig. 24) provide precise formal parallels for Desborough's hybrid house. The geographic range of these structures extended still farther to the east, as surviving examples in Hertfordshire, Bedfordshire, and at Elton in Huntingdonshire suggest.[73]

In fact, hybrid houses were built even in West Cambridgeshire and were thus probably familiar to Desborough as he grew to maturity. Consider, for example, the building in which he was raised, which still stands in Eltisley and bears the date 1612 and the initials of Samuel's parents—James and Elizabeth Desborough—on the lintel over its front door. When first built, it consisted of two large rooms separated by a wall or screen, and a smaller third room (fig. 25). The original front door opened into the stair tower and provided access to the passage. Turning to the left, one entered the smaller of the two main rooms, heated by a chimney along its front wall; this room may have served as the parlor, given that an ornamental oriel window ran up its gable end. To the right was the larger room, most likely the hall, from which was partitioned a smaller service room, perhaps a buttery. Located at the rear corner of the hall was the third room, of one story and open to the rafters. This space was original to the house and must have served as a kitchen or storage room.[74]

An anomaly, the Desborough house in Eltisley resembles none of the plan types that Eden found were common to West Cambridgeshire. But he does note that the period from 1540 to 1620 in the area was "an inventive one and classification is correspondingly unfruitful," with many smaller houses representing both a miniaturization and fragmentation of late medieval forms. In the section of West Cambridgeshire where Desborough grew up, experimentation in domestic design was a cultural constant. With two hearths in the ground floor and two above, the Eltisley house was nothing unusual; almost one in four houses in the village had four or more hearths.[75]

The house stands at the center of a manorial community surrounded by the ridge-and-furrow geometry of open fields. It is one of a number of buildings grouped around an open triangular area now known as "The Green" (fig. 26). The parish church of St. Pandionia and St. John the Baptist, completed in large part by the early fifteenth century, dominates the southern side of The Green. The Desborough house is immediately to the east of the church lot. But between the house and church the Desboroughs contoured a complicated water garden by channeling the slow current of a local stream around the property. The moated waterway is impressive. A ditch almost 40 feet wide and between 5 and 7 feet deep, it began by running some 185 feet along the churchyard fence, continued to the west of the house for 200 feet, another 160 feet to the south, then jogged to the north for 60 feet. The same stream that coursed through the ditches was diverted to fill a pond just to the southwest of the Desborough house and two smaller rectangular ponds arranged symmetrically behind the house (fig. 26, inset). The presence of these

Figure 23. Samuel Desborough's hybrid house and its English antecedents: (a) Desborough house, Guilford, Connecticut, ca. 1641 (scale approximate); (b) house at Stone, North Tawton, Devon, ca. 1570–1610 (after Mercer, *English Vernacular Houses*, fig. 33); (c) house at Kempsford, Gloucestershire, ca. 1600–1630 (after Mercer, *English Vernacular Houses*, 55, fig. 41); (d) house at Colly-weston, Northamptonshire, early seventeenth century, with later one-room addi-tion (after *An Inventory of the Historical Monuments in the County of Northampton*, vol. 6, *Architectural Monu-ments in North Northampton-shire*, 35–36, fig. 48); (e) house at South Farm, Glap-thorpe, Northamptonshire, seventeenth century (after *An Inventory of the Historical Monuments in the County of Northampton*, vol. 6, *Archi-tectural Monuments in North Northamptonshire*, 79, fig. 98). (Drawing by the author)

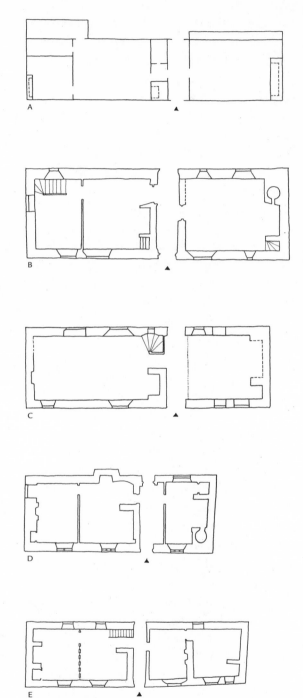

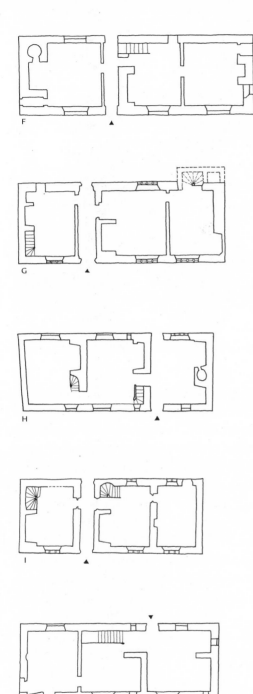

F

G

H

I

J

0   10   20
|ıııııııı| |
FEET

Figure 23 (continued). Samuel Desborough's hybrid house and its English antecedents: (f) house at Fontmell Magna, Dorset, ca. 1580–1620 (after *An Inventory of Historic Monuments in the County of Dorset*, vol. 4, *North Dorset* [London: Royal Commission on Historical Monuments, 1972], xxxvi); (g) Priest's house, Muchelney, Somerset, ca. 1460–80, with rebuildings in the sixteenth and seventeenth centuries (after W. A. Pantin, "Medieval Priests' Houses in Southwest England," *Medieval Archaeology* 1 [1957]: 121, fig. 22); (h) Bennett's house, Bloxham, Oxfordshire, dated 1610 (after Wood-Jones, *Traditional Domestic Architecture of the Banbury Region*, 96, fig. 22); (i) Cromwell Cottage, Hornton, Oxfordshire, ca. 1615 (after Wood-Jones, *Traditional Domestic Architecture of the Banbury Region*, 85, fig. 18); (j) house ("Old Schoolhouse") at Deenethorpe, Northamptonshire, 1660 (after Mercer, *English Vernacular Houses*, fig. 154). (Drawing by the author)

Figure 24. Arthur Grumbold's house, Weldon, Northamptonshire, dated 1654. (Photo: Royal Commission on Historical Monuments [England], © Crown Copyright)

water courses at his parents' Eltisley estate may cast additional light on the "waterhouse" described in the Rossiter plan of Desborough's Guilford farmstead. According to the *Oxford English Dictionary*, a waterhouse may refer to a structure in which water might be raised into a small conduit head or storage container, which could then, through wooden pipes, supply a house with running water. Raised in privileged surroundings and perhaps having heard of the water systems at such East Anglian estates as Ingatestone in Essex, Desborough may have been in the vanguard of a progressive, bourgeois move toward indoor running water that had other early advocates in London, East Anglia, and the Ulster Plantations.[76]

The variety of houses in West Cambridgeshire was evident even in the immediate neighborhood of Eltisley's center. Next to Desborough's 1612 structure stands Green Farm, a mid-seventeenth-century timber structure. In plan, the building consists of a hall with a cross wing on each end (fig. 27a). The peculiar feature, however, is that while typical lowland practice would dictate that the space sharing the chimney with the hall be a parlor, in fact it is a kitchen open to the rafters. Across The Green from the Desborough house stands another dwelling, this one dating from the late fifteenth or early sixteenth century (fig. 27b). Originally consisting of three rooms open to the rafters, it was updated early in the seventeenth century to include a chimney, ceilings, and a new addition for service at one end. When the stack was inserted, however, it was not placed away from the cross passage between the hall and parlor. Rather, it was inserted in the cross passage itself,

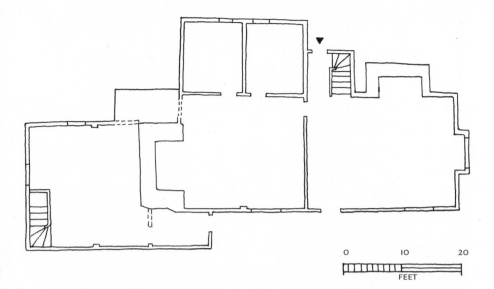

Figure 25. James and Elizabeth Desborough's house, Eltisley, Cambridgeshire, dated 1612 (after *An Inventory of Historical Monuments in the County of Cambridge*, vol. 1, *West Cambridgeshire* [London: Royal Commission on Historical Monuments, 1968], 92–93). (Drawing by the author)

between the hall and the original service space. The cross wing containing the original parlor was therefore demoted in status after the remodeling.[77]

Architectural hybridity was plainly evident in Eltisley's village center and in those nearby counties where Desborough traveled as a young man: Hertfordshire and Bedfordshire to the south, and Huntingdonshire and north Northamptonshire to the west. His family was in fact originally from Desborough in Huntingdonshire, and he knew William Leete in nearby Keyston, both villages close to the Northamptonshire border. His choice of a hybrid plan for his Guilford house carried two associations from West Cambridgeshire. By using a cross passage and placing the hall chimney against it, he referenced a feudal past nostalgically viewed as a community in which the propertied and the propertyless commingled. In this imagined past the obedience of tenants was matched by the largesse of manorial landlords. Coming from a manorial upbringing in Eltisley, Desborough brought this aspiration with him to New England. At the same time, his vision of organic, deferential society was linked to the image of open-field life, which he continued to defend in Connecticut.[78]

Desborough's Guilford house stood at the beginning of a long and diverse history of hybrid architectural forms in colonial New England. Because New England attracted freeholders from many different places in England and brought their ideas of domestic life into dynamic contact, the colonial landscape was more

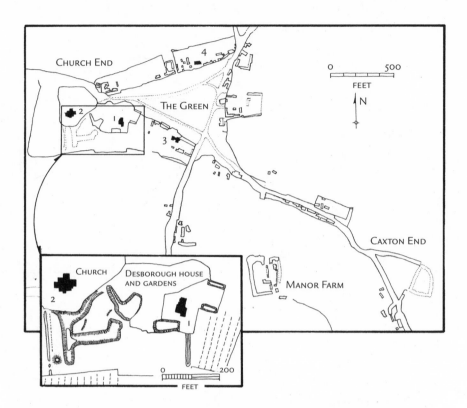

Figure 26. Center of Eltisley, Cambridgeshire, showing town green and surrounding buildings. Key: (1) James and Elizabeth Desborough's house, dated 1612; (2) Parish Church of St. Pandionia and St. John, nave and aisles, ca. 1200; remodeled and extended in the thirteenth century; (3) Green farm, ca. 1630–50; (4) house, late fifteenth or early sixteenth century, with chimney, chamber floors, and extensions at cross wing added in the early seventeenth century. Inset shows detail of original "elaborate water gardens" and moat scheme associated with the Desboroughs' house, early seventeenth century. (After *An Inventory of Historical Monuments in the County of Cambridge*, vol. 1, *West Cambridgeshire*, 90, 96, 97.) (Map by the author)

similar to the Banbury region of Oxfordshire, or the overlap of zones stretching from the Cotswolds up through Northamptonshire, Huntingdonshire, and Lincolnshire, than it was to pure regional strains in, say, either Devon or Kent. The fact that hybridization was an emergent semiotic force across England by the time emigration to New England began allows us to see New World innovations as part of an already established logic of appropriation across regional boundaries.

In Rhode Island, for example, hybrid houses appeared by 1670, as local builders used different English vernacular house forms to their own local ends. The colony's initial planters brought an impressive range of house forms from the English countryside. As early as the 1640s, central-chimney, hall-and-parlor houses

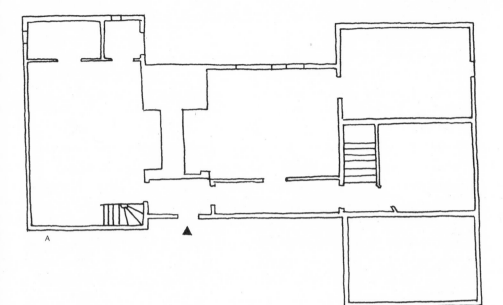

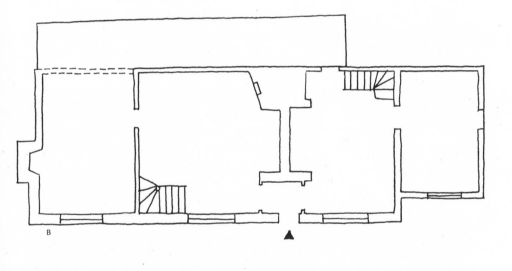

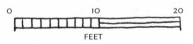

FEET

Figure 27. Hybrid houses in Eltisley, Cambridgeshire: (a) Green Farm, ca. 1630–50; (b) house, late fifteenth or early sixteenth century and later. (After *An Inventory of Historical Monuments in the County of Cambridge*, vol. 1, *West Cambridgeshire*, 94, 95.) (Drawing by the author)

with rear lean-tos similar to those in Massachusetts and Connecticut were already standing. In addition, small, direct-entry houses with end chimneys of stone or brick could be found in Newport, Providence, and Cranston and near Limerock. When these end-chimney structures were extended, new rooms were usually added to one end, resulting in buildings that retained low rooflines but might align one, two, or even three rooms along a single ridge. But these "up-and-back" (lowland zone?) and "low-and-long" (highland zone?) house forms did not summarize the range of architectural options that marked the first-generation Rhode Island landscape. Consider the house built by Christopher Allen in Kingstown about 1703 (fig. 28). The facade chimney and general appearance of the structure seem closely related to extant examples in Devon and the north coast of Somerset, which in plan have three ground-floor rooms (fig. 29); a cross passage entered to one side of the facade chimney gives access to a storage room and to the hall. Beyond the hall, the only heated room, lies a small parlor. In the west of England these houses date from as early as the 1580s but were built through the beginning of the eighteenth century. Originally modeled on aristocratic houses of the early sixteenth century, the facade chimney house at yeoman level in the colonies signaled social pretension and claims on local prestige. Christopher Allen, a slaveholder and wealthy plantation owner, cultivated both.[79]

From these diverse first-generation building traditions sprang new house forms in the decades of the 1670s and 1680s. Thomas Fenner in Cranston, Eleazer Arnold in Lincoln, and Thomas Clemence in Johnston fused the door placement and end-chimney plan of small, direct-entry "highland-zone" houses to the two-story rear–lean-to extension strategy of central-chimney, hall-and-parlor "lowland-zone" houses. Valentine Whitman in Lincoln made a similar stone-ended house two rooms deep but retained the front door in the lobby entry. Benjamin Waterman in Johnston extended his end-chimney, lobby-entry house by building a cross wing. But instead of serving as a parlor, the new room boasted a massive end chimney and oven. The owner of the Waite-Potter house in nearby Westport, Massachusetts, extended his direct-entry, single-cell house by building a lobby-entry structure on the other side of his chimney, resulting in a house with two front doors that may have looked like a center-chimney structure from a distance but was emphatically different once one stepped inside (fig. 30).[80]

During the late seventeenth century new hybrid houses seem to have been restricted to Rhode Island, immediately adjacent areas of Bristol County, Massachusetts, and scattered locations in eastern Connecticut, places where a mix of people from different English regional cultures—among whom were post-1660 West Country immigrants like Christopher Allen—ensured the fusion of diverse architectural traditions and the styles of family government to which house forms had developed in response. But over the next forty years, novel combinations of

Figure 28. James Helme, detail of Christopher Allen's house, ca. 1703, from "Plat of Kingstown," 1727. Ink on paper, H. 25" (63.5 cm), W. 9" (22.9 cm). (Photo by the author, courtesy of the James Helme Plat Map Collection, Special Collections Department, University of Rhode Island)

direct-entry door placements, central-chimney positions, and rear–lean-to locations appeared as new strategies in family structure and religious practice took hold at the margins of settlement in Massachusetts. Hybrid houses appeared on the fringes of Dedham that would become Dover, in small villages in Worcester County, in Deerfield on the northern edge of the Connecticut River valley, and in North Guilford and Stonington along the Connecticut shore (fig. 31).[81] Even though these houses represented new combinations of existing forms, the search for hybrid houses may find even earlier sources. The apparently homogeneous "saltbox" houses of Massachusetts and Connecticut may, in fact, have one mixture at their origin, for although the "complete" form of this house seems to have

Figure 29. House, Clyst Honiton, Devon, ca. 1650–80. (Photo by the author)

its earliest roots in England's southeastern counties and large county towns, the typical New England strategy of attaining that form through two or more segmental additions—beginning often with a "half" house and then doubling it within a single generation—was rare in England's lowland zone. Rather, it probably owes a debt to the "unit system" of house extension, suggesting that the commonality of partible inheritance under customary law in the New England colonies may have forced different members of the same family to build additions that would allow them to live alongside one another (fig. 32). In many instances only a central chimney could effectively separate bitter siblings.[82]

GUILFORD: RELIGION AND ROSSITER

Perhaps the walls, sense of social exclusivity, and protection of private property derive from the specific location and role of Desborough in Guilford's early social structure and economy. Historian John J. Waters has described eighteenth-century Guilford as "marked by strong patrilineal, English peasant mores" that emphasized age as a criterion of authority, the importance of birth order in awarding children property, and the greater economic value of sons than daughters. Early Guilford, he argued, was "a world with ritualistic perambulations of boundaries, burdensome responsibilities, and an ordering of society to be part and parcel of the nature of things." Hierarchy was implicit. The town depended on the wisdom of its leaders, and if they remained in control of local political and exchange

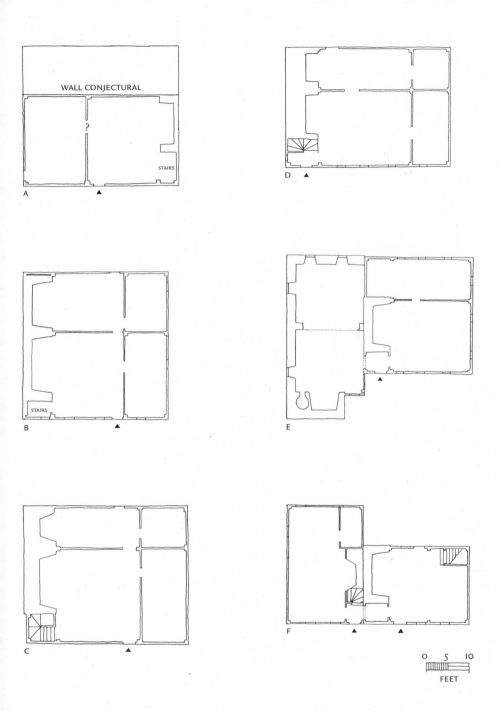

WALL CONJECTURAL

?

STAIRS

A ▲

D ▲

STAIRS

B ▲

E ▲

C ▲

F ▲ ▲

0   5   10

FEET

Figure 30. Hybrid houses in Rhode Island and adjacent East Narragansett Bay: (a) Thomas Fenner's house, Cranston, Rhode Island, 1677 with later additions; (b) Eleazar Arnold's house, Lincoln, Rhode Island, ca. 1687 with added rear wing, ca. 1730–40; (c) Thomas Clemence's house, Johnston, Rhode Island, ca. 1680–90; (d) Valentine Whitman's house, Lime Rock, Rhode Island, ca. 1698; (e) Benjamin Waterman's house, Johnston, Rhode Island, ca. 1700–1715; (f) Waite-Potter house, Westport, Massachusetts, ca. 1684 with addition of ca. 1710–20. (Drawing by the author)

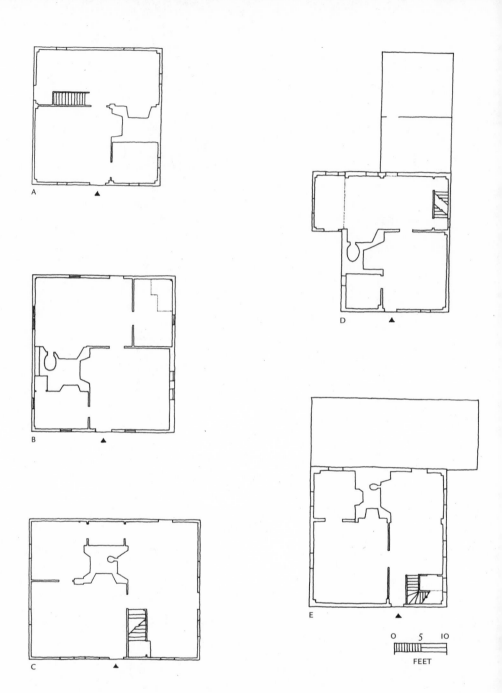

Figure 31. Hybrid houses in eighteenth-century Massachusetts and Connecticut: (a) Joseph Chickering's house, Dover (originally Springfield parish of Dedham), Massachusetts, by 1747; (b) reconstructed plan, David Saxton's house, Deerfield, Massachusetts, 1761 (some partitions and chimney configuration conjectural; after J. Ritchie Garrison, *Landscape and Material Life in Franklin County, Massachusetts, 1770–1860* [Knoxville: University of Tennessee Press, 1991], 160, fig. 7.10); (c) Gershom Wheelock's house, Shrewsbury, Massachusetts, 1754; (d) John Norton's house, North Guilford, Connecticut, 1690s and later (now destroyed); (e) William Whipple's house, Stonington, Connecticut, ca. 1750. (Drawing by the author)

Figure 32. Ebenezer Jenks's house, Pawtucket, Rhode Island, ca. 1680–1700. (Photo: Society for the Preservation of New England Antiquities)

relations, "Guilford existed in high autonomy." As Waters maintains, "it ran itself."[83]

Waters was sensitive to the different ways in which the long shadow of seventeenth-century patriarchal rule continued to shape family life and agricultural labor over the next century. The conservative religious texture of the town supported the persistence of patriarchy. In Guilford, Henry Whitfield modified the form of church polity common to other New England congregations. John Davenport's New Haven church, for example, followed established practice in England and in Massachusetts Bay and elected a "ruling elder" or lay leader whose judgment in issues of ecclesiastical government complemented that of the minister. Whitfield's congregation refused to designate such a ruling elder. Writing to Ezra Stiles in 1770 "with regard to the church in Guilford," Timothy Ruggles explained why "they never had, and upon principle never would, admit a ruling elder":

Although in all other things Mr. Whitfield and Mr. Davenport and their churches exactly agreed and practised, yet in this they were quite different. I have made diligent inquiry into the subject many years ago, with old people who were personally acquainted with the first members of the church. They all invariably agree, that as Mr. Whitfield was never ordained in any sense at Guilford, but officiated as their pastor in virtue of his ordination in England; so neither he nor the church would allow of a ruling elder: and the ancient tradition in the church here was, that New-Haven, and afterward other churches in the colony, conformed their judgment and practice to Mr. Whitfield's and his church's judgment, who were strictly Congregational.[84]

Because a high percentage of Guilford's first-generation planters had migrated from England along with their minister, his legitimacy in the pulpit was never questioned, and therefore no official ordination in Guilford occurred. But note Ruggles's language: Whitfield himself was against admitting a ruling elder, perhaps because it would have lessened his total authority in church and community affairs—and as ministers lost power over the course of the seventeenth century, many came to reconsider Whitfield's early autonomy in a positive light. Clearly, Henry Whitfield was a subtle political leader who realized the power of the pulpit in maintaining social hierarchy, deferential relations, and an organic theory of society that placed the wealthy, the landed, and the learned at the "head" of state and their lesser neighbors in dependent positions.

Despite its refusal to designate a ruling elder that might compromise Whitfield's total judicial authority, Guilford's orthodoxy still found official support in New Haven, where Davenport actively encouraged a strict adherence to Calvinist principles of church government and lay discipline. From an ecclesiastical point of view, the location of New Haven on the western periphery of English settlement in the region and the lack of any surveillance over local religious practices from either the Crown or Boston allowed Davenport to enforce an orthodoxy without parallel elsewhere in colonial New England. According to Isabel Calder, New Haven was "settled by ultra-conservative Puritans, unrestricted by royal charter, far removed from the ecclesiastical organization of England," and "served as a laboratory in which Puritan theories of ecclesiastical and civil organization might be tested." But New Haven's centrality in the colony meant that Davenport's views had a wider impact. Schismatic or heretical sects, for example, were systematically excluded from all towns in the New Haven colony when the general court in 1656 ordered "that no Quaker, Ranter, or other Heretick of that nature, be suffered to come unto, nor abide in the jurisdiction, and if any such rise up among ourselves that they be speedily suppressed and secured for the better prevention of such dangerous errours."[85]

Looking back in 1770, Ruggles reaffirmed his argument for the ultimate similarity of Guilford and New Haven in matters of church discipline. "The church of Guilford and New-Haven in all other things were one in opinion and practice," he maintained. "Members were admitted by relations [or experiences], and by holding up the hands of the brethren. The conformity was uniform."[86] Despite a period in the early 1660s when settling a minister to replace John Higginson proved divisive, the Guilford church in fact remained strictly Congregational through the end of the eighteenth century and was admitting members by open profession of faith or "owning the covenant" as late as 1762, long after most other New England churches had abandoned the practice as untrustworthy.

Arguing for the seamless web of patriarchy, inheritance, and land and remarking on the range of buildings, gravestones, and tax lists that await the historian, Waters stated that "Guilford was a town of *consensus* in a land of 'Steady Habits.'"[87] This image may emerge from the eighteenth-century records and the persistent conservatism of local religious practice. But if so, then it did not spring automatically from easily identified seventeenth-century roots. In fact, first- and second-generation Guilford society was far from being a sleepy agricultural village defined by its continuity with English "peasant" communities. For one thing, some of its residents differed sharply with prevailing patterns of authority and deference. Take Bray Rossiter, for example, the man who purchased the farmstead from Desborough in 1651 and drew its plan. Beginning in 1659, when John Higginson, who had succeeded Henry Whitfield, left Guilford, Rossiter became embroiled in a series of bitter and divisive controversies that followed when, as Ruggles described, the town "fell into confusion by diversity of religious opinions." The confusion centered on Higginson's successor. Rossiter was lobbying hard for Josiah Cotton, son of the eminent Boston minister and his own son-in-law. The town instead asked John Bowers, then living in New Haven, to come and preach on trial. Rebuffed by this slight to his son-in-law, Rossiter moved with a few other families to settle Killingworth, north of Guilford and on the other side of the border with the Connecticut Colony, where he remained until 1664. In so doing, Rossiter allied himself with such inhabitants of Guilford as John Meigs, a contentious man whom Guilford's political leaders, including William Leete, blamed for instigating the secessionist group. In their eyes, Meigs, "whose activity & businesse upon this Acct. is said to be so great & grievous to some," was a man in 1663 "found guilt of sundry enormities unjust dealing & false speaking."[88]

Although he lived in Killingworth, Rossiter remained a property holder in Guilford. He returned periodically to make his opinions on local politics known. In November 1661 he made one such trip, and his petty objections to the town's considerate treatment of Bowers reveal his temper over town taxes being raised to support him. "Mr Rossit[e]r obiected against Mr Bowers his continuing here as a temporary supply as formerly," the town clerk duly noted, "unlesse he would serve as cheape as any would doe in that way, & that ye full p[e]riod of his time might be pr[e]fixed, makeing further obiection against ye writing made betwixt ye freemen w[i]th some others, & Mr Bowers for his continueing here in yt worke till we could accord & ye pr[e]vaile for an other to supply in his stead." [89] He went on to complain that a town rate should not be used to support Bowers. Dung belonging to the town had disappeared from the minister's lot, rent for the barn on the minister's lot had not been paid, and "Clapboards taken away from the meeting house [were] not accounted for." Early in 1662 Rossiter was back in court, this time to answer charges that he had not paid his town rate on time. Arguing that he was a physician and therefore excused from taxes, he failed to convince the authorities. In short order a constable arrived and attached two of his cows to cover his back taxes. In defense of his father, son John greeted the constable with these words: "May he not resist a theife, when he comes into the yard to take away any cattle or goods, he would knocke him down."[90]

Bray Rossiter was sensitive to claims on common property in the name of private interest. His actions, perhaps, portray him as a commonwealthman committed to the collective will before his own. Yet as his defense of son-in-law Josiah Cotton's candidacy for the Guilford pulpit demonstrates, he saw what was good for the community *in terms of* his own interest. His political contentiousness was grounded in his own life history. Born in 1610 at Combe St. Nicholas in Somerset, he had an upbringing almost as privileged as Desborough's. It was also crucial to his contentiousness in Guilford. His father, Edward Rossiter (1575–1630), had been the sole inheritor of a free tenancy in the manor of Combe St. Nicholas. Of twenty-five ratable heads of household living on the manor in 1593, he was the only one taxed on land. As an independent landholder in a manorial village, Edward was an anomaly. He owed no rents, had the legal right to claim a coat of arms, and was a powerful member of the local gentry in south Somerset. He was also one of only two West Country residents to be appointed stockholders in the Massachusetts Bay Company in London. As such, he knew Matthew Craddock, Theophilus Eaton, John Endicott, and others central in the plantation effort. Yet Edward's success in local society may have come at the expense of community approval; in the early years of the seventeenth century he was taken to court by his less wealthy neighbors for failing to maintain ditches adjacent to his property. He was also accused of a greater sin—attempting to enclose a portion of his share in the commons—and when confronted lashed out in defense of his own prerogative.[91]

In 1630 Edward Rossiter, along with twelve family members—including his sons Nicholas, Hugh, and Bray—sailed to Dorchester, Massachusetts, where he was awarded two hundred acres of land for himself and fifty additional acres of land for each person in his group, totaling eight hundred acres. Influential in mercantile and political affairs, he quickly established a sizable estate in Massachusetts. When his father died suddenly in October 1630, Bray remained in New England while his brothers returned to Combe St. Nicholas. He must have found himself with little to keep him in Dorchester, since in 1639 he sold to William and

Edward Hutchinson the farm he had inherited from his father, including a "farme house & other buildinges thereunto adjoyning and all the gardens yardes and out-houses."[92] That same year, with other early West Country emigrants, he left Dorchester for Windsor, Connecticut, where he received a large house lot near those of other leading families on the Hartford Road near the village center. He was Windsor's first town clerk as well as its only physician. Precisely where Rossiter learned medicine is unclear, although Ezra Stiles reported that he had "taken three degrees" in England before emigrating in 1630. As clerk and physician, Rossiter came in periodic contact with political and mercantile leaders elsewhere, including Edward Hopkins and George Wyllys in Hartford, Theophilus Eaton in New Haven, and William Leete in Guilford. Perhaps hearing promises of expanding mercantile wealth in New Haven Colony during the 1640s and, like other Englishmen of the new professional classes, anxious to move up society's ladder, in late 1651 Rossiter purchased Desborough's large estate in Guilford and moved there with his family the following year.[93]

With contentious, socially mobile individuals like Rossiter in mind, Water's claim that Guilford was a consensual community of New England "peasants" is difficult to sustain for the seventeenth century. An additional factor that shielded Guilford from the benign insularity that consensual order often implies was the frequent movement of people between the town and neighboring New Haven during the 1640s and 1650s, a pattern of migration that further cemented kinship ties. Some individuals saw New Haven as their inevitable destination. Anne Higginson, the sister of Desborough's next-door neighbor John Higginson, moved from Guilford to work as a servant in the household of Governor Theophilus Eaton. John Parmelee was in Guilford in 1639 but moved to New Haven by the mid-1650s. Others, after living in the Quinnipiac port, moved away, perhaps in search of greater land holdings. Henry Goldham, in New Haven early in the 1640s, moved to Guilford and married Susannah Bishop by 1645. George Bartlett was in Guilford in 1641, in Branford in 1649, and back in Guilford by 1651. Desborough himself had lived in New Haven for two years before settling in Guilford in 1641.[94]

The presence of headstrong individuals like Rossiter and the frequent migration between towns contributed to a third reason why Guilford resists being typified as consensual: the material signs of ambition and ostentation that characterized New Haven's early merchant elite extended to embrace Guilford in the divisive effects of a nascent consumer culture. Just as it had religious tenets in common with New Haven, Guilford through its leading families was closely tied to neighboring New Haven's early commercial promise and the ambition of its established merchants, including Stephen Goodyear, Richard Malbone, and Theophilus Eaton. With past experience and continuing connections in London and Boston, they planned to develop the mouth of the Quinnipiac River and the adja-

cent area of Long Island Sound—with rich hinterlands providing furs and timber—into a major trading port. From an imperial perspective, they would also
place a protective political wedge between the Dutch in New York and established
English towns in the lower Connecticut River valley. Eaton was particularly aware
of New Haven's strategic location for subverting New Amsterdam's unchallenged
control of the fur trade. As he explained to John Winthrop, "A cloud nerely seemes
to threaten us from the West. We lately built a small [trading] house within our
owne limits (if at least we have any interest in these parts, and that the Duch be
not lords of the countrye, for they write this plantation in New Netherland). I
thinke I may safely say we have not yet traded 20 skinns of beaver in it, from the
first to this day, yet the Duch talke of hundreds nay thousands of skins."[95]

THE SHORT LIFE OF FASHION

With early Guilford and New Haven linked through religion, demography, and
colonial politics, their commercial connections merit closer examination. Initial
signs suggested that New Haven might show signs of God's grace. By 1644 merchants Eaton, Goodyear, and Malbone had financed and begun construction of a
"small ship of about one hundred tons." The vessel was completed and, according
to John Winthrop, "was laden with pease and some wheat, all in bulk, with about
two hundred West India hides, and store of beaver and plate, so it was estimated
in all at five thousand pounds." In January 1647 it set sail for England, "the harbor
being then so frozen as they were forced to hew her through the ice near three
miles." When this vessel disappeared at sea, its impressive cargo totally lost and
nearly seventy people drowned (including Goodyear's wife), the energy of the
Quinnipiac port began to sag. As Winthrop stated, "there fell a sore affliction
upon the country." A second ship and then a third rolled off the ways in New
Haven by 1648, but their freight lacked the optimism of the initial venture. A glim-
mer of renewed economic vigor appeared in 1656, when John Winthrop Jr., attracted by the promise that Connecticut's "black sand" held for iron production,
moved his household to New Haven. But he abandoned the project by 1660, when
his election as governor of the Connecticut Colony forced relocation to Hartford.
After that, New Haven's local economy, and with it the economy of Guilford, remained stagnant for the next century.[96]

In the early 1640s, however, a few New Haven households enjoyed a standard of
living and style that rivaled those of any contemporary English colony. Some of
these men—Theophilus Eaton, Stephen Goodyear, Richard Malbone, and Isaac
Allerton—were merchants. Others, including Thomas Gregson, who died when
the ship sank in 1647, were magistrates. Finally, minister Davenport also main-

tained an impressive mansion. Ezra Stiles recalled Davenport's dwelling in 1794: "[It] had many apartments, and thirteen fireplaces, which indeed I myself remember, having frequently, when a boy, been all over the house." Edward R. Lambert stated in 1838 that the house was "built in the form of a cross; with the chimney in the center." When the house appeared on the 1748 view of New Haven, it consisted of a central block with cross wings—most likely later additions—added at either end. Because Davenport moved to Boston in 1667 and died there two years later, no inventory records the earliest configuration of the structure.[97]

Eaton's house, described in detail in his 1657 room-by-room inventory, is at once more promising and more puzzling. Once again, Stiles in 1794 and Lambert in 1838 commented on its appearance. Stiles: "Gov. Eaton's house . . . had nineteen fireplaces, and many apartments." Lambert: "It was built in the form of a capital E, was large and lofty, and had 21 fireplaces." Based on their comments, Norman M. Isham suggested that Eaton's mansion originally was more like a manor house than an ordinary yeoman's dwelling. Perhaps he had Eaton's pretensions in mind. He was a merchant of great wealth and assumed aristocratic bearing in Davenport's London congregation at St. Stephen's, Coleman Street, a member of the Massachusetts Bay Company in London, and New Haven Colony's first governor. Yet Isham seems to have overestimated its size based principally on Lambert's report, by which time the building already had been extended from a large central-chimney structure to an E plan with cross-wing additions at either end (fig. 33). Based on the rooms mentioned in Eaton's 1656 inventory, the house contained, excluding the garret, only eight rooms, five of which had hearths—if the presence of such objects as andirons, fire dogs, spits, and fire tongs are a reliable index. The "21 fireplaces" cited by Lambert in his 1838 description—and followed by Isham and Brown in their fanciful reconstruction in *Early Connecticut Houses*—could only have resulted from subsequent additions to the original structure.[98]

The detailed probate inventory of the governor's estate nonetheless remains a useful portrait of one New Haven merchant's household in 1657. One of its principal rooms was called the "greene chamber" and contained such en suite appointments as a "greene cubberd cloath," "6 greene cushions," "a greene carpet fringed," and "a set of greene currtens & vallans fringed & laced" enclosing a "downe bed: 4 pillowes, & a feather bed bolster" worth an additional seven pounds. Complementing the green chamber was a "blew chamber" furnished with valuable bedding, stored textiles, and a "blew rugg." The house contained one room called "Mrs. Eaton's chamber," indicating perhaps that the French custom of husbands and wives maintaining separate sleeping chambers, a fashion already filtered through stylish London households, also held sway in elite colonial households. Some of the furnishings in Eaton's house were undoubtedly imported from England, but many of the forms, ranging from chests to chairs to

Figure 33. "Southwest view of Governor [Theophilus] Eaton's house," New Haven, Connecticut, by ca. 1640. From Edward R. Lambert, *History of the Colony of New Haven, before and after the Union with Connecticut* (New Haven: Hitchcock and Stafford, 1838), 52. (Photo: Historical Society of Pennsylvania)

cupboards, were being made by the 1640s in New Haven by such immigrant London-trained woodworking artisans as William Gibbons, William Russell, and Lawrence Ward, using techniques common on London furniture of the period.[99]

The influence of New Haven's elite households and their material prosperity on the early inhabitants of Guilford emerged in a variety of ways. When the initial planters of Guilford arrived in New Haven in 1639, they brought with them Davenport's son, at once suggesting their close and trusted relationship with Davenport in London prior to emigration. Whitfield, through his connections in the church and court in London, had already met Eaton and Davenport. Domestic furnishings in seventeenth-century Guilford were also drawn from fashionable ideas then circulating in England. Joined stools and chairs boasted columnar turnings as crisp and architecturally correct as any in London. Cupboards, including an example that belonged to Joseph Eliot, Jared's father, presented similar turnings and impressive "torus" moldings, large rounded bands at their midpoints that had antecedents in stylish late-sixteenth-century court furniture (fig. 34). Desborough's domestic complex may even have owed a debt to the merchant's premise that set Eaton's New Haven mansion in relation to his "counting house" and his "warehouse."

Wealthy merchants, magistrates, and ministers in New Haven and Guilford used such props to create a theater of dominance that at once drew lines of association to their English metropolitan associates and separated them from their less wealthy

Figure 34. Cupboard, Guilford, Connecticut, 1650–60, owned originally by Rev. Joseph Eliot. From Wilimena H. Emerson, ed., *Genealogy of the Descendants of John Eliot* (New Haven: Tuttle, Morehouse, and Taylor Press, 1905), facing p. 102.

neighbors. Elites knew from experience that if social privilege became more an issue of worldly possessions than bloodline, their own positions would grow increasingly precarious as underlings obtained commodities and imitated their gentle styles. Enclosed domestic compounds like those built by Eaton and Desborough allowed for a comfortable embrace of commercial capitalism, but, by suggesting the persistence of a quasi-feudal, organic social order, they conveniently legitimized keeping the uninvited from seeing their material possessions too closely.

MODEL FARMS

Desborough's Guilford estate owed both a symbolic and formal debt to the bawn, the fortified English house, and the courtyarded urban residence, yet the date of its construction and the detail it provides concerning the functional relationship of house, adjacent outbuildings, and courtyards suggest a third implicated place:

enclosed farmsteads that arranged buildings around one, two, or three courtyards to maximize the farmer's efficiency in labor and to protect animals, crops, and implements. Like their urban counterparts, these farmsteads were English vernacular forms densely overlaid with references to Italian and French architectural ideas. By the last quarter of the sixteenth century, connected farm complexes were common in East Anglia, especially in larger market towns that, like Chelmsford in Essex in the early 1590s, were situated close enough to London's food markets to gear crops and planting schedules toward market production (fig. 35).[100] These enclosed compounds were built earliest in the southeastern counties where individual production for the London market supported the early enclosure of land. They soon provided important models for farmers throughout England, especially as a rising generation of agrarian theorists included architecture on their critical agendas.

One of these writers, Gervase Markham, described a model farm as consisting of buildings distributed in well-ordered fashion around distinct courtyards. In *The English Husbandman* (1613), Markham offered guidance on everything from a proper building site to the exact position of structures and rooms:

> You shall plant the face, or forefront of your house upon the rising of the Sunne, that the vigor of his warmth may at no time depart from some part thereof, but that as he riseth on the one side, so he may set on the other. You shall place the upper or best end of your house, as namely, where your dining Parlor and cheifest roomes are, which ever would have their prospect into your Garden, to the South, that your buttery, kitching and other inferiour offices may stand to the North, coldnesse bringing unto them a manifold benefit. . . . Now you shall further understand that on the South side of your house, you shall plant your Garden and Orchard, as wel for the prospect thereof to al your best roomes, as also because your house will bee a defence against the Northerne coldnesse, whereby your fruits will much better prosper.[101]

After thus outlining the proper siting of a house in terms of exposure and pleasant views, Markham detailed the relationships he thought appropriate between service buildings:

> You shall on the West side of your house, within your inward dairy and kitchin court, fence in a large base court, in the midst whereof would be a faire large Pond, well ston'd and gravelled in the bottome, in which your Cattell may drinke, and Horses when necessitie shall urge be washt. . . . On the North side of your base-court you shall build your Stables, Oxe-house, Cow-house, and Swine-coates, the dores and windowes opening all to the South. On the South side of the base-court, you shall build your Hay-barnes, Corne-barnes, pullen-

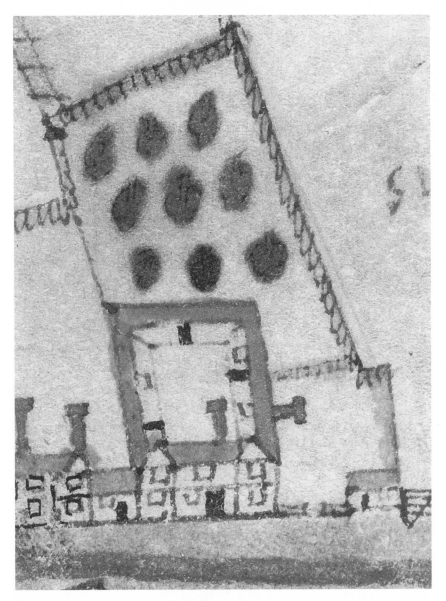

Figure 35. John Walker, detail of courtyarded farmstead from map of Chelmsford, Essex, 1591. (Photo: Essex Record Office)

houses for Hennes, Capons, Duckes, and Geese, your French Kilne, and Malting flowres, with such like necessaries.[102]

Drawing on personal familiarity with mixed farming practices in the south and east of England, Markham championed the ideal order that enclosed courtyards lined with neatly aligned service structures could give to a farmstead. The advice he offered and the courtyards he described would be helpful to farmers bringing in and processing grain crops but also to yeomen trying to control herds of animals as they entered and exited the stead for marking, milking, and ploughing and, finally, to meet the slaughterer's knife.

Markham's vision was shared by other agrarian theorists such as Leonard Mascall, John Norden, Richard Gardiner, and John Worledge. These men derived their arguments from an enthusiastic reading of Continental writers who coupled faith in the classical Romans' systematic but essentially aristocratic approach to farming with a nostalgic belief that it was only through country living and the simplicity of "rustic life" that virtue could be rediscovered in an increasingly urbanizing and class-fracturing European society. Continental authors such as Conrad Heresbach, whose *Rei Rusticae libri quatuor* (Cologne, 1570) had been translated into English by Barnaby Googe and published in London in 1577, or the work of Frenchmen Charles Estienne and Jean Liebault stimulated among conservative freeholders a new commitment to the reclamation of land, to experimentation with new plough types, and, ultimately, to increasing England's annual crop yields so that its economy would be less reliant on foodstuffs imported from the Continent. And lest landowers should feel the social distance between them and their tenants too great, Worledge even supplied English readers with a brief "Rustic Dictionary" to help them communicate with hired labor.

Read in the context of New World social mobility and aristocratic pretension, the work of Estienne and Liebault warrants more detailed examination, since an English translation of their principal text, *Maison Rustique; or, The Countrey Farme* (London, 1600), was the first book containing precise architectural advice known to have been in New England. It was in the London library of the Massachusetts Bay Company by 1629, a collection that Theophilus Eaton transferred to Boston in June 1637. John Winthrop Jr. acquired his own copy while in London in 1630. Robert Child probably used Winthrop's book when he was in Boston in the mid-1640s, for in the book on husbandry he published under Hartlib's name in 1651 he told readers that they may read "a large *Treatise* of the *Countrey-Farmer*" for additional instructions on the cultivation of meadow grasses.[103]

Like Gervase Markham, Estienne and Liebault offered advice that evinced their enthusiasm for ancient treatises, including the early Roman texts of Varro, Palladius, Columella, and Cato the Censor. Admitting that a contemporary building site would not be "so comodious as that great husbandman *Cato* doth desire it," they still argued that it "must be provided & foreseen above all other things that it have the benefit of a good aire." Concerns over good air and prevailing winds prompted more particular suggestions about outbuildings and farm layout: "If there be ever a hill, build upon the edge thereof, making choise to have your lights towards the East: but if you be in a cold countrie open your lights also on the

South side, and little or nothing towards the North, if it be not in your barnes where you put your corne or such other things, as are subject to the weasell and other vermine. Over against the North you shall procure some row or tuft of trees for to be a marke unto you of your place, & defense also for the same against the northerne windes in the winter time."[104]

Estienne and Liebault situated their prescription for the ideal enclosed farmstead within a theory of agrarian production grounded in classical example. The efficient layout of farm buildings led to efficiency of action, which then led to profit and power. "The goode Roman husbandman saith," they maintained, "that a housholder must so diminish the charges of everie thing by his labour, as that he may evermore have mo[r]e things, and more to sel then to buie, and that he everie day become[s] more strong and powerfull then his field." Conditioned by a common faith in classical virtue, their view of Roman farming was off the mark, especially as it assumed that a constant increase in efficiency was part of the Roman system. In fact, Roman farming was a system of leisured aristocratic landlords and slaves or tenants who worked the land intensively. As George Fussell has argued, "most wealthy Romans professed an admiration for the simple life of their peasant ancestors of the remote past, but were careful to surround themselves with luxury and to refrain from farm work." Georgic virtue derived from the immense pleasure of watching somebody else work, knowing that the spectacle of classical agrarian virtue was piling up profits in the landowner's coffers. The model farm layout Estienne and Liebault then describe is clearly organized by courtyards enclosed by impressive walls and lined with smaller work buildings, and the courtyard, "containing two acres square, shalbe compassed in with a wal of eighteene inches thicke, and tenne foot high from the ground, for the resting of your buildings upon that are within."[105]

Elsewhere Estienne and Liebault's text makes it clear that the courtyard should best be divided into a base court (or service area) and a forecourt, at the very least. The precise functions of the "smaller work buildings" inside the walled perimeter of the base court are similar to those of the buildings lining Desborough's "great Court": separate houses for oxen and cattle, horse stables, a separate box for newborn calves, a dog house. Like the Desborough property and its English and Irish cousins, the French walled complex is entered through ceremonial gates whose function links the demands of farm business to the protection of private property. "In the midst of the walle, and in the forepart, which is the part lying upon the sun-set, you shall make your gates and their porch, and in like manner a cover over head, to keepe the said gates from the sun and raine, which otherwise would beat full upon them and overthrow them, as also for the speciall use of your selfe and your familie, as to give them place and shelter in the time of raine, or when they please."[106] Having defined the exterior plan of the complex, Estienne and

Liebault turned to the domestic structures. With late-sixteenth-century French aristocratic farmsteads as their apparent model, they distinguished between two building types based on the requisite social segregation of farm labor from the immediate presence of the landowner. Hence, *Maison Rustique* charted distinct spatial contours for the "farmer's lodge" (meaning the tenant who oversees actual cultivation) and the genteel country house of the landowner.

The plan offered for the farmer's house reveals a modest dwelling composed of a kitchen, two small service rooms (a "dairie house" and a "house of office or vaulted room, which shal also be for the huswifes use and serve for a spence," or pantry) adjacent to the kitchen, and four other ground-floor rooms: "the farmer's bed-roome, and one other joyning to it for his maide-servants and children, and a third joyning close unto it, for to keepe foule linnen," and a "fourth which shalbe sufficient large, and the doore to goe into it shall stand in the court without, and it shall serve for fewell, working tooles, and other necessaries." Describing the interior layout of the farmer's kitchen, Estienne and Liebault specify that "to the end that all his friendes and servants may at all times easilie bestow themselves therein; the oven shalbe set without the roome having the mouth in the inner side of the chimney of the said kitchin, and lower then the mantle-tree, not far above the hearth."[107] Hired domestic hands were thus part of the farmer's immediate social circle. Extending the farmer's house and approached through the same passage were spaces for animals and additional workmen of lowly status. The "farmer's lodge" was derived from a pan-European architectural tradition that relied on a cross passage to separate people from animals while still uniting them under a single roof. This house helped give shape to the "base court," a zone that supported necessary economic production and softened the boundaries between animal husbandry and the control of labor.

The country seat of the landowner derived from vernacular prototypes that relied on a transverse cross passage to articulate the major functional zones of daily activity. The main house passage separated the principal kitchen and service spaces from rooms commonly restricted to the landlord's family and private acquaintances. The house that emerges from Estienne and Liebault's text is almost identical to rural English examples dating from about 1600 to 1650, and to Samuel Desborough's Guilford dwelling:

> In the place right over against the porch of the farme, shall open the doore of your owne house, which by a staire of eight steps at the most, shall bring you to the first storie of the same: the entrie whereinto shall be like unto a plaine vacant alley of an indifferent widenes, with an outcast at the further end, upon the garden. . . . Upon the right hand of this entrie shalbe your kitchin, storehouse, buttery, and a place of recourse or lodging for two or three serving men.

. . . Upon the left hande of the saide ally or entrie shalbe your hall, through which you shall enter into your chamber, and out of your chamber into your wardrobe and inner chamber. . . . You shall make your fairest lightes and frames towards the east upon your garden, reserving onely halfe windowes for the side lying upon your court, seeing they serve for no other thing, but that you may have an eie upon your folke, and to see who be commers and goers to your lodging.[108]

Extant *gentilhommières* in France, especially in the regions of the Loire Valley, Picardy, and Normandy closest to England and with which English textile and wine merchants had close trading ties, show that the architectural theory adumbrated by Estienne and Liebault in *Maison Rustique* was a clever combination of enthusiasm for the ancients with contemporary, vernacular materials drawn from the surrounding countryside. By drawing upon local buildings, the familiar contours of which people of different social ranks could still claim as "their" tradition, Estienne and Liebault fashioned a neofeudal landscape that served to legitimize an idyllic communal and deferential past, in which social ranks were fixed and social order remained static.

As reform-minded English farmers looked to Italian and French sources for models of efficient planning—indeed, the French connection established by Estienne and Liebault is so strong that it almost qualifies as a fourth implicated place in our New World landscape—they masked their business dealings in the rhetoric and imagery of nostalgia. Since ancient pastoral virtue was the husbandman's crop, they urged England to remain rural and dedicated to "country life," albeit a country life more and more calibrated by market demands. Gervase Markham, a champion of the capitalist land market that drove enclosure movements across England, designed a "model" house (fig. 36) for English yeomen that was decidedly old-fashioned, combining a Renaissance H plan with an open "great hall" (despite the rear small chimney added), cross passage and "skreene," and chambered cross wings of the postmedieval Wealden house.[109] Markham's design, at once for houses and society, offered conservative counsel wrapped in the lessons of classical discipline. It linked a backward longing for social hierarchy to the value of civic virtue in an advancing capitalist culture. The popularity of books by Markham and by Estienne and Liebault reminds us that while Puritans wanted a holy commonwealth, they wanted one in which lines of authority were manifest. "In all times some must be rich some poor," advised John Winthrop in 1630, "some highe and eminent in power and dignitie; others mean and in subjeccion."[110] By incorporating vernacular designs in their model farms, members of the gentry could effectively tie the commercializing present to the classical past and subsume current social tensions in an evoked allegory of ancient virtue.

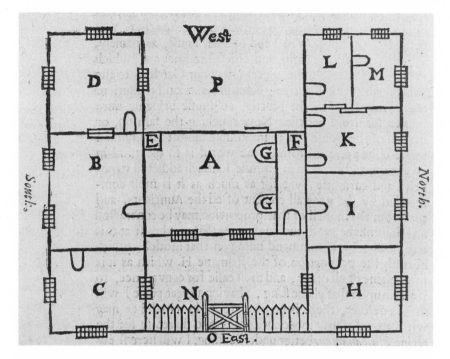

Figure 36. Gervase Markham, "The Modell of a Plaine Country Mans House." From Gervase Markham, *The English Husbandman, Drawne into Two Bookes, and Each Booke into Two Parts* (London: William Sheares, 1635), 24. Key: (A) great hall; (B) dining parlor "for entertainment of strangers"; (C) parlor closet "for the Mistresses use, for necessaries"; (D) lodging off parlor; (E) staircase to rooms above parlor; (F) staircase to servants' rooms above kitchen and buttery; (G) screen; (H) larder; (I) buttery; (K) kitchen; (L) dairy house; (M) milk house; (N) fence; (O) gate; (P) pump. (Photo: Winterthur Library)

Because enclosed farmsteads were built by substantial farmers who were attuned to market production and, in many cases, who also had close contacts with or family relations among merchants in London, Norwich, Poole, Exeter, and Bristol, their diffusion across England was remarkably rapid. At Fosten Green in Kent one farmer arranged a stable with hayloft and a tenant laborer's cottage as dependencies of his own three-room, lobby-entry house. Placed at right angles to the dwelling, the service wings framed an open forecourt. At Caxton, a small West Cambridgeshire village immediately adjacent to Eltisley, another landowner constructed a three-sided farmstead extending from his house along the town street. The new farm-planning literature probably played a key role in the rebuilding of the large demesne farms, or "bartons," in Devon during the first three decades of the seventeenth century. The landholdings of these bartons in many instances were consolidated prior to the Norman Conquest, but the original houses were upgraded and, with the addition of new barns and shippons, "improved" into larger courtyarded complexes during the early Stuart years. The presence of large courtyards marked the expanding significance of cattle herding and dairying to large landholders in the upland pasture regions of the West Country, and scattered references in seventeenth-century deeds and probate records suggest how common courtyarded residences were in that region. A house at Axminster in Devon, for example, had a "walled forecourt [that] led into the dwelling," and one at nearby Bondleigh had "two close[d] courts." Requisite outbuildings—barns, shippons, brew houses, and bake houses—surrounded these courts. In Alphington, one Devon farmer in the late 1670s proudly described his enclosed complex as comprising "4 houses: hall and parlour under one roof, kitchen and malt house under another, the third a barn, [and] the fourth a shippon with a new stable and a corn chamber which I have built."[111]

LOCAL IMPROVEMENTS

The origin of these "improved" courtyarded farmsteads and merchant premises in an agricultural literature both market-oriented and neofeudal raises a final question about possible antecedents for Desborough's domestic compound. Were any courtyarded farmsteads built in seventeenth-century New England—and more particularly in Connecticut—that would have provided Desborough a New World rural model for his own enterprise? John Smythson's 1622 drawing for Mr. Diball is again useful, as it links earlier Italian and French courtyarded houses to a house designed by John Winthrop Jr. soon after his return from London in late 1635 (fig. 37). The purpose of the structure, planned for Saybrook, was to serve as a protective rural retreat for one of a group of highly placed Puritan lords and gentlemen—including Lord Brooke, Lord Saye and Sele, John Pym, Sir Arthur Hesilrige, and Sir Richard Saltonstall—in the event that they were forced to leave England for political refuge. Undoubtedly Winthrop had seen newly built London town houses that integrated Continental design fashions. In 1951 Garvan argued that the Saybrook dwelling clarified the connection between London Renaissance dwellings and the bawn. Indeed, Winthrop, educated at Trinity College in Dublin, had passed through Ulster in early 1635 and had been entertained there by Sir John Clotworthy, a Devon gentleman in county Antrim who was a leading spokesman for the New English planters, farmed land in the proportion of the Drapers' Company, was an ardent follower of Samuel Hartlib, and claimed the firebrand Puritan intellectual John Pym as a brother-in-law. Winthrop had firsthand contact with the bawn tradition while in the Ulster Plantations.[112]

While in England, however, he also visited the ancestral manorial home of the Winthrops at Groton, Suffolk. Initially built by his great-grandfather Adam in the

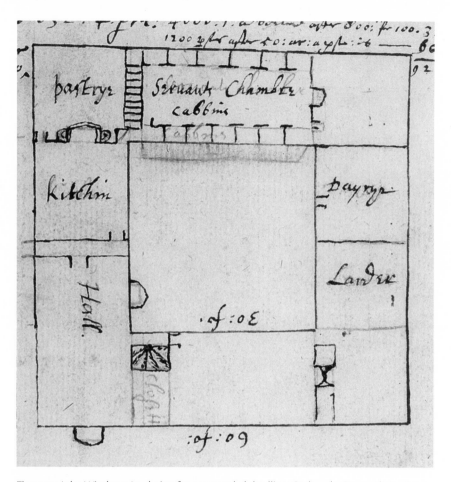

Figure 37. John Winthrop Jr., design for courtyarded dwelling, Saybrook, Connecticut, 1635. (Photo: Massachusetts Historical Society)

late 1540s and much improved in the late 1580s and 1590s (fig. 38), the farmstead consisted of a central courtyard area surrounded by a series of outbuildings very similar to those Winthrop designed for the Saybrook residence: brew house, bake house, dairies, larder, and a "folkes chamber," or rooms for hired hands closely related to the "servants' chamber" with its enclosed, built-in bedsteads or "cabbins" at Saybrook. The plan of the Groton farmstead was not made until John Winthrop III (1681–1747), a professor of natural science at Harvard, visited the place in 1728. Although by then the facade of the ancient house had been updated, the arrangement and designation of outbuildings still demonstrated a close similarity to both the Saybrook plan and Desborough's farmstead in Guilford.[113]

Another drawing by John Winthrop Jr. suggests that the Saybrook structure probably derived more from rural English farmsteads like the one at Groton than

Figure 38. John Winthrop III, plan of Groton house, Groton Manor, Suffolk, England, 1728. (Photo: Massachusetts Historical Society)

from fortified structures in Ulster. Winthrop had acquired a copy of Estienne and Liebault's *Maison Rustique* while in London in 1630, providing a compelling literary source for the Saybrook complex. When compared with the floor plan of the courtyarded residence, this second drawing of the site suggests that the house was placed in relation to a large barn and a smaller granary to form a farmstead surrounded by pallisade fencing. If the two drawings are superimposed, the probable layout of the entire Saybrook complex emerges (fig. 39). Seen in this fashion, the "inner" courtyard was only one of three such enclosures—the second being an "outer" yard between house and the street, the third a rear work or kitchen yard—and thus resembled the organization of the English example at Ingatestone and, more to the point, Desborough's later complex in Guilford. This evidence indicates that Winthrop's Saybrook complex also drew on the equally complex mixture of English and Continental ideas then available in designs for London town houses and rural capital farmsteads. The similarity of Winthrop's Saybrook compound to the plans of defensive structures in Ulster drives home a simple point that archaeologist E. M. Jope made almost thirty years ago: "These bawns *were really farm enclosures*, and contained the necessary buildings, a stable, brewhouse and bakehouse, storehouses, gardens, and probably quarters for servants."[114]

REFASHIONING FARMS

However, if Samuel Desborough's Guilford compound was derived in part from agricultural theory of the late sixteenth and early seventeenth century, one final question remains. What existing agrarian landscape was it trying to reform? The relative success of authors such as Heresbach, Estienne and Liebault, and Markham in reshaping the local contours of England's agricultural economy rested on the willingness of husbandmen to see the wisdom that both ancient learning and its careful application contained, and then change their ways. At the turn of the seventeenth century, the news on that front was not good. As John Norden despaired in 1607, "We have, indeed, a kind of plodding and common course of husbandry hereabouts." Land was exhausted through constant, monotonous cropping. Attempts to reclaim land through ditching and fertilization were spotty at best, and calls to reorganize farmsteads in order to maximize efficiency and protect the value of productive labor usually went unheeded. From the ranks of these "plodding" yeomen came most immigrants to early New England. In 1622 Richard Cushman observed that on farms near Plymouth "all spoils, rots, and is marred for want of manuring, gathering, ordering." Along with land-extensive husbandry techniques, most seventeenth-century New England yeomen failed to

an Acre

yarde

Hall

Kitchin

Closet

parlor

servants Chamber Cabins

barne

Lanter

Figure 39. Conjectural view, John Winthrop Jr.'s 1635 design for Saybrook courtyarded dwelling in relation to entire farmstead layout. (Drawing by the author)

0   25   50

FEET

enforce a clear spatial segregation according to task. In Reading, Massachusetts, for example, town leaders may have had this failure in mind when they advised in 1649 that, owing to "there being manni accidentes in the Countree by fire, to the great damning of many, by joining of barnes or haystacks to dwelling houses," they were ordering that all barns and haystacks be at least six poles, or ninety-nine linear feet, from any dwelling. The prohibition argues how common the attachment of these buildings must have been.[115]

Not all New England yeomen were ploughing in the dark, however. A few shared Desborough's enthusiasm for classical agricultural literature. Richard Muzzey of Ipswich willed his "dun mare" and "my horse book" to his son Joseph in 1642, and when Joseph fell ill in the summer of 1680, he, in turn, bequeathed to his son "my book of Government of Cattell Lenard Mascall." Frequent citations to "Markham," such as the "Markam & 10 smal bookes" listed in the inventory of Rebecca Bacall in 1655, are less revealing, as they might refer to his *Cheape and Good Husbandry* (1623), *Farewell to Husbandry,* or many other volumes he wrote on a wide variety of topics, including *The English Housewife.* The references to these writers are infrequent in early New England, suggesting they appealed principally to residents of New England who, like Miles Standish, had gentle upbringings. In Plymouth Colony Standish had a copy of "the Countrey ffarmer" appropriately listed alongside "homers Illiads" in his library in 1656. He had probably acquired the Estienne and Liebault volume when business took him to London in 1626. Perhaps Standish's zeal for the book's advice led to a remarkable reordering of Plymouth's disheveled townscape. The next year Isaack De Rasieres visited Plymouth and found that each family's house lot now "had gardens *enclosed* behind and at the sides with clapboards, so that houses and *courtyards* are arranged in very good order."[116]

Given the emphasis in *Maison Rustique* on the proper planning and alignment of country estates, Standish may have used the book himself when he left Plymouth in 1633 to begin developing his rural estate in nearby Duxbury. The house he built, excavated by archaeologist James Hall in 1863–64, shows clear evidence of linking sophisticated concepts of site layout and remembered vernacular houses from Standish's Lancashire home near the Welsh border (fig. 40a). The house consisted of two ranges of rooms placed at about a forty-five-degree angle to each other; they connect only at one point. The top range consisted of three rooms, one of which was heated by a large hearth. This range is pierced by two exterior doors and a third that connects it to the lower building. The lower range has two heated rooms, each with an exterior door, and two additional rooms: a square one lying between the two heated spaces, and a small anteroom adjacent to the linkage between the two structures. Based upon surviving houses in areas of northeastern Wales that at one end originally housed cattle (fig. 40b, c), it is possible that Standish's structure did the same; one of the two right-hand rooms in the upper range would have been the likely location for a byre. James Hall's site drawings show that while other living spaces were properly underpinned with stone, this area had wooden footings, suggesting perhaps that it only had to satisfy "creature comforts," and not human ones.[117]

In New England, however, domestic structures that housed people and animals under common roofs were rare. More prevalent in much of England at the time of emigration was a farmstead that relied on two principal buildings: a barn for the processing of grain crops and a cow house for the sheltering of cattle during the winter months and for daily milking. Farmers from the midlands and southern counties of England were principally responsible for transferring this division of functions to New England. In 1652 in New Haven, Henry Bishop was brought into court to answer charges that he had abused a servant named Samuel Andrews; in his defense, Bishop said, "The boy hath bine so lazie that he could not make him . . . chop wood nor draw water nor serve the cattell, but he would doe mischiefe, breake his bucket, and let cattell into his barne and spoyle his corne," implying that Bishop's animals normally lived apart from his grain stores. The next year a writ from Essex County, Massachusetts, plainly describes a "barn and hay in it, with the cow house." A decade later, the 1663 inventory of John Fish of Sandwich mentions a "beast house," and the inventory of his near neighbor Thomas Dexter includes "the outhousing a Barne & Cowhouse" worth ten pounds in 1686. A 1725 reference to a "cowhouse" in Hartford, Connecticut, recalls that community's East Anglian roots.[118] The need to house grain apart from animals, to keep bread away from blood, persisted through the third generation.

The segregation of processed grain from livestock was a rule that Desborough's enclosed farmstead also enforced; recall that he had an "oxe stall," two stalls for cattle, and a stable for "the horses." By the late sixteenth century the multiplication of small service structures on farms in England's midland and southeastern counties already gave them a scattered, disorganized appearance. In the late 1570s William Harrison proudly claimed, "The mansion houses of our country towns and villages . . . are builded in such sort as generally as that they have neither dairy, stable, nor brewhouse annexed unto them under the same roof (as in many places beyond the sea and some of the north parts of out country) but all separate from the first and one of them from another."[119] What Desborough accomplished was a skilled integration of change and continuity. The distinction between his farmstead and those of his less "theoretically" inclined Guilford neighbors was that his buildings were carefully aligned in courtyards to organize related activities conveniently close at hand, while still preserving the segregation of tasks in discrete

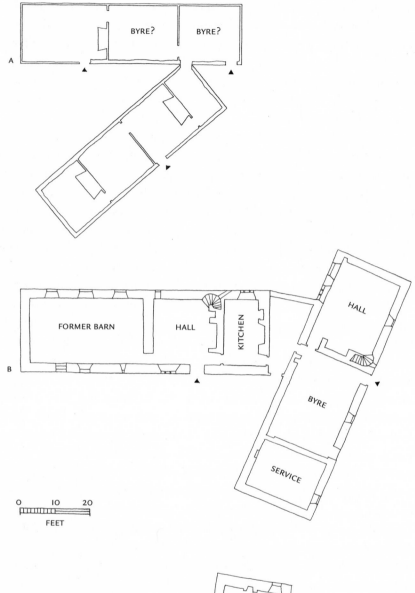

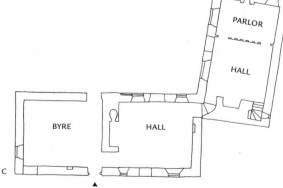

A

BYRE? BYRE?

FORMER BARN HALL KITCHEN HALL BYRE SERVICE

B

0   10   20
FEET

PARLOR HALL BYRE HALL

C

buildings. As the argument went, convenience would save him time, increase the level of surplus value for market, and generate a profit.

A LAYERED LANDSCAPE

Samuel Desborough's enclosed farmstead in Guilford can be understood most fully by reconstructing the complex ways it implicated other places that emerged when patterns of transmission, collisions of feudal and capitalist agrarian ideologies, and ambivalent admixtures of antimodernism and improvement intersected in seventeenth-century Connecticut. From his enclosed residence, Desborough expanded into the countryside, purchasing additional grazing land in Guilford's hinterlands. While the abstract rhetoric of conversion and defense argued that his farmstead offered a bawnlike sanctuary from divine affliction and satanic evil, the concrete rhythms of economic life demanded that it also function as an administrative and processing center for his real estate acquisitions and his entrepreneurial attempts at livestock raising. The careful divisions of space demonstrate that Desborough was concerned with controlling his economic resources and maintaining authority over a limited, rigorously subdivided environment. Offering largesse to locals in his hybrid hospitality zone, Desborough was actually banking on his role as a second-level commercial supplier of grain and livestock to New Haven's export trade until he, with news of Cromwell's growing popularity, returned to England to play a part in the new dispensation.

The interpretation I have offered of Desborough's domestic compound accounts for lines of social class, economic ambition, and religious belief that converge in the production and symbolic meaning of household space. The mercantile underpinnings of enclosed domestic space in England and in northern France prior to the invasion of Ulster are especially significant, since these architectural references to nascent market capitalism are most frequently omitted while scholars argue over the defensive purposes of New World bawns. But Desborough's farmstead was more than simply an example of a "bawn" mentality coming to material fruition in the New World. It epitomized, implicated, and visually referenced a remarkably complex tradition of profane architecture: defensive com-

Figure 40. Miles Standish's house and its Welsh antecedents: (a) Standish house foundation, ca. 1633–50 (after James Hall, manuscript map of excavations on site, 1864, Pilgrim Hall, Plymouth, Massachusetts); (b) Old Castle–upon–Alun, St. Brides Major, Glamorganshire, ca. 1580–1620 (after Peter Smith, *Houses of the Welsh Countryside: A Study in Historical Geography* [London: Royal Commission on Historical Monuments, 1975], 207, fig. 114a); (c) Llanddegyman-fawr, Llanfihangle Cwm Du, Breconshire (after Smith, *Houses of the Welsh Countryside*, 206, fig. 113c). (Drawing by the author)

plexes in the English hinterlands, with roots extending back to peles and tower houses in the Scottish marchlands; town residences anchored in the Renaissance (and through these to mercantile premises in both the Old World and the New, monastic complexes, inns, and theaters); and enclosed farmsteads (and their submerged implication of social segregation in buildings, of agricultural literature that drew upon classical concepts, and of French vernacular farmsteads).

The French, Italian, and Irish connections, including rural *gentilhommières*, town house complexes, Renaissance pattern books, agricultural treatises, and the native Irish *badhún* tradition, highlight a paradox of English Puritan culture: it relied heavily on exoticized cultures whose religious beliefs were anathema to the Cromwellian moment, and it drew selectively from architectural and landscape innovations expropriated on the illicit margins of England's empire while also condemning the dangerous, transgressive qualities of the "papist," the "heathen," the "wild Irish," and the "savage" peoples that were their source.[120] Multiple meanings reverberate within its enclosing walls: military outpost in a hostile universe; metaphysical microcosm of a walled, heavenly city; classical garden perfect in its nostalgic reference to the lost ancient world of feudal obligation and static social rank; efficient commercial machine in the calculus of an expanding imperial market that defined "cultural others" only to devour them, that articulated alien aesthetic systems only to appropriate their power.

As its material metaphors refracted upon one another, Desborough's farmstead mixed the rhetoric of Christian conversion with the architecture of capitalist efficiency. It blurred the boundaries between a protected pastoral utopia and an expanding market economy. It articulated the tension in early New England culture between feeling located in a bounded metaphysical landscape of heavenly correspondences and, at the same time, discovering a sense of existential dislocation in the shifting, irregular terrain of a world increasingly mediated by the figure of the merchant-trickster and the magic of commodities.

An uneasy sense of colonial dislocation bothered Jared Eliot in the 1750s when he looked back and considered the dark, century-old enclosed farmstead that was next door during his youth. From his perspective, the dense overlay of English associations that Desborough's estate brought to mind was precisely the problem. As *Essays on Field Husbandry* makes clear, Eliot believed that agricultural reform would lead to political transformation in the American colonies. Not all of his activities necessarily signaled change. He realized the value of land—whether fertilized or not—and was careful to protect his own property rights in Guilford, which like other towns had seen its common lands repeatedly subdivided to accommodate the needs of succeeding generations. In May 1723, Eliot was one of thirty petitioners who asked the General Assembly of Connecticut for assistance in establishing titles to ancient lands still held in common that were already under siege.[121]

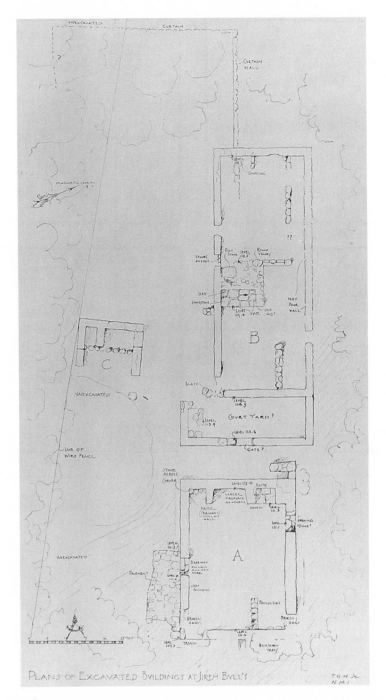

Figure 41. Norman K. Isham, site plan of excavations at Jireh Bull House, South Kingstown, Rhode Island, 1917. Ink on paper. (Photo: Rhode Island Historical Society, no. Rhi X3 8473)

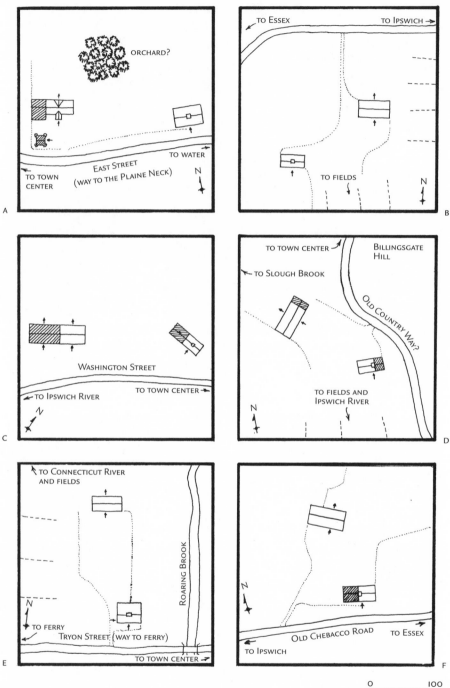

With a keen interest in soil chemistry and the transformation of nature through experimental knowledge, Eliot was fascinated by alchemy. He had studied medicine with Joshua Hobart of Boston and Southold, who, according to Ezra Stiles, had been "initiated an adept" while in England in 1656. Eliot informed Stiles that in 1717, as Hobart lay ill in Southold, he "sent for him in his Deathbed, to come over to L[ong]. Isl[an]d, that he ought impart to him some Secrets in Physic and Chemistry which he had never communicated," but the weather made Eliot's crossing impossible.[122] Thus, Eliot combined an empiricist's distrust in the "ancients" — "an Ounce of Experience is better than a Pound of Science," he stated in his first essay — and an alchemist's faith in the transmutation and perfectability of matter. For adepts in search of the "philosopher's stone" this meant transforming lead into gold. For Eliot, it meant turning a profit from the thin soils and rocky fields of New England. In 1762 one Rhode Island man thanked Eliot for his "Hints abo't the Transmutation of Iron from Black Sand."[123]

Part minister and part magus, Eliot belonged to a scientific utopian tradition that stretched back to include the seventeenth-century English reformers he admired. Like Samuel Hartlib, Eliot was trying to link political reform, capitalist progress, and moral improvement. He did so by separating himself from authors in the Continental or classical mold — Markham, Mascall, Gardiner, Estienne and Liebault — who had accepted the teachings of ancient Greek and Roman authors as received truths without verification through actual experiments in field husbandry. "Our Reasonings and Speculations without Experience are delusory and uncertain," he claimed. Eliot instead followed a new generation of "scientific" Puritan writers beginning with Gabriel Plattes, who sent his *A Discovery of Infinite Treasure, Hidden since the Worlds Beginning* (1639) to John Winthrop Jr. and Robert Childs in Boston shortly after its publication. Plattes, along with Ralph Austen and Walter Blith, argued that only the empirical study of soils, fertilizers, and planting schedules would lead to agrarian and Puritan social reform. These commonwealthmen, imbued with the scientific millennialism of the 1640s and 1650s, publicly renounced the classical teachings of Aristotelian and Platonic tradition as irrational and ill suited to England's actual climate and geography. Blith even opined in his popular treatise *The English Improver, Or a New Survey*

Figure 42. Open farmsteads in colonial New England: (a) Daniel Cushing's farmstead, Hingham, Massachusetts, by 1693 (although of early timber construction, granary or "corn barn" may date from as late as 1783, when first mentioned on town rate list); (b) Giddings-Low farmstead, Essex (formerly Chebacco parish of Ipswich), Massachusetts, before 1702; (c) Joseph Gould's farmstead, Topsfield, Massachusetts, ca. 1710; (d) Matthew Stanley's farmstead, Topsfield, Massachusetts, before 1718; (e) Joseph Hollister's farmstead, South Glastonbury, Connecticut, by 1720; (f) Samuel Giddings's farmstead, Essex, Massachusetts, ca. 1690–1730. (Drawing by the author)

of Husbandry (1649) that texts like that by Estienne and Liebault were "of little use to us."[124] But even experimental reformers could mix their sources. As he ghost-wrote *Samuel Hartlib His Legacie* in 1651, Robert Child informed readers that they "may reade a large *Treatise of the Countrey-Farmer*" for additional instruction on the cultivation of meadow grasses, referring here to the same copy of *Maison Rustique* that John Winthrop had loaned him when he was in Boston in the 1640s.[125]

For Eliot the historical disjunction of "ancient" and "modern" was thematically central to understanding why, when his gaze turned to his own contemporaries in Guilford, "all their former Experience and Knowledge was now of very little service to them." Only after the overdetermined and limiting implications of colonial places like Samuel Desborough's enclosed farmstead were exorcised could people be free of "all their former Experience" and the limitations they placed on action. Only after people stopped assembling farmsteads by adapting odd structures to the task of a profitable household economy would their lives improve. Consider, for example, the country estate built in South Kingstown, Rhode Island, by Newport merchant Jireh Bull (fig. 41). Built at some point between about 1660 and its destruction in 1676, it reused an old small house as an outbuilding ("C") and placed it and another stone end-chimney structure ("A") in linear alignment to the main house ("B") to articulate both a farmyard and a probable "court yard" between the principal dwelling and its adjacent dependency ("B" and "A," respectively). Archaeological excavations undertaken by Norman M. Isham in 1918 suggest that these separate structures, in the fashion of Irish bawns and Desborough's Guilford farmstead, may have been linked by an enclosing stone wall.[126]

Raised amid farmsteads informed by the logic of defined courtyards and the limitation of enclosing walls, reformer Eliot favored the adaptive freedom that "open" farmsteads, with no enclosing walls or perimeter buildings to limit economic possibilities, might afford in a changing agricultural economy. These farm plans, in fact built by New England yeomen from the beginning of settlement (fig. 42), suggest that a more dispersed planning strategy allowed optimistic farmers to add new buildings and smoothly accommodate new husbandry practices should markets change and need arise.

Open farmsteads contained one building that Eliot viewed as an exemplary local innovation born neither of hidebound "tradition" nor of outmoded Continental theory. On each of them, a single barn sheltered both livestock and crops. New England yeomen seem to have worked out this new building type experimentally, at first retaining the English "cow house" even as they outfitted it with a threshing floor and with lofts for the storage of fodder. When John Roe of Duxbury sold his farm in 1642, it included a "cow house that had a floor over . . . of eight or nine boards" for the storage of grain. Ralph Partridge, also of Duxbury,

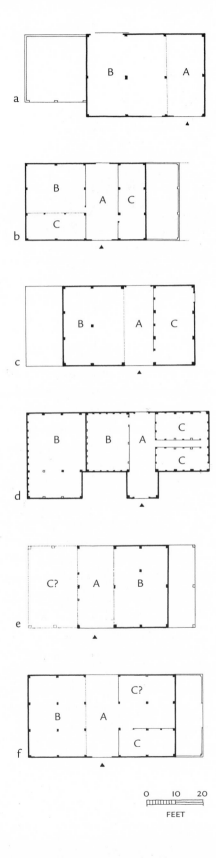

Figure 43. Barns in colonial Massachusetts, showing structures of three, four, and five bays with later additions indicated: (a) John Cogswell, Essex, by 1735; (b) Matthew Stanley, Topsfield, by 1718; (c) Cressy barn, Essex, ca. 1730–40; (d) Daniel Cushing, Hingham, ca. 1679–96; (e) Joseph Gould, Topsfield, by 1710; (f) Giddings-Low farm, Essex, by 1702. Key: (A) threshing floor; (B) hay mow; (C) byre. (Drawing by the author)

0   10   20
FEET

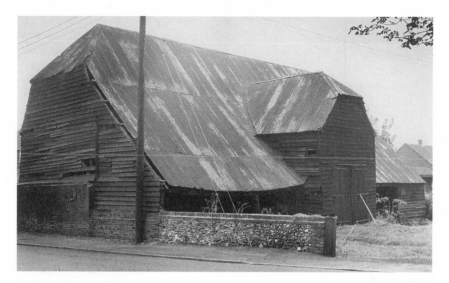

Figure 44. Aisled grain barn with entry porch, ca. 1620–40, near Dedham, Essex. (Photo by the author)

had stored "over the Cow House 1 bushell & an halfe of Corne" in 1658.[127] Certainly a concern for efficiency, intended in part to reduce the cost of maintaining separate structures in Springfield's harsh winter climate, informed John Pynchon's 1652 decision to pay two local men "by ye Removing my Cowhouse to ye Barne." Once it was removed, however, New England yeomen seemed ambivalent about what, exactly, to call the new structure. When Walter Blackbourne sold his Roxbury estate in July 1639, it contained a "Cow house or barne set up but not quite finished." Between the late 1670s and the early 1730s, New England yeomen built barns that combined on the ground floor a large hay mow, central threshing floor, and areas for milking and bedding cattle (fig. 43). An expansive loft provided extra room for fodder. Like houses, these barns often had lean-tos added if more space was quickly needed. On his land in Wethersfield, Connecticut, George Wyllys in 1644 described how he had "built on it a barne as long & wide as that of [his] at hartford, wth a leanetoo all along the one side of it, though it [had] no porch."[128]

Husbandmen like Roe, Partridge, Pynchon, and Blackbourne may not have actually invented the idea of the mixed-function barn but instead combined two English building forms to create a new solution to the problem of how to reduce costs while still engaging in mixed agriculture. They drew upon the accepted form of the grain barn across much of southern England; a central threshing floor and drive-through separated large hay mows on either side. A projecting porch might

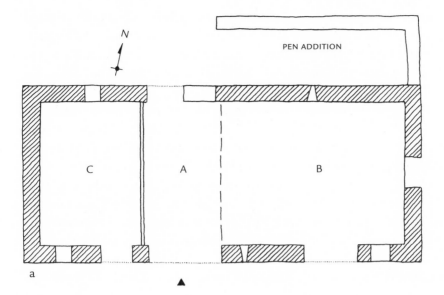

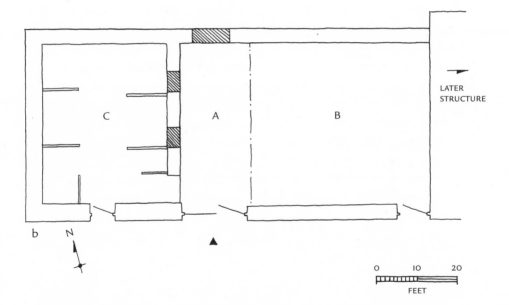

Figure 45. English bank barns with combined housing for crops and livestock: (a) High Birk Howe, Lancashire, late seventeenth century; cross-hatching indicates original fabric; (b) High Hallgarth, Lancashire, ca. 1680–1710; cross-hatching shows original openings in wall surface. After field notes by Tim Whittaker and plans by Martin Higgins, 1984. Key: (A) threshing floor; (B) hay mow; (C) byre. (Drawing by the author)

shelter farm carts as they were unloaded (fig. 44; compare with 43d). This lowland barn form was then fused to a concept transferred to New England by migrants from the hilly area of England's southern Pennines in West Yorkshire. There, and in nearby areas of England's Lake District and Northumberland, bank barns consolidated the housing of animals and grain processing, albeit it usually on two different levels. But in the flatter contours of the Eden Valley, both animals and crops were placed on the same floor, separated by the threshing floor, suggesting that England's northern counties provide the likely source for the dual-function barn often thought to be a New England innovation (fig. 45). In 1941, architectural historian James Walton discovered seventeenth-century barns in that area that, under one roof, "include the shippon where the cows were housed, and the actual barn [i.e., grain storage] itself."[129] Thus the barn in early New England linked the efficiency of the dual-function northern English bank barn with the single-story logic of the southern English barn. In early New England animals and crops, on either side of a central threshing floor, shared a single floor. This represented a merging of English regional practices that New England yeomen "experimented" with until a hybrid form emerged that precisely suited the local climate and type of mixed husbandry they practiced.

By contrast, Desborough's domestic complex emphatically continued the English custom of segregating livestock and crops in distinct buildings and defined the limits of its own possible expansion. Inherently more conservative and from an earlier moment in English political economy, it argued that agrarian resources and property, rather than being fluid and experimental, were fixed and in need of protection. The relatively close placement of Desborough's house to his cattle stalls and barn demonstrates this protective function; he could maintain effective surveillance over his possessions by keeping them all at close range. By enclosing the entire farmstead in surrounding walls, Desborough could defend and restrict access to his property from social inferiors and imagined cultural Others. This is one reason why Jared Eliot in the late 1740s remembered the place next door as somehow retrograde.

REGENERATION

Eliot championed farmsteads, however modest, that arranged a house, outbuildings, and a dual-function barn to be adaptive to the fluidity of agrarian capital that was always within reach to the new farmer-entrepreneur willing to experiment. For Eliot, the minister, alchemist, physician, and scientific theorist, the "transmutation" of colonial society from a collection of litigious individuals into a utopian nation, where self-interested citizens could be as perfect as gold, demanded a landscape of new vernacular forms suited to Americans' own needs. Only then "it may be said," he stated, with an eye on the limitations of colonialism's cultural empire, "that in a sort, *they began the World a New*."[130] When that New World emerged, its places would be saturated by implicated meanings.

I MERVAILE HOW THAT

OLD WITCH KNOWES EVERY

THING THAT IS DONE IN

MY HOUSE.

—ELIZABETH NICHOLSON,

SALEM WITNESS

2 Embodied Spaces

THE AUTOPSY

Human bodies have many meanings. On March 23, 1662, Elizabeth Kelley, an eight-year-old girl in Hartford, Connecticut, cried out that she was being tormented and "pinched" by Goodwife Ayres. As her small body pitched and rolled under the woman's invisible grasp, Elizabeth complained to her father, "Help me, help me, Goodwife Ayres is upon me, and she chokes me, she kneels on my belly, she will break my bowels, she pinches me, she will make me black and blue. Oh father will you not help me." Her agony lasted three more days. On Wednesday morning, "the last words she spoke was, Goodwife Ayres chokes me, and then she was speechless" and died. In many ways, Elizabeth Kelley's case resembles those of the "afflicted" in other New England towns in the seventeenth century: a young child from a modest household falls ill and lays the "cause" of her pain at the feet of an established local matron—in this case one suspected of being in league with Rebecca Greensmith, Mary Sanford, and Katherine Palmer, neighboring women already accused of having practiced "arts inhibited and out of warrant" during the preceding decade. But the Kelley case differed from other incidents in one respect: Bray Rossiter was called from Guilford to perform an autopsy, and his record of the procedure is the first written synopsis of a medical postmortem examination in early New England.

As I have described in the previous chapter, Rossiter received his medical training in England, probably in the early 1630s, just as professional surgeons trained in Padua, Paris, and Leiden were laboring to establish an empirical understanding of the human body in London and Oxford. Rossiter's careful description of Elizabeth Kelley's bodily wounds and trauma suggests a physician whose close understanding of musculature and internal organs came from time spent in the anatomical theater, appreciating the body as a spectacle of revelation. In his examination of "John Kelley's child at the grave," six points struck him as curious. His first concern was that "the whole body, the musculous parts, nerves and joints were all pliable, without any stiffness or contraction, the gullet only excepted. Experience of dead bodies," he noted with experimental precision, "renders such symptoms unusual." His second point demonstrates that he "opened" the corpse itself to view: "From the costal ribs to the bottom of the belly in the whole latitude of the womb, both the scarf skin and the whole skin with the enveloping or covering flesh had a deep blue tincture, when the inward part thereof was fresh, and the bowels under it in true order, without any discoverable peccancy to cause such an effect or symptom." With the child's interior cavities exposed, Rossiter then noticed that "no quantity or appearance of blood was in either venter or cavity as belly or breast, but in the throat only at the very swallow, where was a large quantity as that part could well contain, both fresh and fluid." Rossiter recorded that Elizabeth's blood was thus in "no way congealed or clodded, as it comes from a vein opened, that I stroke it out with my finger as water." This strange detail appeared in his next note: "There was the appearance of pure fresh blood in the backside of the arm, affecting the skin as blood itself without bruising or congealing." Finally, two other discoveries merited comment: "The bladder of gall," Rossiter wrote, "was all broken and curded, without any tincture in the adjacent parts." "The gullet or swallow was contracted, like a hard fish bone, that hardly a large pease could be forced through."

Although the autopsy's graveside location was unusual, Rossiter's careful empirical observations led him to conclude that Elizabeth had died of witchcraft. Each of his points strikes a familiar chord in the period's cultural construction of witchcraft and the invisible battle of God's elect and Satan's minions: a body in which rigor mortis had never set in; the strange blue "tincture" of the epidermis but the "fresh" hue of subcutaneous tissue; and the special diagnostic care given to the gullet, blood, and gall bladder. Rossiter's findings suggested that the normal signs of death were awry. Joseph Marsh, one of the Kelleys' Hartford neighbors, had also noticed strange signs as Elizabeth's body was prepared for the coffin: "The child was turned over upon the right side and so upon the belly, and then there came such a scent from the corpse as that it caused some to depart the room, [such] as Gregory Wolterton and George Grave." But after the child was "turned again and put into the coffin, John Kelley desired them to come into the room again to see the child's face": "and then we saw upon the right cheek of the child's face a reddish tawny great spot, which covered a great part of the cheek, it being on the side next to Goodwife Ayres where she stood." On the basis of an empirical dissection of Elizabeth Kelley's body as an object of professional expertise, combined with his previous "experience of dead bodies," Rossiter reached the conclusion of witchcraft. As he phrased it at the beginning of his report, "All of these 6 particulars underwritten I judge preternatural."[1]

Elizabeth Kelley's opened body, in fact, revealed two bodies that in the early 1660s were struggling for visibility and continuing validation. One was a metaphysical body open to the will of God, the movement of planets, and the shifting balance of the four cardinal humors and their elements: the hot, cold, dry, and moist states of blood, phlegm, black bile, and yellow bile. It was a besieged body, the site of "remarkable providences," preternatural interventions, and epidemic diseases sent by God to punish mortal transgressions. Her frame was an emblem of divinely sanctioned hierarchy, of affliction and punishment, magic and countermagic. It was anchored in an ontology that saw in human bodies evidence of heavenly design. It was also an emphatically hierarchic body, with the head, limbs, hands, and feet invoking and defining a system of meaning that bound church, civil society, and individuals in a unified vision of deference and devotion. Perhaps Rossiter found this body narrated in the pages of Francisco de Valles's *In libros Hippocratis de morbis popularibus commentaria* (Cologne, 1588), a massive compilation of symptoms and diagnoses assembled from the ancient texts of Galen and Hippocrates that Edward Hopkins of Hartford had given him prior to 1652. The narrative of his autopsy, in fact, discursively reproduces the hierarchy. After detailing the condition of the ribs, belly, and bowels, he moved to the "gullet" and then, for the final proof of maleficium, turned to "the child's face" and the telltale red spot on her cheek.

At the same time, however, Elizabeth Kelley's corpse revealed a second body, this one defined through spectacle and scalpel, the "demonstrations" and tools of professional surgeons. This body was enclosed by its own internal rules and systemic linkage of muscles, nerves, circulation, respiration, and digestion and was precisely mapped in the new writings of Andreas Vesalius, Charles Estienne, William Harvey, and Thomas Willis. This body was defined through experiment, not revelation. Freed from the strange pull of planetary alignment, it instead moved in a new material economy of sensate, mechanical objects floating in a sea of related objects, each identical and therefore substitutable for one another. In this chapter, I argue that seventeenth-century covenant theology and the aesthetics of communion undergirded the overlapping metaphoric meanings of the hierarchic body. Covenant theology had some radical implications, but these were typically excluded in a theory of government that saw Christ as the "head" of the church and the father as "head" of the family. The interlocking meanings of the covenant of grace and the "federal" or national covenant effectively fused the purity of

God's free gift of salvation to the power that came from a coercive emphasis on good works in congregations and communities. I also argue that as the objectified or enclosed body, shaped in part by the linked "enlightened" discourses of experimental medicine and a capitalist economy experimenting with the containment of risk, became more of a substitutional unit, it helped to promote among working people a new force for social leveling in the first half of the eighteenth century. This source of leveling also resuscitated those radical but almost forgotten strands of social thought deriving from the covenant of grace—including an ardent millennialism, an antiauthoritarian strain developed in opposition to the federal covenant, and an animating spiritism—that advocates of hierarchy had almost eclipsed.

HEAVENLY MANSIONS

The hierarchic, besieged body Rossiter revealed in his autopsy of Elizabeth Kelley was saturated by the poetics of Saint Paul's first letter to the Corinthians. In that letter, the apostle offered the pivotal reading of the body as a metaphor for the rank order of power and privilege that Christ had instituted in the early church:

> For as the body is one, and hath many members, and all the members of that one body, being many, are one body: so also is Christ . . . For the body is not one member, but many. If the foot shall say, Because I am not the hand, I am not of the body; is it therefore not of the body? And if the ear shall say, Because I am not the eye, I am not of the body; is it therefore not of the body? If the whole body were an eye, where were the hearing? If the whole were hearing, where would the smelling? But now hath God set the members every one of them in the body, as it hath pleased him. And if they were all one member, where were the body? But now are they many members, yet but one body. And the eye cannot say unto the hand, I have no need of thee: nor again the head to the feet, I have no need of you. Nay, much more those members of the body, which seem to be more feeble, are necessary: And those members of the body, which we think to be less honourable, upon these we bestow more abundant honour; and our uncomely parts have more abundant comeliness. For our comely parts have no need: but God hath tempered the body together, having given more abundant honour to that part which lacked: That there should be no schism in the body; but that the members should have the same care for one another. And whether one member suffer, all the members suffer with it; or one member be honoured, all the members rejoice with it. Now ye are the body of Christ, and members in particular.[2]

In the same letter, he extended the metaphor from members of Christ's body to occupants of his architectural imagination. "For we are labourers together with God: ye are God's husbandry, ye are God's building. According to the grace of God which is given to me, as a wise master-builder, I have laid the foundation and another buildeth thereon. But let every man take heed how he buildeth thereupon. For other foundation can no man lay than that is laid, which is Jesus Christ." In Saint Paul's second letter to the Corinthians, he continued the description, stating, "For we know that if our earthly house of this tabernacle were dissolved, we have a building of God, an house not made with hands, eternal in the heavens. For in this we groan, earnestly desiring to be clothed upon with our house which is from heaven."[3]

These verses established God's temple or tabernacle as a body that is a living house, a house the elect will one day exchange for a perfect eternal dwelling. For New England Puritans the body of the faithful appeared in the shape of the meetinghouse, with its seating arrangement that placed men on one side and women on the other, or members of leading families near the front and children, servants, and Native Americans at the rear. With more prominent families at the meetinghouse's "head"—that is, closest to Christ's holy word as it moved through the mouth of the minister—and their lesser neighbors behind them in a posture of abject dependency, each worship service reenacted the emblematic house-body as a static pattern of hierarchic relationships. Heirs to an English Puritanism heavily influenced by Pauline rhetoric, New England's faithful used the metaphoric language of bodies and buildings at many points during the seventeenth and eighteenth centuries. Josiah Rossiter, whose father performed the Kelley autopsy, informed his cousin Rowland Cotton of the deaths of several ministers in 1703, reminding him "to Remember what brittle tabernacles we carry about w[i]th us in this world."[4]

The tabernacles that Rossiter referenced had their source in Saint Paul's letters and in the "language of Canaan" that wrapped the Puritan meetinghouse in bodily discourse. Edward Taylor described the foundation of the Westfield meetinghouse in 1679 as the "Living Stones for this Spiritual Temple," and Cotton Mather explained "[t]hat all the *Furniture* of the *Temple*, Seen by *John*, in the Heavenly *World*, is introduced, as *Living*." The task of building a new meetinghouse from living stones stood metaphorically for building a living social body, an act in which all members of a covenanted community were morally obliged to contribute their efforts toward the maintenance of hierarchic but static positions. Thomas Hooker used the house frame as a model for society and warned, "If the parts be neither mortised nor braced, as there will be little beauty so there can be no strength. Its so in setting up the frames of societies among men, when their mindes and hearts are not mortified by mutuall consent of subjection to one another, there is no expectation of any successeful proceeding with the advantage of the publicke." When Hooker's son Samuel died in 1697, Taylor continued the architectural analogy to praise previous generations of the Hooker family. "Your Grandsire were a Chiefe Foundation Stone In this Blesst Building," while Thomas was a "Chiefe Good Builder" who helped lay the sacred underpinnings of the New Israel.[5] The living stones of the Puritan congregation rested on its seven "pillars," or citizens responsible for ensuring the continuing health of the social body. Each pillar represented the moral rectitude, political leadership, and often the control of property necessary to assert and sustain a congregation. They were the bedrock support of the congregation, just as Christ was the pillar within each converted individual. In September 1655, Michael Wigglesworth composed a "pillar to the prayse of his grace," drawing his text from 1 Sam. 7:12, the story of how Samuel erected a memorial stone in the ground to praise the Lord for helping the Israelites defeat the invading Philistines. Samuel named this stone Ebenezer, "saying, Hitherto hath the LORD helped us." In the sketch Wigglesworth made to illustrate his verse, the Ebenezer stone—surrounded with the passage "Hitherto the Lord hath holpen me"—is transformed into a Puritan pillar (fig. 46).[6]

With houses and bodies metaphorically fused, people extended the analogy to suggest the heavenly mansion or perfect house that the souls of the elect would inhabit after death in the sanctified city that Revelation promised would arrive on earth following the Last Judgment. The house-body metaphor was elaborated in anticipation of heavenly salvation. It appeared, spread across the providential landscape of Massachusetts Bay, on mileage markers that urged travelers to prepare for death even as they walked among the living. One marker placed in 1710 on the Boston road in Wenham (initially called Enon) textualized the site with a passage from Job: "I Know that tho wilt bring me to death and to the house appointed for all living" (30:23). Increase Mather reassured readers that resurrection was a time when the bodies of the regenerate would be destroyed so their souls, released, could dwell in the house of the Lord. "This earthly house must be dissolved," he argued, "that is the bodyes of gods children, that theire soules now dwell In as in a house, an earthly house the body is, and It must bee dissolved by death." But, he continued with borrowed Pauline language, "wee have a *building of God*, another house that is to say, the bodies that our soules shall dwell In after the resurrection And which at last shall dwell In the heavens eternally, and we earnestly desire to be cloathed upon with *our house which is from heaven*." Cotton Mather was more emphatic about the contrast between this house and the next. "The walls of the *clay House*," he insisted, "having been beaten down by the Blows of *Death*, all ye Verminous Leprosy of animated mischiefs Lodged & fastened there, will be forever done away; The *New House*, into which they have now entred, will have nothing of it."[7]

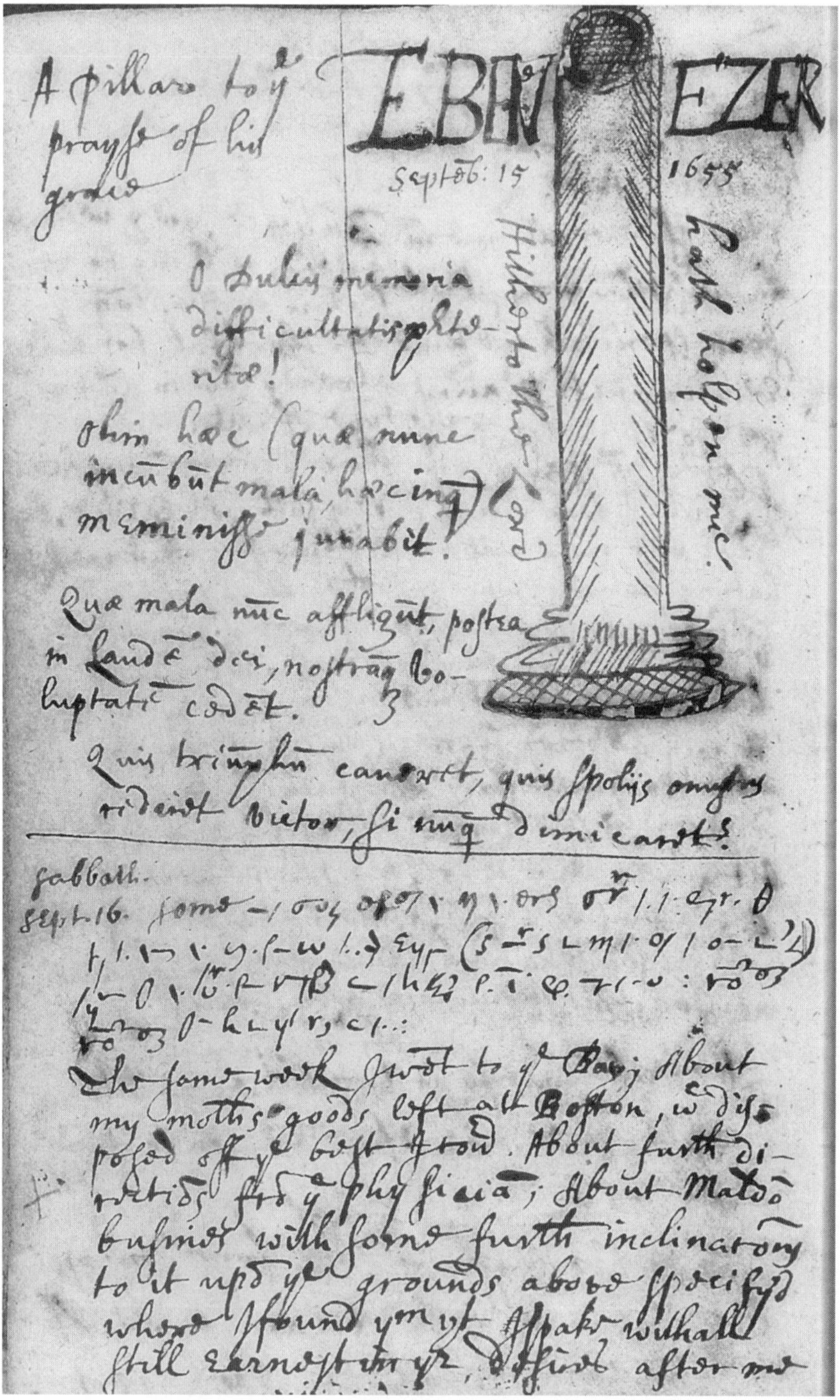

Figure 46. Michael Wigglesworth, "A pillar to the prayse of his grace," September 15, 1655. (Photo: Massachusetts Historical Society)

The heavenly mansions anticipated in sermons were located in the perfect "City of God" that Revelation promised would descend upon the earth with the second coming of Christ. Cotton Mather was sure that the mansion would be revealed to the saints as "A CITY, that has a *wall great & High*, having *Twelve Foundations*, with *Twelve Gates*; A CITY, consisting of *pure Gold*, Exceedingly Burnished; and having its *Foundations garnished with all manner of precious stones*; and ye *Twelve Gates* Entire pearles: A CITY that has *no need of the Sun or the Moon to shine in it*; for the *Glory of God Lightens it, and the Lamb is the Light of it*: The *Length* & the *Breadth* and the *Heighth* of the CITY, equal; each being *Twelve Thousand Furlongs*: or Fifteen *Hundred Miles*, every way, in each of the Three dimensions."[8] A vision of an ideal landscape (fig. 47), hovering just beyond sight, seems so clearly a projection of metaphysical belief that we barely pause to question how "real" early New Englanders might have thought it. Yet Cotton Mather no doubt spoke for many when he defended not only its existence but also its substantiality. "It is a *Material City*," he wrote adamantly.

> For . . . *creatures*, as they cannot Live out of the World, which is replenished with *Matter*, so, neither can they Live out of *Matter*. . . . But insist upon it if you please, that it be an *Ethereal City*. And Lett ye *Matter* be so rich, & so fine, & so splendid that *Gold* and *Gems* are Little better than shadows of it. I object [to] nothing in *That*. *Spiritualize* ye matter as much as you please, But if you think, a *Visible City*, of a *cubical* Form, is too *corporeal* a Thing, yett you must allow, That there will be a *place* of Reception For *Bodies*, and in this *place* those *Bodies* must be so much *Together*, that they may *converse* w[i]th one another, and maintain an admirable *order* among them. Now since there must be such a *place*, and o[u]r God has told us, '*tis a City*, and Showes us the *shape* of it, I know not, why we should be fond of having ye place to which He Leads His *Redeemed*, any other than *A City of Habitation*. This do I take to be that *Holy City*, *whereof we read, That ye many Bodies of the Sleeping Saints*, which Rose & Came out of the *Graves* after the *Resurrection* of our Saviour went . . . after they had *Appeared unto many* here.[9]

When their earthly houses crumbled, the faithful would simply move into the house and city of God, which they envisioned as complete with furniture, streets, and blessed neighbors. Mather's adamant faith in the materiality of the afterlife may, through Saint Paul, have been influenced by the beliefs of the ancient Hebrews in a similarly tangible Heaven. According to historian of religion Charles Harris, if "eternal life implies, as to a Jew it does, the most perfect and satisfying life imaginable, it must imply a life lived *in the body*, and *in a material universe*, both of which, however transfigured and glorified, must still be thought of under the category of matter." When we read Mather's vision of streets in the New

Figure 47. View of the heavenly Jerusalem. From Joseph Fletcher, *The History of the Perfect-Cursed-Blessed Man* (London, 1628), 34. (Photo: The Huntington Library, San Marino, California)

Jerusalem paved with gold, therefore, "we are not meant to think of disembodied spirits existing in *vacuo*, but of visible human bodies gloriously arrayed, and of real sensible things corresponding in the heavenly sphere to what we should call beautiful music, beautiful literature and poetry, beautiful architecture, and beautiful scenery." Meditating on Heb. 10:5, Edward Taylor stated, "Thy Body is a Building all like mine, / In Matter, Form, in Essence, Properties."[10]

When the mortal body dissolved and the "glorious body" rose, what was its configuration in heaven? If Cotton Mather was correct in arguing that the City of God is a "Material City," then resurrected bodies were material as well. But was one's heavenly body qualitatively altered from its familiar earthly materiality? Did scars disappear? Was perfect sight restored? These were questions that had plagued medieval theologians and snared them in tedious doctrinal debates. Samuel Sewall was still embroiled in similar issues in 1714. On a circuit court journey to Plymouth he, Judge Nathaniel Thomas Jr., and Paul Dudley, attorney of the province, debated the nature of heavenly embodiment to fill in extra evening hours:

Last night at Mr. Thomas's had Discourse about the Body. Mr. Dudley maintained the Belly should not be raised, because he knew no use of it. I maintained the Contrary, because Christ saw no corruption. Saints shall be conformed to Him. The Creator in his infinite Wisdom will know what use to make of them. *Dudley*. What use of Tasting, Smelling?
Sewall. Tis possible the bodies of the Saints may have a Fragrancy attending them.
Dudley. Voice is Laborious.
Sewall. As much Labour as you please, the more the better, so it may be without Toil, as in Heaven it will be. I dare not part with my Belly, Christ has Redeemed it; and there is danger of your breaking in further upon me, and cutting off my Hand or Foot. *Obsta Principiis*. Wee'l Continue this Action to the next Term.[11]

Sewall's language asserts the importance of anticipating that one's eternal body will be in the image of Christ's perfect body. The restoration of a complete, symmetrical body in heaven was believed by some to be foreshadowed by the "preparations" for the "great exchange" one's body made during old age. John Winthrop Jr., a man whose skills in medicine were widely admired and trusted in New England, reassured an aging Roger Williams in 1664 that he had heard of a "minister of the North of England" who, "in his very old age, (the particular number of his yeares I doe not perfectly remember, but I thinke it was above an hundred,) the head was againe covered with youthfull haire, & he had new teeth, and having used for fourty yeares before to read with his spectacles, could afterward read the smallest print with his old renewed eyes, without the help of any glasses."[12] In anticipation of the resurrection, the body regained the perfection that time had eroded. It would rise, materially, to its appointed heavenly mansion, a utopian house that placed no burdens on its resident, a "balanced" house with symmetrical rooms and streets for the restored and risen elect.

The play of metaphors linking the body and its death to buildings is an imaginative practice common to many past and present cultures. Each imagines the human body differently and uses it as a model for architectural forms in varying ways. Societies as diverse as Renaissance Venetians, the Dogon of Mali, the Batamalliba of Benin, the Berbers of Morocco, and the Sumba, Balinese, Bima, and Donga peoples of Southeast Asia have all conceptualized the house through bodily metaphor and vice versa.[13] As such, the house and body have long attracted poets and essayists who recognized their performative possibilities.

Writers who seized upon the metaphor often referred to the skeletal aspects of houses. Robert Underwood's 1605 verse poem entitled *A New Anatomie. Wherein the Body of a Man is very fit and aptly (two wayes) compared: 1 To a Household. 2 To a Citie* directly likens "the Timber-worke" of a house to its "bones." John Donne described how "The rafters of my body, bone / Being still with you, the Muscle, Sinew, and Veine, / Which tile this house, will come again." Robert Herrick added that the "body is the Soules poore house, or home / Whose Ribs the Laths are, and whose Flesh the Loame." The "loame" or plaster that Herrick describes was the flesh that covered up the carcass of the house. Joseph Moxon defined a "Carcass" as "the Skeleton of an House, before it is Lath'd and Plastered." Richard Neve, borrowing Moxon's diction for his own treatise on house construction in 1703, defined the carcass as "The Timber-work (as it were the Skeleton) of a House, before it is Lathed or Plaister'd."[14] New England writers also stressed the transient nature of the skeleton and its covering of flesh. Anne Bradstreet described her aging body as "my Clay house mouldring away," while Edward Taylor allowed that "I but an Earthen Vessell bee," "a Mudwall tent, whose Matters are / Dead Elements, which mixt make dirty trade." The particular names for individual framing members, as parts of the skeleton, also suggest bodily discipline: post head, collar, shoulder, hip, "prick post," and foot. In sum, the materiality of a house and of its accompanying language—its timbers, tiles, laths, and bricks—functioned as signs of Christ's perfect body as a model of a "loving" social order. Seeking help through prayer, Taylor humbled himself through self-abasement and architectural imagery: "I'm but a Flesh and Blood bag: Oh! do thou / Sill, Plate, Ridge, Rib, and Rafter me with Grace."[15]

Beyond the metaphoric treatment of the skeleton (frame), the analogies that tie the form of the body—its limbs, organs, and features—to architectural models are detailed and systemically precise from the late sixteenth century through the early eighteenth. Perhaps the most agile and extended play in bodily metaphor emerges in Underwood's *New Anatomie*. In keeping with his ambitious subtitle, Underwood begins by addressing the city as an anatomical construct and quickly equates "a Cittie large, of bigness such, / as if the World had beene: / A thousand thousand Houses there."[16] The city can only be measured in terms of houses, and houses can only be assessed as they reflect bodily parts and proportions. For my purposes Underwood's text is especially useful, since he augmented an impressive array of architectural spaces and functions with marginal notations that state exactly what bodily member he was discussing.

The cross-passage house initially built by Samuel Desborough in Guilford, Connecticut, provides a good place to begin interpretation. In the previous chapter I described its basic form. At its "heart," in the middle of the house was the hall, a room that combined a variety of daily functions. In some parts of northern England the hall so aptly summarized the human figure that it was known simply as the "housebody." As early as 1542 Andrew Boorde argued that the hall was the central bodily feature in the system of correspondences the house represented. "Make the hall under such a fasshyon," he suggested, "that the parlor be anexed to the *heade* of the hall. And the buttery and pantry be at the *lower ende* of the hall, the seller *under* the pantry, sette somwhat *abase*; the kychen set somwhat *abase* from the buttery and pantry, commyng with an entry by the wall of the buttry, the pastry-howse & the larder-howse anexed to the kychen."[17] Boorde was undoubtedly using a large gentry house for his bodily model, but his basic oppositional assumptions are clearly revealed. At either end of the hall are its "head" and its "dependent members." The parlor, at the house's head, is clean, bright, and dry and used by the family on ritual occasions and for polite conversation. Beneath the hall, at its lower extremities, are spaces that are dirty, dark, and damp and used by tenants, women, and servants in their daily labor routines.

Although its exact interior arrangement, room sizes, and chimney locations derived from diverse antecedents found throughout the hybrid area between England's highland and lowland zones that Desborough pressed into service in creating his own theater of hospitality, his house clearly descends from the three-room medieval form popular among substantial property owners across England until the late sixteenth century. This house was characterized by service and storage room(s), or in the north and west of England a byre for cattle, separated from a hall and parlor chamber by a cross passage or, alternatively, a "screen" or wall (fig. 48). Admittedly, Desborough's domestic layout varied in details from Boorde's prescribed plan. Part of its parlor chamber was partitioned to provide a "buttery" or storage room that we might have expected, following Boorde's advice, to find adjacent to the kitchen at the lower end of the structure. But the Guilford property nonetheless articulated the symbolic contours of pollution and danger present in the domestic environment, segregated specific tasks and people, and charted contours of domestic economic activity reaching from the household's "head" to the dependent members lying below.[18]

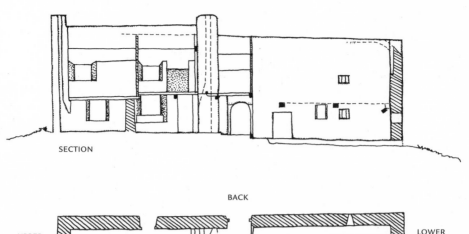

SECTION

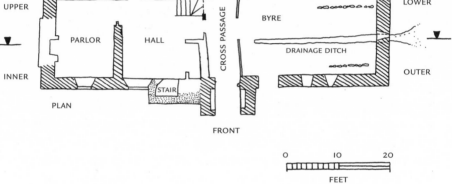

BACK

UPPER

PARLOR | HALL | CROSS PASSAGE | BYRE

DRAINAGE DITCH

LOWER

INNER

STAIR

PLAN

OUTER

FRONT

0   10   20

FEET

Figure 48. Sanders longhouse, Lettaford, Devon, early sixteenth century, with social and topographical directions indicated. This surviving long house, rare because its byre has never been converted to a kitchen, retains the medieval three-room configuration (after N. W. Alcock, M. Laithwaite, and P. Child, "Sanders, Lettaford," *Proceedings of the Devon Archaeological Society* 30 [1972]: 227). (Drawing by the author)

   The English medieval house materialized the hierarchic body in clear terms. Based on whether one stood in the service room(s) or in the hall and parlor, one was either "below the passage" (or entry) in the lower, "animal" end of the house or "above the passage" in its upper, "civilized" end. In *Maison Rustique; or, The Countrey Farme*, Charles Estienne and Jean Liebault guided the reader into the cross passage (or "ally") of their model house and toward its upper end: "Upon the left hande of the saide ally or entrie shalbe your hall, through which you shall passe into your chamber: and out of your chamber into your wardrobe and inner chamber: and at the end heereof, if the bodie of your house shall have compassed in place enough, you shall make a chamber to lodge strangers [in England the "solar" chamber], the way into, as also out of which, shall be by a turning staire on that side toward the court; so that strangers may be at their libertie, not molesting or troubling you by their passing in or out."[19]

As this passage implies when describing a small room next to the wardrobe at the extreme upper end, spaces reserved for the head of household and his immediate family were also termed "inner," whereas working areas lower in the house were classified as "outer" rooms because of their less socially restrictive atmosphere and closer proximity to the "ally" or passage. If we add these terms to Boorde's statement that the "cellar" is more "abase" than the rooms over it, the bodily logic of the English medieval house emerges. Built of sensate material, it surrounded its occupants and visitors with basic bodily oppositions with social and political meanings: one followed the hierarchic nature of the body itself, while the other referenced the dialectics of inner and outer self. Mikhail Bakhtin claimed the distinction as an essential axis of medieval experience. "In the medieval picture of the world," Bakhtin stated, "the top and the bottom, the higher and the lower, have an absolute meaning in the sense of space and values." This is the precise opposition that existed between the different social extremes of the house. "Every important movement was seen and interpreted only as upward and downward," he continued, "along a vertical line. All metaphors of movement in medieval thought and art have this sharply defined, surprisingly consistent vertical character. All that was best was highest, all that was worst was lowest."[20] The oppositional logic of domestic order described here, when added to period nomenclature, suggests that Desborough's postmedieval, hybrid modification of the three-room house really concealed two structures within its walls: an upper-inner house and a lower-outer house. These two houses were functionally and socially distinct. After reviewing the country farmer's need to keep the side of his house containing the kitchen, buttery, and servants' quarters separate from the side where he and his family lived, Estienne and Liebault remained concerned that distinct privies be provided "for the necessarie use of everie [one] of the *two saide bodies of the house*."[21]

If all the house-body analogies from Underwood's *New Anatomie* are collated and compared with a surviving three-room house, the resulting image is impressive for its detailed representation of the doubled human figure in material substance.[22] The cross passage or screen corresponds to the waist that connects the lower body to the upper; it is a passage between the two bodies that one enters through the front door or mouth. Turning into the lower body, one enters the kitchen, defined by Underwood as the "place from the Groines to the Midrife." Here are various vessels or "bowels"—perhaps hogsheads or tubs—full of food "which long there, did not stay." Underwood explains this more clearly: "For things that bad, and noysome were, / this *Kitchin* did convay / By *Gutters, Holes,* and *Channels* so / that every thing was seene / within this *Kitchin* for to be / both hansome, sweete, and clean." In the margin Underwood states that gutters and holes refer to "The Yard & the Fundament" (penis and anus), which allow polluted waters and solids to pass through the end of the house into a channel cut in the ground. Although not in a kitchen per se, a similar hole cut through the lower or "fundament" end of a byre in a Devon longhouse allowed manures to be pushed outside (fig. 49). The walls or "sides" of the house-body are covered with a strange "*Matter* (like I know not what)" that Underwood likens to the "kidnies." This matter is then encrusted with "filthy Gravell, Sand, and Stone" or the "Collicke and stone" that frequently caused trouble by being "A stopping to the Cundits, that / the Water [urine] could not pass." Also in the kitchen were several objects representing abdominal organs. "A Pott hunge boyling there," presumably over a hearth (though no hearth or chimney is mentioned in Underwood's poem per se), represents the "stomacke." Under the stomach, instead of a fire, "a Fountain did appear," representing the liver. From this liver-fountain flows a "redd liquor" or blood that then runs "into every part" of the house through "veines." Finally, next to the liver-fountain lies a small spring, the "Gaull," which, if it overflowed, "made the House in every part, / all yellow for to show / As if it were with Saffron dide." Underwood's treatment of the kitchen as the "lower" body contains several key body parts: the bowels, urine, penis, anus, stomach, kidneys (with "collick" and stone), liver, blood, and gall bladder.

As he cataloged the "lower" parts of the house-body, Underwood was here extending a discourse on bodily regulation that extended in England back at least to Boorde's *Compendyous Regyment.* In addition to commenting on the hierarchy of spaces within the house, Boorde had warned potential builders to keep their houses clean. He called special attention to bodily waste. "There must be circumspection had that there be not about the howse or mansion no stynkynge dyches, gutters, no canelles," of the sort that Underwood's "yard" pointed toward. "Permyt no common pyssynge place aboute the howse," Boorde continued, and "let the common howse of easement be over some water or elles elongated from the howse. And beware of emtynge of pysse-pottes, and pyssyng in chymnes, so that all evyll and contagyous ayres may be expelled, and clene ayre kept unputryfyed. And of thynges let the buttery, the cellar, the kitchen, the larder-howse, with all other howses of offyces, be kept clene, [so] that there be no fylth in them, but good & odyferous savours." The emphasis here is on cleanliness and on the polite management of bodily waste, an issue that Boorde, as a physician, felt was central to the health of individual bodies and society as a whole. His utterances on bodily management, however, had politics as their subtext.[23]

From the body's lower end Underwood moves to the hall, "devided from the *Kitchen* with a / Thinne and slender wall." The hall, traditionally a room used for meals and gatherings around a central floor hearth, contains two vital organs: the

Figure 49. Detail of byre end gable, Sanders longhouse, Lettaford, Devon, early sixteenth century, showing drain hole in masonry wall at ground level. (Drawing by the author)

heart and the lungs. The heart is a seat, "like unto / a Throne of Maiestie: / Or to a Chair of Estate." This heart-throne, "in colour somewhat redd," is the social heart of the family and the preferred position of the patriarch. And "About this roiall Seate" was a bellowslike "thing in substance light"—the lungs—that ventilated the heart ("Hale in the cool and tender air"), and if it stopped, then "the seate and all the house, / do presently decay." Underwood claims that air circulates from the lungs "by a long / and slender Pipe" that stretches from the hall "unto the Turrets reach," or the house's head. From one perspective, Underwood seems to be looking up from the floor to the roof structure of an open hall; his claim that "I did behould and see / A short and hollow Pillar-plaste [placed] / upon its topp to be" seems to be referring to the architectural pillar that medieval carpenters fashioned in the crown-post roof structures used in many open halls (fig. 50). Underwood terms this pillar the "necke," which "was framed with many Ioynts" and supported the house's head or roof turret. In an obscure reference, he then suggests the neck pillar is hollow and contains "Two long and slender Cundits," the windpipe and the "throate gell." He may be referring here to the chimney as a pipe, since elsewhere he links the chimney to respiration by likening it to the house's nostrils, or claiming that breath is "very like to Smoake." This pipe then emitted "a very sweete and sounding noyse" or the voice. Finally, atop "the upper end of all this hollow pillar" stands a "turret" representing the house's head.

At this point Underwood's system of correspondences becomes momentarily difficult to follow; bodily metaphors were occasionally interchangeable in the playfulness of metaphysical poetics. The imagery of pillars, pipes, and turrets certainly suggests the upward vertical movement of the medieval house's open hall. Underwood implies the upright verticality of the house-body when he observes that "Two Pillars framed like an Arch" (presumably in the cellar) form the foundation as the house's "two legs & thighes." But when Underwood states he opened a door and saw into the turret, we are again brought down to earth and reminded that "turret" suggested not only a tower projecting from the upper reaches of a building but also, more figuratively, the head or upper end of any body. The turret could easily refer to the extreme upper end of the house-body. From the hall, another door or mouth leads into a ground-floor parlor chamber; through this mouth, Underwood states, he could see into the head. Looking into the mouth, he "saw a mill therein" — or teeth. The mill itself is unusual, since neither "winde nor water, horse nor hand / did cause it for to goe." It grinds "What so for man is meete to eat" but does not rely on regular millstones to accomplish its task. Rather, the grinding mechanism "framed is of bone." Above the "mill chamber" is an upstairs room or "little chamber," noted as "the place where the Braynes lie."

In the upper room at the upper end of the house-body, Underwood's language becomes very specific. The upper chamber "over head is seelde with Bone like Ivorie," a layer of bone he likens to the skull. The brain itself is represented by a bed, which "(in Pallet wise) doth lie upon the floore." Dreams and portents occurring during sleep took on qualities of prophecy and revelation. Sleep was conceived as a time of dangerous vulnerability to invisible forces. Thus, the metaphoric linkage of the bed and the brain is logical. But in Underwood's poem the bed is "Bewrapped in a Sheete of Lawne," a covering equated with "the thin web which wrappeth in the Brayne." The bed (brain) was placed in the middle of the upper chamber. Between it and the front of the house, "Lustie and young *Invention*" sits, as a counterpart of the "forehead." Behind the bed "an Ancient man doth lie, / Who many things doth beare in mind, / they call him *Memorie*." And from the bed per se arose Wit: "It is his common guise, / Much company for to frequent, / and in his table talke, / To argue there of many thinges, / to make his *Clapper* walke."

The clapper represents the house's tongue and has a mixed meaning. One derives from the common use of the term to describe a talkative person's tongue. "That Clapper of the Divell," one author explained in the late 1630s, is "the tongue of a scould." In early modern England and New England, scolds were commonly

Figure 50. Crown post, roof of solar wing, Moat Farm, Combs, Suffolk, fifteenth century. (Photo: Royal Commission on Historical Monuments [England], © Crown Copyright)

perceived as troublesome women, whose fondness for gossip and rumor could both set neighbors "by the ears" with partial truths and make maintaining family discipline difficult for their husbands. Thomas Adams summarized prevailing beliefs when he stated that "woman, for the most part, hath the glibbest tongue. . . . She calls her tongue her defensive weapon, [but] a firebrand in a frantic hand doth less mischief." Scolds spoke in a variety of styles, from "murmuring," "slighting," and "affronting" to "reviling" and "railing" in a high-pitched shriek. The noisiness of a scold's tongue perhaps reminded weary listeners of the clapper of a bell. Yet a gristmill also had a clapper, which was a device used to shake the hopper so grain would fall down to the millstones. This last meaning links the tongue back to the mill (or teeth) in the ground-floor parlor and also makes clear how important it is for a household's head to ensure proper "government of the tongue" among lesser bodily members.[24]

Underwood's treatment of the exterior facade of the house-body is more formulaic. He identifies glass windows as the eyes, hinged casements in each window as eyelids, and pentices over the windows as eyebrows. An open space on the exterior above the eyebrows he likens to the brow or forehead, perhaps the part of the facade directly before the upper chamber, the frontal section of which he also likens to the forehead. With this final analogy, Underwood's verbal image of the human house is complete. But others soon followed in his tracks and again sought to strengthen the validity of the house as a metaphor of social order to support a unified monarchical culture early in James I's reign. Drawing perhaps from Underwood's 1605 publication but also surely from earlier Elizabethan tropes, Thomas Dekker argued that "the *Head* is a house built for *Reason* to dwell in: and thus is the tenement fram[e]d. The two Eyes are the glasse windowes, at which light disperses it selfe into every roome, having goodly pent-houses of haire to overshaddow them." Drawing perhaps on earlier ethnographic accounts of Native American housing, Dekker explained that "as for the nose, tho some (most injuriously and improperly) make it serve for an Indian chimney, yet surely it is rightly a bridge with two arches, under which are neat passages to convey as well perfumes to aire and sweeten every chamber, as to carry away all noisome filth that is swept out of uncleane corners." Like Underwood and the metaphysical poets in both England and New England, Dekker equated the entrance to the house with the human mouth. "The cherry lippes open like the new painted gates of a Lord Maiors house," he commented, "to take in provision." And like Underwood, he also stated that "the tongue is a bell, hanging just under the middle of the roofe, and lest it should be rung out too deepe (as sometimes it is when women have a peale) whereas it was cast by the first founder, but onely to tole softly, there are two even rowes of Ivory pegs (like pales) set to keep it in."[25] And both Underwood and Dekker, traveling as they did in circles of English learning informed by Italian humanism, may have known of such structures as the Casa dei Mostri in Rome (fig. 51), which carries the human figure into a literal treatment that borders on parody and a grotesque emphasis on bodily orifices.

As I have already suggested, house-body analogies as complex as those described by Underwood appeared in early New England in the dense metaphors of poetry by Edward Taylor and Anne Bradstreet, of sermons by the Mathers, and in the terse entries of Samuel Sewall's diary. Indeed, a brief sample of house-body analogies from early New England shows their clear derivation and playful variation from English tradition: the roof is the head, cupola the brain, laths the ribs, plaster the flesh, clapboards the skin, windows the eyes, door the mouth, threshold the lips, door lintel the tongue, chimney the breast, hearth the heart, and fire the soul and womb (fig. 52).

ARCHITECTURAL PATHOLOGY

Other practices in early New England testify to the personification of ordinary houses. The house-body received medical attention, as it inscribed a pathology of upper and lower segments that tied domestic space to contemporary anatomical theory. Like Bray Rossiter, most New England people adhered to a more or less syncretic system of medical beliefs drawn from Aristotelian and Galenic theory, Paracelsian and alchemical lore, and assorted scraps of post-Baconian "new science"; the coexistence of diverse medical traditions, each of which constructed the body in different terms, argued the body's semiotic multiplicity. The dominant emblem of the body in Galenic (and Paracelsian) medicine was the house, an image that represented the movement of heavenly planets, the houses of the ancient zodiac, and the bodily segments—the different elements, humors, limbs, organs, and moods—they influenced. God controlled planetary motion. People believed that divine will was the ultimate cause of bodily affliction. "Lett us, look upon SIN as the *Cause* of *Sickness*," cautioned Cotton Mather in the introduction to his own book on medical theory, *The Angel of Bethesda.* "There are it may be, *Two Thousand Sicknesses*: And indeed, *any one of whom [is] able to crush us!* But what is the Cause of all? Bear in Mind, That *Sin* was that which first brought *Sickness* upon a *Sinful World*, and which yett continues to *Sicken* the World, with a World of Diseases. Sickness is in short, *Flagellum Dei pro peccatis Mundi.*"[26]

In Galenic theory, disease struck when the heavenly house lost its inherent balance and symmetry. Imbalance resulted from either too much or too little of one of the four humors—blood, phlegm, black bile, and yellow bile—each of which was believed to be "a moist and running body, into which the meate in the Liver is converted, to the end that our bodyes might be nourished by them."[27] Others

Figure 51. Casa dei Mostri, Rome, Italy, ca. 1600. (Photo by the author)

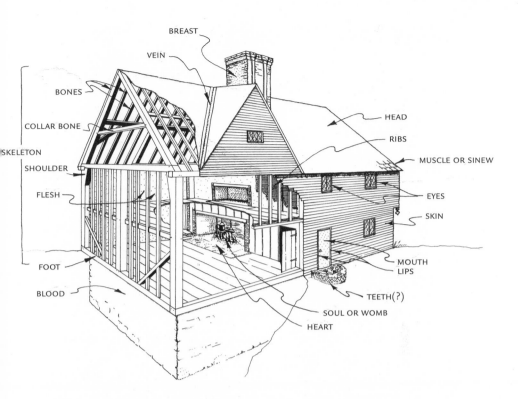

Figure 52. The human house and its parts in seventeenth-century New England. (Drawing by the author)

followed when the body's "tempers"—the properties of being cold or hot, and wet or dry—were upset. Robert Underwood relegated these humors and tempers to the pots, fountain, and red liquor that flowed around the kitchen hearth at the "lower" end of the house; their source was a fountain that represented the liver. Tobias Cohn, a physician writing in Venice during the early eighteenth century, did the same in his remarkable juxtaposition of the body and a hierarchically ordered town house. His engraving in many respects follows Underwood's mapping of the house's bodily parts. Windows with pentices over them are its eyes, an opening with doors represents the mouth. The entire house stands on an arch, similar to the "two legs and thighs" of Underwood's poem. In Cohn's house, too, a fountain in the lower story shows the circulation of humoral liquids to elsewhere in the structure. Above the fountain are a boiling pot, representing the stomach, and an alembic, or still, probably the house's heart (fig. 53).[28]

When physicians diagnosed patients and administered remedies, they concentrated their efforts on those places of the body most vulnerable to disease: the head, including the mouth and eyes, and the heart. The eyes were important in di-

Figure 53. Organs of the human body compared to parts of a house. From Tobias Cohn, *Ma'aseh Toviyah* (Venice, 1708). (Photo: National Library of Medicine)

agnosis. The heart, through which flowed all "vital spirits" that spread "natural heat" throughout the body, was often the ultimate target of medication, much of which was administered through the mouth. One seventeenth-century individual even described the heart as a "hearth supporting a vital fire," that fire being the hot property of the blood itself.[29] Thus the parts of the human house fit together in ways that make sense in terms of medical theory. It is comparatively easy for us to see the logic in equating windows with eyes, doors as mouths, and clapboards as skin covering the skeleton of the house. We can also see bones as equivalent with studs and rafters, sills with feet, the roof with the head, and plaster with flesh. Yet as parts of the human body, did these also conform to the logic of contemporary medical theory? Did the human house "work" the same way as the body?

To answer these questions, we must explore in brief the connections recognized by seventeenth-century people between different parts of the body. In his *Almanack of Coelestial Motions for the Year of the Christian Epocha 1678*, John Foster provided the accepted astrological formula for the connections between the planets and their attributes, and the body as a set of interconnected segments. "The *Head* and *Face* the *Ram* doth crave, / The *Neck* and *Throat* the Bull will have, / The loving *Twins* do rule the *Hands*, / The *Brest* and *Sides* in *Cancer* bands." Foster's verse continues to include the remaining signs of the zodiac and the parts of the body they govern: the Lion (heart and back), Virgo (bowels and belly), Libra ("reyns" and loins), Scorpio (genitals), the Archer (thighs), Capricorn (knees), Aquarius (legs), and Pisces (feet). Foster offers this list moving from head to foot and thus ensures that the astrological concept of medicine reproduces the hierarchic Christian body.[30] Each of these segments, linked to planetary position, had specific humoral qualities. Not every part of the segmented body detailed by Foster had a corresponding part of the human house (hands are noticeably absent), but some linkages are apparent.

According to Foster's verse and consistent with Underwood's earlier text, the head is controlled by the Ram, whose attributes "Are Melancholly, Earthy, and Dry." Melancholy, defined as "dark" because of its association with the depressive moods of black bile, could be overcome by the inherent brightness of the brain. "Melancholicke," wrote William Vaughan, "which through the blacknesse thereof, doth darken the light of the understanding (which is seated in the braine, and there-hence as a candle imparts light unto the whole body)." Taylor's reference to the cupola of a house as "my brain pan turrit" therefore derived from a recognition that a cupola allows light to brighten the darkness of a roof just as the brain permits light to brighten the melancholy darkness of the head. At the other extreme, the "cellar," literally the lowest part of the house-body, was in New England associated with blood, which, "because it watereth all the body, and giveth nourishment unto it: out of which likewise issue the vitall spirits," was thought to be the foundation of life itself. Unlike melancholy, the sanguine humor was dominated by air, a "pleasant element" that "tended upward moderately." In Underwood's poem blood is associated with the kitchen's lower position and emerges from a fountain on the hearth to flow throughout the house. In addition, the cellar was dominated by the base of the chimney stack, whose width was sufficient to support the hearth. Like the heart, the hearth could rekindle the blood's heat and sustain the entire body.[31] Inherently hot and moist, the blood-cellar was seen as any humoral space might have been seen — as profoundly sensitive to its exact opposite. The roof (earthy or cool and dry) and cellar (hot and moist), or the parlor and kitchen, at opposite upper and lower ends of the house, were not only opposed in their social function. They were also opposed in terms of medical theory and their intrinsic elemental properties.

If the house-body malfunctioned, it could also be rebalanced by administering an opposite remedy. Ailments of the stomach, for example, which was thought to be cold and moist, could be soothed by mint, which was intrinsically warm and dry. The body could also be balanced by adjusting temperature and ventilation of the house so as to bring about an opposite effect. "He must use cold things to keepe away the heat," one authority claimed, "and hot things to expell the cold. He must adde dry things to moyst, and moyst to dry." If a room was too drafty and moist, "depart thence into another place. . . . For oftentimes it is seene, that sicke folkes doe recover their former health onely by change of aire. But if the aire be corrupt, and that a man cannot remove thence very quickly, he must artificially rectifie it by perfuming his Chamber with Iuniper, Rosemary, Bay tree, or with wood of Aloes: and then by sprinkling vineger here and there in his chamber." People who experienced the black moods of melancholy "must have lightsome chambers and [have] them often perfumed." Or, "if it be in Sommer, that the Aire be too hot and sultrie . . . and that the patient is affected with some ague or with some other burning disease, hee must be placed in some lower roome or some coole chamber, where the heat of the Sunne comes not to forcibly. In Winter time let fire correct the raw and cold aire, specially for them, that be afflicted with cold sicknesses. For such, a close warme roome must be prepared, secured from winds, where a good fire may be made."[32]

Like a human body, the house was symbolically fed and sometimes even dressed. Incised "teeth" on the edges of doorstones suggest that houses were occasionally offered food (fig. 54). Because individuals in seventeenth-century New England believed that sin collected at the thresholds of houses and that transgression often focused on bodily orifices, these geometric carvings represent teeth that symbolically helped "chew" the manna offered to the house in propitiation of sin. Dressing the human house also endowed it with specific bodily qualities. Costume articulated the key bodily orifices of the house, a point that Balthasar Gerbier advised his English readers in 1662. "As the best Ornaments of a Face appears at first sight by the Eyes, Mouth, and Nose," he claimed, "so doth the best qualities of a perfect Building, by Windowes, and Doores well placed, as also by a large, magnificent, commodious, and well-set Staircase." Accordingly, decorative barge boards that ran along the gable end of the house set off the roof much as wide ruffed collars proclaimed the separation between head and torso in fashionable dress (fig. 55). Piercings in the body of the house were similarly symbolically elaborated through decorative treatment. Doors (mouths) were embellished with incised lines, compass work, and decorative moldings. Windows (eyes) were sometimes "cullered" or capped with decorative pediments and molded surrounds. Inside the house, the hearth (heart) received even more attention, as chamfered moldings, incised geometric patterns, or swirls of bright paint made fireplace lintels visually arresting. Inside the fireplace opening, in the chimney's "throat," patterned brickwork and bands of decorative painting embraced the flame, or soul of the human house. The mantel above the hearth, decked with bright pottery and shimmering plate, was a garment that covered or protected the hearth entrance just as a mantle shields the body from inclement weather. In fact, interior furnishings of all sorts were conceived of as clothing on the house's body, a point that Bruno Ryves made clear when he described the plundering of royalist houses by sectarian radicals in England in 1642 as "disrobings."[33]

A LIVING SPRING OF POWER

If metaphysical writers, medical theory, and analogies of feeding and dressing naturalized the house-body as inherently hierarchic, covenant theology and the aesthetics of communion legitimized it as an emblem of Christ's perfect body. Saint Paul's epistles, contemporary sermons, and metaphysical poetry described the heavenly mansion that visible saints would exchange for their broken clay houses. For New England's Puritans, the house stood finally as a metaphor of the body of the spiritually elect community, as John Winthrop suggested when he discussed "our Community as members of the same body." As a sign of their corporate existence, members of a congregation or the "same body" celebrated the "birth" of newly completed houses with the driving of a pin to complete a final joint. Leading citizens were invited to undertake this symbolic gesture that signaled the house's skeleton had received the blessing of those near society's "head." The birth of a new house warranted a feast to mark its incorporation into community life. Joshua Hempstead noted that when his son-in-law raised his house in New London in 1747, he "had I Supose 200 people there." One afternoon in 1754, Hempstead went to see John Winthrop's "great house Raised & Stayed till night. there was a great many People & many Spectators beside [the] Labourers. they finished the Body of the house all but the Roof."[34]

House-bodies were symbolically charged and thus proper objects of festive celebration in seventeenth-century New England because people believed that God's handiwork was most complete in the symmetrical perfection of the human form. The appreciation was not limited to ministers and poets. Elated after the birth of

Figure 54. Denticulation on doorstones associated with Richard Dummer's house, Byfield Parish, Newbury, Massachusetts, diorite: (a) side view of stone, ca. 1643 (see fig. 63b); (b) top of stone, dated 1636; (c) top of stone, dated 1690. (Drawing by the author, courtesy of Smithsonian Institution, Gift of Mr. and Mrs. Stephen Twaddell)

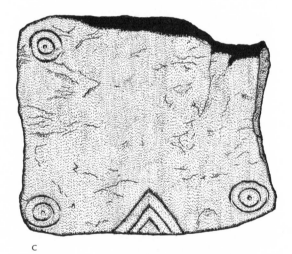

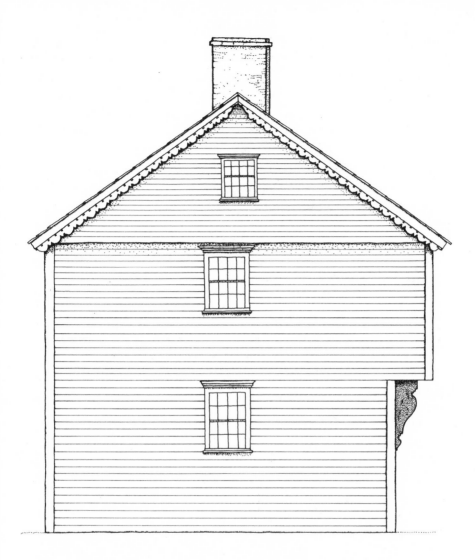

Figure 55. Conjectural view of end gable with decorative eave trim boards, John Sheldon's house, Deerfield, Massachusetts, ca. 1696–98. (Drawing by the author)

his son William in 1695, carpenter John Paine of Eastham on Cape Cod marveled at the divine form of children, saying, "They are of comely proportion in wit & limbs hence holy david taking notis of the curious workmanship of his body in the comly parts & proportion thereof brake forth into this expression. I will praise thee for I am fearfully and wonderfully made." In the confluence of joy, fear, and wonder, Paine believed he apprehended beauty itself, which he termed "that sweet correspondence and orderly usefulness the Lord first implanted in the order of things." He sensed the immanence of a power that, in the words of John Preston, an English theologian avidly read in New England, "consists in a conformity of all the parts." John Winthrop was more precise when he pronounced that "The *being of a thing* . . . lies in the perfection of parts, not degrees; a child of a year old is as truly a man, and as well compact, as one of sixty." "Being" was permanent, immutable, without flaw. It was the manifest presence of divine order visible to believing mortal eyes and a key criterion of aesthetic judgment. Cotton Mather summarized the underlying concept: "Our Face is a Seat which has much of the Divine Image and Wisdom appearing in it." The being of a thing, that which fueled its existential vitality and transcendent spirit, emerged as an object—a sermon, poem, house, or body—invoked God's perfection and offered its eternal beauty and stabilizing wisdom to counter the mad entropy of nature and human society.[35]

By implication, a house possessed "being" if, in its bodily form and articulated "conformity of parts," it invoked the divine beauty of Christ's figure. In 1665 Boston merchant John Saffin copied an "Epistle Concerning Jesus Christ taken out of Humane history" into his notebook. At many points in his writing Saffin defends the authority and wisdom of biblical teaching and demonstrates his conviction that perfection can only be attained through imitation of Christ. For Saffin, this had specific material meaning, and he took pains to record Christ's bodily appearance:

> A Man of stature some what tall and Comely, with A very Reverend Countenance such as the beholders may both Love and feare his haire of the Collour of a Philbird full Ripe and plaine allmost downe to his Eares from his Eares Downward somewhat Curled & more greyant of Collour waveing about his shoulders in the middest of his head goeth a seame or partition of his haire After the maner of the Nazarits his forehead very plaine and smooth, his face without Spott, or wrinckle beautified with Red. his Nose & mouth so formed as Nothing could be Reprehended his Beard somewhat thick agreeable in Collour to the haire of his head, not of any great length but forked in the midest, of an Innocent look, his Eyes grey and quick in Reproveing his voice terrible in Admonishing Courteous and faire spoken pleasant in speech mixed with gravety it canot be Remembred that any have seen him Laugh, but many have seen him weep; in proportion of Body well shaped & straight his hands and Arms right Delectable to behold in speaking very temperate modest and wise A Man for his Singular Beauty surpassing the Children of Men.[36]

As John Foster had done, Saffin's description proceeds from the hair down through the forehead, nose, mouth, and voice to the hands and thus inscribes Christ's body as hierarchic. Yet the "right Delectable" image Saffin had of Christ provided a basic index of divine presence in the material world. Christ's "being," at once aesthetic and political, was a recognized paradigm of perfection and authority in other aspects of social life. Symmetry, balance, and a conformity of parts were aesthetic principles that invoked divine order to sustain Christian communities on earth. Sustenance was key. Edward Taylor imagined Christ's perfect body and realized that "Here is a *Living Spring of power* which tapt / All-doing influences hence do flow." When a form was suffused with the power drawn from this "living spring," Taylor considered it "full," and the logical source of all "fullness" existed in Christ ("All fulness is in thee my Lord, and Christ, / The fulness of all Excellence is thine"). The language derives from the twin experiences of satisfaction at the communion table: supping on the "living spring" of Christ's power, the communicant becomes "full" and renews the bliss of "being" in the "conformity of parts" of the covenanted community—and of dwelling as a member in Christ's body. For Cotton Mather, the church "consists of the whole number of the elect, that have been, are or shall be gathered into one under Christ, the head thereof, and is the spouse, the body, the *fulness of him that filleth all in all.*"[37]

The figure of "fullness," as an inseparable fusion of sensual and intellectual satisfaction in having feasted on (or married) the body of Christ, suggests that an aesthetics of communion underlay not only social order but also architectural embodiment. Edward Taylor implied the metonymy of Christian embodiment and the human house when he referred to taking the sacrament as a type of construction: "Oh! wondrous strange. Angells and Men here are / Incorporated in one body tite. / Two kinds are gain'd into one mortase fair. / Me tenant in thyselfe Lord, my Light. / These are thy body: thou their head, we see / Thou fillst them first, then they do fill up thee."[38]

From the sacred landscape the aesthetics of communion extended into secular structures and argued for their symbolic unity. Early New England houses with forms that clearly articulated the distinct parts that constituted their totality—how the door (mouth) related to the position of the chimney (breast), the location of the fire (soul) within the breast, and how exposed framing members (skeleton) articulated the segmentation of bodily members (e.g., lean-tos betrayed interior functional hierarchies, jettied overhangs signified breaks in floor levels and internal function)—were those that, in their "fulness," owned the most being or power as affecting presences in early New England culture. Seen in this light, the so-called organic nature of early New England houses, with their legible facades and side elevations and rambling additions, was guided by an aesthetic grounded in the poetics and politics of communion and covenant theology. Where clearly segmented houses persisted until the late eighteenth century, as they did in the Connecticut River valley (fig. 56), they signaled the persistence of an organic, deferential concept of the social and political body that retained the hierarchic body of Christ as its key cultural metaphor.

Figure 56. House, Amherst, Massachusetts, ca. 1770. (Photo by the author)

COMMUNION AND CONSUMPTION

The promise of unifying love in a "well-knit" community or family and the aesthetics of communion conveyed mixed messages. They seem to have supported the very kind of public interest in consumer goods that motivated the building of "mansions" that appeared at times to outstrip an individual's actual position in local society. The act of participating in the sacramental communion "feast" ran parallel to and intersected symbolically with the business of "consuming" in the wider, market economy expanding throughout the Atlantic world. For some, feasting on the sacrament provided assurance of a "commodity" or comfort in spirit that promised the additional material comfort of divine grace. But for others it raised feelings of unworthiness and fear. As David D. Hall has observed, ministers reminded their congregations of Saint Paul's words in 1 Cor. 11:28–29: "But let a man examine himself, and so let him eat of that bread, and drink of that cup. For he that eateth and drinketh unworthily, eateth and drinketh damnation to himself, not discerning the Lord's body." Jane Colman Turrell hesitated in taking steps toward the sacrament. Her "Fears were great lest 'coming unworthily she should eat and drink Judgement unto her self.'" Others shared her apprehension and would not "sit down" and "feast" at the Lord's Table while they still felt tensions with neighbors or factional strife within the church. They felt unworthy if they sensed they were not living in the unified body of the faithful.[39]

While admitting a sense of collective fear and a desire for spiritual safety, the increasing hesitancy of people in late-seventeenth-century New England churches to take the sacrament may suggest a deeper ambivalence over the destabilizing side of cultural consumption, the "ethic of hedonism" that threatened the boundaries of propriety as people increasingly relied upon consumer goods to play with fluidity in social relations. Did consumption sustain the Christian community, or did it erode the pillars that gave it strength? People were not sure. But their frequent use of clothing to effect strategies of social masking and movement suggests that their fear of communion may in part have been a subtle means of resisting complete enclosure in the hierarchic, corporate body of Christian government. As early as 1637, John Winthrop received a letter from an anonymous English correspondent who claimed he had heard "that many in your plantacions discover much pride." It seems that many people in Winthrop's "Citty upon a Hill" had already been writing to England for lace and "likewise for cutt-worke coifes; & others, for deep stammell dyes; & some of your owne men tell us that many with you goe finely cladd, though they are free from the fantasticalnes of our land."[40]

Clothing was one commodity with a transformative potential that could undercut the structure of authority in civil society. Attempting to curb the use of clothing as a strategy of misrepresentation, the Massachusetts General Court in 1651 complained that "intollerable excess & bravery hath crept in uppon us, & especially, amongst people of mean condition." What would happen to social order if all "men . . . of meane condition, educations, & callinges should take uppon them the garbe of gentlemen, by the wearinge of gold or silver lace, or buttons, or poynts at theire knees, [or] to walke in great boots; or women of the same ranke to weare silke or tyffany hoods or scarfes"? A confusion of voices. Social inversion. Political anarchy. They promptly ruled that no person could wear any gold or silver lace or buttons, silk hoods or scarves, or "any bone lace above two shillings per yarde" unless their "visible estate" exceeded two hundred pounds. Connecticut passed a similar ordinance, charging that "excess in apparel amongst us is unbecoming a wilderness condition and the profession of the gospell, whereby the riseing generation is in danger of being corrupted." What would happen if the winds of fashion blew men's long hair too freely? Long hair, full wigs, and white powder were signs of a confusion in identities the Puritan hierachy could not accept. Cotton Mather lauded John Eliot's view that "for men to wear their hair with a luxurious, delicate, feminine prolixity; or for them to preserve no plain distinction of their sex by the hair of their head and face; and much more for men to disfigure themselves with hair that is *none of their own*" was an affront to God. As Mather recounted Eliot's life story, "the hair of them that professed religion, long before his death, grew too long for him to swallow; and he would express himself continually with a boiling zeal concerning it, until at last he gave over, with some regret complaining, 'The lust is become insuperable!'"[41]

From an official perspective consistent with Saint Paul's concept of "callings," members of an orderly community in theory would consume and self-fashion in a manner appropriate to their ordained social station and not beyond it. Sumptuary laws, however, failed to dissuade people from using consumer goods for precisely the opposite purpose—to experiment with alternative social identities and reconfigurations of power. Thirty women were "presented" at Springfield court in 1673 as persons of small estate who "use to wear silk contrary to law." Three years later, sixty-eight people from five Hampshire County towns, "some for wearing silk and that in a flaunting manner, and others for long hair and other extravagancies," appeared in court. Perhaps clothing attained its greatest liquidity of value and potential to exchange social identities when it was fused with money itself. Merchant James Russell of Charlestown walked through that town's streets sporting a pair of shoe buckles decorated with "Arab[ian]: pennys."[42]

People held back from the sacrament because it represented a set of conflicting values that seemed both dangerous and irresolvable. Should one sit down at the Lord's Table and join Christ's body if, as Saint Paul warned, the price of such bliss might be damnation? Should one hold back—accept baptism but refrain from communion—and, in so doing, be part of a "mixed" or "halfway" congregation? Finally, a conflict of beliefs arose as people consumed the sacrament, which fixed them explicitly in the mystical body of Christ and implicitly in the hierarchic political body of civil society, and consumed in the marketplace, which allowed them to test the limits of social rank by assuming the boots, hoods, buttons, and lace of superiors they both envied and mocked.

The sacrament raised a still more destabilizing fear that afflicted the Puritan imagination. Despite a clear renunciation of literal transubstantiation in church doctrine, Puritans feared that in feeding on the body and blood of Christ, while sharing in a blessed act of consumption, they risked practicing a kind of symbolic cannibalism. Class exploitation had long been expressed in English culture as one group's literal dismemberment and consumption of the other. John Winthrop argued in 1630 that the "riche and mighty" should nurture qualities of "love, mercy, gentleness, and temperance" and "not eate upp the poore."[43] Popular uprisings inverted the metaphor, as the poor feasted on the fatted bodies of the rich. But in the colonial imagination the specter that cannibalism was a ubiquitous practice shared by all Native Americans recast the meaning of dismemberment. The Puritans projected their fear of consumption gone awry within English culture onto the New England Indians, transforming them into literal cannibals that subverted bodily order.

Conservative critics considered consumerism a disease of English society by the 1630s. Like any illness, it made its victims feel unworthy, disgusting, and infected. Perhaps it was to renounce the corrupting influences of the commodity life that led colonists to leave "their Patrimonies, Inheritances, plentiful Estates, and settlement of Houses well Furnished" and "come into this Desert, & unknown Land, and smoaky Cottages, to the Society of Cursed Cannibals, (as they have proved to be) and at best wild Indians." In discussing the culinary habits of coastal Algonkian peoples, John Josselyn announced, "All of them are Cannibals, eaters of humane flesh. And so were formerly the Heathen-*Irish*, who used to feed upon the Buttocks of Boyes and Womens Paps. It seems it is natural to Savage people to do so." Any New England colonist who had heard such tales about the Indians but remained skeptical could find confirmation of the Irish connection in Nathaniel Ward's *Simple Cobler of Aggawam in New England.* In a special section called "A Word of IRELAND," that author reminded readers that "these Irish [were] anciently called *Antropophagi*, [or] maneaters," and as such represented "the very Offal of men, [the] Dregges of Mankind, [and the] Reproach of Christendom." Suggestions that the Irish and Native Americans practiced cannibalism, inevitably fueled by the many tales about "wild men" then current in European folktales, were taken as proof that these peoples indeed had descended to the lowest state of barbarity. As the projected negation of their own disease, the Puritans were sure that cannibalism could also infect others. Roger Williams informed John Winthrop that the Pequots had joined forces with the "Mauquawogs or Mohowawogs which signifies men eaters in their language," and "these canibals have bene all the talke these 10 dayes, & the Nanhiggansicks are much troubled at them." Williams worried about the Mohawks' incursion into eastern Connecticut: "I sadly feare if the Lorde please to let loose these mad dogs, their practice will render the Pequ[o]ts canibals too."[44]

With no evidence to suggest that the Massachuset, Mohawk, or Pequot ever practiced cannibalism, these statements reveal more about the fears and ambivalent feelings of the English than about the Native Americans. Eager to define their national body in terms of the putative deformity of those they colonized, English planters viewed the American Indians precisely as they had the Irish, through a complicated screen of biblical admonition and quotation, technological condescension, ethnographic reportage, adventure novels or "fictions," and popular beliefs that had no basis in observed fact. The perception and vernacular theory of the colonized landscape in the era of emergent novelization were thus conditioned and mediated by providential jargon and fantastic narrative at every turn. What seems clear is that accusing the Native Americans of cannibalism through narrative discourse enabled the English conveniently to deny tendencies toward the consumption of others they had recognized in their own culture of colonialism. Occasionally, however, the cannibalistic savagery within Puritan civility surfaced with unabated rage and made denial more difficult. In 1677, a group of Marblehead women literally dismembered two Native American prisoners in the street. As one spectator told the story, "With stones, billets of wood, and what else they might, they made an end of these Indians. We were kept at such distance that we could not see them till they were dead, and then we found them with their heads off and gone, and their flesh in a manner pulled from their bones."[45]

POLITICAL BODIES

At the same time that the symbolic extension of the body into buildings served metaphysical ends and grounded, through communion, the English body in Christ's perfection, it also worked to represent the monarch and the nation as local and material and blurred the dynastic with the architectural. The phrase "house of Stuart" suggested the symbolic saturation of the king's presence as both royal and mystical body, his blood lineage, and the dependent members of his embodied subjects. Any approach to the cultural meanings of bodily discourse in colonial New England must be grounded first in the contested cultures of early modern England from which colonial plantations both emerged and established their economic and political identities. In addition to its particular architectural meaning, the body served as a pivotal metaphor of the English nation-state. The consolidation of a corporate mythology at the imperial center was necessary to sustain administrative coherence and ideological consent in pursuit of "natural" resources, a labor supply, the conversion of native peoples, and marketable commodities in overseas colonial possessions. Given the need for a unified national mythology, the figure of the body politic was firmly established in Elizabethan society, and, at least until Hobbes and other materialist thinkers began a systematic assault on its value in the mid-seventeenth century, the trope remained a concise representation of corporate legitimacy and political authority.

As Ernst Kantorowicz has argued, the concept attained such power because it fused and diffused through the person of the monarch the perfect body of Christ and the political body of civil society. The metaphor is historically complex, with roots deep in the fertile writings of Plato, Aristotle, the Roman Stoics, Saint Paul's letters to the Corinthians and Ephesians, and Augustinian theology. As English churchman John of Salisbury developed the metaphor in his *Policraticus* (1159), "the place of the head in the body of the commonwealth is filled by the prince, who is subject only to God and to those who exercise His office and represent Him on earth, even as in the human body the head is quickened and governed by the soul." Other members of society figure as other bodily parts. Members of the Senate occupy the polity's heart. Judges and governors are its eyes, ears, and tongue, economic advisers its intestines, and husbandmen "correspond to the feet." Bodily metaphors were part of England's intellectual history and political discourse and anchored its political economy in figures of Christian perfection and love. Bodies of perfection, bodies of love. The words suggest the utopian longings of certain English political philosophers. They also recall the communal closeness of the small Puritan towns constructed in New England, however problematic attaining that social intimacy might have been.[46]

As John of Salisbury's text makes clear, metaphors of embodiment had entangled English political thought and religious life since at least the twelfth century. The concept of an organic English society gained power in the sixteenth century as the influence of Italian political theory and classical republicanism reached Albion's shores, and bodily metaphors were revived anew from medieval churchmen in order to naturalize the new political rhetoric to the ancient English constitution. A pivotal elaboration of bodily metaphors, however, came in the late sixteenth and seventeenth centuries, as England's imperial expansion overseas occurred alongside a dramatic intensification of domestic inequality, social alienation, and political unrest that accompanied the uneven cultural impact of commercial capitalism.[47] As the inherent risks of dynamic commercial capitalism became apparent and the threat of dismemberment at foreign hands (the Spanish, the French, the Irish) increased, the political and religious discourse of hierarchic embodiment intensified. Between 1550 and 1600 the prescriptive value of the body grew more precise, aided by more exacting maps of bodily function provided by surgeons. As its official uses grew more serious, Elizabethan dramatists found in the body a convenient target for their literary play and transformed such issues as transvestism, mistaken identities, civility in the colonies and savagery at home, and satirical masques of royal embodiment into performances drenched in metaphor, ribaldry, and political subtlety. As bodies domestic, foreign, and feigned were posing new problems of regularity and regulation in the nation state, the language of embodiment (and disembodiment) as a commonwealth became more highly disciplined.

In early modern English culture the timing of the intensification of bodily metaphors was key and demonstrates a contemporary concern for anchoring a reflexive view of society in a material sign just as the contours of that society—the nature of authority, the workings of the banking system, doctrinal disputes between religious sects, the intermingling languages of market and theater—were becoming more and more abstract. From Henry VIII's break with Rome until the literal dismembering of the social body with the execution of Charles I in 1649, the body represented a means of conceiving structural relationships, the presence of diseased or corrupt members in need of symbolic surgery or amputation, and the possibility of achieving a healthy nation-state in which the monarch's material body was suffused with God's grace. The bodily metaphor thus identified a prevailing concept of a deferential but static social hierarchy in which specific members had their destined places and roles to fill. Architectural theorist John Shute argued in 1563 that as social beings, men and women may, "like as the members of mans body[,] be divers in number, and have according to their diversitie divers and peculier properties so is it in a good and well setteled comen weale: in whiche ther is no office so base, or handie worke so simple whiche, is not necessary and profitable for the same. And as the members of the body doing without impedimentes their naturall duties, ye whole body is in an helthful hermonye, & able to performe all that belongeth to the same. So is it in a publike weale whe[n] all men in their calling, do labour not onely for their owne gayne, but also for the profit and comoditie of their Countrie."[48]

Drawing freely on Pauline rhetoric that would soon become particularly evocative to English Puritans, Shute described the powerful image of the state-as-static-body that shaped territorial expansion and internal political discipline in the sixteenth and early seventeenth centuries. Health and harmony follow from a universal acquiescence to one's assigned place. Authors such as Shute, James Chillester, Thomas Floyd, Barneby Barnes, Robert Greene, Thomas Dekker, and Nicholas Breton developed the metaphor to great precision, outlining the particular social creatures thought to correspond to the respective parts of the social body. A typical list might include likening the king (or queen) to the head, counselors to the eyes and ears, lawyers to the lungs, yeomen to the ribs, craftsmen to the hands, and laborers to the feet. Invariably, mercantile riches and even money were conceived as the blood (or alternatively the fat), while irresponsible members such as libertines were, as Robert Greene argued, the social body's "Gangrena . . . a disease incurable by the censure of the Chirurgians."[49] As Englishmen discovered in 1649, diseased and corrupt members could be removed by death. The body, in other words, reserved the right to protect its balanced health by cutting off diseased members, including the head itself.

Like the Pauline concept of "every man to his calling," discourse of the body was politically conservative. It claimed that hunger for movement among lower social ranks was not in the best interest of the smooth, organic function of the body as a whole. On this last point, no single English text was so precise (and witty) in its critique than William Averell's satirical pamphlet *A Mervailous Combat of Contrarieties* (1588), in which members of the body revolt against one another in dialogue form, "malignantlie striving in the members of mans bodie, allegoricallie representing unto us the envied state of our flourishing Commonwealth." Writing in the year of the Armada's defeat with a keen distrust of Spanish papists and the imagined threat they posed to English social order, Averell inverts the normal practice of giving voice only to the prince, or "head" of state. Instead his dialogue, "wherein the extreame voices of this present age are displayed against Traytors and Treasons," allows the Tongue, Hand, Foot, Belly, and Back to vent their anguish. Distrust of other members' motives emerges quickly. The Tongue, always cast as the body's troublemaker, addresses the Hand and Foot. "Like fooles we have made the Belly and Backe our Lords," the Tongue begins, "with great labour we get and provide all things may please them: poore soules we have no rest, sometimes the Belly commaundeth one, sometime the Backe another, one saith to ye Foote, arise some meate, prepare mee some dainties, fetch me some wine, Lay the table, the day passeth, the time goeth, and I have eaten nothing."[50]

Hearing the Tongue rehearse the inequalities present in the system, the Hand concurs. "In the Winter I suffer cold," the Hand states, while "in the Summer I endure heat, my joynts are benummed with the one, and dryed with the other I labor day & night to procure for thee both what I can & yet they are never satisfied." A lesser dependency, the Hand's fate is to serve and not be served and to prosper only at the whim of the superior members. Yet the Hand's complaints pale beside the lament of the Foot, the member whose lot in the commonwealth is the most downtrodden. "How do I trott up and downe," the Foot complains, "and as a Porter togeather with my Fellow, am forced to beare up the rest of the members. Whatsoever must be had, I am the Messenger to fetch it, is there fine apparell fashionable for the Backe? be it never so farre, I must trudge for it. . . . I thinke my burden heavier then Aetna, the waight of the Heavens upon the shoulders of Atlas, with griefe heerof my boanes consume, my synewes shake, my humors dry up, and my joynts quake, like as when two weake Pillars beare uppe the burden of a heavie house."[51] Finally, the Tongue stirs up enough bile to get the Hand and Foot to go on strike against the Belly and Back, whom Averell offers as stock types of consumers who live by the sweat of social inferiors and who "devour" food and accumulate apparel at an alarming rate. They prosper as they wrest commodities from the labor of lesser members.

At this point the conservative, engorged Belly counters with the same argument offered by Shute; members should support one another in a corporate and "well-knit" whole. "What greater misery can happen in this life," the Belly asks, "then when as in a naturall body, where the members should serve each others onely denie their ayde unto the body, but conspire also the death of the same: by meanes of which, not the body alone dooth consume and pine away, but the members themselves doe consequently perish. . . . I know not what hath moved my fellow members to this conspiracie, for my part I have naturally fedde them, and lovingly nourished them all, yet they complaine."[52] What moved them to such a conspiracy, of course, were gross inequalities in livelihood and comfort that emerged as the profits flowing into England's commercial coffers were distributed asymmetrically. The attraction of bodily discourse within Italian republican political theory derived in part from the fact that it provided English merchant capitalists and engrossers of land with overlapping screens of classical virtue and Christian piety, through which they could gaze at the imperial expansion and domestic upheaval to which their own activities actively contributed.

At this point, the Belly denounces the Back for being "the pillar of pryde, the waster of wealth, and the window opening to all wickedness." The Back counters by accusing the Belly of gluttony. All is in chaos now, as Averell's self-dismembering body begins to dissolve into a burlesque of genteel order. The entire dialogue begins, rises, and falls without a single representative utterance from the head, who mysteriously makes no appearance at all in the text. Averell is arguing that all of this discord occurs beneath the nose of the prince, without his or her necessarily being aware of the embittered dissent of dependent members. Finally, as Belly and Back intensify their trade in insult, the Hand and Foot agree to call off their strike, admit that their allegiance to the corporate body was subverted by the Tongue's seductive monologue, and confirm their earlier place of dependence on the nourishing protection of the Belly. Harmony is restored.[53]

COLONIES, COLLECTIONS

The discourse of the harmonious and balanced body politic lies at the heart of the naturalization of national mythology during the seventeenth century. Averell's contented Belly appealed in exactly this language: "What greater misery can happen in this life, *then when as in a naturall body . . .*" Although Underwood's *New Anatomie* of 1605 was in some ways a defense of the metaphysical house-body connection, it actually was written as a thinly veiled polemic in defense of hierarchic political embodiment at the beginning of James I's reign. As the language of bodily restoration used by Shute, Averell, and Underwood referenced the optimistic political economy of nascent capitalist growth, another body served as a foil, a negated site for projected amputations and the silenced, dismembering qualities of social upheaval. The rhetoric employed by explorers, writers, and missionaries to exoticize and then domesticate the bodies of conquered colonized peoples warrants close inspection, because Englishmen projected their own negative bodily images—images of rampant sexuality, lack of self-discipline, slovenliness, filth, disease, an unregulated tongue—onto native peoples. They viewed these "deformed" bodies as emblems of political fragmentation and inversion.

The projective process was gradual, lasting from the mid-sixteenth through the opening of the eighteenth century. As the Tudor and Stuart courts and the courtesy-book world sought to transform the taken-for-granted terrain of eating, gesturing, grooming, and polite speaking into an emulative discipline, they destabilized and implicitly critiqued the existing body image of the English bourgeoisie.

As Norbert Elias has pointed out, courtesy books continued a medieval tradition of providing "mirrors for princes" to teach young rulers how to govern. They helped hone the fine manners and polish necessary to cultivate court alliances and advance in national (and international) politics and were, in fact, more about governing the conduct of others than about primping over one's own posture. From the publication of Thomas Elyot's *The Boke Named the Governour* in London in 1531 to the release of Eleazer Moody's *The School of Good Manners* in New London, Connecticut, in 1715 (and later), these books classified such habits as picking teeth, talking with one's mouth full, stooping, or moving erratically as indicative of poor breeding and social inferiority. Moody's book addressed New England children. "Make not a noise with thy Tongue, Mouth, Lips or Breath, either in eating or drinking." "Spit not forth any thing that is not convenient to be Swallowed." "Spit not, Cough not, nor blow thy Nose at Table." "Grease not thy Fingers or Napkins more than Necessity requires." The rule of civility followed the logic of Mosaic law; both were predicated upon "thou shalt nots." With this negational process under way in English culture in the metropolis and colonies alike, it is not surprising to hear New England planters project the same baggage onto the Native Americans, finding them dirty, infested by lice, and smeared with animal fat. In their dances, Daniel Gookin reported, they used "great vehemency in the motion of their bodies." With few exceptions, the Massachuset, Pokanoket, Narraganset, Mohegan, Pequot, Quiripi, and Abenaki peoples had become by 1640 less cultures than darkened reservoirs of the projected turmoil and negated desires of their colonial overlords. Theirs was a tragic erasure of subjectivity that already had occurred in those places in Africa and Ireland where the English had planted.[54]

Erased subjectivity resulted in part from the fact that the English used the Native Americans in two ways simultaneously and thereby placed them on colonized terrain that was constantly shifting. One use recalls the Englishman's projection of inner fears of treason, savagery, and laziness onto the Welsh and Irish, his transforming of politically subjugated cultures into dumping grounds for inner suspicions, instabilities, and hatreds. Perhaps the planter's violence against and distrust of cultural Others resulted from what Winthrop Jordan has termed a "blackness within" English culture. As scorned and debased objects of the Briton's psychic instability and economic zeal, Africans appeared in Elizabethan drama and in witchcraft narratives as the "Black-a-Moor," the erotic rebel, the "Aetheopian" Satan, the African slave, the "Negro" witch, the colonized figuration of suppressed desire, and chattel property.[55]

The blackness within English culture derived from the uncanny recognition that shadows cast by commercial capitalism's uneven growth, engrossed profits, and mercantile self-fashioning existed as still obscure traces within the self, shadows where the ethics of Christian charity encountered the conversion of black flesh into treacherous devils, market ciphers, and transatlantic cargo. Discussing this alterity of embodied subject formation, Tzvetan Todorov maintains that "we can discover the other in ourselves, [and] realize we are not a homogeneous substance, radically alien to whatever is not us." Yet to recognize that the Other exists in oneself or to admit that "I am an other" does not explain the social strategies for denying precisely that realization. One technique commonly used in early modern English society was to identify a group within one's own society that could be marginalized to serve as the projected negative reading of oneself—women for men, the "mad" for the "normal," the propertyless for the landed, rural people for the urban middle class. More commonly, an outside culture served the same purpose. As Todorov suggests, exotic colonized peoples were "unknown quantities, outsiders whose language and customs I do not understand, so foreign that in extreme instances I am reluctant they belong to the same species as my own."[56]

The projection of internal instabilities onto marginal social groups was already evident by the mid-sixteenth century, when internal colonies of Gypsies, stigmatized as "Egyptians," were publicly accused of counterfeiting and deceiving people through fortune-telling. By 1575, there were an estimated ten thousand Gypsies living in England. Their migratory trades, sallow complexion, and unfamiliar language conjured a series of prompt categorical judgments by the native English. Gypsies were a pack of thieves, petty cutpurses, filthy "cony-catching" rogues, speakers of an incomprehensible antilanguage, an argot of Romany and English. But what brought the wrath of popular judgment against the Gypsies was their nomadic existence and outright rejection of land as a basis of citizenship, an attribute that promptly raised comparisons between them and the native Irish. Many English working people felt an awkwardness of movement in public, a sense of dis-ease due in part to bodily injury, weaknesses caused by chronic illness, and an implicit awareness that only aristocrats could move with inner grace. These self-doubts they projected onto the Gypsies, the Irish, the Scots, and the Welsh—groups, in other words, that were viewed as deformities on the English body social. A pamphlet describing Welsh military practices offered a pornographic parody of drill postures common to the "unregulated" Welsh heathens. It portrayed them as feminized, lower bodies within the empire (fig. 57). If, as the Gypsies discovered, to be an internal colony was to be dangerous, what the Welsh found was equally true. It meant being reduced to a stereotype of weakness and emasculation.[57]

In New England the established images of Africans and Irish coalesced in the bodily meanings of the American Indians, suggesting their superimposition in the English colonial imagination. When Mercy Short of Salem described the "Divel" that visited her during her possession in 1692, she admitted he had the "Figure of

Figure 57. English caricatures of Welsh bodily comportment. From *The Welsh-Mans Postures, Or, The True Manner how her doe exercise her company of Souldiers in her own Countrey in a warlike manners with some other new-found experiments, and pretty extravangants fitting for all Christian podies to caknow* [*sic*] . . . *Printed in the yeare. When her did her enemy jeere* (London, 1642), title page. (Photo: British Library)

A Short and Black Man," but "hee was not of a Negro, but of a Tawney, or an Indian colour."[58] As English people arrived in New England, some already had a mental image of the Native Americans based on early published reports or propaganda tracts. Most planters, however, formed their cultural images of the first Americans from the look of their costume, posture, hair, and skin. Given the fondness of the English middle class for judging an individual's level of moral improvement on the basis of public self-control and symbolic enclosure exerted upon the body, the Native Americans' conduct came under particularly close inspection. What the English discovered were contradictions that struck at the core of colonial stability.

A number of early reporters agreed that the bodies of Native Americans were deformed, prone to violent and contortive gestures, and only drawn into acceptable form when disciplined by Christian conversion. John Eliot discovered they had no knowledge of medicine. "They have no skill in physick, though some of them understand the virtues of sundry things, yet the state of mans body, and skill to apply them they have not," he observed late in 1647. Even so sympathetic an observer as Gookin recorded in 1674 that the Massachuset people used "black and white paints; and [made] one part of their face of one colour; and another, of another, very deformedly." The painting of women's faces during mourning rituals drew comments that revealed racial comparison. "The women, in the times of their mourning, after the death of their husbands or kindred, do paint their faces all over black, like a negro."[59] As these observations suggest, some Englishmen classified American Indians according to the same indexes of external behavior that informed their classification of Africans, Irish, and other peoples marginalized under the process of English imperial expansion. The encounter of English people with the deformed bodies of the New World was filtered through a long history of monstrosity within European popular culture, including the fascination with tales of the sexual perversion and utopian freedom of wild men and wild women. Native peoples in New England filled a role for the objectified Other that somehow dwelled already within the reviled, suppressed selves of English colonists. Planters who lived out the collapse of the "out there" with the "in here" were reviled indeed, because in so doing they crossed a crucial cultural boundary. Writing to Winthrop in 1637, Roger Williams condemned the action of "William Baker of Plymmouth," who went to live among the Pequot and was "turned Indian in nakednes & cutting of haire, & after many whoredomes, [was] there married." But Baker had less "turned" savage than admitted the savagery within his own culture. This is what worried Williams. "This fire brand with those Pequots may fire whole townes."[60]

Even as the English viewed Native Americans as debased objects of disgust, they transformed them into moral beings worthy of emulation and imitation. Roger

Williams's comments in *A Key into the Language of America* (1643) represent this position most fully. He views the Narraganset people as a pristine, prelapsarian race not yet corrupted by the sin and materialism of European society. He explores "their Persons and parts of body," "their nakednesse and clothing," "their paintings." Each category testifies to his belief in the crucial importance of the body as an index of the Narraganset's location on the continuum from savagery to civility. Williams drew attention to Native American bodily deportment in order to make specific points to his readers in England and Massachusetts Bay. Consider his comments on hair. "Some cut their haire round, and some as low and as short as the sober English," he observes, "yet I never saw any so to forget nature it selfe in such excessive length and monstrous fashion, as to the shame of the English Nation, I now (with griefe) see my Countrey-men in England are degenerated unto." For Williams, comparing Europeans with native peoples entailed a radical leveling of assumed cultural superiority. "Nature knows no difference between Europe and Americans in blood, birth, bodies, & c. God having of one blood made all mankind . . . and all by nature being children of wrath."[61]

The apparent sympathy some colonists felt for the Native Americans had been rehearsed in the Ulster Plantations. Some English planters used the apparent poverty of Irish domestic housing in order to "savagize" their alien culture. But others felt that native housing practices were actually superior to their own domestic designs. As Edward Howes explained to John Winthrop Jr. in 1632, certain construction techniques he had encountered in the colonized terrain of England's expansion seemed better than their own work: "I conceive the manner of buyldinge in Ireland, vizt. to frame the howse and reare it, then with loame & strawe tempered together, to daube both out side & inside to a foot thicknes or more, to be very stronge and warme." Howes was critical not only of construction techniques. He missed the open halls of medieval houses that in Ireland survived without having been "improved" and ceiled over. "I like well the old English and still Irish buyldinge," he argued, "where the roome is large, & the chimney or herth in the middest; certainly thereby ill vapour & gnatts are kept out, lesse firinge will serve the turne, and men had then more lusty and able bodies then they have nowe." Yet other colonists felt that the wigwams of the Massachuset and Narranganset people were reminiscent of "the ancient halls of England," cooler, more comfortable, and more encouraging of social interaction and good fellowship than English frame housing of the day. Of course Howes's language betrays a basic assumption that Roger Williams had avoided—namely, the sure knowledge that what the Irish (or the American Indians) had in 1632 the English had by 1560 already advanced beyond, and this strange warp in time was a sign that the English nation was more advanced and thus favored by God.[62]

On the one hand, ethnocentric vision enabled the English to conflate New England Indians with Africans and Irish. On the other, the cultural politics of Williams's utopian critique exalted the Native Americans as a source for the renewal of English civility. Between stereotype and dissent lay two other techniques through which the colonists attempted to define, enclose, and control cultural Others. The techniques were closely related. One was an imaginative process that Puritans in both old and New England saw as the necessary act of "unmasking" exotic peoples in order to apprehend and judge the worthiness of their "true" or "inner" selves.

The business of unmasking was everywhere in early modern English culture. Unmask the Quakers. Unmask the Irish papists. Unmask the Indian heathen. Yet stripping away the mask of strangeness assumed, paradoxically, that the Puritans had already internalized the language of the very theater they had repeatedly denounced as evil since the 1580s and succeeded in closing in 1642. Sitting in judgment of the "authentick" feeling of the unmasked performer in the theater of conversion narratives, they sought to remain in control of bodily representation as detached bourgeois critics. English culture as a whole may have relied on the theater as a place and performance to test the fluidity of values that defined the capitalist market economy of the expanding empire. Puritans, however, believed that official sanction of the public theater blurred the transparency of the body as an emblem of fixed rank and semiotic stability, and they insisted that the sanctimonious language of the antitheater movement would shape their encounters with masked, exotic peoples that stood in their way in the New World. Confrontations with alternate bodies in the colonies provide a new, overlooked perspective on the "market as theater" argument, since part of the Puritans' distrust of subversive masking at home derived from the emergent politics of cultural domination in a creolizing world. They viewed imperial expansion as part of a change in the meaning of public performance; this demanded a strange combination of discovery and amnesia. As Julia Briggs has argued, "perhaps the very centre of the theatrical experience is an anomalous one, for the performance challenges the audience to believe and disbelieve simultaneously, to involve themselves in what they see and be self-forgetful, and yet to let the play work upon them, involve them, even change them."[63] Puritans exchanged one mask for another. Encountering a Native American was in some ways like meeting an actor.

On this point Roger Williams betrayed his orthodox, antitheater position even as he revealed his abiding hope that the Native Americans might one day be converted to the transparency of God's "Truth." After introducing readers in his "Generall Observations of their paintings" to the Narraganset words for various colors and different types of earthen pigments, Williams concludes his word list with the American Indian phrases for "You spoile your Face" and "The God that made you will not know you." He digresses to indict, through the perceived falseness of Native American bodily adornment, the history of such deceptive imagery in England itself. "It hath been the foolish Custome of all barbarous Nations," he claimed, "to paint and figure their Faces and Bodies (as it hath been to our shame and griefe, wee may remember it of some of our Fore-Fathers in this Nation.) How much then are we bound to our most holy Maker for so much knowledge of himselfe revealed in so much Civility and Piety? and how should we also long and endeavour that *America* may partake of our mercy?"[64]

For Williams the established medieval image of everyday life as a theater of God's judgments or the mise-en-scène of divine revelation and emblematic discourse eclipsed the artificiality of mortal stagecraft. Because the New Israel was the grand stage for the unfolding of God's Word, he felt it was necessary to rid it of any artificiality. For this reason Williams's text, while perhaps borrowing occasional phrases from More's *Utopia*, draws more consistently from Phillip Stubbes's *The Anatomy of Abuses* (1583), a standard source for antitheater rhetoric wrapped in scriptural citation. Williams worried that Native American tattoos and other body markings were distracting deformities, that the Narraganset language permitted its speakers to say the same things in several different ways, and that American Indians could apparently change names as frequently as actors assume new identities on stage. Other Puritan clerics drew support from antitheater tracts in countering bodies whose boundaries threatened the straitened contours of English manhood. Tearing a page from William Prynne's *Histrio-Mastix: The Player's Scourge, or, Actors Tragedy*, Cotton Mather extended the antitheater critique to women. He cautioned them in *Ornaments for the Daughters of Zion* against the sacrilege of painting their faces. If the Puritans had successfully curbed the duplicity of the English stage in 1642, the potential for artifice in the New Israel presented a novel challenge.[65]

If Native Americans threatened the boundaries between authentic and artificial experience, their cultural alterity would be defined and controlled through appropriation of native material culture into English households. This was the second technique—the collection of American Indian material culture in order to possess metonymically their culture and history. Struck by the strength, strong design, and high standard of workmanship of select artifacts, English settlers soon integrated them into their households. In the 1620s Robert Cushman described a snare set by Pokanoket hunters near Plymouth as "a very pretty device, made with a rope of their own making and having a noose as artificially made as any roper in England can make, and as like ours as can be." Cushman also found a small Algonkian basket "very handsome and cunningly made." By 1637 William Palmer of Duxbury owned "ii Indian Treyes," likely baskets of flat-woven fiber or bark stitched together with porcupine quills. In the 1670s John Josselyn noticed, "The *Indians* make use of their Quills, which are hardly a handful long, to adorn the edges of their birchen dishes, and weave (dying some of them red, others yellow and blue) curious bags or pouches, in works like *Turkie-work.*" The precise sources of English appreciation for the aesthetics and utility of Native American objects are not easy to discern. Perhaps some individuals, like Josselyn, had seen artifacts collected by early explorers for aristocratic sponsors or specimens sent back to the Royal Philosophical Society by such colonial members as Cotton Mather and Joseph Dudley. Still others may have heard of or actually seen the Virginia Indian that James I had "collected" to roam alongside deer and peacocks in his menagerie (fig. 58).[66] As they compared Native American snares, baskets, and woven hemp bags with familiar nooses and woven turkey work, colonial commentators revealed that the native objects they seemed to appreciate most were those for which fairly direct English equivalents were recognized.

The fondness for Native American wares increased over the late seventeenth and early eighteenth centuries. By the late 1720s Mohegans, Pequots, Nihantics, and Narragansets in southern New England had been drawn into the cash economy bottoming chairs and producing baskets and selling them as itinerant traders. By the 1740s the Schagticoke and Mahican peoples of western Massachusetts and Connecticut had also been drawn into the cash nexus as petty producers. Their wares seem on occasion to have been bought and resold in urban centers in which distance, perhaps, made the artifacts especially attractive as traces or fetishes of erased native societies. Boston retailer Daniel Pecker had "2 Indian Bows and Arrows" in his shop in 1750. Boston widow Mary Pace kept "1 Indian Bark Box" in her small house in 1752. In 1758 merchant Joseph Prince owned an "Indian Bow[,] Arrow & pipe," while shopkeeper and jeweler Abiel Walley had for sale the prize trophy: "a large white transparent Pebble sett in silver to hang by way of Privment at a Sachem's Breast." Listed along with other jewels available for purchase, this seems to have been intended for merchants or politicians in need of a token for trade or treaty with native peoples. Perhaps it was destined for ritual exchange with the eastern Abenaki, whose land claims and keen economic sense as participants in the fur trade made them frequent visitors to eighteenth-century Boston. But given its precise description and its association with a native leader, Walley's object may have been collected by him and kept on display for curious visitors to his shop. A fondness for Native American aesthetics—of seeing in their objectified selves something besides the projected disorder of English culture—was not restricted to the wealthy or the highborn. We can just as easily imagine Boston tallow chandler Benjamin Frobisher sitting up at night, pouring over the engraved illustrations in the two volumes of "Lahanton's Voyages to America" he owned at his death in 1762.[67]

Figure 58. "The Young Man from Virginia," watercolor, 1614. From Michael van Meer, *Album Amicorum*. (Photo: Edinburgh University Library, Manuscript Collection, shelfmark La.III.283, fol. 254r)

DEFORMITY, MONSTROSITY

In meeting the challenge of native bodily alterity, Roger Williams and Cotton Mather undertook to deny subjectivity to New England Indians using other, sometimes conflicting, tactics. They sought to diffuse the potential power of specific native individuals by casting "heathenism" in the glaring light of evangelical Christian piety, a move that inevitably placed Native Americans in the dark shadow of savagery. At the same time they attacked the exclusion of native peoples from public roles in market society as a means of criticizing the debauchery and backsliding of English culture generally. For example, smoky wigwams were to English eyes certain proof of Native American depravity. But John Wilson in 1651 could only marvel at "a faire house" which the same people "have built after the *English* manner high and large . . . with chimnies in it" when visiting the "new *Indian* Towne" John Eliot was organizing at Natick. Surprisingly, the building had "no *Englishmans* hand in it, save that one day or two they had an *English* carpenter with them to direct about the time of rearing. . . . They are building English houses for themselves," Wilson wrote approvingly, "mean while living in wigwams."[68]

The English wanted Native Americans to remain childlike. They also wanted them to lead productive lives contributing to the market economy. This program of simultaneous paternalist critique and commercial domestication was fully in place in English culture by the mid-seventeenth century. It appears in the catalog of bodily infractions recorded by John Bulwer in *Anthropometamorphosis. Man Transform'd: Or, the Artificial Changling.* Bulwer's volume opens with a complex emblem showing, as he explains, "The high Commission from Heaven granted for the triall of the Artificiall Changling upon the matter of Fact, touching Man's Transformation" through "all the Artificiall Retortions, Native Alienations, and Absurd Transfigurations of the Humane forme" (fig. 59). Having revealed his abiding hostility to bodily modifications of any and all sorts, Bulwer nonetheless proceeds with lurid fascination to catalog a remarkable range of aberrations. The book, a programmatic attempt to see bodily deformation as an imperial spectacle, is composed as a play in twenty-three acts. Each act covers a particular set of worrisome mutilations exercised by the world's peoples on their bodies. Beginning with "Certaine fashions of the head" around the world, the book then moves to hair, "Eye-brow rites," through "Mouth-fashions and Orall monstrosities" and "Lip-fashions" until the reader finally gets down to "Leg and foot Fashions." Bulwer therefore may have set out to survey the "artificial changeling" throughout the world, but his sequence of narrative acts once again reproduces the hierarchic body of the English nation and of Christ as the ideal figure. As it does so, however, Bulwer's enthusiasm in compiling a world inventory of bodily mutations suggests the degree to which he, like other Puritans, was fascinated by the very desires their own faith and social standing demanded they renounce. Although he claims to abhor theatricality, he chose the form of a play to inform and to parody his own project.

Bulwer's exhaustive ransacking of published travelers' reports and explorers' diaries and his inclusion of orally transmitted stories indicate the extent to which internal English political affairs drew upon colonized peoples as a vehicle for critique at home. Published just two years after Hobbes's *Leviathan,* Bulwer's treatise constituted a Puritan attack on the philosopher's renunciation of Aristotelianism and, more specifically, on his articulation of artificiality as a basic and constant quality of personal representation. "A *person,*" Hobbes had argued, "is the same that an *actor* is, both on the stage, and in common conversation; and to *personate,* is to *act,* or *represent* himself, or another." Such a view no Puritan could long endure, since it directly threatened the sanctity of calling and place in God's patterned creation. Hobbes licensed the artificial stagecraft of public citizenship. Bulwer condemned it as morally corruptive, stating in a passage on cosmetics that "in adorning and setting forth the Body differs nothing from the ostentation of Stageplaies, and is no lesse indecent then fiction in manners."[69]

Bulwer surveys a startling array of meditations on techniques of bodily modifi-

Figure 59. The heavenly spectacle of "Anthropometamorphosis." From John Bulwer, *Anthropometamorphosis. Man Transform'd: Or, the Artificial Changling* (London, 1653), frontispiece. (Photo: Library Company of Philadelphia)

cation, including those used by midwives "to draw and force the bodies of Infants into fantastick shapes." Yet throughout his many anecdotes and thundering indictments, Bulwer pays specific attention to bodies as metaphors of the political state of a particular people; perhaps his own recent experience of England's cultural decapitation led him to explore the topic. As a result, he is particularly attentive to the shape of heads—bodily symbols of monarchy, after all—in different cultures. The Portuguese, he argues, along with Belgians and Egyptian women, have long heads, while Brazilian men have flat heads. Each of these qualities bespeaks a specific attribute, as with the French, who "are observed to have their Heads somewhat Orbicular, to which their disposition and Naturall temper is Analogicall."[70]

Given his stature as a parliamentarian writer after the decapitation of Charles I, Bulwer displayed a keen interest in the social customs and intelligence of so-called headless peoples. Curiously, his catalog provides a metaphoric trace of "republican" political bodies existing as exotic models on the margins of empire, in which rule derives legitimacy only at the behest of parliamentarian agreement and not at the whim of an exalted, corrupt monarch or "head." Bulwer turns to these groups and, drawing upon secondary authorities, provides important details. "Ancient writers," he maintains, "have spoken of Acephali, or a headlesse Nation. Mela writes that the Belmii are Headlesse, and have all the parts of their counteneance upon their Breast." He then invokes Mandeville to argue that on the Island of Dodyn "there are Men that have no Heads, and their Eyes are in their Shoulders, and their Mouth is on their Breast." For final support he turns to the case of the Ewaipanomi, whom Walter Raleigh "saith are a strange headlesse Nation . . . a Nation of People, whose Heads appear not above their Shoulders, which though it may be thought a meere Fable, yet for my own part I am resolved it is true" (fig. 60).[71] Drawing upon the established sixteenth-century figure of the body as the model of the state, Bulwer searched the world for native models that rejected the king's "head." He found bodies on the colonized periphery of Europe whose symbolic forms legitimized the "headless" parliamentary government then controlling England's metropolitan center.

Bulwer's reading of deformed bodies as emblems of deformed nations articulated the great concern provoked in early modern English culture by deformity. What did it signify, for example, when Bulwer noticed that "many humane bodies" "appeared without feet"? A deformed nation? A similarly deformed political economy? Perhaps. People were extremely sensitive to bodily deformation and its possible meanings. In 1648 Obadiah Govis appeared in Salem court for "unclean speeches and practices," including the opprobrious words: "Goodman Spooner had gotten but a crook-legged girl." Mary Grant of Rowley landed in Ipswich court in 1680 "for striking Elizabeth Mighill and upbraiding her for her deformi-

Figure 60. An acephalous, or "headless," tribe of Indians in the New World. From Levinus Hulsius, *Kurtze Wunderbare Beschreibung* (Nuremberg, 1599). (Photo: The Huntington Library, San Marino, California)

ty of body and other provoking words," including, according to two witnesses, having called her "a crooked-back slut and a theif," and for giving her "a box on the ear." Bodily deformity suggested association with Satan. Boston merchant John Saffin noted that there are "some women so hansom that onely their faces and splay feet, have made them be accused for Witches."[72]

Saffin's words suggest a third possible interpretation of bodily deformity. Perhaps it tokened an angry God. No cases of deformity raised the specter of national dismemberment and divine wrath more powerfully than those involving monstrous births. People flocked to the scenes of "remarkable" deliveries, since they brought into congruence popular fears concerning affliction, evil, women, unanticipated freaks of nature, and implied distortions in political economy. Freaks of nature raised questions of divine purpose. Were misshapen animals and humans a sign of God's displeasure? English scientist and virtuoso Robert Boyle pondered an answer as he examined the "Monstrous Head" of a newborn colt late in the 1650s (fig. 61). According to Boyle, after he "went into the Stable where the *Colt* lay, and got the Head hastily and rudely cut off," he examined its distorted facial features with exacting care. He spent time examining its eyes, and discovered "that the *two Eyes* were united into one *Double Eye*, which was placed just in the

Figure 61. Head of monstrous colt. From Robert Boyle, "Observations upon a Monstrous Head," *Philosophical Transactions* 1 (1665–66), facing p. 78. (Photo: Special Collections, Van Pelt–Dietrich Library, University of Pennsylvania)

middle of the Brow, the Nose between wanting." The bone structure itself was malformed. "The two Eye-holes in the Scull were united into one very large round hole, into the midst of which, from the Brain, entred one pretty large *Optick Nerve*, at the end of which grew a great *Double Eye*." Boyle noted this doubleness in detail. "That is, that *Membrane*, called *Sclerotis*, which contained both, was one and the same, but seemed to have a *Seam*, by which they were joined, to go quite around it, and the fore or pellucid part was distinctly reparated into two *Cornea's* by a white *Seam* that divided them." To make the eye — or eyes? — even more problematic, "it had four Eye browes." Finally, just above it, "in the midst of the Forehead," Boyle found a "very deep depression, and out of the midst of that grew a kind of double Purse or Bagg . . . containing little or nothing in it." A useless double bag? He concluded that "it seemed to be a production of the matter designed for the Nose, but diverted by this Monstrous Conception."[73]

Boyle's description of the monstrous colt concentrates on the problematic either-or, or doubled quality of the animal's distorted features. Linked to the brain by a single nerve, the apparently one eye conceals two corneas. The putative presence of two eyes is again doubled in the four eyebrows. The strange nasal formation is a "double" purse or bag, suggesting again the indeterminacy of this mutated specimen. If animal monsters could challenge God's ordained "conformity of parts," human monstrous births posed even graver interpretive difficulties. Caricatures of human deformity circulated in local legends and as penny broadsides, such as the images (one headless) of two remarkable births near Faversham in Kent in 1615 (fig. 62). In Massachusetts Bay, the close attention given to monstrous births reveals the extent to which people used them both to conjure God's will and to estimate the state of civil disorder within the colony. On February 15, 1681, Samuel Sewall reported in Boston: "There is a child born near the north Meeting-House, which hath no Tongue at all; or the Tongue grown fast to the roof of the Mouth; one finger too much on one Hand, and one too little on the other: And the Heels right opposite one to another, the Toes standing to the Right and left outward." The infant's bodily entanglements were certainly noteworthy, but Sewall was struck also by the dangerous proximity of the birth and the meetinghouse, of deformity and the sacred geography of the visible saints. Was this a sign? Thirty years later his interest in such births was still keen when he took special pains to visit a pair of twins attached at birth (a "two-headed monster") that had recently died.[74] To regard these monstrous bodies as portents of God's hidden will, as just punishment for transgressions past, continued an earlier tradition that had reached its zenith with the monsters delivered from Mary Dyer in October 1637 and Anne Hutchinson in September 1638.

John Winthrop recorded the Dyer and Hutchinson cases in great detail. Because each woman adhered to beliefs that threatened the Puritan orthodoxy de-

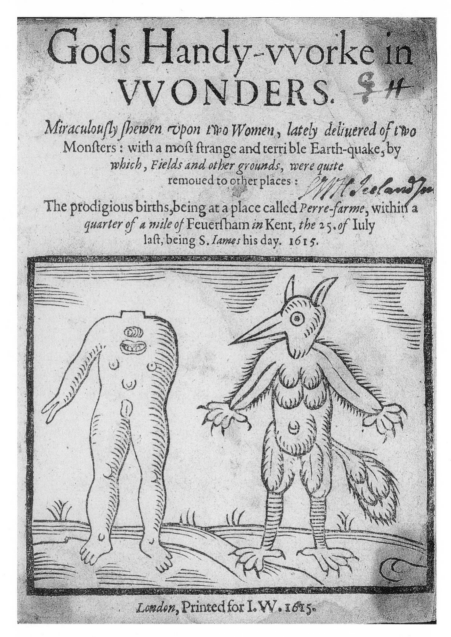

Figure 62. Remarkable births at Faversham, Kent, 1615. From *Gods Handy-worke in Wonders. Miraculously shewn upon two Women, lately delivered of two Monsters . . .* (London, 1615), title page. (Photo: The Huntington Library, San Marino, California)

fined by such ministers as John Cotton, John Wheelwright, and John Davenport—Dyer was a leading Quaker whose husband was a London merchant, and
Hutchinson, also the wife of a London merchant, had been exiled from Boston
after the Antinomian crisis in 1637—Winthrop watched each carefully and stood
ready to interpret details of their births as heavenly portents. One of his descriptions of Dyer's delivery sounds surprisingly like Bulwer's discussion of an exotic
race. It was "so monstrous and misshapen, as the like hath scarce been heard of: it
had no head but a face, which stood so low upon the brest, as the ears (which were
like an Apes) grew upon the shoulders." The child was thus headless, and additional details suggest that "monsters" were narrated as deformed inversions of
bodily order. "The navell and all the belly with the distinction of the sex were,"
Winthrop observed, "where the lower part of the back and hips should have been,
and those parts were on the side [where] the face stood."[75]

When he described Hutchinson's birth, Winthrop felt that the monstrous
forms indicated the extent of her heresy:

> Mistris Hutchinson being big with child, and growing towards the time of her
> labour, as other women doe, she brought forth not one, (as Mistris Dier did)
> but (which was more strange to amazement) 30. monstrous births or there-
> abouts, at once; some of them bigger, some lesser, some of one shape, some of
> another, few of any perfect shape, none at all of them (as farre as I could even
> learne) of humane shape. . . . And see how the wisdome of God fitted this
> judgement to her sinne every way, for looke as she had vented mishapen opin-
> ions, so she must bring forth deformed monsters; and as about 30. Opinions in
> number, so many monsters; and as those were public, and not in a corner men-
> tioned, so this is now come to be knowne and famous over all these churches,
> and a great part of the world.[76]

For Winthrop, Hutchinson's schismatic religious practices had disrupted the
Christian vision of a "well-knit body" whose members were connected by the
clear lines of "mutual love" and common faith that together revealed a divine
purpose. So when Winthrop received Dr. John Clarke's handwritten diagnosis of
the Hutchinson case, he viewed it a representation of social confusion. Of the
"several lumps" in the aborted tissue, Clarke stated, "Every one of them [is] greatly confused, and if you consider each of them according to the representation of
the whole, they were altogether without form." They were, in contrast to Winthrop's vision of a holy commonwealth, "so confusedly knit together by so many
several strings" and "were so snarled one with another" that it was difficult to discern any order at all.[77]

In moving from monstrous bodies to deformed ideas that violated the seamless
perfection of Christian embodiment, Winthrop was on solid intellectual ground

that had been charted at least as early as Richard Eden's 1555 translation of *The Decades of the Newe World of West India,* drawn principally from the writings of
mariner Sebastian Cabot. In that text, one of the first published in English on
places and peoples in the New World, one section dealt explicitly with the causes
and significance of monstrous births, in relation to both religion and the social
conduct proper to the English nation-state. The conclusion demonstrates that
Winthrop was merely following accepted wisdom in the Dyer and Hutchinson
cases:

> Consyder ageyne that disorder of the partes is a deformitie to the hole. One
> hath well interpreted that such monstrous byrthes signifie the monstrous and
> deformed myndes of the people mysshapened with phantastical opinions, dis-
> solute lyvynge, licentious talke, and such other vicious behavoures which mon-
> strously deforme the myndes of men in the syght of god who by suche signes
> dooth certifie us in what similitude we appere before hym, and thereby gyveth
> us admonition to amende before the day of his wrath and vengeance. What de-
> formed beastes are more monstrous then lyinge, rebellion, strife, contention,
> privie malice, slaunderynge, mutterynge, conspiraces, and such other dev-
> ilysshe imaginations. But O Englande whyle tyme is gyven thee, circumcise thy
> harte. Put to onely thy good wyll, and thou mayste fynde grace and favoure to
> recover thyne aunciente bewtie whych hath so longe been defaced.[78]

From the perspective of Winthrop's gender and class, monstrous births represent
inversions of a clearly defined patriarchal social order, an order with one set of
rules and a pronounced hostility to violations of these monologic principles.
What stands out in many narratives of monstrous births, however, are bodily fig-
urations that subvert and offer alternatives to prevailing theories of patriarchal
social order.

Winthrop described the Dyer monster with a sense of awe derived from the infant's grotesque appearance and its symbolic alterity. "The arms and hands," he
noticed, "with thighs and legges, were as other childrens, but in stead of toes, it
had upon each foot three claws, with talons like a young fowle." In 1639 John Josselyn offered a similarly worried version of what other paradigm of order the Dyer
birth might portend, stating, "It was (it should seem) without a head, but having
horns like a Beast, and ears, scales on a rough skin like a fish called a Thornback,
legs and claws like a Hawke, and in other respects as a woman-child." Josselyn also
recalled reading about one case in Brussels from 1564 in which "a sow brought
forth six pigs, the first whereof . . . had the head, face, arms and legs of a man, but
the whole trunk of the body from the neck, was of a swine, a sodomitical monster." Looking back in 1659, John Hull recalled that Mary Dyer's child was "a
hideous monster, part like a man, part like a fish, part like a bird, part like a beast,

and had no neck: it had scales, claws, and horns."[79] Political bodies with "mixed" natures were also equated with hideous, deformed births. Worried by the "two-headed" body of the English state in 1647, when both Parliament and Charles I claimed rule, Thomas Peters wrote to John Winthrop, "We need the continuance of N.E. prayers fore the cure of our monstrous distraction."[80]

John Winthrop Jr. wrote immediately to his friend Edward Howes in London concerning the two monstrous births. Predictably, Howes responded in 1639 by linking them again to the false knowledge of Christ at issue in the Antinomian controversy two years earlier. "Where is there such an other people then in New England?" he asked, "that labours might & maine to have Christ formed in them, yet they would give or appoynt him his shape, & cloath him too." Continuing, his language reveals a central tension in colonial politics. "It cannot be denied but we have conceived many monstrous imaginations of Christ Jesus, the one imagination says loe, here he is; the other says loe, there he is; *multiplicitie of conceptions*, but is there any one true shape of Him? and if one of many produce a shape, tis not the shape of the sonne of God / man but an uglie horridd Metamorphosis."[81]

Howes put his finger directly on the very question that vexed Winthrop the elder. If one admits an aesthetic and politics of "multiplicitie" into an operating colonial political economy based upon "republican" theories of the federal covenant, what will become of social order? Of economic gain? Of labor discipline? Of religious unity? Monstrous births galvanized popular attention in colonial New England precisely because they raised the problem of symbolic and social multiplicity in a community that stressed transparency and uniformity. If Christ represented the type of human perfection and the hierarchic body upon which an orderly society should be modeled, Mary Dyer's child, described by John Eliot as "a woman, a fish, a bird, & a beast all woven together," could only have represented a radical order of political embodiment, a modality in which a diversity of interests might counter the authority of Winthrop's "well-knit" community.[82] Similarly, if the head was the recognized type of authority and power, the birth of a two-headed monster must have signified political alterity.

HOUSEHOLD BODIES

Alterity in the political body followed when two heads appeared where one was expecting to reign supreme. A confusion of precisely this sort emerged in one final context: the household. Here, despite frequent references scholars make to "patriarchal authority" and formulary advice manuals such as William Gouge's *Of Domesticall Duties* (1622), women effectively vied with men for control over the household itself. The image of the "house-body" and its accompanying language play a central role in demonstrating that patriarchal mandate was never absolute. Cracks within its image of order admitted ambiguity and resistance. The house-body was a gendered body.

The productive acreage that surrounded the house consisted of male spatial domains. Fields were often also named for laboring bodily parts, such as the "neck" field, the "back" field, the "backsides," or the "Bauld Pate Meadow" mentioned by Edward Jackson of Cambridge Village (Newton) in his 1681 will. A large stone marker cut between 1636 and 1650 once marked the boundaries of Richard Dummer's farm in Newbury, Massachusetts, and fixed the male line of the "house of Dummer" in space and time (fig. 63a). Barns in which productive capital, such as crops and livestock, was processed and stored (or, in urban shops, retail goods) were also arenas controlled by men.[83]

Yet within the house, women ruled. A doorstone made for the Dummer house shows the face of Frances Burr Dummer flanked by incised geometric flowers, hearts, and a sunburst (fig. 63b). Although years of exposure to the elements have obscured detail, her mouth seems to be slightly open, suggesting she was represented in the act of speaking. The edges of the stone were cut with a serrated pattern that resembles teeth, again suggesting that the entry zone, including the door, threshold, lintel, and doorstone, served as the mouth, lips, tongue, and teeth of the house and had the power symbolically to address visitors. But if Frances is speaking, what might she be saying? Surviving English examples provide suggestions. At Harleyford in Buckinghamshire, inscriptions on thirty-one houses provided a silent dialogue between homeowners and seem to have articulated the values of local women during the seventeenth century. "If Thou Speakest Evil of Thy Neighbour, Come Not Nigh the Door of This House." "Peace on Earth, Goodwill Towards Women." "An Obedient Wife Governs Her Husband."[84]

The central place of women in the household's body gains support in New England from the metaphoric correspondence of the chimney, hearth, and fire to the breast, heart, womb, and soul of the house. Women worked constantly at the hearth, tending fires and performing the many tasks associated with their heat: cooking food, processing soap, dying cloth, rendering offal from a late November slaughter. Each move at the hearth called for adjustment to crane, jack, pot, trivit, draft, kindling, coal. As one proverb of the period put it, "A woman can never go to the hearth without tampering with it," for in tending the flame she symbolically tended the soul of the house. Edward Taylor made the connection in worrying over the state of his soul: "My Fireless Flame! What Chilly Love, and Cold? / In measure Small! In Manner Chilly! See. / Lord blow the Coal: Thy Love Enflame in mee." He asked God to put new life in his soul and directed God's aid to his hearth. "But oh! if thou one Sparke of heavenly fire / Wilt but drop on my hearth; its holy flame / Will burn my trash up." As the emblem of the soul, seventeenth-

Figure 63. Figural stones associated with Richard Dummer's farm, Byfield parish, Newbury, Massachusetts, diorite: (a) front view of boundary marker with man's body, probably representing Richard Dummer, ca. 1636–50; (b) top view of stone with face of woman, probably representing Frances Burr Dummer, ca. 1643; (c) related floral sprays and decoration on front edge of doorstone, dated 1640. (Drawing by the author)

century women associated fire and ovens with pregnancy. A contemporary belief in Lincolnshire held that a woman could be impregnated by fire if a red-hot spark or cinder burned her apron above the knee. Cotton Mather even recommended a prayer for women to repeat during labor: "Therefore now let it please thee to Bless the House of thy Hand-Maid."[85]

That early New England houses metaphorically extended a woman's breast, heart, womb, and soul to the chimney, hearth, and fire and allowed women to speak symbolically for the household argues that the house was an arena of female authority. But why should this have been the case in New England more than in England itself? True, the house slogans at Harleysford were suggestive, but recall that Robert Underwood made no such analogies to female breasts, wombs, and souls in his architectural anatomy. Why not? One reason might be that men realized, as Richard Dummer likely did, that women who were granted some control over domestic affairs would be "deputy husbands" and wield that authority in service of the corporate estate. Consider the classification of household space alone. While women may have been relegated to cooking hearths in rear lean-tos, the centrality of the kitchen and women in orienting other spaces and social activities emerges in the 1678 inventory of Edmund Browne of Sudbury. Besides a parlor, "middle room," and "lower westernmost room," the house contained a kitchen, a "roome next ye kitchin," "ye little roome by ye kitchen," a "roome over ye Kitchen," and, finally, "ye roome, over ye roome next [to] ye Kitchin." Was this Mr. Browne's house, or Mrs. Browne's? In 1714 the inventory of Aaron Berlow in Rochester, Plymouth County, included "the Back Lentow," "the next partition In the Lentow," another "next partition In the Lentow," and still another "Next partition in the Lentow," making a total of four work spaces along the rear of the dwelling. In some extant houses lean-to work spaces extended so far that they projected beyond the ends of the structure per se, subverting the desire to conceal the messy activities of women's domestic work behind the polite facade of patriarchal control.[86]

This licensed inversion of gender roles in seventeenth-century households was sometimes announced publicly on the exterior of the house itself. The lintel of a porch dated 1649 on Wood Lane Hall in Sowerby, Yorkshire, clearly shows the effigy of the wife *above* that of her husband. A sculpted drip molding over the main entrance to Richard Gough's house (ca. 1660) on Wem Road in Myddle, Shropshire, seems to show effigies of Gough and his wife, Joan, beneath that of their newborn son Richard (fig. 64).[87] The strategy was, in a sense, transparent. By granting "goodwives" more authority in private than in public, husbands believed women would be more complicit in the cultural hegemony of patriarchal privilege and thus in their own subordination.

Another reason why men permitted women control over their household affairs may relate to New England's specifically "Puritan" construction of male identity. Perhaps they were at times more sympathetic than commonly perceived. Puritan patriarchy implied the integration of a feminized role in which men, as "brides" of Christ, sat down at communion, as at a marriage feast, to celebrate their roles as "handmaidens" of the Lord. Ministers, surely committed to the defense of patriarchy, also likened themselves to women's breasts from whom their congregations "may receive the sincere milk of the Word"; they urged their flocks to "suckle at the breasts of both Testaments" (fig. 65). Psychologically, Puritan men were thus both patriarchs and strangely submissive, individuals who at once denied inner conflicts over having been "spoiled" and "feminized" in childhood, and found in "feminine" emotional dependence a sense of personal affirmation. As David Leverenz has suggested, for seventeenth-century men "female imagery provided a transformational vocabulary satisfying desires for dependence while denying ambivalence in fantasies of regressive union."[88] As a result of the femi-

0   3   6
INCHES

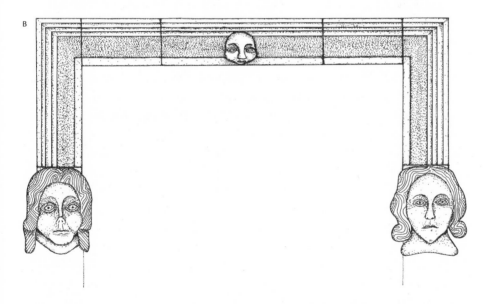

Figure 64. Anthropomorphic piercings in seventeenth-century English houses: (a) faces of wife and husband on porch lintel, Wood Lane Hall, Sowerby, Yorkshire, 1649 (after Christopher Stell, "Pennine Houses: An Introduction," *Folk Life* 3 [1965]: fig. 7, facing p. 17); (b) faces of wife, husband, and probably firstborn son on window lintel, Richard Gough's "Cheife House," 24 Wem Road, Harmer Hill, Myddle, Shropshire, ca. 1660 (after Madge Moran, "Re-Erecting Houses in Shropshire in the Late Seventeenth Century," *Archaeological Journal* 146 [1989]: 546–47). (Drawing by the author)

Embodied Spaces   177

nized construction of patriarchy and their own emotional dependence on that construction, men may have felt some empathy and compassion in granting partial subjectivity to their wives.

Evidence, perhaps, of the ambiguous gendering of Puritan men may exist in the indeterminate gendering of such central architectural elements as the chimney. Robert Underwood's *New Anatomie* specifically cited the "yard" or penis of the house as its only genital feature. It was likely in the same end of the house as the chimney, the hearth of which contained the stomach, liver, and gall bladder. Despite the fact that Edward Taylor repeatedly glossed the chimney, hearth, and flame as the heart, breast, and womb of the woman, a competing claim from colonial New England complicates the argument. A specifically male identity for the chimney was argued in 1634 in Maine, when John Winter affirmed, "I have built a house heare at Richmon Island that is 40 foote in length & 18 foot broad within the sides, besides the Chimnay & the Chimnay is large with an oven in each end of *him*, & *he* is so large that we Can place our Chittle [kettle] within the Clavell [lintel] pece. We can brew & bake and boyle our Cyttell all at once in *him* with the help of another house that I have built under the side of our house."[89]

Winter's purposeful use of the male pronoun may derive from a common belief, described in early almanacs and medical texts, that "heat"—a sign of both productivity and reproductive capacity—was a male quality. Writing to her husband, Anne Bradstreet described her children as "those fruits which through thy heat I bore." Reversing their own typical association with land, men viewed women as fields in need of "improvement" on their own estates and referred to sexual intercourse as agricultural work—an act of "breaking" ground, ploughing, planting seed, cultivating. Preparing for a trip to England, William Byrd of Virginia commented in 1729 that his wife, like his fields, "must be content to *lye fallow* til I come back." Another man added that "howses where no woemen bee are lyke desarts or *untilled land*."[90] Like land that refused to yield, women who suffered tillage without producing were categorized as "barren."

With the precise gender of the house indeterminate, the question of how to naturalize the house as a hierarchic body that contained women as subordinate members had no easy answer. One technique for containing women lay in the design of the New England "saltbox" house itself. It was made for the task. It was a house that announced the sanctity of the nuclear family and ordered space so that the family's head could efficiently maintain ideal surveillance over the dependent members of his body. It ensured proper family government, a point the town of Hadleigh in Suffolk recognized when it ordered in 1619 that no more than one family should dwell in a house and no one "shall devide or parte any Cottages or dwelling houses" for purposes of rental.[91] The front of the house presented an image of order and control to the public way. The lobby entry prevented unwant-

Figure 65. Isaac Johnson stone, Charlestown, Massachusetts, 1702. (Photo by the author)

ed guests from entering the family's "body" per se. Lean-tos allowed people to move kitchens and domestic work spaces to the rear of the structure, so that cooking, domestic textile processing, and butchering could be carried out in the rear yard away from the prying gaze of passersby. Rear entries ensured that domestic servants and informal backyard visits would remain hidden.

In both England and New England a public face of order was essential to maintaining family government and gender relations. John Norden's *The Surveyor's Dialogue* phrased the question precisely in 1607: "And is not every Mannor a little common wealth, whereof the Tenants are the members, the land the body, and the Lord the head?" In transplanting the organic language of republican political theory to family discipline, husbands were indeed the "heads" of their family's body; wife and children were lower extremities. Petitioning to have a jail sentence shortened in October 1670, Boston tailor William Turner commented that an additional stay would "be the utter ruine of my headles[s] family." In 1755, Esther Edwards Burr described her state when her husband was away: "I am in the glooms two, half *ded*, my *Head* gone. Behead a person and they will soon *die*." But as the saltbox house plan relocated and "incorporated" the kitchen, formerly placed at the house's "lower end," at its "rear," it sustained the image of family self-discipline only by demoting women, cooking, and kitchen conduct from the "lower" but publicly visible end to the socially invisible "backside" of the domestic body.[92]

Women had not always been incorporated so fully within the body of the house. As explored in the previous chapter, English medieval dwellings with hearths only in the hall often lacked separate kitchen hearths. The third room "below the passage" was usually a storage room not used for the preparation of food. Instead, on many freeholds a detached small building near the house served as an external kitchen and allowed women their own spatial domain—an early "separate sphere" that actually permitted them and their children a good deal of autonomy. Although the dimensions and interior appointments of these out-kitchens varied widely in relation to the wealth and household size of the land-owner, a late-fourteenth-century, timber-framed example from Little Braxted, Essex, is approximately twenty-two feet square in plan and fifteen feet high at the eaves, lit by two unglazed mullioned windows, and entered by a decorated door-way along one side. Smoke exited through vents cut in the roof. Like the Little Braxted example, which remained in use until about 1575–1600, enough external kitchens survived in England to have been familiar to New England colonists.[93]

They were also built in New England, although their distribution is highly re-stricted. Always a source of radical critique of Puritan family government and re-ligious embodiment, people in Rhode Island employed external kitchens along-side their hybrid houses. As late as 1698 Epenetus Olney in Providence had a kitchen with a cellar underneath that clearly stood apart from his dwelling house. The other high concentration of external kitchens was in Boston, where by the early 1680s the town actively encouraged their construction in order to minimize the threat of fire. In 1681, for example, the estate of Joseph Gillam in Boston con-tained "the dwelling house out kitchen part of a shed being already divided, with an Orchard & garden, A wharfe & all the Land belonging to sd. houses" valued at £675. The carpenter's contract to build the Latin schoolmaster's house in Boston in 1701 specified a house and a separate "Kitchin of Sixteen foot in length & twelve foot in bredth with a Chamber therein." In October 1707, John Mico constucted "a timber Building for a Kitchen of 19 foot long 18 wide & 15 stud with a flatt Roof to stand about 15 foot distant from the Southerly side of his New house lately Erect-ed." The persistence of a separate work space for women may correlate in Boston with the relative autonomy that social historians have noticed among female mer-chants and retailers.[94]

Yet these examples from Rhode Island and Boston were exceptions that proved the rule. After the turn of the eighteenth century, kitchens located in rear lean-tos were the norm throughout New England. The incorporation of the woman's principal work domain into the body of the hierarchic house signaled a new form of gender enclosure and segregation that placed women and children even further under the watchful eye of the husband/father. As Cotton Mather observed in 1725, women "ly[e] very much Conceal'd from the World, and may be called *The Hidden Ones*," especially in rural towns.[95]

ENTERING, POSSESSING

But houses were no place to hide, for either women or men. God afflicted houses as He did bodies, attacking their vulnerable points to test the frailty and transience of earthly vessels. Ordinary people searched for signs of divine purpose and personal grace in "remarkable providences" and concluded that God smote the houses of ordinary men and women as punishment for manifold sins. In 1657 Michael Wigglesworth awoke to find his house in Malden invaded by insects. "There is yet an other afflicting thing," he confided to his diary, "and that is a multitude of great black buggs which do swarm all over the hous no room nor place free, no cupboard, pot, & c. like Pharoah's froggs. And they eat all kind of food and we apprehend they have eaten some cloaths also. I am loath to make a discouragement (though a great affliction) because I hope it may be removed in some measure by plaistering the chimneys and stopping their holes, or els by building new chimneys of brick. or if there be no remedy by building a hous in another place."[96]

The very next year God struck John Phillips's house in Marshfield with lightning. When the smoke thinned and the smell of brimstone abated, Phillips was discovered "dead on the hearth . . . without any motion of life." But only certain parts of his bodily house were damaged. "Many bricks of the chi[m]ney were beaten downe the principle Rafters split the battens & lineing next [to] the chi[m]ney in the chamber broken, one of the maine posts of the house into which the summer was framed torn in to shivers & great part of it carried severall rods from the house, the dore where the ball of fire came downe Just before the sd Phillips was broken downe, one of the girts or sumer aforesd being a dry oake was into peices wonderfully taken." In 1668 John Hull heard that "a man at Ipswich repeating a sermon," who, "because it was darkish, stood at a door or window, as a flash of lightning stunned him," was not hurt. A bible under his arm was also spared, except that "the whole book of Revelation was carried away."[97] The entire scene recalls an image entitled "Man's life is short & full of miserie," in which an aged man prays, surrounded by rain and lightning. A ravenous lion and dog eagerly await his death, which itself is signaled by the destruction through fire and earthquake of his human house (fig. 66).

Figure 66. "Man's life is short & full of miserie." From Fletcher, *History of the Perfect-Cursed-Blessed Man*, 26. (Photo: The Huntington Library, San Marino, California)

There were other instances of God's providence revealed through assaults on human houses—lightning, hail, and "lithobolia," or strange incidents in which stones were mysteriously hurled at their roofs and sides. As ministers who traded on interpreting God's hidden will to their flocks pointed out, thunder was one of New England's special tokens. From Cotton Mather's point of view, "New-England hath been a countrey signalized with mischiefs done by thunders," and the frequent "falling" of thunders on meetinghouses and ministers' houses was added proof of their providential meaning. Thunder was, in Mather's words, "Brontologia Sacra," or God's voice heard on earth. Earthquakes were similarly charged. In his account of the 1727 earthquake, minister James Allen of Brookline recalled, "All on a sudden our Houses shook as if they were faling to pieces, and this was attended with a great Noise." In 1755 John Tudor survived an earthquake in which "the tops of many Chimneys was thrown down, [and] Thousands of Bricks Slaites & c. Scatter'd in the Streets" of Boston. His conclusion: "Blessed be God for preserving us & our dwellings."[98] The house-body was a common site that God chose to manifest his will through human affliction, a point the clergy used to bolster their traditional critique of growing too attached to superficial worldly wealth.

Assaults on houses and bodies were a central feature of witchcraft. If holding back from communion represented an unwillingness on the part of some to merge into the enclosed, corporate metaphor of Christ's body, so, too, did witchcraft. Those accused of practicing witchcraft were typically old, unmarried or widowed or were women whose independent control of real property made them the focus of distrust, animosity, and hostility in their communities. From individuals pushed to the edges of the body social came forces that inverted and contorted polite embodiment beyond recognition. The drama of misshapen figures is most developed in stories about possession, when witches and Satan took symbolic control of someone's body and recast it in a malefic image. In 1688 the children of John Goodwin, a Boston mason, suffered the torments of invasion, and Cotton Mather's narrative of their difficulties suggests the power of bodily alterity that evil could effect:

Som times they would be deaf, sometimes dumb, and sometimes blind, and often, all this at once. One while their tongues would be drawn down their throats; another while they would be pulled out upon their chins, to a prodigious length. They would have their mouths opened into such a wideness, that their jaws went out of joint; and anon they would clap together again with a force like that of a spring lock. The same would happen to their shoulder blades, and their elbows, and handwrists, and several of their joints. . . . Their necks would be broken, so that their neck bone would seem dissolved unto them that felt after it; and yet on a sudden, it would become stiff again so stiff that there was no stirrings of their heads; yea, their heads would be twisted almost round; and if main force at any time obstructed a dangerous motion which they seemed to be upon, they would roar exceedingly.[99]

From entering the actual bodies of victims, it was a short step in metaphor for a witch or demon to enter their houses and wreak havoc at similar bodily points. Consider the strange series of events that in 1679 transpired in the Newbury

household of William Morse. Morse testified that flying sticks and stones bar-
raged the roof of his house, that furniture danced in midair, and that the locked
front door was useless: "We heard a grete noyes of A hoge in the house," Morse
wrote of the incident, "and I aros and found a grete hoge in the huse and the dore
being shut I opened the dore the hoge running vilently out" (fig. 67). He became
still more worried when the shoemaking tools and leather he had in a window disappeared, only to come flying down the chimney in disarray moments later. The
chimney malfunctioned badly, with other objects coming down and into the
house as often as they went up and out.[100]

Similar mishaps took place at George Walton's house in Portsmouth, New
Hampshire, in 1682 and at the Hartford house of Nicholas Desborough in 1683.
Walton's house, the target of a "stone-throwing devil," was pelted by rocks from
every conceivable direction. As at Morse's, objects also began to dance in midair
and to disappear and reappear at will. There was a distinctly topsy-turvy quality
to some of what happened: a cheese jumped from its press and crumbled on the
floor; a piece of iron appeared stuck into a wall with a kettle hanging from it; several cocks of hay somehow were lifted up and settled in trees near the house.
Things that belonged on tables refused to stay put: "The Pewter and Brass were
frequently pelted, sometimes thrown down upon the Ground. . . . So were two
Candlesticks, after many hittings, at last struck off the Table where they stood, and
likewise a large Pewter Pot, with the force of these Stones. Some of them were
taken up hot, and (it seems) immediately coming out of the Fire; and some
(which is not unremarkable) having been laid by me upon the Table along by cou-
ples, and numbred, were found missing." But note where in the house things went
awry. A gate was ripped off its hinges. Stones came into "the Entry or Porch of the
House." Glass windows were shattered; a spit was carried up the chimney, came
back down, and was then thrown "by an invisible hand" out a window. Desborough's Hartford house was also surrounded by a cosmic storm, as stones, "pieces
of earth," and "cobs of Indian corn," again hurled by an "invisible hand," came
"sometimes thro' the door, sometimes thro' the window, sometimes down the
chimney, and sometimes from the floor of the room (tho' very close) over his
head."[101]

The material world spun out of control. Barns burned when no fire was visible.
Houses blew down. Chairs flew around rooms. Morse, Walton, and Desborough
concluded their houses were bewitched—and for good reason. In folk tales in old
and New England, witches often attacked houses at their weak points or their
bodily openings. They entered and left houses by their chimneys, slipped miraculously through keyholes, and passed nonchalantly through doors and windows
well secured by terrified homeowners. When a wizard passed the hearth, the fire
would crackle and blaze, as the soul of the house was threatened with eternal

Figure 67. William Morse in his bewitched house. From Robert Burton [Nathaniel Crouch], *The Kingdom of Darkness: Or, the History of Daemons, Spectres, Witches, Apparitions, Possessions, Disturbances, and Other Supernatural Delusions*, 4th ed. (London, 1728), 2. (Photo: The Connecticut Historical Society)

damnation. As "piercings" in the thin membrane that separated the world of interior artifice from the dangerous exterior universe of entropic nature and divine affliction, these places also served as passages between the visible and invisible worlds. Witches attacked precisely the crucial bodily openings in the house—the door (mouth), window (eyes), chimney or hearth (heart)—that defeated the premature enclosure and complete regulation of the upright body. As Robert West has observed, "the simple popular conception was that demons entered the body through its orifices, ordinarily with bewitched or unblessed food, or, if to a devotee, perhaps through the ignoble parts."[102]

Witchcraft narratives abound with house-body analogies. In 1597 Alice Goodridge of Stapenhill, Derbyshire, bewitched a cow that then ran to her house and, "scraping the walls and windows," demanded entrance. In New Haven in 1655 three young girls heard a witch making a "great fumbling at the chamber door." Doors and windows seem to have been favorite targets. According to Joseph Marsh of Hartford, young Elizabeth Kelley saw Goodwife Ayres invisibly enter her house and screamed, "There she comes over the mat." In Stratford, Connecticut, in 1692, accusations made against Hugh Scotia included that "he also sayd ye devell opened ye dore of eben booths hous made it fly open and ye gate fly open."

That same year a Salem man recalled that when his son was ill in 1680, as Bridget Bishop "Came oftener to the hous he grew wors & wors: as he would be standing at the door would fall out & bruis his fase upon a great Step Stone as if he had been thrust out bye an invisible hand."[103]

Narratives represent windows (eyes) as more vulnerable than doors (mouths). In the 1656 case against Eunice Cole in Hampton, New Hampshire, two local women were puzzled when they heard "something scrape across the boards of the windowe." Joseph Safford of Salem claimed that Bridget Bishop's familiars escaped through a window too small for the witch herself. "Rising erly in the morning and kindling a fir in the other Room," Safford recalled, "mi wife shricked out I presently Ran into the Room wher my wife was and as soon as ever I opened the dore my [wife] said ther be the evill one take tham wherupon I Replyed whar are thay I will take them if I can shee said you wil not tek them and then sprang out of the bed herselfe and went to the window and said thar they went out thay wer both biger than she and thay went out ther but she could not." In an interrogation of Mary Lacey in July 1692, the Salem justices asked how she had gotten into Timothy Swan's bedchamber. "W'ch way did you gett in?" they asked. "The Divel helped us in at the window," she answered. In one popular book on witchcraft, spirits assemble in midair over a house, a figure flies in a window, and another dances in a chamber supported by unseen forces (fig. 68).[104]

Finally, witches were associated with the chimney of the house-body and its "opening" at the hearth. Elizabeth Knapp of Groton claimed in 1671 that the devil had urged her to murder family members, neighbors, and her own children, "especially the youngest—tempting her to throw it into the fire, on the hearth, into the oven." In Connecticut Abraham Fitch claimed that Elizabeth Clawson came into his chamber invisibly one night in 1692. "I saw a light abut the bignes of my too hands glance along the sommer of the house to the harth ward, and afterwards I sawe it noe more." That same year in Salem, Eleazar Keyser saw strange apparitions in his chimney. "Being in my own house, in a Roome without any Light," he explained, "[I] did see very strange things appear in the Chimney. I suppose a dozen of them. w'ch seemed to mee to be something like Jelly that used to be in the water and quaver with a strainge Motion, and then quickly disappeared soone after which I did see a light up in the chimney aboute the bigness of my hand some thing above the bar w'ch quivered & shaked, and seemed to have a Motion upward upon Which I called the Mayd, and she looking up into the Chimney saw the same, and my wife looking up could not see any thing, soe I did and doe very Certainly Concider it was some diabolicall apperition."[105]

Although narratives suggest that doors (mouths), windows (eyes), and the chimneys and hearths (breast/heart/womb/soul) were attacked most often, other parts of the house also proved vulnerable to witches. Hannah Perley of Salem stat-

Figure 68. Spirits flying over house, entering house through window, and hovering in midair in chamber. From Joseph Glanvill, *Saducismus Triumphatus; or, Full and Plain Evidence Concerning Witches and Apparitions* (London, 1681), facing. p. 180. (Photo: Houghton Library, Harvard University)

ed that Elizabeth How "appared to her throug[h] a crevic of the clabourds" (metaphorically, meaning a cut in the skin). Mary Brown of Reading deposed against Sarah Cole of Lynn, charging, "My self and children have often heard lik the throwing of stone against the house and the creatures crying like catts upon the Roffe of the house."[106] This could be done directly—by flying in a window, for example—or it could be done through the use of image magic, using small dolls or "poppets" the witch could secrete in the hidden places of her own house-body, often in small corners or small "holes." In Cutchogue, Long Island, two such poppets discovered behind original walls of Benjamin and Anna Horton's house (ca. 1659 and later) may be similar to the ones that John Blye and his son William found in 1685 while helping "take downe the Cellar wall of The Owld house" in Salem where Bridget Bishop had once lived (fig. 69). According to the Blyes, they "in holes of the s'd owld wall Belonging to the s'd sellar found Severall popitts made up of Raggs And hoggs Brusells w'th headles pins in Them, w'th the points out ward."[107]

COUNTERPRACTICES

With a world of demons, witches, and portentous fires announcing God's wrath and threatening their bodies, New England Puritans took various steps to minimize risk of deformity and death. The most obvious was to attack or disembody the witch herself through countermagic. But witches often had superhuman strength and were not easy to challenge. Although their deformities—crooked backs, lying tongues, haglike faces—may have represented dangerous inversions of regulated, hierarchic embodiment, they were nonetheless expected to yield to the logic of the political body. Cut off the head, and destroy the source of power and control. Such was the assumption young Elizabeth Kelley may have made in 1662. In the middle of her "fits," Elizabeth was heard "saying Goody Ayres torments me, she pricks me with pins, she will kill me. Oh father . . . get the broad axe and cut off her head, if you cannot get a broad axe get the narrow axe and chop off her head."[108]

Most attempts to amputate deformed parts of malefic bodies sought to effect material change in a dangerous situation. And there were people in early New England experienced in occult arts. In 1652 someone overheard John Bradstreet of Rowley say that "he had read in a book of magic, and that he heard a voice asking him what work he had for him." One Caleb Powell offered in 1679 to help Elizabeth Morse's husband rid the house of spirits, saying that "he had understanding in Astrology and Astronomy and knew the working of spirits." Ministers encouraged those afflicted by the magic of cunning women and conjurers to pray, hop-

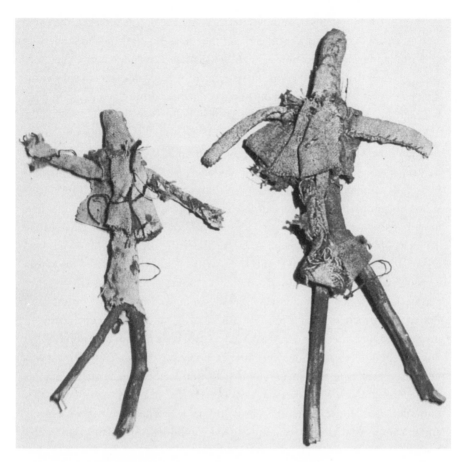

Figure 69. Cloth poppets discovered behind original walls of Benjamin Horton's house, Cutchogue, Long Island, late seventeenth century. (Photo: Society for the Preservation of New England Antiquities)

ing faith in Christ would shield them from Satan's power. But to combat invisible oppressors some people turned to countermagical techniques, which offered a means of symbolically regaining control and restoring the balanced political economy of the body. These techniques conflicted creatively with church doctrine in shaping the lived experience of a syncretic popular faith.[109]

Direct evidence of countermagical strategies is scattered unevenly and demands caution in interpretation. Much has been written about the "magic guarding" of the house in Western culture, but much of it is antiquarian and fragmentary and, beyond arguing that houses somehow needed protection, lacks interpretive cohesion. If we look at these techniques from the perspective of the house-body metaphor, however, the scraps of documentation make a new kind of sense. Vulnerable points or piercings in the house as a metaphor of the body needed protection through medical, religious, and architectural means. Spirits attacked the same orifices where disease and sin collect, and they were as worrisome to carpenters and yeoman farmers as to ministers and magistrates. Anyone's house could become a theater of divine affliction and magical force. The same fears that drove individuals to value the protection of church ordinances drove them to guard symbolically the house that represented the family's body.[110]

To guard against arbitrary disaster, people carefully planned the time when they built their houses: by the season, the position of the moon, the schedule of holy days, and, perhaps for a wealthy individual planning a large or ostentatious house, the stability of local class relations. In 1692 Samuel Sewall in Boston consulted his minister to make certain the moment was appropriate to build a new brick house. "I asked Mr. Willard," he remarked of the occasion, "whether the Times would allow [one] to build an house," referring perhaps to his own role as a magistrate in the Salem witchcraft trials. Willard must have calmed his apprehensions, for construction moved apace. Once moved in, he and his family held a private fast to offer thanks for their new lodgings: "Mr. Willard begins with Prayer, and preaches from 2 Chron. 34. from Luke 1, 50, and then concludes with prayer. . . . I appointed this day to ask God . . . [to] bless us in our new house." Yet doubt crept into Sewall's mind when his new house was "violated" at its most vulnerable points during a storm in 1695. "Mr. Cotton Mather dined with us, and was with me in the new Kitchen when this was; He had just been mentioning that more Ministers Houses than others proportionably had been smitten with Lightening; enquiring what the meaning of God should be in it. Many Hail-Stones broke throw the Glass and flew to the middle of the Room or farther. . . . I got Mr. Mather to pray with us after this awfull Providence; He told God He had broken the brittle part of our houses, and prayd that we might be ready for the time when our Clay-Tabernacles should be broken." Three years later, in a pious reversal of the poppet's image magic, Sewall placed cherubim heads at the gates to his property, believing they would endow the house with protective forces. The presence of cherubim on other artifacts in early New England houses suggests that a concern for protecting the body was widespread. A small cherubim guarded prized textiles in a chest (fig. 70); another, painted on the summer beam in the hall of a house near Little Compton, Rhode Island, looks down on the vulnerable hearth and recalls Abraham Fitch's description of Elizabeth Clawson, disembodied in a small ball of light, moving along the "sommer" of his house and disappearing in the chimney.[111]

Various objects were thought to have protective powers in safeguarding a house, but only a few material remains are well documented. Zerubabbel Endicott placed a horseshoe and a small iron eel-spear trident on different "bones" or framing members of his house in Danvers (fig. 71). Because they were found af-

Figure 70. Cherubim carved on central panel of joined chest, Connecticut, ca. 1680–1720. (Photo by the author)

fixed to the structural members underneath original weatherboarding, they may have been placed there when his house was erected, about 1681. The horseshoe was nailed to the exterior surface of a corner post next to the front door, and the spear trident rested over a door on top of a first-floor girt near the front chimney post. These two posts marked the front of the chimney bay and were in close proximity to both the front door and the hearth.[112]

Others buried objects in the cellar and chimney walls of their structures as construction proceeded. John Farrington, a Lincolnshire farmer who settled in Dedham in the late 1630s, laid a spoon up in his cellar wall, believing that the presence of a metal object in his foundation would give added strength to his house (fig. 72). In England and in New England shoes were concealed behind walls, above windows, under floors, in roofs, and in chimney stacks. In vernacular practice, boots and shoes had been used to conjure and contain the devil, and when placed in walls near windows, doors, or under hearths, they might trap an evil spirit as it was trying to enter the house. Shoes were likened to a firm foundation and steadied the body of the house against evil spirits.[113] As gestures that strengthened, guarded, and blessed the house-body, each of these otherwise obscure features affirmed the house as a living being.

Throughout England in the sixteenth and seventeenth centuries, people buried small "witch bottles" under their thresholds or hearths or laid them up in the wattle-and-daub work over the door a witch was most likely to enter. Some bottles were glass and filled with colored threads, bones, hair, nail parings, and even cloth hearts pierced with pins. In East Anglia and London the most frequent type of witch bottle was a Bellarmine jar, its bulbous shape commonly buried beneath the hearth to protect against witches who might come down the chimney. When placed in the ground inverted and filled with cloth hearts, sharp metal implements, and the urine, hair, and nail parings of a bewitched person, these bottles were believed to simulate bladders that would give the witch sympathetic abdominal spasms and ultimately cause death.[114]

One Suffolk man complained that "his Wife had been a long time in a languishing condition, and that she was haunted by a thing in the Shape of a Bird that would flurr near her face, and that she could not enjoy her natural rest." Concluding she was bewitched, he sought the advice of an aged local healer. The old man visited his wife, observed her condition, and quickly advised him, "Take your Wife's Urine . . . and cork it in a Bottle with Nails, Pins and Needles and bury it in the Earth." Shortly after doing so, "his Wife began to mend sensibly and in a competent time was finely well restored. But there came a Woman from a Town some miles off to their house with a lamentable Out-Cry that they had killed her Husband." She was mistaken, they claimed, since they had never seen her or her house and had never met her husband. But the woman in her anguish insisted, and "at

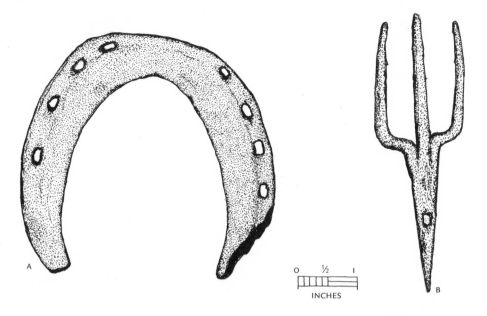

Figure 71. Countermagical objects from Zerubabbel Endicott's house, Danvers, Massachusetts, ca. 1710–30: (a) horseshoe, found nailed to front face of original southwest corner post under clapboard, tips facing up; (b) trident or eel spear, recovered from on top of an end girt between entry bay corner post and chimney post at rear of chimney stack. (Drawing by the author)

last they understood by her that her Husband was a Wizard, and had bewitched this Man's Wife, and that this Counter-Practice prescribed by the Old Man which saved the Man's Wife from languishment, was the death of that Wizard that had bewitched her."[115]

If not buried beneath the hearth, witch bottles were associated in some way with the chimney, since they were intended to prevent witches from entering the house. After a series of stone-throwing attacks in 1682 that, like the pelting of William Morse's house, focused on the door, windows, clapboards, and roof, a group of Portsmouth Quakers promptly "did set on the Fire a Pot with Urine, and crooked Pins in it, with [the] design to have it boil, and by that means to give Punishment to the Witch, or Wizard (that might be the wicked Procurer or Contriver of this Stone Affliction) and take off their own, as they had been advised." In 1692 Roger Toothaker, a Billerica physician, described how his daughter had killed a witch using a similar technique. According to Toothaker, his daughter knew how to use a witch bottle if "there was a certaine person be witched and said person complained of beeing afflicted by another person, that was suspected by ye afflicted person." Her method was simple, and again focused on the chimney area. She "gott some of ye afflicted persons urine and put it into an Earthen pott and stopt

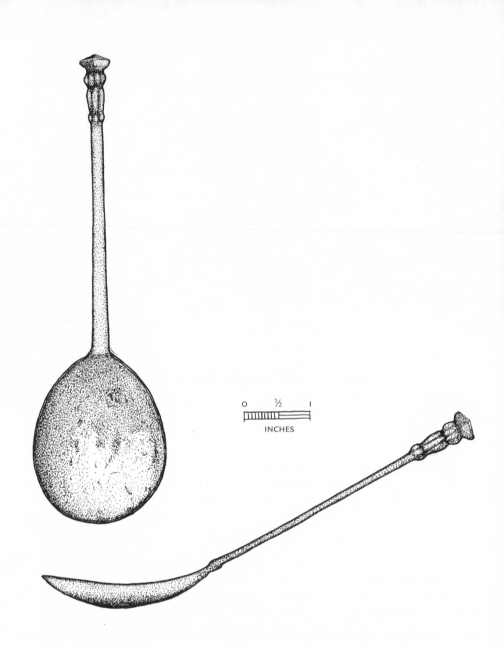

Figure 72. Latten spoon, ca. 1620–60, recovered in 1865 from chimney base of John Farrington's house, Dedham, Massachusetts. H. 6¾" (17.1 cm), W. at spoon 2 1/16" (5.2 cm). (Drawing by the author, courtesy of the Dedham Historical Society, Gift of Mrs. Keziah Farrington)

said pott very close and putt said pott *into* a hott oven, and stopt up said oven and ye next morning said *childe* was dead." Still others, especially colonists from England's northern and western counties, may have carved their chimney posts with designs that would prevent a witch from crossing the threshold, lined their chimneys with salt-glazed bricks, or put salt in small niches built into a chimney jamb because they believed that salt could ward off demons and purify the house.[116]

ANOTHER NATURE

There was conflict, to be sure, over the morality and efficacy of these and other "countermagical" practices. Some people swore by their value and rationalized their efficacy by explaining it in practical terms. Others indicted them, arguing that they represented a fondness for those "meer superstitions" the clergy warned against. An ambivalence over the efficacy of countermagic strategies may have been common. As a heated argument at William Morse's Newbury house in 1680 over the appropriate use of a horseshoe makes clear, the functional and conceptual interdependence of these two strains in daily practice and belief continually intertwined. But the clergy's critique of "superstition" found persuasive confirmation through the marketplace. Long before John Locke theorized the sensory basis of human understanding and knowledge, a London merchant named Lewis Roberts stated in 1635 that in the commercial world, the only knowledge that could be trusted was that which the merchant established on the basis of firsthand sensory contact with commodities. An individual could know the value of textiles, for example, only if he or she had internalized an understanding of the feel and texture of cotton, wool, and silk and knew how variations of the weaving technique affected their finish, their softness. "Empirical" knowledge, it seems, was actually first theorized by merchants—and understood by their clients—and only then codified by the philosophers.[117]

A related transformation that undercut the metaphysical power of the housebody in early New England culture was a gradual shift in how natural philosophy and professional medicine defined the body itself. Galenic and Paracelsian theorizations of anatomy, with their explicit commitment to the interrelations of heavenly correspondence, astrological influence, and humoral balance, did not remain a static inheritance from classical antiquity and late medieval Europe. Under the looming impact of Vesalius's anatomical engravings of the 1540s, English physicians tempered their classical book training with empirical observations of how specific treatments affected patients. One English physician whose writings particularly interested Cotton Mather was Thomas Sydenham. A clinician as well as a scholar, Sydenham rejected the administration of drugs without first closely observing a patient's symptoms at bedside. As a result of his methods, Sydenham argued in the 1680s that disease in general was not caused by a generic state of humoral imbalance. Rather, he suggested that each disease represented a separate and distinct bodily disorder and demanded localized instead of general treatment.

Sydenham's work represents an attempt to rethink the articulation of body and belief within the existing framework of classical medical theory. His work enabled later thinkers, such as Boston's Zabdiel Boylston and Mather himself, to explore the body as a systemic machine governed by its own internal motions rather than as a set of conjoined parts subject to heavenly movements. Unlike Sydenham, whose interest in symptoms never demanded he break from Galenic texts, Boylston and Mather explored outright the causative principle of disease. Mather argued the existence of small "animals" (protozoa and bacteria) that live on plants and mammals and, when spread from body to body by "winds" or physical contact, spread disease. Seeing these "animals" under the microscope, Mather began in the late 1680s to doubt the entirety of the Galenic system. If germs rather than sins were the cause of disease, then why all the concern for planetary movement and humoral imbalance? His investigations with Boylston led him to a further question. Could these germs also be a means of actually preventing sickness?

An outbreak of smallpox in Boston gave them an chance to test the theory in 1721. Smallpox was the most virulent disease that New England ever had to confront, but its precise cause remained unknown. During the first two decades of the eighteenth century, Mather had read reports in the *Transactions* of the Royal Philosophical Society of successful inoculations performed by folk healers in Turkey and China. He had also heard of similar treatments in West Africa from his own slave, Onesimus. With these reported successes in mind, Boylston and Mather inoculated 274 individuals with smallpox. Only 6 of his patients died, and probably not from the pox.[118] Proud of their new work, minister Mather was shocked when local Bostonians reacted with fear, throwing "grenadoes" through his windows and threatening to destroy his property.

The precise details of local reaction to the 1721 Boston inoculation remain unknown. Presumably, many people felt that inoculation was senseless, since it was tantamount to actually giving someone the disease. Yet an inoculation riot in Marblehead in December 1730 suggests other anxieties. The controversy surrounded the active support given to inoculation by Edward Holyoke, the town's leading intellectual and president of Harvard College, and a circle of émigré Bostonians gathered in Holyoke's Second Church congregation. Holyoke had been among Mather's patients in 1721, and he insisted that inoculation was the way to protect the town against an outbreak of smallpox that had begun claiming lives in August 1730. But Holyoke and his supporters encountered strong opposition to the procedure. At a meeting held in early October, Marbleheaders voted not to sanction inoculation unless everyone in town could be treated, which was not possible. Still, like Holyoke, some residents—including schoolmaster Richard Dana, justice of the peace Stephen Minot, merchant John Tasker, and wealthy tanner and trader Joseph Blaney—had gone to Boston in 1721 and strongly favored inoculation. Confronted by their power and apparent self-determination, disgruntled townsmen made these men realize their views ran counter to the public will.

According to one observer, fifty armed men threatened to "pull down" both Dana's and Minot's houses, while one angry fisherman swore he would "knock the Sheriff's brains out." In the widening gulf that separated merchant princes from local artisans and fishermen, class differences were everywhere obvious. Inoculation cost money, and therefore the wealthy were more likely to consider it an option. Yet rumblings deeper than class antagonism ran through the crowd. What really set the mob against the likes of Minot, Dana, Tasker, Blaney, and others of the pro-inoculation group was their shared social background. They were all transplanted Bostonians with profitable ties to large seaports beyond the narrow bounds of Marblehead Harbor. As Christine Leigh Heyrman has observed, these men "made their money by encouraging dependency on bigger ports and indebtedness at home." Through their actions, the Marblehead "mob" announced their rejection of leadership that cultivated outside alliances while ignoring concern for the common good at home. Men like Minot and Tasker "exercised no restraint in the pursuit of private will and interest" and therefore broke the covenant of deference and obedience that had always supported hierarchic social relations in the town.[119]

Phrased differently, the Marblehead inoculation riot entered a wider debate concerning how the social body itself should be imagined. Active support for inoculation was perceived as potentially dangerous because it implicitly advocated an understanding of the human body as an enclosed, self-contained, and self-regulating mechanism. Consider, for example, how Cotton Mather theorized the body when he narrated the 1721 Boston inoculation campaign. "Since the Animal Body is a *Machine*," he wrote, "and Diseases are nothing else but its Particular Irregularities, Defects, and Disorders, a Blind Man might as well pretend to Regulate a Piece of Clockwork . . . as a Person ignorant of *Mathematicks* and *Mechanism* . . . to cure Diseases, without understanding the Natural Organization, Structure, and Operation of the *Machine*, which he undertakes to regulate."[120]

Because the mechanical metaphor had, among other sources, fairly recent roots in Hobbes's *Leviathan* (1651), a text universally loathed by Puritan divines for its demystifying critique of the Bible, it may seem unusual for Mather to be using it here. Yet he was by no means alone. Late in the seventeenth century Samuel

Willard viewed all of creation as a machine, observing that "every wheel in this curious watch moving aright and what less than Infinite wisdom, could so contrive and compose this?"[121] For Mather and Willard what kept the mechanical metaphor "safe" was their belief that God was the master mechanic, the watchmaker above all watchmakers in this clockwork universe. Yet the clergy's adoption of a mechanical metaphor for society and for the human body did have pivotal implications that may have worked in the opposite direction. It suggested that the body, ordered now by the internal motion of "animals," was enclosed within itself, governed by its own internal systemic law, hidden from the shifting position of planets, astrological signs, and, gradually, providential intervention. It is no mere coincidence that the "man of signs" ceases being a serious illustration in almanacs and descends to an amusing relic of popular lore just when the inoculation controversies are severing the body from the heavens. By 1747, almanac writer Nathaniel Ames lampooned "the People's Ignorance" in clinging to a belief "that human Creatures should have actual Society and Communion with spiritual Daemons," calling such a belief a "strange Thing." He also ridiculed the long association between bodily deformity and the socially deforming practice of witchcraft. "If there be an old *Woman* in a Parish prodigious ugly, her Eyes hollow and red, her Face shrivel'd up, that goes double, and her Voice trembles, she is a Witch forsooth; but the handsome young Girls are never suspected: as tho' Satan took a Delight in the Dry Sticks of Humane Nature, and would select the most neglected Creature in the humane Species to be his *Privy-Counsellor*."[122]

More worrisome to fishermen and artisans in towns like Marblehead and Boston was a perception that once the human body was scientifically mapped, the individual soul might somehow disappear among the engravings and theories that found little or no difference between one person's anatomy and another's. As flesh opened to reveal underlying bones, blood, and muscle, the body-as-machine metaphor represented all bodies as essentially identical and therefore as substitutable objects in the enlightened discourse that narrated new medical discoveries in the language of mercantile theory (fig. 73). The "experimental" approach to anatomy had implicitly embraced this position as soon as Vesalius published his *De humani corporis fabrica* (1543), and certainly by the time Rossiter was dissecting Elizabeth Kelley's corpse in 1662. Yet as Rossiter's autopsy concluded, Kelley's body was both a hierarchic, covenanted body and a mechanical one, its tissues yielding completely to neither paradigm.

As the Marblehead inoculation riot demonstrated, by 1730 New England's social body was splitting into two epistemic segments. It is difficult to align these segments with actual social groups. Merchants seem to have favored the metaphor of the self-regulating, mechanical body, as it legitimized their control of a self-regulating market economy. The town's laboring people distrusted this view com-

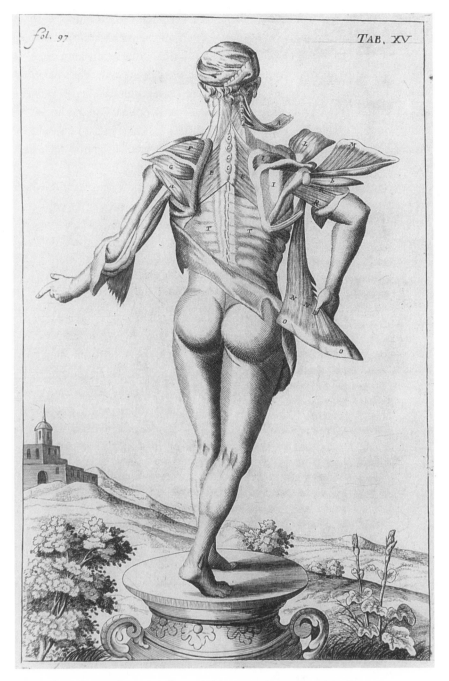

Figure 73. The human figure revealing underlying musculature. From John Browne,
A Complete Treatise of the Muscles as They Appear in [the] Humane Body, and Arise in Dissection
(London, 1681), plate 15. (Photo: Medical College of Philadelphia)

pletely. It might convert them to interchangeable ciphers in a calculus of production and profit. In England's West Country, from which many Marbleheaders had emigrated, the 1720s were a time of dramatic change in the textile industry. One English critic, defending the prerogative of clothiers in the Wiltshire woolen industry, pointed to a concern shared by Marblehead's laboring families: "The Value of Labour has its Ups and Downs . . . the same as any other Commodity."[123] By maintaining the open, providential body, fear of divine affliction would be matched by a faith that at least before God they were distinctive individuals with souls that could not be given a market value.

The point is a delicate one. It is easy to overestimate both the extent to which the body was being "mechanized" and "commodified" in late-seventeenth- and early-eighteenth-century New England and the degree to which laboring people distrusted the implications of inoculation. Most physicians remained confirmed followers of the ancient masters, despite their mastery of dissection and ownership of surgery tools; local lay healers remained unaffected by empirical anatomical study, although arguably their work had long been informed by close observation and modification. And after the Marblehead melee of 1730, inoculation per se no longer provoked riots. Undoubtedly Rossiter knew of Vesalius's experimental work and probably also the anatomical text that Charles Estienne had published in 1545. Although Estienne's *Tres libri de dissectione partium corporis humani* (1545) did not challenge the Galenic and Aristotelian inheritance as openly as did Vesalius's *De humani corporis fabrica*, it nonetheless argued that it provided "not verbal description alone but rather visual representation of (even) the minutest things," drawn from the actual dissections by the French surgeon Rivière of "what was necessary, such as bones, ligaments, nerves, arteries, veins, muscles . . . in which subject he has had much experience."[124]

RADICAL IMPLICATIONS

When Bray Rossiter examined the corpse of eight-year-old Elizabeth Kelley, he found two bodies that referenced competing epistemologies. Her open, emblematic body announced the hierarchy of church and state, stabilized through its projection into the everyday experience of architecture, the unifying aesthetic of communion, the promise of Saint Paul's writings, and arguments about politics and national consolidation using exotic bodies and colonized peoples. William Averell's "lower members," by talking back to the belly and the back, threatened to invert the perfect order of Christian embodiment by demonstrating how vulnerable its members could be to factional dispute and conflict. Indeed, Averell's discordant dialogue suggested one antibody that Rossiter "discovered" in Elizabeth

Kelley's corpse, a body that inverted Christ's perfect frame through witchcraft. The strange appearance of fresh blood in her corpse, the contracted "gullet or swallow," and the "tawny great spot" on her face were bodily signs of maleficium conflicting with—and thus confirming—Christian order. The body of Canaan not only enclosed the discourse of upright behavior defined through the growing literature on bodily management in civil society but also implied its upending, an inversion the bodies of exotic peoples and monstrous births made apparent. As Michel Foucault has suggested, the dominant body and the resistant body are interior to each other.[125] As narratives of monstrous births and witchcraft both demonstrate, these bodily inversions cleared a site for an alternative aesthetic of multiplicity, of mixed bodies.

Elizabeth Kelley's closed, mechanical body, defined through new medical science and experimental anatomy as a substitutional unit, moved in a market of meanings where secular and sacred exchange was common. In seventeenth-century England the rise of experimental surgery had in part constituted the body as a commodity. Under the scalpel of a unifying theory of science, all bodies were systemically alike beneath the outer layer of skin. And as Ruth Richardson has demonstrated, the search by physicians for legally obtained corpses needed to teach anatomy had created a market in dead bodies by the mid-seventeenth century.[126] The progress of experimental dissection in New England had apparently progressed to a point where, in 1676, Samuel Sewall attended a dissection in Boston conducted by three area physicians. In a manner consistent with the English trade in recently executed criminals, the corpse was that of a Native American who had been hanged the previous day for arson. Sewall commented that one of the attending surgeons picked up the heart "in his hand, and affirmed it to be the stomach."[127] Although on the surface this suggests an inability to identify inner organs properly, it may indicate that playful inversion and joking had already invaded the anatomy theater. The procedure was likely a parody dissection, meant to suggest shortly after the conclusion of King Philip's War that American Indians were not correctly "embodied." The confusion of heart and stomach once again recalls Averell's dialogue of bodily parts assuming roles beyond their assigned place. The dissection was a lesson in how to objectify the deformed bodies of those they had finally conquered.

The dissection also shows how the two bodies mixed together, constituting each other even as they seemed to be coming apart. The Native American's body was clearly an object, a corpse as commodity. But it was being used to reveal, through parody, the continuing validity of the hierarchic body and its inversion by cultural Others. Like Elizabeth Kelley's limp frame, it demonstrates the close interdependence of metaphysics and the marketplace. Consider, for example, how fully the practice of piety could prepare one for the world of disembodied objects common in consumer societies. As Victor Harris has argued and as the concrete metaphors of Edward Taylor demonstrate, Puritans thought by projecting their own image into the physical world and then contemplating it as a separate object, a self-contained and disembodied artifact moving among other apprehended objects. The style of piety itself predisposed Puritans to embrace commodities, since they were emblems of their own externalized selves.[128]

Empirical science also found what Edward Howes had in 1639 termed "multi-plicitie" or "mixed" bodies to be a pivotal concept in dealing with the physical world. What had been a subversive idea in popular religion proved essential in science. In 1687 Charles Morton assembled a text called *Compendium physicae* to use in teaching physics at Harvard College. According to Morton, "a Mixt is a natural body consisting of Elements (as matter) and the form of a mixt. Mixture is the Union of Elements alt[e]red (sayes Aristotle), [altered] not corrupted; for the Elements remain in the mixt bodyes but their Qualities are so broaken by the mutual reaction of contraries, and their matter so divided into minute parts, and Shuffled together that they are not discernable apart in any mixt body."[129] Morton has here appropriated the essence of what constituted the dangers of hybridity or dialogism in hierarchic Puritan bodies—a concept that invoked two-headed metaphoric challenges to centralized authority—and pressed it to serve his morally neutral scientific interests.

A final intermingling of metaphysics and marketplace warrants attention. If working people were challenged by the vision of a mechanical, self-regulating economy, they could appropriate it to their own ends. What interests me are the connections that seem to have existed between the culture of experimental medicine and the culture of commodities—in which working peoples' various bodies and their labor value were transformed into identical shapes whose output was calibrated by the strange, unifying logic of the cash nexus. Viewed from one perspective, labor loses out. But from another, the logic of the anatomy theater and the commercial economy argued that everyone was the same, leveled under the surgeon's knife.

The inherent radicalism of this realization drew strength from the long history of covenant theology. As New England Puritans understood the concept, it subsumed a necessary and contractual tension between the covenant of grace and the "federal" covenant of works. The gift of Christ's spirit was an inner or "effectual calling" that came at the expense of exemplary civic duty and public obedience. This was the orthodox doctrine. Yet in actual practice laboring people embraced an Antinomian strain of piety that ran counter to the covenant of works and the structures of obedience and social division it sustained. As Perry Miller suggested, "Antinomian" references a collection of vaguely related sects—"Anabaptists, Quakers, Ranters, Levellers, or what-not"—in order to point out the mystic spiritism or "common belief that the union of the elect with the Holy Ghost is immediate and intimate," at their core. Spirit mystics stressed the continuity of divine revelation at the logical expense of established institutional means of grace. Gortonists in early Rhode Island opposed any magistracy made up of "men [who] make themselves Gods . . . by ruling over the bodies and estates of men." According to Philip F. Gura, "to Gorton . . . and other spiritists who moved to the Leveller camp," during the stormy years of the 1640s and 1650s, "the equality of all men was so literal a fact that deference to a hierarchic system, civil or religious, denied the priesthood of all believers." In their rejection of "hireling" ministers, Quakers also faced charges of social leveling from an apprehensive orthodoxy. John Eliot, who based his *Christian Commonwealth* on the empirical millennialism of his praying Native American communities in Massachusetts Bay, found England's Fifth Monarchists extremely receptive to his outline of a government derived from Scripture rather than from English common law.[130]

The history of radical mystic spiritism within New England Puritanism meant that it was always a "mixed" body with a "multiplicitie" of opinions defining both orthodoxy and heterodoxy. What these strains of radical faith did was provide a repertoire of dissent within the church, a repertoire that extended through New England's Baptists, Sabbatarianists, and Rogerenes. At times the language of these groups echoed earlier English sectarian movements: Diggers, Muggletonians, Ranters, and Seekers. In New England the repertoire of radical millenarianism, fueled by the cross-class appeal of New Light enthusiasm during the Great Awakening and the identicality of bodies in science and commerce, combined to make a new kind of homegrown social leveling during the first half of the eighteenth century. The aim of this local radical enlightenment shared with alchemy a faith in the possible transmutation of one material (or social order) into something more refined. Just as Jared Eliot had found so promising his attempt during the early 1760s to turn black sea sand into iron, artisans would embrace the liberal politics of the "secrets" of freemasonry as a means of linking evangelical enthusiasm to social transformation. As mixed bodies and social multiplicity appeared everywhere, the problem was how to transform the political system to protect effectively the lives of laboring people, including those artisans and fishermen who in Marblehead had threatened to pull down houses and knock out brains. As a self-proclaimed "Student of Astronomy and Astrology" in Rhode Island rephrased the politics of rebuilding society in 1752, the challenge was "to make New Bodies out of old shapes."[131]

THE CROWD PARTICULARLY LIKES
DESTROYING HOUSES AND OBJECTS:
BREAKABLE OBJECTS LIKE WINDOW
PANES, MIRRORS, PICTURES AND
CROCKERY; AND PEOPLE TEND TO
THINK THAT IT IS THE FRAGILITY OF
THESE OBJECTS WHICH STIMULATES
THE DESTRUCTIVENESS OF THE CROWD.

3 Attacking Houses

IT IS TRUE THAT THE NOISE OF DES-
TRUCTION ADDS TO ITS SATISFACTION;
THE BANGING OF WINDOWS AND THE
CRASHING OF GLASS ARE THE ROBUST
SOUNDS OF FRESH LIFE, THE CRIES OF
SOMETHING NEW-BORN. IT IS EASY
TO EVOKE THEM AND THAT INCREASES
THEIR POPULARITY. EVERYTHING SHOUTS
TOGETHER; THE DIN IS THE APPLAUSE
OF OBJECTS.

—ELIAS CANETTI, *CROWDS AND POWER*

THE HANGING

A diary entry: August 14, 1765. "This morning," wrote John Tudor late that evening, "was discovered hanging on the great Trees at the South end of Boston the Effigies of And[rew] Oliver Esqr. as Stamp Master & a Large Boot with the Divel coming oute of the top. . . . The effigies hung all Day," he continued, "and towards evening a number of people assembled, took down the effigies carr[i]ed them throw the Town as far as the Townhouse, then March'd down King Street, and then proceeded to Oliver's dock, pulled down a New Brick Building caled the Stamp Office, belonging to the s[ai]d Oliver & carried the Wooden part of it up to Fort Hill and with Shouting made a Bonfire of it with s[ai]d Oliver's Fence which stood near s[ai]d Hill." The mischief and destruction climaxed in a public attack on Oliver's brick dwelling house, a sumptuously decorated Georgian mansion in the South End. Having successfully destroyed his office and uprooted his fence for kindling, Tudor reported, the mob "then surrounded Mr Olivers House, Broke his Windows & entred the House & destroyed [a] great part of the Furniture & c."[1]

Tudor's terse evocation of this complex event leaves many questions unanswered. There can be no doubt that the attack on Andrew Oliver's house, as one of a series of such assaults that occurred during the stormy Stamp Act months of 1765, was a precisely targeted strike at an individual securely identified with the "corrupt," "diseased," and unconstitutional policies of the British Crown. Yet much more than care in selecting and justifying victims was at work. In recent years the study of crowd actions and the analysis of riots have demanded that cultural historians take into account the divergent political, economic, and moral perspectives of participants. Mobs move with more than one mind. Competing agendas can roil beneath the seamless surface of a single crowd at work. To this end, the study of crowd actions has also grown more precise by drawing on theories of performance borrowed from folklore and symbolic anthropology. The Stamp Act riots in 1765 that saw the sacking of Andrew Oliver's house are a case in point. The contours of social tension and political debate that shaped popular protests in eighteenth-century New England derived from a combination of nascent (or worsening) class conflict, a fear that "placemen" in colonial administrations would compromise the property rights of working men and women, and suspicions among Congregationalists that the Anglican court party would use the church to help centralize imperial authority in its own hands.[2]

Andrew Oliver was only the first victim in a series of house assaults that "afflicted" Boston in 1765 and such towns as Newport, New London, Norwich, Windham, New Haven, Durham, Providence, Plymouth, Duxbury, and Scarborough. Nor were these outbreaks confined to New England; they also happened in New York City, New Jersey, North Carolina, Philadelphia, and the British West Indies.[3] A gap exists, however, in our understanding of what transpired at street level, especially how worsening economic circumstances contributed to a growing labor consciousness among working people, and how they staged their critique of class prerogative through the performance of key cultural metaphors in public spaces. We still have not penetrated, in other words, the symbolic underpinnings of popular violence in eighteenth-century experience.

John Tudor's brief narrative raises several questions. One concerns context and necessarily demands a summary description of the basic social relationships, political alliances, and moral grievances made apparent by attacks on the Boston houses of Andrew Oliver, Charles Paxton, William Story, Benjamin Hallowell, and Thomas Hutchinson. Another set of questions engage issues of form and social participation. Why did these assaults take the particular shape they did? Why hang and burn an effigy? Why parades to celebrate the effigy's mock funeral? Perhaps most perplexing, why did these events culminate in violent, destructive attacks on material possessions? Doors were split open with axes, partitions crashed, family portraits slashed, feather mattresses disgorged onto the street, mirrors shattered, important public and private papers mutilated. A third and final set of questions explore alternative provisional meanings. Was such enthusiastic destruction licensed once its target had been carefully defined, or was this mayhem itself a type of symbolic performance that made specific sense to its perpetrators and victims? If so, how did these events—consisting of warnings, effigy hangings, mock funerals and parades, the actual assaults on the buildings themselves, and then pious claims by the victims for remuneration for damages sustained—function as metaphor?

PEOPLE IN TRANSIT

Context and causation demand consideration first. Different problems plagued Boston over the course of the eighteenth century. The steady economic downslide the town witnessed between 1690 and 1760 had many causes. A slump in maritime trades after the Treaty of Utrecht, a dramatic increase in the number of immigrants to the port city, and a lack of liquid specie were contributing factors. These difficulties were made worse by the appearance in town of a coterie of provincial bureaucrats or local court party whose extravagant tastes, access to cash from sources in London and Bristol, and skillful intermarriage with daughters of established Boston merchants brought cries of resentment from laboring people. As one observer explained in 1720, artisans "are Squeezed and Oppress'd, to Maintain a few Lawyers, and other Officers of the Courts, who grow rich on the Ruins of their Neighbours, while [a] great part of the Town can hardly get Bread to satisfie Nature." The control of property by wealthy merchants had, by the 1760s, grown into a distorted concentration of almost one-half of all productive capital in the hands of the richest 5 percent of the town's taxable residents.[4]

Meanwhile, Boston's population changed. It had grown steadily during the expansionist years of the previous century but leveled off by the 1720s and actually dropped over the next few decades as work vanished. During the first quarter of the eighteenth century, the stability of the local population was affected as working people assuming a market for their labor arrived in town. These new arrivals exerted new pressures of competition and price warfare on established artisans and led, on the one hand, to an exodus of skilled workers from Boston during the middle decades of the eighteenth century, a decentralization of skill that by the 1740s concerned many of the town's residents. "Our Butchers who used to be Thirty in number are now Reduced to four or five," they cried, and "our curriers are gone out of Town"—to name just two of the many trades that fled the port city.[5] By contemporary estimates a quarter of the town's adult workforce left in search of more secure markets elsewhere. Yet, on the other hand, as economic conditions worsened between the 1740s and the 1760s, these pressures led other laboring people—like shoemaker Ebenezer Macintosh, for example—to increasingly radical political action: petitions to protect their interests, published price lists, and house attacks. What factors urged some men and women to leave, while others remained to play roles in the countertheater of colonial insurgency?

In the century between 1660 and 1760, high taxes, spiraling inflation, and increasing social stratification hit Boston's artisans hard, the impact of which was intensified by a rate of immigration so fast that one scholar termed it "the invasion of New England." The total population of Boston increased from about three thousand in 1660 to almost seventeen thousand in 1740. New arrivals from England, other British colonies in North America, and New England's troubled hinterlands surely contributed to this dramatic rise. And since many of the immigrants were skilled artisans looking for work, they posed unanticipated problems for Boston's mechanics. Many immigrant artisans were poor, a high percentage came with families, and they soon exhausted available poor relief. A 1679 town ordinance announced, "Strangers admitted into this colony may not be forced upon this towne." In 1714 the town again emphasized "that no person whatsoever, Comeing from any other Town or place to dwell or Reside in this Towne at any time" could remain unless he or she obtained the permission of the selectmen, secured a certificate of residency from the town clerk, or posted bond to absolve the town of any financial liability on his or her behalf. The stream of immigrants proved too violent, however, and in a tone of reconciled defeat the town in 1738 realized it was "the Receptacle of almost all the Poor that come into this Province, by reason that most Foreigners fix here," and in turn petitioned the provincial assembly for financial relief.[6]

While migration into Boston during most of the seventeenth century seems to have been slow and steady, its pace quickened in the 1690s. After an initial influx of French Huguenots, the first decade of the eighteenth century brought scores of lower-class English and Irish migrants. If Cotton Mather was right in saying 1711 was "a Time of more than ordinary Resort of Strangers" to Boston, the signing of the Treaty of Utrecht in 1713 opened the floodgates. Between 1710 and 1720 alone, Boston's population increased by almost 40 percent. New hoards of residents strained local housing and food supplies. In 1718 one observer reported, "These confounded Irish will eat us all up," and another added, "I wish their coming so over do[es] not prove fatall in the end." Six years later, as immigrants kept arriving, another resident claimed, "[The] *Strangers have devoured our Strength*."[7] The tide rose until the early 1730s, when, along with Boston's faltering economy, the rate of immigration began a steady decline. Between 1660 and 1740, the social position of working artisans grew more precarious as the town's ability to enforce admittance regulations gradually weakened. Of 74 arrivals reported between 1660 and 1680, the selectmen warned 71 (95.9 percent) to leave. Between 1720 and 1740, 440 arrivals stood better than a one in three chance of remaining (73.9 percent warned out, 26.1 allowed to stay). Although this decline in warning-out rates may have been due in part to difficulties in enforcing laws during a period of rapid population growth, it also may reflect a basic weakening of local artisanal influence on town government. Immigration persisted. In 1756 the selectmen noted,

"Of Late [a] great Number of Strangers have come into this Town from diverse places," and in 1769 local workers claimed that if fewer immigrants were present, their "own Townsmen would be imployed in the stead of Strangers."[8] Who, exactly, were these "strangers"? Did most of them come from abroad, as contemporary accounts suggest? If not, how influential was migration from the middle colonies or from rural New England? Did immigration hurt some trades more than others? Of 959 immigrants recorded in town records and selectmen's minutes, the trades and geographic origins of 231 (24.1 percent) are known. This group can help us address specific qualities of artisans arriving in Boston.

Overall, transatlantic migrants account for 123 (53.2 percent) of the group. Just over half were English, one-half again of whom were definitely from London (table 1). Not demonstrably present prior to the turn of the eighteenth century, Irish migrants accounted for almost one-third of all arrivals between 1700 and 1740. Individuals from Scotland and France made up the remaining few in the group. The social composition and geographic origins of this second Great Migration differed greatly from those of the Puritan migration between 1620 and 1640. In the first exodus, artisans from rural English counties prevailed. Skilled workers from London were rare in first-generation New England towns, accounting for only 3 to 5 percent of the heads of households in most settlements, if present at all.[9] But now came urban artisans used to urban competition, ready to stand their ground in the colonial port.

In keeping with existing laws, some mechanics came with estates sufficient to satisfy the town's fears about vagrancy and poor relief. In 1736 an English "printer of Linnens" who was worth two hundred pounds arrived, and in 1744 James Atkinson, a London watchmaker and "Gentleman of a Good Character," landed, "having brought with him upwards of Five Hundred Pounds Sterling." Others offered specialized trades that indulged the whims of the colonial elite. In 1729 a Glasgow wig maker and a London brush maker started in business, followed in 1737 by a "Printer of Painted Paper" able to decorate walls in the latest London taste. The very next year a London tailor specializing in the "Sale of English Goods" set up shop. To satisfy the needs of a growing provincial bureaucracy, Caleb Phillips, a "Teacher of Short Hand" from London, began tutoring privately in 1727.[10]

Financially secure, Atkinson and Phillips were unusual. An overwhelming majority of transatlantic arrivals were neither propertied nor specialists for whom Boston's established creole elite or its new generation of imperial bureaucrats provided a ready market. A majority worked in the building and cloth trades, followed by metalworkers and leather workers, including tanners, shoemakers, glove makers, and harness makers. As they cut prices to compete with established artisans, profits plummeted and native unemployment quickly rose. "It is not prof-

Table I. Trades Practiced by Transatlantic Migrants to Boston, 1660–1740

Place of Origin:	England			Scotland	Ireland	France	Total	
	London	Bristol	Not Spec.					
Trade	No.	No.	No.	No.	No.	No.	No.	(%)
Woodworking/ building	10	7	8	—	8	—	33	(26.9)
Leather	7	2	2	—	6	—	17	(13.8)
Cloth	9	4	8	1	7	1	30	(24.4)
Metal	5	1	5	—	8	—	19	(15.4)
Service*	2	—	1	1	4	1	9	(7.3)
Food/drink	3	1	1	—	1	—	6	(4.9)
Unskilled	1	1	1	—	—	—	3	(2.4)
Other	2	—	1	—	3	—	6	(4.9)
Total	39	16	27	2	37	2	123	(100.0)

Sources: BTR, 1, 2; *BSR*, 1, 2, 3; Ethel Stanwood Bolton, "Immigrants to New England, 1700–1775," *EIHC* 63 (1927): 177–92, 267–84, 365–80; 64 (1930): 411–26, 521–36; 67 (1931): 89–112, 201–24, 305–28; "Vessels Entering Boston, 1714–16," in *A Volume of Records Relating to the Early History of Boston, Containing Miscellaneous Papers*, Record Commissioners Reports, vol. 29 (Boston: Municipal Printing Office, 1900), 229–42.
*Includes barbers, gardeners, schoolteachers, language instructors, haberdashers, tobacconists

itable to the Publick, to have *too many* of any *particular Trade* or *Calling*," wrote one concerned observer. "*Supernumeraries* are *hurtful* not *serviceable* to the Publick; 'twould be better they were imploy'd in other business." Aware of the danger that too many "supernumeraries" or overlapping competitors might cause, selectmen on occasion warned specific newcomers not to enter trades already overcrowded. In 1715, for example, a London distiller named William Cutlove arrived in town exactly at a point when Boston's own distilleries were struggling prior to the 1717 establishment of trade with the West Indies. Realizing that Cutlove would cause further tension among disgruntled Boston distillers, the selectmen told him to depart "in as much as more of that Imployment is not needfull in this Town." Others, however, were harder to convince. One arrival in 1678 "sayd he will stay in the towne despite of any or complaine to England." In 1762 two single Scots shoemakers landed, announced their "design to settle in this place," and adamantly refused to move on.[11]

Artisan migrants from British colonies outside New England were fewer in number and less of a direct threat; fifty-three individuals constituted 22.9 percent of newcomers with known trades and places of origin (fig. 74). Of these, workers

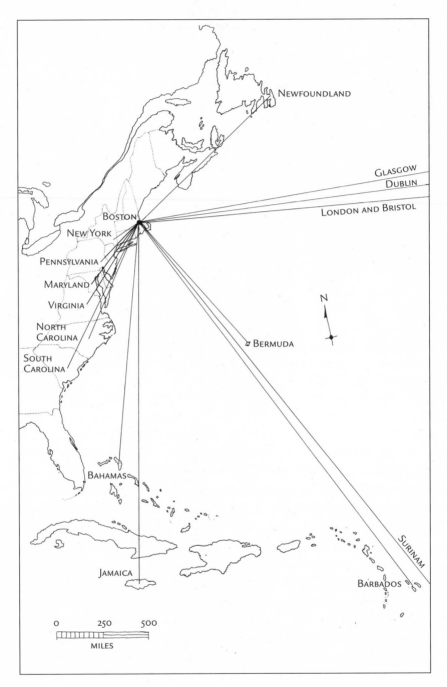

NEWFOUNDLAND

GLASGOW
DUBLIN
LONDON AND BRISTOL

BOSTON
NEW YORK
PENNSYLVANIA
MARYLAND
VIRGINIA
NORTH
CAROLINA
SOUTH
CAROLINA

BERMUDA

N

BAHAMAS

SURINAM

JAMAICA

BARBADOS

0   250   500
MILES

Figure 74. Places of origin of artisan migrants to Boston from other British North American colonies, 1660–1740. (Map by the author)

from New York, North Carolina, and the British Caribbean accounted for a clear majority (table 2). Some migration to Boston was linked to the short but intense depressions that wracked New York and Philadelphia between 1720 and 1740, economic calamities that produced a long-distance "strolling poor" that ranged over great distances in its search for work. More than a few migrants must have left their own cities looking for greener fields, but once they arrived in Boston, they soon left. Edward Drinker, for example, left Philadelphia in 1730 to ply his joiner's skills in Boston, but he was back in his hometown four years later.[12]

Not all workers had a place to which they could easily return. Consider James Fitzgerald, a wandering worker who in 1738 informed Boston authorities "that he came from Philadelphia in March last, that he has travelled from thence to this Town by Land, that he came hither about Four months ago, that for Six weeks or more next after his coming to Town he lodg'd at the House of John Keefe, [and] that he is by Trade a Leather breeches maker."[13] Or William Beauford, whose story presents a life like Fitzgerald's but suggests even more the transience and apparent aimlessness of some eighteenth-century workers. Asked for information by Boston's selectmen in 1737, Beauford, then aged sixty, told them that "he was born at Blanford in [Dorset] from whence he went to Newfoundland and followed the Fishery, that about Five years ago he came into this Town with Capt. Giles Hall, that he has tarried here about a Week, and then went into the Countrey where he has wrought for his living whilst he was capable of Working, sometimes at One place, sometimes at another." Like Fitzgerald, Beauford had moved from place to place, an oft-repeated account that may have left the selectmen unmoved. Beauford added bodily infirmity to gain more sympathy: "but that he is now fallen Lame in his Hands whereby he is rendered unable to Support himself by Labour any longer . . . [and] That he came into this Town the last Night from _____ where he had been about One month." The officials remained unconvinced.[14]

The image of Beauford picking up jobs as they came along, of living "sometimes at One place, sometimes at another," and finally admitting defeat to a tired, broken body conflicts with the common picture of the eighteenth-century master working in proud self-sufficiency in a well-lit shop with dutiful apprentices nearby. Lameness is a theme common to other artisans' life stories. Shortly after being ordered to leave Boston in 1711, Peter Rubine told local officials that "he is by Trade a Mason & that haveing been Subject to fitts & now weak in his hands, & that he belongs to Philadelphia and came Lately from thence to Road Iseland, & that from thence he came by Land into this Towne About a moneth Since."[15] Both Beauford and Rubine may have migrated to Boston in order to avoid the embarrassment of being unable to contribute to the economic health of their towns, friends, or families. Although lameness may have been a figure of occupational weakness, it came from sacrificing one's body to the cruel work of one's craft. Among the la-

Table 2. Trades Practiced by Intercolonial Artisan Migrants to Boston, 1660–1740

Place of Origin:	New York	Pennsylvania	Maryland	Virginia	Carolinas	British Caribbean	Newfoundland & Nova Scotia	Total	
Trade	No.	No.	No.	No.	No.	No.	No.	No.	(%)
Woodworking/ building	4	1	1	1	2	1	2	12	(22.7)
Leather	2	3	—	1	—	1	1	8	(15.1)
Cloth	3	1	1	—	1	2	2	10	(18.9)
Metal	2	1	—	—	3	1	—	7	(13.3)
Food/drink	2	1	—	—	—	1	—	4	(7.5)
Service	1	1	—	2	—	—	—	4	(7.5)
Unskilled	1	—	—	—	1	—	3	5	(9.4)
Other	1	—	1	—	—	1	—	3	(5.6)
Total	16	8	3	4	7	7	8	53	(100.0)

Sources: BTR, 1, 2; *BSR*, 1, 2, 3; Ethel Stanwood Bolton, "Immigrants to New England, 1700–1775," *EIHC* 63 (1927): 177–92, 267–84, 365–80; 64 (1930): 411–26, 521–36; 67 (1931): 89–112, 201–24, 305–28; "Vessels Entering Boston, 1714–16," in *A Volume of Records Relating to the Early History of Boston, Containing Miscellaneous Papers*, Record Commissioners Reports, vol. 29 (Boston: Municipal Printing Office, 1900), 229–42.

boring classes, it also may have been a badge of virtue that easily warranted public support.

If we look at the trades intercolonial migrants practiced, mechanics in the building and cloth trades again dominated, followed by metalworkers and leather workers. In general they sought work in the same trades as did migrants from England and Ireland. As early as 1675, "Hugh Price Playsterer . . . came from Maryland" to pry his way into the then constricted Boston building trades. In 1680 "John Tompson, Tayl[o]r, came from Virginia who[se] parents & relations are Roman Catholicks." James Batteson, a clockmaker, from Pennsylvania, came in 1707. In 1715 James Thompson left Jamaica and announced upon landing in Boston that he was ready to start "carying . . . books into ye country to Sell." The next year cooper Richard Sprague arrived from Surinam. Patrick Jourdain, a hatter, arrived from Maryland in 1727. Although it had slowed to a trickle during the Seven Years' War (1756–63), the current of immigration was still flowing in 1760 when "Mr. Robb," a Philadelphia sugar baker, arrived with the hope of reviving an industry that his native city had largely usurped during the previous decade.[16]

Even though immigrants from abroad and elsewhere in the colonies accounted for three-quarters of all arrivals to Boston between 1660 and 1740, Boston's working people may have most resented newcomers from New England's hinterlands. As early as 1663 the town realized that country folk were using their marketplace to vend produce, complaining that because of those "whoe bring goods into the Towne and make saile thereof, [and] who depart out of the Towne . . . before any raite is made . . . the trade of our Inhabitants is much impared."[17] Crushed by high provincial taxes, city dwellers believed they were not only paying their fare share but also shouldering financial burdens that their rural neighbors could have eased. Portraying country people as mercilessly tight-fisted ingrates who profited as the city grew poorer, urbanites in 1738 pointed to the self-interest of farmers, "who by the Indulgence of this Town are grown Rich, and well Able to help Us under Our present difficulties." Two years later, a Hingham man proved the point when he tried to sell a bad lot of shingles to a Boston housewright. The tension between city and country even surfaced in the popular press. One Boston author dipped his pen in vitriol and asked, "How happy are you in the Countrey, who have your Milk and Honey of your own, while we depend on the ready Penny from day to day?"[18]

Urban bitterness met rural resentment of equal intensity. Impatient with Boston's failure to govern its growing ranks of poor laborers, the surrounding towns of Suffolk County tried unsuccessfully in 1726 to have Boston partitioned off as a county unto itself. Rural life was far from bucolic. Pressed by hardships in their own towns, forty-six (83.9 percent) of the fifty-five rural migrants that arrived in Boston from 1660 to 1740 were from Massachusetts or its Maine territory (table 3). Unlike those from abroad or other colonies, rural migrants came in greatest numbers after 1720, as increased population density and inheritance delays upset the calm contours of agrarian villages. Between 1720 and 1740, for example, the mean price of an acre of land in the Chebacco parish of Ipswich rose by more than 40 percent; the price of choice house lots nearly doubled. In 1749 there were almost sixty people per square mile on the village's land. "Many of our Old Towns are too full of Inhabitants for Husbandry," wrote the Reverend John Wise, "many of them living upon small Shares of Land."[19]

Land shortages and inflated values were rampant in many older towns in Massachusetts and Connecticut. One way out for many people meant leaving farming and working full-time at one of the subsidiary trades they had picked up as seasonal by-employment. Another way out was to join the ranks of the poor that worked their way from town to town. In many instances, the former inevitably led to the latter, and once a countryman took to the highway, all roads seemed to have led to Boston. Thomas Trott spoke for many rural arrivals to the city when he explained in 1714 "that he hath removed from one Town to another and [was] unsettled untill he settled at Roxbury and dwelt there for more [than] one year together, and that About five moneth Since, he came from thence and hath Resided here in Boston." And many poor women, eager to escape the shrinking opportunities in their hometowns, no doubt envied Mary Brock, a Scituate woman

Table 3. Trades Practiced by Artisan Migrants from Rural New England to Boston, 1660–1740

Place of Origin:	Massa-chusetts	Connect-icut	Rhode Island	New Hampshire	Maine	Total	
Trade	No.	No.	No.	No.	No.	No.	(%)
Woodworking/ building	4	—	1	—	—	5	(9.1)
Leather	14	—	—	—	4	18	(32.7)
Cloth	10	1	1	—	—	12	(21.9)
Metal	4	—	—	1	1	6	(10.9)
Food/drink	1	—	—	—	—	1	(1.8)
Service	1	2	1	1	—	5	(9.1)
Unskilled	2	—	1	—	—	3	(5.4)
Other	3	—	—	—	2	5	(9.1)
Total	39	3	4	2	7	55	(100.0)

Sources: BTR, 1, 2; BSR, 1, 2, 3; Ethel Stanwood Bolton, "Immigrants to New England, 1700–1775," *EIHC* 63 (1927): 177–92, 267–84, 365–80; 64 (1930): 411–26, 521–36; 67 (1931): 89–112, 201–24, 305–28; "Vessels Entering Boston, 1714–16," in *A Volume of Records Relating to the Early History of Boston, Containing Miscellaneous Papers*, Record Commissioners Reports, vol. 29 (Boston: Municipal Printing Office, 1900), 229–42.

who in 1715 told Boston officials she had moved to the city "in order to Learn a Trade."[20]

Although Trott's destinations at each move are unknown, most rural New England artisans in the seventeenth and eighteenth centuries moved frequently but seldom ranged far from the town of their birth. Of fifty-five rural tradesmen whose trades and places of origin are known, twenty-two (40.0 percent) traveled less than fifteen miles to reach the colonial capital (table 4). Boston drew many of its migrant artisans from the immediately adjacent towns of Dorchester, Roxbury, Milton, Charlestown, and Cambridge (fig. 75). In much the same way that seventeenth-century London drew short-range migrants from towns in nearby Sussex and Surrey, Boston promised nearby artisans a wider labor market while still allowing them to remain within a familiar circle of kinship ties. The largest single concentration (32.7 percent) of rural New England migrants worked in the leather trades, most of them as shoemakers. In 1704 Peter Patey left his cobbler's bench in Haverhill for Boston. Patrick Corbin came from Lynn to make shoes in 1717, as did John Cullerer from Milton. In 1728, Hull cordwainer Ambrose Tower opened up a shop after having given security to the town.[21] While some long-distance New England migrants also joined the leather trades, a greater percentage of them went

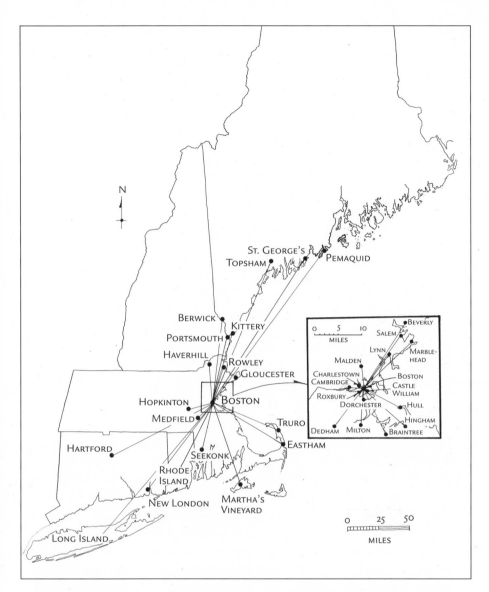

Figure 75. Places of origin of artisan migrants to Boston from rural New England, 1660–1740. (Map by the author)

into retailing or service work or performed unskilled labor. Perhaps some of them had known only farming prior to arriving in Boston. Without question, workers from rural New England towns who went to Boston added to the already over-crowded leather and cloth industries.

If we combine the data on which trades were most affected by the immigration of strangers between 1660 and 1740, we see that native Boston mechanics faced

Table 4. Distances Traveled by Artisan Migrants from Rural New England to Boston, 1660–1740

Trade	Less than 15 Mi. No.	15–30 Mi. No.	31–60 Mi. No.	Greater than 60 Mi. No.	Total No.	(%)
Woodworking/ building	4	—	1	—	5	(9.1)
Leather	8	5	5	—	18	(32.7)
Cloth	7	2	1	2	12	(21.8)
Metal	2	1	1	2	6	(10.9)
Food/drink	1	—	—	—	1	(1.8)
Service	—	1	2	2	5	(9.1)
Unskilled	—	2	1	—	3	(5.5)
Other	—	3	—	2	5	(9.1)
Total	22	14	11	8	55	(100.0)

Sources: BTR, 1, 2; BSR, 1, 2, 3; Ethel Stanwood Bolton, "Immigrants to New England, 1700–1775," EIHC 63 (1927): 177–92, 267–84, 365–80; 64 (1930): 411–26, 521–36; 67 (1931): 89–112, 201–24, 305–28; "Vessels Entering Boston, 1714–16," in A Volume of Records Relating to the Early History of Boston, Containing Miscellaneous Papers, Record Commissioners Reports, vol. 29 (Boston: Municipal Printing Office, 1900), 229–42.

new competition no matter what their calling (table 5). Artisans in the building, cloth, and leather trades were hit hardest. Metalsmiths also felt the pain of new competition. In sheer numbers, migrants from England and Ireland made their presence known evenly throughout the building, leather, cloth, and metalworking trades and added to the ranks of retailers and service workers. Migrants from other British colonies contributed to the same trades, while newcomers from New England's hard-pressed hinterlands dominated additions to the leather trades. Broad patterns are, of course, abstractions from lived experience. How did this new, often intense competition affect established artisans?

DEFENDING SKILL

The sensitivity of tradesmen in Boston to increased pressure from immigration and competition may be assessed by examining their strategies for controlling the labor market even as it was being cast within the larger framework of commercial capitalism: petitions submitted to the town and provincial governments asking for official control of their trades, forms of collective action they initiated, and the

Table 5. Trades Practiced by Artisan Migrants to Boston, 1660–1740

Place of Origin:	Other Countries		Other Colonies		Rural New England		Total	
Trade	No.	(%)	No.	(%)	No.	(%)	No.	(%)
Woodworking/ building	33	(26.8)	12	(22.7)	5	(9.1)	50	(21.6)
Leather	17	(13.8)	8	(15.1)	18	(32.7)	43	(18.6)
Cloth	30	(24.4)	10	(18.9)	12	(21.8)	52	(22.5)
Metal	19	(15.5)	7	(13.3)	6	(10.9)	32	(13.8)
Food/drink	9	(7.3)	4	(7.5)	1	(1.8)	14	(6.1)
Service	6	(4.9)	4	(7.5)	5	(9.2)	15	(6.5)
Unskilled	3	(2.4)	5	(9.4)	3	(5.4)	11	(4.8)
Other	6	(4.9)	3	(5.6)	5	(9.1)	14	(6.1)
Total	123	(100.0)	53	(100.0)	55	(100.0)	231	(100.0)

Sources: BTR, 1, 2; BSR, 1, 2, 3; Ethel Stanwood Bolton, "Immigrants to New England, 1700–1775," EIHC 63 (1927): 177–92, 267–84, 365–80; 64 (1930): 411–26, 521–36; 67 (1931): 89–112, 201–24, 305–28; "Vessels Entering Boston, 1714–16," in A Volume of Records Relating to the Early History of Boston, Containing Miscellaneous Papers, Record Commissioners Reports, vol. 29 (Boston: Municipal Printing Office, 1900), 229–42.

radical implications of diversification across different trades. When seen as part of a single process—the defense of skill—these techniques suggest that a distinct "labor consciousness" began to emerge gradually in Boston beginning in the late seventeenth century. Requests for official restraints, for instance, although coming most often from specific trades or tradesmen acting in isolation, appeared as early as the 1640s. Sporadic attempts to form trade companies—by the shoemakers and coopers in 1648, the coopers again in 1668, and the hatters in 1672—focused on the failure of new arrivals to honor the apprenticeship system. In their 1668 petition to incorporate, the coopers protested the "injury of many Parents too Eagerly desiring the Advancement of their Children to . . . a calling & to bee masters before they attaine to sufficient yeares & discretion to receive & obtaine the full mistery thereof." If these ill-trained children became working coopers, they would be not only "more fitt to bee taught then to teach others or well governe themselves" but also the type of men who "for their private advantage are willing to engage, to teach theire full Art in a yeare or two . . . breaking all the Laudable Customes & Experiences of our nation that have judged seaven yeares time little enough to learne well such a mistery. Such raw-workemen," the coopers warned, "are swarming & increasing." A total of sixty-four individuals signed the petition, a few of whom—like John Freake and Anthony Checkley—were prosperous merchants who realized their own fortunes might increase if better hogsheads could minimize risk in transit.[22]

The coopers were probably not alone among Boston's skilled workers in meeting in the 1660s. The building trades may have organized in some fashion as early as 1661, when a "Carpenters Hall" appears in the inventory of Boston innholder Evan Thomas. Most likely used for trade meetings, this room suggests that carpenters gathered for guildlike periodic discussions closed to other artisans. Nor were they, along with Boston's coopers, shoemakers, and hatters, alone in the British colonies in their attempts to institute corporations for their own protection. In New York in 1667, carters petitioned to be granted a monopoly, asking, in their words, for control "in [the] form of a Guild like the Weigh-house laborers," a privilege they were allowed and kept until they were officially disestablished in 1684.[23]

Petitions for the redress of grievances came more forcefully when workmen from more than one trade acted in their common interest. As early as 1660 artisans representing different trades succeeded in pressuring the town to make seven-year apprenticeships mandatory, but the number of violations recorded suggests enforcement of the code proved difficult at best. With no guarantee of a full apprenticeship, the quality of work might drop and the prosperity of producers decline. Artisans waited. The town did nothing. Finally, they took matters into their own hands. In 1675 nine shipwrights were taken to court "to answer for theire forcible taking John Langworthy upon a pole & by violence carrying of him from the North end of Boston as far as the Town dock; which occasioned a great tumult of people; meeting there with the Constable who did rescue him." Asked why they had mistreated Langworthy, the offenders "declared theire ground of so acting towards him was for that hee was an interloper & had never served his time to the trade of a Ship carpenter & now came to worke in theire yard." Although these zealous guardians of skill went on to acknowledge that they understood that the undercutting of apprenticeships and the admittance of strangers "were usuall in England," they refused to allow such liberties on this side of the Atlantic. In making the intruder "ride the stang"—a variation of the skimmington theme in popular punishment for moral transgression—they drew upon a repertoire of ritual protest that linked them firmly with the unofficial culture of England's laboring classes.[24]

In 1677 the combined difficulties of regulating apprenticeships and restricting new arrivals led Boston artisans to file a joint petition protesting a lack of official intervention on their behalf, a theme echoed in a second petition in 1696. The 1677 document, purposefully submitted as the town was both recovering from a devastating fire the previous year and still feeling the pains of King Philip's War, was signed by 129 tradesmen. By "preventing unskillful workmen" from opening shops, they hoped to save the apprenticeship system and eliminate the type of "stranger" who, after "hireing or buying a Servant" rather than train an apprentice, "Drawes away much of the Custome from his Neighbour which hath been Long Setled, & [who] in reality is much more the deserving man."[25] The 1696 petition, signed this time by 241 individuals, asked for a repeal of a 1679 ordinance that all new buildings in Boston had to be built of brick for reasons of fire safety. Carpenters realized that brick-building codes would always be enforced at their expense. And because most tradesmen could not afford to build brick structures, they felt the law would keep younger Boston men from getting a start and prevent established workmen from expanding existing facilities. In the petition, artisans blamed both new arrivals and their dispassionate wealthy neighbors for the scarcity around them. "If we have not Speedy redress and relief herein," they warned, "many of us that are antient Inhabitants and Children of the first Planters and Settlers of this place must either be forced for a Subsistence and Livelyhood to Leave our Country . . . or else to become Tenants to Forraigners that have come among us, & with their moneys, have purchased houseing and Lands, Or att best to our Rich and Wealthy Neighbours, who are Sometimes telling us, That if wee cannott comply with the Law we must Sell our Lands, which is a very hard and unreasonable thing."[26]

Offered twenty years apart, these petitions show skilled artisans from different trades in league with supportive merchants protesting interests vital to their collective welfare. Although no official response to either petition survives in the records, they are useful in clarifying which trades felt most pressed during the last quarter of the seventeenth century. Members of the building, cloth, and leather trades dominated among the signers of the 1677 petition (table 6). By 1696 the focus of participation shifted slightly from these trades as metalworkers, service workers, retailers, and producers of food and drink increased. In 1691, for instance, the licensed "drawers of wine" in Boston had protested that "there are a very great number that draw without either aprobation of ye selectmen or allowance or authority." Among the subscribers who claimed to feel "very much wronged" were five women: Jane Keen, Elizabeth Watkins, Elizabeth Jackson, Mercy Lawrence, and Dorothy Cresson. Without doubt, the tense years of the last quarter of the seventeenth century mobilized those women who worked as innholders, many of whom were widows who had no other means of support. In 1698 Mary Burnsdell, explaining that her "husband has been Long absent from her," and she "haveing five Small Children, and a mother neer forescore years of age, & therefore unable to provide for her selfe, and all these depending upon your Petitioner for maintenance," asked for a license to sell liquor. By the turn of the eighteenth century, women were also active as small brewers and distillers. In 1701, for example, widow Leah Baker and her widowed sister Judith Clark petitioned for "Setting up of a Still and Improveing the Same in ye Said Bakers house." They were permitted to do so, provided that she "inlarge the hearth of the Chimney with brick and Case the Mantle tree & Ceil the floor next thereto." Clark was then licensed to sell the "Cordiall waters" they made "out of doors." By 1750 observers noted that "the Business of retailing Tea, Coffee, & c. is mainly carried on by Widows and persons in low circumstances, who, generally, very hardly get a poor subsistence."[27]

MARKETS AND WORK

Petitions fell on ears not attuned to economic pressures on laboring people and the need to ensure their health by maintaining an open and fluid social structure. They fell on ears that echoed with the Pauline concept of calling and the static relationship between social classes it sustained. Certainly the "each man his calling" approach to political order was conservative in that it insisted that society functioned best when knowledge was rigidly segregated by a division of labor. Rationalizations of such schemes appeared as early as the 1590s, when Gervase Markham argued that such a system resulted in higher-quality products: "A man generally scene in all things," he maintained, "can be particularly perfect in none." In 1771, five years before Adam Smith's *The Wealth of Nations* first appeared, William Henry Drayton revealed to the laboring men and women of the American colonies the hegemonic process that had long legitimized keeping people at work in a single trade. "The industrious mechanic, [is] a useful and essential part of society," Drayton claimed; "a society cannot subsist without them. But, friends! every man to his trade: a carpenter would find himself somewhat at a loss in handling a smith's tools, and he would find himself but in an awkward situation on a cobbler's bench. When a man acts in his own sphere, he is useful in the community, but when he steps out of it, and sets up for a statesmen! [*sic*] believe me he is in a fair way to expose himself to ridicule, and his family to distress, by neglecting his private business."[28] Drayton connected the moral vision implicit in keeping tradesmen in their proper places to an abstract promise of increased productivity and increased wealth. A rigid division of labor would guarantee sufficient work for the laboring classes, and their higher-quality products would ensure accumulation that supported an essentially static and rigidly hierarchic social structure. At least in this social order employers (and rulers) in theory were obliged to protect the livelihoods of workers in exchange for their submission and peonage. In this world, labor's value seemed secure in being morally located.

This world, however, was unfortunately not the one in which colonial artisans spent much time. As they suffered, Boston's mercantile elite argued that relief would come only if they allied themselves more closely to the economic policies

Table 6. Occupational Participation in Petitions of 1677 and 1696

Trade	1677		1696		Total	
	No.	(%)	No.	(%)	No.	(%)
Woodworking/ building	56	(43.4)	89	(36.9)	145	(39.2)
Leather	19	(14.7)	22	(9.2)	41	(11.1)
Cloth	28	(21.7)	17	(7.1)	45	(12.2)
Metal	1	(0.8)	16	(6.6)	17	(4.6)
Service	2	(1.6)	6	(2.5)	8	(2.1)
Food/drink	2	(1.6)	15	(6.2)	17	(4.6)
Unskilled	—	(—)	1	(0.4)	1	(0.3)
Other*	6	(4.6)	32	(13.3)	38	(10.2)
Unknown	15	(11.6)	43	(17.8)	58	(15.7)
Total	129	(100.0)	241	(100.0)	370	(100.0)

Sources: "The 1677 Petition of the Handycrafts-men of Boston," fac. repr. in *Bulletin of the Public Library of the City of Boston*, whole ser. 12, no. 95 (January 1894): 305–6; "Petition of Boston Inhabitants in 1696, That the Law Relating to Building in Brick Be Repealed," *NEHGR* 16 (1862): 84–87.
*Consists of retailers (shopkeepers, mariners, petty merchants)

advocated by their London counterparts. Untroubled by devalued currency, England's upper classes prospered as they succeeded in freeing markets from protective restraints. From their point of view, labor was just another commodity. "Labour is like everything else," wrote one English theorist in 1733; "it rises or falls according to the Proportion that there is between the Demand and the Quantity then in the Market; all Restraints are unjust." Mercantilist policy worked to regularize the economy and generate profits by regulating laboring people as calculable ciphers of supply and demand.[29]

In the morally neutral game of calculation and self-regulating markets, any hard specie generated in the colonies was routinely sent back to England to cover a mounting provincial debt. As a result, artisans commonly received part of their pay in goods, a custom that was still widespread in rural areas but since the late seventeenth century had never been fully tolerated by tradesmen in Boston's more aggressive commercial environment. "Where *Coin* is scarce," one man claimed in 1682, "Merchants and Shop-keepers, undersell one another; and pitifully help themselves, by beating down Craftsmen." Getting hard money was the goal, but few players could score. Contemporary estimates vary on how much of an artisan's pay was actually in cash instead of goods or bills of credit. One writer in 1719 claimed that workmen were paid "with half Money and half Goods." This estimate may have been close to the norm, as Edward Wigglesworth claimed the next year that "Gentlemen . . . turn off their Workmen with two thirds instead of one half Goods," implying that the latter was more usual. John Colman claimed that "more than three Quarters of the Payments are made by Barter and Exchange of one Commodity for another." There was an alternative, of course. In 1703 James Barnes, a Boston goldsmith, was caught in the act of "making and Stamping with French Kings Armes Sundry Peices of Mettal & emitting the same at the value of a penny each."[30]

Because workers only received anywhere from 25 to 50 percent of their pay in cash, their economic freedom was constricted. There was a coercive aspect to this part-cash, part-goods pay system that exploited the reciprocal obligations of creditors and debtors to maintain the social structure during a period of economic crisis; it supported the same vision of a static social hierarchy that mercantilism did. Merchants and shopkeepers paid craftsmen with a small amount of cash and either promissory notes or goods. As a result of the notes, artisans often had to wait weeks or more for full payment. When stonemason Henry Christian Geer contracted to repair the masonry on Faneuil Hall in 1761, he "agreed to wait for his pay, as the other Tradesmen, imploy'd on said Building have engaged to do." In 1764 the workers had not yet been satisfied, and the town met to "consider the Petition of . . . Tradesmen employ'd in repairing Faneuil Hall, praying that the Town would grant them some relief on account of the length of Time, they have already and are still like to be out of the Money due to them."[31]

If patrons did not use notes to put off payment entirely, they paid with useless commodities that could not be used to produce additional income or to maintain a decent living. Merchants and shopkeepers paid workmen with a small amount of paper currency and made up the balance with imported textiles and domestic goods that forced artisans to appear perversely prosperous. The town pondered the dilemma in 1735: "The Nature of Our Trade exposes the Inhabitants to appear in extravagant Garbs, Who would gladly avoid the same, were they to receive Money in lieu of their Labour, Manufacture and Trades: But . . . they cannot be paid but in Notes to Shops which cannot be avoided." A few successful merchant-producers were able to insist on a partial cash advance, but they were the exceptions. Some Boston artisans even lowered their prices if cash payment was in the offing; in other cities workmen gave discounts of 5 to 8 percent for hard cash. And while not from Boston, evidence suggests that the system may even have cut down on productivity; a South Carolina watchmaker commented in 1766, "I spend more time in collecting . . . money than in earning it." While retailers were thus keeping artisans in check, master craftsmen limited the opportunities of journeymen by limiting the payment they received to patterns, jigs, and materials that would ensure continued dependency on the shop. The end result of this difficult pay structure was plenty for few and poverty for many. Although the first Boston almshouse had been rebuilt in 1682 specifically for people who were "aged & incapacitated for labour," by 1740 its residents included tailors, shoemakers, mop makers, and nailers whose luck had run out. One recent scholar has termed "vicious" the perilous credit economy in which artisans worked. By 1691 one Boston resident already saw it as "a Moral Madness."[32]

LABOR RESPONDS

As advocates of free trade sought to transfer this English view of labor and its attendant strategies to the streets of colonial Boston during the 1730s and 1740s, they met resistance. In fact, as early as 1719 a pamphleteer had championed the establishment of a regulated public market in the town, saying it would put an end to the engrossing of retail goods by greedy retailers, promote "*Vertue* and *Good Morals*" among the citizenry, guarantee a schedule that would attract visitors from rural towns, save the time that many petty producers spent hawking their wares to little profit, and protect poor inhabitants from the forestalling of goods and price gouging by hawkers. A regulated market, the writer argued, would keep prices of consumables down through competition, improve the material lives of laboring men and women, and bring into the market more liquid specie. Working artisans remained suspicious, however, and during the 1730s and 1740s they began to resist the apparently flawless logic of commercial capital. A market might also flood the town with cheap, ready-made English goods, undercut their own production, and drive them out of business. Hard cash would be siphoned off and disappear. The moral reform that lurked in the language of market advocates made it clear they wanted to eliminate undesirable hawkers, butchers, tanners, and unruly journeymen and retain closer watch over proper conduct while preventing independent tradesmen from selling their wares as they might see fit. By the late 1730s artisans had the unexpected support of nearby farmers, who worried that imported foodstuffs might undercut the value of their fresh produce in Boston. Targeting the merchant supporters of free trade, a "Number of Persons Unknown" in 1737 demolished one of Boston's market houses and crippled another. According to local reports, the market breakers were dressed up as clergymen, suggesting the claim they made to moral judgment and the zeal of their deliverance. Advocates of the market were outraged and offered a reward for the offenders. Their broadside, however, brought only an anonymous note revealing the extent of popular support for the minister-vandals. "Those good Fellows that are for pulling down the Market," it read, "will show you a Hundred men where you can show One. . . . We have about Five Hundred Men in Solemn League and

Covenant to Stand by one another, and can procure above Seven Hundred more of the same Mind. . . . It will be the hardest Piece of Work that ever you took in Hand, to Committ any man for that Night's Work."[33]

The language here—especially concerning the "Five Hundred Men in Solemn League and Covenant"—is particularly rich. On the one hand, it suggests that Boston's laboring people remembered when, in 1704, two blacksmiths, a carpenter, and a wine cooper had been apprehended and harshly imprisoned for being part of a "Combination of divers Persons in the . . . wicked Design of Forgery and Deceit" in counterfeiting bills of credit. They perhaps knew also of recent developments in the west of England, where secret "combinations" had strengthened the resolve of workers in the textile industry. In 1725 merchants and traders in Tiverton in Devon worried that "the Woolcombers and Weavers . . . have combined and formed themselves into Clubs, and unlawful Assemblies; and have taken on themselves an arbitrary Power to ascertain their Wages in their respective businesses and trades."[34] Yet the attack on the market implied still more.

The choice of the target was itself a difficult one, as it brought to public light the clouded and disappointed relationship that Boston's artisans had encountered in the marketplace for almost a century. In 1656 subscriptions were taken to support the market beneath the new town house, and artisans at that point had signed on optimistically. Of a total of 118 subscribers, the occupations or "callings" of 112 (94.9 percent) can be determined (table 7). Surprisingly, only 24 (21.4 percent) of these subscribers were merchants, while the remaining were artisans representing more than a dozen trades. Shoemakers alone enlisted as many names as did merchants; along with an additional 18 craftsmen in the woodworking and building trades, they accounted for 42 (37.5 percent) signatures on the document.[35]

Yet by 1677, as we have seen, their expectations had been undercut, compressed, denied. More than forty of the artisans who had signed the market subscription had left town without a trace. But five others, including coopers John Coney and John Lowell, joiner Henry Messenger, felt maker John Clough, and carpenter Ralph Carter, put their names to the 1677 complaint over inadequate enforcement of full apprenticeships and the failure of the town to police new competition from immigrant "strangers." Five more names on the 1677 document were sons of market subscribers; Carter's wife, Ann, had also signed the market list. It is possible to interpret the early attempts at guilds and the rumblings of Boston's artisans in the 1660s as signs that they simply could not play in the open market they eagerly supported; so many sour grapes may have colored their grievances. Yet the opposite is more likely. Boston's ambitious merchant community, not sizable in 1656 and thus wanting to create common cause with laboring people for the short term, expanded rapidly in the years following the institution of mercantilism after 1660. Their peculiar energy and development of family-based networks began to

Table 7. Occupational Participation in Subscription List for Market/Town House, 1656

Trade	No.	(%)
Woodworking/building	18	(15.2)
Leather	24	(20.4)
Cloth	11	(9.2)
Metal	9	(7.6)
Food/drink	12	(10.2)
Merchant*	24	(20.4)
Service**	6	(5.1)
Unskilled	—	(—)
Other***	8	(6.8)
Unknown	6	(5.1)
Total	118	(100.0)

Source: Walter Kendall Watkins, "Subscription List for Building the First Town House," *Bostonian Society Publications* 3 (1906): 105–49.

*Includes one retail shopkeeper and three mariners

**Includes one painter, bookseller, apothecary, tobacconist, surgeon, and boatman

***Includes two widows, two planters, and one magistrate, "gentleman," and lawyer

squeeze artisans out of the open market by the late 1670s.[36] From one perspective, attacking the market house, which was to be publicly "regulated" and therefore subject to political interests, implied coming to terms with loss.

At the same time, the convenient glossing of the idea of the combination using the powerful New England term "covenant" implied the wellspring that religion may have supplied to the laboring class's subversive strategies and millenarian political views. Here there were degrees of religious dissent defined against the closure of institutional orthodoxy; there was no single position for the opposition. Perhaps most moderate was the secession of numerous artisans, among others, from Boston's First Church following John Davenport's arrival in the pulpit in 1667. Davenport had proven his unwavering orthodoxy in New Haven and brought that conservatism to Boston. His church did not extend full communion to individuals who had not "owned" the covenant and publicly witnessed Christ's saving presence; he adamantly refused the terms of the Half-Way Covenant of 1660, which allowed invitation to membership of individuals who had only been baptized. Declension over the Half-Way Covenant was primarily political; without full membership there was no franchise. One could be taxed but, unless a full member, not have a vote in local elections. Two years later, an anti-Davenport minority split from the First Church and established a new congregation with more relaxed membership rules under minister Samuel Willard. Within the debates that roiled with the formation of the Third Church, however, came charges of an "anti-ministerial spirit" to which the new congregation's active artisans may have contributed; at least seven of its standing members in 1677 signed the petition of grievances.[37]

This was a moderate path for artisans toward increased political participation. They could remain within the congregational fold and known rhythms: plain-style sermonics; a recognized hierarchy of laity, deacons, and clergy; a familiar liturgy. Other laboring people, however, sought more radical critiques of the established church. Boston artisans had long been participants in religious sects deriving their attraction and evangelical appeal from loose associations with Antinomianism, or an emphasis on the mystic spirituality of inner grace as a free gift from Christ. For artisans, the covenant implied more an enthusiasm for the covenant of grace and less regard for the contingent demands for obedience and servility required by the complementary concept of the "federal" or "national" covenant; events in the 1630s and 1640s make such an emphasis apparent. Boston thatcher William Townsend and Nathaniel Briscoe, a Watertown tanner, were disarmed for supporting Anne Hutchinson in 1637. So were tailors Thomas Savage and Richard Wayte, shoemaker George Burden, and cooper Edward Rainsford. Tanner Nicholas Easton, who went to Rhode Island with Hutchinson, taught "that every of the elect had the Holy Ghost and also the devil indwelling," wrote John Winthrop; "another, one Herne, taught, that women had no souls, and that Adam was not created in true holiness, etc., for then he could not have lost it." In 1643 joiner Stephen Fosdick was excommunicated from the Charlestown church for reading "Anabaptist books."[38]

Artisans like Fosdick played a central role in nascent Anabaptist gatherings. In 1644 Thomas Painter, a Boston carpenter who had already moved on to Hingham, was brought to court "for saying that our baptism was antichristian." Winthrop worried that "Anabaptistry [had] continued and spread in the country," despite every effort to crush it. But people selectively embraced elements of Antinomianism, Anabaptism, Quakerism, and even the Fifth Monarchy movement because they suggested a path to Christ that was direct, unmediated, and routed outside the social discipline and doctrinal mediation of the official clergy. Tanner Briscoe went to England in 1652 and wrote back, "I am to go down into the country very shortly to dispute the points of freewill, and universal redemption, and spiritual baptism, and seeking, and some other points," showing that English sectarian beliefs were sometimes directly linked to mystic spiritists in New England. By the 1660s, just as merchants were tightening their grip on the marketplace, artisans embraced new alternatives of religious practice. Between 1655 and 1670, the "Anabaptist heresy" in Charlestown and Boston was organized by wheelwright Thomas Goold, tailor William Turner, potter Edward Drinker, shoemakers John

Russell Jr. and Benjamin Sweetser, and housewright John Johnson. The sect reached an early climax of dissent in 1666, when John Farnum, a Boston joiner, stormed out of Increase Mather's Second Church after a dramatic confrontation during which the joiner genuflected to the minister, or "made a Legg to him in a way of scorn & derision before the church."[39]

In 1679 Boston Baptists built a meetinghouse on land donated by two believers, one of whom was cooper Ellis Callendar. Two years earlier Callendar, along with fellow Baptist and tailor Turner, had signed the 1677 petition seeking government protection. Artisan politics and radical religion intertwined, their strands extending into the eighteenth century in different ways. By 1718, when Callendar's son Elisha became the first minister of Boston's Baptist church, three of its deacons were still metalworkers. Yet already things were changing. The younger Callendar had gone to Harvard and was the first professional minister to the Baptist congregation. The tradition of lay preacher and the abhorrence of "hireling" clergy, a point that joiner Farnum had taken up with Mather, had yielded to a perceived need for socially respectable leaders if new converts were to be attracted in the competitive ecclesiastical marketplace. With the ordination of Jeremiah Condy to the Baptist pulpit in 1730, the church grew more theologically liberal and still closer in style and politics to Boston's conservative orthodoxy. As Carla Pestana has observed, by the time of the market attack in 1737, "the Baptists had moved so far from the tradition of artisan preachers and lay leadership that they had become literally unable to function without an ordained minister."[40]

The decline of lay control over evangelical religion helps to explain why laboring people, confronting a temporary vacuum for the expression of radical millenarian belief and mystic spiritism in the Antinomian and Anabaptist traditions, dressed up as preachers when they pulled down the market house. Like early Anabaptists in the Low Countries, they fused theatricality to rebellion. In this violent morality play about the market's immorality, they placed themselves in the vanished local role of artisan-preachers, itinerant illuminists, called by a collective spiritual force to destroy the material sign of unrestrained commercial capitalism and wage millennial war on prices they could not control. Four years after the market attack, Boston's caulkers voted that they would no longer accept notes for shop goods as compensation, warning that "Numbers of other Artificers and Tradesmen" would do likewise. In 1744 Boston's master carpenters agreed on a standardized price list. In 1747 local tanners set costs for "green Hides" and "Shoe leather" and volunteered to "keep down the Price of all sorts of Tan'd Leather." By the mid-eighteenth century, workers in all of Boston's major trades had set prices. Radical religious critique, linking the covenant to the combination, played a key role. Yet in asserting control of labor value and refusing to adapt it as Boston's economy declined at midcentury, master artisans risked pricing themselves out of work. In 1750, one man explained that "the Reason that building in Boston is so *dear* . . . is, from the Combinations of several Head Carpenters, Bricklayers, etc. who have established certain Rules of Work." The hesitancy of these trade leaders to bend with market demands contributed to the departure of some journeymen and the political radicalization of many others.[41]

If popular violence was one way to surface on the horizon of public opinion, a more subtle but influential reaction to the combined pressures of inflation, a credit economy, and increased competition from "strangers" beckoned. Artisans could diversify production and increase the number of trades they actually practiced. For many urban workers, the security of diversified production represented the only hope of remaining independent and self-employed in the face of overcrowding, undercutting of apprenticeships, and a lack of protection by local government. They seized the right to expand into available labor markets. Diversification occurred in two ways. The most common and easiest to accomplish involved moving into a closely related craft that relied on the knowledge, materials, techniques, and social connections already familiar to the worker. Such expansion was well under way in Boston's first decades of settlement. In 1671 William Parsons, a Boston joiner, was making a ship. In 1677 William Baker, working as a carpenter, a sawyer, and a pump maker, had good reason to sign the petition indicting new arrivals for driving him from trade to trade. In 1736, the selectmen granted Theophilus Shove permission "to Exercise his Calling of a Glazier and Joyner." But others, perhaps with additional working capital in hand or a conveniently placed relative, branched out into trades completely unrelated to the calling of their apprenticeship. Brazier John Dolbeare, for instance, embarked in 1724 on the "Dressing of Leather" to pick up extra work.[42] Although they differed in the breadth of tasks in which they engaged, artisans who diversified still counted on the purposeful application and extension of their skill to succeed. For these workers, diversification did not erode their reputation as people whose lot in life depended on productive labor.

Diversification entailed violating the clear separation of trades that had long guided the actions of Boston's artisans in defending their livelihoods against outside encroachment. Recall the language of the 1660 apprenticeship act, the 1668 coopers' complaint, and the 1677 petition. Why would they violate that separation now? It did allow some horizontal movement in a paralyzed economy. But diversification was not merely a hedge against disaster. As it countered the Pauline concept of calling—the static social view advocated by Drayton, for example—diversification was also politically radical. It argued that any person could fill the place of another. If a carpenter worked as a blacksmith, or a brazier as a tanner, precisely what "place" did these men occupy? What was their "calling"? From one perspective, the implied interchangeability suggested that they could be "anyplace."

Such a view also sounds complicit with the aims of a displacing commercial capitalism and the experimental science it enveloped as part of its enclosing discipline. Yet from another point of view, the interchangeability and equality of working people was a pivotal concept in the articulation of labor consciousness in colonial New England, for diversification suggested that people occupied no fixed places. A carpenter could be a brazier, a tanner a retail merchant. As early as 1677 William Gilbert was both a cordwainer and a merchant. In 1739 Robert Hewes, a prosperous Boston tanner, asked the town for permission "to put up a Stall . . . for the Sale of Meat." Recognizing that people had no fixed position in society and thus in terms of either horizontal or vertical movement were actually "no place," diversification contained within it the germ of a leveling radicalism that derived directly from the lived experience of the laboring classes. Not read in books or adopted from Whig orators, it was an "empirical" leveling force.[43]

Artisan politics deployed along many fronts. Despite a selective embrace of protectionist trade actions, dispersed acts of violence, and the radical implications of diversification, Boston's laboring people still played the part of looking to their gentle imperial leaders for "guidance" in economic affairs. But despite legal precedents in town ordinances and past attempts to exert control still within memory, little came. Basking in the warm glow of his victory at Louisbourg in 1745, Governor William Shirley assured the working people of Boston, "Whenever it may be in my power to contribute towards reviving the decay'd trade . . . I shall gladly Embrace the Opportunity." But his promises, like those of his cronies, were empty. In response, laboring people escalated the rhetoric of their discontent: "Our Rates run so high that . . . many that have but a House to live in and Health to follow their Callings are Rated higher than Country Gentlemen that can buy Twenty such," they cried. "We . . . have Our Bread & Water measured out to Us by those Who Riot in Luxury & Wantonness on our Sweat & Toil and be told perhaps by them, that We are too happy, because We are not reduced to Eat Grass with the Cattle."[44]

RANGES OF DWELLING

The "riot" of "Luxury & Wantonness" made apparent the gross disparities of economic scale that Boston artisans saw everywhere around them. Surfaces of loss and despair, of control and discipline, of dark urban scarcity and allegorical country gardens met every gaze and grew more frequent between 1660 and 1760. A world of difference separated the size and expense of household spaces of laboring people from those of the merchants. A property that cooper Barrett Dyer sold to widow Anne Foot in 1746 suggests the size and shape of artisan housing.

Fronting on busy Marlborough Street, it consisted of the house, a small work yard, detached rear kitchen, and garden that stretched an impressive sixty-two feet beyond to the estate's rear boundary. A drawing made to accompany the sale shows one other feature, a small shed or "gallery" that provided shelter at ground level and a storage chamber above between the dwelling and the rear kitchen (fig. 76). As in England, these passages could be an integral part of a structure's original build, or they could be added at a later point to complete the linkage between the house and kitchen. In 1708, for example, the town allowed Jonathan Waldo "to Erect a Timber building for a Lodging Chamber of 12 foot square and 7 Studd with a flat roofe Over a passage way between his Dwelling house & Kitchen nigh the Conduit at the Lower end of Union street in Boston."[45]

Title research reveals that Dyre's house had previously been described in an indenture of 1683, when Thomas and Joseph Robinson, a cordwainer and cooper, respectively, agreed to subdivide the house they had jointly inherited from their father. In the indenture, Thomas received "the Northernmost End of the sd Dwelling house Messuage or Tenement . . . Containing one large Cellar, One low Room and Shop therein and Stairway up to the Garrett, One Chamber Fronting to the Street and One Garrett. Also One small Kitchen behind the sd part of said house with a Chamber over the same, and another small Chamber that lyeth between the Chamber that Fronts to the Street, and the said Kitchen Chamber with the Closets Garretts or Cocklofts belonging to the same, with the free privilege of the Well in the Yard and of the passage way into the said Yard." For his share, brother Joseph received the "Southernmost part of the aforesaid Messuage Tenement or dwelling house . . . Containing One Cellar, One large Low Room and Closet or small Kitchen adjoyning and Shop fronting to the Street with Two Chambers and the Stair Case and Chamber at the head of the Stairs and Garretts over the same."[46] With the property facing east onto Marlborough Street, Thomas received the northern half of the house, including the detached rear kitchen (and connecting shed or "gallery" segment), and Joseph the southern half of the house. Within the half house each brother inherited, they had to dedicate one room— presumably the ground-floor room closest to the street—as a shop. Whether their father, Thomas, also a cooper, had placed his shop in a similar position remains unclear. His inventory, taken after his death in 1665 or 1666, describes the same structure that Dyre sold to the widow Foot in 1746 and values the house and land at £310. It also confirms that he owned one set of fireplace equipment, suggesting the presence then of only one working hearth.[47] Thus, despite the location of the house and its subsequent development over time, cooper Robinson's house may have been typical of seventeenth-century houses of the sort many artisans lived in. It may have offered little beyond basic necessity, but it was owned outright, a freehold property.

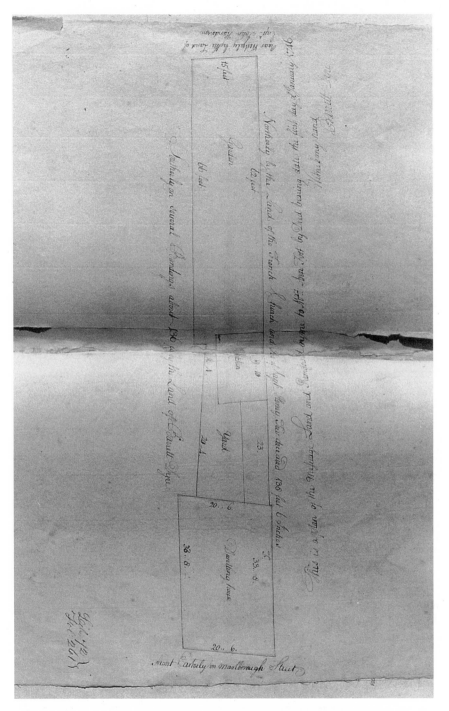

Figure 76. Survey of house with detached kitchen and connecting gallery or shed, made for sale of property by cooper Barrett Dyer to widow Ann Foot, Marlborough Street, Boston, 1746; originally house of cooper Thomas Robinson, by 1665. (Photo by the author)

Beginning in the 1690s, however, artisans began to lose economic ground and often rented rather than owned their houses and shops. A close examination of a property developed by Stephen Greenwood, a Boston shipwright who, through a strategic marriage turned merchant-entrepreneur, begins to make this problem visible. In March 1711, as part of a debate concerning his nephew's rightful access to a small piece of land "intermixed" with his own, Greenwood petitioned the governor to stop the inheritance. Greenwood's estate was, by his description, "Situate at the Northerly End of Boston Lying in an Iregular forme as Decypherd in a plan herewith Offered." The surviving plan indicates various buildings, passages, and a garden space arranged at the north end of Fish Street (fig. 77). According to the 1712 report of the appraisers sent to adjudicate the probate case, the property was judged "to be worthe. Vizt. The Old House Wood Yards & Land at one hundred & fourty pounds The rowe of Shops At One hundred & Twenty pounds: The Shoomakers Shop in the said Row at Thirty pounds." The property has a complex social history in its own right. The "old house" shown likely predates 1650, and the "Brick House" is the same structure Greenwood's father (Nathaniel) mentioned when he stated in his 1684 will: "I give & bequeath my new Brick house, with halfe the garden & halfe the Yard."[48] By his own death in 1722, Stephen Greenwood had almost completed construction of a large new brick house on the property marked in 1711 as simply "Old house plott," a project aided by the large inheritance that came to the Greenwood estate through the death in 1707 of his wife Elizabeth's father, wealthy brewer Robert Bronsdon. By that time, therefore, the side passage actually gave access to three interconnected houses built between about 1650 and 1722.

What concerns us are the shops arranged on the Greenwood property along Fish Street, including the "Shoe-Makers Shop," a triangular "smal Shop," and a small structure labeled "Benja: Browne," presumably for the person to whom it was then let. The shops are small and obviously rented from Greenwood; so much emerges from a 1721 deed that describes them as "the Shop which Samuel Saxton formerly Rented and the land belonging to it and the Shop wch Benjamin Brown formerly Rented adjoyning the aforesd Shop on the South Side [of Fish Street] with the Land thereunto belonging." Stephen Greenwood's inventory taken the year following refers to them as "The Three Brick Tenements & the Land thereto belonging fronting & bounded on Ship street" and values them at £450.[49] His placement of these three shops in close proximity to form a row of commercial properties was by no means unusual. In 1708 Edward Hutchinson had a "Row of New Shops . . . nigh his Dwelling house in Fish Street at the North End of Boston"; Habijah Savage three years later received permission "to erect with Timber a building for Shops of 80 foot long 20 foot wide and 15 foot high on the North side and 11 foot high on the South side," the roof of which he soon modi-

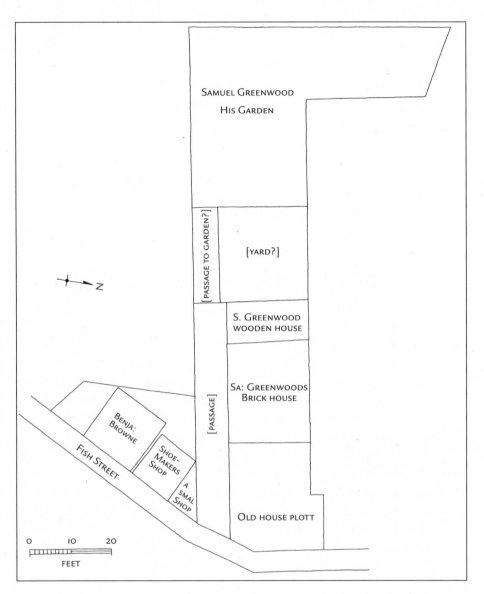

Figure 77. "Plan of Lots in Boston owned by Stephen Greenwood and Nathaniel and Mary Henchman, 1711," Fish Street, Boston, Massachusetts. (Drawing by the author)

fied from a shed to a pitch angle to ensure the better drainage of rain and snow.[50]

It is difficult to know the exact contribution to the domestic economy that rental properties offered to a landlord. Fortunately, a comprehensive inventory of all rental properties was made by the Boston selectmen for the year 1707; for each rental property, the census includes the name of the lessee, the number of taxable polls in the rental property, the number (if any) of "Negroes" on the premises, the annual rent for the property listed, and the name of the landlord(s) associated with the property. Overall, the census was impressive: 274 taxable polls were living in rental properties, including 209 as town residents, 38 "men at sea," and 27 "more in Expeditions." In addition, inhabitants of rental properties included 76 widows, 33 "poor women," and an additional 36 black men, 29 black women, and 10 black children. Altogether, the census of renters in Boston included 458 souls who paid landlords for the roof over their head, a figure that would climb rapidly if it included the wives and children of the 274 taxable polls. The rental properties were themselves owned by a variety of landlords. Some were widows ("old mrs Moores," "mrs Wakefeild Midwife," "mrs Flack very poor," "Flora Mackartys"), others officers of the church ("Deacon Barnard," "mr Allins minister"). Upwardly mobile artisans rented to poorer ones; William Dummer owned a house "in the present Tenure of Moses Aires of Boston Housewright" when he moved to rebuild it in 1720. In 1739 joiner John Davis asked the selectmen for "leave to admit mr Robert Banning pewterer, an under tenant, in the shop he hath lately Leased from the Select men, Vizt. Number Six in Dock Square."[51]

Artisans most frequently rented houses and shops from merchants, some of whom must have owned small clusters of rental buildings that resembled Stephen Greenwood's row of shops. One "Collo. Hutchinson," for example, held leases on "Mary Earle Senr. & her Daughtr Shop," "Edwd Eades house & shop," "Wm Willett house & shop," "Robt. Sharp Shop & house," "Joseph Gray Shop," and four additional houses, one of which he lived in himself. Dr. Jonathan Clark rented "Erasmus Stevens Shop No 1," "John Buttler house & shop," "Samuel Gardner Shop," "Thos Cole Shop," "and Jno. King Shop." Merchants who rented to artisans sometimes had social roots in artisan families from whom they had worked to distance themselves. Thomas Fitch, the son of a cordwainer who had extended his skills as an upholsterer and interior decorator in the 1690s, became a leading merchant with correspondents and factors in New York, Philadelphia, and London. Upon his death in 1736, Fitch held mortgages on 120 Boston properties and was due £14,000 in debts and £1,185 in outstanding rents from twenty-one Boston rental properties (many of them let to artisans); he owned more than 22,000 acres of land in thirty-four towns and had household goods valued at £3,400.[52]

The development of a large merchant's premise took years and demanded the gradual consolidation of real estate holdings to amass a single large property that contained wharfage, access to public streets, necessary stores, barns, rental housing, and the principal residence. Stephen Greenwood's premise in the North End only reached its final form after thirty years of work. Wharfinger Jabez Hatch fashioned a mercantile complex at Windmill Point in Boston's South End between 1743, when he purchased his first piece of real estate in the area, and his death in May 1763; his property came to more than £3,400, including four ships and four black slaves. His premise included three major wharves, two dwelling houses (his own and one in which his daughters lived), a store, and six rental "tenements." Hatch's complicated estate was not settled until 1786, when a plan of the complex was drawn to clarify the division of property (fig. 78).

What makes Hatch's premise unusual is that he assembled pieces of it largely from artisans who needed cash more than they needed to own land. Hatch assembled this estate in at least four steps. In late 1743, he purchased some tidal flats to the east of Sea Street from currier Jonathan Loring for £200. These flats became the two wharves lying to the east of Sea Street shown on the plan. In March 1745, he purchased for £750 a house and land from William Wheeler, a mason and lime burner. The Wheeler purchase lay two or three lots to the west of the flats he purchased two years earlier. Two additional purchases allowed him to fill in the space between. In 1749 Hatch secured from mariner William Miller "certain house land wharffe and flatts thereto belonging," being his own "mansion" house, the wharf, and flats lying along the southern side of Beach Street, for £2,010. The quality of this house must have been high indeed to warrant such a price; it probably had been built by merchant Joseph Marion in the late 1720s. The remainder of the land and buildings finally came in a purchase in April 1758, when Hatch paid the Loring heirs for "all that peice of Land with the Buildings thereon" stretching from Sea Street west to the tract Hatch had gotten from Wheeler. A currier who perhaps had entertained thoughts of developing this site for a tannery in the late 1720s, Jonathan Loring himself had assembled this tract from separate agreements with a shopkeeper, shoemaker, cooper, and potter. Before he left for Charlestown in 1727, the entire area seems to have belonged to the potter Philip Cutler.[53]

His estate assembled, Hatch divided it into three general zones. To the west along Beach Street and farthest from the docks were the family's residences, with rear yards and gardens extending to the north property line. The dock or wharf zone was occupied with shipping, the cartage and loading of stores and freight, and the arrival of any strangers by boat. In between, Hatch placed his store and rental properties as social buffers between the rough play of seaborne trade and the protected interiority of household life. He maintained "six Wooden tenements" for rental; one shared a wall with the store, while the other five were divided among two adjacent buildings across a small yard. Access to rental housing was through narrow passages; solid lines on the plan suggest the passages did not connect with the rear yards of the family's houses. Even after Hatch died, his widow, Mary, continued to enlarge the property with new purchases from the executors of Philip Cutler and William Wheeler in 1765.[54]

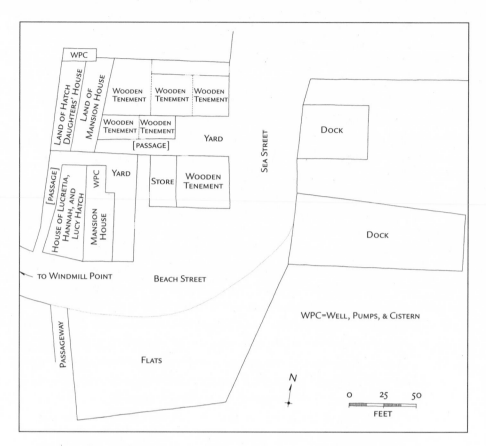

Figure 78. Jabez Hatch's premise, South End, Boston, 1743–63. (Drawing by the author)

DARKNESS AT THE CENTER OF TOWN

Having purchased much of his land for cash from artisans, Hatch became prosperous in part because working people were desperate for hard money and eager to leave town. Many in key trades like shipbuilding and butchering responded to underemployment and poverty by moving to outlying village centers, hoping that their smaller markets might be more stable. Looking back in 1743—the year Hatch began acquiring his property—artisans saw that while the town's total taxable population had dropped by 15 percent in the previous five years, local taxes during the same period had risen nearly 30 percent. "Our Trade in general at this Day," they announced, "is not above One half that it was in 1735." Distilleries, the cod fishery, and trade to the West Indies and to London had reached low ebbs. To make matters worse, although "the greatest Advantage this Town reaped from that Trade was by Ship Building which employed most of Our Tradesmen . . . that is now reduced so that whereas in 1735, Orders might arrive for Building Forty Sail of Ships, there has been as yet Orders for Two." Within a year, "the Trade of Building Houses" was "in a manner Stagnated" as well. "The Middling Sort of People are daily decreasing," complained one observer, noting, "Many of them [are] Sinking into extream Poverty—That not only the Trade is visibly decreasing, but many honest Tradesmen are without Employ." An almanac summarized the problem: "So much Finery, so much Poverty."[55]

Discordant notes echoed through Boston's waterfront. In the 1750s, Jabez Hatch was plotting how to get from the Loring family a crucial piece of real estate that would cement the integrity and energy of his dockside complex. In the 1750s, artisans aching from four decades of hardship identified the trades whose ranks had thinned from outright desertion. "The Removal of Shipbuilding, sinking of the Distillery & Sugar Works here, the killing [of] Meat and Manufacturing the Hides and Skins out of Town, have thinned Our Numbers above a Thousand Rateable Men," they claimed, or roughly one-sixth to one-fourth of the town's adult male population. Each of these industries was critical because it subsumed adherent crafts, as fears over the flight of the shipwrights clearly revealed. "In the whole not less than Five or Six Thousand Tons of Shipping were Built Annually in the Town," artisans observed, but activity had slackened dramatically during the 1740s. By the early 1750s an estimated three-quarters of all ships were being built in Newbury, with others coming down the ways at Salem, Portsmouth, or Scituate on the banks of the North River. The drop in Boston's business was multiplied, since the trade "necessarily Employed and brought into Town a great number of Shipwrights, Blacksmiths Shipjoyners Ropemakers, Blockmakers, Sailmakers, Riggers, and other Labourers as well as Sailors, all which mainly resided in Boston, and added to their numbers and Wealth, and help't to pay the Towns proportion of Taxes."[56]

The failure of the shipbuilding industry had threatened before, notably at the end of Queen Anne's War in 1713, when the need for warships disappeared and brought work to a standstill. By 1722, Boston newspapers advertised that artisans willing to go to Charleston, South Carolina, would "find employment enough . . . by reason of the great want of Artificers there."[57] The distillery business also pulled out, although it had only been part of Boston's economic armature since about 1700. Revenues came as imported molasses and raw sugar left as marketable rum, spirits, and sugar loaves for other British colonies. In exchange Boston obtained grain, meat, turpentine, skins, fish oil, and bills of credit. But between 1720 and 1750, sugar houses and distilleries had also sprung up in New York City, Philadelphia, and, more worrisome, New England towns like Plymouth, Salem, Newbury, Watertown, Medford, Newport, and Providence. Their own neighbors were draining off trade that Boston had once alone enjoyed. With "that Trade . . . in a very languishing Condition," Bostonians in 1750 smelled a conspiracy of rural towns to undercut the urban port: "there is a profess'd design of some in the Neighbouring Governments, to strip them as far as possible of the trade they have had from their Foundation."[58]

The removal of the slaughtering industry to surrounding towns hammered a final nail in Boston's economic coffin. Only twenty years earlier, "Hides & Skins were then almost wholly Tanned, Curryed & Manufactured in Town." With the major transformation of animal skins into workable leather centralized, "the Shoemakers in the Country were mainly Supply'd with Leather from hence, and great numbers of Shoemakers in Boston, had large Employ in making Shoes for People living in the other Towns of the Province; But the very reverse is the Case now, hardly a single Bullock is killed by an Inhabitant of Boston, nor is One quarter if an Eighth part of the Hides belonging to the Meat consumed by the People in Boston, Tanned & Manufactured here, Our Shoemakers *what few We have*, are Obliged to go into the Countrey for their Leather, and a great number of Shoemakers who live in the Country, have large Employ from Boston." Indeed, by the early 1760s cordwainers who had left Boston formed an impressive circle of shoe towns around the aching metropolis, villages that pulled workers out of Boston in great numbers. George Robert Twelves Hewes tells us he headed for Lynn as soon as he could successfully flee Boston in 1775. His search for work was assisted by the many émigré Boston cordwainers he met when he arrived in town. Within a few years, urban-trained shoemakers working in towns like Lynn and Salem were sending piecework back into the city in a dramatic reversal of normal practice.[59]

Between 1720 and 1760, Boston's shipbuilding industry declined by 90 percent, its distilling business by 66 percent, and its butchering and leatherworking trades by 86 percent. At least the close of the Seven Years' War promised a ray of hope that the economy might recover and that most artisans might remain in town. It did not last. As soon as the peace came, so did yet another wave of new arrivals eager to find a place in a desperate social geography. Between March 1763 and August 1765 a total of ninety-eight working people came, representing a wide variety of trades and diverse points of origin. John Peck, Joseph Peirce, and Josiah Metwick, all carpenters, came from Nova Scotia. A tailor and weaver arrived from Philadelphia. A shoemaker stepped off a boat from Annapolis, and a cooper disembarked from Martinique. This group of immigrants varied in some ways from earlier ones; a sizable group had left Halifax looking for better work, people from Cape Breton met tradesmen from Glasgow in the streets of Boston. Artisans also came from diverse small islands in the Caribbean — Granada, Guadeloupe, Barbados, and St. Christopher (fig. 79). With the decreased threat of warfare in colonial New England, people from elsewhere in the British empire thought Boston might be worth a gamble. They lost. A large majority vied for entry into the building and

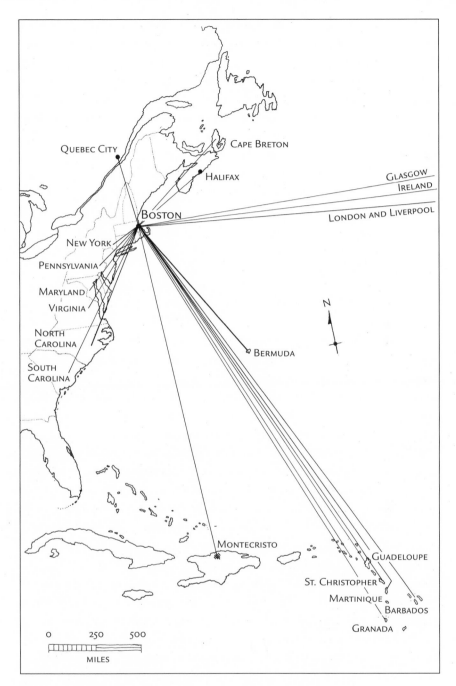

Figure 79. Places of origin of artisan migrants to Boston from other British North American colonies, 1763–65. (Map by the author)

cloth trades, both sectors of the local economy that had always been hit hard by the arrival of strangers (table 8). The prospects of carpenters like Peck, Peirce, and Metwick had been complicated by the new ordinances outlawing timber construction and shingle roofs in the town that followed in the wake of a calamitous fire in March 1760 that, in addition to laying waste to more than four hundred houses, completely wiped out many artisans. One boatbuilder submitted a claim for damages "of what I Lost in the line of Bots and tules and Stuf as neere as I Can Cercolate was the hole tenn Pound thirteen & eight pence." His was one of thirty-four claims submitted by people whose trades can be determined, including curriers, coopers, laundresses, braziers, glaziers, a pewterer, and others.[60] Where could people turn? What could they do?

A FAMILIAR KIND OF TERROR

Perhaps it was the recent memory of seeing their own houses, possessions, and livelihoods go up in smoke that changed things. The house attack proved particularly useful to laboring people hard pressed by increasing poverty, a breakdown in the apprentice system, the growing futility of petitions, the despair of depopulation, the zeal of rural towns to draw off their labor and money, and the radicalism of diversification and collective crowd actions. It made sense to boatbuilders and carpenters racked by rents and ruined by the 1760s fire. It made sense because economic difficulties were complicated and intensified by political debate. Crown policies concerning taxation and import duties (the Sugar Act and Revenue Act in 1764 and Stamp Act in 1765, for instance) and the alarming wealth of some provincial Tory officials seemed a direct threat to liberties already eroded. The educated leaders of anti-Crown activities worried that the republican freedoms fostered by parliamentary strength and England's "mixed constitution" would be corrupted by a power-hungry, degenerate, engrossing court party bent on consolidating its own authority. Harvard-trained lawyers like John Adams or radical Whigs like James Otis may have quoted Blackstone, Addison, and Bolingbroke, but the working people of Boston translated the language of imperial critique into their own very direct terms. They abhorred men like Oliver, Story, Paxton, Hallowell, and Hutchinson, less because of their support for specific imperial decisions than because these men put private interest ahead of public good.[61]

As a form of festive violence intended to shame targeted individuals for moral transgression, the house attack was a complex blend of inherited custom and participants with different reasons for joining the fray. Its historical roots extend back in Anglo-American culture at least to 1612, when angry London mobs attacked a Shoreditch brothel on Shrove Tuesday. On the same holiday in 1617 several houses had their windows smashed by brickbats and their roofs torn off. During the English Civil War, militant Puritans periodically attacked the mansions of prominent royalists and high church officials, trashing their furniture and slashing family portraits in a collective reimagining of legitimate providential history. In the summer of 1642 parliamentarians attacked the dwellings of royalists Richard Mynshall in Bourton, Buckinghamshire, and John Lucas in Colchester, Essex. The former incident opened with Mynshall's own departure from his house to visit the king, so no one was at home to resist the onslaught of destruction, which began when Cromwell's soldiers broke open the dwelling and, "with their swords, they most treacherously pierce[d] through in diverse places" a portrait of Charles I. "And not content to wound him in that representation . . . they whet their tongues against their sovereign, using traiterous and scornful language against him." They then raided his cellars, appointing a wine steward to first sample his bottles, since "in a saucy imitation of greatness they will not drink without a Taster." Then "they breake open his Library and the place where he kept his Evidences; they seize on all the Bills, Bonds, Deeds, Evidences, Writings and Books which they find whether Sir *Richards* or his friends." Having gathered his papers and legal records relating to his legitimate claims on property, "some of these they take away with them, some they tear in peices, some they binde in bundles and make them serve instead of fuell both to heat Ovens and to rost meat for their Supper." Finally, their eyes turn to his dwelling itself. "The house itselfe escapes not their fury: wanting Ladders to come at the Lead [roof], they supply the defect with the Rackes broken downe from the Stables." Once they were up on the roof, the dark play accelerated. "They rip up the Lead and carry it away, they teare downe the walls of the houses with spades and Mattocks, they dig up the lower roomes, hoping there to find more Treasure: they breake the windowes, doores, wainscot, Seelings, glasse, they take away all Iron barres, Casements, Locks, Keyes and hinges."[62] At Lucas's Colchester estate the next week the mob's fury extended still further: "to shew that their rage will know no bounds, and that nothing is so sacred and venerable which they dare not to violate, they breake into Saint Giles his Church, open the Vault where his Ancestours were buryed, and with Pistols, Swords, and Halberts, transfix the Coffins of the dead."[63]

These instances of ritual pillaging set a forceful example in early modern English popular culture: planned attacks on strategically selected targets, a concern to dishonor family lineage through the literal dismantling of their visible estate, an attempt to lay bare the transgressive qualities of a specific individual by (as was said in the Mynshall case) "disrobing" his house, and a marked concern by the mob to repossess legal documents that denied them subjectivity in propertied circles of local society. The early modern origins and popular uses of house assaults extended beyond England. In an event widely published in England immediately

Table 8. Trades Practiced by Artisans Arriving in Boston, March 1763–August 1765

Place of Origin:	Britain			Ireland	British Colonies		
	London	Glasgow	Liverpool		Carib.	Carols.	Maryld
Trades							
Woodworking/ building	3	1	—	1	—	—	1
Leather	—	1	1	—	—	—	1
Cloth	1	1	—	—	2	1	2
Metal	1	1	—	—	—	—	2
Service*	—	—	—	—	1	—	—
Food/drink	—	1	—	—	—	—	2
Unskilled labor	—	—	—	—	—	—	—
Other**	—	—	—	—	—	—	—
Total	5	5	1	1	3	1	8

Source: "Vessels Entering Boston" (March 16, 1763, to August 14, 1765), in *A Volume of Records Relating to the Early History of Boston, Containing Miscellaneous Papers*, Record Commissioners Reports, vol. 29 (Boston: Municipal Printing Office, 1900), 245–68.

after Cromwell assumed control, the Italian fishmonger-hero Masaniello had led mobs in Naples in revolt against Spanish rule in 1647 over an imposed food tax that cut deeply into the lives of poor Neapolitans. For a brief interlude Masaniello led a topsy-turvy state in which prisoners went free, the poor gorged on foodstuffs hoarded by the rich, and laboring people destroyed the houses of local imperial authorities.[64]

While Masaniello's heroic republican exploits were praised by Puritans in New England, the "mobbings" in Boston in 1765 could have drawn on the powerful grip the Sacheverell riots in London in March 1710 held on the New England imagination. When a Whig-majority House of Commons found Anglican minister Henry Sacheverell guilty of crimes against the state for preaching on Guy Fawkes Day, people took to the streets of London's West End. They targeted evangelical and dissenting meetinghouses, the Bank of England, and the houses of Whig clergymen and political leaders. In New England these riots were memorable because they were so worrisome; the mob had moved in support of the established church, while wrecking the properties of evangelical and sectarian Whigs for whose political philosophy and religious beliefs the New England clergy had offered unilateral support. Cotton Mather recounted how "an High-Church Mob was raised, by some Incendiaries; who did horrid Things, and pull'd down six Presbyterian Meeting-houses . . . and were proceeding to pull down the

British Colonies			French Colonies		Rural NE		Total	
Penna.	N.Y.	Halifax & N.S.	Quebec	Caribbean	Conn.	R.I.	No.	(%)
3	8	10	—	2	7	—	36	(36.8)
—	1	2	—	1	3	—	10	(10.3)
4	—	9	—	—	—	1	21	(21.4)
—	1	3	—	1	—	—	9	(9.2)
—	—	1	—	—	—	—	2	(2.0)
1	—	6	1	—	—	1	12	(12.2)
—	—	4	1	—	1	—	6	(6.1)
—	—	2	—	—	—	—	2	(2.0)
8	10	37	2	4	11	2	98	(100.0)

*Includes bookkeeper

**Includes painters

Bishop of *Salisburies* House." Worried by these attacks on ministers' houses, Mather lamented "the endless Outrages" committed by the London mob.[65]

There were also more homegrown versions of the house attack. In 1661 in Guilford, Connecticut, physician Bray Rossiter was upset when his son-in-law was not chosen as the town's second minister. As Ezra Stiles recounted the event, when Rossiter in protest staged a siege of the town common with men from neighboring Killingworth, locals "beset old Dr. Rosseter's house & would have shot him because of his being a Presbyterian." In 1690, "200 or 300 of the rabble" attacked the Roxbury house of one Mr. Paige at midnight, searched the premises unsuccessfully for Joseph Dudley, the inscrutable president of the provincial council, "broke open" the structure, "smashing his windows," and then vanished into the night. And in New Haven on July 30, 1765—just two weeks before Andrew Oliver's Boston mansion was attacked—eight students at Yale assaulted "the College Mansion where the President and fellows lived." The students seem to have been acting in support of Naphtali Daggett, a professor of divinity who openly suspected President Thomas Clap of excessive New Light leanings and political corruption. At the students' trial on August 27, the day after a long night of destruction in Boston that had culminated in the ransacking of Thomas Hutchinson's house, the prosecution claimed that "with Evil Intent" the students "did with Strong hand burst and take off the gates of the yard of the mansion house and Carry away and with Screaming and Shouting did in furious violence throw into said House Numbers of large stones with Cattles Horns into the windows of said House." The offenders pleaded guilty, dutifully paid nominal fines, and were released. But Clap, disoriented by the affront to his authority and polished reputation, eventually resigned his office.[66]

Instances of personal property being destroyed in New England must have been frequent enough that a law was passed as early as 1715 "For Preventing Damage to the Housing and Estate within the Several Towns of this Province," an ordinance that cited the frequent breaking of glass windows, throwing of stones and snowballs, and throwing down fences and other enclosures. Coming only one year after the passage of the riot act in England, this law may have been inspired as much by colonial legal reform as by an actual increase in house attacks early in the eighteenth century. But a 1723 ordinance repeated the sanction against destroying fencing, expressing particular concern for those "ill-minded persons," who, "as well in the night time as in the day (being disguised and painted), have pillaged and committed great spoil in the cedar swamps and other lands, and have laid open the inclosures of particular persons by destroying the fences about them." The law promised severe punishment for "any person or persons having their faces black'd, painted or any ways disguised." These ordinances apparently could not keep people from masquerading in public. A final decree in 1752 outlawed "any persons, being more than three in number, and being arm'd all or any of them with sticks, clubs or any kind of weapons, or disguised with vizards, so called, or painted or discolored faces, or being in any other manner disguised, shall assemble together, having any kind of imagery or pageantry with them, as a public shew." Bonfires were also outlawed in the same session.[67]

FIRE IS CRIED IN A CITY AT MIDNIGHT

House attacks began with a signal, a rumor, or, for night raids in Boston, despite its danger (or perhaps because of it), a bonfire at a prominent location near the center of town. On the night of Monday, August 26, 1765, the night of the attacks on the houses of Paxton, Story, Hallowell, and Hutchinson, "there was some small Rumor that Mischeif would be done that Night; but it was in general discarded. Towards Evening Some Boys began to light a bonfire before the Town house, which is an usual Signal for a Mob: before it was quite dark a great Company of People gathered together crying Liberty and Property, which is the usual Notice of their Intention to plunder & pull down an House." In another case, the sight of a bonfire led to a reinforcing "peculiar whoop and whistle [which] was observed to be sounded from various quarters, which instantaneously drew together a number of disguised Ruffians . . . armed with clubs, staves, & c."[68] Such were the signs that trouble was afoot.

Why was the bonfire itself such a potent signal of impending mob violence? For one thing, fire had been recognized in seventeenth-century New England culture as a sign of God's displeasure with a sinful people. Since it assumed providential meanings during King Philip's War, fire had grown to be a powerful symbol of judgment, punishment, and cleansing, apocalyptic deliverance. When at least forty-eight English houses in Providence were leveled and another one hundred damaged in 1675, Mary Pray reflected, "We once were as Rich as any town within 40 miles of us Round about But now are the poorest of al towns." The same was true in Springfield, where a devastating two-day raid in October 1675 saw the loss of thirty-three houses "and close to as many barns" (table 9). Even John Pynchon, the overlord of the Connecticut Valley in Massachusetts, felt the sharp sting of economic loss. "The Lord hath spared my dwelling house," he told his son, no doubt congratulating himself on building in brick. "But my barns and out-housing are all burned down, and all my corn and hay consumed." There had been warnings of God's displeasure. In 1667 people in Malden heard loud noises "like musket shott discharging very thick" and heard "the flying of the Bullets which came singing over their heads." Then they heard the sound of drumbeats. That same day farmers at Scituate heard "the running of troops of horses." A monstrous birth at Woburn in 1670 startled townspeople and ministers throughout the colony. It was a sign their society was deformed. Guns, drums, bullets, horses, deformed bodies: here were sure signs of a coming conflict.[69]

Afflictions signified divine displeasure because fire and flames represented damnation to the besieged bodies of God's elect. They brought to mind Satan, Hell, and the attendant agonies of eternal torment. According to an eyewitness of the November 19, 1675, raid on Pawtucket, "two nights before the Indians had assaulted a Gentlemans House about break of day with much Violence . . . striving to Fire the House several times, by tying Pine-splinters or long Poles in a Bunch fired, and held up [to] the Shingles." By igniting shingles they were firing the muscles or sinews of the human house, elements that gave the house strength and resiliency. Ministers were sure that divine displeasure lay beneath such bodily assaults. "Behold how great a matter a little fire kindleth," wrote Increase Mather in Boston. "This fire which in *June* was but a little spark, in three months time is become a great flame, that from East to West the whole Country is involved in great trouble, and the Lord himself seemeth to be against us, to cast us off, and to put us to shame, *and goeth not forth with our Armies.*" The laity followed the clergy in believing God's wrath had been stirred against them, but they sometimes located the cause of His fiery anger in the temporal injustices committed by mortal magistrates. Joseph Gatchell of Marblehead claimed in December 1675, "Ye Cause of ye

Table 9. Reported Destruction of Houses and Barns during King Philip's War, 1675–1676

Date of Raid	No. of Houses	No. of Barns	Town
[1675] June 24	23 ("one-half")	—	Swansey
28	18	—	Providence
[29]	"most"	—	Rehoboth
	"diverse"	—	Taunton
July 8	30 ("all")	—	Dartmouth
	"all"	—	Middleboro
August 2–4	20+	—	Brookfield
September 3	25	—	Deerfield
(?)	1	—	[Casco Bay?]
October 1–3	"all"	—	Saco
	22	—	Black Point
4–5	33 ("and close to as many barns")	—	Springfield
November	1	—	Sudbury
	"most"	—	Narragansett
December 2	"all"	—	Quonsickamuck
16	1	—	Kingstown
19	1	—	East Greenwich
[1676] January 27	1	—	Patuxet
February 10	"all"	—	Lancaster
21	50+	—	Medfield
28	11	11	Weymouth
March 12	1	—	Plymouth
13–14	57 of 63	—	Groton
14	5	5	Northampton
17	"all but 1"	—	Warwick
20	"remaining"	—	Narragansett
26	"all"	—	Marlborough
	"all"	—	Simsbury
28	66	many	Seaconk
	40	30	Rehoboth
29	30	—	Providence
April 7(?)	1	—	Chelmsford or Andover
19	"remaining"	—	Marlborough
20	19	19	Scituate
21	"most"	—	Sudbury
27	1	—	Rehoboth
May 6	17	17	Bridgewater
11–13	18	7	Plymouth
	"remaining"	—	Nemasket
30	12	12	Hartford

Table 9. (continued)

Date of Raid	No. of Houses	No. of Barns	Town
July 11	2	—	Taunton
19	all but 5	—	Swanzey
Total 44 raids	516+	101+	34 towns

Sources: Contemporary texts reprinted in Richard Slotkin and James K. Folsom, eds., *So Dreadfull a Judgment: Puritan Responses to King Philip's War, 1676–1677* (Middletown, Conn.: Wesleyan University Press, 1978), and in *King Philip's War Narratives*, March of America Facsimile Series No. 29 (Ann Arbor, Mich.: University Microfilms, 1966).

Note: The chronology of events has been adjusted to that in Slotkin and Folsom, *So Dreadfull a Judgment*, 46–52. The raids included above are those that can be substantiated in more than one source and thus do not take into account the raids at "*Grantham* and *Nashaway* all ruined but one house or two," the "Great spoil made at *Hadley* . . . [and] *Hatfield*," and other incidents at Westfield, Hingham, and Braintree that are cited without specific sites or the specific losses suffered in N.S., "A True but Brief Account of our Losses sustained since this Cruel and Mischievous War began," (N.S. II) in *King Philip's War Narratives*, 13–14. Additionally, the total houses and barns cited here err on the low side, owing to the many references to "all," "many," or "most" of the buildings in a town being destroyed.

Judgments of God upon us by Reasons of ye wars was their murthering of Quakers." The providential significance of Native American attacks intensified when they ran amid the flames to destroy town records, as they did in Providence in 1675 and in Andover in 1698. They were destroying the chronicle of the New Israel, a history of mythic importance. A Native American absconded with the pulpit cushion from the Andover meetinghouse that same year, and its absence symbolically undercut the ritual of reading Holy Scripture that secured the sacred body of covenanted society.[70]

As had been the case in England, the burning of houses also suggested the Apocalypse was imminent, that Christ's kingdom might soon arrive on earth to deliver the saints from evil in a purifying firestorm. Flames lit the sky with eschatological signs; the burning of houses metaphorically figured the burning of the bodies of the faithful. Cotton Mather detailed the progress of fire during the Apocalypse, explaining that the burning of the world would mark its final destruction before the second coming of Christ. "When, *Fire! Fire!* is cried in a City at midnight," he stated, "it affrightens ye Inhabitants: But what will ye cry of, *A World on Fire!* The inexpressible Anguish, and Horror, and consternation, that a *Woeful World* will be thrown into!" Searching through the Old Testament, Mather found his text in Ps. 21:9–10: "*The great* HALLELUIA comes on, with a *Confla-*

gration. . . . Thou'st make them as a FIERY OVEN, *in the Times of thy wrath:* Th'ETERNAL *in His Great wrath will swallow them wholly up: And the* FIRE *irresistably shall quite devour them all.*" And in the terror of Revelation he discovered the prediction affirmed. "But concerning the *Burning* of *This World*, and what shall follow thereupon," he argued, "what can be more astonishing, than what we have in the XXIV chapter of those prophecies. Read a Little of them, and be astonished! — Behold, The Lord maketh the Earth Empty, and maketh it waste. — The Earth shall be utterly Emptied, & utterly spoiled. — The Earth is defiled under the Inhabitants thereof; *Therefore ye* CURSE *has devoured ye Earth, and they that dwell therein are desolate: Therefore the Inhabitants of ye Earth are* BURNED, *and few men Left.*"[71]

Fueled by the memory of King Philip's War, the providential interpretation of house fires continued throughout the seventeenth century and deep into the eighteenth. In 1698, Cotton Mather recalled the great fire in Boston in 1678 and wrote, "Ah, Boston! Thou has seen the vanity of all worldly possessions. One Fatal morning, which laid fourscore of thy dwelling-houses, and seventy of thy warehouses in a ruinous heap, not nineteen years ago, gave thee to read it in firey characters." After viewing the damage done by the Boston fire of 1760, John Tudor called it a "grevos Judgment" indeed. His words reassert fire's role in providential judgment and deliverance and recall the playful language of yeoman John Sharpe of Muddy River, whose report after the conclusion of King Philip's War that "wee are yet in our habitations thro' Gods marsi" created a double meaning that would have pleased Robert Underwood and Edward Taylor.[72]

"A MOCK SHOW, REPRESENTATION, AND TRAGICAL SCENE"

Bonfires may have used various implicated meanings to frame the opening act of house attacks. But the opening act itself focused on effigies, hanging in trees, twitching in a quick breeze. Workers prepared and hanged effigies under cover of darkness. The effigy of Andrew Oliver met with "the surprize and joy of the public" when it was discovered hanging from what would soon become the Liberty Tree in Boston's South End. Accompanied by a boot (symbolizing John Stuart, earl of Bute, one of George III's most despised cronies) painted with a "Greenville" sole (mocking George Grenville, chancellor of the Exchequer), the scene was acknowledged to be "a spectacle" that "continued the whole day without the least opposition, tho' visited by multitudes."[73] In other towns similar effigies were hanged. In Newport the effigy of Dr. Thomas Moffatt had "a boot hung over the Doctor's Shoulder with the Devil Peeping out of it." In Providence on September 5, "some of the people there (struck with patriotic behaviour in support of their

Brethren at Newport,) . . . suspended the effigy of the Rhode Island Stamp-man over the great bridge there and it hung all the next day." In New London, effigies were "suspended in the Air, on a Gibbet, between 20 and 30 Feet from the Ground."[74]

Beyond the immediate resemblance between an effigy and the person it imitated, the use of effigies carried deeper implications in eighteenth-century society. Effigies reverberated across layers of association and evocation. Their official use had long been recognized as a way to exalt and commemorate individuals who had died in service of their country. Any visitor to Westminster Abbey is familiar with figures remembered through effigiation: ecclesiastical leaders, members of the royalty, military heroes whose deeds had safeguarded the English constitution. In most instances, these effigies or monuments were simply placed over the tombs of the deceased following their funeral. In other instances, movable three-dimensional copies of rulers and military heroes focused popular commemoration. But in some cases in early modern Europe—in the public burial of the *auto da fé* in Valladolíd during the Inquisition in 1558, for example—a fully dressed effigy was held aloft on a pole and preceded the coffin during the ceremonial procession from church to graveyard. If effigies commonly memorialized political and religious leaders, the use of comical or parodic effigies to mock an individual represented an inversion of established norms. In an illustration for Samuel Butler's *Hudibras* showing the popular festivities accompanying England's return to a free Parliament early in 1660, William Hogarth showed a stuffed effigy in just such a lampooning posture (fig. 80). Suspended for all in the street below to see, "Some on the Sign Post of an Ale house / Hang in Effigie on the Gallows, / Made up of Rags to personate / Respective *Officers* of *State*."[75]

Symbolic inversion was itself an established practice, drawn from a number of diverse sources that contributed to the logic of effigiation in popular protest. As memorials of living people, effigies were commonly believed to have sympathetic magical powers. They were thus related to the cloth poppets used by witches to afflict their victims; their potential was very "real." The use of effigies also derived from traditional English harvest festivals, during which two figures—one a godlike spirit (as in the Devil) and the other its human embodiment (as in Oliver)—appeared alongside each other in a ritual doubling of opposed yet interdependent forces. Effigies were sometimes hanged in order to inflict symbolically upon the stuffed or wooden figure a punishment the "real" person rightfully deserved. Thus effigy hangings represented the execution of a sentence pronounced on a "criminal" who had since escaped. Animals could serve as stand-ins for specific individuals and be executed in their absence. In London, for example, a stridently Protestant crowd shaved a cat to look like a priest, dressed it in mock clerical vestments, and hanged it in a gallows near Cheapside. The processional use of ef-

Figure 80. William Hogarth, "Burning ye Rumps at Temple-Barr," sketch for plate II from series for Samuel Butler's *Hudibras*, 1726. (Photo: The Colonial Williamsburg Foundation)

figies in New England riots borrowed some English elements—especially the use of motley clothing held aloft on poles—from village skimmingtons and rough music that used parodic transvestism to ridicule and excommunicate sexual offenders symbolically (fig. 81).[76]

Few contemporary images show what effigies actually looked like in eighteenth-century New England. They seem to have been of two types—full-body effigies that were hanged, paraded through town, and ceremonially cremated, and those in which a grotesque wooden head alone was held aloft on a pole. An engraving from the *Boston Gazette* in 1766 shows the full-body effigies of Lord Bute and George Grenville hanging from a gallows, chained to a devil who extends a copy of the Stamp Act for their mutual inspection and approval (fig. 82). Bute is dressed in the tartan and kilts of a Highland Scots chieftain, undoubtedly a reference to the culture that had provided both a pretender to the Crown and a long

Figure 81. William Hogarth, "Hudibras Encounters the Skimmington," engraving, plate 3 of series for Samuel Butler's *Hudibras*, 1726. (Photo: The Colonial Williamsburg Foundation)

history of antipathy to royal prerogative. Grenville wears the shoes, socks, breeches, coat, and tricorn hat of an ordinary citizen, suggesting that in effigy his exalted status may have been brought down to match that of the Boston crowd. New England effigies satirizing Bute clearly derived in part from images that circulated widely in the English popular press during the early 1760s. Bute's undue influence over George III's taxation policies and his apparent control over other ministers at court made him a favorite target of cartoonists. One satirical print of September 1762 portrays him as a fraudulent "state quack," with an emblematic black boot supported on a pole at his side. Another shows an effigy of Bute burning while surrounded by tradesmen—including a butcher with ax and apron, a yeoman farmer with spade, and a chimney sweep with his brush—celebrating his demise in the wake of his despised 1763 Cider Tax (fig. 83). At the same time, hanging Bute in effigy was undoubtedly a symbolic reversal of his own careful manipulation, as with marionettes or stage dummies on strings, of governmental officials (fig. 84). A suggestion that the Boston effigies may also have referenced the aggrandized style of some Harvard graduates emerges in one anonymous note, stating, "It is supposed by some people, that the effigies exhibited in this town on Wednesday last (ACTUALLY or VIRTUALLY) originated in Cambridge, from this remarkable circumstance, that the very breeches were seen upon a gentleman of that town on commencement day."[77]

An engraving of 1770 shows the use in Boston of a pole-and-head effigy figure. A crowd of young boys attending the effigy has posted it in the ground in front of the store of merchant Theophilus Lillie, trying to frighten him into honoring the nonimportation agreement. Lillie's face is exaggerated into a defiant, belligerent

Figure 82. Effigies of John Stuart (Earl of Bute) and George Grenville, 1766. (Photo: Rare Books and Manuscripts Division, The New York Public Library, Astor, Lenox, and Tilden Foundations)

sneer, his wig is pulled back into a tight knot, and pendant strips of cloth fall from his neck (fig. 85). There is no single source for this type of effigy. It seems to be a fusion of three different popular traditions. Held aloft on a pole, making it frighteningly gigantic in scale, it draws on full-figure commemorative effigies like those raised during the Valladolíd procession. It also derives from the vernacular practice of posting the head of a vanquished victim on a pole. New England Puritans could recall numerous instances when decapitated bodies represented decapitated social bodies. In New Haven in 1639 a Quiripi Indian was captured and "accordingly his head was cutt off the next day and pitched upon a pole in the markett place." The high theater of Charles I's execution was seared into the memory of Puritans, and in 1676 the bloody exhibition of King Philip's head met travelers on the road leading into Plymouth. Finally, the Lillie effigy may have been a grotesque play on the liberty pole with cloth cap—a device that implies the imagined presence of a head—made popular during the "*North Briton* no. 45" Wilkesite crisis of April 1763, a blow against Bute and the threat of tyranny with great support in New England.[78]

An enormous grotesque figure appeared in West Haven, Connecticut, in September 1765 and registered in parodic form widespread antipathy to Connecticut's stamp master, Jared Ingersoll, who lived in nearby New Haven. According to a newspaper report, it was "a horrible Monster of a Male Giant, twelve Feet high, whose terrible Head was internally illuminated." The head was likely made of

The SCOTCH YOKE; or Englifh Refentment.

A New SONG. To the Tune of, *The Queen's ASS.*

OF *Freedom* no longer, let *Englifhmen* boaft,
Nor *Liberty* more be their favourite Toaft;
The *Hydra* OPPRESSION your *Charter* defies,
And galls *Englifh* Necks with the *Yoke* of EXCISE.
    The Yoke of Excife, the Yoke of Excife,
    And galls Englifh Necks with the Yoke of Excife.

In vain have you conquer'd, my brave Hearts of Oak,
Your *Lawrels*, your *Conquefts*, are all but a *Yoke*;
Let a r—f—ly PEACE ferve to open your Eyes,
And the d—n—ble Scheme of a CYDER-EXCISE.
    A Cyder-Excife, a Cyder-Excife,
    And the d—n—ble Scheme of a Cyder-Excife.

What though on your *Porter* a Duty was laid,
Your *Light* double-tax'd, and encroach'd on your Trade;
Who e'er could have thought that a BRITON fo wife,
Would admit fuch a Tax as the CYDER-EXCISE!
    The Cyder-Excife, the Cyder-Excife!
    Would admit fuch a Tax as the Cyder-Excife!

I appeal to the Fox, or his Friend JOHN A BOOT,
If tax'd thus the *Juice*, then how foon may the *Fruit*?
Adieu then to good *Apple-puddings* and *Pyes*,
If e'er they fhould tafte of a curfed EXCISE.
    A curfed Excife, a curfed Excife,
    If e'er they fhould tafte of a curfed Excife.

Let thofe at the H——m, who have fought to enflave
A Nation fo glorious, a People fo brave;
At once be convinc'd that their Scheme you defpife,
And fhed your laft Blood to oppofe their EXCISE.
    Oppofe their Excife, oppofe their Excife,
    And fhed your laft Blood to oppofe their Excife.

Come on then my Lads, who have fought and have bled
A Tax may, perhaps, foon be laid on your Bread;
Ye Natives of *Worc'fter* and *Devon* arife,
And *ftrike* at the Root of the CYDER EXCISE.
    The Cyder-Excife, the Cyder-Excife,
    And ftrike at the Root of the Cyder-Excife.

No longer let K——s at the H——m of the St——e,
With fleecing and grinding purfue *Britain's* Fate;
Let Power no longer your Wifhes difguife,
But *off* with their *Heads* --- by the Way of EXCISE.
    The Way of Excife, the Way of Excife,
    But off with Heads --- by the Way of Excife.

From two *Latin* Words *ex* and *fcindo*, I ween,
Came the *hard Word* EXCISE, which *to cut off* does mean,
Take the Hint then, my Lads, let your Freedom advife
And give them a *Tafte* of their fav'rite EXCISE.
    Their fav'rite Excife, their fav'rite Excife,
    And give them a Tafte of their fav'rite Excife.

Then tofs off your Bumpers, my Lads, while you may
To PITT and Lord TEMPLE, Huzza, Boys, Huzza!
Here's the King that to tax his poor Subjects denies,
But Pox o' the Schemer that plann'd the EXCISE.
    That plann'd the Excife, that plann'd the Excife,
    But pox o' the Schemer that plann'd the Excife.

Figure 83. "The Scotch Yoke; or English Resentment," broadside, London, April 1763. (Photo: British Museum)

Figure 84. "The Wire Master and His Puppets." From *Political Register* 1 (1767), facing p. 129. (Photo: British Museum)

Figure 85. "The Life, and Humble Confession of Richardson, the Informer," broadside, Boston, 1770. (Photo: Historical Society of Pennsylvania)

wood and supported on a pole, as was the Lillie effigy. However, the West Haven giant combined different features drawn from English popular culture of the period and common to festive violence of the day. "This giant seemed to threaten Destruction to every Person and Thing around him, which raised the Resentment of a Number of stout Fellows, who constantly pelted him with Stones till he fell." The ritual attack and chase completed, the giant "Assailants" then surrounded him, "soon took him Captive, and triumphantly drove him about a Mile in the Town, attended with the discordant Noise of Drums, Fiddles, and taunting Huzzas." The music echoed with the cacophonous strains of the skimmington. "The People then directed their Course towards a Hill called Mount Misery. There the Giant was accused, fairly try'd and condemned by a special Jury and an impartial Judge, as an unjust intruder, a Patron of Ignorance, a Foe to English Freedom, & c. and was sentenced to be burnt. The Sentence was accordingly executed, amidst the joyful and loyal Acclamations of near three Hundred Men, Women and Children."[79]

Rough music or "discordant Noise," a mock funeral on "Mount Misery" (a reference to Golgotha?), a crowd stoning an effigial target, and loud jeering and cheering: each of these elements tied the West Haven event to charivari (recall the "Cattles Horns" thrown through the windows of the Yale president's house), political satire, popular justice, and religious processionals. But they also linked it to the eschatology of Revelation. The key referent is the fact that the giant "was mounted on a generous Horse groaning under the weight." The horse, often misshapen by the weight of its burden, recalled the prophetic vision of apocalyptic famine, disease, and death. According to one source, once he beheld the West Haven giant, Ingersoll "now had a clearer idea than ever he had before of that passage in Revelation which described Death on a pale horse and Hell following him." For stamp master Ingersoll, the pale horse represented the opening of the seal of his social death. The image reappeared in Lebanon, Connecticut, the very next year, this time connecting social suffering to the skimmington. "By setting him & causing him to ride astride a certain White Horse thro' the streets where his offense was most notorious," the colony felt it could bring John Allyn Jr., already found "guilty of great miscarriag[e]s and Abuses towards his own Wife," to a proper "Sence of Shame."[80]

Effigies used in house attacks also invoked the laughable costumes worn by participants in Pope's Day contests and by seasonal mummers. Loose-flying clothing, perhaps derived from ragged motley dress, and a parson's hat adorn a stampmaster effigy in Portsmouth, New Hampshire (fig. 86). In Windham, Connecticut, effigial costume made the same use of stylistic opposition in late August 1765: "on the morning of the 26th instant, a certain ever memorable and most respectable gentleman, made his appearance in effigy, suspended between the heavens and the earth, (as an emblem of his being fit for neither) he was cloathed in white and black, with a view to represent the great contrast of his character." When the Newport mob did its work on September 26–28 of that year, some men were attired "in muffled big coats flapped hats and bludgeons," perhaps playing on the foppish clothes artisans were forced to take in payment for goods.[81]

The performative effects of gesture, style, and costume of effigies were heightened by intertextual allusions to elements of related festive forms. In skimmingtons offenders were forced to ride in a cart to the place of their mock execution; in Newport, "amidst the Acclamations of the people," the effigies of Martin Howard Jr., Thomas Moffatt, and stamp master Augustus Johnston "were paraded through the streets [of Newport] in a cart with halters about their necks, and then hung on a gallows in front of the Colony House on the Parade."[82] Effigies fused diverse folk dramatic traditions—the doubling of masks, the flexibility of sympathetic magic, and hilarious lampooning of leading citizens—into a single figure that directed them to an individual who had violated local customary codes. The power of the effigy lay in the comedic terror it struck in onlookers'

Figure 86. Effigy of stamp master being stoned by crowd, Portsmouth, New Hampshire, 1765. From John Warner Barber, *Interesting Events in the History of the United States* (New Haven, 1829). (Photo: Metropolitan Museum of Art)

souls. In Durham, Connecticut, in September 1765, just such an effective effigy was created when a small group of people did "begin a Procession with an Image . . . representing [Benjamin Gillam] . . . figured and fashioned in the Likeness of a Man and habited in dolefull frightfull & dismall Hue."[83]

The representational power of an effigy was intensified through written messages attached to its body. According to one report, Andrew Oliver's effigy had a label pinned to its breast that read "in praise of liberty" and "denouncing vengeance on the subvertors of it." Another observer claimed that while its right arm bore the telltale initials "A. O.," its left arm revealed the message "*What greater pleasure can there be, / Then to see a* Stamp-Man *hanging on a Tree.*" The first report also stated that underneath the effigy another message appeared: "HE THAT TAKES THIS DOWN IS AN ENEMY TO HIS COUNTRY," while the latter saw "a Paper before it, on which something to his Effect was wrote in large Characters": "*Fair Freedom's glorious Cause I've meanly quitted, / _____ For the Sake of Pelf, / But ah! the Devil has me outwitted, / And instead of* stamping *others, have* hang'd *myself. / P. S. Whoever takes this down, is an Enemy to his Country.*"[84]

In Newport the effigies of Howard, Moffatt, and Johnson all wore inscriptions, ranging from brief notes to extended indictments. On Johnson: "THE STAMP-MAN." On Moffatt's breast: "THAT INFAMOUS, MISCREATED, LEERING JACO-BITE DOCT'R MURFY." His hand held a letter, addressed "To that Mawgazeene of Knowledge Doct'r Muffy in Rhode Island," while his arm read, "If I had but Rec'd this Letter from the Earl of Bute But One Week sooner." Finally, a strip of paper stuck to the mouth of the effigy lamented, "It is too late Martinius to Retract, for we are all Aground."[85]

This last text was anything but cryptic to onlookers in Newport's central parade ground; it referred to Martin Howard Jr., for whose effigy the crowd had reserved the most extended scurrilities. The mob had its reasons for this. Earlier in 1765 Howard had published *A Letter from a Gentleman at Halifax*, a pamphlet whose haughty Tory tone was taken as insulting to his fellow Rhode Islanders. Howard was particularly hard on Newport's merchants, whom he portrayed as unable to deal with the complex negotiations and calculations that world trade demanded. "To comprehend the general trade of the British nation," he maintained, "much exceeds the capacity of any one man in America, how great soever he may be. Trade is a vast, complicated system, and requires such a depth of genius, and extent of knowledge, to understand it, that little minds"—here referring to the minds of most local merchants—"attached to their own sordid interest, and long used to the greatest licentiousness in trade, are and must be, very incompetent judges of it." Having with the "Halifax" letter alienated himself from Newport's powerful merchants, individuals who helped to model the mob's critical agenda, Howard found his own effigy bearing a more detailed text than his fellows victims. On the breast of his effigy: "THAT FAWNING, INSIDIOUS, INFAMOUS MIS-CREANT AND PARACIDE MARTINIUS SCRIBLERIUS." On his right arm: "CURS'D AMBITION AND YOUR CURSED CLAN HAS RUIN'D ME" and, lower down, "WHAT THO' I BOAST OF INDEPENDENCE POSTERITY WILL CURSE MY MEMORY." And if all this were not yet enough, some passersby had written on one of the posts of the effigy's mock gallows: "We have an Heriditary Indefeasible Right to a Halter, Besides we Encourag'd the Growth of Hemp you know," this last a reference to Howard's sarcastic suggestion that hemp growing might prove better for Rhode Island's trade than grain, horses, or maritime supplies. On the other gallows post were these words: "That Person who shall Efface this Publick Mark of Resentment will be Deem'd an Enemy to liberty and Acordingly meet with Proper Chastisement." Beneath these two inscriptions, also tacked onto the gallows, were the words and chorus of a "New Song (made upon the Occasion)":

He who for a Post of Base sordid Pelf
His Country Betrays, Makes a Rope for himself.
Of this an Example, Before you we Bring
In these Infamous Rogues, Who in Effigy Swing.

Huzza my Brave Boys, Ev'ry man Stand his Ground
With Liberty's Praise, Let the Welkin Resound
Eternal Disgrace On those Miscreants Fall
Who Through Pride or for Wealth, Wou'd Ruin us All.

Let us Make wise Resolves and to them stand strong
Your Puffs and your Vapours will Ne'er last Long
To Ma[i]ntain Our Just Rights, Every Measure Pursue
To Our King we'll be Loyal, To Ourselves we'll be True.

Those Blessings Our Fathers, Obtain'd by their Blood
We are Justly Oblig'd to Our sons to make Good
All Internal Taxes let us then Nobly spurn
These Effigy's First, The Next The Stamp Papers Burn.
   Chorus
Sing Tantarara, Burn All, Burn All
Sing Tantarara, Burn All.[86]

Attached to the mouth of the West Haven giant was a label that announced Jared Ingersoll's hope that he might be freed from the "giant" of the Stamp Act that threatened to consume him. Written in the name of "Antonius," the following quoted speech was put literally into Ingersoll's mouth, transforming him into a figure lifted from a political cartoon: *"Behold a Giant vile and base | (Ye humane Powers deplore my Case!) | Has got me under; and keeps me so | That I can hardly creep or go. | His weight is most intolerable; | To bear it I'm no longer able. | When'er I neigh, or grieve or cry | He scorns to pity me, poor I!"*[87] In each case, the label with the "speech" of the effigy was attached to parts of the body that were symbolically charged. As was the case with the Oliver and Moffatt effigies, attaching words to the breast meant associating them with the heart, the seat of the soul and truth. The right arm offered words with the appearance of strength and confidence in character, and the left played with that appearance. The body of the effigy was discursively constituted.

MOCK FUNERALS

After effigies had been swinging for a day and were dead for festive purposes, they were cut down and prepared for their ritual immolation, the next major act in this unfolding street theater. Mock funerals for dead effigies drew crowds of onlookers who turned into participants as the processions moved through the streets; a coffin can be seen preceding the stamp-master effigy in the busy scene in Portsmouth. In New London, "when there was a prodigious concourse of people gathered, the effigies were taken down, and carried through the town, attended by a large procession," and burned, invoking the power of fire to level social distinction through judgment, to purify a corrupt world, and to focus resistance to authority; recall the anarchic advice of the "New Song": "Burn all, Burn all . . . Burn all."

In Boston, the mock funeral procession and cremation marked the demise of Andrew Oliver's effigy. "About evening a number of reputable people assembled, cut down the said effigies, placed it [*sic*] on a bier, and cover[ed] it with a sheet." Having prepared the body for its deliverance, the designated pall bearers "proceded in a regular and solemn manner, amidst the acclamations of the populace through the town, till they arrived at the courthouse, which after a short pause they passed, proceeding down King-street soon reached a certain edifice then building for the reception of stamps, which they quickly leveled with the ground it stood on and with the wooden remains thereof marched to Fort-hill, where kindling a noble fire therewith, they made a burnt-offering of the effigies for those sins of the people which had caused such heavy judgments as the STAMP Act &c. to be laid upon them."[88]

Note the particular pathway the procession followed through Boston's crowded center. It traced a complete rectangular route that took them past the courthouse, the seat of official justice at which their "short pause" seemed like a sneer of contempt, through the merchants' district on Cornhill, past the Old South meeting-house, up to the old burial ground, and, finally, back to where they started after passing by the Anglican churchyard. The procession asserted plebeian control of public space between the principal zones of secular and sacred moral judgment (the town house, courthouse, Old South, and the burial ground) and certain liminal areas where power was effectively suspended (the territories of merchants and Anglicans). As it walked this rough grid, the procession was reclaiming steps already traced by the funeral processions of elite families for almost a century. In 1727, for example, retail merchant Benjamin Walker watched the funeral of magistrate Penn Townsend: "A very large funeral Came From his house down Queen Street & Down King Street round ye Town house & so up to ye New burying ground." In 1742 Peter Fanueil's "very large funerall" procession "Came Down Queen Street went down Kings street below the Town house & Turn'd up the southside [of] The Town house went Thro Cornhill & so up School street [past the Old South meeting house] & Carried Into Kings Chapel . . . & Then carried to ye Common burying place in Wall Tomb." The mock funeral procession took the mob past the mansion houses of many leading citizens, suggesting that the house assault would be a symbolic rehearsal of death. By tracing a grid in the middle of a town plan dominated by linear thoroughfares, the procession transformed a linear merchant city shaped for the efficient communication of goods and services into an orthogonal city, the angular geometry of which momentarily evoked biblical visions of heaven's perfect order and the "loving" proximity of the Christian covenanted community that earlier planners had experimented with in New Haven and Cambridge in the mid-1630s. They were inscribing a leveling layer of popular sacred meanings on an avowedly secular and hierarchic landscape.[89]

Effigies hanged and mock funeral parades completed, some attacks mysteriously stopped. Their participants apparently were satisfied that their display of displeasure had already made its point; that is, by "killing" an effigy—by tearing out its eyes and tongue, disgorging its stuffing, and either hanging or beheading it—they had symbolically murdered the person represented. Yet in other cases the violence continued as crowds attacked the actual houses of their victims. The first event in the sequence of Boston assaults was the attack on Oliver's house on August 14, the birthday of Sir Robert Walpole, a figure widely portrayed as epitomizing the image of the Machiavellian court minister bent on consolidating his own interests in court at colonial expense. Having first destroyed Oliver's small brick office on the waterfront (from which it was feared he was going to sell the dreaded stamps), the crowd moved against his stable, coach house, and chaise. They approached his house. No one was home. Careening through the front door, they smashed his windows and mirrors, splintered his furniture, drank his private stock of fine wines, and then reduced his ornamental garden to stubble. They burned his private papers. A quick study, Oliver promised the next morning that he would resign his post.[90]

On August 26, the crowd struck in sequence, having targeted at least four houses for their night's work; some rumors said as many as fifteen were slated for demolition. At the first, the residence of Charles Paxton, commissioner of the provincial courts, a fast-talking landlord told the mob that Paxton was not at home and succeeded in buying off the crowd with a round of drinks at a local tavern. From the tavern, as Governor Francis Bernard later explained it, the mob went to the house of William Story, deputy registrar of the Vice-Admiralty Court, a building that "stood near the Town House" in the center of Boston. There, according to Bernard, the mob "Broke the Windows of the House and Office, destroy'd & burnt part of the Goods scattered & burnt most of the papers in a Bonfire they made in King Street near the House." By Story's own account of the damages, the mob successfully destroyed "almost every glass window in the front part of his house and the windows and doors of his Office tho' the same were well locked or bolted making a thorow fare from the Street thro his office into the other part of his dwelling destroying and damaging [a] great part of his household furniture and carrying out of his office all the files and records of the said Court of Admiralty all his private papers books and every thing that was in his office most of which were consumed to ashes or otherways destroyed and lost." The mention of the crowd's destruction of the Court of Admiralty records suggests that Boston merchants keen to erase any proof of their smuggling activities may have been behind some of the destruction specifically targeted at Story's house.[91]

The crowd then surrounded the dwelling of Benjamin Hallowell, comptroller of the customhouse. With little delay, they "Broke down the Fence & Windows of his Dwelling house, & then entered the House, Broke the Wainscot and great part of the Furniture & c. and carried of[f] 30£ Sterling in money & c." Having finished off two fine buildings, the mob turned and "proceeded with Shouts to the Dwelling House of the Honl. Thos. Hutchinson Esqr. Lieut Governor," an impressive neo-Palladian mansion on a quiet street in the North End (fig. 87). Built by his grandfather, merchant John Foster, the house boasted large end chimneys, a roof balustrade, and a cupola from which Hutchinson could no doubt gain a panoramic view of the town and people below. Earlier that summer, Hutchinson expressed his position of paternal oversight: "I am the patron of those people who cannot help themselves."[92] He had offered laboring people no help at all.

The pulse of the crowd quickened when the mansion appeared. They "enter'd in a Voyalent manner, broke the Wainscot, partitions, Glasses, & c.; broke & distroy'd every Window, Broke, tore or carr[i]ed of[f] all the Family's Apparel, Jewels, Books & c. and Carr[i]ed off about 900£ Sterling in Cash, they worked hard from 8 O'Clock on the House, Fences & c. till about 12 or one O'Clock; when they got on top of the House and cut down a large Cupola, or Lanthorn which took up their Time till near Daylight, leaving the house a mear Shell." The intensity of the destruction was palpable. Crowds rushed in the front door, ran up the stairs to the chambers, to the roof. From the street people appeared in broken windows, pitching stylish chairs and looking glasses to the pavement below. The 1780 attack on the New Gaol at Newgate (fig. 88) and the burning of Joseph Priestly's household furnishings during the Gordon riots conveys the sense of violence, vertigo, and dark play that pervaded the scene (fig. 89).[93]

The next day, money was scattered in the streets of Boston's North End, family papers were blowing in the breeze, and cracked fragments of mahogany furniture littered the yard. Hutchinson himself described the assault in dramatic terms.

In the evening while I was at supper & my children round me somebody ran in & said the mob were coming. I directed my children to fly to a secure place & shut up my house as I had done before intending not to quit it but my eldest daughter repented her leaving me & hastened back & protested she would not quit the house unless I did. I could not stand against this and withdrew w[i]th her to a neighbouring house where I had been but a few minutes before the hellish crew fell upon my house with the rage of devils & in a moment with axes split down the door & entred my son being in the great entry heard them cry damn him he is upstairs we'll have him. Some ran immediately as high as the top of the house others filled the rooms below and cellars & others remained without the house to be employed there. . . . Not contented with tearing off all

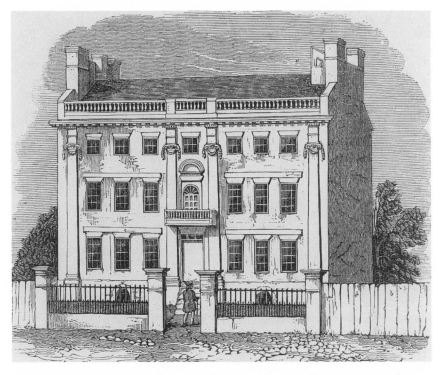

Figure 87. Thomas Hutchinson's house, Garden Court Street, North End, Boston. Built by his grandfather, merchant John Foster, ca. 1686, attacked in 1765, and finally taken down in 1834. From the *American Magazine of Useful and Entertaining Knowledge* (February 1836). (Photo: Society for the Preservation of New England Antiquities)

the wainscot & hangings & splitting the doors to pieces they beat down the Partition walls & altho that alone cost them near two hours they cut down the cupola or lanthern & they began to take the plate and boards from the roof & were prevented only by the approaching daylight from a total destruction of the building. . . . Such ruins were never seen in America.

Ruination made the wrecked mansion an instant tourist attraction. Hutchinson himself marveled at how "people came in from many parts of the country, to view the ruins of the lieutenant-governor's house, out-houses, garden, & c., and, from the shocking appearance, could not help expressing a disapprobation of such acts of violence."[94] At the very least, it was a "classical" ruin. But why did people find themselves strangely attracted by the site of Hutchinson's dead, violated house?

The attraction was partly due to Hutchinson's own life and public persona. He was well educated, moved with grace, spoke with ease, had traveled abroad. As a learned gentleman interested in economic theory, he had also championed the

Figure 88. "The Devastations occasioned by the Rioters of London firing the New Gaol of Newgate, and burning Mr. Ackerman's furniture & c June 6 1780." (Photo: British Museum)

cause of "hard money," or a currency backed by silver specie, since the monetary crisis in the early 1740s. Distrusted by rural farmers and urban artisans alike, this policy regularly saw liquid specie being sent back to London to retire colonial debt, leaving the middling and lower orders with no currency. Hutchinson combined classical erudition with faith in the centralizing cultural force of the British empire. His actions validated the centralizing order and symmetry of what James H. Bunn has termed the "aesthetics of British mercantilism." Yet when people gathered to gawk at the tattered remnants of Hutchinson's life, the sense of awe they shared at witnessing the creation of an instant social ruin was an expression of a particularly colonial antiaesthetic that saw in popular violence a sublime source of liberating pleasure and a means of critiquing the very kind of cultural dependency that mercantilism defined.[95]

House-attack narratives are remarkable summaries of the violence with which individual property was destroyed. Yet three nagging questions remain. One focuses on the "who" of crowd actions, the "they" of Hutchinson's account. Who participated in the attacks? The answer lies in the mixed popular reaction to the proclamation of the Stamp Act itself, that mandate of April 1765 ordering that all paper goods—writing paper, marriage licenses, diplomas, and newspapers— would have a stamp or duty imposed on them. Although some protesters— wealthy merchants who had profited as smugglers—found the stamps and other

Figure 89. Charles Joseph Hullmandel, "The sacking of Dr. Priestly's house," lithograph, after painting of 1791. (Photo: Reproduced by Permission of Birmingham Library Services)

recent policies (the Sugar Act and Revenue Act in 1764) damaging, poorer people saw the act more as a chance to air a long list of grievances they had been forming for decades.[96] The mob in colonial New England thus consisted of educated, wealthy Whigs whose hatred for the Stamp Act may have been due as much to their own self-interest as to a taste for country politics, as well as radical artisans impatient with economic hardship.

A second question is more difficult to answer. How did these members of the "mob" establish a critical agenda that offered at least an image of "collective action"? For one thing, propertied Whig merchants and radical artisans shared an attachment to the intersecting politics of covenant theology and republican ideology. But each group seems to have emphasized different ideas within these complicated concepts. Both the covenant and republicanism contained arguments for the defense of power and property and for the utopian leveling of social distinctions; they index systems of intellectual thought driven by dialectical tension. As we have seen, some artisans emphasized the covenant of free grace; distant echoes of Antinomianism and Anabaptism registered a belief that evidence of grace or "effectual calling" came strictly from the movement of the spirit in every individual. These same artisans spoke the republican language of James Harrington, envisioning a millennial polity that would restore Christ's kingdom, unify body and soul, and guarantee property rights to all. The social horizon of artisan politics was not entirely distinct from the radical spiritualism of Gerrard Winstanley, for whom social justice on earth was fused to the resurrection of Christ in universal spirit. In contrast, Boston's educated leaders generally argued for the republicanism of Bolingbroke, a republicanism that honored nostalgic claims of deference and prerogative and emphasized the continuing validity of the "orthodox" or federal covenant, in which civic duty and public obedience were evidence of justification. Merchants gathered in Charles Chauncy's First Church to hear him speak for liberal theology. Artisans left stranded by the Baptists' support of Chauncy often belonged to the more evangelical Third Church, where they were drawn in the early 1740s to itinerant preachers. They flocked to hear the firebrand James Davenport, who in an effort to lead people away from the distractions of worldly goods had already convinced hearers in New London to throw their clothes and furniture on a bonfire, using the judgmental force of the jeremiad to fuel radical republican ideology. In 1742 Chauncy cautioned that itinerants like Davenport and George Whitefield were trying to "destroy all property, to make all things common, wives as well as goods." As Philip F. Gura has suggested, the programs of such New Light itinerants as Davenport "were indeed comparable to those of the radical sectarians of the 1640s and 1650s, and by their challenge to the established social and ecclesiastical norms they, too, threatened to turn the world upside down, and at a time more suited to the reception of such liberating ideas."[97]

In gross terms, then, Whig merchants and radical artisans were striving for different ends, moving in a group that with one careening body concealed divergent interests. Governor Bernard understood this complex issue in precise terms. Once the August 14 attack on Andrew Oliver's property had been carried out—an attack that prominent menders of the Whig "Boston caucus" had fittingly planned while attending the festival in honor of George IV's birthday on August 12—Bernard, worried that the "Principle People of the Town publicly avowed & justified the act," attributed the violence to the fact that "Everything that for years past had been the Cause of any popular discontent was revived; & private resentments against Persons in Office work'd themselves in & endeavoured to execute themselves under the Mask of Public Cause."[98] What were the resentments?

RESENTMENT I: A THEATER OF DOMINANCE

Popular resentment focused first on the visible signs of gross social inequalities that had turned some of Boston's streets into promenades of pomp and puffery. As we have seen, economies of scale had long separated the domestic lives of laboring people from those of merchants, magistrates, and ministers. But when the mob attacked Hutchinson's mansion, they were calling particular attention to the fact that he lived in very different kind of dwelling, the form of which contrasted sharply with the house of cooper Barrett Dyre and smaller rental properties. Hutchinson's house made the change in fashion and architectural scale obvious; its cruel symmetry, cool brickwork, and classical pilasters gave new meaning to the importance of maintaining regulated public facades in Boston's commercial community. Constructed earliest in Boston, then adopted in ports like Newport, Salem, Marblehead, and Portsmouth and by merchants at their country estates, these new structures tethered the taste and power of England's local aristocracy and middling merchants to the nervous shuffle of place and politics along the colonial periphery. By 1700 the streets of Boston and Charlestown were dotted with neo-Palladian mansions distantly modeled on the rural villas of ancient Rome. But these homegrown "Georgian" houses were not visibly torn from pages of Andrea Palladio's *Four Books of Architecture*. They instead translated architectural ideas from the English countryside and secondary ports into distinctly local New England terms. These points of imagined departure for colonial mimicry are significant, however, and suggest the connections contemporaries made between nostalgia for an always-about-to-disappear ancient republican virtue and the neo-Harringtonian politics of England's "true Whig" country party in the opening years of the eighteenth century. Built initially by colonial merchants who occupied a novel zone between the *ancien régime* and courtly culture, these houses made apparent a weakness in existing social structure and a group of people actively seeking to turn it to their advantage.[99]

Three aspects of Georgian houses signaled change in the representational work that ordinary houses accomplished. Their facades were perfectly symmetrical, split down a central axis. The bilateral symmetry made it difficult to tell from the exterior where the parlor, hall, dining room, or kitchen might be. Whereas older, asymmetrical houses revealed the locations of living spaces, Georgian houses concealed them. While Palladio's distant prototypes may have suggested the disposition of four rooms of precisely the same dimensions on each floor (the "four-square" plan), the interior arrangement of most houses entailed some disequilibrium as people retained earlier patterns of social use behind the public mask of external symmetry. Hutchinson's house was two rooms deep, as was the ground floor of merchant William Clark's house. Built about 1712 in the North End close to Hutchinson's residence, Clark's dwelling contained a "Hall," "Dining Room," "Little Room," and a "Kitchen." These room names, especially the retention of a "little room" for storage at the rear of the house, suggest differences in the function and size of his four downstairs rooms; familiar spatial distinctions continued even as the rigors of formal symmetry tried to minimize their presence. The tightly disciplined facades of Georgian houses imposed a mask of unknowability over these internal variations. These were houses of masks, disguises, facades, unknowable people. Plying the open seas of commercial risk, commercial traders understood that maintaining a competitive edge often entailed the humiliation of public exposure; as Thomas Dekker and John Webster had penned a century before, "he that would grow damn'd rich, yet live secure, Must keep a case of faces." Georgian houses worked to minimize exposure, to make their owners unknowable through the disguised skin of facades and faces. Georgian houses were thus paradoxes. They materialized a crisis of representation their bourgeois owners had helped to shape.[100]

Their plans introduced a central hall that moved people and goods through with efficiency and a minimum of disruption. Like the earlier cross-passage house Samuel Desborough built in Guilford, this central hallway ran straight from front to back and permitted easy access to rooms on each side; like the small lobby entries in central-chimney houses, the central hall provided access to the stairs leading to the second floor without having to cut through a room. But similarities with earlier house forms end here. The central hall in the neo-Palladian house was much wider than the old cross passage and much deeper than either the lobby entry or added entry porch. It usually contained a staircase. It was well designed for keeping people waiting, making an entrance, and attenuating the theatrics of hospitality. The number of rooms on a given floor was highly variable. As the uneven sizes of William Clark's rooms suggest, individuals combined the veneer of public balance with the incorporation of what rooms and sizes seemed appropriate to their needs.

Although merchants like John Foster and William Clark may have arranged four rooms on a floor, more common were houses that contained one room on each side of the central hall and a back kitchen. Many people seemed hesitant to build houses that cut too grand a figure, afraid that rumors of inappropriate public ostentation might spread. Ministers throughout New England seemed particularly anxious about what other people thought, and they preached restraint from the pulpit to convince themselves as well as their parishioners of the virtue that issued from self-control. In 1715, minister Stephen Williams paused while having a new house built to consider local criticism of the building. "I heard my neighbor Brooks is uneasy because of my house being so stately," he worried. "I have heard of others who speak meanly and reproachfully of me. God forgive them and help me heartily to do it." Similar concerns plagued Ebenezer Parkman of Marlborough when his new dwelling house began to rise in June 1751: "Lieutenant Tainter was very Sharp upon me about the pride of Ministers, when he saw the Window Frames—and tho I reprov'd him, for the unseasonableness of it, being before such a Number of Strangers, yet I endeavour'd to let him know that I was myself griev'd that the windows were so large and I have often said it that I wish'd they were less." Construction continued through the following autumn, with neighbors constantly coming and going to check on its progress. Finally, on November 1, 1751, the verdict came in. Joseph Woods, Parkman's timber supplier for the job, "exclaims against my New House and thinks that it is too big, and that it is too high, He thinks there needed to be no Chamber over the room we were sitting in etc., etc."[101]

With critical comments that might injure reputation hanging in the balance, many people used the central hall to focus the arrangement of two- and three-room plans. In both cases the familiar contours of the seventeenth-century house remained influential, including the placement of working kitchens to the rear of the structure. These plans were built by ministers and by artisans eager to associate themselves for purposes of business and anticipated upward mobility with the mercantile set. Glazier Moses Peirce built a Georgian house with a two-room plan on an irregular lot in North Square in 1711. Consisting of one room on either side of a narrow stair passage and chambers above, the house relied on hearths built into its rear wall (fig. 90a). Conceptually, this house is the front half a fully developed four-room, internal-chimney structure. Boston's Third Church built three-quarters of this plan in 1710 for its minister, Ebenezer Pemberton; here the rear kitchen shared a chimney with a front room (fig. 90b). That same year brickmason Ebenezer Clough built another three-room Georgian plan on Unity Street in the North End. In this structure, however, the rear kitchen has been enlarged by stealing space from the smaller of the two front rooms (fig. 90c). These vernacular Georgian houses all have rooms of unequal sizes, thereby retaining familiar asymmetries in how rooms were used and which rooms mattered more. Unlike William Clark's three-story mansion, these were two-story structures. Each of these houses argues that although Georgian houses were at times grand, people exercised formal restraint to keep the critical gaze of neighbors in check. They were masks that concealed life within but revealed the privacy so cherished at the core of bourgeois existence.[102]

Finally, these houses marked a change in the bodily figure cut in the landscape. Central-passage structures, though their plans were markedly different from the earlier house-bodies we have examined, were still interpreted using the same metaphor. According to Palladio himself, "an edifice may be esteemed commodious, when every part or member stands in its due place and fit situation, neither above nor below its dignity and use. . . . Beauty will result from the form and correspondence of the whole, with respect to the several parts, of the parts with regard to each other, and again to the whole: that *the structure may appear an entire and compleat body*, wherein each member agrees with the other."[103] Yet the cultural organization of the body being referenced had changed. The plans of the houses built by Foster, Clark, Peirce, Pemberton, and Clough moved people and goods

Figure 90. Center-hall or Georgian houses in early-eighteenth-century Boston: (a) Moses Peirce's house, North Square, ca. 1711–12; (b) Ebenezer Pemberton's house (Third Church parsonage), planned in 1705, built in 1710 (after plan by Thomas Dawes, 1770; fenestration pattern not given in original); (c) Ebenezer Clough's house, Unity Street, 1710–11. (Drawing by the author)

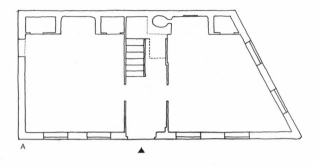

A

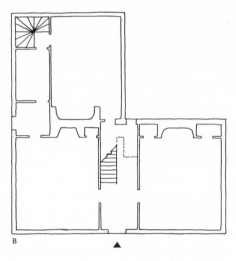

B

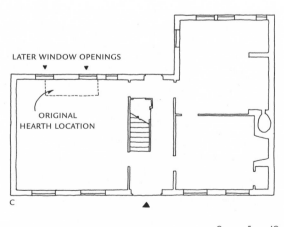

LATER WINDOW OPENINGS

ORIGINAL
HEARTH LOCATION

C

0   5   10
FEET

with mechanical ease. Central passages permitted predictable circulation. Symmetrical masks kept the self-contained logic of this house-body closed to public view. The Georgian house figured forth a body, but it was the closed, experimental body of the new science, not the open, besieged body that witches could invade at will.

Laboring people also resented the frequency with which wealthy Boston merchants built a second Georgian house at their country estate. This touched a nerve rubbed raw since the early 1720s, when artisans complained about country towns siphoning off the port's wealth and revenues. By 1750 urban merchants had built large houses in towns as far afield as Medford, Milton, Lincoln, and Cambridge (fig. 91); with these large mansions as their models for domestic modernization, local versions appeared everywhere in New England: Danvers, Worcester, Scarborough, Kittery, Deerfield, Hadley, Springfield, and Hartford—to name but a few. And when new merchants arrived in Boston, at times they refused to settle in town at all, passing directly to a life on a country estate. Consider, for example, the country estate built by merchant Isaac Royall in Charlestown (later Medford) in the 1730s. Born in Maine, he had profited in the sugar and slave trades in the West Indies. In 1732 he returned to Massachusetts from Antigua and bought the Ten Hills farm that had originally served as John Winthrop's rural retreat. When he acquired the property, a brick house constructed in the late seventeenth century was still standing on the site, along with a barn, and down the road stood another barn next to "A Tenement," or house for a farm tenant (fig. 92). Over the next few years Royall reworked the structure and surrounding landscape completely. What rose in its place was a colonial plantation, complete with an "out kitchen" in which at least thirteen house slaves worked and may have lived, articulating in a "dependency" of the house their position as social dependents in Royall's household (fig. 93). It would have fit as seamlessly in Virginia or Antigua as in Medford.[104]

Royall's plantation represents the first documented impact of a new generation of English agricultural reform. In his library when he died in 1739, just as his house was being finished, Royall had a copy of John Mortimer's *Whole Art of Husbandry*, which he apparently read, reread, and put into practice. Mortimer enjoined readers to avoid placing walled enclosures that directly linked cattle and poultry yards and courtyards to the principal dwelling, favoring instead estate plans that looked outward into nature and located protected yards for animals adjacent to the house at a polite distance. Mortimer glossed in the language of aesthetics why Jared Eliot objected to Desborough's Guilford estate: it looked inward and viewed capital as fixed and in need of protection, rather than being expansive and adaptive to changing regimes of production. Royall made sure that his barn was not "annoyingly" close to the house and even gave it a new separate entrance

Figure 91. Country estates in
Boston's hinterlands: (a) Peter
Tufts's house, Medford, ca. 1688;
(b) William Shirley's house,
Milton, ca. 1747–56; (c) John
Vassall's house, Cambridge, 1759.
(Drawing by the author)

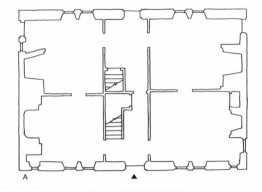

A

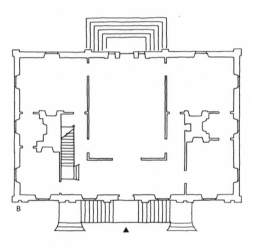

B

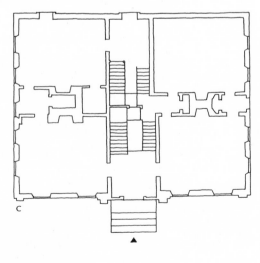

C

0   5   10

FEET

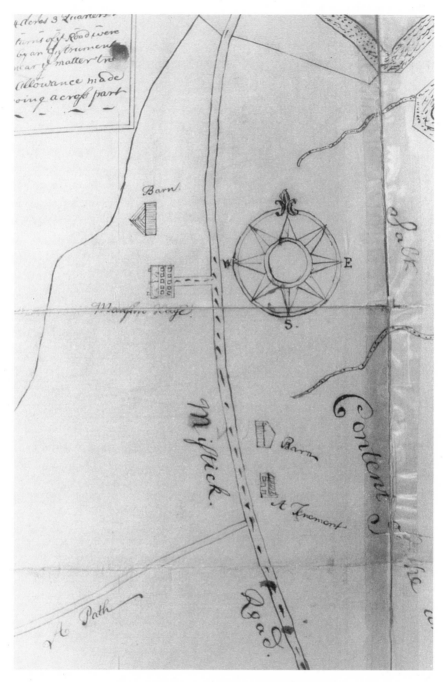

Figure 92. "A Plan of a Farm purchased by Maj[or] Isaac Royal of ye Heirs of ye Late Lt. Governor Usher . . . Scituate in Charlestown," October 1732. (Photo by the author)

Figure 93. Garden (rear) elevation of Isaac Royall's house, Medford, Massachusetts, ca. 1733–38. (Photo: William French, ca. 1880–1920, courtesy of the Society for the Preservation of New England Antiquities)

from the "Mystick Road" to further segregate farm labor—and the stable, pigeon house, and corn house—from the fictive allegorical scene he was contriving. Royall embraced Mortimer's thoughts on the type of view that a country house should offer. "If on thy native Soil thou dost prepare / T'erect a Villa, thou must place it there / Where a fine Prospect does itself lend into a Garden." Behind his house, away from the street, Royall planned a landscape garden complete with a path leading to a raised summer house (see fig. 94). According to Mortimer, the garden's middle walkway, a direct axial continuation of the house's central hall, should "terminate in the best prospect your situation should afford." Atop his prospect hill, Royall placed a summer house crowned by a figure of Mercury (fig. 95). He could retreat there to read his copies of *Tacitus*, the "*Duke of malborough his Life*," the *Specta[c]le of Nature*, the *Establishment of Brittans among ye Gauls*, and the *History of the Revolutions of ye Romans Republick*. Narrating his way through high republican theory to his summer house and back, Royall could almost forget that the river across his fields was the Mystic and not the Thames.[105]

Relying on Mortimer as a source for Royall's plantation has its limitations. While the book may have conditioned his placement of the garden and prospect hill, it may obscure aspects of farm planning that Royall may have drawn from the wider culture and shared with individuals who never consulted an English authority for advice. Alongside the rising popularity of Georgian facades as masks that separated people from their neighbors, barns and houses were increasingly disassociated. Royall's estate is symptomatic of a new insistence that the "clean" realm of polite landowners be radically disjunct from the polluted zone of animals and unprocessed crops. As had Royall, by 1748 minister John Prentice of Lancast-

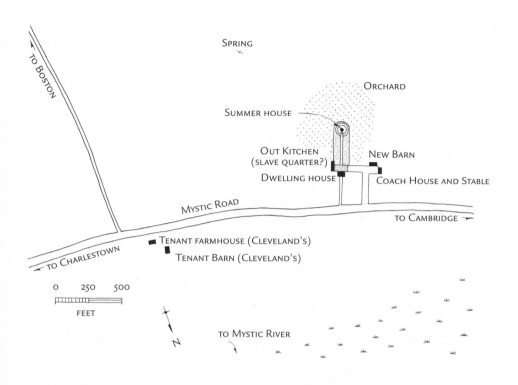

Figure 94. Plan of Isaac Royall's estate, by 1738. After map by F. P. Helyar, Radcliffe Seminar, July 1985, based on 1732 deed survey (see fig. 92) and Royall's 1739 estate inventory; buildings recorded in 1739 but of unknown location included "Pidgen House," "Corn house," three "Old Barnes," and "2 Small Do. of Cleveland." (Drawing by the author)

er employed an entrance for his house that was clearly distinct from the path that led to the barn; the path leading from the house down to the road was 150 feet long and 8 feet wide, and the two structures were 380 feet apart (fig. 96a). A more common strategy for effecting the same disjunction retained the single approach from the road that was typical of seventeenth-century farmsteads but placed house and barn perpendicular to each other, with the house always in front of the barn, as John Cogswell in Essex accomplished by 1751 (fig. 96b).[106] Now the Georgian farmhouse masked the entire estate, while snapping the symbolic connection that had long tied it to the barn. With one move the historical tissues binding the two structures, which may be traced chronologically back to the house and barn having parallel ridgelines, to their being in linear alignment, and, finally, to the symbolic unification of humans and animals under a single roof, had been severed. Georgian sensibilities brought opposites together in a delicate balance, playing an insistence on cultural segregation and boundaries off against a fantasy of classical allegory and temporality of lost perfection regained.

Figure 95. Summer house, Isaac Royall's estate gardens, Medford, Massachusetts, by 1738. (Photo: William French, ca. 1890–1900, courtesy of the Society for the Preservation of New England Antiquities)

RESENTMENT 2: CLAIMS DENIED

Houses could not contain all the resentment that working people had in store for Hutchinson, Oliver, and Hallowell. After the devastating fire that ruined houses, shops, and working lives, Hutchinson chaired the committee that oversaw the evaluation of claims for restitution. Oliver was the secretary of the committee and often visited properties to assess firsthand the extent of property loss. Many arti-

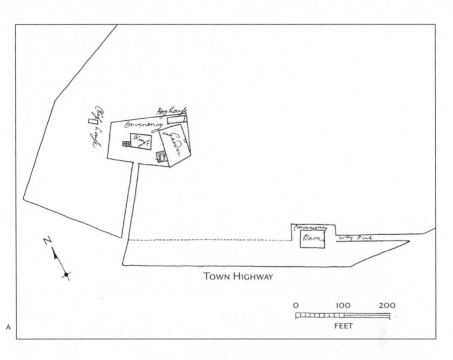

TOWN HIGHWAY

0   100   200

FEET

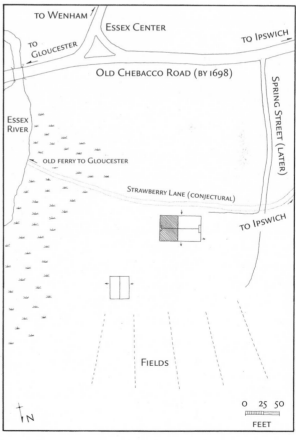

TO WENHAM

ESSEX CENTER

TO
GLOUCESTER

TO IPSWICH

OLD CHEBACCO ROAD (BY 1698)

ESSEX
RIVER

SPRING STREET (LATER)

OLD FERRY TO GLOUCESTER

STRAWBERRY LANE (CONJECTURAL)

TO IPSWICH

FIELDS

Figure 96. Georgian farm layouts: (a) separate entrance plan, John Prentice's farm, Lancaster, Massachusetts, by 1748; (b) single entrance plan, with barn perpendicular to house, John Cogswell's farm, Essex, Massachusetts, ca. 1751. (Drawing by the author)

N

0   25   50

FEET

B

sans felt they were sorely mistreated in the process. Thomas Allen, a Boston shingle maker, lost £38 but was reimbursed for £5. Tailor William Baker submitted claims for £288 and received £36. Two woodcarvers jointly petitioned for £490 in damages but received only £65. Tanners were universally squeezed out. Officials did not appreciate the fragrance of their work, and denying any claims to rebuild submitted by tanners was a sure way to speed their departure. If out-migration by artisans had already started, it was now unavoidable. The government was virtually telling them to go. Women were among those who lost property in the 1760 claims game, especially widows of artisans who were trying to continue to run their husbands' shops and compete for business. Mary Cross included "2 Sett of Coopers Tools" worth £60 and "Sundry Chalk Scoars that I had" when she submitted damages of £365. Cross got £48, virtually a suggestion that she give up any attempt to stay in business. Eleanor Clay was running an impressive shoemaker's shop. Along with "3 shoe makers seats Hammers & Other Shoemakers Tools" valued at £10, she had in stock "Nine Dozn. English soles at £10 p Dozn." (£90), "15 pr men's double Channel pumps at 70 [shillings]" (£52), "10 prs. Ditto Turned pumps at 60 [shillings]" (£30), and another £16 worth of men's shoe lasts made in both England and America. Clay was making fancy shoes, of the double-pump sort that Hutchinson and Oliver might have been wearing as they read her claim. She asked for £282. They gave her £37. Finally, Margaret Rogers lost "a shoe Makers seatt wth all the Tools" and "1 side sole leather" when her shop burned. She wanted £254 to recoup her losses but only managed to get £2.[107]

There was resentment smoldering here for Hutchinson and Oliver, enough to blow down their houses easily. These losses were further aggravated when members of the claims committee gave awards to their cronies that called for no reduction in the amount requested. Benjamin Hallowell lost his house in the South End in the fire, as did Oliver. Both structures were rebuilt entirely, new bodies rising phoenixlike from ashes. Hutchinson further announced that a "New Street of forty feet wide should be laid open from King Street to the Eastward of Mackrel Lane to run to Mr Hallowells House in Battery March," ensuring that the customs official would have swift and easy access between his South End residence, the customhouse, the town house, and Dock Square. The fire provided an opportunity for the committee to straighten old crooked streets and better adapt them for the unimpeded movement of goods and traffic. Modifying the dimensions and directions of roads demanded that the committee delicately request property from the sides of certain house lots. Plans to widen Leverett's Lane to 28 feet "at Deacon Salter's (or 30 feet if Mr Salter shall be consenting to it)" were slowed because Salter was apprehensive of having his land seized.[108]

Some of Boston's merchants made common cause with artisans because increasing regulation and surveillance had jeopardized efforts at smuggling basic to their livelihood. Hutchinson believed that a coterie of merchant-smugglers had manipulated the mob for their own interest, and claimed that merchant John Rowe later admitted to stirring "up the mob to attack the houses of the Custom House officers . . . and the Chief Justice." Three years after the attacks Charles Paxton, still worrying about what would happen to his reputation if his having "Suffered the indignity of being burnt in Effigie should be made Public," also criticized the manipulative role played by Boston merchants in the various acts of insurgency that had erupted during the 1760s. Writing to Lord Townsend, Paxton stated that "the merchants . . . seem to have taken all government into their hands and are combined or confederated to compel Parliament to do what they would have them." For Paxton, the resentment merchants felt toward having their operations-as-usual interrupted by inconvenient "Stamps" translated into a concerted attempt—the language of artisan "combinations" here describes merchants—to orchestrate political events. The merchants, Paxton concluded, "are perfect Tyrants over who will not approve their measures."[109]

The unleashing of frustrated anger at the scale and anonymity of Georgian houses, the betrayal of urban loyalties by merchants building country estates, the disinterest of government in stabilizing the shifting place of labor, the seizing of private property for street projects no one had requested, and the government's preferential treatment of imperial placemen like Hallowell fanned the embers still glowing from the imposition of the Stamp Act. These were the "private resentments" that allowed house attacks to get out of hand. But many targets for popular violence were possible. Our third and final question still remains—why houses?

BREAKING AND ENTERING

The popular objection to the masklike qualities of Georgian houses suggests they were the vilified symbol of a standard of living unattainable by working people. The household surroundings of the "rabble" were far below the level of material comfort enjoyed by Hutchinson, whose house, one contemporary claimed, "from its structure & inside finishing seemed to be from a Design of Inigo Jones or his Successor," John Webb. Hallowell's house, too, was reportedly "fitted & furnished with great elegance." Perhaps crowd members were seeking vengeance for having suffered through times "when good Honest, Industrious, Modest People, are driven to such streights, as to Sell their Pewter and Brass out of their Houses." On the one hand, angry townsmen may have been turning the violence of dispossession back on landlords who had treated them badly if rent payments were late. Hutchinson's father had used the family mansion as a center for rental operations before his death in late 1739; eight tenements and four artisans' shops meant that each year a dozen properties would be up for renegotiation. And techniques for eviction in colonial New England could be harsh. In 1731 "Madam Winthrop" wanted a tenant off her property in New London and spared no cruelty. "She took Possession & flung out the household Stuff of all Sorts in Every Room & put out al the People." On the other hand, crowd members were likely returning systematic pillage for systematic pillage; using writs of assistance, they complained, customs officials had already rifled private homes with impunity. "Our houses," Bostonians argued, "and even our bedchambers, are exposed to be ransacked, our boxes chests & trunks broke open ravaged and plundered by wretches, whom no prudent man would venture to employ even as menial servants; whenever they are pleased to say they suspect there are in the house wares & c for which the dutys have not been paid." Because of these invasions, they claimed, "we are cut off from that domestick security which renders the lives of the most unhappy in some measure agreeable."[110]

Returning one invasion of domestic property for another had long been a popular strategy to resist official but unwarranted acts of property seizure. Because such scattered acts of housebreaking, vandalism, and burglary posed a threat to property holders, the crime of housebreaking had been officially outlawed in Massachusetts Bay in 1648. A first offense in "breaking up any dwelling house" brought a brand of "B" (for "breaker" or "burglar") on the forehead, a second offense being again branded and whipped, and a third offense was punishable by death. Anyone who "broke house" on Sundays had one ear cut off.[111] The exchange meted out in such punishment was symmetrical: For defacing or fragmenting the bodies of houses, offenders had their own bodies similarly defaced and broken.

In New England people were taken to court to answer charges for breaking into different points of houses. In New Haven in 1644 Henry Hummerston stood trial "for creeping into Captaine Turn[er]'s house att a window [just as would have a witch, as we have seen] in a felonious manner in the time of publique meeting on the Lord's Day," was convicted, and whipped in the marketplace. Others faced accusations of "malicious damage to real estate" and of "injuring and breaking down [a] chimney whereby tenant leaves house" in 1683. People pilfered small amounts of food, clothing, fabrics, and jewelry, a common strategy for redressing inequalities in wealth throughout the seventeenth and eighteenth centuries. In July 1738 a newspaper advertisement in Boston announced that "several Gentlemen of this Town had lately had their Yards and Gardens robbed of wearing Apparel, Kitchen furniture, & c. and advised People to be more careful for the future." Within days three young men living in Boston's North End confessed to the thefts, and returned "many hundred Pounds, in pewter, Linen, & c. among which are many of Mr. Jenner's, Capt. Wendell's, Mr. Faneuil's, and some of Mr. Dennie's Goods, and many other Persons come in as Claimers, who never expected to hear of their Goods again." When found, the goods taken from the merchants had been "deposited in the Hands of the Women" with whom the three were found. Appropriations of surplus property were by no means confined to port towns. In 1754 Elisha Parks of Westfield claimed that Michael Fowler, a local laborer, did "with force & arms feloniously & Burglariously break and enter the Mansion house" of Parks and did "take Stel & carry away Twenty shillings of lawful money," a watch, a pair of leather britches, and one gray wig.[112]

Members of the Boston mob thus felt completely justified in breaking open the house of Thomas Hutchinson. When the episode was over, the mob had in retaliation "emptied the house of every thing whatsoever except a part of the kitchin furniture"—that is, they had stripped the house until its furnishings resembled the very things they had in their own tenements. By emptying houses or pulling entire buildings down, crowds symbolically invoked and playfully reversed a contemporary popular practice in the west of England and in Wales known as the "one-night house." The one-night house tradition held that if an individual successfully erected a house on a piece of common land in one night, then he acquired a freehold right to that land. Though less speedy, the common-law concept of *vacuum domicilium* was similar and had been invoked by English settlers when first appropriating land from the Native Americans; if one built a house on a piece of unimproved land, one had legal right to that terrain, "which," as John Winthrop maintained, "we took peaceably, built a house upon it, and so it hath continued in our peaceable possession ever since without any interruption or Claim . . . which being thus taken and possessed as vacuum domicilium gives us a sufficient title against all men." In the house attacks, the reverse was argued: if you could tear down a house in a single night, its space and contents reverted to common possession. The hesitancy to give up reclaimed property is apparent in how victims' lengthy petitions for remuneration were met by local officials. Confronted by room-by-room listings of objects broken or stolen, the town meeting accused them of inflating values and never paid what was asked.[113]

METAPHORIC MANSIONS

House attacks had a symbolic dimension that both enhanced the magical power of effigies and words to afflict a real person and turned the event into good theater, the "spectacles" that throngs came to witness. To uncover this hidden level of meaning we need to return briefly to the world of postmedieval buildings and the metaphysical belief system of seventeenth-century English people, a belief system that survived at a substrate level into the nineteenth century long enough to influence literary tropes used by Melville and Emerson, among others. The previous chapter details the many metaphoric correspondences linking houses and human bodies. Recall Richard Neve's claim in the *City and Countrey Purchaser* (1703) that the first thing to do when evaluating a house "is to pass a running Examination over the whole Edifice, according to the Properties of a well shapen Man; as whether the Walls stand upright, upon a good Foundation; whether the Fabric be of a comely Stature, . . . whether the principal Entrance be in the middle of the Front, like our Mouths; [and] whether the Windows, as our Eyes, be set in equal Number, and distance on both sides [of] the Entrance."[114]

Or recall the intricate and sustained analogies between buildings and bodies offered by poets and preachers. Anne Bradstreet: my body is "my Clay house mouldring away." Edward Taylor: "I but an Earthen Vessell bee," "a Mudwall tent, whose Matters are / Dead Elements, which mixt make dirty trade." Or Cotton Mather: a grieving widow should remember her dead husband's body as "the forsaken Mansion of the Soul which was dearer to her than the World." Taylor again, imploring God: "Sill, Plate, Ridge, Rib, and Rafter me with Grace."[115] These house-body analogies, already described in great detail from the work of Robert Underwood and many others, suggest why crowds attacked houses the way they did, and they also argue that millennial zeal, grounded in typological thought, was crucial to the logic and rhetoric of successful mob violence. To attack a house was more than a mere lashing out at the material property of the rich and powerful; it was also to destroy symbolically the body of its owner by tearing out its eyes and its tongue, opening its head, and exposing its brain (remember the mob working on the windows, door, roof, and cupola of Hutchinson's house) and, by tearing down interior partitions and throwing broken furniture and mangled household possessions out onto the streets, to publicly disembowel his corpse. The house-body metaphor also helps explain in cultural terms the antipathy to petty housebreakers, individuals who essentially opened other people's bodies to public view and took parts of them away. Their offense was more than merely absconding with material things. The housebreaker laid the body of the house open to view and thus discovered a performative means of resisting the bourgeois enclosure of the body as political and social metaphor. The wages of such activity surely were in kind, as one almanac stated in 1735: "Let thieves beware of Burglary lest we dissect their Bodies and set up their Bones for Skeletons." Two years later a man was hanged at Worcester for housebreaking; the fate of his body is unknown.[116]

A melodramatic and cruel morality play, the house attack reminds us of Hogarth's gruesome 1751 engraving of Tom Nero's body being eviscerated as the "Reward for Cruelty" (fig. 97). Nero began life by torturing small animals with no remorse. But as one contemporary editor of Hogarth's works observed, he soon grew worse, since "continued acts of barbarity are found in time to divest men of their natural feelings; for he that would not hesitate to torture and destroy a harmless, helpless animal, would not, but through fear of the law, scruple to murder a fellow-creature." After finally beating to death a helpless young woman, young Nero is apprehended, convicted of murder, and then hanged at Tyburn. His ultimate reward, perpetrated on his corpse by grave robbers in league with the Royal College of Surgeons, is to be stretched on a stone table and have his body exposed to public eyes. During Nero's depraved youth, people already saw the "Tyrant in the Boy." Yet by his death he received justice for his disregard of others: "Behold and shudder at the ghastly sight! See his tongue pulled from the root, his eye-balls wrung from their sockets, and his heart torn from his body, which the dog is gnawing beneath the table!" Elsewhere, verses commented on "Those eye-balls from their sockets wring, / That glow'd with *lawless lust*." Not surprisingly, symbolic disembowelment through the destruction of their human house-bodies was a fitting form of symbolic folk justice for Hutchinson and the others, who were repeatedly derided in contemporary pamphlets as being placemen in service to a tyrant, "cruel" and "merciless" "oppressors of the weak."[117]

Unwarranted cruelty, even when couched in political language and political debates, violated the moral boundaries of the body social, the established Christian model of proper social order. Recall Thomas Hooker's equation of society and a house frame: "if the parts be neither morticed nor braced, as there will be little beauty so there can be no strength. Its so in setting up the frames of societies among men, when their mindes and hearts are not mortified by mutuall consent of subjection to one another, there is no expectation of any succeseful proceeding with the advantage of the publicke."[118] With this in mind, we can see that the significance of house assaults derived in part from the parallelism of effigy as body, house as body, society as body—a paradigm in which virtue and property must be defended from corruption just as a house's fortitude must depend on the sturdiness of its frame. The parallelism was affirmed in Durham, Connecticut, when a local mob caused the "Image or Effigy to be beheaded & within also a Small Distance of the Persons Dwelling House to be burnt," thus establishing a crucial symbolic connection between the destruction of the effigy, the mock destruction of the person, and then the transference of "personness" to the impending destruction of his or her house. The metaphoric connections again surfaced when the contents of Martin Howard's Newport house were themselves effigied on the parade ground just as if they were the disheveled components of a body. "And first they went to Martin Howards," a newspaper report revealed, "And Broke Every

Figure 97. William Hogarth, "The Reward of Cruelty" (*Cruelty* no. 4), 1751, engraving on paper. (Photo: The Colonial Williamsburg Foundation)

Window in his house Frames & all, Likewise Chairs Tables, Pictures & every thing which Stood before his door & Bro[ugh]t them & *stuck them up on two Great Guns which have been fix'd at the Bottom of the Parade Some Years as Posts*."[119]

FLIGHT, FEMINIZATION, MENDICANCY

Attacking houses offered one way for the mob to peel away the mystifying mask of mechanical control and expose the face behind the facade to public ridicule. The desire to see behind the external mask of Georgian symmetry and order was one reason why, when mobs gathered, they frequently "surrounded" the house designated for mischief. "A large Body of People tumultuously surrounded" the house of Benjamin Wickham, the customhouse officer in Newport. By surrounding it, they would see its owner's public facade as well as his backstage demeanor. A key to this process of exposing the "real" person behind the facade to public shame, and a clue that in almost all cases no one was really after a "real" murder of the homeowner, lies in the fact that all of the targeted individuals were given fair warning to vacate. They were given time to act. By the time the mob reached Andrew Oliver's house, the doors had been barricaded and the house deserted, left as a sacrifice to public will. In this case, it was Suffolk County sheriff Stephen Greenleafe who "being apprehensive that the person of the then Stamp-Master, and his family, might be in danger from the tumult, went and advised them to evacuate the house." Hutchinson also had more than adequate warning. He had first been visited and warned by the crowd immediately after they had done in Oliver's house on the night of August 14. As Governor Bernard explained it (in language curiously reminiscent of witchcraft narratives), he "had been apprized that there was an evil Spirit gone forth against him." Perhaps some signals had gotten crossed, as Hutchinson himself described the confidence he had in his own position; on August 30, he explained, "I came from my [country] house at Milton with my family the 26 in the morning after dinner it was whispered in town there would be a mob at night & that Paxtons, Hallowells, & the custom house & admiralty officers houses would be attacked but my friends assured me the rabble were satisfied with the insult I had received & that I was become rather popular."[120] Yet in spite of all this, he admits that before his house was attacked, "Messages soon came one after another . . . to inform me the mob were coming in pursuit of me." Yet unlike Oliver, who, having been duly alerted, promptly left, Hutchinson refused to muster the provincial cadets in his own defense, despite the fact that such a move would have been legal under the terms of England's Riot Act of 1714 and the local ordinances passed in the intervening decades.[121]

Why such hesitancy? In one sense, it seems out of character, since men like Oliver and Hutchinson may have elected to use the force of a standing army for their own protection. Yet at the same time, these men were Bostonians by birth and shared, if ambiguously, an understanding of how local popular culture worked. In this regard, they were different from Paxton, Story, or Hallowell and thus were more effective victims. They realized implicitly that their only hope of retaining authority depended on their voluntary, symbolic subjection to the "collective will" of the people. Despite their high political positions, they had to undergo the process of ritual shaming and publicly atone before the "rabble" for their "cruelty" in order to continue. Again drawing on the skimmington as a model for moral shaming, the house assault stripped a transgressor of his separable facade and forced him to atone for his sins through voluntary effeminization and public mendicancy.

In the eighteenth century effeminization was closely linked to emasculation. On some occasions we know that attacks on masculinity were effected through physical cruelty and laughter that bordered on violence. In New London, Connecticut, in 1769, a crowd targeted some of the town's tidesmen who had served as informers to Crown officials. They quickly located and held one of the informers, Barnabas Wilson, while others found John Boyd, Wilson's partner in crime, at the house of the local customs collector. Learning he was on the premises, the mob stormed "forcibly into the House, searched everywhere & found [him] on the House Top." They then took Boyd into the street "near the Episcopal Church"—surely the symbol of Anglican transgression—and interrogated him. After learning what they could "about some Rum seized and afterwards stolen at East Hadaam," they turned their gaze back to Wilson and "stripp'd or rather tore off Willson's cloaths and cut off his Hair and then severely whipped him."[122] To be exposed naked in public (like a Quaker) in front of the Episcopal Church (like a Tory) and have one's hair cropped (like a prisoner) was clearly an assault on masculinity. Why was effeminization so effective a form of ritual degradation that it would be incorporated into an attack on a community member deserving of moral shaming?

In the frail theater of colonial masculinity, effeminization reduced a merchant to a lower stage of Otherness than women themselves occupied: freedom abrogated, posture ambiguous, the body besieged. Hutchinson's narrative of the attack suggests in different ways his adoption of a demeanor at once effeminate and ambiguous. Recall Governor Bernard's observation that before the mob arrived, Hutchinson had been told "that there was an evil Spirit gone forth against him." The language of witchcraft reminds us that only witches had the power to penetrate the walls, windows, chimney, and barred doors of human houses. Perhaps Hutchinson was being attacked by a strange mob maleficium, his body passively waiting to be pierced and entered at will. Waiting in his house, he also seemed like a captive of his own body, unable to move until his daughter dramatically intervened. Strangely, he now was in a Georgian dungeon. In a lengthy verse poem, "Captivity Improved into Freedom by the Grace of God," George Withers had a century earlier captured the repentant turn of mind of prisoners as they felt the shackled metaphors binding houses and bodies. "How, the quiet of our lives we trouble / About our *structures* of wood, straw, and stubble; / Which, when our several *Fiery Tryals* come, / Will into smoke and Ashes, quite consume." For Withers, the only freedom with captivity came when one saw one's own body as the site of divine rebuilding. In his captive cell, we can imagine Hutchinson voicing additional verses of the poem. "It made me take into consideration / What I had *Built*, and upon what *Foundation*, / That, I myself, might therein be secure / Although my *Works*, thy flame should not endure. / And, thereof, having an assurance got / The loss of all my *Works* disturb me not: / For, I, a thousand times more pleas'd am grown / With *his on whom I Build*, then with mine own."[123]

Hutchinson's domestic captivity more particularly recalls the patterned action of Puritan captivity narratives: a discourse of violence, steps taken through affliction, and redemption that mirrored the enplotment of the individual's soul as it withstood loss, endured divine judgment, and triumphed in repentance through Christ. Hutchinson was thoroughly familiar with the captivity narrative published by Mary White Rowlandson of Lancaster in 1682. Rowlandson's narrative works by taking the reader through a series of twenty "removes" on her hard forced journey. Like Hutchinson's account, Rowlandson rivets attention by describing the opening attack on her house. "At length they came and beset our own house," she writes, "and quickly it was the dolefulest day that ever mine eyes saw." The Native Americans were scattered on a small hill behind the house, "from which places they shot against the house, so that the bullets seemed to fly like hail." Their assault on Rowlandson's house recalls the malefic racket of "lithobolia," or the tiny stones that witches were said to hurl against human houses to test their strength. As Rowlandson and her children looked back on their dwelling, she cried, "Oh! the doleful sight that [it] now was to behold this house!" Hutchinson opened his account with the rattling frenzy of destruction; his house instantly became a similarly doleful spectacle that people flocked to stare at in disbelief. Rowlandson described the preternatural noise of bullets hitting her house. Hutchinson relates the sound of splitting, crashing, cracking. He also used the strategy of narrating "removes" in a like manner. In his house, someone comes and tells him the mob is coming. First remove: he apparently retreats upstairs with his son, since he recounts the progress of the noise downstairs in detail. Second remove: he leaves house with daughter. Third remove: he fled the architectural carnage, "obliged to retire thro yards & gardens to a house more remote," embarrassed in his "undressed" state.[124]

Hutchinson's physical appearance was a key element in the drama of effeminization. When the mob first arrived, "I had undressed me & slipt on a thin camlet surtout over my wastcoat." He had removed his wig and his jacket and perhaps exchanged buckled shoes for slippers. He was, in fact, waiting for the mob to arrive in a loose, flowing "surtout," a garment with a curiously mixed set of associations in Hutchinson's own culture. The surtout was originally a French term for a garment that offered protection from rain and wind. However, it was also known to have feminine overtones, a fashionable hood (usually with an attached mantle) worn by genteel women since at least 1690. The material of the "thin" camlet, a light blend of silk and goat or camel's hair imported from Turkey, had intimate associations with women's bodies, having been used for female garters in the colonies since at least the 1730s. The overall impression of Hutchinson's cowed demeanor during his third remove is suggested by the relaxed, orientalized, and feminized air suggested by the surtout and turban that merchant Nicholas Boylston donned for his portrait by Copley (fig. 98).[125]

Although the surtout may have evoked feminine attire, Hutchinson himself suggested that was not his intention. In July 1764, when he ordered his surtout from his London tailor Peter Leitch, Hutchinson stated, "I am told the Judges and Lawyers upon the circuits wear a fine camlet surtout cloth colour which they travel in over their black [robes] if so send me one made in the same fashion lined." At some point in the early eighteenth century, then, the surtout seems to have been appropriated from upper-class women for use by England's judicial ranks, who found this costume at once practical and, once "slipt on," helpful in symbolically positioning themselves outside normative social order, in much the same manner that Johan Huizinga argued wigs and medieval gowns also functioned for English judges. According to Huizinga, "judges about to administer justice step outside 'ordinary' life as soon as they don wig and gown," articles that "transform . . . the wearer into another 'being.'"[126] For Hutchinson, then, his "thin camlet surtout" imaginatively linked him, as the chief justice of the provincial Supreme Court, to his English counterparts, but in this instance, he did not place it over judicial robes but used it as had women—to cover their ordinary daily clothing. The day after his house was so illicitly entered, still in rags of retreat, he reported, "I had not cloaths enough in my posession to defend me from the cold & was obliged to borrow from my friends."[127]

Finally, Rowlandson details the "mob" of Native Americans celebrating a successful raid: "Oh the roaring and singing and dancing and yelling of those black creatures in the night, which made the place a lively resemblance of hell." With some members masked or wearing blackface and returned to a "savage" state of nature, the mob cavorting through Hutchinson's central hallway seemed like a replay of Indian madness. Like Rowlandson, Hutchinson created a captivating text to lend significance to the redressive passage of his soul. By implicating the language of both witchcraft and captivity narratives in his own diction, Hutchinson admits that, having lost mechanical control of his bodily facade, his body is now open, besieged by shame and piercing gestures, subjected to the limiting love of covenant politics. Having experienced the forced entry of the "mob" into his house-body, with its implication of political rape of an effeminized male body, Hutchinson felt the sting of moral correction. His shaming was now complete.[128]

By birth, upbringing, and profession a consummate consumer, Hutchinson was now placed in the role of scavenger. "Many articles of clothing & [a] good part

Figure 98. John Singleton Copley, *Nicholas Boylston*, ca. 1769. Oil on canvas, H. 50¼" (127.6 cm), W. 40¼" (102.2 cm). (Photo: Museum of Fine Arts, Boston, Bequest of David P. Kimball)

of my plate," he stated, "have since been picked up in different quarters of the town." The crowd seems to have targeted his precious imported consumer goods as a means of critiquing his apparent distance from the quotidian existence and typical standard of living of laboring people. The list of Hutchinson's lost property reported by Governor Bernard is impressive for its detail and precision and included such items as "a chased gold head of a cane," "a new fashion'd gold chain and hook for a lady's watch," "a pair of ruby earings set in gold, and necklace," a "gauze handkerchief and sattin apron both flowered with gold," "silk shoes, brocaded silk, padufoy, damask lutestring gowns and petticoats," and "silver spoons." According to Hutchinson's own reckoning, other objects that indexed his cosmopolitan tastes were simply smashed: "a very good clock both clock & case broke to pieces and destroyed"; "8 bedsteads all broken to pieces two of them mahogany, bed cloaths, & c., a great part of which are wholly destroyed"; "a very large damask table cloth cut to pieces." The loss of stolen or broken objects came to more than £2,200. Despite his close attention to tracking down and recovering his scattered goods, Hutchinson had to use the courts to recover lost possessions and to make a claim on his suspended authority.[129]

For Hutchinson, the self-proclaimed Tacitus of New England, the results were still more traumatic for what he feared could never be recovered from his house's scattered wreckage; he discovered that the mob had not left "a single book or paper in it & have scattered or destroyed all the manuscript & other papers I had been collecting for 30 years together besides a great number of publick papers in my custody."[130] Governor Bernard, in his summary report to the earl of Halifax on the attack on Hutchinson's house, confirmed the extent of the loss of precious historical records:

> They went to work with a Rage scarce to be exemplified by the Most Savage People. Everything Moveable was destroyed in the most minute manner, except such Things of Value as were worth carrying off, among which was near 1000 Pounds sterling in Specie, besides a great quantity of family plate & c. But the loss to be most lamented is, that there was in one Room kept for that purpose a large & valuable Collection of Manuscripts & Original Papers which he had been gathering all his Lifetime, & to which all Persons who had been in Possession of Valuable Papers of a Publick Kind, had been contributing as to a publick Museum. As those related to the History & policy of the Country from the Time of its settlement to the present & was the only Collection, the loss to the publick is great & irretrievable, as it is to himself the Loss of the Papers of a family, which had made a figure in this Province for 130 Years.[131]

But a report the next day from Providence said outright that Hutchinson's house had been attacked because people did not like *his* version of *their* history. Not only did they destroy his manuscripts materials, but they broke apart the "museum" he had been assembling of New England rarities and then, in a move designed to destroy Hutchinson's personal history of family "effigies," slashed the family portraits that graced his lower rooms, symbolically defacing the cultural memory they encoded. The attack on Hutchinson's papers may also have been intended as a redress of the growing inequality of property control that afflicted working people with special intensity. Such a motive was not lost on Bernard, who noted that the papers in question were those specifically "relating to the claims and titles of this province; all dispersed, stolen and defaced, so that the damage in its consequences may be esteemed publickly as well as privately injurious."[132]

OLD RUINS, NEW FOUNDATIONS

Attacking a house was not merely an act of frenzied vandalism undertaken by mobs once they or their leader(s) had carefully selected an appropriate target for their legitimate hostility. It was an expressive form of planned symbolic violence that called attention to the fact that the victim was no longer acting in a morally responsible way. Like rough music and skimmingtons—and earlier Puritan iconophobic wreckage of "graven images" in established churches—attacks on houses were frontal assaults on people accused of moral transgression. As we have seen, however, the "mob" was a mixed entity, and so house attacks were externalized dismantlings of competing interpretations. The symbolic invocation of the "body" of Whig merchants and lawyers implied the model of coercive dependent relationships between "members" that Saint Paul had outlined in his letters to the Corinthians and that John Winthrop had stressed when he beheld beauty in a "conformity of parts." Yet this body had already accepted a mechanical model, and some of these individuals also lived behind cool Georgian facades. They had no interest in doing away with deference and the linkages between wealth, power, knowledge, and property it appropriately subsumed. What they wanted to accomplish through these symbolic murders, these violent ritual shamings, was to remind their leaders that a mechanical theory of politics and society demanded that each part accomplish its assigned movement. Mechanical metaphors ran with vigor through the veins of eighteenth-century political rhetoric. A rural clergyman in 1720 laid the language at the door of Boston's merchant princes: "'Why,' say the Traders, 'Do but two Things and the Wheels will all be set a moving again.'" Deriding higher taxes and extensions of royal patronage, one citizen worried in 1756 that government might become "merely a ministerial engine." Stamp master Andrew Oliver's brother, Peter, even claimed the "rabble" might behave predictably from a mechanical perspective. "The People in general," he said, "were like the Mobility of all Countries, perfect Machines, wound up by any Hand who might first take the Winch."[133] Philadelphian William Hicks in 1766 even described the English constitution—the great organic artifact of a body politic that Whigs were defending—as a "nice piece of machinery."[134]

Among artisans and the laboring classes, however, house attacks were a means of asserting a very different view of life. From their more radical republican perspective, the commonwealth was emphatically not a mechanism but rather a utopian, millennial fusion of body and soul. They did not look back on the hierarchic, federal covenant of Saint Paul's conservative interpreters and the regressive vision of power relations it demanded. Rather, they looked forward to a new social formation. They wanted to purge the social body of too much money concentrated in one place, that "blood of social politics" that, according to William Petty, "is but the fat of the Body-politick, whereof too much doth as often hinder its Agility as too little makes it sick."[135] Radical republican millennialism informed not only the house attacks of 1765 but also a series of evangelically driven assaults on brothels, in which mobs moved against institutions of symbolic exchange that made immoral conversions of people into interchangeable commodities. In March 1737, for example, a "great number of People" attacked a "House of bad Fame" and "were so irritated as to break all the Glass Windows, and stave in the Doors . . . so that the Woman who kept the same, has been obliged to quit it."[136] They wanted to vilify what they believed was an attempt by those in control of money and power to see society, economy, and the body per se as machines, running according to their own inner laws, protected like Georgian houses by separable facades and detached from providential revelation by slipping gears of form and language. As Governor Bernard feared, from a radical perspective house assaults insisted on *"generall levelling & taking away [of] the Distinction of rich and poor."*[137]

As a form of symbolic violence that mobilized people of all ranks, the house attack in colonial New England performed different kinds of cultural work on a variety of symbolic levels. The element of cruel or dark play in these events "can erupt suddenly" and usually "subverts order, dissolves frames, breaks its own rules, so that the playing itself is in danger of being destroyed." The dark play characteristic of house attacks varies from most other performance modalities in that instead of "breaking though" into a performance frame, or "breaking out" into an assumed fictive role during performance, it often *breaks apart*, or deconstructs, as the action develops.[138] Houses "pulled down" crash to the ground, chairs break in pieces, the mob articulates its own internal differences and goals. Inversion, frame breaking, metacommentary through social entropy, and the parodic quality of momentary self-dissolution are the ludic elements most characteristic of crowd actions in early New England. As one form of festive or playful violence, the house attack defined the individual dwelling as the prime public index of property rights and claims to authority. The concept of "house" itself indexed a complicated set of associations: of household and family, of lineage and rank, of effigies and cultural memory, of divine and earthly embodiment. As a trope for the changing constructed meanings of the human body, the house assumed the symbolic role of representing material consumption as a disease.

The house attack was a symbolic performance that permitted participants on both sides of the facade, each through their own broken-windowed view, to construct speculatively and literally through parody, politics, and social pain the mixed social vision that defined for New England the revolutionary ethos itself: a fluid blend of liberal thought on open markets tempered by fervent millennialism, which tied the interchangeable images and people of the mechanized marketplace to the radical promise of spiritual renewal. This novel combination suggested a way that people in revolutionary New England might productively reread John Cotton's 1651 sermon *Purchasing Christ*. Paradoxically, as it linked buildings, bodies, and political appearances through the purgative process of destruction, the ritual house attack was central in defining what Cotton termed "the sacred rights of Domicil" in the new nation.[139]

THERE IS A SENSE IN WHICH

A POEM OR STORY BEING

SPOKEN, OR MUSIC BEING

PLAYED, EMPHASIZES THE

PRESENCE OF THE SPEAKER

OR PLAYER. WHEREAS A

VISUAL IMAGE, SO LONG AS

IT IS NOT BEING USED AS

4 Disappearing Acts

A MASK OR AS A DISGUISE,

IS ALWAYS A COMMENT ON

ABSENCE. THE DEPICTION

COMMENTS ON THE ABSENCE

OF WHAT IS BEING DEPICTED.

VISUAL IMAGES, BASED ON

APPEARANCES, ALWAYS SPEAK

OF *DIS*APPEARANCES.

—JOHN BERGER,

"PAINTING AND TIME"

ANATOMY LESSONS

In January 1788, a penitent painter named Ralph Earl was released from a debtor's cell in the attic of New York's city hall. He had been incarcerated for fifteen months. He was an artist of proven talent. As a youth, Earl had studied carefully the works of John Singleton Copley, lived in London during the mid-1780s, and basked in the aura surrounding American expatriate Benjamin West. He had already completed a series of impressive portraits of numerous leading citizens in early national New York. As he walked into the light of morning a free man, he met his appointed legal guardian, Dr. Mason Fitch Cogswell. Cogswell was an upstanding New York physician whose membership in the Society for the Relief of Distressed Debtors provided an opportunity both to "administer to the comfort of prisoners, by providing food, fuel, clothing, and the necessaries of life," and to "procure the liberation of such as were confined for small sums, and were of meritorious conduct, by discharging their debts." Because he had known of the painter's skill in taking likenesses, the doctor intervened and secured Earl's freedom.[1]

Cogswell did more than pull Earl from the darkness of debt and enforced discipline. He took him to Hartford, Connecticut, when he moved there late in 1789. In relocating his medical practice to Hartford, Cogswell was in a sense moving back home, having grown up a minister's son in nearby Scotland. As Hartford grew in size and wealth after the Revolution, Cogswell saw a market primed for an ambitious physician. For Earl the move proved more than convenient, as over the next decade he painted a steady stream of local Connecticut landowners, their houses, and their land. Almost without exception, his sitters came from the well-connected ranks of Cogswell's patients. As Cogswell examined the bodies of the gentry and prescribed cures, Earl was busy constructing an alternative anatomy of late-eighteenth-century Connecticut society.[2]

How could a painter possibly make apparent those lines of circulation and nervous connection that one pass of a surgeon's scalpel might reveal? Was a brush like a blade? Of course, the painter laid bare the nervous lines of connection and circulation in the social body, not the literal one. And Earl accomplished one feat that Cogswell could not approach; through the limned appearance of his sitters, Earl in fact oversaw the exact terms of their bodily disappearance, their conversion into substitutional icons that made their painted absence in some ways more powerful than their physical presence. Offering anatomy lessons of this sort placed Earl at the center of a swirl of conflicting images in the early Republic. In the wake of the Revolution competing interests fought over proper government, market growth and direction, and religion. The language of republican ideology focused anew on questions hotly debated before the war. Should property and political privilege be directly linked? How should the quest for an elusive ancient "virtue" relate to markets? Can citizens pursue private gain and not sacrifice the benefits of civil society in the process? How, precisely, are such social and political concerns possibly connected with the symbolic, anatomical art of portrait painting?

A brief summary of recent work in cultural history will help to position Ralph Earl's work in critical terms and suggest why his elite Connecticut sitters were particularly sensitive to the management of disappearances. Earl spent time during the mid-1780s in Benjamin West's London studio and thus would have been familiar with the spell Joshua Reynolds cast over English academic training of the day. According to John Barrell, Reynolds's early lectures to the Royal Academy derived initially from the received aesthetic theories of Richardson and Shaftesbury; he argued that England was a "republic of taste" much like a political republic, with various genres arrayed vertically. History painting was at the head of the tasteful state, and portrait painting closer to its feet. All painting potentially struggled with the problem of the portrayed body. The body as a common central focus of depiction necessarily effaced or occluded differences among people and asserted their generic similarity and ultimate uniformity as national citizens. But to make a painting interesting, Reynolds suggested in his final *Discourses*, interchangeable faces had to vary. However, the representation of "singularity" of bodily detail or individual "character" created anxiety for a discourse of civic humanism, as it indexed an economic model of self-interest at odds with the smooth workings of the collective embodied state. Like little commonwealths, paintings struggled to mediate between the privacy of singular images and spectators imagining a collective public sphere. Style was not about persuasion or rhetorical force; rather, it was a philosophy of action that sought to efface any division between a spectator's uniform public identity as citizen and his or her private identity or interest. But if painting was less rhetorical at heart than politically contemplative, it could also be dangerously ambiguous.[3]

If paintings riveted attention on questions of commonwealth and individual identity, it is possible to puzzle out answers at the level of the family as well as the state; writing in the context of English colonial control over Ireland, as early as 1735 George Berkeley had pondered "whether a nation might not be considered as a family." In a 1987 essay, Margaretta M. Lovell explored what she termed "a puzzling shift" in the composition of early American family portraits. Prior to 1760 group portraits generally revolved around an authoritative father figure, to whom wife and children defer and look for symbolic guidance. But after 1760, the mother gradually becomes the focus of the composition, while her children pleasantly distract a playful father standing near the edge of the canvas, sometimes with his side toward the viewer. Such a shift roughly correlates with historian Lawrence Stone's argument that the eighteenth century witnessed the emergence of affective individualism and "companionate" marriages in which emotional bonds and sentimentality were viewed with a new approval. Fathers could relax as benign protectors rather than create the distance essential to play judgmental patriarchs. Unlike earlier students of American portraits who read portraits as *reflective* of change elsewhere in society, Lovell argued that portraits themselves played a *constitutive* or *transformative* role in social relations. "It is clear that in the mime show of the portrait (as in the newly popular medium of the novel)," she asserts, "certain fictions and ideals are being asserted that helped the early modern family adjust to the status of new economic and social relationships."[4]

Interpreting portraits as affecting presences that assert constructive fictions demands an important shift in approach, from one that views likenesses as "reflections" or "memorials" of social life to one that sees the work deeply implicated in the deferential dialectic of power and consent. Timothy H. Breen intensified the shift in 1990 by connecting portraits to broader processes of self-fashioning in eighteenth-century England and America. From Breen's perspective, too much attention has been paid by previous scholars to stock issues of pose, gesture, and composition. Instead, he directs the viewer to consider the importance of the clothing, wigs, swords, furniture, and the play of sensory surfaces within the confines of the canvas. Breen argues that the fluid image-production characteristic of consumer culture led to a transformed, more private self whose only hope of imagining national citizenship was dependent on a faith—an evangelical belief in the symbolic efficacy of objects to alter social states—that others who owned similar commodities must be kindred spirits. This perspective "directs our attention away from purely aesthetic judgments and encourages us to situate their work within a world of commerce. It helps us to understand how they wove the materials and experiences of everyday life onto a distinctly new set of visual symbols." Breen allows us to see that consumer goods did the same sort of imaginary work in early America as novels, newspapers, and advertisements did in the metaphysics of nationalism outlined by Benedict Anderson. And as Reynolds realized, portraits require us to contemplate the inner tensions and mixed intentions of this national imaginary; they are "interpretations devised by artists and sitters of their place within an imagined Anglo-American society."[5]

These works depict portraits as packed with political ambivalence, as fictive constructions of imagined commonwealths that depend on the metaphysics of the marketplace for grace as well as power. While they reference the discourse of civic humanism, they complicate its elitist intellectual appeal by immersing national citizens in the costume of commerce: silk shirts, creased foreheads, hands lined by work and desire. Each image vibrates with conflicts. In an unanticipated way, disappearance eclipses appearance. Another way of considering this difficult shift focuses on the framing of public representations of time using the notions of continuity and contingency. According to J. G. A. Pocock, the dimension of continuity directs us to the "complex of institutions" that make up a society and, by "transmitting its forms of authority," maintain the legitimacy of those in power. When we consider the dimension of contingency, however, "we become aware of other and less institutionalized phenomena," including groups, ideologies, and everyday actions that oppose the centralizing logic of dominant culture. With contingency, Pocock adds, "we are in the domain of fortune, as it used to be called: of the unpredictable contingencies and emergencies which challenge the human capacity to apprehend and to act, and which may appear either exterior or interior to the institutional structure of society." In the realm of contingent time, "the structure [of society] is seen as striving to maintain itself in a time not created by it, but rather given to it by some agency, purposive or purposeless, not yet defined. It may succeed or fail in maintaining itself; and if it succeeds, this may mean that it succeeds in preserving its own existence in the midst of a history it does not otherwise modify, or that it succeeds in imposing itself on exterior time and re-creating the latter in the image of its own continuity."[6]

If the representation of time was thus split, then Earl's portraits of New England's postrevolutionary, rural elites disappear into the continuity of authority and institutional legitimacy; they move into the continuity of allegorical illusion. They retreat from the contingency of situated citizenship, where dissenting voices challenge their control of political and religious institutions. In the discussion that follows, I argue that Earl's sitters used having a "likeness" made in order to position themselves in the disappeared, continuous time of allegory, a zone within the present tense in which they could deny the politics of everyday life, domesticate the ephemeral to the mythic, calibrate concepts of virtue, and assert a hierarchic national image in the decade following the ratification of the Constitution. They reframed the contingent time of "real" appearance among social inferiors in the past. Seen in such a critical light, Earl's painted anatomy of Connecticut's late-eighteenth-century elite reveals how portraits themselves actively shaped the selective process of remembering and forgetting at the heart of national images and imagination.

Earl's portraits show that although Breen's putative realm of "purely aesthetic judgments" may have been illusory, it nonetheless provided a screen through which a politics of self-interest and class prerogative could be continually allegorized as a "natural" part of national embodiment. But nations are inherently unstable political forms. Revolutions happen. New citizens declare independent states and independent states of mind. Nations are marked by histories of transition and fragmentation, shifting terms of allegiance and membership, and a "wavering between vocabularies." The rhetoric of national affiliation can be treacherously subtle. What are the implications of using words like "the people," "the state," "high culture," and "folklore" during moments of colonial resistance and national consolidation? As Homi K. Bhabha has suggested, these qualities and terms define the nation as one of the "major structures of ideological ambivalence within the cultural representation of modernity," an ideological ambivalence strikingly similar, with its coupling of dreams and danger, to the vision of Englishness John Barrell discovered in the unfolding logic of Reynold's *Discourses*.[7] How, then, did people in Ralph Earl's New England actually *image* the nation as they both defined and lived through its emergence? How did his portraits of elite bodies in Connecticut, Massachusetts, and Vermont represent the ambivalent coexistence of republican virtue and material greed, restraint and danger in their lives? How did these disappearing acts work their magic on space and time?

THE OPERATION

Disappearance begins with appearance in a familiar place. Earl painted Oliver Ellsworth and Abigail Wolcott Ellsworth at Elmwood, their Windsor, Connecticut, home, in 1792 (fig. 99). The scene appears unified. Oliver and Abigail rest serenely amid the confident surroundings of their pastoral country seat. The portrait, however, splits in two, its parts broken by the threshold of a window frame. In the foreground the Ellsworths are surrounded by the acquired stage sets of material prosperity. They pose comfortably in a parlor they recently added to the house. They sit in chairs that were part of a set just acquired from Aaron Chapin of Hartford, the town's premier cabinetmaker, who had been trained in Philadelphia; their acquisition marks the first documented purchase of such refined neoclassical furniture in the Connecticut River valley. Although the Ellsworths were wealthy by Connecticut standards, their clothing is deliberately not avant-garde. It is restrained; it signals their acuity at strategically identifying with social inferiors in a culture acutely critical of ostentation. Part of Judge Ellsworth's extensive library reveals an active pursuit of titles in the provincial book trade. An ornate imported carpet lies beneath their feet. "Their portrait," costume historian Aileen Ribeiro has written, "was the final symbol of their ascendency to a position of political and social leadership."[8]

Beyond the parlor window, in the background, stands the very house in which the Ellsworths sit. In standard painterly convention, the house is rendered not in commodity cross section but for its value as an emblem, as a compressed metaphor representing the rising and hopefully assured permanence of kin, estate, and social embodiment. It is a fixed, transparent symbol of bloodline on the land. It announces an active and powerful present, proclaims a hopeful future, and predicts an accomplished past. Earl was fond of using this painterly trick. It appears in many of his portraits and was imitated by Joseph Steward, among other followers. In another guise the same device had gained popularity during the eighteenth century as people placed pictures of their house and lands as overmantels in polite parlors. An example from the early-eighteenth-century mansion of Boston merchant William Clark survives and shows his impressive brick structure, an elaborate doorway, and the iron fence that protected it from the street. In the early eighteenth century some people even owned chests of drawers with one or two Georgian mansions painted across their front. But the greater number of surviving house portraits suggest an increasing popularity of such split signs or doubled portraiture during the last two decades of the eighteenth century. Under Earl's hand the emblem itself sometimes becomes the subject of play. In his portrait of his cousin Thomas Earle, no horizontal sash intrudes to remind the viewer of the window's presence (fig. 100). Instead, the imaginary window could also be a frame within a frame, presenting the house beyond as a picture hanging, trophylike, in Thomas's interior. Unsure whether the device frames a two-dimensional area or yields to the recession of three-dimensional space, the spectator finds that his or her own location is thus indeterminate.

The semiotic space opened by the window frame articulates the separation of the immediate, private world of commodity accumulation and the quickening speed of changing fashion from the emblematic house-body in the distance, a sign of changelessness. The permeation of New England by imported commodities was nearly complete, as estate inventories and travelers' observations from the

Figure 99. Ralph Earl, *Oliver Ellsworth and Abigail Wolcott Ellsworth*, 1792. Oil on canvas, H. 76" (193 cm), W. 86¾" (220.4 cm). (Photo: Wadsworth Atheneum, Hartford, Gift of the Ellsworth heirs)

area make clear. When Englishman William Strickland set out for western Massachusetts from Albany in late October 1794, he noticed that the countryside he traversed was already saturated with ready-mades. "It is surprising to see how perfectly English, even to the minutest articles, every thing is one meets with in this country to the remotest place we have yet been in," he observed. "The Ladies may be accomodated with every article of the perfume shop fresh imported from London, and . . . earrings might be purchased which the fertile brain of a London Jeweller had invented as lately as the last spring. Of more material accomodations nothing is wanting; of modes and customs, manners of living, and of ideas with few exceptions, all are English."[9] If the availability of consumer goods he observed in New York and western New England was far advanced, it had already penetrated such prosperous Connecticut towns as Hartford, Windsor, Suffield, and New Haven. As commodities turning to the wind of fashion, these objects tried to change people into things. At the same time, the mansions in the distant background of Earl's portraits referenced the memory of mad play of attacked houses, house-bodies, and the house as emblem of family; these icons tried to transform objects into people. The juxtaposition of these implicated worlds focused anoth-

Figure 100. Ralph Earl, *Thomas Earle*, 1800. Oil on canvas, H. 37⅝" (95.7 cm), W. 33⅞" (86 cm). (Photo: National Gallery of Art, Andrew W. Mellon Collection)

er tension in the portrait, one that also evoked revolutionary culture. Writing to Thomas Pownall in 1770, Samuel Cooper admitted, "I could wish with you that we were at all Times wise eno[ugh] to distinguish *Things f[ro]m Persons*, and to place ourselves on the broadest and most constitutional Bottom."[10]

The portrait implies that the Ellsworths live somewhere between the interior realm of private prerogative and the exterior world of public restraint and that their high social rank demands they effectively maintain a tension between the contingency of lived social relations and the continuity of allegorical representation. This doubling of representational strategies suggests why these paintings moved Earl's polite sitters—the Ellsworths, Boardmans, Taylors, and Bostwicks, among others—in an aesthetic sense, for they effectively embodied and intensified the felt tensions that defined the ambiguous moral space that new elites occupied in the late colony or early Republic; as Hannah Arendt suggested, they inhabited "that curiously hybrid realm where private interests assume public significance."[11]

MARKETS AND MANNERS

In the new moral space of residual colonialism and emergent nationalism an abstract concept of virtue conditioned how people perceived the contingency of social relations. How did Earl's elite sitters understand virtue? Although the arguments of intellectual historians, who have explored the concept of virtue in detail, occasionally abstract it from the mundane pressures of daily life, they nonetheless provide a genealogy of the concept. "Virtue" has a complicated history in political discourse. As it developed within classical republican thought, it could mean a devotion to the public good rooted in the willing sacrifice of self-interest to that of the community as a whole, or the practice of relations of equality between citizens engaged in ruling and those being ruled, or the active ruling quality (from the Italian *virtù*) that confronted the vagaries of *fortuna* with the firm resolve of benevolent citizens acting in public. For Montaigne, virtue consisted of moral virtue, Christian virtue, and political virtue, the last of which, J. G. A. Pocock has argued, was "formally unlike the others and entailed a devotion to equality before the laws of the republic."[12] In a specifically American context, Gordon S. Wood has reiterated the essential aspects of virtue in the classical republican tradition. "In a republic . . . each man must somehow be persuaded to submerge his personal wants into the greater good of the whole," he writes. "This willingness of the individual to sacrifice his private interests for the good of the community, patriotism or love of country—the eighteenth century termed 'public virtue.'" Wood even suggests an aesthetic of "frail beauty" for classical republicanism, rooted perhaps in the delicate heroism of public sacrifice.[13]

Perhaps the prescriptive model of sacrificial citizenship was recognized. When an individual failed to act in accordance with such a standard of virtue, the community's trust in that person was violated, and it was up to responsible citizens to make their grievances known through efficient networks of local gossip, public meetings, corrective ritual acts, or in the popular press. A willingness to be virtuous in a republic depended on citizens being allowed to participate in the legitimate authority that ruled them, including participation in property rights. An initial problem lay in ensuring that property and an attendant pursuit of individual freedom be held in check, to keep society safe against the moral corruptions of avarice, wealth, and luxury. One position argued that such a system need not exchange outright new ideas of equality and economic liberalism for the older blessings of prerevolutionary deference. John Adams had stated this position in 1776 with a force that almost all of Earl's sitters later endorsed: "There must be a Decency, and Respect, and Veneration introduced for Persons in Authority, of every Rank, or we are undone."[14]

Adams's call for continuity in social discipline as a basis for the exercise of virtue and political equality echoed unevenly throughout the troubled period of the revolutionary settlement. After independence, the barriers separating virtue from commerce were falling; the free but ordered marketplace appeared more as a source of positive rationality—a regulator of character and a public check on the danger of private passions—than of corruption. We therefore discover a postrevolutionary embrace of the liberating mutability of identity implicit in the consumer revolution by the same public figures who had earlier argued persuasively for the public virtues of restraint and "competency." It suggests the paradoxical and contested nature of "virtue" within their psyches. In the first half of the eighteenth century, republican ideology and the principles of virtue and self-control it encapsulated represented more often a reactionary than a radical ethic. As Michael Zuckerman has suggested, "one function of republican ideas was to enable provincial patriots [like many who after the war sat for portraits] to absolve themselves of responsibility for the untoward aspects of their activities and ambitions. Civic humanism permitted them precisely to project their anxiety for their spiritual safety and ethical identity onto the British, decrying as they did the sinister transoceanic design 'to undermine the moral and economic independence of the colonies.' So long as they concentrated on their assumptive virtue, they did not have to dwell on their eagerness for imported commodities."[15]

The market was republican in that it provided a means for citizens to participate directly in the public sphere and so provided an arena in which questions of moral responsibility and ethical restraint in larger society were pivotal. This understanding stood behind Timothy Dwight's bitter yet puzzled indictment of New Haven's market in 1796. Dwight (1752–1817) was far from being the disinterested observer of the Connecticut scene that the copious objective detail of his posthumously published *Travels through New England and New York* might suggest. The views and descriptive passages of Dwight—president of Yale, descendant of a Connecticut Valley "River God" family, and grandson of Jonathan Edwards—are complex but far from politically neutral. He was an individual whose range of interests and experiences spanned seemingly opposed positions and whose activities regularly interwove pastoral poetry and the aesthetics of high mercantilism.[16]

Dwight defended the ancient virtue of propertied citizens at every turn, found idyllic pleasure while gazing at the georgic triumph of work over nature, and promoted public markets. Of New Haven's hesitancy to adopt a regulated market he wrote, "The greatest evil which the inhabitants suffer is the want of a regular system. A few years since, a new market was established in a convenient part of the town under proper regulation." Regulation and public oversight of periodic exchange was the key issue. Dwight favored regulated markets in part because he feared that peddling, a type of commercial activity that was not public and therefore took place beyond the surveillance of the marketplace, was morally subversive and distracting. In Suffield, he argued that peddlers "who begin life with bargaining for small wares almost invariably become sharpers. The commanding aim of every such man will soon be to make a good bargain, and he will speedily consider every gainful bargain a good one." For Dwight, the unchecked pursuit of the good bargain led to unrestrained self-interest, deception, the dangers of social unrest. "The tricks of fraud will assume in his dealing the same place which commercial skill and an honorable system of dealing hold in the mind of a merchant. Often employed in disputes, he becomes noisy, pertinacious, and impudent." He also worried that participation in an unregulated market could never lead citizens to virtuous lives; he pondered: "There is something very remarkable in the hostility of the New England people to a regular market. . . . Those who buy and those who sell manifest this opposition alike," he observed. Yet despite their resistance to the rational calculus of regular exchange, Dwight allowed, "the fact *is*, however, an epicure may find all of his wishes satisfied without much difficulty in this town."[17] At issue was the guarantee of moral conduct in the public arena, not any concern over the "corrupting" or weakening effects of imported commodities. By advocating regulated market exchange as a proof of virtue and monitor of transgression, Dwight expressed his enthusiasm for what Joyce Appleby has termed the "chaste and venerable classical republicanism distilled by Harrington for English needs and updated by Montesquieu for eighteenth-century readers." This view of the marketplace as theater of moral action provided an apt metaphor to one of the principal authors to whom American patriots more radical than Dwight had turned in support of their cause. According to Thomas Paine's *Dissertation on First Principles of Government* (1795), "The public good is, as it were, a common bank in which every individual has his respective share; and consequently whatever damage that sustains, the individual unavoidably partakes of that calamity."[18]

Ministers and politicians sought to protect citizens from the dangers of wanton luxury by proscribing public conduct itself. Pocock observes that as markets emerged as a moral, rational force, people entered "an increasingly transactional universe of 'commerce and the arts,'" in which a new set of "multiplying relationships more than compensated for the loss of antique virtue by an indefinite and perhaps infinite enrichment of his [or her] personality." Yet "progress in commerce," translated into "progress in the arts," raised a double possibility: "Culture could either expand to embrace new segments of the populace, or, again, it could lead to still more 'corruption of virtue.'"[19] To protect political virtue, people had to cultivate social manners. Manners orchestrated ease, but they also defined levels of social pretension and ambition. As Edmund Burke argued in 1796, "manners are of more importance than Laws. . . . They aid morals, they supply them, or they totally destroy them."[20] Manners included a wide range of symbolic forms, from behavior in public places, to architecture, to table manners, to proper style in conversation. At the time Earl was working, the assumed cultural exclusivity of the eighteenth-century gentry was under siege. A thirst for respectability moved through rural New England society. Abroad on the land came a new fashion for polite houses, popular theaters, local lending libraries, and country newspapers. Cultural entrepreneurs of all sorts found new markets. Manners were more effective than public markets; they inculcated self-regulation as a necessary discipline of virtuous citizens.

Consider Dwight's penned portrait of Oliver Ellsworth, the man whom Earl painted sitting in his parlor while his house waited outside. A series of remarkable but conflicting qualities made him, in Dwight's opinion, a paradigm of power and grace, the landed gentleman of mannerly virtue:

> Mr. Ellsworth was formed to be a great man. His person was tall, dignified, and commanding; and his manners, though wholly destitute of haughtiness and arrogance, were such as irresistibly to excite in others, wherever he was present, the sense of inferiority. His very attitude inspired awe. His imagination was uncommonly vivid, his wit brilliant and piercing, his logical powers very great, and his comprehension fitted for capacious views and vast designs. Intense thought appeared to be his amusement, and he unfolded his views on every occasion with an arrangement singularly clear and luminous. . . . His eloquence, and indeed almost every other part of his character, was peculiar. Always possessed of his own scheme of thought concerning every subject which he discussed; ardent, bold, intense, and masterly; his conceptions were just and great, his reasonings invincible, his images glowing, his sentiments noble, his phraseology remarkable for its clearness and precision, his style concise and strong, and his utterance vehement and overwhelming. . . . To this superfluity of intelligence his moral attributes were peculiarly suited. In private life he was just and amiable. In his manner of living, although possessed of an ample fortune, he blended with a happy propriety, plainness and dignity. Affable, frank, obliging, easy of access, equally sprightly and instructive in his conversation, he was an uncommonly agreeable man. In public life his impartiality, fairness, integrity, and patriotism awed and defied even calumny and suspicion.[21]

Like Dwight himself, Ellsworth was a study in cultural contradiction. His "manner of living" suggests paradoxes within "republican virtue" for Earl's rural elite sitters. Devoid of arrogance, Ellsworth nonetheless made others feel "the sense of inferiority." He was "sprightly and instructive in his conversation" and "uncommonly agreeable" by nature, yet "his utterance [was] vehement and overwhelming" at the same time. "Easy of access," "affable," and "frank," he still organized the world around him from a one-point, hierarchic perspective ("always possessed of his own scheme of thought concerning every subject"), as if the apparatus of the panopticon had merged with his subjective psyche.

Social manners inscribed political virtue. Social manners allow us to look at Earl's body of work and describe an "aesthetics of virtue" as one refraction of their politics. They permit us to consider individuals like Oliver Ellsworth as particularly subtle image makers eager to situate themselves in an allegory of classical republican virtue—as champions of equality, defenders of freehold property rights, protagonists of a classless society, patriots who, like Cincinnatus of old, have sacrificed private interests to the collective will—while at the same time, following John Adams, arguing that authority must not crumble and effectively grafting themselves into a prerevolutionary matrix that linked kinship, church polity, government position, and wealth. Ellsworth, after all, "inspired awe" but was "uncommonly agreeable." He "had vast designs," died "possessed of an ample fortune," but presented "in public life his impartiality, integrity and patriotism." Ellsworth was an aristocrat of the new republican order, and, as John Adams observed, "the state of Connecticut has always been governed by an aristocracy, more decisively than the empire of Britain is. Half a dozen, or, at most a dozen families, have controlled that country when a colony, as well as since it has been a state."[22] The trick facing many of Ralph Earl's sitters was to remain an aristocrat but not to appear aristocratic, to engage the commodity life as an inconspicuous consumer, and to play out unsettling implications of private desire in the theater of public restraint.

CONTINGENCY

Allegory often entails a symbolic displacement or temporal disappearance for purposes of moral instruction or political consolidation. If Earl's portraits, serving as stand-ins for their absent subjects, marked their disappearance into allegory, where did they go? As we shall see, they attempted to fashion a classical republican idyll as the present tense of the nation; they plundered the past for a set of images and props they could use to remain in control of contemporary events. They did so because not all aspects of life in the early Republic yielded to equality and happiness, and by allegorizing the present they could also make certain competing interests and people disappear as well. Hence Earl's portraits manage a kind of double disappearance. Like all portraits they mark the disappearance of the sitter; in the case of these Connecticut portraits, they also attempt to make other people vanish.

The "land of steady habits," Connecticut loses some of its steadiness when we admit that cultural or political consensus had been undercut by the time of the Revolution owing to the combined effects of reactions to church discipline, differing local textures of the Great Awakening, and social fragmentation linked to Loyalist leanings in the early 1770s. Even by then, one historian has argued, "a closer scrutiny of Connecticut on the local level reveals our tidy image of political consensus to be more apparent than real." The irregular fallout, both political and cultural, of the revolutionary settlement was everywhere apparent.[23] Older Connecticut towns displayed little uniformity in material prosperity. Living in the old river towns of Hartford, Windsor, and Middletown, some of Earl's sitters had been raised in landscapes of mixed social references. Central-chimney houses remained dominant, but even artisans in some towns had recently built impressive Georgian mansions, suggesting a desire to play for power and influence in a wider social field.

The appropriation of fashion across class lines in Wethersfield, a town adjacent to Hartford, resulted in a sense of social ambiguity. The town contains forty dwelling houses built before 1790. As built, twenty-nine of these were central-chimney structures, almost all of which were two stories high and had irregularly spaced windows. Twenty-one retained the end-gable door, suggesting, as we have already seen, that coercive rituals of hospitality deriving from postmedieval cross-passage houses continued in Connecticut until the very end of the eighteenth century. Among the owners of these houses were seven artisans, six merchants or mariners, one minister, and one lawyer; on average, these individuals had forty-seven pounds' worth of taxable property the year they began building. Another eleven houses had two chimneys and were built on a Georgian plan. All of these structures had two stories, and all but one were five bays in width. But other features show the extent to which Georgian form was altered when built in Wethersfield. All but one of the houses had irregular window spacing, a far cry from the crisp mathematical proportions of a "typical" Georgian facade. Seven retained the traditional pitched roof; four had a fashionable gambrel roof that symbolically associated them in local terms with the marked authority of public buildings. These owners were, on average, worth eighty-five pounds the year their houses went up. Two of these local Georgian houses even retained the end-gable door; these structures were thus hybrids of postmedieval and neo-Palladian plan and social function. Finally, only three of these Wethersfield mansions boasted an ornamental door frame.[24]

But two of the householders who built Georgian houses in Wethersfield were artisans: joiner Samuel Butler and tanner Isaac Stevens. And their presence lay at the core of the problem for Earl's patrons. Tradesmen in fact disrupted the social landscape of many old Connecticut towns. The rise of artisans to positions of influence in the New England countryside was never common but was immediately visible. After all, these were often the individuals whom the landed gentry paid to construct, decorate, and furnish their own estates. Here was a paradox the withdrawing gentry faced: as they sought to separate themselves from the plebeians beneath them, they effectively put more liquid capital into the hands of the craftsmen whose skills they relied on for markers of social difference. As a result, artisans had more work, attained greater wealth, and invested some of it in new real estate. Some of the images seemed hollow, like so many stage sets for social climbing. Looking at the large houses recently raised in Enfield, English traveler Thomas Anburey noticed in 1789 that "most of them were only one half finished, the other half having only the rough timbers that support the building . . . but as the houses are entirely compleat on the outside, and the windows all glazed, they have the appearance of being finished, but on entering a house, you cannot help lamenting that the owner was unable to complete it." And when the houses were properly finished, not all were as impressive inside as a passerby might have guessed. Visiting Dr. Eliot Rawson in Middletown in 1771, John Adams remarked disdainfully that his house was "handsome without, but neither clean nor elegant within, either in furniture or anything else."[25]

There was more operating here than simply a lack of resources necessary to accomplish a grand house in a single build. Anburey even learned some of it: "Upon inquiry I found, that when a man builds a house, he leaves it in this [unfinished] state till his son marries, when he fits it up for his family, and the father and son live under one roof, as though they were two distinct houses." The large residence was planned to operate as a late-eighteenth-century "unit-system" structure, ensuring that amid the vagaries of partible inheritance at least one child would be sure to inherit and carry on the home place. Even Anburey's observation of the single mansion functioning as "two distinct houses" was accurate; four-room Georgian houses with two internal chimneys were uniformly referred to as "double houses" throughout the eighteenth century. Hence what looked like impoverished theater to the local gentry actually signified a strategy of surviving on the land. These houses, husks of space and social grace, thus were a declaration of faith in material prosperity over time on the part of laboring people. By 1768 a tailor in Glastonbury and a joiner in Farmington had also announced their arrival in "genteel" society by slapping ostentatious pedimented doorways on otherwise humble houses.[26]

Variations in the land itself articulated the social differences at work. Ranging from the extreme northwestern towns of Sharon and Litchfield to the older settlements of Hartford and Windsor along the Connecticut River, and east to include Woodstock, Norwich, and New London, the topography varied between lowland areas in the river valleys and along the coast of Long Island Sound and upland and intervale in the western part of the state and to the east of the Connecticut River valley (fig. 101). Along with topographical differences, although not corresponding to them in any predictable manner, soil types and qualities ranged widely, suggesting varying levels of surplus agrarian output and market engagement. Before the Revolution, these towns differed also in population density, levels of artisanal activity and trade, and the average terms and turnover rates of their deputies to the General Assembly in Hartford. Broadly speaking, established centers of trade and political activity, including Hartford, Middletown, and New Haven, had the longest average terms in office of their legislators. This ensured stability, perhaps, but repeated a prerevolutionary emphasis on the domination of local politics by key families; the clan groups may have changed since the 1770s, but state politics was still family politics. Next in line came secondary inland centers such as Litchfield and Danbury, followed closely by secondary ports and, finally, country towns (table 10). Political stability and local control were greatest in towns with better-quality soil. Indeed, with the exception of hinterland Newtown, the remaining four country towns where Earl's sitters lived had the worst soil in the state. Between 1767 and 1790, pressure intensified for newly opened lands, the settlement of children on inherited property, and access to new sources of water power. Connecticut saw the establishment of twenty-nine new towns. In these new towns the landscape was less confusing than fiercely competitive.[27]

In the existing terrain of markets and morals, Georgian houses and blurred social relations, conflicts over institutional structure and control made apparent the contingency of privilege and power on the maintenance of social discipline. The political antagonisms of the late 1780s, especially during the stormy constitutional debates of 1786–87, climaxed as those in authority (called Federalists, after their belief that social hierarchy and a strong, centralized government would safeguard democracy) found their position openly challenged by a rising opposition group of anti-Federalists, persons of middling rank seeking to consolidate their right to vote and own land. The critical moment for the debate focused on the anti-Federalists' charge that their opponents did not support the framing of a new state constitution guaranteeing basic rights and were in favor of limiting town representation to one assemblyman each, thereby weakening the role of towns in participatory democracy. In 1787 Benjamin Gale pointed out that the Connecticut royal charter of 1662 had never been approved by the freemen and therefore could not be assumed to be an adequate base of a new civil government. In *A System of the Laws of Connecticut* (1795), itself a lengthy defense of the charter, attorney

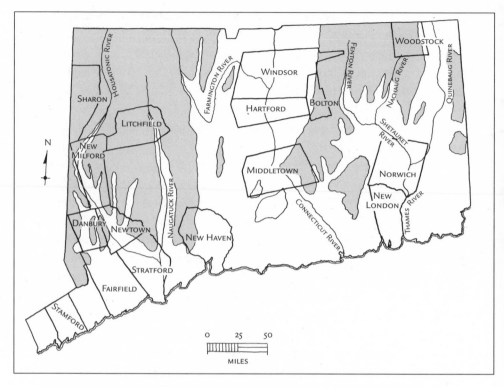

Figure 101. Topography of Connecticut, showing towns where Ralph Earl worked. Key: shaded areas indicate upland terrain of more than 500 feet above sea level; unshaded areas show lowland areas of less than 500 feet. (Map by the author)

Zephaniah Swift countered: "The constitution of this state is a representative republic. Some visionary theorists have pretended that we have no constitution, because it has not been reduced to writing, and ratified by the people. It is, therefore, necessary to trace the constitution of our government to its origin, for the purpose of showing its existence, that it has been accepted and approved of by the people, and is well known and precisely bounded."[28]

Swift argued for an unbroken continuity in civil authority, grounding Federalist prerogative in the 1790s on the legitimacy of the Royal Charter of 1662 and in an irreproachable ethical commitment by the gentry to honor an essentially oral history of republican government. This contrasted, in his mind, with the desire of "the people" to have political systems "reduced to writing" and the attendant assumption that, unless written down, liberties could be easily modified or denied depending on the interests of leaders. Perhaps anti-Federalist farmers recalled Jared Eliot's warning in 1748 that "tradition is a very slippery Tenure, and a slender Pin to bear any great Weight for a long Time." An opposition piece in the *Litchfield Monitor* (1793) attacked the 1662 charter as unfair and inherently elitist

Table 10. Officeholding of Deputies to Connecticut General Assembly, with Ranking for Population and Artisanal Activity, in Towns Where Ralph Earl Worked

	Population Rank	Artisanal Rank	Average No. of Terms	
	(1774)	(1778)	per Deputy	(%)
Principal centers (5)				
Hartford	8	5	6.7	27
Middletown	10	9	10.0	31
New Haven	1	2	6.2	21
New London	4	7	8.0	18
Norwich	2	1	4.2	43
			Mean 7.0	28
Secondary ports (4)				
Fairfield	11	8	5.6	33
Stamford	17	14	6.2	31
Stratford	5	6	4.4	38
Windsor	40	31	5.6	48
			Mean 5.4	37
Secondary inland centers (2)				
Danbury	30	25	4.7	42
Litchfield	29	28	6.7	29
			Mean 5.7	35.5
County towns (5)				
Bolton	65	61	6.0	3*
New Milford	27	26	4.2	41
Newtown	38	44	4.9	51
Sharon	46	51	5.2	42
Woodstock	43	35	5.4	42
			Mean 5.2	44

Sources: Bruce C. Daniels, *The Connecticut Town: Growth and Development, 1635–1790* (Middletown, Conn.: Wesleyan University Press, 1979); town rank orders as calculated on pp. 194–95, drawing for population ranks on 1774 Connecticut census, and for artisanal activity on 1778 industries list, Finance and Currency, 2d ser., V, doc. no. 164, Connecticut Archives, State Library, Hartford; and pp. 200–201, app. 12, "Officeholding Patterns of Deputies to the General Assembly, 1700–1780." N = sixteen towns of the eighteen where Earl is documented as having worked; Easton and Salem were not incorporated by 1780.

*Not included in calculation of the mean turnover rate for this group

and lambasted the new state legislature as hopelessly weak in defending popular rights. "You profess republican principles, but tacitly submit to the ordinances of despotism," opened the attack. "You hold to the rights of man, but have not established the enjoyment of them. . . . But look about you my countrymen; take it up and view it in all its parts and properties, and see if it breathes the genuine spirit of republicanism. You will doubtless find it a *conglomerated mass of heterogeneous principles.* . . . A republican Constitution is a voluntary compact of the people establishing certain fundamental principles by which they will be governed." The battle lines of political and class difference thus drawn, the debate roiled for twenty years. Classical republicans (another term for Federalists) argued that their concept of authority and law was best for "the people," that imaginative national construct par excellence, while anti-Federalists (alternately termed either liberal republicans or Jeffersonian republicans) countered the "natural" legitimacy of hierarchy by saying, as did John Leland in 1801, that Connecticut citizens "have been trained too much in the habit of trusting the concerns of religion and policy to their rulers." Anti-Federalists bridled when they heard noted opponents like Fisher Ames publicly conclude, "Democracy is a troubled spirit, fated never to rest, and whose dreams, if it sleeps, present only visions of hell."[29]

During the 1790s both parties argued the necessity of a free market to the new nation. But as Joyce Appleby has observed, the free market was about more than mere economics, and these two groups differed most profoundly in their opposed theories of civil society. As Dwight's comments on New Haven revealed, Federalists saw in the regulated market one means of inscribing an established system of deference and public virtue that provided a constant check on individual freedom and mobility; their market was implicitly political and in defense of a prerevolutionary concept of social hierarchy. For liberal republicans, however, the market economy suggested an alternative to precisely such a conservative and authoritarian scheme. As Appleby has observed of the Jeffersonian concept of the free market, "here was a system operating independently of politics and, like the physical world, taking its cues from nature" and the liberal intellectual tradition from Bacon to Locke to Smith.[30] By the 1790s individuals like John Leland distrusted the rhetoric of legislators because they saw Connecticut's legal profession as a Federalist club. Liberal republicans painted the Federalists as a clique acting, finally, in its own interest, an indictment that resonated powerfully through the memories of the revolutionary generation.

Liberal republicans distrusted the pivotal roles that Federalists played in Hartford and in such conservative strongholds as Litchfield County in banking and the new insurance business. In 1792 there were no banks in Connecticut. By 1810 there were ten. The amount of investment needed to begin each bank was testimony to the unevenness of wealth and its control by Federalists. In May 1792 the Hartford bank was capitalized at one hundred thousand dollars and the New London bank at fifty thousand. Over the next few years banks opened with equally impressive start-up costs in Middletown, Norwich, and New Haven. The individuals involved included Oliver Ellsworth, Oliver Phelps, and Jeremiah Wadsworth. Insurance companies sprang up alongside banks and often shared leadership. Hartford's first company opened for business in 1794, with firms at Norwich and New Haven following the next year. To these financial interests, one could also add the dominant role played by Federalists in newspaper publishing and book circulation. Wadsworth epitomizes the overlapping roles played by some Federalists in shaping many institutions at once. A merchant, politician, and entrepreneur, he was an active booster of the Hartford Woolen Manufactory Company (1788), a charter member of the Hartford Bank (1792), a full partner in the Hartford Insurance Company, and a skilled model farmer specializing in cattle breeding. Elsewhere, to be sure, occasional ambivalence surfaced concerning the centralization of wealth that banks demanded and the worry among Federalist elites that their grasp on authority might seem too transparent. Near Boston, Fisher Ames warned, "The spirit of banking is a perfect influenza. . . . Intrigue and speculation will probably have their perfect work. I want a bank in my barn-yard, and wish to be erected into a corporation sole, to take deposits of corn, for my pigs."[31]

Closely linked to the debates over authority and public authority in political discourse were conflicts in local religion. With the passage of Connecticut's Toleration Act in 1784, a crack appeared in the exclusionist armor of the old standing order of Congregational clergy and conservative parishioners. Orthodox Calvinism began to lose ground. David Daggett in 1787 witnessed the visible decline of the old standing order, a system in which "the body of the clergy, with a few families of distinction, between whom there was ever a most intimate connection, ruled the whole state," and he ascribed its weakening "to two causes—the increase of knowledge, and the growth of opposition to religion. Knowledge has induced the laity to think and to act for themselves, and an opposition to religion has curtailed the power of its supporters." That same year, New Haven's three Congregational societies included only 26 percent of the adult population. Large congregations of "separates" or postrevolutionary New Lights took hold by 1790 in Middletown, Norwich, and New Milford, the membership of which together accounted for 31 percent of the towns' population, while the Congregationalists numbered 26 percent. By 1800 only 16 percent of Windham's 2,644 inhabitants remained active in the established standing-order congregation, a pale showing against the growing strength of evangelical Baptists, Methodists, and Unitarians. Communities west of New Haven, including Stratford, Newtown, and Stamford, and those to the northwest, such as New Milford and Kent, also had sizable Anglican parishes, in which Masonic lodges with anti-Federalist sympathies were especially active; indeed, an Anglican and tolerationist "Sons of Liberty" party met in New Haven as early as 1755. With their numbers and institutions besieged by resistance and schism, the standing order retrenched and dug in with a renewed sense of hierarchy in the 1790s. In 1799 Timothy Dwight was accused by some of promoting the "ecclesiastical schemes of Calvin and Knox," and lampooned as the "Pope" of Connecticut in 1802. In many of the houses where Ralph Earl set up his easel, defenders of Old Light faith were staunch Federalists.[32]

Problems with organized labor particularly rankled classical republican concepts of social order. In his reverie on New Haven's troubled market economy, Dwight had suggested that some mechanics were "generally prosperous" and capable of taking a respectable place next to others who "deserve credit for their industry and economy." By this he implied that skilled artisans could prosper and remain virtuous if their material comfort was counterbalanced against an appreciation of their proper social place. And such successful tradesmen certainly existed within Dwight's New Haven purview. The 1794 inventory of Joel Booth, a Newtown joiner, rates his estate property at a respectable £386. In 1806 Stephen Trowbridge's New Haven house and cabinetmaking shop, with contents, totaled $6,527, while in 1813 Samuel Houghton of New Haven died possessed of $7,693 worth of property. Yet Dwight reserved his particular disdain for those laboring people who either rejected the moral compass of the market economy or who realized that labor itself was not without power if it made use of its own tactics and economic strategies. Dwight dismissed the former group as consisting uniformly of "that class of men who look to the earnings of today for the subsistence of tomorrow," adding, "In New England almost every man of this character is either shiftless, diseased, or vicious."[33] The latter group, however, was less easily dismissed, since their motives and experiences were more complex and politically more subtle. And, as we shall see, they were directly influenced by transformations in urban labor structure during the previous century.

Consider, for example, what Dwight and other standing-order Federalists encountered in a series of agreements running from 1792 through the 1810s, in which mechanics and laborers alike began organizing in order to retain some degree of autonomy and control over local economies they perceived as run increasingly by Federalist banks, moneylenders, and lawyers. May 1792 brought a statewide petition by more than fourteen hundred laboring men from twenty different towns protesting Connecticut's system of taxation. Although the petition failed to effect any long-term political mobilization by working people, it nonetheless reveals a variety of complaints and social tensions working people shared in common. The petition was itself grounded in a series of protest articles published by Walter Brewster, a young Canterbury shoemaker, in the *Norwich Packet* that April. Thinly veiled as "The Mechanick on Taxation," Brewster identified three sore points in the lives of Connecticut's laboring people. The first was a so-called faculty assessment of five pounds that was arbitrarily tacked onto the assessor's estimate of any artisan's taxable income. A second was that Connecticut's poll tax unfairly burdened any artisans who boarded apprentices or journeymen laborers, who became liable for poll assessments. In Danbury each artisan's poll tax was increased by £24 because of this rule. As James P. Walsh has argued, "artisans made up only 10 percent of the taxpayers but paid taxes on 40 percent of the town's minor polls."[34] Finally, Brewster resented the state's granting of tax monies to support new manufacturing enterprises, such as the Hartford Woolen Manufactory in 1788 and 1790 and the Society for Establishing Useful Manufactures. Such large ventures, he cautioned, would surely flood the domestic market with cheap ready-mades and drive local producers out of business; the implicit reminder of the Luddite riots argued that Connecticut must not be transformed into an American Manchester. Brewster's politics were clear. "Whatsoever is repugnant to the Labouring interest," he maintained, "is also repugnant to the general or common interest of the whole state, which is the labouring interest." To which he added: "The uniform and universal tendency of all laws, in all countries, is to assist those who have property and power against those who have none."[35]

A Canterbury shoemaker articulating economic theory to the "Labouring interest" in order to counter the prerogative of those with "property and power"? Where did such notions and practices come from in rural Connecticut in the late eighteenth century? One answer points to the explosion of local newspaper printing in the decade after the Revolution and the circulation of tracts on political economy from new rural booksellers. Yet another source for radical labor politics in New England's hinterlands during the 1790s had roots in earlier out-migrations of skilled artisans from Boston, a decentralization of skill and labor consciousness by individuals in search of greater access to resources and more flexibility in production. Even in the mid-eighteenth century the exodus was large enough in scale to frighten port town politicians. By 1753 one man complained that the tide "carried from us many of our most Industrious, frugal and provident Inhabitants." In their place, the old seaport city witnessed a proportionate rise in the "number of thoughtless, Idle and Sottish Persons, who have very soon of course, come to be the charge and burthen of the Town."[36] For those who left Boston, what mattered most was what and how they could contribute to new countryside economies.

For their part, skilled urban workers brought changes to rural New England towns during the last half of the eighteenth century. Their abilities shot a jolt of new economic current into country towns whose surplus populations and reliance on part-time by-employment had hindered the growth of local industries. Shortly after rapid decentralization from Boston began in the late 1740s and early 1750s, farmers who had been scratching a meager existence from too little land were able to put aside their ploughs and, sometimes seasonally but often permanently, cast their lot with a more specialized occupation. Many of the workers who left Boston and the large adjacent port of Charlestown seem to have had a distinctly entrepreneurial outlook. In short, they left the city for the profits they believed the hinterlands would yield to those who worked hard. In about 1730, for example, cabinetmaker William Manley left his native Charlestown and moved to Wethersfield. He remained there until 1745, during which time he trained numerous local apprentices and marketed his furniture as far away as Hatfield, Massachusetts. A decade later another Charlestown artisan, chairmaker Thomas Brigden, arrived in Wethersfield and established a shop that lasted for three generations.[37]

Others followed in their wake. In 1766 Jonathan Brooks left the Boston area shortly after completing his apprenticeship as a cabinetmaker and set up a successful shop in New London, Connecticut. Two years later Jonas Locke, a master builder who had probably been trained in Boston, accepted an invitation from Deerfield to design and build a new tower and steeple for the town's meeting-house. Discovering avid patrons—and artisans eager to work under his supervision—Locke remained in the area, building mansion houses for local gentry and starting a business that lasted until his death in 1812. Seeing former Bostonians like Brooks and Locke prospering—and perhaps out-migrants from Manhattan doing the same—Justin Hobart Jr., a native of Fairfield, explained in 1800 why he planned to quit working as a journeyman joiner in New York City: "I don't think I shall work Journey work any Longer *their is no profit in it* I don't Earn but Just Enough to pay my Expenses and I believe I can Doe that in the Country."[38]

If the actions of Brooks, Locke, and Hobart were typical of younger workers who left large but depressed port towns for the promise of hinterland opportunities, the entrepreneurial urge may have been strongest among those artisans who declared their independence in rural shops. It was for Ebenezer Hartshorne, who had migrated to Boston early in the eighteenth century and quickly became one of its leading joiners. During the artisan exodus of the late 1740s he moved to Concord. By the 1760s, Hartshorne had "arrived" as part of Concord's respected citizenry and served as a selectman. He was also one of the few citizens regularly entrusted to handle the intricacies of settling estates. In that capacity, he was frequently accused of stalling or stretching out the probate process in order to exact more money from a decedent's surviving heirs. When local yeomen protested his subtle avarice, he betrayed his own conservative preference for the aristocratic order whose local ranks he had just attained. He thought his neighbors had "A Party Temper of mind." Indeed, Hartshorne believed his accusers were "very good men *in their own business*," but maintained "it is very Improbable they Should understand" the complexities of property distribution. By 1772, Hartshorne proudly called himself a "shop joiner," someone who owned the shop building and the materials but who left work to his journeymen — young Concordians eager to avoid a dull life behind their father's plough.[39]

The decentralization of skill in New England takes on greater meaning when one stops to consider the influences that these artisan-entrepreneurs exerted on rural landscapes like those in which Ralph Earl worked. They brought with them a battery of organizational procedures from the highly specialized and competitive world of Boston's declining trades in the mid-eighteenth century. They brought a strategic knowledge of wage labor and quantity production based on the stockpiling of premade parts for later assembly (known in Boston inventories and surviving artifacts as early as the 1670s), the journeyman's strategy of moving from job to job for work, and the workshop whose efficiency relied on the carefully monitored orchestration of several workers. These techniques, for example, stood behind Hartshorne's Concord operation, the scores of small shops that churned out nails, leather goods, and bobbins in new mill towns, and the brief interregnum from 1790 to 1820 in which the ten-footers of Lynn and Newark supported well-integrated, protoindustrial enclaves.[40]

The most important innovation occurred when the urban organization of piecework collided with the existing structure of seasonal by-employment in rural districts. In New England between 1730 and 1770, skilled urban workers saw an opportunity in rural part-time farming and artisanry to secure inexpensive and reliable labor. After all, farm families had always had secondary trades; the trick lay in organizing the functional diversity of rural by-employment in such a way that each household could make a usable final product. Production would be fast and workmanship high in quality, since farm families already had the rudimentary skills well in hand. Urban experience was what made entrepreneurs like Nathaniel Holmes and Ebenezer Breed seem progressive, since both realized that piecework could be smoothly adapted to schedules of work embedded in the rural household mode of production.

Nathaniel Holmes was a Boston cabinetmaker who succeeded by diversifying out of his trade altogether. Born the son of a Boston joiner and mason in 1703, Holmes apprenticed locally and started his own business during the depressed years of the 1720s. With the help of a strategic marriage, by 1735 he had bought a distillery and by the 1740s was so busy producing and shipping rum that he put down forever his cabinetmaking tools. But during the 1730s, as he was turning his eye to commerce, he paid local turners and japanners for piecework and organized a group of ten joiners to build furniture that he would then sell. Significantly, six of these men lived *outside* Boston: two in Malden, two in Marblehead, and one probably in Plymouth (the location of the sixth cannot be determined). In exchange for financial support, materials, and a guaranteed market, these men produced finished pieces of furniture that Holmes would then collect and sell from his Boston shop. Although he never left Boston before his death in 1774, Holmes provides a clear case of an urban merchant-producer organizing a rural labor force to make completed products ready for market. Ebenezer Breed was a native Lynn resident who worked as a journeyman in Philadelphia in the 1780s. When he returned home to lead Lynn's late-eighteenth-century expansion, he organized an elaborate outwork system that drew upon the skills and seasonal work schedules of rural farmers and of fishermen in towns like Marblehead and Gloucester. As artisans such as Holmes, Breed, and others with urban experience fueled the emergence of urban trade structures in rural New England, there was a dramatic and pervasive reorganization of occupational life in the countryside; between 1760 and 1830, unprecedented numbers of rural people took up nonagricultural work.[41]

RADICAL IMPLICATIONS

The decentralization of skill, a movement necessitated by the harsh economic climate of port towns that forced trained artisans to seek stable labor markets and employment opportunities elsewhere, was a principal means by which capitalist relations of production born in the seventeenth- and eighteenth-century city first entered the rural scene in Massachusetts, Rhode Island, and shoemaker Brewster's Connecticut. The decentralization of skill was rooted in the multiple tensions that derived from the pressures of rapid immigration, the decline of sanctioned legal restraints, the vagaries of diversification, and the severe limitations that mercantile economic theory placed on the circulation of liquid wealth. Throughout the seventeenth and eighteenth centuries, orderly attempts by men and women to gain official protection for their trades yielded to labor actions initiated by and for working people. This steady movement toward self-protection in both city and country had origins in an explicit labor consciousness that emerged during the second half of the seventeenth century. As it brought capitalist relations of production to outlying towns whose economies were still based on barter and domestic production, the decentralization of skill was a vital force both in preparing the countryside for political engagement, industrialization, and proletarianization and in constructing our dominant image of the rural landscape in the early Republic—a territory whose bizarre contours lacked the density of urban experience and the unpredictable rhythms of agrarian life. The landscape of Ralph Earl's Connecticut was just such a contradictory countryside.

At the same time that émigré urban artisans spread capitalist relations of production to the countryside, rural workers developed ways to counteract the emerging structure of work discipline. The movement of skilled workers out of

Boston during the 1750s and 1760s, in particular, had prepared the countryside for labor taking an active political role in the revolutionary cause. Worcester was one place where émigré Boston artisans went. Hence it is no surprise to discover that various artisan groups were meeting among themselves; the blacksmiths of that town drafted their own political position statement in late 1774 in response to a request from Boston's committee of correspondence. "Being deeply impressed with a sense of duty to [their] country," the blacksmiths agreed on a number of issues relative to those for whom they would not work. Chief on the list were "persons who we esteem enemies to this country, commonly known by the name of tories," including anyone "who addressed Governor Hutchinson at his departure from this province," as well as local Loyalists including "Timothy Ruggles of Hardwick, John Murray of Rutland, and James Putnam of Worcester, Esq'rs." The blacksmiths next turned their eyes on anyone who had not already signed the "nonconsumption agreement" and who "shall not strictly conform to the association or covenant agreed upon and signed by the Continental Congress lately convened at Philadelphia." More telling is the blacksmith's agreement that they should not do business with any local artisans who even worked for known Tories: "We further agree that we will not do any work for any mechanic, tradesman, laborer, or others, that shall work for, or in any ways, or by any means whatever, aid, assist, or promote the business, or pecuniary advantage, pleasures, or profits of any of the said enemies to this country." The blacksmiths closed their solemn agreement by calling on their brothers in Massachusetts's other counties to enter into similar covenants. "We earnestly recommend it to all denominations of artificers," they stated, "that they call meetings of their respective craftsmen in their several counties, as soon as may be, and enter into associations and agreements for said purposes."[42] The Worcester blacksmiths may have been atypical in their focus and apparent level of cohesion, yet their awareness of artisanal contributions to the national agenda alerts us to the role that migrating craftsmen, moving from one politicizing place to another, developing contacts both within and across trades, played in linking people together in imagined communities. The political mobilization of the blacksmiths on the eve of the Revolution also suggests that a structure was already in place when artisans in the late 1780s and 1790s turned to collective action to improve their economic and political position.

Following Brewster's essays in defense of the "Labouring interest" in April 1792, Norwich's leading industrialist and popular leader Christopher Leffingwell took up the reform campaign. Although a member of Norwich's leading family and an employer, Leffingwell echoed Brewster's earlier charges of unfair taxation that burdened artisans with arbitrary charges; his own grand schemes for advancement had been thwarted when Alexander Hamilton chose Patterson, New Jersey, over Norwich as the preferred site of his Society for the Establishment of Useful

Manufactures. Leffingwell's own local woolen operation was also denied by the state when it applied to have its workers exempted from the poll assessments. The language of the petition makes clear the agenda:

> Your Memorialists conceive that every kind of discouragement to Mechanical arts is a great injury to the landed interest in this state, and that the Poll Tax and assessment on Mechanicks has occasioned many of the valuable labouring part of its Citizens removing into other States; The assessment on Minor Polls, together with the Military Tax on apprentices has been so heavy a burden on Masters in the Mechanical line, that it has discouraged them from taking Apprentices without considerable allowances from their Parents or Guardians—Such allowances as many worthy Children have lost the benefit of acquiring useful Trades—Your Petitioners beg to suggest that the State of Connecticut is the best calculated for Manufacturing of any State of the Union—That the more labourers there are employed in that way, the greater will be the demand for the produce of the lands for home consumption.[43]

Connecticut's 1792 artisan protest may have joined such individuals as Brewster and Leffingwell in momentary common cause, but the key point on its critical agenda—unfair taxation by the state—seems to have been falsely drawn. But the use of a petition to galvanize labor politics made their views publicly known. And in those towns where Earl's sitters lived and worked, the number of subscribers was remarkably high (table 11). Ultimately, the petition strategy owed its use to Brewster's belief that a community of laboring people existed across the Connecticut countryside and that all workers—independent, apprentices, journeymen, or shop masters—would make common cause over economic exploitation.

Perhaps some of Brewster's perceptions were accurate. Artisans in some towns faced tough times. Geographic mobility among woodworkers in Woodbury, for example, increased at the end of the eighteenth century as specialized artisans arriving from outside displaced locals unable to reorganize production techniques for a larger external market. Such specialization had occurred in such trades as coopering and wheelwrighting during the Revolutionary War years, as local merchants calibrated production of barrels, casks, and wagon wheels to ensure that food and supplies reached the troops. They made a solid living in the process. But as this economic movement occurred, specialties emerged in a diversifying landscape of labor relations. Towns like New Milford, Roxbury, and Bethlehem became coopering centers. As Stamford chair maker Ezra Slason announced in a 1792 advertisement, towns along the lower Housatonic River developed specialties in chair bottoming: "Flags of the best kind and quality—Likewise Rushes of various Kinds . . . are transported from Derby, or the Ferry a little below, and are supposed to be some of the best in the State or County for handsome genteel gentle-

Table II. Subscription Levels to 1792 Connecticut Artisans' Petition in Towns Where Ralph Earl Worked

Date (1792)	Town	Signatures	
		No.	*(%)*
May 2	Norwich	179	(13.2)
5	New London	89	(2.9)
8	Stamford	298	(22.1)
10	New Haven	185*	(13.6)
11	Danbury	63	(4.7)
12	Hartford	78	(5.7)
14	Windham	55	(4.1)
14	Windsor	41	(3.0)
17	Litchfield	61	(4.5)
Sept. 28	Norwich	124	(9.2)
Oct. 12	New Haven	155	(11.4)
Oct. 13	Danbury	68	(5.6)
Total		1,346	(100.0)

Source: Manuscript artisan petitions, Finance and Currency, 2d ser., XIII, pp. 164–91, Connecticut Archives, State Library, Hartford, as reprinted in James Walsh, "'Mechanics and Citizens': The Connecticut Artisan Protests of 1792," *WMQ*, 3d ser., 42, no. 1 (January 1985): 72, table 1. N = ten (New Haven and Danbury each appear twice) of the eighteen towns in which Earl's patrons lived.
*Given as an approximate number

men's parlor chairs—also, a course [*sic*] kind for kitchen chairs may be had."[44] Mobility and turnover increased, specialization geared to external markets increased, and a more visible hardening of boundaries between the trades emerged.

This sense of specific domains within a competitive economy emerged as well in 1792, when the "Cabinet-Makers" of Hartford formally convened "for the purposes of regulating the prices" of their work. In specific terms, they stated, "[We] have formed ourselves into a Society for the purpose of regulating the prices of our work; on the principle of dealing in CASH, and of establishing a uniformity in our trade for the general interest of ourselves and customers." Any instance of deviation from these published prices, the compact continued, "shall be deemed a forfeiture of *word* and *honour*."[45] The house joiners in rural Hatfield, Massachusetts, organized four years later. Like the 1741 Boston caulkers' agreement, the language of these rural manifestos invokes the moral radicalism of laboring people immersed in the process of assembling fragments of millenarian political thought and Antinomian mystic spiritism into a coherent force for critiquing the steady progress of merchant capital. What is still more remarkable is how soon the idea of using price lists for self-protection emerged in Connecticut's countryside. In Boston, as we have seen, the appearance of price lists climaxed in the 1740s and early 1750s. Yet as early as 1759 joiner Timothy Loomis of Windsor, Connecticut, made up a personal price list for furniture and carpentry work that he kept concealed within the pages of his ledger, suggesting once again that rural artisans kept fully abreast of urban trade reforms.[46]

After artisans for more than a century had humbly submitted petitions to court and colony officials to better their economic lot, their rural price lists represented a key step in asserting the prevailing liberal economic perspective of "Labouring interests." Left on their own by Federalist civil authorities, labor groups stepped in to claim an active role or class-based agency in the marketplace. In 1825, a Charlestown, Massachusetts, hatter named Fisher Hartshorn arrived in Woodbury, Connecticut, to set up work but died shortly thereafter of smallpox. When the town refused to bury him in the common burying ground, the hatters in the town did so under the cover of darkness. Finishing their task at midnight, they erected a monument that shows the degree of labor consciousness that bound their group together: "This monument is erected by the Society of Hatters, to the memory of their brother, Fisher Hartshorne" (fig. 102).[47]

CONTINUITY

With conflicts over political ideology, religious tolerance, and labor actions complicating their clean vision of a hierarchically ordered society, Federalist elites began in the mid-1780s to counter the confusion by constructing themselves into an allegory of republican virtue. One way they did this entailed anchoring the legitimacy of their own mansions in biblical typology. Congregational minister Daniel Foster preached a sermon in Worcester in 1789 that referenced Jesus exploring "the silent mansions of the dead" and argued, following Isaiah, that "He has bought the grave, it is no longer a prison, but a house, yea, his inner chamber, here the saints of the Most High God may rest in hope, till the last grand revolution." Following established tradition, references to heavenly houses supported their invocation of a bodily ideal for organic social structure, with wise (now Federalist) leaders at its head and dependent, content members (dissenters) at its hands and feet. Despite the fact that, as we have seen, during the 1760s numerous mob actions broke out in Norwich, New Haven, West Haven, Windham, New London, and Durham and after the Revolution buildings in nearby Massachusetts were attacked during Shays's Rebellion, Connecticut Federalists attempted to erase popular memory of class tensions within their bodily vision of republican order. De-

Figure 102. Hatter's monument to Fisher Hartshorne, Woodbury, Connecticut, 1825. From John Warner Barber, *Historical Collections of Connecticut* (New Haven: printed by the author, 1836), 505. (Photo: The Connecticut Historical Society)

scribing the comportment of people at general elections—traditionally a time when rowdiness might break out in a public square—Dwight claimed the following:

> One of the judges of the Supreme Court of the United States was present, a number of years since, at this election. As he was conversing with the governor, he said, "Pray, Sir, where are your rabble?" "You see them around you, Sir," said the governor. "Rabble, Sir," said the judge, "I see none but gentlemen and ladies." "We have no other rabble," said the governor, "but such as you see." "You astonish me," replied he. "Why, Sir, when General Washington took the oath of office in the balcony of the assembly house in Philadelphia, the chief justice, who administered it, could scarcely be heard at the distance of ten feet on account of the noise and tumult of the yard below. Among the thousands who are present, I do not discover an indecorum. These are your rabble, Sir? Well, I say, that the inhabitants of Connecticut are the only people within my knowledge who understand the nature of an elective government."[48]

Allegory denies full self-recognition in exchange for imagining one's social being as a transparent sign. In political terms, however, it is not equivalent to nostalgia. Nostalgia locates the present in the past, whereas allegory insists upon the continuity of past with present, of one event with the next, and shapes a mythology of community without rupture or contingency.[49]

But that mythology is hardly seamless. Allegory shares one quality with its close cousin, cultural hegemony; in their zeal to provide a language and imagery for the cultivation of consent, they leave cracks, intrapsychic lesions where the terms of domination turn inward and confront elites with sudden recognitions of what they have repressed in the process of consolidating power. The studied surface of grace and virtue grew distorted in jarring and arresting moments when Earl's Federalist elites recognized in a perceived social inferior aspects of themselves that lurk restlessly and surface with surprise and suddenness. These moments of recognizing the Self in the Other cut a doubling, reflexive figure. As Freud phrased it in his essay "On the Uncanny," they involve "the doubling, dividing, and interchanging of the self." Confrontations with the uncanny in Earl's Connecticut articulated both the splitting of the national subject and the split sign of the nation's time. They remind us that unanticipated moments of recognition—of seeing the repressed Self in the suppressed Other—could always interrupt the allegory of national emergence; as my own narrative technique will suggest, such uncanny encounters upset the symmetrical surface of New England society that Earl's patrons were shaping. They remind us also that any nation attains coherence in part on the basis of what its dominant cultural classes and their institutional interests attempt to "forget" or render strategically invisible. This has always been a crucial element in theories of nationalism. Ernest Renan pointed out the intricate dialectic of selective memory and selective amnesia in 1882. "Forgetting, I would even go so far as to say historical error, is a crucial factor in the creation of a nation," he argued, "which is why progress in historical studies often constitutes a danger for the [principle of] nationalism. Indeed, historical inquiry brings to light deeds of violence which took place at the origin of all political formations, even of those whose consequences have been altogether beneficial. Unity is always effected by means of brutality. . . . The essence of a nation is that all individuals have many things in common, and also that they have forgotten many things."[50]

The aesthetics of allegory and rupture are manifest clearly in the landscapes Earl created for his sitters. "Landscape" is a densely laden word. It can have many meanings: utopian, spectral, sociological, or the quotidian visual inventory of fields and fences, hills and houses. Any landscape, however, constructs a space-time or chronotopic dimensionality, and these are the twin axes manipulated selectively in the allegorical aesthetic of Earl's portraits. Continuity in space assumed one or two well-recognized forms necessary for the cultivation of order and deference: the grid and concentricity. These disciplines were made more apparent when their rigor broke to admit singular natural "wonders," a term that recalls the way that seventeenth-century intellectual discipline was realized in the sudden rupture of a "wonder," or token of God's immanence in human society. The pattern imposed by the grid is familiar through Dwight's obvious praise for

New Haven's nine squares and has deep resonances in designs for classical cities, military encampments, colonial plantation towns, and John Davenport's utopian anticipations of the heavenly city in the early 1640s.[51]

The one-point perspective of the concentric plan warrants closer study. It informs Dwight's "View from Greenfield Hill" (of which John Warner Barber said, "No other spot in Connecticut can show such a commanding, extensive, and beautiful prospect"), the layout of new mercantile centers like New Milford, and William Strickland's 1794 description of Rocky Hill. "This station," Strickland observed, "commands an extensive view of a rich and high[ly] diversified country in every direction. . . . A country as well cloathed, with as beautifully waving and wooded an outline as ever was seen, is here more thickly settled with the neat mansions of comfort and independence than the most boasted spot in our own Island. . . . On this rock the boasted morals, the enlightened policy of the N[ew]: England States, on their virtues rest the character, the fate of America, and their virtues originate in the universal knowledge and education of the people. Here, I may confidently assert, Englishmen may be contemplated in their greatest, most exalted character." The shared rhetoric is one of control. If a view "commands" the surrounding countryside and the people working in it, it is "extensive" and beautiful. Hierarchy craves the distant, disengaged view.[52]

The concentric landscape could be literally circular, with spheres of decreasing order and authority spinning outward from a central focus, or it could be linear in arrangement. In the latter case, a single town street would grant priority of place to institutional and important private structures at its midpoint, while one would encounter lesser structures as one approached each end of the thoroughfare. Accentuated by enclosures of well-tended, private freehold property, these linear examples appear in the distance in Earl's Connecticut. Consider the landscape we see as an emblem of public virtue through the window in Earl's 1791–92 portrait of Samuel Talcott of Hartford (fig. 103). In the foreground, his land—including in the immediate foreground a right of passage through his property that he granted in 1761, thereby "sacrificing" private interest to public convenience—is well fenced, his fields glowing in the rosy light of anticipated profit. His property extends to the Connecticut River, shown with distant buildings crowding its gentle banks. But does this peaceful vision actually represent all of Talcott's holdings? Far from it. In 1797 Talcott owned an additional sixteen hundred acres of land and a total of six houses that he had rented out to agrarian tenants. So while he was a man of "public virtue," he was at the same time a landlord who had inherited the property that now provided him an independent income. A similar scene appears in the view of New Milford center in the background of Earl's 1789 portrait of Daniel Boardman (fig. 104). Beyond the meandering path of the Housatonic River lie neatly fenced fields on Boardman's large farm, with house and outbuildings ar-

Figure 103. Ralph Earl, *Samuel Talcott*, ca. 1791–92. Oil on canvas, H. 71¼" (181 cm), W. 53¾" (136.5 cm). (Photo: Wadsworth Atheneum, Hartford, the Ella Gallup Sumner and Mary Catlin Sumner Collection Fund, endowed by Mr. Joseph T. Hall in honor of Mrs. John Lee Bunce)

Figure 104. Ralph Earl, *Daniel Boardman*, 1798. Oil on canvas, H. 81⅝" (207.3 cm), W. 55¼" (140.3 cm). (Photo: National Gallery of Art, Gift of Mrs. W. Murray Crane)

Figure 105. Ralph Earl, *Landscape View of Old Bennington*, 1798. Oil on canvas, H. 36½"
(92.7 cm), W. 59¾" (151.8 cm). (Photo: The Bennington Museum, Bennington, Vermont)

rayed in good order. In the distance the steeple of the Congregational meetinghouse rises to assert the growing prosperity and spiritual alignment of the town.

Earl used this concept of landscape most fully in his 1798 view of Bennington,
Vermont, a village with straggling entry and exit zones (fig. 105). Past a foreground of orderly and precisely managed fields, fields that look "agrarian" but
were actually the site of a bloody revolutionary battleground, Earl draws in detail
the mansion house of Governor Isaac Tichenor. Behind the governor's house and
garden lie the county courthouse (center), the brick armory (left), and the impressive house (right) of another local notable, David Robinson. Faced with disorder and the visible presence of "outliers," Earl emphasized the town's dense,
more tightly packed center and, in so doing, described the structured interdependence of private wealth and public institutions that enlivened the early national
economy. From this central focus of power, concentric rings of lesser buildings,
lesser people, and poorer land spun outward. An 1836 watercolor sketch by John
Warner Barber shows a similar deposit of official buildings at the center of Fairfield, Connecticut: courthouse, church, and jail, all seats of power, judgment, and
discipline (fig. 106). Indeed, each of Earl's town views is marked by the existence
of a high symbolic center at the heart of its social organization. He argues, therefore, for the persistence of hierarchic town plans and the centrality of deference in
the new republican social order. As Edward Shils has commented, "In all societies,
the deference system is at its most intense and most continuous at the center. The
high concentration of power and wealth, the elaborateness of style of life, all tes-

Figure 106. John Warner Barber, "East View of the Court House, Church and Jail," Fairfield, Connecticut, ca. 1820–35. Pencil sketch with ink wash. (Photo: The Connecticut Historical Society)

tify to it and call it forth."[53] Many late-eighteenth-century Connecticut towns made use of a raised center to announce the presence of a republican form of government, relying on a plan continuous with the nucleated village scheme of the seventeenth century. As William Strickland observed at Rocky Hill in 1794, "Here numerous places of worship [are] the only ostentatious buildings in view, [and] preserve the parent in the paths of order and morality."[54]

Strickland's attention to churches and their central role in the political system in Connecticut towns is significant for, among other reasons, the modest, local light it casts on recent meditations on centers and peripheries in nation-states. Benedict Anderson has suggested that under dynastic or monarchical rule (including that of imperial states), "high centers" are the invariable pivot point of power, a power derived in part from the imagined identification of the king with divine forces. In states with high symbolic centers, boundary zones between them remain "porous and indistinct, and sovereignties faded imperceptibly into one another." When republics assert a "modern conception" of national topography, their "state sovereignty is fully, flatly, and evenly operated over each square centimetre of a legally demarcated territory."[55] Their boundary zones are firmly marked, and porosity disappears.

What, then, are we to make of the persistence of high centers in the early national landscape of Connecticut? Certainly they were within one state (itself bounded from its neighbors) and related to a distant, highly secular national capitol. Yet Anderson's imputed high center in imperial monarchies has now been radically dispersed. And in republican Connecticut, many towns have high centers still articulated by the interbred dynasties of local merchants, magistrates, and ministers. Dispersed high centers indeed marked the topography of this national republican polity. Perhaps a new consolidation of boundaries in republics need not occur at the expense of high symbolic centers, especially when a new secular government may sacralize itself through their intentional perpetuation.

The landscape of high symbolic centers persists, too, because it provides a key metaphor, suitably stylized through architectural decoration, for the surveillance necessary to ensure public order. To see and not be seen: that is the question that many Federalist elites pursued, ensuring a continuity in social policing that we normally ascribe to Puritan towns. Nathaniel Hawthorne, a keen student of seventeenth-century cultural practices surviving into the mid-nineteenth, caught exactly this image in his short story "Sights from a Steeple." The narrator of the story provides an intoxicating summary of what can be seen from the high center. "In three parts of the visible circle, whose centre is this spire, I discern cultivated fields, villages, white country seats, the waving lines of rivulets, little placid lakes, and here and there a rising ground that would fain be termed a hill." The aesthetic of the distanced view is directly reminiscent of Dwight's descriptions of Connecticut towns. Looking down from his perch, Hawthorne's narrator continued his survey. "Yonder is a fair street," he observed, "extending north and south. The stately mansions are placed each on its carpet of verdant grass, and a long flight of steps descends from every door to the pavement. . . . The door of one of the houses, an aristocratic edifice, with curtains of purple and gold waving from the windows, is now opened, and down the steps come two ladies, swinging their parasols, and lightly arrayed for a summer ramble."[56] From the imaginary vantage point of Hawthorne's Salem, these details seem exact, as exact as they might for any town with impressive buildings and citizens interested in public architecture. Yet what is striking about this description, and Dwight's, is the emphasis on churches, distant views, large houses, and the virtuous, well-behaved people that dwell within. There is no poverty from this dizzying height, no rejection of unifying allegorical truth from this distance.

The concentric landscape of virtuous, republican yeomen was largely a selective perpetuation, conceptually speaking, of an earlier landscape of hierarchic values; indeed, the "historicity" of the early nucleated plan was largely an invented tradition of this period. Close to the center of the towns—across from the church spire, next to the courthouse steps—are the large, fashionable houses of new local leaders eager to gloss their recent accessions to power with recent accessions to taste. In the next concentric ring come large, two-story houses of an earlier vintage of village gentry, forming the parade of polite structures on either side of the town's high street. Mixed among them, moving outward, are the surviving large frame houses from the late seventeenth or earlier eighteenth century, with plans that include halls, parlors, central chimneys, and rear lean-tos added later. Finally, at the margins of settlement are modest, one-story cottages of poorer residents. But such mean structures are overlooked in the selective, amnesiac vision of the allegorical landscape. Instead, the dominating logic of concentric spaces is confirmed in Dwight's various (and frequent) comments about typically prosperous landscapes. In the center of Suffield, for example, he noted "the houses on both sides of the street are built in a handsome style and, being painted white (the common color of houses in New England) and in the midst of lots universally covered with a rich verdure and adorned with flourishing orchards, exhibit a scene uncommonly cheerful." In the parish called "Upper Houses" in Middletown, he stated that because the houses "are generally well built . . . the whole place wears an air of sprightliness and prosperity," an air no doubt bolstered by the fact that an "advantageous trade is carried on by the inhabitants, particularly with the West Indies."[57]

RECOGNITION: SECRET MURDER

The rational public sphere of virtue and sacrifice was shattered by the irrationality of brutal, mass murders. The landscape itself had always forced startling place-names and associated events to mind, reminding us that "peaceable kingdoms" were not always placid. At the sleepy heart of Winsted's west village was "Mad River." On the east side of Farmington was perilous "Rattlesnake Hill," while South Glastonbury's benevolent fields were cut by "Roaring Brook." Places associated with noise, violent movement, and human passion had always marked the cultural contours of local memory. But no mental map could have prepared Connecticut's orderly society of yeomen for the brutal clubbing and burning of a family in Judea (now Washington) in Litchfield County in February 1780, or the "mad" and "roaring" (the adjectives recall witchcraft narratives) horror of the Beadle mass murder in Wethersfield in 1782. One local observer summarized the feelings of dislocation the violence caused: "This town has been the theater of one of the most atrocious murders committed in New England."[58] Or who would have suspected, almost a century after Salem, that Thomas Goss of Barkhamsted would accuse his wife of witchcraft in October 1784 and then murder her in cold blood?

The recognition of unanticipated violence within the new nation posed a new challenge: How should citizens of the Republic imagine the inner workings of the "secret murderer"—that is, a person like Wethersfield retailer William Beadle, whose established pattern of behavior offered no clues to the cruelties he committed. "'Tis very natural for you to ask," one chronicler of the Beadle tragedy observed in 1783, "whether it was possible a man could be transformed from an affectionate husband and an indulgent parent to a secret murderer, without some previous alteration, which must have been noticed by the family or acquaintance? Yet this was the case in this instance, there was no visible alteration in his conduct." Established techniques of shaping the meaning of murder amid the pain of community loss of course continued. Public executions, complete with scaffold confessions, pleas for forgiveness, and prayers for the about-to-be-departed soul continued to draw crowds through the end of the century. In Hartford in June 1797, "as there had not been an execution in this place for a considerable number of years," an estimated six thousand to ten thousand spectators appeared at the hanging of an Irish murderer.[59] But criminals like William Beadle were cold blooded, irreligious, apparently remorseless. They articulated new contradictions and raised new questions. How could a loving father be so cruel? How could a peaceful man harbor such inner torment and not show it? Or more worrisome still: Were there signs that *we* should have seen? Could *we* have stopped the atrocity before it began?

The new genre of the horror narrative arose to help answer the question. As Karen Halttunen has suggested, these quasi-novelistic treatises challenged the accepted Enlightenment concept of the liberal subject reliant on reason, sentiment, and environmental surrounds as safeguards of public virtue.[60] The "secret murderer" was recast as a moral monster, someone whose deed was so heinous that it could not be accommodated within existing understandings of sin and human nature. Because there was no prior "sign" of their cold-blooded meditations, the cases of criminals like William Beadle suggested that within each apparently rational human being an unpredictably brutal act might be brewing. Calls for classical virtue and sacrifice were in part constituted by fear of their dramatic subversion. Social discipline and an emergent cult of horror were closely intertwined.

MAPS

Supporting the historical continuity of a concentric geography within the unifying gaze of local elites at the center of public life was the importance of enclosed property and its proper ordering. Republican virtue was continuous with the aesthetic of enclosure often associated with seventeenth-century republican thought. Listen to Timothy Dwight on the landscape of Worcester County, Massachusetts:

> In no part of this country are . . . the enclosures of stone so general, and everywhere so well formed. These enclosures are composed of stones merely laid together in the form of a wall and not compacted with mortar. An eye accustomed to the beautiful hedges of England would probably regard these enclosures with little pleasure. But emotions of this nature depend much on comparison. There are no hedges in New England, those which formerly existed having perished by some unknown misfortune. Few persons, therefore, who see these walls will be able to compare them with hedges. A great part of what we call beauty arises from the fitness of means to their end. This relative beauty these enclosures certainly possess, for they are effectual, strong, and durable. Indeed, where the stones have a smooth, regular face and are skillfully laid in an exact line with a true front, the wall independently of this consideration becomes neat and agreeable. A farm well surrounded and divided by good stone walls presents to my mind, irresistibly, the image of a tidy, skillful, profitable agriculture, and promises to one within doors the still more agreeable prospect of plenty and prosperity.[61]

Dwight recasts the political economy of enclosure in aesthetic terms. The pursuit of "a tidy, skillful, profitable agriculture," a practical system already defined by "the fitness of means to their end," is equated with "a great part of what we call beauty." His view of improvement's inherent morality derived from a puritanical emphasis on things—land, horses, children, a strong will—that were sufficiently "broken" and enclosed by fences and "love." The propertied elite of New England had always championed the vision of "a farm well surrounded and divided"—an enclave of production and family discipline at once protected from one's social inferiors and planted with a watchful eye trained on the vagaries of the capitalist marketplace—since the seventeenth century; recall Samuel Desborough's obvious fascination for enclosure and the neat arrangement of farm buildings. At the turn of the nineteenth century, Dwight may have cast the calculus of wealth in the language of the sublime, but he was still working through aesthetics to direct the politics of conduct.

Dwight's attention to the look of the landscape draws attention to a second technique used by Earl's Federalists to bolster their high central place in the social environment: the new science of geography. Geography, especially of the sort offered by Jedidiah Morse in his books *American Geography* (1789) and *American Universal Geography* (1796), or by Nathaniel Dwight in his influential *A Short but Comprehensive System of the Geography of the World* (1796), proved an effective means of organizing the known world into a patterned, hierarchic mental map with the reader at its high, omniscient center. Geography and maps had proven essential in expanding the boundaries of the English empire in the sixteenth and seventeenth centuries and the colonized peoples they subsumed. When New England geographers Morse and Dwight began publishing, it was also with an eye to shaping commonsense instruction in public schools and naturalizing the concentricity of the enclosed, high-centered world. According to his preface, Morse believed that "Europeans have been the sole writers of American Geography, have too often suffered fancy to supply the place of facts, and thus have led their readers into errors, while they professed to aim at removing their ignorance." From his point of view, only an American could accurately describe the imagined topography of the early Republic. As he claimed, "Since the United States have become an independent nation, and have risen into Empire, it would be reproachful for them to suffer this ignorance to continue; and the rest of the world have a right now to expect authentic information."[62] Because maps present themselves as value-free but have a long history as instruments of political expansion and consolidation, the popularity of Morse's and Dwight's texts suggests the role that cartography played in establishing an image of an "authentically" bounded nation, a nation whose metaphysical terrain had been mapped as the "Sacred Geography of God's Kingdom" by Cotton Mather in the early 1720s and by Ezra Stiles in the 1770s. Stiles even described a meeting he held "of young Men of my Congregation at my hous," at which he "gave them a View of the terrestrial Globe with a Lecture on the Scripture Geography."[63] From this perspective, when geography books or globes appear as details in Earl's portraits of Noah Smith in Bennington (fig. 107), Nehemiah Strong, or Sherman Boardman, they serve as powerful emblems of a high-centered, panoptic reader arguing the limits, the metaphysical contours, and the important memory sites of the imagined community.

RECOGNITION: SAVAGIZED SAINTS

When they encountered scattered groups of remaining native peoples living on the margins of towns and fields, Connecticut's elites saw in themselves a construction of the "savage" Other. Ever since the 1637 English attack on the enclosed native town at Pequot, relationships between the two groups had been hard, with the former exploiting the latter at every possible turn. While small local native societies continued to live in different places throughout Connecticut, the progress of Christianization in Connecticut had affected them deeply. By the time of the Revolution almost all native peoples in Connecticut were practicing Christianity, with educated leaders such as Samson Occum and Joseph Johnson, both Mohegan, having been trained by Eleazar Wheelock. In contrast with the

Figure 107. Ralph Earl, *Noah Smith*, 1798. Oil on canvas, H. 64¼" (163.2 cm), W. 42¼" (107.3 cm). (Photo: Art Institute of Chicago, Goodman Fund, 1956.126)

property holdings of whites, native peoples in Connecticut, as at Natick in Massachusetts, lived in a state of unrelieved poverty. As early as 1761, Wheelock summarized the Mohegan's material lives with disgust: "They would soon kill themselves with Eating and Sloth," "they are used to set upon the Ground," "they are used to live from Hand to Mouth (as we Speak) and have no care for Futurity," and "they have never been used to the Furniture of an English House, and dont know but that a wineglass is as strong as an Handloom." His words could have come from the mouth of a seventeenth-century missionary. Little had changed. Whites assessed the Native Americans' progress toward "civility" using domestic life and technology as a primary index. Even Occum's house, undoubtedly one of the finest among the Mohegan because of his high status within the community, and far from the wigwams that Ezra Stiles recorded at Niantic in 1761, was still small when compared with the mansions of Earl's sitters— although its unabashed "Englishness" must have surprised them nonetheless (fig. 108). English disgust of native practices translated into fear as white people recalled how immediately prior to the Revolution native lay leaders, including Occum, Johnson, and David Fowler, held prayer meetings at which representatives of different local groups attended, including Mohegan, Tunxis, Quiripi, Pequots, Narranganset, Nihantic, and Montauks from eastern Long Island. Along with the scattered members of the newly formed society at Schagticoke in New Milford, these associations between local native groups suggested to whites a new "confederacy" (an ethnocentric political term, to be sure) that focused Native Americans more on their own political organization than on assimilation. The Indians were probably struggling to position themselves so the white man's revolt against English tyranny might bring about a postcolonial emergence in their lives. Other whites worried when reports from Connecticut missionaries in Pennsylvania came with news of violence against life and property. In 1785, for example, Joseph Meacham of Coventry told his neighbors that while "he had been preaching at Susquehannah for a considerable time," he "was so unfortunate as to be driven from his possessions their by the Indians," and "that his property was destroyed by them."[64]

Still more surprising and perplexing to Connecticut's standing-order elites was the evangelical style of worship preferred by the Native Americans. Evangelical preaching, with an "enthusiastic" emphasis on bodily movement, oral exhortation from the heart rather than memorized texts from the head, and spontaneous witnessing to the movement of the spirit, was consistent with native religious practices and attracted the

Figure 108. "Sampson Occum's House in Mohegan, Montville," ca. 1760–92. From Barber, *Historical Collections of Connecticut*, 240. (Photo: The Connecticut Historical Society)

concern of elites anxious to discourage any form of worship that might undermine the established authority of the Congregational ministry. Native communicants not only wanted a more emotive style of worship; they were also drawn to itinerant New Light preachers because they objected to the standing order's so-called hireling ministry. When Joseph Fish, the Congregational minister at North Stonington, tried to preach among the nearby Pequots, he discovered that they had already been converted by Separate Baptists, since ministers from that church sanctioned trances, visions, and emotional expressions in a manner that was consistent with their own cultural experience.[65]

But native worship practices did not end with any easy conformity to the theatricality of recognized New Light or Separate style. Both Occum and Johnson were widely respected among Native Americans for their adherence to Old Light sermonics and prayer, with its customary emphasis on self-abasement, worthlessness, and reliance on God's mercy alone and an adherence to close biblical exegesis. Within this customary code, however, individuals like Occum and Johnson found opportunity for subversion, as they attenuated rituals of public self-abasement as strategic ways of manipulating white leaders to their own purposes. One of the functions of the language of self-abasement, expressed often through the groveling discourse of petitions to members of Connecticut's government, therefore, was to turn claims of total, abject subservience to their own advantage, creating an antistyle of coded critique. Despite dire poverty, people like Johnson and Occum had learned to manipulate Connecticut's elite, and the inversive, if momentary, effects were profoundly disorienting.[66]

POINTS OF VIEW

Mapping New England's terrain with painted landscapes provided an alternative to written geography lessons and a screen memory that rinsed labor disputes from view. In 1800 Thomas Denny of Leicester, Massachusetts, asked Earl to paint a view of southern Worcester County "looking east from Denny Hill." The resulting picture celebrates the virtues of an agricultural economy in which work and beauty merge (fig. 109). Framed by graceful elms in the foreground, teams of harvesters mow, rake, rick, and load hay. Animals munch happily in a fenced meadow. A pair of ladies take a stroll, reveling in the georgic aura of the scene. Fields and stone walls lead the viewer's eye across a landscape broken only by small buildings—houses, a church steeple, the bell tower of a small mill. The mill may be small but it is key, as it signals Denny's own deepening involvement in the industrialization of the countryside. He ran a machine card manufactory. According to Denny's friend Anna Henshaw, he commissioned the view because he was about to move into a new home and "wanted to take with him a picture of the view that he was so familiar with since childhood," a view that resulted, according to Henshaw, in a "most splendid panorama view from Denny Hill, which embraces the surrounding country, dotted with the white houses of the inhabitants and a dozen or more churches. At the northwest is seen Leicester village situated on a hill equal, if not superior in height, about two miles travelling distance. . . . In the northeast in a valley are hills and dales, woodlands, plots of grass, and arable fields, delightfully diversified."[67] But in looking backward through time, it was also a view that symbolically reversed the very process of economic and social change in which Denny himself was playing an energetic, transformative role. Earl's picture pushes the industrialization of Leicester and other villages nearby to the background and instead highlights an agrarian mythology already deeply affected by scientific husbandry and whose profitable days were numbered. Still, ploughing matches locally referred to as "Agrarian Games" continued uninterrupted, for as one letter writer named Georgicus wrote in 1825, "There is an obvious analogy between the ploughing sports and the ancient Greek Games."[68]

The beauty Dwight witnessed in gridded and concentric landscapes was confirmed by its formal reversal in places and things that offered affronts to allegorical virtue. Here Dwight's comments on Northampton are especially revealing.

Figure 109. Ralph Earl, *Looking East from Denny Hill*, 1800. Oil on canvas, H. 45¾" (116.2 cm), W. 79⅜" (201.6 cm). (Photo: Worcester Art Museum)

Compared with the neat grid of his own New Haven or the prim, high centers of yeoman towns in the countryside, the town "is built on ten streets, proceeding from the center with no very distant resemblance to the claws of a crab, only somewhat less winding and less regular," he observed. "It has been said that they were laid out by cows and that, wherever these animals when going to feed in the forests made their paths, the inhabitants located their streets. . . . A considerable number of the houses are ordinary; many are good; and not a small proportion are handsome. They are, however, so scattered in the different streets as to make much less impression where they are presented at a single view. None of the public buildings are handsome."[69] By critiquing the disorderly appearance of scattered or "crablike" settlement, the Yale president again revealed the unbroken continuity of planning dicta from two centuries earlier. Towns with plans of patterned concentricity—of streets and houses moving outward from meetinghouse, tavern, and the houses of leading citizens (i.e., merchants, magistrates, and ministers)—inscribed the legitimacy of hegemonic deference on the face of the land. By contrast, scattered settlements could only reveal a dangerous mixing of stations, or a flagrant disregard for the visible hierarchy of proper rule. Lost on these views was the fact that such differences in town layout might have distinct regional—rather than moral—origins in England, a point that Joseph S. Wood has made clear. They might also be the result of the impact that different class interests had on town appearance—of working people needing direct routes of access through one another's fields, regardless of lofty ideas of enclosed, classical forms. But to

Dwight and others, towns lacking in any centralized geography of authority seemed like "nowhere" in a phenomenological sense. To Dwight they seemed almost locationless, as they did to the Marquis de Chastellux when he approached Voluntown in October 1780. He observed "only a certain number of houses, dispersed over a great space," and when he could, he asked for directions. "How far is it to such a town?" he asked a local. "You are there already," he was told. John Warner Barber, when he described rural Salem, Connecticut: "There is no *place* in the town which may be considered a village."[70] Without concentricity, there was simply no "there" to be found.

The flow of rank and privilege emblematized in the gridded or concentric town plan occasionally broke to admit the sublime novelty of a natural wonder. Near Northampton Dwight encountered a waterfall. "A cataract," he allows, "is of course a romantic and delightful object." In this case, he observes, "When a spectator approaches the falls, he is presented with an object at once singular and beautiful, a sheet of water spread over an inclined plane of 230 feet, floating most elegantly in thousands of perpetually changing, circular waves, and starred with an infinite multitude of small fluctuating spangles. Until I visited this spot," he admitted, "I knew not that it was possible for water to become so beautiful an object."[71]

What this encounter with the waterfall does is bring us face to face with the aesthetic counterpoint to the patterned discipline of high centers within the allegorized landscape: variety. Dwight himself used this term with care, as when he noted a "grove of pines" near the cataract that "lends its gloom to vary the landscape." Or when he described the vista of Chatham, Connecticut, in the distance: "Beyond the river rise the fine slopes of Chatham, covered with all the varieties of culture, orchard, grove, and forest, and interspersed with well-appearing farmhouses. These grounds, and indeed the whole assemblage and arrangement of the objects which form the landscape, are fashioned with an exquisite hand, and delight the eye of every traveller."[72] Or, veering from the public way in the orderly precinct of South Glastonbury, Barber commented on the value of juxtaposition as a key to romantic sensibility: "The first appearance of this village strikes the traveller with an agreeable surprise: considering the general face of the land in this section of the town, he is not prepared to find in such a short distance from the main road, such a romantic and beautiful specimen of interesting scenery [as Roaring Brook]."[73] Variety and assemblage together indexed a romantic aesthetic that derived from the cultural writings and rebellion against Enlightenment rationality of such figures as Vico, Rousseau, and Herder. In political terms, variation from established norms and assemblage of fragmentary experience played a key role in arguments for cultural relativism and in fueling nationalist movements. For Connecticut Federalists, in aesthetic terms, they could also be deployed strategically as a means of organizing the inherent difficulties of cultural dissensus and shaping places and people by means of assigned temporalities.[74]

TIME SHIFTS

How did this symbolic placement in time work? Connecticut elites created social inferiors not only by locating them in a marginal geographic position but also by imposing upon them various dimensions of pastness, usually conceived of as a slowness or stasis contrasted with the speed and dynamism of the national present they themselves occupied. The assignment of alternative "time zones" was crucial to the nationalist imaginary the Federalists worked to maintain; Anderson has argued that the particular form of allegory necessary to national emergence is the articulation of temporal simultaneity, a crucial collapse of a millennial future and a selection of useful ancestors into the "instantaneous present." This is what Earl's sitters affected. Take the popularity of Morse's *American Geography* as emblematic of this elision. Morse assigns both new states and old towns to the same moment; he then uses maps to bolster his own historical account of the way America's political geography had formed. Indeed, Morse's survey may have provided a direct model for Dwight's own travelogue, a text that traced the Federalist view of the landscape in narrative form. Like Dwight and his own father, a Windham County clergyman, Morse was a minister himself, the standing-order mainstay of Charlestown, Massachusetts. He believed fervently in the imminent arrival of an era of Christian peace, worked to spread his millennial vision among citizens who remained indifferent to organized religion, and would play a leading role in the Second Great Awakening. Morse's maps, therefore, represented the fusion of historical selection and eschatology that Anderson, glossing Walter Benjamin, described as the "messianic" time in which "the term 'meanwhile' cannot be of real significance."[75]

Using maps, narrative discourse, and their own estates, Federalist elites created within the historicity of everyday life in the early Republic a means of "destructuring" time and representing other cultural subjects as inhabiting temporal locations discontinuous with their own. Perhaps their flexibility in deploying differential time placements derived from the experience some of their group had had with satire, dramatic reversal, and a Shandean use of what literary historian Adam Mendilow has termed the "time shift," as members of the club of Yale graduates and young Federalists known as the "Hartford Wits." Certainly the circle of literati around John Trumbull in Hartford—including Earl's guardian and mentor Mason Fitch Cogswell, Timothy Dwight, Joel Barlow, and Richard Alsop—knew of the Shandean tropes in *M'Fingal* and, as writings in *The Anarchiad* (1786–87) and *The Echo* (1791) make clear, were devotees of Sterne's temporally complex fiction.[76]

Whatever its specific genealogy, allegory functioned to legitimize social difference by arranging people into time zones. Listen to Benjamin Silliman's description of rural virtue in the parish of Avon, Connecticut, in 1798:

> It was an interesting remnant of primeval New England manners. The people, evidently agricultural, had scarcely departed from the simplicity of our early rural habits; the men were not parading in foreign broadcloth, nor the women flaunting in foreign silks and muslins; but they appeared in domestic fabrics, and both men and women were dressed with simplicity. I do not mean that there were no exceptions, but this was the general aspect of the congregation, and, from the smallness of the house, although there were pews, it seemed rather a domestic than a public religious meeting. The minister corresponded admirably with the appearance of the house and congregation, as far as antiquity and primeval simplicity were concerned, but he was highly respectable for understanding, and sustained even in these humble circumstances, the dignity of his station. He was an old man, with hoary locks, and a venerable aspect, a man of God, of other times.[77]

Even dialect could be used to frame a distinct temporality, as when William Strickland in Coventry in November 1794 noticed "by their speech" that the residents of the town were "a colony" from the West Country perceived as a static survival surrounded by more dynamic neighbors.[78]

As commerce accelerated in Connecticut near the close of the eighteenth century, many towns could not match the speed of urban transformation in places like Hartford or Norwich or the intensity of expansion into hinterland communities in the northwestern towns of New Milford, Sharon, or Litchfield. Timothy Dwight described Wethersfield, for example, as falling behind. It "has not kept pace with the general improvement of the country," he judged, and seemed decades behind its burgeoning neighbor, Hartford. In 1802 Governor John Treadwell separated the pace of farming from that of capital advancement still more dramatically. "The farmer is thrown into the shade," he claimed, and "he feels that riches, as the world goes, give pre-eminence . . . with heavy steps returning from the fields, he sees with pain the powdered beau rolling in his carriage . . . and feels himself degraded."[79] Farm people in the countryside walk with "heavy steps," as if in some suspended, slumberous trance. Mercantile characters, by contrast, roll along at a brisk, predictable speed. Shandean humor and economic advance are linked by a single thread: timing is everything.

Country people had their own view of this divide. The small town was knowable terrain. People recognized their responsibilities and realized that mutual obligations were not only inescapable but often claustrophobic. The speed and anonymity of large towns were strange but euphoric releases. In June 1790, Julia Cowles left her native Farmington to go to school in Middletown. A young single woman, she had been forewarned to avoid the "pleasures of the world and its fashionable enjoyments." But still she hesitated, stating, "I am so strongly attached to my native place that it is not without some regret that I leave it. From these calm scenes of pleasure, into a busy crowd of extravagant people."[80] For Cowles and her family, Middletown's accelerated flow of people, goods, and money was not incomprehensible; it was dangerous. Fashion is a cruel clock, an entrancing but arbitrary index of temporal discontinuity that functions politically.

Earl's Federalist patrons fashioned landscapes that situated them in distinct temporalities as well. They could shape the present in a very immediate way by arranging buildings, moving land, sponsoring road- and bridge-building projects, and constructing public spaces through which they could move with a theatrical sense of self-assuredness. But redesigning the built environment entailed a compromise with the classical republican virtues they had long regarded as aesthetic anchors. There was a felt need to inscribe the historical inequality of market capitalism in a convincing historical fiction. As Jeremiah Wadsworth of Hartford explained the issue to Strickland in November 1794, "We are true republicans, too wise to be misled by names, too honest to make a figure at the expense of our creditors[,] too good politicians to desert established principles, *or follow the fancies of the day*."[81] They often chose to use poetic metaphors of landscape to naturalize what Bhabha has termed the "rhetoric of national affiliation and its forms of collective expression."[82]

Passages in Timothy Dwight's pastoral poem "Greenfield Hill," for example, turn on positive images of light, socially visible marks on the landscape, and classical temporality. On images of light, lightness, and unrestrained freedom, for example: "Where, in light gambols, healthy striplings sport, / Ambitions learning builds his outer court." Or consider the visibility of the Greenfield Hill Academy, the building where Dwight himself taught while minister in the village: "Where yonder humble spire salutes the eye / Its vane slow turning in the liquid sky." Finally, Greenfield Hill, the village in which Earl himself lived during his years in Connecticut, appears as a reverie of classical allusion: "Little he knew, though much he wish'd to know, / Enchanted hung o'er Virgil's honey'd lay, / And smil'd to the despient Horace play, / Glean'd scraps of Greek; and, curious, trac'd afar, / Through Pope's clear glass, the bright Maeonian star."[83]

Through the ordering of the landscape and through Ralph Earl's portraits, the second-generation "standing order" of conservative Connecticut society in fact moved into three temporalities that allowed them both to discipline their social inferiors and to vary sufficiently that discipline so its coherence and purpose remained implied, elusive: the zone of an imagined return of a lost Arcadia or gold-en age; the zone of retreat into aristocratic, customary codes; and the temporality of the emblematic self. The first of these temporalities, as we might expect given that republicanism acknowledged roots in classical forms, involved the construc-tion of a fashionable, but essentially antimodernist, theater of virtue through ar-chitecture and domestic furnishings. Some revolutionary theorists had believed that patriotic Americans could "recover lost innocence" in the promise of an Ar-cadian return, a rediscovery of forgotten knowledge. Samuel Stanhope Smith in 1778 wrote to James Madison that a new nation could be forged by "recalling the lost images of virtue: contemplating them, and using them again as motives of ac-tion." And critics of Thomas Paine argued, not entirely without reason, that his enormous popularity was because he "had promised Americans a golden age if they became republicans."[84]

ET IN ARCADIA SUMUS

Earl's elite Federalists managed their mythic return to classical perfection in part by rebuilding the popular landscape. Older landscapes, like those of Wethersfield, Windsor, and Middletown, needed to be critically updated to ensure the rearticu-lation of social distinction that had been blurred between 1760 and 1790. Rebuild-ing also promised to erase the scars on the landscape left by the Revolution itself, when British colonial troops laid waste to particular areas of the New England countryside. Most compelling to Earl's sitters living in such eastern Connecticut towns as Salem, Woodstock, Norwich, and New London was the dramatic level-ing of nearby Rhode Island between 1776 and 1779. The destruction recalled and exceeded the area's property losses during King Philip's War a century earlier; 192 houses, 45 stores, 32 stables, 30 privies, and assorted farm structures lay in smol-dering ruins as the British pulled out of Newport (table 12). The destruction had an immediate impact on Connecticut. On the one hand, some large property owners in eastern towns were Newport merchants directly touched by the dam-age. Godfrey Malbone, for example, was a wholesale merchant with a pew in Trin-ity Church in Newport and a country estate in Brooklyn that boasted its own Trinity Church, a small structure Malbone designed in 1770 that functioned al-most like a private estate chapel.[85] On the other, a Federalist rebuilding would help people forget the pain of political transformation itself. It might make radical im-plications of revolution disappear.

Public buildings decked in neoclassical detailing announced the Federalist re-building campaign. The Connecticut statehouse in Hartford (fig. 110), designed by Boston architect Charles Bulfinch in 1792, drew on the suggested hierarchic de-

Table 12. Buildings Destroyed in Rhode Island during the British Occupation, 1776–1779

Building Type	No.	(%)
Barn	13	(2.9)
Chaise house	8	(1.9)
Crib	19	(4.3)
Dwelling house	192	(43.5)
Little house	12	(2.8)
Outhouse	15	(3.4)
Privy	30	(6.8)
Shop	37	(8.7)
Stable	32	(7.3)
Still house	9	(2.3)
Store	45	(11.6)
Other*	30	(7.7)
Total	441**	(100.0)

Source: "Revolutionary War Claims for Damages, 1776–1781," General Assembly Papers, Rhode Island State Archives, Providence, Rhode Island.

*Includes a variety of building types that, when taken alone, occur in such small numbers as to account for less than 1.0% of the total sample: dairy houses, hen houses, "cold houses" (or spring houses), bake houses, "grane houses," pump houses, wash houses, and wood houses common to farmsteads; also included are wheel houses, longhouses (part of rope-making facility), rum houses, sugar houses, fishing houses, tar houses, spermacaeti works, market houses, and screw houses found in the center of Newport.

**Of N = 441 structures, 390 (88.4 percent) were in Newport, and the remaining 51 (11.6 percent) were scattered throughout the towns of Bristol, Jamestown, Middletown, North Kingstown, and Portsmouth and on Prudence Island.

ployment of Doric, Ionic, and Corinthian columns familiar from architectural pattern books. Its facade was a hybrid face, contrived by Bulfinch by fusing the academic classicism of Somerset House in London with the elevation of John Wood's Liverpool town hall, two structures he studied while traveling in England in 1786. Other public buildings were similarly impressive. According to Timothy Dwight's eye, the bank of Hartford "is of brick, eighty-five feet long. Its whole front of thirty-six feet is covered by a simple Tuscan portico, of four columns and two pilasters, built of dark brown freestone." The new Litchfield County courthouse designed in 1795 by architect William Sprats even had a small Georgian house plan built into its entry chambers (fig. 111).[86] The aura of historical and critical legitimacy that pervaded new public institutions was quickly co-opted by aspiring individuals, as new vernacular houses, monuments to imagined public virtue, sprang up with similar neoclassical facades. The house of Oliver and Abi-

Figure 110. Charles Bulfinch (architect), John Leffingwell (master builder and contractor), and Elisha Sage (master mason), Connecticut State House, Hartford, Connecticut, 1792–96, as shown in detail of Joseph Steward, *Jeremiah Halsey*, ca. 1796. Oil on canvas, H. 43¾" (111.1 cm), W. 38¾" (98.4 cm). (Photo: The Connecticut Historical Society)

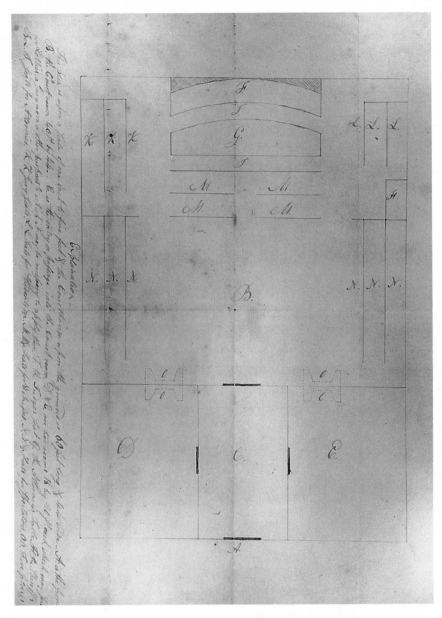

Figure III. William Sprats, plan for Litchfield County Courthouse, 1795–96. Ink on paper.
Explanation along left side of plan reads: "This plan is upon a Scale of one inch to five feet
& the Courthouse upon the ground is 60 feet long & 44 wide. — A. is the front. B. the Courtroom, 40 ft. by 44. C. is the entry or passage into the Courtroom. D. & E. are two rooms
16 by 20 ft. each, which may serve for Lobbies, a Jury room or other purposes to which it may
be necessary to apply them. F. the Judge's Seat. G. the Attorney's Table. H. the Sheriff's Box.
I. Seats for Attornies. K. K. Jury Seats. L. L. Seats for Students. M. M. Seats for Witnesses.
N. N. Seats for Spectators. O. O. Fireplaces." (Photo: Litchfield Historical Society)

gail Ellsworth, our original protagonists, is a case in point. Built initially in 1781 on land inherited from Oliver's father, David, the structure gained a new parlor wing in 1788. In that same year Ellsworth also planted thirteen elm trees (each symbolizing a new state) on the property and renamed the estate "Elmwood." Thomas Hayden, a local contractor and self-proclaimed architect, was responsible for the design work. By the 1820s the house had also acquired a portico in front of the added wing and is now recognized as a fine example of "Federal" design; our name for the style is politically exact.

The Ellsworths were by no means alone. The demand for classical landscapes as part of the allegory of Arcadian return to the present grew so rapidly that professionals like Hayden, Lavius Fillmore, or Sprats (active in Farmington, Litchfield, and New Milford) could market their singular mastery of archaeological truth. Hayden, for example, supplied a new mansion house for John Watson, a successful merchant in East Windsor Hill, in 1788–89, the drawings for which survive and demonstrate his skill with the draftsman's pen. Without doubt, Hayden relied for such details on the ready stock of motifs available in his small architectural library; at his death in 1817 he owned volumes described as the "Practical Builder" and a "Bench Director."[87]

In other towns neoclassical buildings also signaled the combination of moral improvement, social advancement, and a reference to the ancient, golden age of an imagined classless, virtuous society. Elijah Boardman's new house in New Milford was exactly this type of monument. In his 1789 portrait of Boardman, Ralph Earl playfully reversed the terms of the split-sign predicament so evident in his portrait of the Ellsworths. Now we are standing in the sphere of the rational marketplace (his retail dry-goods shop in New Milford), looking back over a threshold (with a trompe l'oeil trick of double doors to draw attention to that boundary) into his private, protected realm of imported fabric and dry goods (fig. 112). Boardman and his brother Daniel ran their dry-goods store out of the old Bostwick house (next door) from 1781 until about 1792, at which point, having both married, they built a new shop structure (the one in which we, as viewers of the portrait, are standing) and an impressive mansion house typical of Sprat's work (fig. 113, at left). The house still stands in New Milford and resembles, especially in the projecting portico with its distinctive use of four columns supporting an entablature beneath a large Palladian window, other Sprats-attributed structures in Litchfield and Farmington.

The choice of a neoclassical structure by Boardman makes particular sense. As Rodney C. Loehr has suggested, the storekeeper was "the intermediary with the outside world and facilitated the change from self-sufficiency to commercial farming." As Boardman fueled the engine of agrarian capitalism, he chose a public front that bathed his activities in the soft Arcadian light of republican virtue.

Figure 112. Ralph Earl, *Elijah Boardman*, 1789. Oil on canvas, H. 83" (210.8 cm), W. 51" (129.5 cm). (Photo: Metropolitan Museum of Art, Bequest of Susan W. Tyler, 1979)

Figure 113. Ralph Earl, *Houses Fronting New Milford Green*, ca. 1796. Oil on canvas, H. 48" (121.9 cm), W. 54⅛" (137.5 cm). (Photo: Metropolitan Museum of Art)

Occasionally the neoclassical design vocabulary extends more fully to include de-tails familiar from the architectural treatises of William Halfpenny, Batty Langley, and others, books owned by these architects and other local carpenters eager to play in the new market. A steady demand in Connecticut stood behind the supply of six such titles in the Hartford bookshop of Hudson and Goodwin in 1788.[88]

Three other allegorical houses were also popular among Earl's sitters. One was a house with a formally articulated inner courtyard, suggested by the small image of a balustraded entry portico on Daniel Boardman's house in New Milford (fig. 114). Another consisted of a large central block flanked on either side by small "hy-phens" or dependency passages; such an arrangement shows clearly in Earl's epic view of the New Milford house Jared Lane "improved" about 1791–92 after inher-iting it from his father-in-law, Lazarus Ruggles (fig. 115), or in the equally ambi-tious house of Judson and Mabel Ruggles Canfield in nearby Sharon (fig. 116). Fi-nally, a third plan option included a central block, hyphens, and fully developed out-offices, completing the ideal five-part plan of the English country house. Buildings of this sort were occasionally built in prerevolutionary New England

Figure 114. Ralph Earl, detail of Daniel Boardman's house in New Milford, in *Daniel Boardman*, 1798. Oil on canvas, H. 81⅝" (207.3 cm), W. 55¼" (140.3 cm). (Photo: National Gallery of Art, Gift of Mrs. W. Murray Crane)

Figure 115. Ralph Earl, *Landscape of the Ruggles Homestead*, 1796. Oil on canvas, H. 38" (127.3 cm), W. 52" (92.7 cm). (Photo: Corporate Art Collection, Reader's Digest Association)

Figure 116. Ralph Earl, *Landscape View of the Canfield House*, ca. 1796. Oil on canvas, H. 34⅝" (88 cm), W. 72⅛" (183.2 cm). (Photo: Litchfield Historical Society)

Figure 117. Overmantel from the Elisha Hurlbut house, Scotland, Connecticut, by 1772. (Photo: © 1994 Sotheby's, Inc.)

when the initial craze for rural retreats had swept the countryside beginning in the 1730s; although no longer extant, the impressive structure built by 1767 in Scotland, Connecticut, by Elisha Hurlbut looks more like a Virginia plantation house than an English country mansion (fig. 117).[89] A similar symmetrical building appears in the background of Earl's portrait of Captain John Pratt of Middletown (fig. 118). Pratt's mansion appears anomalous for New England and re-

Figure 118. Ralph Earl, *Captain John Pratt*, 1792. Oil on canvas, H. 46½" (118.1 cm), W. 38½" (91.4 cm). (Photo: Dallas Museum of Art, Gift of the Pauline Allen Gill Foundation, 1990)

sembles at first glance another plantation scheme; because it is atypical of any surviving Connecticut houses, some scholars have felt it may have been a fanciful design cooked up by Earl to fill in the background of the portrait in proper English style. Arguably, however, this was not the case, as a very similar structure built by Governor Roger Griswold in Lyme in the 1790s still exists (fig. 119). Both structures appear unusual because of the way they have retained elements of seven-

Figure 119. John Warner Barber, "South View of the Gov[ernor Roger] Griswold House, in Lyme," ca. 1820–35. Pencil sketch with ink wash. (Photo: The Connecticut Historical Society)

teenth-century domestic design and grafted them onto a five-part plan. Each house is only three bays wide, and not the more common Georgian five-bay design. In addition, the central block of each house retains a conservative central chimney common to earlier New England houses, while fusing it to an essentially Georgian plan. Although it lacks the small roof gable shown on the front of Pratt's house, Griswold's has hyphens a full two stories in height. In both instances, the piercing of the end gables of the dependent out-offices is identical. In both instances, again, the desire to build a grand estate was balanced against the necessary retention of formal elements with which locals might readily identify.

The Federalist rebuilding of the countryside in Connecticut was continuous with its transformation in nearby Massachusetts. In Princeton in southern Worcester County, near Thomas Denny's card mill and close to Earl's own ancestral village, magistrate and gentleman farmer Moses Gill built an impressive estate on a small hill overlooking the village center. With an appropriate distance between him and surrounding souls, Gill enclosed an ornate Georgian mansion and service dependencies within a neat ornamented fence (fig. 120). To the left of the house stands a stable and private office; to the right small structures overlook a garden politely planted in parterres and decorative trees. According to the *Massachusetts Magazine* in 1792, the "honourable proprietor must have great satisfaction in seeing improvements so extensive, made under his eye, under his own direction, and by his own native industry." Mowers in the foreground, interchangeable with those working on Thomas Denny's hillside, are doing the real

Figure 120. "View of the Seat of the Hon. Moses Gill Esq. at Princeton, in the County of Worcester, Massa[chuset]ts," 1792. From *Massachusetts Magazine* 4 (November 1792). (Photo: Society for the Preservation for New England Antiquities)

work. The scene recalls Dwight's passage through the same area in late 1796, when he admired the regularity of stone walls in the area and concluded that it "presents to my mind, irresistibly, the image of a tidy, skillful, profitable agriculture, and promises to one within doors," someone like Moses Gill, "the still more agreeable prospect of plenty and prosperity."[90]

Connecticut's propertied elite argued their legitimate claim to republican virtue as well by retreating to the temporality of "customary" comforts and ancestral homesteads that supported the "natural" basis of civil authority. In Earl's portraits, the emblematic detail of the ancestral claim to property and deference appears most strikingly in the field behind William Floyd (1793). Floyd, the distinguished scion of a Long Island gentry family, signer of the Declaration of Independence, and longtime legislator at both state and national levels, returned to Long Island in 1783 to find his estate in disarray. The portrait shows the house as a last refuge, a final claim to the customary time of prerevolutionary deference and gentility (fig. 121). A building with a related function, the old Wyllys mansion in Hartford, appears in the background of Earl's portrait of Polly Wyllys Pomeroy (fig. 122). Undoubtedly because of its being adjacent to the famous Charter Oak, the Wyllys house was shown in early September 1781 to traveler Anburey as a romantic relic, who remarked: "We were shewn, among other things, the following curiosities; an house built in the year 1640 of American oak, the timbers of which

Figure 121. Ralph Earl, detail of house from *Colonel William Floyd*, 1793. Oil on canvas, H. 47⅛" (119.7 cm), W. 35½" (90.2 cm). (Photo: Independence National Historical Park, Philadelphia)

were yet sound, and almost in a state of petrifaction."[91] The Wyllys mansion—and the Charter Oak itself—were pivotal sites in what was then emerging as a distinctly Federalist tourist route. During the debates in 1786–87 over the legitimacy of the 1662 charter, Federalists had stood by the inherent "democracy" and "republican" principles of the royal charter, while anti-Federalists cried in response that it gave preference to the interests of the propertied elite. Icons of customary time were thus powered by their association with images of hierarchic gradations in social structure and enforced the sanctity of high symbolic centers within the new mixed republican polity.

RECOGNITION: POVERTY IN ARCADIA

In many country towns, although most houses remained unaffected by neoclassical fashion, they nonetheless charted a comfortable (if conservative) evolution from asymmetrical structures with rear lean-tos through larger frame houses with kitchen ells added at the rear. Occasionally the apprehension of outmoded or archaic dwellings amid the assumed progress of improvement reminded those who considered themselves "civi-

Figure 122. Ralph Earl, detail of house from *Polly Wyllys Pomeroy*, ca. 1791–92. Oil on canvas, H. 38½" (97.8 cm), W. 32" (81.3 cm). (Photo: Wadsworth Atheneum, Hartford, lent by Colonel Philip S. Wainwright)

lized" how fragile the narrative of civilization could be. One log house that survived in Easton, Connecticut, until 1937 consisted of a single thirteen-by-seventeen-foot room with a ceiling and plastered walls, a beaten earthen floor, and a pitched roof. It was one type of building seen in the 1790s as decidedly substandard and backward (fig. 123). In 1794 Henry Wansey encountered a similar although larger building in Windsor: "I now saw a log house, for the first time; it was about thirty feet long, and six feet

Figure 123. James Bennett's house, log with frame additions, Easton, Connecticut, ca. 1780–1800. (Photo: Society for the Preservation of New England Antiquities)

to the roof; and consisted of logs or poles, with the bark on, laid upon each other; at the four corners, where the logs crossed, they were notched together, and nailed; and the interstices were plastered up with loam. I soon saw ten or twelve little heads peeping out at window and door." And despite the fact that a large number of such mean and crowded structures were recorded in the Direct Tax of 1798, by the late eighteenth century the log house provided a strange reminder of earlier "garrison" houses built to provide defense during the initial decades of settlement at the margins of English expansion. The seaweed-thatched winter huts of oyster workers along the Connecticut shoreline, such as the rows built on Poconoc Point in Milford, reminded some commentators of the drafty, impermanent shelters built from earliest settlement or, worse still, of Quiripi wigwams (fig. 124). According to John Warner Barber, who visited Milford to sketch these structures in the opening years of the nineteenth century, these were impermanent buildings used on a seasonal basis. "There is a street containing about 15 or 20 huts of this description covered with sea weed," he observed, and "about 50 or 60 persons, engaged in the oyster business, reside in these habitations during the winter months, and four or five have their families with them." In a characteristically romantic turn, Barber aestheticized these structures as "quite novel in their appearance."[92]

These substandard houses were only supposed to last a short while

Figure 124. John Warner Barber, "Oyster Houses on Poconoc Point," Milford, Connecticut, ca. 1820–35. Pencil sketch with ink wash. (Photo: The Connecticut Historical Society)

before they were replaced with more comfortable frame houses. In the early 1780s the Marquis de Chastellux described exactly this sequence with a house a farmer had upgraded on the road from Farmington to Litchfield: "This dwelling, which at first was no better than a large hut formed by a square of the trunks of trees, placed one upon the other, with the intervals filled by mud, changes into a handsome wooden house, where he contrives more convenient, and certainly much cleaner apartments than those in the greatest part of your small towns."[93] The persistence of these structures in the 1790s raises questions about the assumed progress in a propertied republic toward permanent houses as a sure index of attained prosperity and bourgeois propriety. It was one thing to realize that such flimsy structures were standing a century before; Sarah Knight encountered such a house in southern Rhode Island in 1704: "It was supported with shores enclosed with Clapboards, laid on lengthways, and so much asunder, that the Light come thro' every where; the doore tyed on with a cord in the place of hinges'[.] The floor bare earth; no windows but such as the thin covering afforded. . . . The family were the old man, his wife and two Children; all and every part being the picture of poverty." But it was worse to realize they were still being commonly built in marginal towns throughout New England. In 1771, for example, fifty-three "log camps" were standing in North Yarmouth, Maine, seventy-one more in

Boothbay, and eighty-one in Pownalborough. Those in Boothbay, "of Chiefly Round logs," were "mostly without chimneys and . . . the Inhabitants are very poor"; the Pownalborough examples were "poor buildings & mostly without clabboards & shingles & many of them without Chimneys."[94] These houses—log or boarded, but commonly viewed as emblems of poverty and the lower orders—came out of the imagined past to invade Connecticut's early national present, reminding some that the distance between attained "civility" and the "savagery" of poor English and Native Americans alike was not fixed permanently.

FRAGMENTS AND SOULS

Landscapes, buildings, and portraits each played a role in constructing time as one means of defining class difference while maintaining an apparently flexible political arena. As Elias Canetti has pointed out, "the regulation of time is the primary attribute of all government," and any "new power which wants to assert itself must also enforce a new chronology; it must make it seem as though time had begun with it." Earl's painted anatomy of Connecticut in the 1790s defines the contradictory time of the emergent nation. His portraits couple the ancient past to the entrepreneurial present while leaving behind the terrain of local exchange, limited means, and economies of kinship riven by ecclesiastical politics. In so doing, they call attention to the way in which time is shaped within the portrait and demonstrate that the power of the visual image is contingent upon what it excludes. Portraits always reveal disappearances. According to John Berger, "had pictorial art not possessed this power—the power to speak with the language of timelessness about the ephemeral—neither priesthoods nor ruling classes would have had any use for it." Portraits harness the authority of timelessness to address the passing and the ephemeral; they appropriate the practice of local memory to the politics of national amnesia. Through visual art specific groups perfect a concept of regularized, allegorical time, but such perfection always entails the imperfection and wreckage of alternative temporalities valued by others.[95]

Federalist temporalities of a vanished Arcadia and retreat to customary codes found a final complement in the transcendent temporality of the emblematic self. This sign of time becomes apparent in the seemingly stark "realism" of many portraits by Ralph Earl and his contemporaries. It is easy to dismiss the occasionally flat stares and errors in academic perspective or proportion that we call "startling realism" as the result of either a poor artist or an entrepreneur just doing quick work. And there were artists working in the northern states at the close of the eighteenth century and in the early nineteenth who seem to have been after little more than a ready market and some tasteless clients. In 1825 John Vanderlyn looked back over his career and admitted to his nephew, "Were I to begin life again, I should not hesitate to follow this plan, that is, to paint portraits cheap and slight, for the mass of folks can't judge of the merits of a well-finished picture." The same view was current in some of the towns in northwestern Connecticut that Earl visited in the 1790s. Shortly after his arrival in New Milford in 1796, one of the painter's local allies advertised his skills in the Litchfield newspaper. "We feel a pleasure in making this communication," the announcement began, and it promptly went on the defend his abilities. "Many gentlemen in this vicinity, having been disappointed of his services, and several of our friends being driven to accept of the paultry *daubs* of assuming pretenders." Earl was reasonable, they concluded, his "price for a Portrait of full length is *Sixty Dollars*, the smaller size *Thirty Dollars*." To be sure, Earl had spotted a ready, if not uniformly discerning, market among his Federalist patrons and exploited it thoroughly. He was a keen entrepreneur, and Stephen Kornhauser's painstaking tests of his canvases reveal that he at times even added "sugar of lead" to his pigments to help speed up their drying time; the quicker one picture was done, the sooner the next one might begin. Additionally, Earl's patrons were also busy with their own projects and no doubt appreciated that the taking of their likeness took only minimal time from their schedule; such seems to have been the case for Oxfordshire minister James Woodforde, who noted in 1775, "After prayers I went . . . to have my Profile taken of by a Lady who is come to town and who takes great likenesses. I was not above a minute sitting for the same."[96] Yet neither Earl's business acumen nor the athletics of his production schedule offer clues to why his clients—people who were, after all, well educated, well traveled, widely read, and scrupulously self-critical— actually *liked* his work.

Fortunately, in Earl's case we know that he was master of two styles at once. In New York in 1791 Earl changed his style for urban patrons who demanded the softer modeling of form of academic tradition. But back in Connecticut the very next year, he switched to a style marked by long rather than short brush strokes, a restricted palette, and full-length rather than one-half portraits, simplifications that somehow offered his rural clientele the portraits they found compelling. The question becomes less one of how inept or opportunistic an itinerant rural limner might have been than what the local definition among Earl's sitters of the preferred, full-length "likeness" was that made its style so desirable and recognizable. I argue that the reasons have nothing to do with the tired topic of "realism" in early American art at all, but instead everything to do with the practice of piety.

A key clue emerges in a 1795 letter written by Mary Breed of Norwich to Dr. Cogswell, Earl's guardian and mentor, in Hartford. Upon her death bed, Breed asked to sit for a final portrait: "I wish very much to have my likeness taken. . . .

My earnest request is that if you know of a limner that would take a likeness . . . (I do not want a picture without) that [you] encourage him to come to Norwich." The wording of this missive is ambiguous in emphasis. One could understand Breed to mean "I do not want a picture without it being a good likeness." Yet as she approached the finality of death, the moment of heavenly translation and the "great exchange" of an earthly body for heavenly raiment, Breed more likely meant that she wanted a "likeness," meaning an effigy or "memorial" that not only captured her "picture without"—that is, her external or "outer self"—but also was emblematic of her essential soul, her "inner" being. Or, to use terms chosen by Esther Edwards Burr in the early 1750s, Breed wanted her likeness to somehow bring into fusion and represent the collapse of "my Best Self"—the exterior, acting, transactional self—into "my Other Self," or inner soul that was the divine spark of life itself.[97] What Breed was after was an image that held out the promise of disappearance in final unification: in symbolic terms, the unification of inner essence and outer appearance; in personal terms, the unification of mind and body; in medical terms, the unification of body parts that were being diagnosed separately and treated as if they were interchangeable commodities circulating in a disembodied market.

Bodily dislocations already were common in Connecticut portraits, perhaps because Earl relied on, as had Copley, a "layman," or wooden mannequin with hinged joints, to model the bodies of his sitters (fig. 125). Writing to his brother-in-law in 1774, Copley stated that "the Life" must be used when painting heads, hands, and feet, but for costume details one could use "Drapery sett on the layman." This method could result in stiff figures that resembled one another closely except for personal details of face or hands. In 1738 one English text complained of common portrait painters that "when the Face was finished, they had no further Regard to the Life, but chose a Posture, at Pleasure, out of Drawings or Prints, without considering whether it suited the Person," or even "whether the Head match'd the Body." Reynolds concurred, claiming that most painters "have got a set of postures, which they apply to all persons indiscriminately." In Connecticut the substitutability of one body for another obtained still stranger results. When Earl's protégé Joseph Steward composed his portrait of Eleazer Wheelock in the mid-1790s, he asked Ludovicus Weld to sit for the lower half of the body, implying perhaps that for practical purposes the body was already being mechanized, considered as much a series of interchangeable fragments as were Eli Whitney's gun parts. The interchangeability of parts and experiences played a key role in early national imaginings.[98]

In one remarkable instance we have contemporary evidence of a psychic split between inner self and outer mask. In 1771 Ezra Stiles wrote a lengthy commentary in his diary on the portrait Samuel King had recently finished of him (fig. 126).

Figure 125. *A Lay Figure*. From Crispijn Van de Passe, *La Prima-[Quinta] Parte della Luce del Dipengere et Disegnere* (also known as *'tLight der teken en Schilderkonst*) (Amsterdam, 1643–44). (Photo: National Gallery of Art Library, Rare Book Collection)

Disappearing Acts   367

His reflection is the most detailed contemporary "reading" of any surviving portrait, and he worried that the portrait be constructed to convey the nature of his "mind" (the inner self) as well as his "face" (the outer, public persona). On August 1–4 of that year, Stiles records, "This day Mr. King finished my Picture. He began it last year—but went over the face again now, & added Emblems & c." Stiles was no doubt picky as a client and demanded that the painter rework parts of the portrait that either displeased him or failed to convey through iconographic detail a didactic meaning. Thankfully, Stiles continues: "The piece is made up thus. The effigies sitting in a Green Elbow Chair, in a Teaching Attitude, with the right hand on the Breast, and the Left holding a preaching Bible. Behind & on his left side is a part of a Library—two Shelves of Books—a Folio [i.e., lower] shelf with *Eusebij Hist. Ecc.*, Livy, DuHalde's Hist[or]y of China, and one inscribed Talmud B., Aben Ezra, Rabbi Selomoh Jarchi in hebrew Letters, and a little below R. Moses Ben Maimon Moreh Mevochim." This impressive collection of titles was complemented by his listing of remaining volumes: "On the other shelf are Newton's Principia, Plato, Watts, Doddridge, Cudmorth's Intellectual System; & also the New England primaeval Divine Hooker, Chauncy, Mather, Cotton."[99]

Stiles then states why each volume is essential to the total image of himself. "I have selected the Books to my Taste," he allows, but he goes on to clarify his choice of rabbinical titles: "By these I denote my Taste for History. . . . I prize this Learn[in]g only for the scattered Remains of the antient Doctrine of the Trinity & a suffering Messiah, preserved in the Opinions of some of the Rabbins before Christ." His English titles provide a "good Idea of evangelical apostolic pastors" and "all the Mythology of the fabulous Ages, which I conceive to have originated from primeval Revelation to the Originals of all Nations." After decoding one or two more emblematic details—a "black spot" signifying "the Receptacle of the fallen Angels & the finally wicked," and a tall wooden pillar with representations of the Newtonian and Pythagorean systems, the Trinity, and a "Cluster of Minds whose central Tendencies are turned off from God to Earth, self & created good"—Stiles reveals his portrait's place in articulating an inner realm and a public image: "These Emblems are more descriptive of my Mind, than the Effigies of my Face."[100]

In such a context, the idea that Earl was so good at painting portraits that he could "start them with life" suggests that his ability to draw out and represent the sitter's interiority as part of the total image seen on the picture plane, to create a single image that emblematized the reunification of the sitter's inner and outer selves, was essentially modeled on the utopian unification of identities commonly represented as happening in death. This helps to explain why painters in rural places like Connecticut, where the force of the standing order remained strong despite the 1784 Toleration Act, often flattened their sitter's faces or, as in the case of

Figure 126. Samuel King, *Ezra Stiles*, 1771. Oil on canvas, H. 33½" (85.1 cm), W. 27½" (69.9 cm). (Photo: Yale University Art Gallery, Bequest of Dr. Charles Jenkins Foote, B.A., 1882, M.A., 1890)

John Brewster Jr.'s *Lucy and Her Son George*, painted their faces with ethereal, disengaged expressions (fig. 127). Their faces say, "I am not solely of this world." Their eyes open to the blinding light of revelation, providential wonders, visions of Christ's kingdom. When these humble but wild countenances are taken into account in portraits by Earl, Brewster, or Rufus Hathaway, the resulting expressions are almost entirely unrelated to the mimetic veracity or tedious, bourgeois realism

Figure 127. John Brewster Jr., *Lucy Knapp Mygatt and Her Son George*, 1799. Oil on canvas, H. 54" (137.2 cm), W. 40" (101.6 cm). (Photo: Palmer Art Museum, The Pennsylvania State University, University Park, Gift of Mrs. Nancy Adams McCord)

of Copley or West. Rather, their features implicate the representations of soul effigies, rising to meet their maker on gravestones throughout the New England countryside (fig. 128). And the relative lack of "realistic" details of facial hair, double chins, or warts in Earl's portraits—say, in contrast to those by Copley—suggests that Earl's bodies, perhaps idealized in order to heighten their stature, also may have been "restored" in preparation for salvation.[101]

The power of soul effigies to represent the final, blissful collapse of outer mask into inner self was reinforced by generational continuity in religious life. The prescribed use of portraits and gravestone images harkened back to late-seventeenth-century pronouncements on what sorts of images were appropriately "religious" or "civil." In 1672 Samuel Mather, in a revealing comment on what was permissibly excluded from the Second Commandment's ban on graven images, had argued that "the Civil use of Images is lawful for the representation and remembrance of a person absent, for honour and Civil worship to any worthy person." Like gravestones, portraits served to keep the genealogy of public service and personal salvation in constant view. The sober face and stiff posture of Earl's early portrait of Roger Sherman already suggested the abstract souls that inhabited the region's landscapes of memory (fig. 129). Earl allowed Sherman to combine the distant, iconic stare of the public gravestone with a resolute "singularity" of individual character; the cracks at the corners of his mouth, skinny legs, and awkward hands make his disappearance pragmatic, direct, arresting. Sherman's corporeal stiffness, rather than being dismissed as his own genetic physical awkwardness, also suggests that the movements, the bodily styles, of Connecticut's standing order may have been due to their studied attempts to fuse inner soul with the *gravitas* of public deportment. Thomas Anburey commented on Connecticut elites in the early 1780s. "Puritanism and a spirit of persecution are not yet totally extinguished," he noticed. "The gentry of both sexes are hospitable and good-natured, with an air of civility in their behaviour, but constrained by formality and preciseness; even the women, though easiness of carriage is peculiarly characteristic to their nature, appear here with much stiffness and reserve: they are formed by symmetry, handsome, and have delicate complexions; the men are tall, thin, and generally long-visaged."[102]

Why would Earl's worldly Federalist subjects want to have their inner and outer selves merged in the transcendent temporality of a decidedly "nonrealist" likeness? Precisely because their commercial activities opened a dangerous gap between piety and profit that could undermine moral authority. Experienced in commerce and political geography and in assembling identities from the abstract signals floating in commodities, "portrait people" like Oliver Ellsworth and Elijah Boardman worked hard to minimize the kind of financial risks that might publicly expose too great a rift between their private and public selves.

A

B

Figure 128. Soul effigies on New England gravestones: (a) detail of William Wolcott stone, South Windsor, Connecticut, 1749; (b) detail of Jennet Crage [Janet Craig] stone, Princeton, Massachusetts, 1776; (c) detail of Luke Roberts stone, King's Chapel burial ground, Boston, Massachusetts, 1780; (d) detail of Dorothy Walker stone, Brookfield, Massachusetts, 1804. (Drawing by the author)

RECOGNITION: SPECULATIVE SELVES

Leading citizens of the land of steady habits exposed an inner instability during the land speculation madness of the late 1780s and 1790s. The steadiness and sheer political clout of Earl's sitters derived principally from mercantile activities, in shipping, domestic trade, military supply, milling, and real estate. The pursuit and sale of land had quickened as the northwestern and northeastern hinterlands of Connecticut were settled and developed in the years following the Revolution. Elijah Boardman, for example, as the grandson of New Milford's first minister, was blessed with land and status from birth. Like his father, he added additional acreage to the family's local holdings as they came on the market. But Elijah, trained

C

D

as a retail clerk and dry-goods merchant, was aware of money's generative power. In 1795 he joined the Connecticut Land Company and bought
major tracts in Ohio's Western Reserve, including the present towns of
Medina, Palmyra, and, modestly, Boardman. Such speculation was dangerous, since it demanded an outlay in capital premised on a rewarding
return once settlement progressed and the land was sold off as individual
house lots. But as Timothy Dwight put it, "the splendor of the object fascinated the eye of every rash adventurer, and vast purchases were made
by various individuals." For those who, like Boardman, could invest with

Disappearing Acts   373

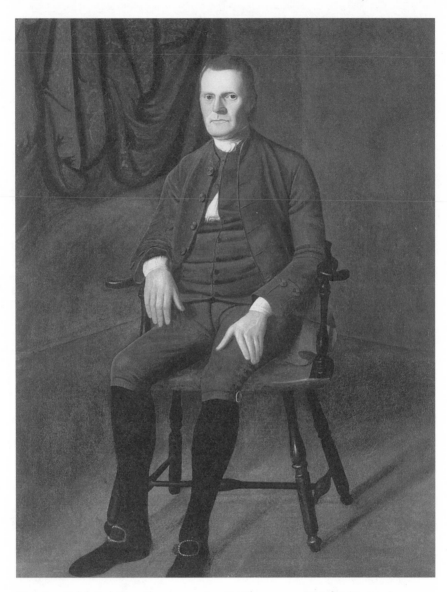

Figure 129. Ralph Earl, *Roger Sherman*, ca. 1775–76. Oil on canvas, H. 64⅝" (164.2 cm), W. 49⅝" (126.1 cm). (Photo: Yale University Art Gallery, Gift of Roger Sherman White, B.A. 1899, LL.B. 1902)

cash and adequate collateral and either sell quickly or afford prolonged ownership, the risk was predictable. As for those who invested heavily on credit, Dwight reports they "generally became bankrupts."[103]

The difficulty came when too many players got caught up in the game. According to Dwight, "the market was glutted; the price fell suddenly;

and those who had bought before this fall and were obliged to sell in order to make payments were often unable to obtain more than a moderate part of what they had given. In the course of buying and selling, the chain of purchase and credit was extended through a great multitude of individuals, and involved most of them in common ruin." Postrevolutionary land speculation was thus a "bubble" scheme similar to the South Seas stocks that had rocked the English imperial economy in the 1720s. Some people, like "entertaining, sagacious and successful trader" Oliver Phelps of Suffield, even invented their own scrip to handle credit transactions more smoothly, and "his own paper formed a kind of circulating medium." Dwight explained the peculiar passion of speculation in terms of social development:

> In certain stages of society the expectation of enterprising men may, with little difficulty, be raised to any imaginable height. Fortunes, they will easily believe, may be amassed at a stroke, without industry or economy, by mere luck, or the energy of superior talents for bisness. These talents every sanguine man will arrogate to himself, and on this luck he will rely without fear. The prize, he assured, will fall on him; and the twenty thousand blanks by which it is ominously surrounded will be drawn by others. That others have failed of success while attempting to acquire instantaneous wealth, he will indeed acknowledge, but he will show you that the failure was owing to that want of genuine skill, or caution from which himself is happily exempted.[104]

Seemingly rational people fell prey to a strange inner irrationality when confronted with the possibility of rapid wealth and equally fast social ascent. The consequences were clear. On the one hand, Dwight's objection seems grounded in his patrician disdain for the violation of social hierarchy. If people were successful in their financial scheming, commoners could end up with real economic and political power. Yet on the other hand, Dwight was concerned for the overall prosperity of Connecticut. As cash and credit were consumed by speculation, local exchange systems slowed to a crawl. "The commerce of Middletown," Dwight perceived, "has long been considerable, but, I think, has obviously declined within a few years past. The first cause, both in time and efficacy, of this evil was, if I mistake not, what has been proverbially called in this country speculation."[105] The "evil" for Dwight was simpler still: people speculating in lands were, at the risk of a deferential social structure, also speculating in personal identity.

Earl's portraits reveal an inner schism in the lives of his New England patrons. A split emphatically did exist between their "soul" and the carefully masked facades they manipulated for social ends in their mercantile lives, their hospitality lives, their traveling lives, their legal lives, their medical lives, and their political lives. Their identities were speculative. And if the allegory of republican virtue, the disappearance into the dimension of temporal continuity, demanded that public figures serve as emblematic embodiments of imagined collective values, any appearance of slippage between inner conscience and outer act must be minimized or, better still, eliminated. What better way to be thus represented than in a "likeness" of oneself in which any duplicitous shifting of social identities was momentarily suspended, their motion stopped? If, as George Kubler has suggested, artistic style is "another way of imposing space upon time and of denying duration under the illusion that successive events are similar events," then the particular style of one's painted disappearance assumes paramount importance as a strategy of shaping consensual communities in an age of capitalist expansion. From this perspective, then, when William Dunlap derisively commented of Steward, a minister turned painter, that "What turned him from the cure of men's souls, / to the caricaturing of their bodies, I never learned," he was missing the essential point, namely that by limning a full "likeness" and not just "a picture without," one could minister precisely to the gap between the varied actions of the mortal body and the blissful peace of the immortal soul.[106]

Hovering between this world and the next, between the concrete challenge of everyday life and the amnesia of national allegory, Earl's portraits of Federalist leaders in Connecticut placed them in the ambivalent pedagogic terrain of the "instantaneous present" in the last decade of the eighteenth century. The Federalist elites who had Ralph Earl paint portraits of their buildings and bodies shared basic assumptions about social order with their Congregational ancestors. Like them, they envisioned a mythic nation largely in fulfillment of seventeenth-century promises of a New Israel. Like them, they conceived of the body as a metaphor of social hierarchy that was divinely sanctioned. And like them, they saw different "capacities" among individuals that warranted assigned distinctions of rank. Earl's Connecticut sitters concurred with Fisher Ames's distrust of "democracy," with John Adams's keen defense of privilege, and with William Hubbard when he claimed that "it is not then the result of time or chance, that some are mounted on horse-back, while others are left to travell on foot," and "that some have with the Centurion, power to command, while others are required to obey."[107]

The 1790s were not the 1670s, however, and enough had changed in New England's colonial culture to make allegory a level of symbolic action that disenchanted Federalists found both necessary and attractive. As I have suggested, alternative versions of history and uncanny recognitions of the Self in the Other rested uneasily, impossibly, within the continuous flow of allegory and disappearance. As Bhabha observes, "the distracting presence of another temporality that disturbs the contemporaneity of the national present" establishes a productive rupture for new, more inclusive political formations; in late-eighteenth-century Connecticut, the zone of contingency was so pressing that it was institutionalized and on its own became "a continuous transmission of legitimacy" that elites could simply not escape.[108] The moments of "recognition" that interrupted the flow of national narration—and that occasionally have interrupted my narrative as well—reveal how powerfully elites were reminded by the Other that lived within the Self that their lives were now forever tied to the time of contingency and the world of daily, uncomfortable appearance.

THE EXCITEMENT OF

COMMODITIES IS THE

EXCITEMENT OF POSSIBILITY,

OF FLOATING AWAY FROM

THE PARTICULAR TO TASTE

THE RANGE OF AVAILABLE

LIFE. THERE ARE TIMES

WHEN WE WANT TO BE

AFTERWORD # Metaphysics and Markets

ALIENS AND STRANGERS, TO

FEEL HOW THE SHAPE OF

OUR LIVES IS NOT THE ONLY

SHAPE, TO DRIFT BEFORE A

CATALOG OF POSSIBLE LIVES.

—LEWIS HYDE, *THE GIFT*

COMMERCE AND CHRIST

I have argued that concerns over relations of authority and resistance emerged in New England culture with clarity and force whenever material representations of the body came under scrutiny. These representations were always indirect; they came as metaphor, symbol, gesture, or discursive reference that in turn brought other indirect representations to mind, making moments when authority was exercised or contested rich with the poetics (and politics) of implication. A final concern warrants further attention, in part to suggest a conclusion but also to work toward an opening for new investigations into how structures of implication, including intimation, intensification, temporalities of speed and slowness, metaphoric compression and diffusion, and distraction, make the separation of "metaphysics" and "markets" that so often characterizes studies of colonial societies difficult to maintain. To speak of metaphysics in colonial New England culture, for example, typically means one is studying the discourse and experience of religious practice in the seventeenth century, concentrating on works written by ministers whose interests were served, after all, by arguing a continuity between the visible and invisible worlds. Students of metaphysics talk about remarkable providences, witches, and monstrous births, about affliction, revelation, and grace. The "market," on the other hand, only gets good in the eighteenth century. Trade is extensive, mercantilism of unquestioned strength, and talk of "consumer revolutions" rivals discussion of political upheaval.

These worlds were never separate, their historical progress never linear. The commodification of culture asserted by market forces was always incomplete and, as the house attacks I have described demonstrate, bore an enchantment as intensely metaphysical as any witchcraft narrative. Perhaps one way to make the point is to examine an assumption many early American historians implicitly hold dear: namely, when Puritan communities encountered commercial capitalism, Puritanism lost. The process may have been gradual, the emergence of a commercial economy in New England locally textured, but port towns like Boston, Salem, Marblehead, and Newport discovered earlier than rural villages that merchants spawned more wealth, a new distance between rich and poor, faith in upward social mobility, new ethnic enclaves, and the polite material trappings of English gentility. Against such ready signs of earthly reward, ministers argued that merchants and unregulated trade would undermine the deferential, organic community and religious asceticism that had shaped New England's distinctive social cohesion. So runs the litany of decline.[1]

The "community breakdown" model of New England history, as Christine Leigh Heyrman has termed it, has different points of origin. One was the impact of generational change in the last half of the seventeenth century. As immigrant elders approached death, they worried at the hesitancy of children to gain full communion; their children accepted baptism but approached the sacrament with consummate caution. Interpreting the arrival of a new generation of ambitious English merchants after 1660 as a sign of worldly depravity, an aging ministry railed in jeremiad after jeremiad against the poverty of piety among the second generation. Thomas Breeden, the first of these new traders to land in Boston, was so fashionably dressed in "a strange habit with a 4 Cornerd Cap instead of a hat" and "Breeches hung with Ribbons from the Wast downw[ard] a gr[ea]t depth, one row over another like shingles on a house," that local boyes greated him "from one end of the street to the other calling him a Devill."[2] Another reason why the declension model has opposed religion and commerce derives from a belief that the latter represented a new liberal individualism, a freedom that triumphed as the Revolution exposed the limits of the Puritan organic-hierarchic social structure. But enough of this critical cant; Heyrman suggested that commerce, far from leading to community decline, seems in Marblehead and Gloucester to have validated and enlivened structures of religious authority and church membership already in place. What Heyrman discovered openly challenged common approaches to metaphysics and markets. Commerce made visible the presence of Christ.[3]

The subtle connection of sacred and secular bodies was nothing new in seventeenth-century New England. It had deep roots in the medieval church's troubled efforts to define and then contain the first expansion of the economic sphere during the late twelfth century. Architectural historian Otto von Simpson has argued that "we do not easily realize to what extent the religious and the economic spheres interlocked in those days. The age of the towering pilgrimage churches and cathedrals was, economically speaking, the age of the great fairs. It is well known how powerfully these recurrent markets—spasmodic concentrations of the economic life of entire regions—stimulated the development of the medieval city."[4]

The challenge was to spark commercial activity while at the same time retaining a means of limiting mercantile growth. As Von Simpson pointed out, the church realized that sponsoring fairs and trade guilds of artisans was in its interest. Some of the fairs, such as the Lendit of Saint Denis, were established to honor relics of saints, while others, including one at Chartres, were important for the sale of religious souvenirs and devotional objects. A ready supply of skilled artisans under the church's patronage in guilds and confraternities assured the steady progress of ecclesiastical building projects. Because of these intertwined interests, the sacred terrain of the church was cut through with secular pursuits. Stained glass windows of the Virgin were gifts of butchers, weavers, bakers, and petty merchants. At Chartres markets were held within the Cloister itself, with individual merchants setting up stalls in front of the canon's houses. Fresh produce was hawked under the southern portico of the cathedral itself. As von Simpson maintained, the worlds of belief and business were fused: "Masons, carpenters, and other craftsmen gathered in the church itself, waiting for an employer to hire them. Even the selling of food in the basilica was not considered improper if carried on in an orderly fashion. At one time the chapter had to forbid the wine merchants to sell their product in the nave of the church, but assigned part of the crypt for that purpose, thus enabling the merchants to avoid the imposts levied by the Count of Chartres on sales transacted outside. The many ordinances passed by the chapter to prevent the loud, lusty life of the market place from spilling over into the sanctuary only show how inseparable the two worlds were in reality."[5]

The connection of the two worlds in medieval towns during the twelfth century grew tighter and more intense over the succeeding centuries and grew to be as characteristic of small parish churches in the countryside as it was of great cathedrals in European cities. Under the front porch of the church in Regensburg in 1520 hung tools, baskets, and shoes, among other market goods, even as pilgrims exalted the Virgin Mary in response to a rising reformation tide (fig. 130). A map of Chelmsford, Essex, in the early 1590s shows the church and market square on continuous ground (fig. 131), and a surviving sixteenth-century market house at Thaxted, Essex, sits directly beneath a parish church perched on a small hill overlooking it. In these towns the marketplace lay directly in front of the church. The same arrangement marked central public spaces in colonial Charlestown, Boston, and Salem, where each town placed its first meetinghouse directly adjacent to its central market space. Parishioners had to tiptoe through commerce to reach religion.[6]

Figure 130. Michael Ostendorfer, *Pilgrimage to the Blessed Mary at Regensburg*, engraving, 1520. (Courtesy Hamburg Kunsthalle, Kupferstichkabinett; photo: Elke Walford, Hamburg)

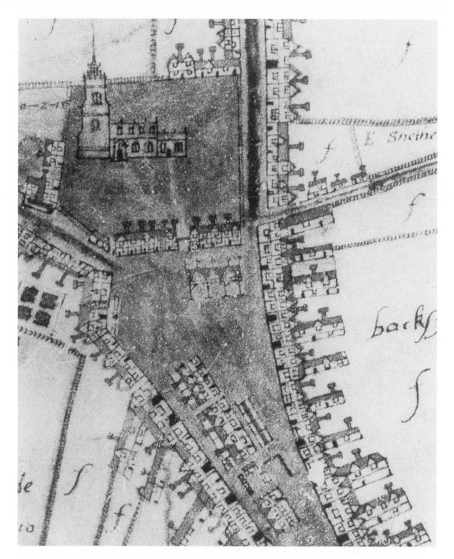

Figure 131. John Walker, detail of marketplace and church area from map of Chelmsford, Essex, 1591. (Photo: Essex Record Office)

In these situations, however, which realm of symbolic exchange is really watching over the other? The interlocking nature of religious practice and commodity exchange was not without an organizing dynamic, a directional flow. Von Simpson was careful to observe this dynamic in his discussion of fairs and cathedrals. "The fairs," he wrote, "are inseparable from the religious life of the Middle Ages; indeed *they originate in it.*"[7] Similarly, the persistence of an earlier metaphysical perspective shaped ways that people in New England encountered commerce. "In both Gloucester and Marblehead," Heyrman states, "the survival or resurgence of a communitarian culture limited the impact of commercial development. The profit motive did not dissolve the bonds of communal cohesion of the social strength of Puritanism; instead, personal ties, customary practices, and religious values shaped the conduct of commercial activity. . . . Rather than being at odds with the ideals of Puritanism or the ends of communitarianism, commercial capitalism coexisted with and was molded by the cultural patterns of the past."[8]

What do these statements suggest about buildings and bodies in colonial New England? First, the marketplace likely emerged from the world of the church and its corporate, customary ethos. Commerce remained symbolically tied to the metaphysical world of death, rebirth, and eternal life and perhaps still presents a window or eye on the enchanting possibility of transcending oneself through contract and exchange. Commodities, anthropologist Arjun Appadurai has argued, have no existential priority in our world, despite frequent attempts to represent them as "mechanical products of production regimes governed by laws of supply and demand." Rather, their definition as such is entirely contingent on specific situations of exchange, each of which presents a mixture of "socially regulated paths and competitively *inspired* diversions."[9] Throughout its long social life, any object might be diverted to function as a gift in one transaction, an object of loan or customary barter in another situation, and a commodity in a third. Or owing to the overlapping temporalities of implicative signs, the same object, at different levels of apprehension and perception, may have veered at once toward emblem and commodity, the ideal poles of exchange in colonial New England.

Contemporary discourse asserting the anticipated material comforts of heaven made the nervous course of metaphoric wavering apparent. Worried that anxiety over salvation and communion was encouraging rather than discouraging an embrace of worldly goods, ministers appropriated the language of the marketplace to lead people to God. The heavenly mansion, as perfectly symmetrical as a Georgian house, overflowed with remarkable possessions. Imbuing the sensate world with spiritual significance, ministers urged parishioners to "spiritualize the most Earthly objects that are before [them]," as there were "Numerous Lessons of *Morality*, which by the Help of the *Analogy* between the *Natural* and *Spiritual* World . . . we may learn from them."[10] Lay readers found advice on how to practice this imaginary art in books. Richard Baxter, an English minister whose works circulated in New England, urged individuals to contemplate familiar objects "to quicken your affections, by comparing the unseen delights of Heaven with those smaller which you have seen and felt in the flesh." The faithful in early New England subjected their houses, bodies, and interiors to ruthless inspection, using objects of all sorts to index the progress of grace among them. As Edward Taylor's eye swept across his inventory of metaphoric furnishings, he found that the cabinets that merchants used to protect valuables reverberated as protective containers of the soul's value: "Oh! That my Soule, Heavens Workmanship (within / My Wicker'd Cage . . . / Might be they Cabbinet, Oh Pearle of Price / Oh! let thy Pearle, Lord, Cabbinet in mee. / I'st then be rich! nay rich enough for thee." Resurrection itself became a contractual relationship in which salvation was exchanged for the individual soul as a cipher of God's grace. "Lord, make my Soule Thy Plate / . . . Then I shall be thy Money."[11]

By the last quarter of the seventeenth century, ministers envisioned the "new house" of heavenly embodiment with the sharpened precision of a cloth merchant. It was a city-palace with streets of gold and walls of crystalline transparency. Taylor imagined its interior decor as a "Bright Jasper Hall Walld with translucid gold" and "Floors pav'd with Pearls." He conjured furnishings in equal detail, concentrating often on God's heavenly chair, "A Golden Throne whose Banisters are Pearles, / And Pomills Choicest Gems: Carbuncle-Stayes / Studded with Pretious Stones, Carv'd with rich Curles / Of Polisht Art, sending out flashing Rayes." He even imagined how food was prepared in the next house. Manna, that "Soule Sweet Bread," was made "On Heavens high Dresser Boarde and thoroughly bak[e]d."[12]

Samuel Sewall also had precise visions of the next world. In 1675 he dreamed he was climbing a long stair, until "at last I came to a fair chamber with goodly lodgings." Its appointments were not what he expected. Having roomed with Edward Taylor at Harvard College and no doubt having had conversations about the afterlife, he may have shared the poet's vision of gold and pearls. But to his diary Sewall confided a more literal and doltish approach to the problem. "Amazed I was," he recalled, "not being able to conceive how furniture should be brought up those stairs so high." Nearly two decades later he visited a friend who was living in a house filled with expensive furnishings. Lying awake at night and thinking of his neighbor's "commodity," he admitted the furniture "led me to think of Heaven the House not made with hands, which God for many Thousands of years has been storing with the richest furniture (Saints that are from time to time placed there), and that I had some hopes of being entertain'd in that Magnificent Convenient Palace, every way fitted and furnished. These thoughts were very refreshing to me."[13]

It is perhaps easiest to see the appropriation of marketplace language and the attenuation of material descriptions of the heavenly mansion as attempts on the part of an anxious clergy to graft religion onto the burgeoning growth of commercial capitalism. Since Puritan ministers had first appeared in public in England during the late sixteenth century, after all, they had been accused of adopting the demeanor of merchants even while they tried to demonstrate their differences. William Perkins, perhaps the most orthodox of Puritan theologians, admitted in a Sturbridge Fair sermon in 1593 that "everyone brings hither something to be sold." And while most merchants hawked earthly goods, "the merchandise I bring . . . is from heaven and all the earth cannot yield it: and as it is from heaven, so it is of a heavenly virtue and will work that which all the wealth in this fair is not able to do."[14]

John Cotton, who migrated from Boston in Lincolnshire to become a leading minister in Boston, Massachusetts, traded in mercantile metaphors in his 1651 sermon "Purchasing Christ." The sermon as a whole eventually urges people to buy Christ in strictly indirect, metaphoric terms. "Christ is to be purchased, not so much by money," Cotton warned, "as chiefly this purchase must be made by parting with all those many and strong Lusts, and Corruptions, and sinnful rebellions of heart, by which we keep off Christ from comming into our hearts." But Cotton nonetheless began by setting forth "three Cases in which money must be layd out, or else Christ cannot be had, and in refusing to lay out money, we refuse life in him." One case is particularly strong in its use of commercial language. "But secondly," he wrote, "there is another time, namely, when in the case of persecution the market of Christ goes at so high a rate, that a man cannot have Christ with any comfort in his soule, or peace to his Conscience, or purity of heart or life, unlesse he hazzard all his estate, or a good part of it: In buying and selling of a precious commodity, a good Chapman will have it what ever it cost him: So Christ is sometimes at an higher, and sometimes at a lower rate, but whatever he costs him, he will have him."[15]

Perkins and Cotton were adepts in the alchemy of borrowed language. Yet these sermons do not show them tailoring religion to the coattails of an accelerating commerce. Rather, by strategically drawing the discourse of merchants into their own pulpit performances, they were attempting to attract merchants by demonstrating that the church took care to speak in terms they understood. In the early decades of Puritan reform, incorporating wealthy merchants into the fold had political advantages as well; the attempt to use material metaphors freely was a continuous theme in Puritan sermonics that many have interpreted as a sign the clergy was buckling to commercial interests. The opposite was more the case. The crisis over charity in late-seventeenth- and early-eighteenth-century New England brought the same borrowing of language to the fore. In 1712 John Barnard of Marblehead preached in language that recalls Perkins and Cotton. He urged wealthy merchants that "their greatest business" was "securing" a place in heaven, and the best way for traders to pursue "where our greatest interest lies" was through charity. Ministers argued that if the wealthy gave to the less fortunate, by "doing good" to others they would strengthen their own "natural" position at the pinnacle of the social order. Maintaining charity, the clergy argued, assured that God's immutable order for a hierarchic society—their own key fiction—would remain fixed. In making this argument, ministers were not interested solely in bolstering their own position by co-opting economic language. Instead, as Heyrman observes, "ministers shored up the credibility of merchant leadership less through overt justifications than by their denial that social change was actually taking place."[16]

Motive established, ministers in the early eighteenth century forwarded the "charity sermon" as a new genre and urged merchant-communicants to engage in benevolent activities that would put the poor to work in schools and factories funded by their own contributions. The charity sermon typically positioned the wealthy merchant as an agent for an "enterprising deity," while the "chief parties to the charitable transaction were no longer donor and recipient, but instead the affluent middleman-benefactor and a revenue-hungry God." Listen to Samuel Willard's attempt, merging strangely the language of rational calculation with that of feudal obligation, to enlist the philanthropist-broker's involvement in charity: "We owe it to God, who is our Land-Lord, and it is part of the Quit-Rent which he expects of us; and that in this way we shall be under the Blessing. . . . We hereby engage God to be our Paymaster; and have good security that we shall not be losers, but great gainers in the foot of the Account." Or in a more precise calculation of cost and investment, Cotton Mather's appeal to merchants: "But indeed, after the Stupendous Transactions of the Great Day, throughout all the Days of Eternity, still all our present Acts of Liberality, will be lying by us, like so many Good Bills of Exchange; which our merciful God will be forever Owing and Paying . . . yea, after more than millions of Ages, we shall make a greater Gain of the poor than Joseph did of a Famine in the Days of Old."[17]

Charity sermons preached by New England ministers seemed to sanction liberal economics even as they used it to corral the expanding contours of commercial prerogative. Still attempting to live up to the ideals of their grandfathers, third-generation ministers concentrated on stimulating charity because they believed it was their duty to shape a society at whose "head" stood the wealthy and privileged merchant prince. What worried ministers in the early eighteenth century was that merchants seemed to be shirking the responsibility to lead and govern that had always accompanied privilege. By stressing charity as a way for the merchant to purify his money and overcome the taint of immorality that clouded him in the public eye, ministers discovered a way to authorize property and its accumulation as one means of determining social status. But they only did so in an effort to perpetuate a conservative theory of a hierarchic social body, a figure that would have been familiar to Perkins and Cotton a century before. Here again, ministers relied on the language of commerce and commodities to drive home a metaphysical claim. Cotton Mather's dogged assurance that heaven will be a "material city" was therefore consistent with a perceived desire to cajole merchants into the fold with language that at once proselytized and legitimized.

The metaphysics of Georgian houses make the point directly. In the Connecti-cut River valley, for example, local gentry typically marked the formal entrance into the inner realm of treasured commodities with a doorway of exaggerated scale and mannerist proportion (fig. 132). These were portals, as we have learned through the recollections of Catherine Sedgwick, through which only the socially elect could pass. Once inside, however, the chosen few enjoyed a sensory world of earthly delights, the familiar and exotic fruits of merchant capital. Yet the social separation the portal proclaimed was forceful only as it grounded class division in legitimizing religious imagery. The social distance separating the Dwights, Stod-dards, or Williamses from their local supplicants in this world metaphysically sig-naled the ordained segregation of those souls elected for salvation and the glories of the heavenly mansion. Also approached through a gate or portal, the "Bright Jasper Hall Walld with translucid gold" and "Floors pav'd with Pearls" that poet Edward Taylor foresaw promised material delights only a similarly elect group could experience. Gravestones in the area frequently employed the "portal of death" as a key iconographic element. The souls of the dead cross through literal thresholds (fig. 133) and appear, eyes blinded, as they pass through portals into the world beyond (fig. 134). "Death is the portal to eternity, and carries men over to an unchangeable state," wrote Samuel Willard in 1726.[18] And anticipations of the heavenly mansion's perfect symmetry in death and of coming glory stood behind not only the balanced symmetry of merchants' houses but also the local gentry's penchant for "crown-topped" doors (portals to heavenly), "crown-topped" high chests (for heavenly raiment), and "crown-topped" looking glasses (in which to glimpse one's sacred image).

SACRED COMMODITIES: A DIGRESSION

Since the eighteenth century the contiguity of metaphysics and markets has sur-faced frequently, if uncomfortably. Marx admitted that the commodity form, born of the rational market and the alienation of labor value under conditions of divided labor in production, kept one foot planted in metaphysical terrain. Em-bodied work retains a trace of the sacred. Or to use the language Marx himself offered, a language that has received far less attention than it deserves, the com-modity is "abounding in metaphysical subtleties," it "transcends sensuousness," and, while perhaps as a "social hieroglyphic" it cryptically references the very so-cial relations of production it masks, it has a "magic" or "mystical character" that has strange parallels with the workings of the spirit in material things in colonial New England. Here is Marx on the contortive nature of commodities:

Figure 132. Doorway, Samuel Porter's house, Hadley, Massachusetts, ca. 1760–65. (Photo by the author)

Figure 133. Joseph Manning and Elizabeth Manning stone, Ipswich, Massachusetts, 1784. (Photo by the author)

It is absolutely clear that, by his activity, man changes the forms of the materials of nature in such a way as to make them useful to him. The form of wood, for instance, is altered if a table is made out of it. Nevertheless the table continues to be wood, an ordinary, sensuous thing. But as soon as it emerges as a commodity, it changes into a thing which transcends sensuousness. It not only stands with its feet on the ground, but, in relation to all other commodities, it

Figure 134. Detail of Martha Welch stone, Storrs, Connecticut, 1773.
(Photo by the author)

stands on its head, and evolves out of its wooden brain grotesque ideas, far more wonderful than if it were to begin dancing of its own free will.[19]

And here is shoemaker William Morse, attempting to capture in words what happened in his Newbury, Massachusetts, house in 1680:

> I saw the andiron leap into the pot and dance and leap out, and again leap in and dance and leap out again. . . . Also I saw the pot turn itself over and throw down all the water. Again, we saw a tray with wool leap up and down and throw the wool out, and so many times. . . . Again, in the morning, a great stone . . . did remove from place to place; we saw it. Two spoons [were] throwed off the table, and presently the table was thrown down. . . . Again, my wife [had] her hat taken from her head sitting by the fire by me. The table [was] thrown down again; my spectacles were thrown from the table almost into the fire.[20]

In both texts, furniture dances and confounds the mastery of human action as things assume the role of active, personified presences. In one case, the subtle spell of fetishism catches desire in the artificial illusion that a living person exists on the "other side" of the inert object's fragile walls. In the other, the equally treacherous trance of witchcraft offers the danger that the Devil is in one's house, in one's body, and manipulating objects from the "other side" of the conceptual plane separating the invisible from the visible world. In both Marx and Morse, the object threatens with the power of revelation and reveals the further contiguity of the human body and God in the production of objects: cities, houses, cabinets, money itself.[21]

In colonial New England objects could suspend people between life and death, poised precisely at the purchase point of transformation that minister Cotton called "purchasing Christ." Although it addresses commodities in contemporary supermarkets more than in early modern commerce and may thus seem marginal to my historical project, Don De Lillo's novel *White Noise* approaches the poetics of commodities in a way that supports my argument. De Lillo observes that supermarkets, where we daily encounter products, packages, and our spiritual vacuity, are able, paradoxically, to reconnect us with the transcendent. In one scene, Murray Siskind, a visiting professor of popular culture, meets Babette. As Jack Gladney, Babette's husband, eavesdrops on their conversation, he hears Murray say to her: "Tibetans believe there is a transitional state between death and rebirth. Death is a waiting period, basically. Soon a fresh womb will receive the soul. In the meantime the soul restores to itself some of the divinity it lost at birth. . . . That's what I think of whenever I come in here. This place recharges us spiritually, it prepares us, it's a gateway or pathway. Look how bright. It's full of psychic data."[22]

By having Murray speak these words, De Lillo repositions the world of commodities in a contemporary culture that long ago abandoned any serious pursuit of religious life. Since Marx we have been aware of the role that commodities play as fetishes, or the promise that mass-produced objects make to connect consumers imaginatively with a specific and unified social being on the other side of their bodies. Attracted to the promise of social connection through the possessed object to an anticipated creator, the consumer is disappointed when the object, itself the end product of a divided labor process and alienated value, fails to fulfill the imagined contract. From this perspective, the commodity fetish serves to fragment human connection. It repeatedly offers but repeatedly sunders the possibility of connection.

This is not how commodities and supermarkets work in De Lillo's fictive space. Here, commodities offer an opening to rethink the implied poetics of commercial capitalism. From this perspective, commodities represent not a premature closure but a portal through which we may apprehend spiritual concerns immanent in exchange. Contingent on both their sensory existence and their invocative or immanent power, commodities are instead a means of reaching through substance to interrogate belief. For Murray Siskind, the world of commodities is coterminous with revelation itself. "Everything is concealed in symbolism, hidden by veils of mystery and layers of cultural material," he comments. "But it is psychic data, absolutely. The large doors slide open, they close unbidden. Energy waves, incident radiation. All the letters and numbers are here, all the colors of the spectrum, all the voices and sounds, all the code words and ceremonial phrases. It is just a question of deciphering, rearranging, peeling off the layers of unspeakability."[23]

But what is all the "psychic data," with its voices, codes, phrases, and colors, preventing most of us from discovering? What, precisely, is "unspeakable" in the marketplace? The answer, political theorist Thomas L. Dumm suggests, is death. "The supermarket," he maintains, "is our repository of death, a warehouse of the 'things' we people eat. It has the sanctity of a graveyard; one can hear a certain hush underneath its bustle. This silence reflects our collective realization that the supermarket serves as the contemporary site of the religious impulse, the place where 'intimacy is given external form.' . . . The supermarket not only operates to commodify life, but also to create a dystopia of danger." Dumm's argument ultimately leads elsewhere, since he wants to suggest that shopping, as a practice through which people encounter a discourse that is at once commercial and political, is metaphorically linked to torture, especially when we pause to consider not only what shopping does *for us* but *to us* as well. For my purposes in this book, however, his connection of the marketplace to religious beliefs surrounding death affirms De Lillo's interpretive insights and, more obliquely, recalls Marx's aside that the "mystery of commodities" is composed of "all the magic and *necromancy* that surrounds the products of labor on the basis of commodity production." And his emphasis on commodities having death at their metaphoric core recalls the sense of social loss that figured prominently in Marx's theory of commodity fetishism. Dumm even ventures an analogy that recalls von Simpson's discussion of economy and architecture: "When I enter the supermarket I think of the vestibule of a church. I become acutely aware that I am traversing a liminal arena."[24]

The perspectives of Marx, Appadurai, De Lillo, and Dumm are external to the culture of early New England as it was lived, but not to my culture as I write. In different ways, they suggest that metaphysics and markets continually constitute each other; the relationship is fully dialectical. Commodities can be flattened neither into secular indexes of an expanding market calculus nor into banal strategies of display by cultural elites worried about status; in the end, Earl's patrons settled for fictions of themselves that mimed soul effigies, portraits of death "started to life" under the painter's hand. Commodity fetishism is not about memorializing loss but a story of how the market opens the metaphysical to popular contemplation.

THE GREAT EXCHANGE

Perhaps the work of revelation related buildings and bodies as people in colonial New England struggled to contain a key cultural anxiety: the exact moment when their risen souls would face eternal judgment. At this determining moment when, in both transactional and translational terms, they faced something they called the "great exchange" or the "work of transformation," individuals were led to contemplate a single existential question that had haunted their lives: *What will the value of my soul be?* Anxiety about the afterlife was as intense as that over communion, and the similar fear of being "unprepared" or "unworthy" made this single great transaction the central metaphoric structure of the culture. After leading you through the implied meanings of buildings from sixteenth-century farmhouses to Georgian mansions and through the contested implications of the human body, as empirical science challenged Pauline doctrine, I conclude that given this pivotal anxiety afflicting all souls, commercial exchange itself served as a means of exploring in both "transcendent" and "sensuous" terms the problem of resurrecting value; William Goodwin of Hartford in 1653 described the death of a friend: "He accomplished that greate worke of exchanging this life for a better."[25] Engaging the market, in concrete terms, demanded that individuals survive or perish in a maze of trivial decisions, know flawed goods from valuable ones, and acquire sufficient surplus to persist despite shifts in money supply or trade balances. In metaphoric terms, the market and its flow of commodities allowed people to explore central ontological issues of death, judgment, resurrection, and eternal life.

The market was thus alive with metaphysical implications: valuation, judgment, covenant, loss. At question in the marketplace, however, was a diffusion of symbolic power similar to that which transferred the anthropomorphism and "living stones" of the church outward into the human houses of pious yeomen. Let me reverse the normal terms of the "declension" argument, in which religion finally capitulates to capitalism. What if potentially every commercial transaction reverberated—some more, others less—with the enormous metaphoric power of the "great exchange"? If this were the case, at various purchase points consumers could act *in loco Dei*, assuming upon themselves the position of being the ultimate judge of the exchange at hand. Yet while being arbiters of value might be an authorizing act, it might also have been unnerving. From their symbolic vantage point of the ultimate Judge, the same individuals could see themselves as "thing-like" in the very transaction they were viewing from above. The process of commodity exchange therefore involved a double vision of omniscient "person" and objectified "thing," a strange mix of euphoric power and depersonalized distance. A purchase (or loan, barter) could therefore leave an individual feeling at once glorified and polluted, excited and exhausted; for evangelical Puritans already skilled at self-objectifying critical meditation, commercial transactions aroused deeply conflicted religious feelings of elation and disgust, authority and debasement, power and worthlessness. The double vision of consumption lay behind New England Puritans' simultaneous need for and rejection of markets and is a central problematic in any culturally specific analysis of commodity fetishism in colonial America.

Somehow, however, theorizing the metaphysics of the marketplace by dissecting the problem of commodity fetishism in a new way is less an explanation than an indication of where new work could usefully lead. Finally, many of the objects discussed in this book undercut easy dichotomies that gloss the imagined polarity of a metaphysical and a market culture. As Edward Howes suggested in 1639, they are bodies with a "multiplicitie" of possible interpretations, Charles Morton's "mixts," our hybrid cultural forms and processes. One way to approach the analysis of objects and texts suspended between metaphysical and mercantile exchange systems could begin with the distinction often drawn between "preindustrial" production, with artisans making houses, chairs, shoes, and cloth in their own shops for local clients, and the awakening "industrial economy," with rationalized structures of wage labor, centralized manufacture, and large capitalization that perhaps began in earnest during the early 1790s. Increasingly, however, we are discovering that labor practices such as pieceworking and the stockpiling of interchangeable parts were in place among Boston joiners, turners, and blacksmiths by 1670. With putting-out strategies in place this early, the intermediate concept of "protoindustrialization," used by American historians to describe "transitional" qualities of rural economies, may be appropriate to suggest a middle, intermingled stage of by-employment that enabled families caught between cycles of agricultural depression to engage in handicrafts. Craft production was directed not merely to local clients but, organized through piecework and final assembly by larger shops in Boston or Salem, sought to market objects over a wide area.[26]

The concept of protoindustrialization is suggestive because it complicates the reductionist dualism of "emblem" versus "commodity" that often invades our analysis of "metaphysics" and "markets." The zone of protoindustrial culture defines an intermediate field of always incomplete transformation. In this book I have attempted to describe the utter contingency of metaphysics and markets in colonial New England culture and to interpret in each chapter the rich interplay among objects that were never exclusively either emblem or commodity. To be honest, I found emblems tricky enough. As Rosemary Freeman has argued, for Elizabethans the cohesion of medieval allegorical thought had already cracked, and emblems were "fragments of the old allegorical ways of thinking still present in men's minds, but present only as fragments and not co-ordinated." Arguably, since emblem books peaked in popularity just as Elizabethan commerce was accelerating, commercial exchange itself may have provided the semiotic cohesion that "coordinated" these scattered signs of religious piety for popular consumption. The long shadow of the emblem also risks a false totalization of meaning, as Emerson revealed in his transcendental paean to the promise of human unity. "We are symbols and inhabit symbols," he wrote, "workmen, work, and tools, words and things, birth and death, all are emblems."[27]

Fragmented or total, the emblem's historical trajectory was far from pure. Its commitment to a single iconic value suggests it was always implicated in, reacting to, the liquidity of market relations. The use of the term "commodity" in recent critical theory is equally worrisome, since not every reified, deallegorized, or transactional object or text necessarily qualifies. As I have suggested, there were (are?) buildings and bodies that hover between the emblematic evocations of heavenly pattern and the transactional demands of the market. They partake in both logics but are completely neither; as Edward Taylor suggested, the cabinet— representing at once the merchant's treasure box of valuables and Christ's treasure house of souls—relied upon exactly this conflation of referential worlds.

Perhaps a contingent process of "protocommodification" accompanied protoindustrial production in colonial New England, marking objects of socially indeterminate value. With production organized *partially* through piecework and *partially* through the integrity of master-apprentice shop relations, protocommodities were artifacts of the hybrid social connections that informed their production and distribution. Importantly—and this is where they differ from Marx's canonical definition of the commodity form—the labor value of protocommodities was never fully alienated. And if the protocommodity was (only partly) a stand-in for social ties that were (only partly) broken, then what order of partial, incomplete fetishism might it imply? Protofetishism? Perhaps. It seems an apt term for the intermediate, incomplete, awakening kind of hybrid symbolic work they performed. In colonial New England, buildings and bodies brought people before mysteries of existence, and revealed ways that existence itself was mystified.

NOTES

ABBREVIATIONS USED IN THE NOTES

AC   *The Antinomian Controversy, 1636–1638: A Documentary History,* ed. David D. Hall. Middletown, Conn.: Wesleyan University Press, 1968.

AQ   *American Quarterly*

BSR, 1   *A Report of the Record Commissioners of the City of Boston, Containing the Records of Boston Selectmen, 1701 to 1715.* Boston: Rockwell and Churchill, 1884.

BSR, 2   *A Report of the Record Commissioners of the City of Boston, Containing the Records of Boston Selectmen, 1716 to 1736.* Boston: Rockwell and Churchill, 1885.

BSR, 3   *A Report of the Record Commissioners of the City of Boston, Containing the Records of Boston Selectmen, 1736 to 1742.* Boston: Rockwell and Churchill, 1886.

BSR, 4   *A Report of the Record Commissioners of the City of Boston, Containing the Selectmen's Minutes from 1742–43 to 1753.* Boston: Rockwell and Churchill, 1887.

BSR, 5   *A Report of the Record Commissioners of the City of Boston, Containing the Selectmen's Minutes from 1754 through 1763.* Boston: Rockwell and Churchill, 1887.

BSR, 6   *A Report of the Record Commissioners of the City of Boston, Containing the Selectmen's Minutes from 1769 through April, 1775.* Boston: Rockwell and Churchill, 1893.

BSR, 7   *A Report of the Record Commissioners of the City of Boston, Containing the Selectmen's Minutes from 1776 through 1786.* Boston: Rockwell and Churchill, 1894.

BTR, 1   *Second Report of the Record Commissioners of the City of Boston [Boston Town Records, 1634–61].* Boston: Rockwell and Churchill, 1877.

BTR, 2   *A Report of the Record Commissioners of the City of Boston, Containing the Boston [Town] Records from 1660 to 1701.* Boston: Rockwell and Churchill, 1881.

BTR, 3   *A Report of the Record Commissioners of the City of Boston, Containing the Boston [Town] Records from 1700 to 1728.* Boston: Rockwell and Churchill, 1883.

BTR, 4   *A Report of the Record Commissioners of the City of Boston, Containing the Boston [Town] Records from 1729 to 1742.* Boston: Rockwell and Churchill, 1885.

BTR, 5   *A Report of the Record Commissioners of the City of Boston, Containing the Boston Town Records, 1742 to 1757.* Boston: Rockwell and Churchill, 1885.

BTR, 6   *A Report of the Record Commissioners of the City of Boston, Containing the Boston Town Records, 1758 to 1769.* Boston: Rockwell and Churchill, 1886.

BTR, 7   *A Report of the Record Commissioners of the City of Boston, Containing the Boston Town Records, 1770 to 1777.* Boston: Rockwell and Churchill, 1887.

BTR, 8   *A Report of the Record Commissioners of the City of Boston, Containing the Boston Town Records, 1778 to 1783.* Boston: Rockwell and Churchill, 1895.

CSM *Pub.*	Colonial Society of Massachusetts, *Publications*
Cummings, *FHMB*	Cummings, Abbott Lowell. *The Framed Houses of Massachusetts Bay, 1625–1725.* Cambridge: Harvard University Press, Belknap Press, 1979.
Dwight, *Travels*	Dwight, Timothy. *Travels in New England and New York,* ed. Barbara Miller Solomon. 4 vols. Cambridge: Harvard University Press, 1969.
ECQCR	*Records and Files of the Quarterly Courts of Essex County, Massachusetts,* ed. George Francis Dow. 9 vols. Salem, Mass.: Essex Institute, 1912–75.
EIHC	*Essex Institute Historical Collections*
Hull Diary	"The Diaries of John Hull, Mint-master and Treasurer of Massachusetts Bay." *Transactions and Collections of the American Antiquarian Society* 3 (1857): 109–318.
MA	Massachusetts Archives, Boston
Mather, *Diary*	Mather, Cotton. *The Diary of Cotton Mather,* ed. Worthington Chauncy Ford. 2 vols. In Massachusetts Historical Society, *Collections,* 7th ser., 7–8 (1912).
Mather, *Magnalia*	Mather, Cotton. *Magnalia Christi Americana; Or, the History of New England.* 2 vols. Hartford: Silas Andrus & Son, 1853–55.
MBR	*Records of the Governor and Company of the Massachusetts Bay in New England,* ed. Nathaniel B. Shurtleff. 5 vols. Boston: Commonwealth of Massachusetts, 1853–55.
MHS *Coll.*	Massachusetts Historical Society, *Collections*
MHS *Proc.*	Massachusetts Historical Society, *Proceedings*
NEB	*New England Begins: The Seventeenth Century,* ed. Jonathan L. Fairbanks and Robert F. Trent. 3 vols. Boston: Museum of Fine Arts, 1982.
NEHGR	*New England Historical and Genealogical Register*
NEQ	*New England Quarterly*
NHTR	*Ancient Town Records,* Vol. 1: *New Haven Town Records, 1649–1662,* ed. Franklin Bowditch Dexter. New Haven: New Haven Colony Historical Society, 1917.
OTNE	*Old-Time New England*
PMA	*Post-Medieval Archaeology*
SCPR	Suffolk County Probate Records, Suffolk County Courthouse, Boston
Sewall, *Diary*	Sewall, Samuel. *The Diary of Samuel Sewall,* ed. M. Halsey Thomas. 2 vols. New York: Farrar, Giroux & Straus, 1973.
Sewall, *Letter-Book*	Sewall, Samuel. *The Letter-Book of Samuel Sewall.* 2 vols. In Massachusetts Historical Society, *Collections,* 6th ser., 1–2 (1886).
SWP	*The Salem Witchcraft Papers: Verbatim Transcripts of the Legal Documents of the Salem Witchcraft Outbreak of 1692,* ed. Paul Boyer and Stephen Nissenbaum. 3 vols. New York: DaCapo, 1977.
TAMS	*Transactions of the Ancient Monument Society*
Taylor, *Poems*	*The Poems of Edward Taylor,* ed. Donald E. Stanford. New Haven: Yale University Press, 1977.
UF	*Ulster Folklife*
UJA	*Ulster Journal of Archaeology*
VA	*Vernacular Architecture*
Winthrop, *Journal*	*John Winthrop's Journal "History of New England,"* ed. James K. Hosmer. 2 vols. New York: Charles Scribner's Sons, 1910.
WMQ	*William and Mary Quarterly*

1. On "verbal limning" and "topiary poems," see Norman K. Farmer Jr., *Poets and the Visual Arts in Renaissance England* (Austin: University of Texas Press, 1984), 5–10 ("A Defense of Poetry: The Theory of Visual Thinking"), 66–67, 70. Quoted from Paolo Lomazzo, "The Second Booke of the Actions, Gestures, Situation, Decorum, Motion . . . of Pictures," in *A Tract Containing the Artes of Curious Paintings*, trans. Richard Haydock (London, 1598), 4–5, in Farmer, *Poets and the Visual Arts*, 2.

2. *Oxford English Dictionary*, 2d ed., s.v. "implicate," "implication," "implicative," with historical meanings.

3. *BTR*, 6:305.

4. On Hobbes and the early-seventeenth-century roots of associationism, see John Archer, "The Beginnings of Associationism in British Architectural Esthetics," *Eighteenth-Century Studies* 16 (1983): 241–61, and Archer, "Character in English Architectural Design," *Eighteenth-Century Studies* 12 (1970): 339–71. For recent work that suggests connections of architecture and colonization in another context, see Gwendolyn Wright, *The Politics of French Colonial Urbanism* (Chicago: University of Chicago Press, 1991).

5. M. M. Bakhtin, "Epic and Novel," 11–12, and "Discourse in the Novel," in M. M. Bakhtin, *The Dialogic Imagination: Four Essays*, trans. Michael Holquist and Caryl Emerson (Austin: University of Texas Press, 1981), 293–94; John Bullokar, "To the Courteous Reader," in *An English Expositor: Teaching the Interpretation of the Hardest Words Used in Our Language* (London, 1616), as quoted in Tetsuro Hayashi, *The Theory of Lexicography, 1530–1791* (Amsterdam: John Benjamins B. V., 1978), 35.

6. David D. Hall, "A World of Wonders: The Mentality of the Supernatural in Seventeenth-Century New England," in *Seventeenth-Century New England*, ed. David G. Allen and David D. Hall (Boston: Colonial Society of Massachusetts, 1984), 241; David D. Hall, *Worlds of Wonder, Days of Judgment: Popular Religious Belief in Early New England* (New York: Knopf, 1989), 75; Stuart Hall, "Notes on Deconstructing 'The Popular,'" in *People's History and Socialist Theory*, ed. Raphael Samuel (Boston: Routledge and Kegan Paul, 1981), 228. Compare with the comments on "appropriation" and strategies of transmission in popular culture in Roger Chartier, "Appropriation as Culture: Popular Culture Uses in Early Modern France," in *Understanding Popular Culture: Europe from the Middle Ages to the Nineteenth Century*, ed. Stephen Kaplan (Ithaca, N.Y.: Cornell University Press, 1984), 233.

7. On metaphoric compression, see Simon Schama, *The Embarrassment of Riches: An Interpretation of Dutch Culture in the Golden Age* (Berkeley and Los Angeles: University of California Press, 1988), 143; Mary Douglas, *Natural Symbols: Explorations in Cosmology* (New York: Pantheon, 1982), 47–48.

8. Peter Hulme, "The Spontaneous Hand of Nature: Savagery, Colonialism, and the Enlightenment," in *The Enlightenment and Its Shadows*, ed. Peter Hulme and Ludmilla Jordanova (New York: Routledge, 1990), 16–35.

9. On the shifting definition of performance in early modern England, see Jean-Christophe Agnew, *Worlds Apart: The Market and the Theater in Anglo-American Thought, 1550–1750* (New York: Cambridge University Press, 1986), 83. On performance as expressive and moral frame, see Dell Hymes, "Breakthrough into Performance," in *Folklore: Performance and Communication*, ed. Dan Ben-Amos and Kenneth S. Goldstein, Approaches to Semiotics, no. 40 (The Hague: Mouton, 1975), 13–20; Richard Bauman, "Performance," in *Folklore, Cultural Performances, and Popular Entertainment*, ed. Richard Bauman (New York: Oxford University Press, 1992), 41–49; and Richard Bauman, *Verbal Art as Performance* (Prospect Heights, Ill.: Waveland Press, 1984). I expand on these qualities of performance and their ramifications for folklore and folklife in Robert Blair St. George, "Folklore," in *A Companion to American Thought*, ed. Richard Wightman Fox and James T. Kloppenburg (Oxford: Blackwell, 1995), 239–41.

10. On Ramus and the education of the New England clergy in the "dichotomies" of dialectic logic, see Perry Miller, *The New England Mind: The Seventeenth Century* (Cambridge: Harvard University Press, Belknap Press, 1982), 115–53. Francis A. Yates, *The Art of Memory* (Chicago: University of Chi-

cago Press, 1966), 232–33. Mather, *Magnalia*, 2:48–49. On this debate, see also Francis A. Yates, "Lodovico Da Pirano's Memory Treatise," in Yates, *Renaissance and Reform: The Italian Contribution* (London: Routledge and Kegan Paul, 1983), 259–72; the use of site references by Ramus is discussed in John C. Adams, "Ramus, Illustrations, and the Puritan Movement," *Journal of Medieval and Renaissance Studies* 17, no. 2 (Fall 1987): 205. See also John Morgan, *Godly Learning: Puritan Attitudes towards Reason, Learning, and Education, 1560–1640* (Cambridge: Cambridge University Press, 1986), 106–12.

11. Winthrop, *Journal*, 1:77. Edward Winslow, *Good Newes from New England* (1624), in *Chronicles of the Pilgrim Fathers of the Colony of Plymouth, from 1602-1625*, ed. Alexander Young (Boston, 1844; reprint, Baltimore: Genealogical Publishing Co., 1974), 367.

12. Hubbard quoted in William Dana Orcutt, *Good Old Dorchester: A Narrative of the Town, 1630–1893* (Cambridge, Mass.: John Wilson & Sons, 1893), 59–60. On New England legends still referencing the landscape of revelation in the nineteenth century, see, for example, Samuel Adams Drake, *A Book of New England Legends and Folk Lore* (Boston: Roberts Brothers, 1884).

13. Allan R. Pred, "Space as Historically Contingent Process," in *Place, Practice, and Situation: Social and Spatial Transformation in Southern Sweden, 1750–1850* (Totowa, N.J.: Barnes & Noble, 1986), 6. See also Allan R. Pred, "Power, Everyday Practice, and the Discipline of Human Geography," in *Space and Time in Geography: Essays Dedicated to Torsten Hägerstrand*, ed. Allan R. Pred (Lund: C. W. K. Gleerup, 1981), 30–55; Edward W. Soja, "The Spatiality of Social Life: Towards a Transformative Retheorisation," in *Social Relations and Spatial Structures*, ed. Derek Gregory and John Urry (New York: St. Martin's Press, 1985), 90–127; Hilda Kuper, "The Language of Sites in the Politics of Space," *American Anthropologist* 74, no. 3 (June 1972): 411–25; Arjun Appadurai, "Introduction: Place and Voice in Anthropological Theory," *Cultural Anthropology* 3, no. 1 (February 1988): 16–49; and the essays gathered in *Space, Identity, and the Politics of Difference*, ed. James Ferguson and Akhil Gupta, special issue of *Cultural Anthropology* 7, no. 1 (February 1993).

14. Susan Stewart, "Lyric Possession," *Critical Inquiry* 22, no. 1 (Autumn 1995): 62–63.

15. See Caroline Bynum, "Why All the Fuss about the Body? A Medievalist's Perspective," *Critical Inquiry* 22, no. 1 (Autumn 1995): 2–6 and its footnotes. The "body criticism" scene is a current industry; see Marcel Mauss, "Techniques of the Body" (1936), *Economy and Society* 2, no. 1 (February 1973): 70–88; Douglas, *Natural Symbols*, 65–81; Michel Foucault, *The History of Sexuality*, vol. 1, *An Introduction*, trans. Robert Hurley (1976; New York: Vintage, 1990), 77–133; Bryan Turner, *The Body and Society: Explorations in Social Theory* (Oxford: Basil Blackwell, 1984); and Peter Brown, *The Body and Society: Men, Women, and Sexual Renunciation in Early Christianity* (New York: Columbia University Press, 1988).

16. Cotton Mather, *A Pillar of Gratitude. Or, A Brief Recapitulation, of the Matchless Favours, with which the God of Heaven hath Obliged the Hearty Praises of His New-England Israel* (Boston, 1700), 5, 30. See Philip S. Haffenden, *New England in the English Nation, 1689–1713* (Oxford: Clarendon Press, 1974), 38–71.

17. Here I am adding to the debate charted in Homi K. Bhabha, "Of Mimicry and Man: The Ambivalence of Colonial Discourse," in his *The Location of Culture* (New York: Routledge, 1994), 85–92; see also Frantz Fanon, "The Pitfalls of National Consciousness," in *The Wretched of the Earth*, trans. Constance Farrington (New York: Grove Press, 1963), 200–202.

18. Emanuel Downing to John Winthrop, [Summer] 1645, in MHS *Coll.*, 4th ser., 6 (1863): 64–65.

CHAPTER ONE

1. Jared Eliot, *Essays upon Field Husbandry in New England and Other Papers, 1748–1762*, ed. Harry J. Carman and Rexford G. Tugwell (New York: AMS Press, 1967), 11, 17, 20, 33, 89.

2. See George Lyman Kittredge, "Dr. Robert Child the Remonstrant," CSM *Pub.* 21 (1919): 103–8, for his persuasive argument that Child was the author of the "Large Letter concerning the Defects and Remedies of English Husbandry written to Mr. Samuel Hartlib" that formed the bulk of Hartlib's

book. For specific instances of New England being brought into the discussion of English agricultural reform, see [Robert Child], *Samuel Hartlib His Legacie* (London, 1651), 24, 46, 47.

3. On the role of gatehouses in linking the imagery of authority to rituals of arrival and entry in early modern English culture, see Peter Smith, *Houses of the Welsh Countryside: A Study in Historical Geography* (London: Royal Commission on Historical Monuments, 1975), 230–31, and Richard Neve, *The City and Country Purchaser and Builder's Dictionary: Or, the Compleat Builder's Guide* (London, 1703), 143–44. Ann Leighton, *Early American Gardens: "For Meate or Medicine"* (Boston: Houghton Mifflin, 1970), 376–78. On a possible etymology for "biere hag," see Joseph Wright, ed., *English Dialect Dictionary*, 6 vols. (New York: G. P. Putnam Sons, 1898–1905), 1:475, 3:15. On "haggards" as small areas near Irish houses where hay is stacked on "prepared foundations of stones and heather or bushes" that "draw the wind in under" and hasten its rapid drying, see E. Estyn Evans, *Irish Heritage: The Landscape, the People, and Their Work* (Dundalk: Dundalgan Press, 1942), 98.

4. Charles M. Endicott, "Memoir of Governor Endicott," *NEHGR* 1 (July 1847): 215.

5. The plan, along with Hoadly's manuscript notations, is on the back cover of Joannis Petri Ayroldi, *Francisic Vallesii Couarrubiensis in Libros Hippocratis de Morbis popularibus Commentaria . . .* (Cologne, [1588]), in the collections of the Watkinson Library, Trinity College. I am indebted to Jeffrey Kaimowitz, curator of rare books at Trinity, for allowing me to examine it in detail. This volume, published under Ayroldi's name, is identical to Francisco de Valle, *In libros Hippocratis de morbis popularibus commentaria* (Cologne, 1588).

6. Bernard Christian Steiner, *A History of the Plantation of Menunkatuck and of the Original Town of Guilford, Connecticut* (Baltimore: printed by the author, 1897), 412–13. Accession book, vol. 1, gift no. 904044, Henry Whitfield State Historical Museum, Guilford, Conn. I am indebted to Michael McBride for letting me examine the 1904 tracing and the accession book.

7. Accession book, vol. 1, no. 904048, Henry Whitfield State Historical Museum, listed as "Possible superstructure Rossiter diagram (no. 387) by Mr. Isham." Gift of Norman M. Isham, Providence, July 14, 1904. The Isham drawing is dated October 12, 1903. See also Norman M. Isham and Albert F. Brown, *Early Connecticut Houses* (Providence, 1900; reprint, New York: Dover Publications, 1965), 97–124.

8. "A Book of the Terryers of all the Divided landes in Guilford according as they were at first Division . . ." (April 10, 1648, and later; hereafter cited as "Guilford Terriers"), 1 (1648–85): 1 ("A terryer of all the landes of Mr Samuell Desborow lyeing in Guilfford as followeth"; emphasis added); Guilford Town Records, Book C, 56, both in Town Hall, Guilford, Connecticut. "Extracts from Ruggles' MS. History," MHS *Coll.*, 1st ser., 10 (1809): 96–97.

9. On the religious climate in Eltisley and West Cambridgeshire generally, see Margaret Spufford, *Contrasting Communities: English Villagers in the Sixteenth and Seventeenth Centuries* (London: Cambridge University Press, 1974), 227–38, esp. map, 235. For biographical details on Samuel Desborough, see James Savage, *A Genealogical Dictionary of the First Settlers of New England, Showing Three Generations of Those Who Came before May, 1892, on the Basis of the Farmer's Register*, 4 vols. (Boston, 1860–62; reprint, Baltimore: Genealogical Publishing Co., 1969), 2:41–42; "Letter from John Maidston to John Winthrop, Governour of Connecticut" [March 24, 1659], MHS *Coll.*, 3d ser., 1 (1825): 197. Ralph D. Smith, *The History of Guilford, Connecticut, from Its First Settlement in 1639* (Albany: Joel Munsell, 1877), 120, points out that Desborough, along with Theophilus Eaton and William Leete, was instrumental in establishing New Haven Colony in 1643.

10. *Records of the Colony and Plantation of New Haven, from 1638 to 1649*, ed. Charles J. Hoadly, 2 vols. (Hartford: Case, Tiffany, & Co., 1857), 1:96, 275. Quoted in Steiner, *History of the Plantation of Menunkatuck*, 49. Additional biographical information on Desborough is in *The Dictionary of National Biography*, ed. Leslie Stephen and Sidney Lee, 22 vols. (London: Oxford University Press, 1937–38), 5:855.

11. "Guilford Terriers," 1:1; Guilford Town Records, Book C, 56; inventory of Bryan [Bray] Rossiter, taken November 6, 1672, New Haven Probate Records, 1, pt. 2:32 (n.p.), microfilm collection, Connecticut State Archives, Hartford. Inventory of Josiah Rossiter, New Haven District Probate Records,

4:391–92 (taken March 5, 1715), microfilm collection, Connecticut State Archives; see also "Guilford Terriers," 1:1.

12. The thirteen acres constituting Bray Rossiter's home lot at his death are specified in the list of property transferred to his son in "Guilford Terriers," 1:1 (entry of March 11, 1672), and confirmed later in "A Terier of all the Land Belonging to Josiah Rosseter of gilfor," in "Guilford Terriers," 2 (1686–1715): 5 (entry of November 16, 1710). Josiah Rossiter took over the cattle quickly after his father's death and registered his earmark with the town on April 7, 1674 (Guilford Town Records, Book C, 107).

13. Will of Josiah Rossiter, New Haven District Probate Records, 2:389–90 (written January 24, 1715–16).

14. "Guilford Terriers," 5 (1731–37): 89, 108 (deed of February 19, 1732/3). On August 25, 1723, Timothy Rossiter, then of Durham, Connecticut, sold to his brother "one Tract of parcell of Land Scituate lying & being in Guilford . . . Containing by Estimation Ten Acres" for thirty pounds; "Guilford Terriers," 3 (1719–27): 174.

15. Joel Helander, Guilford town historian, interview with author, Guilford, Conn., August 12, 1992. Helander recalled that Walker Nettleton of Guilford always maintained that the Desborough estate was located on the knoll where the post office was built. On the spring, Beverly Anderson, interview with author, Guilford, Conn., August 13, 1992. A description of Guilford's early roads is available in Steiner, *History of the Plantation of Menunkatuck,* 211–12.

16. Anthony N. B. Garvan, *Architecture and Town Planning in Colonial Connecticut* (New Haven: Yale University Press, 1951), 31–44; Philip S. Robinson, *The Plantation of Ulster: British Settlement in an Irish Landscape, 1600–1760* (New York: St. Martin's Press, 1984), 129–49. For documentary and pictorial records on these and other plantations of the London Companies, see James Steven Curl, *The Londonderry Plantation, 1609–1914* (Chichester, Sussex: Phillimore & Co., 1986). Barnaby Rich, *A Short Survey of Ireland, Truely Discovering Who It Is that Hath So Armed the Hearts of that People, With Disobedience to Their Princes* (London, 1609), 2.

17. John Reps, *Tidewater Towns: City Planning in Colonial Virginia and Maryland* (Williamsburg: Colonial Williamsburg Foundation, 1972), 10–20; Nicholas P. Canny, "The Ideology of English Colonization: From Ireland to America," *WMQ,* 3d ser., 30, no. 4 (October 1973): 573–76; and Ivor Noël Hume, *Martin's Hundred* (New York: Knopf, 1982), 236–38. These works stand in debt to Howard Mumford Jones, "Origins of the Colonial Idea in England," *Proceedings of the American Philosophical Society* 85, no. 5 (September 1942): 448–65, and David Beers Quinn, "Sir Thomas Smith (1513–1577) and the Beginnings of English Colonial Theory," *Proceedings of the American Philosophical Society* 89, no. 4 (December 1945): 543–60, and, later, the more detailed discussions in David Beers Quinn, *The Elizabethans and the Irish* (Ithaca, N.Y.: Cornell University Press for the Folger Shakespeare Library, 1965), 24–33, 106–22. In recent years debates have shown caution in regards to Quinn's thesis. See the summary of positions in Nicholas P. Canny, *Kingdom and Colony: Ireland in the Atlantic World, 1580–1800* (Baltimore: Johns Hopkins University Press, 1988), 5–17, 31–68; and for the views of contemporaries (especially Francis Bacon), see Raymond Gillespie, *Colonial Ulster: The Settlement of East Ulster, 1600–1641* (Cork: Cork University Press, 1985), 219–22. More recently, Ann Rosalind Jones and Peter Stallybrass have pointed out the ways in which the native Irish—in their hair, dress, language, and sexuality—emblematized disorder and an evident need for the English colonizer's yoke; see their "Dismantling Irena: The Sexualizing of Ireland in Early Modern England," in *Nationalisms and Sexualities,* ed. Andrew Parker et al. (New York: Routledge, 1992), 157–71.

18. The original sections of the Whitfield house masonry show that yellow clay mortar was used, not lime; see J. Frederick Kelly, *The Henry Whitfield House: 1639, Architect's Journal* (Guilford: Henry Whitfield State Historical Museum, 1939), 4, 32; Isham and Brown, *Early Connecticut Houses,* 184–85. On stone houses in the Ulster Plantations, see Philip S. Robinson, "Vernacular Housing in Ulster in the Seventeenth Century," *UF* 25 (1979): 15–17. See also Alan Gailey, *Rural Houses of the North of Ireland* (Edinburgh: John Donald, 1984), 46–54, and Desmond McCourt, "A Seventeenth-Century Farmhouse at Liffock, County Londonderry," *UJA,* 3d ser., 35 (1972): 48–55.

19. The Walter Smith measured drawings are reproduced in Smith, *History of Guilford,* following p. 16; see also the early description of the building's unaltered state on 16 n. On fortified houses being constructed as part of the stone wall enclosing a bawn, see Garvan, *Architecture and Town Planning,* 31 n. 34. The original configuration of the Whitfield house in Guilford may be assumed from evidence presented in Kelly, *Henry Whitfield House,* and in Sarah Langley, "Archaeological Work on the Grounds of the Henry Whitfield House Museum," *Connecticut History* 23 (April 1982): 56–60. Examples from the north of Ireland parallel the Whitfield house plan closely; see E. M. Jope, "Moyry, Charlemont, Castleraw, and Richhill: Fortification to Architecture in the North of Ireland," *UJA,* 3d ser., 3 (1960): 111, and D. M. Waterman, "Some Irish Seventeenth-Century Houses and Their Architectural Ancestry," in *Studies in Building History: Essays in Recognition of the Work of B. H. St. John O'Neil,* ed. E. M. Jope (London: Odhams Press, 1961), 255, 258–60, 273. See also the 1670 enclosed farm complex at Stratford, Virginia, discussed in Fraser D. Neiman, "Domestic Architecture at the Clifts Plantation: The Social Context of Early Virginia," in *Common Places: Readings in American Vernacular Architecture,* ed. Dell Upton and John Michael Vlach (Athens: University of Georgia Press, 1986), 314.

20. On the skinners' and salters' buildings, see Thomas Phillips, *Londonderry and the London Companies, 1609–1629* (Belfast: His Majesty's Stationery Office, 1928), plates 25, 27, facing pp. 133, 145. The examples at Ardtarmon and Castlederg are discussed, respectively, in Waterman, "Some Irish Seventeenth-Century Houses," 268–69, and D. M. Waterman, "Sir John Davies and His Ulster Buildings: Castlederg and Castle Curlews, Co. Tyrone," *UJA,* 3d ser., 3 (1960): 90–92. On the Irish landholding and his connection with John Preston, see Desborough's will of September 1680, in Henry F. Waters, "Genealogical Gleanings in England," *NEHGR* 51 (July 1897): 356. For a list of the merchant members of the Massachusetts Bay Company who were also members of the London livery companies—including such figures as Robert Keayne, Matthew Craddock, and Samuel Vassall—see Frances Rose-Troupe, *The Massachusetts Bay Company and Its Predecessors* (Clifton, N.J.: A. M. Kelley, 1973), 130–61.

21. On Castle Doe and its construction, see Brian Lacy, ed., *Archaeological Survey of County Donegal: A Description of the Field Antiquities of the County from the Mesolithic Period to the Seventeenth Century A.D.* (Lifford, Donegal: Donegal County Council, 1983), 356–58.

22. On social gradations in housing and materials in the Ulster Plantations, see Robinson, "Vernacular Housing in Ulster in the Seventeenth Century," 11–23, and Brooke S. Blades, "'In the Manner of England': Tenant Housing in the Londonderry Plantation," *UF* 27 (1981); 39–56; "On the Disorders of the Irishry" (1572), quoted in Canny, "Ideology of English Colonization," 584. Nicholas Pynnar, "Pynnar's Survey of Ulster," in *Hibernica: Or, Some Ancient Pieces Relating to Ireland,* ed. Walter Harris (London: John Milliken, 1770), 166. On the skinners' plantation, see Nicholas F. Brannon and Brooke S. Blades, "Dungiven Bawn Re-Edified," *UJA,* 3d ser., 43 (1980): 91–96, and Nicholas F. Brannon, "A Lost Seventeenth-Century House Recovered: Dungiven, Co. Londonderry," in *Pieces of the Past: Archaeological Excavations by the Department of the Environment of Northern Ireland, 1970–1986,* ed. Ann Hamlin and Chris Lynn (Belfast: Her Majesty's Stationers Office, 1988), 81–84.

23. "Preface in the Form of a Petition from Sir Thomas Phillips to King Charles I," in Phillips, *Londonderry,* 18. On the politics of displacement and quick reliance of the English on native Irish labor and rents, see T. W. Moody, "The Treatment of the Native Population under the Scheme for Plantation in Ulster," *Irish Historical Studies* 1, no. 1 (March 1938): 59–63, and W. H. Crawford, "Landlord-Tenant Relations in Ulster, 1609–1820," *Irish Economic and Social History* 1 (1975): 5–21. For information on the exploitation of forests, see Eileen McCracken, *The Irish Woods since Tudor Times* (Newton Abbot, England: David and Charles, 1971).

24. Raphael Holinshed, *The Historie of Ireland from the First Inhabitation thereof unto the Yeare 1509* (London, 1577), 28r.

25. Quoted in Quinn, *Elizabethans and the Irish,* 166, 168.

26. Philip S. Robinson, "The Spread of Hedged Enclosure in Ulster," *UF* 23 (1977): 57–58, cites instances of enclosure in 1622 and 1641; "Preamble of the Londoners' Charter Granted by His Majesty 2d

March 1614," as quoted in "Preface in the Form of a Petition from Sir Thomas Phillips to King Charles I," in Phillips, *Londonderry*, 16.

27. "Preface in the Form of a Petition from Sir Thomas Phillips to King Charles I," in Phillips, *Londonderry*, 19.

28. Bernard Bailyn, *The New England Merchants in the Seventeenth Century* (Cambridge: Harvard University Press, 1979), 35–36. On New England Puritan backers of anti-Irish expeditions, see the individuals listed in "Adventurers for Ireland" for 1641 in Raymond Phineas Stearns, "The Weld-Peter Mission to England," CSM *Pub.* 32 (1933–37): 203–4. *MBR*, 1:17; John Saffin, *John Saffin, his Book (1665–1708); A Collection of Various Matters of Divinity, Law, & State Affairs Epitomiz'd both in Verse and Prose* (New York: Harbor Press, 1928), 64.

29. William Wood, *New England's Prospect*, ed. Alden T. Vaughan (London, 1634; reprint, Amherst: University of Massachusetts Press, 1977), 111; John Josselyn, *An Account of Two Voyages to New-England* (London, 1675), in MHS *Coll.*, 3d ser., 3 (1833): 300. Parallels between Irish and Native Americans were first introduced and summarized in Jones, "Origins of the Colonial Idea in England," 453–54. Edward Winslow and William Bradford, "Relation or Jornall of the Beginning and Proceedings of the English Plantation settled at Plimoth in New-England," in *Chronicles of the Pilgrim Fathers of the Colony of Plymouth, from 1602–1625*, ed. Alexander Young (Boston, 1844; reprint, Baltimore: Genealogical Publishing Co., 1974), 210–13; Edward Winslow, *Good Newes From New England* [1624], in Young, *Chronicles of the Pilgrim Fathers*, 364.

30. Roger Williams, *A Key into the Language of America* (1643), ed. John J. Teunissen and Evelyn J. Hinz (Detroit: Wayne State University Press, 1973), 150; Wood, *New England's Prospect*, 84; Winslow, *Good Newes from New England*, 365; Martin Pring, "A Voyage Set Out from the Citie of Bristoll" (1603), in *Early English and French Voyages Chiefly from Hakluyt, 1534–1608*, ed. Henry S. Burrage (New York: Charles Scribner's Sons, 1906), 348. For a "native" Irish example of such a mantle, see the costume worn by the Irish kern Rory Og Ó More in a woodcut (ca. 1575) in Quinn, *Elizabethans and the Irish*, plate 10.

31. William Morrell, "Morell's Poem on New England" (ca. 1625), MHS *Colls.*, 1st ser., 1 (1792): 135. On "booleying," or the seasonal migration to summer pastures for dairying, see Evans, *Irish Heritage*, 52; Robinson, "Vernacular Housing in the Seventeenth Century," 1–7; and F. H. A. Aalen, "Transhumance in the Wicklow Mountains," *UF* 10 (1964): 65–72. See also the plan of a probable sixteenth-century example in Philip S. Robinson and Brian B. Williams, "The Excavation of a Bronze Age Cist and a Medieval Booley House at Glenmakeeran, County Antrim, and a Discussion of Booleying in North Antrim," *UJA*, 3d ser., 46 (1983): 32, fig. 4. Thomas Morton, *New English Canaan* (Amsterdam, 1637; reprint, Boston: Prince Society, 1883), 134.

32. See the example illustrated in Caoimhín Ó Danachair [Kevin Danaher], "Representations of Houses on Some Irish Maps of c. 1600," in *Studies in Folk Life: Essays in Honour of Iorwerth C. Peate*, ed. Geraint Jenkins (London: Routledge and Kegan Paul, 1969), 96, plate 4; compare with the form of the Pequot "fort" overrun by the English in 1637, in Neal Salisbury, *Manitou and Providence: Indians, Europeans, and the Making of New England, 1500–1643* (New York: Oxford University Press, 1982), 223.

33. *NHTR*, 24.

34. According to Matthew Grant, who in 1654 described the construction of the palisado, it was built "about 1637—years, when the English had war with the pequit Indians; our Inhabita[n]ce on Sandy Bank gathered themselves neerer together from their Remote Dwelings, to provide for their Safety" (Grant, "A Book of Town Ways in Windsor," Office of the Town Clerk, Windsor, Connecticut, ca. 1654–1700). On New Haven's sacred meanings, see John Archer, "Puritan Town Planning in New Haven," *Journal of the Society of Architectural Historians* 34, no. 1 (March 1975): 140–49.

35. Salisbury, "Red Puritans: The 'Praying Indians' of Massachusetts Bay and John Eliot," *WMQ*, 3d ser., 31, no. 1 (January 1974): 33. For town plans of Londonderry and Coleraine, see Curl, *Londonderry Plantation*, 55, 76.

36. John A. Goodwin, *The Pilgrim Republic: An Historical Review of the Colony of New Plymouth* (Boston: Houghton Mifflin, 1920), 230–31; *NHTR*, 224, 233. Sidney Perley, *The History of Boxford, Essex County, Massachusetts* (Boxford: printed by the author, 1880), 63; Guilford Town Records, Book C, 18. I am indebted to James Sexton for this reference. On garrison houses in New England, see Cummings, *FHMB*, 92–93, and Stuart Bartlett, "Garrison Houses along the New England Frontier," *Monograph Series* 19, no. 3 (April 1933): 253–67. In my interpretation of the Whitfield house corner opening I follow the drawings done by the Smiths in the 1850s; they knew the original evidence better than anyone.

37. Quoted in Penry Williams, "The Northern Borderland under the Early Stuarts," in *Historical Essays 1600–1750, Presented to David Ogg*, ed. H. E. Bell and R. L. Ollard (London: Adam and Black, 1963), 15. See also W. R. Kermack, *The Scottish Borders (with Galloway) to 1603* (Edinburgh: Johnston and Bacon, 1967), 7–23, 31–44, 62–71.

38. The 1715 description of a "peel" house is quoted in Wright, *English Dialect Dictionary*, 4:353. On English antecedents for the bawn, see Waterman, "Some Irish Seventeenth-Century Houses," 261–63.

39. On the locations of bastles shown in figure 11 and plans of the houses at Tarset, Otterburn, Hepple, Elsdon, and Upper Denton, see H. G. Ramm, R. W. McDowall, and Eric Mercer, *Shielings and Bastles* (London: Her Majesty's Stationers Office, 1970), 17, 86, 88, 89–90, 91–92. The Haltwhistle structure, with a corner cannon embrasure similar to that at the Whitfield house, is illustrated in M. W. Barley, *Houses and History* (London: Faber and Faber, 1986), 250.

40. For suggesting the Scottish connection I am indebted to Matthew H. Johnson of the University of Durham (letter to author, June 1, 1993). On late medieval houses in Scotland, see Brian K. Davison, *The Observer's Book of Castles* (London: Frederick Warner, 1979), 77–99, 118–23, and P. A. Faulkner, "Domestic Planning from the Twelfth to the Fourteenth Centuries," *Archaeological Journal* 115 (1958): 150–83.

41. Davison, *Observer's Book of Castles*, 12.

42. See Robin McDowall, "The Westmoreland Vernacular," in *Studies in Architectural History*, ed. William A. Singleton (York: St. Anthony's Press for the York Institute of Architectural Study, 1956), 129–31. The Hartland example is illustrated and discussed in E. M. Jope, "Cornish Houses, 1400–1700," in Jope, *Studies in Building History*, 215.

43. I am indebted to Emerson Baker for information on the Arrowsic site (letter to author, June 13, 1986); see Baker, "Archaeology Reveals the Manor of Fort Christian," *Old York Historical Society Newsletter* (Summer 1986): 1, 6, and Leon Cranmer, "Cushnoc: An Example of Non-Traditional Seventeenth-Century New England Architecture," *Kennebec Proprietor* 5, no. 2 (Winter 1988): 4–12. Compare the Clarke and Lake plan with those of Devon farmhouses along the edges of Dartmoor discussed in Michael Havinden and Freda Wilkinson, "Farming," in *Dartmoor: A New Study*, ed. Crispin Gill (Newton Abbot, England: David & Charles, 1970), 174–81.

44. Common West Country antecedents for the Desborough house are suggested in M. W. Barley, *The English Farmhouse and Cottage* (London: Routledge and Kegan Paul, 1961), 104, fig. 16 (type D1), 111, fig. 18 (no. 7); Eric Mercer, *English Vernacular Houses* (London: Royal Commission on Historical Monuments, 1975), 55–59 and figs. 33, 41, 42; *An Inventory of Historical Monuments in the County of Dorset*, vol. 2, *South-East*, pt. 1 (London: Royal Commission on Historical Monuments, 1970), 87; *An Inventory of Historical Monuments in the County of Dorset*, vol. 3, *Central Dorset*, pt. 2 (London: Royal Commission on Historical Monuments, 1970), 152–53; *An Inventory of Historical Monuments in the County of Dorset*, vol. 4, *North Dorset* (London: Royal Commission on Historical Monuments, 1972), xxxvi, 23.

45. Cyril F. Fox, *The Personality of Britain* (Cardiff: National Museum of Wales, 1932). For general overviews of English domestic architecture that follow Fox in reproducing the "highland-lowland" cultural division, see W. G. Hoskins, "Introduction: Farms and History," in *History from the Farm*, ed. W. G. Hoskins (London: Faber and Faber, 1970), 15–16; M. W. Barley, "Rural Housing in England," in *The Agrarian History of England and Wales*, vol. 4, *1500–1640*, ed. Joan Thirsk (Cambridge: Cambridge University Press, 1967), 696–766; and Mercer, *English Vernacular Houses*, although Mercer's more crit-

ical approach varies in places from the orthodox interpretation. For extensions of the "zones" to convergences in colonial New England, see Robert Blair St. George, "'Set Thine House in Order': The Domestication of the Yeomanry in Seventeenth-Century New England," in *NEB*, 2:165–72. For critical comments on the way the zones have been used in agricultural history, specifically in the influential work of Thirsk and her myriad followers, see George Homans, "The Explanation of English Regional Differences," *Past and Present* 42 (February 1969): 18–34.

46. Quoted from Richard Carew, *Survey of Cornwall* (London, 1723), in W. G. Hoskins, "The Rebuilding of Rural England, 1570–1640," *Past and Present* 4 (November 1953): 45; William Harrison, *The Description of England*, ed. George Edelen (Ithaca, N.Y.: Cornell University Press, 1968), 195–201 (emphasis added).

47. Sydney E. Jones, *The Village Homes of England*, ed. George Holmes (London: Studio, 1912), 4, 5, 8, 10; J. Archibald, *Kentish Architecture as Influenced by Geology* (Ramsgate, England, 1934); and Olive Cook and Edwin Smith, *English Cottages and Farmhouses* (New York: Studio Publications, 1955), frontispiece. See also J. T. Smith, "The Concept of Diffusion in Its Application to Vernacular Building," in Jenkins, *Studies in Folk Life*, 73.

48. Hoskins, "Rebuilding of Rural England," 44–59, reprinted in W. G. Hoskins, *Provincial England: Essays in Social and Economic History* (London: Macmillian, 1963), 131–48; and W. G. Hoskins, "An Excursus on Peasant Houses and Interiors, 1400–1800," in W. G. Hoskins, *The Midland Peasant: The Economic and Social History of a Leicestershire Village* (London: Macmillan, 1957), 283–310. On economic change at the national level, see Joan Thirsk, *Economic Policy and Projects: The Development of a Consumer Society in Early Modern England* (Oxford: Clarendon Press, 1978), 133–57. For early-seventeenth-century surveys of domestic housing, see Eric Kerridge, "Surveys of the Manors of Philip, First Earl of Pembroke and Montgomery, 1631–1632," *Wiltshire Archaeological Society Record* 9 (1953), and "A Survey of the Manor of Settrington," ed. H. King and A. Harris, *Yorkshire Archaeological Society Record Series* 126 (1960).

49. Robert Machin, "The Great Rebuilding: A Reassessment," *Past and Present* 77 (November 1977): 32–56, first opened Hoskins's thesis to revisionist research. For studies that link rebuilding cycles to local economic change, see, for Dorset, Robert Machin, "The Mechanism of the Pre-Industrial Building Cycle," *VA* 8 (1977): 815–19, and Robert Machin, *The Houses of Yetminster* (Bristol, England: University of Bristol, Department of Extra-mural Studies, 1978); for Devon, N. W. Alcock and M. Laithwaite, "Medieval Houses in Devon and their Modernisation," *Medieval Archaeology* 17 (1973): 100–125; N. W. Alcock, *Stoneleigh Villagers: 1597–1650* (Warwick: University of Warwick, Department of Open Studies, 1975); and N. W. Alcock, "The Great Rebuilding and Its Later Stages," *VA* 14 (1983): 45–48; for Yorkshire, Barbara Hutton, "Rebuilding in Yorkshire: The Evidence of Inscribed Dates," *VA* 8 (1977): 819–24; for southeast England, J. L. M. Gulley, "The Great Rebuilding in the Weald," *Gwerin* 3, no. 3 (June 1961): 126–41; Philip Crummy, "Portreeve's House, Colchester and a Method of Modernizing Essex Houses in the Sixteenth and Seventeenth Centuries," *PMA* 10 (1976): 89–103; and Matthew H. Johnson, "Rethinking the Great Rebuilding," *Oxford Journal of Archaeology* 12 (1993): 117–25. For an economic argument for rebuilding in colonial America, see Cary Carson, Norman F. Barka, William M. Kelso, Garry Wheeler Stone, and Dell Upton, "Impermanent Architecture in the Southern American Colonies," in *Material Life in America, 1600–1860*, ed. Robert Blair St. George (Boston: Northeastern University Press, 1988), 113–58.

50. On changes in room use and quantity, see M. W. Barley, "A Glossary of Names for Rooms in Houses of the Sixteenth and Seventeenth Centuries," in *Culture and Environment: Essays in Honour of Sir Cyril Fox*, ed. I. Ll Foster and L. Alcock (London: Routledge and Kegan Paul, 1963), 479–501.

51. Harrison, *Description of England*, 195–201.

52. On the insertion of chimney stacks into highland zone houses, see Mercer, *English Vernacular Houses*, 50–59; Barley, *English Farmhouse and Cottage*, 108–25.

53. Mercer, *English Vernacular Houses*, 58.

54. On the apprenticeship of children and the function of "tribalism" in early New England, see Ed-

mund S. Morgan, *The Puritan Family: Religious and Domestic Relations in Seventeenth-Century New England* (New York: Harper and Row, 1966), 168–74.

55. On lowland chimney placements, see Mercer, *English Vernacular Houses*, 62–65; Barley, *English Farmhouse and Cottage,* 62–77; and R. T. Mason, *Framed Buildings of the Weald* (Horsham, England: Coach Publishing Co., 1964), 45–54; see also R. C. Watson, "Parlours with Exterior Doors," *VA* 6 (1975): 28–30. For an English example of the two-door facade, see P. S. Spokes and E. M. Jope, "The Priory, Marcham," *Berkshire Archaeological Journal* 57 (1959): 86–91. I interpreted Winthrop's Ten Hills farmhouse as a two-door structure in St. George, "The 'Three Cranes' Tavern: Sources in English Vernacular Architecture," site report for Public Archaeology Labs, Inc, Providence, R.I. (February 1988).

56. For the English regional origins of Guilford's early settlers, see Charles Edward Banks, *Topographical Dictionary of 2885 English Immigrants to New England, 1620–1650,* ed. Elijah Ellsworth Brownell (Philadelphia, 1937; reprint, Baltimore: Genealogical Publishing Co., 1969); research summarized in John J. Waters, "Patrimony, Succession, and Social Stability: Guilford, Connecticut, in the Eighteenth Century," *Perspectives in American History* 10 (1976): 132–33, and in David Grayson Allen, "Both Englands," in *Seventeenth-Century New England,* ed. David Grayson Allen and David D. Hall (Boston: Colonial Society of Massachusetts, 1984), 72. For useful cautions on the biases of Banks's compilation, see Martin J. Bowden, "Culture and Place: English Sub-Cultural Regions in New England in the Seventeenth Century," *Connecticut History* 35, no. 1 (Spring 1994): 71–76. On patterns of building in the Wealden area of Kent that supplied most of Guilford's immigrant colonists, see Mason, "The Architectural Topography of South-East England," *TAMS,* n.s., 21 (1976): 32–44; John M. Harding, "Timber-Framed Early Building in Surrey: A Pattern for Development, c. 1300–1650," *TAMS* 37 (1993): 117–46; and Barley, *English Farmhouse and Cottage,* 62–66, 133–38.

57. For assistance with interpreting the Austin-Lord house, I am indebted to Abbott Lowell Cummings, Frank Demers, and Robert F. Trent; for another early eastern Massachusetts example, see the John Webb house in Dracut, illustrated in Ernest George Walker, *Walkers of Yesteryear* (Washington, D.C.: Ransdell, 1937), 63. For an early use of the end-gable door in the Connecticut River valley, see the engraving of the William Stoughton house (dated 1669) in Henry R. Stiles, *The History and Genealogies of Ancient Windsor, Connecticut: Including East Windsor, South Windsor, Bloomfield, Windsor Locks, and Ellington, 1635–1891,* 2 vols. (Hartford: Case, Lockwood and Brainard, 1891), vol. 1, facing p. 141. Samuel Davis, "Journal of a Journey from Plymouth, Massachusetts, to Connecticut" (1789), MHS *Proc.,* 1st ser., 11 (1871): 14, and *Life and Letters of Catherine M. Sedgewick,* ed. Mary E. Dewey (New York: Harper Brothers, 1871), 49–50. Gailey, *Rural Houses of the North of Ireland,* describes an analogous tension between front lobby entry and end-gable direct entry in the Ulster provinces: "The front door is seldom opened. Indeed, I have visited other comparatively 'ambivalent' houses where the front door had not been opened for years, and in one or two instances I have seen front doors no longer capable of being opened" (228). See also the comments on the end-gable door remaining where a cross passage had been eliminated (ca. 1690) in Neiman, "Domestic Architecture at the Clifts Plantation," 307–8.

58. Edward Howes to John Winthrop Jr., in MHS *Colls.,* 4th ser., 6 (1863): 500.

59. On demographic change in England between 1550 and 1700 and London's changing image during the period, see Peter Clark and Paul Slack, *English Towns in Transition 1500–1700* (Oxford: Oxford University Press, 1976), 46–96, esp. 87, 91–92; I borrow the useful descriptive terms "subsistence" and "betterment" from their argument. Quoted from Andrew P. Appleby, *Famine in Tudor and Stuart England* (Stanford: Stanford University Press, 1978), 113. See also A. L. Beier, "Social Problems in Elizabethan England," *Journal of Interdisciplinary History* 9, no. 2 (Autumn 1978): 203–21.

60. Clark and Slack, *English Towns in Transition,* 92, 93. On demographic upheaval and local adaptation in Kent, see Peter Clark, "The Migrants in Kentish Towns, 1580–1640," in *Crisis and Order in English Towns, 1500–1700,* ed. Peter Clark and Paul Slack (London: Routledge and Kegan Paul, 1972), 121–22; W. K. Jordan, "Social Institutions in Kent, 1480–1660," in *Essays in Kentish History,* ed. Margaret Roake and John Whyman (London: Frank Cass, 1973), 87–89; see also C. W. Chalklin, "The Rural

Economy of a Kentish Wealden Parish," *Agricultural History* 10 (1962): 29–45, and comments in John Patten, "Patterns of Migration and the Movement of Labour in Three East Anglian Towns," *Journal of Historical Geography* 2 (1976): 118–21.

61. Peter Eden, "Smaller Post-medieval Houses in Eastern England," in *East Anglian Studies*, ed. Lionel M. Munby (Cambridge, England: W. Heffer & Sons, 1968), 86–87.

62. The precise chronology of the lobby-entry house remains a subject of debate. On the house at Kneeshall, see Mercer, *English Vernacular Houses*, plate 37; and Anthony Quiney, "The Lobby-Entry House: Its Origins and Distribution," *Architectural History* 27 (1984): 456–66, esp. 457, fig. 1c, where he illustrates the plan of the Kneeshall structure. For the "plott" of the Moneymore house, see Philip S. Robinson, "'English' Houses Built at Moneymore, County Londonderry, c. 1615," *PMA* 17 (1983): 52, fig. 3. On specific lobby-entry structures, see H. M. Colvin, "Haunt Hill House, Weldon," in Jope, *Studies in Building History*, 223–28; Cecil Hewett, "Some East Anglian Prototypes for Early Timber Houses of America," *PMA* 3 (1969): 100–121; R. H. Cake and Elizabeth Lewis, "Paulsgrove House and Seventeenth-Century House Plans in Hampshire and West Sussex," *PMA* 6 (1972): 160–74; on Welsh examples, Peter Smith, letter to author, March 20, 1986. Because of his stress on the emergent middle class's quest for privacy, I believe that Hoskins, "Rebuilding of Rural England," failed to extend its argument to a sufficiently wide sector of society; see Barley, *English Farmhouse and Cottage*, 60; Elizabeth Lewis, "New England Salt Boxes," *VA* 8 (1977): 838–40; and Barbara Hutton, "Timber-Framed Houses in the Vale of York," *Medieval Archaeology* 17 (1973): 87–99. On the Fairbanks house and its carpenters, see Cummings, *FHMB*, 22–24; conversation of Cummings and author, August 3, 1996.

63. For a challenge to the consequences of seeing the "zones" as representing culturally pure spheres, see the cautionary remarks on the issue of "Celtic" versus "Anglo-Saxon" origins in Mercer, *English Vernacular Houses*, 47 n. 3. For an argument that the "longhouse" is actually an "early west European" form and not "Celtic" at all and has a more complex genealogy than earlier scholars such as Iorwerth Peate and Cyril Fox initially thought, see Eric Mercer, "'Domus Longa' and 'Long House,'" *VA* 2 (1972): 9–10; N. W. Alcock and Peter Smith, "The Long House: A Plea for Clarity," *Medieval Archaeology* 16 (1972): 145–46; and Gwyn I. Meirion-Jones, "The Long House: A Definition," *Medieval Archaeology* 17 (1973): 135–37, and "The Long House in Brittany: A Provisional Reassessment," *PMA* 7 (1973): 17. On Hoskins and his liberal distaste for national planning in cities and for popular culture in general, see David Matless, "One Man's England: W. G. Hoskins and the English Culture of Landscape," *Rural History* 4, no. 2 (October 1993): 188, 190–94. An exception to the rural preferences of architecture scholars is Roger Leech, *Early Industrial Housing: The Trinity Area of Frome*, Royal Commission on Historical Monuments (England), Supplementary Series 3 (London: Her Majesty's Stationery Office, 1981).

64. On the appropriations of housing cited here, see P. J. Tester, "A Medieval Hall-House at North Cray," *Archaeologia Cantiana* 87 (1972): 9–14; B. H. St. John O'Neil, "Some Seventeenth-Century Houses in Great Yarmouth," *Archaeologia* 95 (1953): 141–80; Anne Padfield, "Lucas Farm," *Historic Buildings in Essex*, no. 3 (November 1986): 6–7, 12; and *An Inventory of Historical Monuments in the County of Cambridge*, vol. 1, *West Cambridgeshire* (London: Royal Commission on Historical Monuments, 1968), 15. See also Hutton, "Timber-Framed Houses in the Vale of York," 88–89, fig. B; E. W. Parkin, "The Ancient Buildings of New Romney," *Archaeologia Cantiana* 88 (1973): 124–25; and Cecil Hewett, "Aisled Timber Halls and Related Buildings, Chiefly in Essex," *Transactions of the Ancient Monument Society* 21 (1976): 45–99, and "The Smaller Medieval House in Essex," *Archaeological Journal* 130 (1973): 172–82. The extreme hybridity of housing in early-seventeenth-century London has not yet been approached as such, since the rural bias of the highland-lowland zone model rendered urban spatial practices as nonessential and interpretively unmapped. Correcting the problem could easily begin with the precise architectural plans in *The London Surveys of Ralph Treswell*, ed. John Schofield, Publication no. 135 (London: London Topographical Society, 1987).

65. On the highland-zone origins of the Whitfield house plan type, see Henry Glassie, *Folk Housing in Middle Virginia: A Structural Analysis of Historic Artifacts* (Knoxville: University of Tennessee Press,

1975), 75. The "open" quality of this design that Glassie sees as a sign of sociability also made it ideal to appropriate and reuse for various tasks of architectural surveillance—almshouses, workers' houses, and slave dwellings—that all emerged in the seventeenth century. For the social and design context of the Allen house, see Dell Upton, "Vernacular Domestic Architecture in Eighteenth-Century Virginia," *Winterthur Portfolio* 17, nos. 2–3 (Autumn 1972): 104.

66. For a view (ca. 1645) of Jones's arcades in Covent Garden, see "The Piazza in Covent Garden," in Arthur Hind, *Wenceslaus Hollar and His Views of London and Windsor in the Seventeenth Century* (London: John Lane, 1922), plate 47. On Coleraine's piazzas, see Philip S. Robinson, "Some Late Survivals of Box-Framed 'Plantation' Houses in Coleraine, County Londonderry," *UJA*, 3d ser., 46 (1983): 134–35. The arcaded fortification is illustrated in Thomas Raven, "A Plat of a Fortification in Lieu of That in the Market-Place in the City of Londonderry" (1622), in Phillips, *Londonderry*, facing p. 5.

67. Mark Girouard, "The Smythson Collection of the Royal Institute of British Architects," *Architectural History* 5 (1962): 160, fig. III/19; Mark Girouard, *Robert Smythson and the Elizabethan Country House* (New Haven: Yale University Press, 1983), 273.

68. Sebastian Serlio, *The Five Books of Architecture* (London, 1611; reprint, New York: Dover Publications, 1982); for biographical information, see Myra Nan Rosenfeld, *Sebastiano Serlio (1475–1555): An Exhibition in Honor of the Five Hundredth Anniversary of His Birth* (New York: Low Library of Columbia University, 1975), 1–6. French plans are illustrated in Pierre LeMuet, *Maniere de bastir pour touttes sortes de personnes* (Paris, 1623); see also M. Jurgens and P. Couperie, "Le logement à Paris aux XVIe et XVIIe siècles: Une source, les inventaires après décès," *Annales* E.S.C. 17, no. 3 (May–June 1962): 488–500; Raymond Alexandre Quenedey, *L'habitation rouennaise: Etude d'histoire, de geographie et d'archaeologie urbaines* (Rouen: Lestrigant, 1926), 317–19, figs. 66, 69; and P. Parent, "L'architecture privée a douai, du moyen age au XIXe siècle," *Révue de Nord* 2 (1911): 265–84.

69. On the impact of Continental architectural concepts on English domestic planning, see Michael Laithwaite, "Totnes Houses, 1500–1800," in *The Transformation of English Provincial Towns, 1600–1800*, ed. Peter Clark (London: Hutchinson, 1984), 93–94; Robert Taylor, "Town Houses in Taunton, 1500–1700," *PMA* 8 (1974): 63–79. A. C. Edwards, "Sir John Petre and Some Elizabethan London Tradesmen," *London Topographical Record* 23 (1972): 71, 83–84; for the 1566 plan of Ingatestone Hall, see Frederick W. Emmison, ed., *The Art of the Map-Maker in Essex, 1566–1860*, Essex Record Office Publication no. 4 (Chelmsford, England: Essex County Record Office, 1947), plate 6. For a discussion and conjectural plan of Hewett's house, Pishiobury Park, at Sawbridgeworth, see J. T. Smith, *English Houses, 1200–1800: The Hertfordshire Evidence* (London: Royal Commission on Historical Monuments, 1992), 57–60. The emergence of courtyarded estates in Ireland is discussed in Waterman, "Some Irish Seventeenth-Century Houses," 252.

70. For medieval courtyarded plans in England, see W. A. Pantin, "Medieval English Town-House Plans," *Medieval Archaeology* 6–7 (1962–63): 202–39, and Vanessa Parker, *The Making of King's Lynn: Secular Buildings from the Eleventh to the Seventeenth Century*, King's Lynn Archaeological Society, vol. 1 (London: Phillimore, 1971). The obvious debt that courtyarded merchants' complexes owe to inns is detailed in W. A. Pantin, "Medieval Inns," in Jope, *Studies in Building History*, 166–69. For the debt that theaters owe to inns in Elizabethan and Jacobean England, see Charles Jasper Sisson, *The Boar's Head Theatre: An Inn-Yard Theatre of the Elizabethan Age*, ed. Stanley Wells (London: Routledge and Kegan Paul, 1972), and the revisionist study of Herbert Berry, *The Boar's Head Playhouse* (Washington, D.C.: Folger Shakespeare Library, 1986), 94–105. In the context of courtyarded open theaters, an unsuccessful attempt by Edward Harfleite to play Shakespeare's *As You Like It* for the Commissioners of Enquiry in an Ulster merchant's bawn in May 1628 seems logical; see Phillips, *Londonderry*, 119–20. The economic role of the Alberti family in England, with implications for how ideas in Leon Battista Alberti, *The Ten Books of Architecture*, trans. James Leoni (London, 1755; reprint, New York: Dover Publications, 1986) first made it to London, is suggested in G. A. Holmes, "Florentine Merchants in England, 1346–1436," *Economic History Review*, 2d ser., 13, no. 2 (December 1960): 193–208.

71. *Note-Book Kept by Thomas Lechford, Esq., Lawyer, in Boston, Massachusetts Bay, from June 27,*

1638, to July 29, 1641 (Cambridge, Mass.: John Wilson & Sons, 1885), 56–57, 156–57; Hutchinson purchased Desborough's estate when he departed for Windsor in 1639. SCPR, 9:14, 72. The relationship between republicanism and mercantile ideology is described in J. G. A. Pocock, *The Machiavellian Moment: Florentine Political Thought and the Atlantic Republican Tradition* (Princeton: Princeton University Press, 1975), and localized in Robert Brenner, "The Civil War Politics of London's Merchant Community," *Past and Present* 58 (February 1973): 53–107. On Robert Keayne's ordeal, see Bailyn, *New England Merchants*, 41–44.

72. Eden, "Smaller Post-medieval Houses in Eastern England," 90; and Peter Eden, *Small Houses in England, 1520–1820: Toward a Classification* (London: Historical Association, 1969), 27–29; Eden also argued, following Wood-Jones, that "hybridization began early" (27) — in Oxfordshire at least by 1607. See Raymond B. Wood-Jones, "The Banbury Region: Minor Domestic Architecture before 1600," *TAMS*, n.s., 4 (1956): 133–46, later expanded in Raymond B. Wood-Jones, *Traditional Domestic Architecture of the Banbury Region* (Manchester: Manchester University Press, 1963). See also Derek Portman, "Vernacular Architecture in the Oxford Region in the Sixteenth and Seventeenth Centuries," in *Rural Change and Urban Growth, 1500–1800: Essays in English Regional History in Honor of W. G. Hoskins*, ed. C. W. Chalklin and Michael Havinden (London: Longman Group, 1974), 135–38, and R. A. Cordingley, "British Historical Roof Systems — a Classification," *TAMS* 9 (1961). On the changing meanings of hybridity, emphasizing the implications of commercial sites for narrative performance, see Deborah A. Kapchan, "Hybridization and the Marketplace: Emerging Paradigms in Folkloristics," *Western Folklore* 52, nos. 2–4 (April–October 1993): 303–26.

73. For postmedieval houses in Northamptonshire, which, like Oxfordshire, was a key county in England's so-called limestone belt for hybrid forms, see *An Inventory of the Historical Monuments in the County of Northampton*, vol. 6, *Architectural Monuments in North Northamptonshire* (London: Royal Commission on Historical Monuments, 1984); M. V. J. Seaborne, "Cob Cottages in Northamptonshire," *Northamptonshire Past and Present* 3, no. 5 (1964): 215–30; and John Stearne, *The Northamptonshire Landscape: Northamptonshire and the Soke of Peterborough* (London: Hodder and Stoughton, 1974), 214–219. On the Buckden and Elton houses, see *An Inventory of the Historical Monuments in Huntingdonshire* (London: Royal Commission on Historical Monuments, 1926), 38–39, plate 47.

74. The Desborough house in Eltisley is described in *An Inventory of Historical Monuments in the County of Cambridge*, vol. 1, *West Cambridgeshire*, 92–93, plate 77.

75. Eden, "Smaller Post-medieval Houses in Eastern England," 75; Spufford, *Contrasting Communities*, 43, map 7.

76. On Eltisley, its town plan, and the relationship between its key buildings, see *An Inventory of Historical Monuments in the County of Cambridge*, vol. 1, *West Cambridgeshire*, 90, 96, 97. The *Oxford English Dictionary*, 2d ed., 12:172, defines "water house" as "a building in which water is raised from a river or well into a 'conduit-head' or reservoir to be conveyed by means of conduits or pipes for domestic use." The earliest reference in the *OED* dates from 1681 and describes "A Delightful Water house adjoyning to the Bowling Green." This late-seventeenth-century use, along with the presence of such a structure on Desborough's property, undoubtedly derives from the embourgeoisement of earlier interior plumbing schemes at a courtly level; see the plumbing plan (ca. 1566) made for Ingatestone Hall in Essex illustrated in Emmison, *Art of the Map-Maker*, plate 6; see also the earlier flushed toilet scheme offered in John Harington, *A New Discourse of a Stale Subject, Called the Metamorphosis of Ajax* (London, 1596). On the 1622 scheme to supply water to every planter's house on the drapers' plantation at Moneymore, see Robinson, "'English' Houses Built at Moneymore," 60. Alternatively, the "waterhouse" on Desborough's Guilford property may refer to either the "privey house" or the "Stoned well" mentioned in the 1732/33 deed marking the passage of the property from Joshua Stone to Andrew Ward; both are unaccounted for on the Rossiter plan. "Guilford Terriers," 5 (1731–37): 89, 108 (deed of February 19, 1732/33).

77. On the two Eltisley structures, see *An Inventory of Historical Monuments in the County of Cambridge*, vol. 1, *West Cambridgeshire*, 94, 95.

78. The presence of open-field agriculture in early Guilford is signaled by the attempts of small groups of farmers, subsequent to initial land grants, to enclose small tracts of land on a cooperative basis; see Allen, "Both Englands," 72. Writing of the breakup of the communal farming at Plymouth in 1627, Neal Salisbury has stressed a darker reason why open-field farming would also be valued by elites—"as a means of exercising a closer watch over those who had threatened to strike out on their own" (Salisbury, *Manitou and Providence*, 142).

79. On the range of vernacular housing in early Rhode Island, see Antoinette F. Downing, *Early Homes of Rhode Island* (Richmond: Garret and Massie, 1937), and Norman M. Isham, *Early Rhode Island Houses* (Providence: Preston and Rounds, 1896). For the Allen property, see James Helme, "Plat of Kingston" (1727), Elisha R. Potter Papers, Rare Book Library, University of Rhode Island, Kingston, R.I. For capsule summaries of the houses shown on the Helme plat and their owners, see William Davis Miller, *Early Houses of the King's Province in the Narragansett Country* (Wakefield, R.I.: privately printed, 1941), 12–13; Miller's documentary information is generally accurate, but his drawings of the houses vary greatly from those by Helme. A structure that early photographs and a sketch in Edwin Whitefield, *The Houses of Our Forefathers in Massachusetts* (Boston: A. Williams and Co., 1880), unpag., suggest also had a facade chimney was the Caleb Carr house on Jamestown Island; its large stone chimney fell in 1886. See Downing, *Early Homes of Rhode Island*, 20–22, and [Charles E. Preston,] *The First Movable Church: The Chapel of the Transformation, Conanicut Island, Diocese of Rhode Island* (Newport: F. W. Marshall, 1899), 96–99. The history of the earlier form of the facade chimney house is discussed in Barley, *English Farmhouse and Cottage*, 112. For variants of the three-room, facade-chimney type in Devon, see the 1535 rectory in Kentisbeare in W. A. Pantin, "Medieval Priests' Houses in South-west England," *Medieval Archaeology* 1 (1957): 127–28. A probable direct-entry, single-cell house with stone end chimney, built about 1705, was documented by Robert F. Trent in Preston, Connecticut, as it was being disassembled in March 1984 (letter to author, April 18, 1984).

80. On hybrid houses in early Rhode Island, see St. George, "'Set Thine House in Order,'" 2:167, and Upton, "Architectural Change in Colonial Rhode Island," *OTNE* 69, nos. 3–4 (Winter–Spring 1979): 18–33. On specific hybrid structures, see John Hutchins Cady, "The Thomas Clemence House (c. 1680)," *OTNE* 39, no. 1 (July 1948): 17–24; Russell Hawes Kettell, "Repair and Restoration of Eleazer Arnold's Splendid Mansion," *OTNE* 43, no. 2 (October–December 1953): 29–35; Helme, "Plat of Kingston" (1727), illustrates Ichabod Sheffield's house. The preference for retaining the linear plan may also have been linked to folk beliefs about how house form conditions social practice; according to E. Estyn Evans, *Irish Folk Ways* (London: Routledge and Kegan Paul, 1957), "the long rectangular shape was sanctioned by custom and preserved by superstition; a house, to be 'lucky,' must not be more than one room wide. 'Widen the house,' I have heard it said, 'and the family will get smaller'" (41).

81. On the John Norton house in North Guilford, see J. Frederick Kelly, "The Norton House, Guilford, Connecticut," *OTNE* 14, no. 3 (January 1924): 122–30; for information on the Seth Pratt house in Shrewsbury, Massachusetts, I am indebted to Holly V. Izard (letter to author, May 15, 1990). The Stonington example is described somewhat in Victor E. Scottron, "Forge Farm," *Connecticut Antiquarian* 37, no. 2 (December 1985–Summer 1986): 17–18.

82. Cummings, *FHMB*, 23, states that 82 of 144 standing pre-1725 houses in Massachusetts began as small houses and were subsequently enlarged. On the unit system in England and its relationship with different inheritance strategies, see J. T. Smith, "Lancashire and Cheshire Houses: Some Problems of Architectural and Social History," *Archaeological Journal* 127 (1970): 168–73; Robert Machin, "The Unit System: Some Historical Explanations," *Archaeological Journal* 132 (1975): 187–94; K. L. Sandall, "The Unit System in Essex," *Archaeological Journal* 132 (1975): 195–201; and Colin A. Gresham, "Gavelkind and the Unit System," *Archaeological Journal* 128 (1971): 174–75. For an argument that would place the Standish house (fig. 40a) in the unit system tradition, see *An Inventory of the Ancient Monuments in Glamorgan*, vol. 4, *Domestic Architecture from the Reformation to the Industrial Revolution*, pt. 2, *Farmhouses and Cottages* (London: Her Majesty's Stationery Office, 1988), 438–40.

83. Waters, "Patrimony, Succession, and Social Stability," 139, 140.

84. "Extract of a Letter from Rev. Mr. Ruggles, Author of the History of Guilford, to Dr. Stiles" [June 21, 1770], MHS *Coll.,* ser. 1, 10 (1809): 92.

85. Isabel MacBeath Calder, *The New Haven Colony* (New Haven: Yale University Press, 1934), iv; *Records of the Colony or Jurisdiction of New Haven, from May, 1653, to the Union,* ed. Charles J. Hoadly (Hartford: Case, Lockwood and Co., 1857–58), 217.

86. "Extract of a Letter from Rev. Mr. Ruggles," 92.

87. Waters, "Patrimony, Succession, and Social Stability," 141 (emphasis added).

88. Steiner, *History of the Plantation of Menunkatuck,* 170, notes that Rossiter served in the capacity of a surveyor between 1656 and 1660, so he was evidently skilled at measuring land and drawing boundaries. "Petition against planting at Kenilworth" [Killingworth], Towns & Lands, ser. 1, vol. 1, Connecticut State Archives, Hartford.

89. "Extract of a Letter from Rev. Mr. Ruggles," 92. Guilford Town Records, Book C, 187 (November 10, 1661). On the controversy, see also Calder, *New Haven Colony,* 87–88; and Smith, *History of Guilford,* 92–94.

90. Guilford Town Records, Book C, 187 (November 10, 1661). For the 1662 case, see Steiner, *History of the Plantation of Menunkatuck,* 102.

91. Winthrop, *Journal,* 1:28 n. 3, 37. For biographical information on Edward Rossiter, see Meredith B. Colket, "Edward Rossiter, Colonist of Dorchester, Mass., and the Rossiter English Lineage," *NEHGR* 138 (1984): 12–13; and Meredith B. Colket, "Edward Rossiter," *American Genealogist* 13 (1937): 145–51.

92. *Note-Book Kept by Thomas Lechford,* 157.

93. Biographical information on Rossiter is available in Ralph D. Smith, comp., "Dr. Bryan (or Bray) Rossiter of Guilford, Conn., and His Descendants," *NEHGR* 55 (1901): 149–54; Colket, "Edward Rossiter, Colonist of Dorchester," 12–13; Savage, *Genealogical Dictionary,* 3:577; and Smith, *History of Guilford,* 41. Information on Rossiter's house lot and activities in Windsor is in *The Memorial History of Hartford County, Connecticut, 1633–1884,* ed. James Hammond Trumbull, 2 vols. (Boston: Edward L. Osgood, 1886), 2:501–7, 557.

94. Savage, *Genealogical Dictionary,* 1:130–33; 2:269; 3:359.

95. Theophilus Eaton to John Winthrop, August 6, 1646, in MHS *Colls.,* 4th ser, 6 (1863): 346. Calder, *New Haven Colony,* vi.

96. Calder, *New Haven Colony,* 158–64. Linked as it was to New Haven's economic downturn, the decline of Guilford was also probably one reason why Desborough's farmstead remained in use until razed by Pendleton.

97. Ezra Stiles, *A History of Three of the Judges of King Charles I* (Hartford, 1794), 63; Edward R. Lambert, *History of the Colony of New Haven, before and after the Union with Connecticut* (New Haven: Hitchcock and Stafford, 1838), 52; for the 1748 map of New Haven, inscribed "Plan of the City of New Haven Taken in 1748," see David Grayson Allen, "*Vacuum Domicilium*: The Social and Cultural Landscape of Seventeenth-Century New England," in *NEB,* 1:29.

98. New Haven Probate Records, 1:69–75, Connecticut State Archives, Hartford. Stiles, *History of Three of the Judges,* 63, and Lambert, *History of the Colony of New Haven,* 52–53; on the tentative furnishing plan of the Eaton house based on his 1657 inventory, see Isham and Brown, *Early Connecticut Houses,* 101, 106.

99. On the connections between New Haven furniture and London production, see Patricia E. Kane, *Furniture of the New Haven Colony: The Seventeenth-Century Style* (New Haven: New Haven Colony Historical Society, 1973), 7–8, 81–84; and Robert F. Trent, "New England Joinery and Turning before 1700," in *NEB,* 3:503, 505, 524–26.

100. For market farms, see Frederick W. Emmison, ed., *Catalogue of the Maps in the Essex Record Office, 1566–1855,* Essex Record Office Publication no. 3 (Chelmsford, Essex: Essex County Council, 1947), frontispiece and plate 6b. The Chelmsford map of 1591 illustrates the Bishop's Hall manor owned by Sir Thomas Mildmay in the parish of Chelmsford, a busy center along the road from London to Norfolk and Suffolk. For additional discussion, see the catalog entry on this document by Allen in *NEB,*

1:18, no. 7, and Frederick W. Emmison, "A Survey of Chelmsford, 1591," *Transactions of the Essex Archaeological Society*, n.s., 23 (1942–45): 133–40.

101. Gervase Markham, *The English Husbandman*, ed. John Dixon Hunt (London, 1613; reprint, New York: Garland, 1982), sigs. A5, B1.

102. Ibid., sigs. B–B1.

103. Julius Herbert Tuttle, "The Libraries of the Mathers," *Proceedings of the American Antiquarian Society*, n.s., 20 (1909–10): 271. "A booke called The French Countrey Farme" is noted as being donated to the library of the Massachusetts Bay Company in Salem on April 13, 1629. [Child], *Samuel Hartlib His Legacie*, 50. Charles Estienne, in particular, was already well established as a printer, known for his edition *De Dissectione*; see K. B. Roberts and J. D. W. Tomlinson, *The Fabric of the Body: European Traditions of Anatomical Illustration* (Oxford: Clarendon Press, 1992), 166–87.

104. Charles Stevens [Charles Estienne] and John Liebault [Jean Liebault], *Maison Rustique; or, The Countrey Farme*, trans. Richard Surflet (London, 1606), 5, 8.

105. Ibid., 18–19, 21. George E. Fussell, *The Classical Tradition in West European Farming* (Rutherford, N.J.: Fairleigh Dickinson University Press, 1972), 37. On the "fortress"-like quality of French domestic architecture and its role in defining "physical space to achieve social and psychical distance," see Susan G. Carlisle, "French Homes and French Character," *Landscape* 26, no. 3 (1982): 13, 23. See also Joseph Stany-Gauthier, *Petits chateaux et manoirs de France* (Paris: Charles Massin, 1958).

106. [Estienne and Liebault], *Maison Rustique*, 21.

107. Ibid., 22. See the related plans illustrated in Harold Donaldson Eberlein and Roger Wearne Ramsdell, *Small Manor Houses and Farmsteads in France* (Philadelphia: J. B. Lippincott & Co., 1926), 110 (La Ferme la Cugnie, Pas de Calais), 120 (La Ferme de la Haie, Neuchâtel, Pas de Calais), 143 (La Ferme du Manoir, Hesdigneuil, Pas de Calais).

108. [Estienne and Liebault], *Maison Rustique*, 23.

109. The similarity of Markham's model house plan to H-plan houses being built in Ireland by English settlers also argues for the neofeudal, aristocratic motive; see the description of "Oldbawn," a house built about 1635 by Archdeacon Bulkeley at Tallaght, County Dublin, in H. G. Leask, "Early Seventeenth-Century Houses in Ireland," in Jope, *Studies in Building History*, 250. On open-hall houses, see Mercer, *English Vernacular Houses*, 8–22; on the Wealden house in particular, see Mason, *Framed Buildings of the Weald*, 27–29, 37–41. On the complex diffusion of Continental theories on market agriculture, see George Fussell, "The Classical Tradition in West European Farming: The Sixteenth Century," *Economic History Review*, 2d ser., 22, no. 3 (December 1969): 547–49.

110. John Winthrop, "A Modell of Christian Charity," in *The Puritans*, ed. Perry Miller and Thomas H. Johnson, 2 vols. (New York: Harper and Row, 1963), 1:195.

111. The Fosten Green stead is illustrated in Cook and Smith, *English Cottages and Farmhouses*, plate 106. On the Caxton farmstead, see *An Inventory of Historical Monuments in the County of Cambridge*, vol. 1, *West Cambridgeshire*, 39. W. G. Hoskins, "Some Old Devon Bartons," *Country Life*, September 22, 1950, 912–14 (see especially the aerial view of Westcott Barton at Marwood, Devon [913], and Hoskins's claim that in bartons "there is much of interest in the layout of farm-buildings round a great open court-yard that is typical of large farms everywhere in western Europe where cattle are more important than corn" [914]). The English colonial courtyard plan—more commonly three-sided than four-sided—once introduced into Ireland in the sixteenth and seventeenth centuries, was integrated into Irish vernacular design; see the discussion in Caoimhín Ó Danachair, "Farmyard Forms and Their Distribution in Ireland," *UF* 27 (1981): 68–72.

112. On John Winthrop Jr.'s trips to Ulster and London in 1635 and the Saybrook experiment, see Richard S. Dunn, *Puritans and Yankees: The Winthrop Dynasty of New England, 1630–1717* (Princeton: Princeton University Press, 1962), 65–69; Clotworthy's importance in Ulster politics is explained in Aidan Clarke, "The Government of Wentworth, 1632–1640," in *A New History of Ireland*, vol. 3, *Early Modern Ireland, 1534–1691*, ed. T. W. Moody, F. X. Martin, and F. J. Byrne (Oxford: Clarendon Press, 1978), 266–67.

113. Garvan, *Architecture and Town Planning*, 43–44. The Winthrop plan of Groton Manor is in "Winthrop Deeds, Commissions, 1587–1860," comp. Robert C. Winthrop, vol. 88:16, Massachusetts Historical Society, Boston. On the historical background of Groton Manor, see *Winthrop Papers*, vol. 1, *1498–1628* (Boston: Massachusetts Historical Society, 1929), 7–10. Aids in interpreting specific dialect words on the plan can be found in Walter W. Skeat and A. L. Mayhew, *A Glossary of Tudor and Stuart Words* (Oxford: Clarendon Press, 1914), 217 ("kell"); and Wright, *English Dialect Dictionary*, 2:440 ("folkes"), 3:436 ("kile"), 6:264 ("tumpe yard"), 6:581 ("yeilding house").

114. Jope, "Moyry, Charlemont, Castleraw, and Richhill," 112 (emphasis added). The second Winthrop sketch is reprinted in Garvan, *Architecture and Town Planning*, 126 (lower left).

115. John Norden, *The Surveyor's Dialogue* (London, 1607), 226; Robert Cushman, "Reasons and Considerations Touching the Lawfulness of Removing out of England in the Parts of America," in Young, *Chronicles of the Pilgrim Fathers*, 243. Quoted in Robert R. Walcott, "Husbandry in Colonial New England," *NEQ* 9, no. 2 (June 1936): 233.

116. *ECQCR*, 1:413; 3:413, referring to Leonard Mascall, *Government of Cattell* (London, 1620); Plymouth Colony Wills and Inventories, 2:39, Plymouth County Courthouse, Plymouth, Mass.; "Isaack De Rasieres to Samuel Blommaert, 1628," in *Three Visitors to Early Plymouth*, ed. Ruth MacIntire (Plymouth, Mass.: Plimoth Plantation, 1976), 71 (emphasis added).

117. On the plan of Standish's Duxbury house, see St. George, " 'Set Thine House in Order,' " 2:166, 200. The Hall plan is discussed in James J. F. Deetz, "Plymouth Colony Architecture: Archaeological Evidence from the Seventeenth Century," in *Architecture in Colonial Massachusetts*, ed. Abbott Lowell Cummings (Charlottesville: University Press of Virginia, 1979), 54–55.

118. *NHTR*, 162; *ECQCR*, 1:293; Plymouth Colony Wills and Inventories, vol. 2, pt. 2:17; Barnstable County Wills and Inventories, 1:7, Barnstable County Courthouse, Barnstable, Mass. For a map of the distribution of the word "cowhouse" in Britain, see Harold Orton, "A Linguistic Atlas of England," *Advancement of Science* 27, no. 131 (1970): 89–90.

119. Harrison, *Description of England*, 199.

120. See the similar observation on the stylistic references made by household furnishings in Robert F. Trent, "The Concept of Mannerism," in *NEB*, 3:368: "A central irony in relating the arts of seventeenth-century New England to their continental antecedents lies in the fact that the English settlers of New England, most of them Calvinists by conviction, enjoyed a Mannerist style that had its inception in the extravagant Roman Catholic courts of Italy in the early 1500s."

121. "Towns and Lands," ser. 1, 4:131a, Connecticut State Archives, Hartford.

122. Ezra Stiles, *The Itinerarium of Ezra Stiles*, ed. Franklin Bowditch Dexter (New Haven: Yale University Press, 1916), 364.

123. Eliot, *Essays upon Field Husbandry*, 15; on Eliot's view of Aristotle versus empirical knowledge, see 24. H. W. Robinson of South Kingston, R.I., to Eliot, July 13, 1762, in Eliot, *Essays upon Field Husbandry*, 252. Robinson was no doubt responding to the publication of Jared Eliot, *An Essay on the Invention, or Act of Making Very Good, if Not the Best Iron, from Black Sea Sand* (New York, 1762).

124. On Gabriel Plattes, Ralph Austen, and Walter Blith—their philosophical embrace of Baconian positivism, their political agenda linked to the Puritan revolution, their connections with Samuel Hartlib, Robert Child, and John Winthrop Jr.—see Charles Webster, *The Great Instauration: Science, Medicine, and Reform, 1626–1660* (London: Duckworth, 1975), 465–74, and *Utopian Planning and the Puritan Revolution: Gabriel Plattes, Samuel Hartlib, and Macaria* (Oxford: Wellcome Unit for the History of Medicine, 1979). Walter Blith, *The English Improver, Or a New Survey of Husbandry* (London, 1649), sig. 3r.

125. [Child], *Samuel Hartlib His Legacie*, 50.

126. On the Jireh Bull site, see Norman M. Isham, "Preliminary Report to the Society of Colonial Wars of Rhode Island on the Excavations at the Jireh Bull Garrison House on Tower Hill in South Kingstown," *Rhode Island Historical Collections* 11, no. 1 (January 1918): 3–11. The site of the stead was also clearly marked on a survey done of the area in 1729; see *A Plat of the Land of Capt. Henry Bull at*

Pettaquamscut Drawn by James Helme Surveyor January 8, 1729 (Providence: Society of Colonial Wars of Rhode Island, 1927), 5–17.

127. Plymouth Colony Deeds, 10:86–87, Plymouth County Courthouse, Plymouth, Mass.; Plymouth Colony Wills and Inventories, vol. 2, pt. 1:69–73.

128. On pre-1730 farmsteads and barns, see St. George, "'Set Thine House in Order,'" 2:163–65, 190, and Robert Blair St. George, "The Stanley-Lake Barn in Topsfield, Massachusetts: Some Comments on Agricultural Buildings in Early New England," in *Perspectives in Vernacular Architecture*, ed. Camille Wells (Annapolis, Md.: Vernacular Architecture Forum, 1982), 7–23. On English background, see *Old Farm Buildings in Eastern Sussex, 1450–1750*, pt. 2, *The Farmstead and Barns (Survival and Construction Dates)*, special issue of *Historic Buildings in Eastern Sussex* 3, no. 2 (1982): 35–132; I am indebted to Edward Chappell for this reference. For a reinterpretation of Daniel Cushing's farmstead in Hingham (1679 and later), see Cary Carson, "The Consumer Revolution in Colonial America: Why Demand?" in *Of Consuming Interest: The Style of Life in the Eighteenth Century*, ed. Cary Carson, Ronald Hoffman, and Peter J. Albert (Charlottesville: University Press of Virginia for the United States Capitol Historical Society, 1994), 559–61. "Gov. George Wyllys to [his son] George Wyllys," *Collections of the Connecticut Historical Society* 21 (1924): 66.

129. James Walton, "Some Notes on South Pennine Barn Buildings," *Architectural Review* 90 (July–December 1941): 122. I am indebted to Tim Whittaker for sharing his ongoing research on bank barns in northern England with me. According to Whittaker, barns with cow house or shippon on the same level as crop storage "are if anything more common than bank barns" in areas like the Eden Valley (letter to author, July 28, 1986). For related examples, see the plan of Greenhill bank barn at New Mill, West Yorkshire, in James Walton, "Upland Houses: The Influence of Mountain Terrain on British Folk Building," *Antiquity* 30, no. 119 (September 1956): 143, fig. 1a.

130. Eliot, *Essays upon Field Husbandry*, 7.

CHAPTER TWO

1. All citations are in documents from the Kelley autopsy reprinted in Charles J. Hoadly, "Some Early Post-Mortem Examinations in New England," in *Proceedings of the Connecticut Medical Society, 1892* (Bridgeport, Conn.: Buckingham and Brewer, 1892), 207–17. See also Albert Matthews, "Notes on Early Autopsies and Anatomical Lectures," CSM *Pub.* 19 (1916–17): 273–90. On the training of physicians in early-seventeenth-century England, see Phyllis Allen, "Medical Education in Seventeenth Century England," *Journal of the History of Medicine and Allied Sciences* 1, no. 1 (January 1946): 115–43, and Paul Slack, "Mirrors of Health and Treasures of Poor Men: The Uses of the Vernacular Medical Literature of Tudor England," in *Health, Medicine, and Mortality in the Sixteenth Century*, ed. Charles Webster (Cambridge: Cambridge University Press, 1979), 237–74.

2. 1 Cor. 12:12, 14–20.

3. Ibid., 9–11; 2 Cor. 5:1–2. See S. K. Heninger Jr., "Metaphor as Cosmic Correspondence," in *Medieval and Renaissance Studies: Proceedings of the Southeastern Institute of Medieval and Renaissance Studies, Summer 1967*, ed. John M. Headley (Chapel Hill: University of North Carolina Press, 1968), 3–22.

4. John S. Coolidge, *The Pauline Renaissance in England: Puritanism and the Bible* (Oxford: Clarendon Press, 1970), 23–54; Frank Bottomley, *Attitudes to the Body in Western Christendom* (London: Lepus Books, 1979), 31–43. Josiah Rossiter to Rowland Cotton, April 9, 1703, Miscellaneous Bound Mss., Massachusetts Historical Society, Boston.

5. Edward Taylor, "[The Foundation Day Sermon] Eph. 2.22 In whom you are also builded (up) together, for an Habitation of God through the Spirit," in *Edward Taylor's "Church Records" and Related Sermons*, ed. Thomas M. Davis and Virginia L. Davis (Boston: Twayne Publishers, 1981), 125. Cotton Mather, "Triparadisus," ca. 1720 ms., octavo vol. no. 49, bk. 9, 26, Mather Family Papers 1613–1819,

American Antiquarian Society, Worcester, Mass. Thomas Hooker, *A Survey of the Summe of Church-Discipline* (London, 1648), 188. Taylor, *Poems,* 484.

6. *The Diary of Michael Wigglesworth, 1653–1657: The Conscience of a Puritan,* ed. Edmund S. Morgan (New York: Harper and Row, 1946), 93.

7. James B. Stone, "Ancient Milestones of Essex County," *EIHC* 123, no. 3 (July 1987): 278. Mason Lowance Jr. and David Watters, "Increase Mather's 'New Jerusalem': Millennialism in Late Seventeenth-Century New England," *Proceedings of the American Antiquarian Society* 87, pt. 2 (1977): 381; this second sermon probably dates from about 1687 (p. 363 n. 5). See also Taylor, *Poems,* 126: "Together in thy Person all Divine / Stand House, and House holder." Mather, "Triparadisus," bk. 1, 10.

8. Mather, "Triparadisus," bk. 9, 27–28. The importance of heavenly visions to the typological nature of Puritan town planning is discussed in John Archer, "Puritan Town Planning in New Haven," *Journal of the Society of Architectural Historians* 34, no. 1 (March 1975): 140–49. For other examples of New England towns planned to make the gridded vision of the heavenly Jerusalem appear immanent on earth, see the town maps in Josiah H. Temple and George Sheldon, *History of the Town of Northfield, Massachusetts, for 150 Years* (Albany: Joel Munsell, 1875), 136 (1715), and John Montague Smith, *History of the Town of Sunderland, Massachusetts, 1673–1899* (Greenfield: E. E. Hall & Co., 1899), 18 (1714). See also the related discussion in "Essay on the Laying Out of Towns, & c." (ca. 1634), in MHS *Coll.,* 5th ser., 1 (1891): 474–80.

9. Mather, "Triparadisus," bk. 9, 27. On "material" versus "ethereal" constructions of heaven and for the impact on Puritans of Saint Paul's statements in Eph. 2:22 and 1 Cor. 3:16 that earth is God's "habitation" and "temple" (suggesting the materiality of heaven), see *The New Schaff-Herzog Encyclopedia of Religious Knowledge,* ed. Samuel Macauley Jackson et al., 13 vols. (New York: London, Funk, and Wagnalls Co. 1908–14), 5:180–82 (s.v. "Heaven"). The detailed instruction in Old Testament theology that New England ministers received accounted, in part, for their having a material understanding of heaven. See also Bottomley, *Attitudes to the Body in Western Christendom,* 25–30. For another, more political description of the New Jerusalem, see William Williams to Samuel Sewall, January 22, 1727/8, in Sewall, *Letter-Book,* 2:250–53.

10. C[harles] Harris, "State of the Dead (Christian)," in *Encyclopaedia of Religion and Ethics,* ed. James Hastings, 13 vols. (New York: Charles Scribners' Sons, 1925–27), 11:833–34. Taylor, *Poems,* 158 ("A Body has thou prepared mee").

11. Sewall, *Diary,* 2:747. Four years earlier (1710), Sewall intimated his belief that resurrected bodies could eat; he imagined heaven as a "most . . . magnificent Palace, furnished with the most Rich & Splendid Entertainments; and the noblest Guests are invited to partake of them" (Samuel Sewall, "Talitha Cumi," MHS *Proc.,* 1st ser., 12 [1871–73]: 380).

12. John Winthrop Jr. to Roger Williams, February 4, 1664, MHS *Coll.,* 4th ser., 6 (1863): 530.

13. On anthropomorphism in Western architecture, see Marco Frascari, *Monsters of Architecture: Anthropomorphism in Architectural Theory* (Savage, Md.: Rowman and Littlefield, 1991); Geoffrey Scott, *The Architecture of Humanism: A Study in the History of Taste* (New York: W. W. Norton, 1974); Leonard Barkan, *Nature's Work of Art: The Human Body as Image of the World* (New Haven: Yale University Press, 1975), 117–74; and Kent C. Bloomer and Charles M. Moore, *Body, Memory, and Architecture* (New Haven: Yale University Press, 1977). Webb Keane, "The Spoken House: Text, Act, and Object in Eastern Indonesia," *American Ethnologist* 22 (1995): 102–24, suggests a way of constructing cultural space that is simultaneously material and discursive. On specific African cultures, see Giovanna Antognini and Tito Spini, *Il campo dei segni: Territori funzionali e metafisici di culture africane,* exhibition catalog (Rome: Centro Studio Archeologia Africana, 1990); Suzanne Preston Blier, *The Anatomy of Architecture: Ontology and Metaphor in Batammaliba Architectural Expression* (Cambridge: Cambridge University Press, 1987); on Southeast Asian cultures and architectural bodies, see the overview in Roxana Waterson, *The Living House: An Anthropology of Architecture in South-East Asia* (New York: Oxford University Press, 1990), 129–37.

14. Robert Underwood, *A New Anatomie. Wherein the Body of a Man is very fit and aptly (two wayes) compared: 1 To a Household. 2 To a Citie* (London, 1605), 3; *The Complete Poetry of John Donne,* ed. John

T. Shawcross (Garden City: Anchor, 1967), 111; *The Complete Poetry of Robert Herrick*, ed. J. Max Patrick (New York: W. W. Norton, 1968), 367 (H-865: "The Body"). Joseph Moxon, *Mechanical Exercises, or the Doctrine of Handy-Works*, ed. Benno M. Forman (London, 1703; reprint, New York: Praeger, 1970), 152–66, s.v. "carcass," "hips." According to Richard Neve, *The City and Countrey Purchaser and Builder's Dictionary* (London, 1703), 96, loam is a type of mud used in plastering walls and therefore appropriate to the idea of one's body being a "house of clay."

15. Anne Bradstreet, "As Weary Pilgrim, Now at Rest," in *The Puritans*, ed. Perry Miller and Thomas H. Johnson, 2 vols. (New York: Harper and Row, 1963), 2:579. Taylor, *Poems*, 48–49, 172, 218–19; for Taylor's conception of the "mansion" being the house of the soul on earth, see Thomas M. Davis and Virginia L. Davis, "Edward Taylor on the Day of Judgment," *American Literature* 43 (1972): 52. Taylor's prayer/poem could be inverted, and the house-body analogy might issue forth as a curse. In a court case in 1640, joiner John Davis said he was cursed by the defendant, Anne Hibbens, as follows: she "sayd. that the Timbers. of the Roome would crye for Judgment againyst me." (Samuel Green, "Note-Book of Robert Keayne, and Trial of Mrs. Anne Hibbens," in MHS *Proc.*, 4 [1889]: 315).

16. Underwood, *New Anatomie*, sig. B1. One of many overviews appears in Neve, *City and Countrey Purchaser*, 84; the first thing to do when evaluating a house "is to pass a running Examination over the whole Edifice, according to the Properties of a well shapen Man; as whether the *Walls* stand upright, upon a good Foundation; whether the Fabric be of a comely *Stature*; . . . whether the principal *Entrance* be in the middle of the *Front*, like our Mouths; [and] whether the *Windows*, as our Eyes, be set in equal number, and distance on both sides [of] the *Entrance*."

17. On "housebody" as a common name for the "hall" in Lancashire, see Sarah Pearson, *Rural Houses of the Lancashire Pennines, 1560–1760* (London: Her Majesty's Stationers Office, 1985), 73, 74, 81, 91, 169. Andrew Boorde, *A Compendyous Regyment or a Dyetary of Helth* (London, 1542), in *Works of Andrew Boorde*, ed. F. S. Furnivall, Early English Text Society, Extra Series n. 10 (London: N. Trübner & Co. for the Early English Text Society, 1870), 238 (emphasis added).

18. On medieval plans and their distribution, see J. G. Hurst, "A Review of Archaeological Research (to 1968)," in *Deserted Medieval Villages*, ed. Maurice Beresford and J. G. Hurst (New York: St. Martin's Press, 1971), 104–17. For other works on medieval houses, see Eric Mercer, *English Vernacular Houses* (London: Royal Commission on Historical Monuments, 1975), 8–49; M. W. Barley, *Houses and History* (London: Faber and Faber, 1986), 106–30, 145–67. See also James Walton, "The Open Hearth," *Country Life*, November 26, 1948, 1160–61.

19. Charles Stevens [Charles Estienne] and John Liebault [Jean Liebault], *Maison Rustique; or, The Countrie Farme*, trans. Richard Surflet (London, 1606), 24.

20. M. M. Bakhtin, *Rabelais and His World*, trans. Heléne Iswolsky (Cambridge: MIT Press, 1968), 401. The materialized opposition between low and high, hall and parlor, and "Other" and Self in medieval French and English culture has analogies elsewhere and is common in folk housing traditions across the world; see the distinction between the "hearth room" and the "clean room" in Jan Harold Brunvand, "Traditional House Decoration in Romania: Survey and Bibliography," *East European Quarterly* 14, no. 3 (1980): 295.

21. [Estienne and Liebault], *Maison Rustique*, 24 (emphasis added). For a useful extension of Ernst Kantorowicz's notion of the "king's two bodies" into aesthetics, see David Lee Miller, *The Poem's Two Bodies: The Poetics of the 1590 Fairie Queen* (Princeton: Princeton University Press, 1988); see also R. F. Hill, "Spenser's Allegorical 'Houses,'" *Modern Language Review* 65, no. 4 (October 1970): 721–33.

22. The section that follows is drawn from Underwood, *New Anatomie*, 2–19.

23. Boorde, *A Compendyous Regyment or a Dyetary of Helth*, 236–37.

24. *Oxford English Dictionary*, 2d ed., s.v. "clapper," citing Henry Shirley, *The Martyr'd Souldier, a Tragedy* (London, 1638); Underwood, *New Anatomie*, 15. Thomas Adams, "The Taming of the Tongue," in *The Works of Thomas Adams*, ed. James Angus, 3 vols. (Edinburgh, 1861–62), 3:17. On the dangers of the tongue and its association with the danger and "passions" of women, see Robert Blair St. George, "'Heated Speech' and Literacy in Seventeenth-Century New England," in *Seventeenth-Century New*

England, ed. David Grayson Allen and David D. Hall (Boston: Colonial Society of Massachusetts, 1984), 275–322, and Jane Kamensky, "Words, Witches, and Woman Trouble: Witchcraft, Disorderly Speech, and Gender Boundaries in Puritan New England," *EIHC* 128, no. 4 (October 1992): 286–307.

25. Thomas Dekker, *The Guls Horne-booke* (London, 1609), 14–15.

26. Cotton Mather, *The Angel of Bethesda, an Essay upon the Common Maladies of Mankind,* ed. Gordon W. Jones (Boston, 1724; reprint, Barre, Mass.: American Antiquarian Society and Barre Publishers, 1972), 5. The discussion of Galenic medicine that follows is necessarily abbreviated and simplified, especially given its complicated relationships with both Paracelsian medicine and alchemy.

27. William Vaughan, *Approved Directions for Health, Both Natural and Artificiall,* 4th ed. (London, 1612), 121.

28. Cohn's engraving is put in the context of iatrochemistry and the distillation of spirits in I. Bernard Cohen, *Album of Science: From Leonardo to Lavoisier, 1450–1800* (New York: Charles Scribner's Sons, 1980), 225. I am indebted to Monique Bourke for bringing this reference to my attention.

29. Quoted in John Nef, *The Conquest of the Material World* (Chicago: University of Chicago Press, 1964), 296. On the relationship of the heart to the soul in Galenic theory, see Lawrence Babb, *The Elizabethan Malady: A Study of Melancholia in English Literature from 1580 to 1642* (East Lansing: Michigan State College Press, 1951), 8–9.

30. John Foster, *An Almanack of Coelestial Motions for the Year of the Christian Epocha 1678* (Boston, 1678), unpag.

31. Vaughan, *Approved Directions for Health,* 63, 121, 122. Taylor, *Poems,* 72. Some evidence suggests that masonry houses may have been damp and trapped ill humors; the wife of Offin Boardman disliked her home, the Spencer-Pierce-Little house (ca. 1700) in Newbury, because she "consider[ed] it unhealthy to live between stone walls continually" (Alvin Lincoln Jones, *Under Colonial Roofs* [Boston: G. B. Webster, 1894], 81). In Salem in 1798 a brick house "was demolished from the prejudice against brick houses," a bias related to their retention of moisture (*The Diary of William Bentley, D.D.,* 4 vols. [Salem: Essex Institute, 1907], 2:268). But see this "unhappy prejudice . . . that houses of brick or stone are less wholesome than those of wood" systematically debunked in Thomas Jefferson, *Notes on the State of Virginia,* ed. William Peden (Chapel Hill: University of North Carolina Press for the Institute of Early American History and Culture, 1955), 153–54.

32. See Gordon W. Jones, introduction to Mather, *Angel of Bethesda,* xxiii. Vaughan, *Approved Directions for Health,* 3–4, 5, 122.

33. Taylor, *Poems,* 123: "Sins thick and threefold at my threshold lay / At Graces Threshold I all gore in Sin." See also the connection drawn between thresholds, mouths, and the "Bread of Life" in Taylor's "Meditation no. 8" in Miller and Johnson, *The Puritans,* 2:656h, 656i: "This Bread of Life dropt in thy mouthe doth Cry." Suzanne Preston Blier, "Houses Are Human: Architectural Self-Images of Africa's Tamberma," *Journal of the Society of Architectural Historians* 42, no. 4 (December 1983): 374, 376 n. 19. For examples of other objects being symbolically fed in British folk tradition, see Thomas Davidson, "Plough Rituals in England and Scotland," *Agricultural History Review* 7, pt. 1 (1959): 27–37, describing the Scottish ceremony of "streeking the plough" in which the ploughman was given food and drink and then "a portion was given symbolically to the plough: that is, food was tied or laid on the beam of the plough and drink was poured over it" (27). Balthasar Gerbier, *A Brief Discourse Concerning the Three Chief Principles of Magnificent Building. viz. Solidity, Conveniency, and Ornament* (London, 1662; reprint, Farnborough, England: Gregg International, 1969), 11. On seventeenth-century doors and windows marking points of vulnerability in the human house, see St. George, "'Set Thine House in Order': The Domestication of the Yeomanry in Seventeenth-Century New England," in *NEB,* 2:168, and George Ewart Evans, *The Pattern under the Plough: Aspects of the Folk Life of East Anglia* (London: Faber, 1966), 58–59. Surviving studded exterior doors with decorative nailing patterns include those from the John Turner house in Salem, in *NEB,* 2:205, no. 162, and the Jabez Huntington house, Norwich, Conn., illustrated in J. Frederick Kelly, *Early Domestic Architecture of Connecticut* (New Haven, 1924; reprint, New York: Dover Publications, 1963), 137, fig. 142. For a particularly elaborate joined in-

terior door from the first (ca. 1650–1670?) section of the Oliver Pomeroy Tavern in the Rocky Hill section of Wethersfield, see Robert F. Trent, "Acquisitions," in *Notes and News of the Connecticut Historical Society* 8, no. 4 (July–August 1983), 2–3. Boarded interior doors with two or three horizontal battens survive in greater numbers; see Cummings, *FHMB*, 186, fig. 253. On the coloring of windows in 1681–84, see "Hingham Selectmen's Records," quoted in Arthur Marble ms., unpag., on deposit in office of the First Parish (Unitarian) of Hingham, Mass. [Bruno Ryves,] *Mercurius Rusticus: Or, the Countries Complaint of the Barbarous Out-rages Committed by the Sectaries of this Late Flourishing Kingdome* (Oxford, 1646), 33.

34. John Winthrop, "A Modell of Christian Charity," in Miller and Johnson, *The Puritans,* 1:198. The great exemplar of this tradition was Samuel Sewall, who records numerous instances of driving pins, hammering nails, and assembling timbers in new houses in and around Boston. See Sewall, *Diary,* 1:11 ("Brothers house was raised, at the raising of which I was. Two Pins lower Summer"); 1:277 ("Drive a Nail in Abiel Sommerby's House"); 1:529 ("Drove a Pin in the Ministers House which I found Raising; bolted on the Raisers out of Bishop's Lane before I was aware"). See David D. Hall, *Worlds of Wonder, Days of Judgment: Popular Religious Belief in Early New England* (New York: Knopf, 1989), 217. In the late nineteenth century H. W. Haynes, "Remarks upon Driving a Pin or Nail," MHS *Proc.,* 2d ser., 4 (1887–89): 101–2, attributed this custom to an ancient Roman sign of predestination to death; Halsey M. Thomas, in Sewall, *Diary,* 1:11 n. 6, suggests it was a "gesture of good will and voluntary association." *Diary of Joshua Hempstead of New London, Connecticut, Covering a Period of Forty-seven Years from September, 1711, to November, 1758* (New London: New London County Historical Society, 1901), 482 (entry of June 10, 1747), 634 (entry of August 6, 1754).

35. "Deacon John Paine's Journal," *Mayflower Descendant* 8 (1906): 181. John Preston quoted in Perry Miller, *The New England Mind: The Seventeenth Century* (Boston: Beacon Press, 1961), 215. Winthrop, *Journal,* 2:299 (emphasis added). Cotton Mather, *Ornaments for the Daughters of Zion, Or, the Character and Happiness of a Vertuous Woman* (Boston, 1691), 17.

36. John Saffin, *John Saffin, His Book (1665–1708): A Collection of Various Matters of Divinity, Law, and State Affairs Epitomiz'd both in Verse and Prose* (New York: Harbor Press, 1928), 12–13.

37. Taylor, *Poems,* 147–48, "Without me yee can do nothing" (emphasis added), 165, "The Fulness of the Godhead dwelleth in him bodily." See Sewall to Joseph Dudley, August 10, 1702, in Sewall, *Letter-Book,* 1:274, for a reference to Christ as "the Fountain of Living Waters." On "fullness" as a state in which human impediments disappear in the unity of divine perfection, see Taylor, *Poems,* 44, "In Him should all Fulness Dwell": "Such rich rich Fulness would / Make stammering Tongues speake smoothly, and Enshrine / The Dumb mans mouth with Silver Streams like gold / Of Eloquence making the Aire to Chime." Mather, *Magnalia,* 2:202–3. On the poetics of communion, see Charles Trinkaus, *In Our Image and Likeness: Humanity and Divinity in Italian Humanist Thought,* 2 vols. (Chicago: University of Chicago Press, 1970), 2:633–50.

38. Taylor, *Poems,* 172–73, "Which is his body, the fulness of him that filleth all in all." Quoted in David H. Watters, *"With Bodilie Eyes": Eschatological Themes in Puritan Literature and Gravestone Art* (Ann Arbor: UMI Research Press, 1981), 51; Cotton Mather, *The Temple Opening: A Particular Church Considered as a Temple of the Lord* (Boston, 1709), 10–11. I argue that the aesthetic of "fullness" in Christian embodiment, so remarkably concentrated in the ritual of communion, diffuses outward from the sacraments to other symbolic forms (houses, fields, cities) in a complementary reverse movement to the discussion of the "condensation of symbols" in the Eucharist in Mary Douglas, *Natural Symbols: Explorations in Cosmology* (New York: Pantheon, 1982), 47–48. Here the symbolic power of the sacramental feast "seeps" into everyday life in a myriad of ways, and affected forms can take on the symbolic "charge" of a central nexus of value. For use of identical metaphors of "spring," "fountain," "living waters," and "fullness" in a theory of aesthetic power and phenomenological presence in material culture (with an apparent debt to the play of tropes in English metaphysical poetry?), see Robert Plant Armstrong, *The Powers of Presence: Consciousness, Myth, and Affecting Presence* (Philadelphia: University of Pennsylvania Press, 1982), 69: "Rather than of wholeness, one ought to think of syn-

detism in terms of *fullness*. . . . The power of the syndetic is the power of physical and metaphysical repletion" (emphasis added). Folklorists also make use of metaphysical "fullness" as one aspect of a performance frame; see Dell Hymes, "Breakthrough into Performance," in *Folklore: Performance and Communication*, ed. Dan Ben-Amos and Kenneth S. Goldstein (The Hague: Mouton, 1975), 11–74, and Dell Hymes, "Folklore's Nature and the Sun's Myth," *Journal of American Folklore* 88, no. 350 (1975): 345–69. The "living object" is one that transcends metaphor as phenomenological presence; see Gregory Bateson, *Steps to an Ecology of Mind* (New York: Ballantine Books, 1972), 402: "In human behavioral systems, especially in religion and ritual and wherever primary process dominates the scene, the name often *is* the thing named. The bread *is* the Body, and the wine *is* the Blood." On "Living Bread," see Taylor, *Poems*, 20, "I am the Living Bread."

39. Hall, *Worlds of Wonder*, 157–60. For a contemporary description of communion, largely based on Boston practices of the late 1630s and early 1640s, see William Lechford, *Plaine dealing. Newes from New-England* (London, 1642; reprint, New York: Putnam, 1969), 45–47.

40. Colin Campbell, *The Romantic Ethic and the Spirit of Modern Consumerism* (Oxford: Basil Blackwell, 1987), 58–76; Anonymous to John Winthrop, ca. 1636/37, in MHS *Coll.*, 4th ser., 6 (1863): 450.

41. *MBR*, 3:243–44; *Public Records of the Colony of Connecticut from 1665 to 1678*, vol. 2, ed. J. Hammond Trumbull (Hartford: F. A. Brown, 1852), 283. On the English context of sumptuary laws, see N. B. Harte, "State Control of Dress and Social Change in Pre-Industrial England," in *Trade, Government, and Economy in Pre-Industrial England: Essays Presented to F. J. Fisher*, ed. D. C. Coleman and A. H. John (London: Weidenfeld and Nicolson, 1976), 132–65. Mather, *Magnalia*, 1:540.

42. Sylvester Judd, *History of Hadley* (Northampton, Mass., 1863; reprint, Springfield, Mass.: H. R. Hunting & Co., 1905), 91. Middlesex County Probate Records, 12A:47–57, inventory of James Russell, taken May 16, 1709, Middlesex County Courthouse, East Cambridge, Mass. On the transformative potential of clothes, see *The Miraculous Power of Clothes, and Dignity of the Taylors: Being an Essay of the Words, Clothes Make Men* (Philadelphia, 1772), and the argument in George Foster, "The Anatomy of Envy: A Study in Symbolic Behavior," *Current Anthropology* 13, no. 2 (April 1972): 169–70 ("Objects Causing Envy"). On the larger context of commodity production and the fabrication of popular desire in early modern England, see Eric Jones, "The Fashion Manipulators: Consumer Tastes and British Industries, 1660–1800," in *Business Enterprise and Economic Change: Essays in Honor of Harold F. Williamson*, ed. Louis P. Cain and Paul J. Uselding (Kent, Ohio: Kent State University Press, 1973), 198–226.

43. Winthrop, "Modell of Christian Charity," 195 (emphasis added).

44. Joshua Scottow, *A Narrative of the Planting of the Massachusetts Colony Anno. 1628: With the Lord's Signal Presence the First Thirty Years* (Boston, 1694), in MHS *Coll.*, 4th ser., 4 (1858): 288; John Josselyn, *An Account of Two Voyages to New-England* (London, 1675), in MHS *Coll.*, 3d ser., 3 (1833): 295; Nathaniel Ward, *The Simple Cobler of Aggawam in New England*, ed. Paul Zoll (London, 1647; reprint, Lincoln: University of Nebraska Press, 1969), 67–68; Roger Williams to John Winthrop, October 1638(?), in MHS *Coll.*, 4th ser., 6 (1863): 239; see Stephen Orgel, "Shakespeare and the Cannibals," in *Cannibals, Witches, and Divorce: Estranging the Renaissance*, ed. Marjorie Garber (Baltimore: Johns Hopkins University Press, 1987), 40–67. For a particular approach to cannibalism and colonialism, see Myra Jehlen, "History before the Fact: Or, Captain John Smith's Unfinished Symphony," *Critical Inquiry* 19, no. 4 (Summer 1993): 677–92, esp. 684: "In the colonial situation, the cannibals are ineradicable markers of alterity." But see the debate between Peter Hulme, "Making No Bones: A Response to Myra Jehlen," and Myra Jehlen, "Response to Peter Hulme," both in *Critical Inquiry* 20, no. 1 (Autumn 1993): 179–91.

45. James Axtell, "The Vengeful Women of Marblehead: Robert Roules's Deposition of 1677," *WMQ*, 3d ser., 31, no. 4 (October 1974): 652.

46. See Ernst H. Kantorowicz, *The King's Two Bodies: A Study in Medieval Political Theology* (Princeton: Princeton University Press, 1957), 8–23, 336–83 ("The Crown as Fiction"), and John of Salisbury,

The Statesman's Book of John of Salisbury, trans. John Dickinson (New York: Russell and Russell, 1963), 65; Jacques LeGoff, "Head or Heart? The Political Use of Body Metaphors in the Middle Ages," in *Fragments for a History of the Human Body, Part Three*, ed. Michel Feher (New York: Zone Books, 1989), 122–28. On the utopian body social and its integration into sectarian debates and mercantile progress, see J. C. Davis, *Utopia and the Ideal Society: A Study of English Utopian Writing, 1516–1700* (Cambridge: Cambridge University Press, 1981), 64–167. Kenneth A. Lockridge, *A New England Town: The First Hundred Years* (New York: W. W. Norton, 1970), see pt. 1, "A Utopian Commune, 1636–1686," 3–78.

47. On Italian political influences, see Zera S. Fink, *The Classical Republicans: An Essay in the Recovery of a Pattern of Thought in Seventeenth-Century England* (Evanston: Northwestern University Press, 1945), 28–51; see also David George Hale, *The Body Politic: A Political Metaphor in Renaissance England Literature* (The Hague: Mouton, 1971), 13–17, 20–24. Hale argues that the cross-cultural tendency to imagine the state as a body comes from "man's desire to identify himself with his environment and thereby to control it" (24).

48. John Shute, *The First and Chief Grounds of Architecture Used in All the Auncient and Famous Monuments* (London, 1563), epistle dedicatory.

49. On these authors, see Hale, *Body Politic*, 72–75. See also Stanley Bertram Chrimes, *English Constitutional Ideas in the Fifteenth Century* (Cambridge: Cambridge University Press, 1936), 312–13; F. W. Maitland, "The Crown as Corporation" and "The Body Politic," in *Selected Historical Essays of F. W. Maitland*, ed. Helen M. Cam (Boston: Beacon Press, 1962), 104–27, 240–56, and Kantorowicz, *King's Two Bodies*, 193–257, 419–36.

50. William Averell, *A Mervailous Combat of Contrarieties. Malignantly Striving in the Members of Mans Bodie, Allegoricallie Representing Unto us the Envied State of Our Flourishing Commonwealth* (London, 1588), sig. A1r.

51. Ibid., sigs. A1r, A2v.

52. Ibid., sig. A2v.

53. Ibid.

54. Norbert Elias, *The History of Manners*, trans. Edmund Jephcott (New York: Pantheon, 1978), 70–133; Eleazer Moody, *The School of Good Manners*, 5th ed. (New London, 1754), 6, 7, 8, 9. See also Richard L. Bushman, *The Refinement of America: Persons, Houses, Cities* (New York: Knopf, 1992), 31–38, and Thomas Frederick Crane, *Italian Social Customs of the Sixteenth Century* (New Haven: Yale University Press, 1920), 323–433, 505–54. Daniel Gookin, *Historical Collections of the New-England Indians* (1674), in MHS *Coll.*, 1st ser., 1 (1792; reprint, 1806): 153.

55. Winthrop Jordan, *White over Black: American Attitudes toward the Negro, 1550–1812* (Chapel Hill: University of North Carolina Press for the Institute of Early American History and Culture, 1968), 43–45; Peter Stallybrass and Allon White, *The Politics and Poetics of Transgression* (Ithaca, N.Y.: Cornell University Press, 1986), 9–26; Elliot H. Tokson, *The Popular Image of the Black Man in English Drama, 1550–1688* (Boston: G. K. Hall, 1982), 1–90, 106–19.

56. Tzvetan Todorov, *The Conquest of America: The Question of the Other*, trans. Richard Howard (New York: Harper and Row, 1984), 3. This section is indebted to the insightful discussion of "popular culture and the internal other" in Peter Mason, *Deconstructing America: Representations of the Other* (New York: Routledge, 1990), 41–68; see also Eric Cheyfitz, *The Poetics of Imperialism: Translation and Colonization from "The Tempest" to "Tarzan"* (New York: Oxford University Press, 1991), 22–58; Germán Arciniegas, *America in Europe: A History of the New World in Reverse*, trans. Gabriela Arciniegas and R. Victoria Arana (New York: Harcourt Brace Jovanovich, 1975), 70–86, 105–13; and Stephen William Foster, "The Exotic as a Symbolic System," *Dialectical Anthropology* 7, no. 1 (September 1982): 21–30.

57. On Romanies in early modern England, see Gamini Salgado, *The Elizabethan Underworld* (New York: St. Martin's Press, 1992), 149–64. On early Romany creole, see W. B. Lockwood, *Languages of the British Isles Past and Present* (London: Andre Deutsch, 1975), 242–57; Glanville Price, *The Languages of*

Britain (London: Edward Arnold, 1984), 232–40; and M. A. K. Halliday, "Anti-Languages," *American Anthropologist* 78, no. 3 (September 1976): 570–84.

58. Cotton Mather, *A Brand Pluck'd Out of the Burning* (1693), in *Narratives of the Witchcraft Cases, 1648–1706,* ed. George Lincoln Burr (New York: Barnes & Noble, 1914), 261.

59. John Eliot to Thomas Shepard, September 24, 1647, in *The Clear Sun-shine of the Gospel Breaking Forth upon the Indians in New England* (London, 1648), reprinted in MHS *Coll.,* 3d ser., 4 (1834): 56; Gookin, *Historical Collections of the New-England Indians,* 153.

60. Roger Williams to John Winthrop, January 10, 1637/8, in MHS *Coll.,* 4th ser., 6 (1863): 222.

61. Roger Williams, *A Key into the Language of America* (1643), ed. John J. Teunissen and Evelyn J. Hinz (Detroit: Wayne State University Press, 1973), 130, 133.

62. Edward Howes to John Winthrop Jr., March 26, 1632, in MHS *Coll.,* 4th ser., 6 (1863): 474–75.

63. Julia Briggs, *This Stage-Play World: English Literature and Its Background, 1580–1625* (Oxford: Oxford University Press, 1983), 163. See Jean-Christophe Agnew, *Worlds Aparts: The Market and Theater in Anglo-American Thought, 1550–1750* (New York: Cambridge University Press, 1986), 101–48, and M. C. Bradbrook, *The Rise of the Common Player: A Study of Actor and Society in Shakespeare's England* (Cambridge: Cambridge University Press, 1979), 39–76.

64. Williams, *Key into the Language of America,* 240–41. See also the couplet "Truth is a Native, naked Beauty; but / Lying Inventions are but Indian paints" (241).

65. Mather, *Ornaments for the Daughters of Zion,* 17: "A painted face . . . is a vile affront unto God, for a Woman to deface the Workmanship of the Almighty there."

66. [Robert Cushman], "Mourt's Relation," in *Chronicles of the Pilgrim Fathers of the Colony of Plymouth, from 1602–1625,* ed. Alexander Young (Boston, 1844; reprint, Baltimore: Genealogical Publishing Co., 1974), 133, 136–37; Plymouth Colony Wills and Inventories, 1:56–61, Plymouth County Courthouse, Plymouth, Mass.; John Josselyn, *New-Englands Rarities Discovered* (London, 1672; reprint, Boston: Massachusetts Historical Society, 1972), 17–18. Rosemary Weinstein, "Some Menagerie Accounts of James I," *Transactions of the London and Middlesex Archaeological Society* 31 (1980): 134–35. On collecting American Indian artifacts for cabinets of curiosity during the period, see Arthur MacGregor, "Collectors and Collections of Rarities in the Sixteenth and Seventeenth Century" and "The Americas," in *Tradescant's Rarities: Essays on the Foundation of the Ashmolean Museum, 1683,* ed. Arthur MacGregor (Oxford: Oxford University Press, 1983), 70–97, 108–39, and T. H. Lunsingh Scheurleer, "Early Dutch Cabinets of Curiosities," Arthur MacGregor, "The Cabinet of Curiosities in Seventeenth-Century Britain," and Michael Hunter, "The Cabinet Institutionalized: The Royal Society's 'Repository' and Its Background," all in *The Origins of Museums: The Cabinet of Curiosity in Sixteenth- and Seventeenth-Century Europe,* ed. Arthur MacGregor and Oliver Impey (Oxford: Oxford University Press, 1985), 115–20, 147–58, 159–68.

67. SCPR, 44:419; 47:27–30; 53:261; 55:66; 60:485. On Native American basketmaking and its economic significance, see Trudie Lamb Richmond, "Spirituality and Survival in Schagticoke Basket-Making," in *A Key into the Language of Woodsplint Baskets,* ed. Ann McMullen and Russell G. Handsman (Washington, Conn.: American Indian Archaeological Institute, 1987), 126–43. For an example of Native Americans doing craft work for whites, see *Diary of Joshua Hempstead,* 251: "I went to Nahantic to the Indian Town to get a Squaw to Botom Chairs [for] Brother Talmage" (entry of May 8, 1732).

68. John Wilson to Henry Whitfield, October 27, 1651, in Henry Whitfield, *Strength out of Weaknesse; or a Glorious Manifestation of the further Progresse of the Gospel among the Indians in New-England* (London, 1652), reprinted in MHS *Coll.,* 3d ser., 4 (1834): 177.

69. John Bulwer, *Anthropometamorphosis. Man Transform'd: Or, the Artificial Changling* (London, 1653), frontispiece caption, sig. B2v; Thomas Hobbes, *Leviathan,* ed. Michael Oakeshott (New York: Macmillan, 1962), 125.

70. Bulwer, *Anthropometamorphosis,* sig. B2v, 7–8.

71. Ibid., 21–22. From a discussion of "headless" nations, Bulwer's text moves rapidly into remarkable births and two-headed people, with their implied value as political metaphors that assured En-

glish Puritans in 1651 that the execution of Charles I had been legitimate, since "two-headed" bodies—social and political—were "unnatural."

72. Ibid., 451; *ECQCR,* 1:152; 8:14; Saffin, *John Saffin, His Book,* 64.

73. Robert Boyle, "Observations upon a Monstrous Head," *Philosophical Transactions* 1 (1665–66): 75–85; the engraving faces p. 78.

74. Sewall, *Diary,* 1:52; 2:730. Sewall's relationship with the body remains problematic. See Mary Adams, "The Other Diary of Samuel Sewall," *NEQ* 55, no. 4 (September 1982): 361: "the human body enters the diary again and again—in pieces. . . . The diary is like an infirmary; it lets in the wounded, but it makes no place for the whole. Whole bodies, in fact, hardly ever appear in the diary."

75. John Winthrop, *A Short Story of the Rise, Reign, and Ruine of the Antinomians, Familists Libertines,* 3d ed. (London, 1644), 44–45, in *AC,* 214–15, 280–81. See also the additional (and conflicting) accounts of the Dyer birth by Winthrop that reached England by June 1638, in Valerie Pearl and Morris Pearl, "Governor John Winthrop on the Birth of the Antinomians' 'Monster': The Earliest Reports to Reach England and the Making of a Myth," MHS *Proc.* 102 (1990): 35–37, esp. 29: "Winthrop gives four different locations for the position of the mouth, three locations each for the back and the horns, and two for the site of the navel and the face." It is also clear that Winthrop supplied a (now lost) drawing of the Dyer "monster" with his first letter (22).

76. Winthrop, *Short Story,* 214–15.

77. Winthrop, *Journal,* 1:277; see also Emory Battis, *Saints and Sectaries: Anne Hutchinson and the Antinomian Controversy in the Massachusetts Bay Colony* (Chapel Hill: University of North Carolina, 1962), 346–48.

78. *The Decades of the Newe Worlde of West India,* trans. Richard Eden (London, 1555), in *The First Three English Books on America, [?1511]–1555 A.D.,* ed. Edward Arber (Birmingham, 1885; reprint, New York: Kraus Reprint Co., 1971), 53.

79. Winthrop, *Short Story,* 280; John Josselyn, *An Account of Two Voyages to New-England* (London, 1675), in MHS *Coll.,* 3d ser., 3 (1833): 229–31. Hull Diary, 188–89. On the Dyer birth as a narrative construct, see Johan Winsser, "Mary Dyer and the 'Monster' Story," *Quaker History* 79, no. 1 (Spring 1990): 20–34, and Anne Jacobson Schutte, "'Such Monstrous Births': A Neglected Aspect of the Antinomian Controversy," *Renaissance Quarterly* 38, no. 1 (1985): 85–106. See also K. Park and L. J. Daston, "Unnatural Conceptions: The Study of Monsters in Sixteenth- and Seventeenth-Century France and England," *Past and Present* 92 (1981): 20–54, and Ben Barker, "Ann Hutchinson and the Puritan Attitude toward Women," *Feminist Studies* 1 (1972): 65–96.

80. Thomas Peters to John Winthrop Jr., April 27, 1647, in MHS *Coll.,* 4th ser., 7 (1865): 431. See also the autopsy performed in 1645 on a stillborn infant with a misshapen head in *The Narratives of the Reverend John Fiske, 1644–1675,* ed. Robert G. Pope, in CSM *Pub.* 47 (1974): 49–50.

81. Edward Howes to John Winthrop Jr., April 14, 1639, in MHS *Coll.,* 4th ser., 6 (1863): 505–6.

82. John Eliot to Thomas Brookes, May 19, 1660, quoted in Winsser, "'Monster' Story," 30–31; Eliot, in remembering the Dyer monster, summarized the exhumation of the child's corpse by Winthrop, John Cotton, John Wilson, and "40 persons, more" as "a most hideous creat[ure]. a woman, a fish, a bird, & a beast all woven together. no head, but in the neck 2 great eye holes. the nose with the chin end upward on the forehead (or topp of the neck) 3 hornes. the bellie behind & back before, on wch there were sharp prickes, like as on a thornbacke fethers on diverse parts. hands & feete like a duck, & c. these credible persons (men you know of great integrity) & the rest of the witnesses declared this fully to my self & 1000 of others. that it was famously knowen, as any thing that ever was seen or done in the land & uncontradictable in those places." On the dangers of multiplicity, see Italo Calvino, *Invisible Cities,* trans. William Weaver (New York: Harcourt Brace Jovanovich, 1974), 145 (Perinthia's astronomers may "reveal that the order of the gods is reflected exactly in the city of monsters").

83. "Will of Edward Jackson," ed. John Noble, in CSM *Pub.* 8 (1902–4): 255. The figure of the man, standing still in Byfield at the entrance to "Witch Stone Farm," has long been assumed to be a form of countermagic rather than an emblem of male prerogative with property. See Lura Woodside Watkins,

"The Byfield Stones—Our Earliest American Sculpture?" *Antiques* 84, no. 4 (October 1963): 420–23, and Robert F. Trent, "Boundary Marker" (catalog entry), in *NEB*, 2:191, no. 141; see also J. G. Dent, "The Witchstone in Ulster and England," *UF* 9 (1963): 46–48. On "meerstones" being used to demarcate property boundaries, see *Diary of Joshua Hempstead*, 85 (entry of March 2, 1719), 236 (entry of June 19, 1731). E. Estyn Evans, *Irish Heritage: The Landscape, the People, and Their Work* (Dundalk: Dundalgan Press, 1942), 50, reports that the waste strips or "balks" that ran between patches of cultivated land in Ireland were termed "mearings," "bones," and "ribs." On the anthropomorphic nature of field layout, see A. Hunter Dupree, "The English System for Measuring Fields," *Agricultural History* 45, no. 2 (April 1971): 121–28.

84. Watkins, "Dummer Family," 12. Quoted in S. F. A. Caulfield, *House Mottoes and Inscriptions: Old and New* (London: Eliot Stock, 1902), 53–54.

85. Individuals in seventeenth-century New England conceived of their own hearts as being made of formed earth similar to the bricks used in hearths and chimneys; "poore knobs of Clay, my heart," was how Edward Taylor put it in "Meditation 49," in Miller and Johnson, *The Puritans*, 2:656; Taylor, *Poems*, 5, 157. Donne also conceived of the soul in terms of fire and wrote of "the flame / Of thy brave Soule, that shot such heat and light / . . . and made our darkness bright." (*Complete Poetry of John Donne*, ed. Shawcross, 32.) E. Estyn Evans, *Irish Folk Ways*, 58–59, discusses the Irish folk belief that the soul of the house exists in the flame at the hearth and that "the soul goes out of the people of the house" when the fire dies; "when the smoke dies out of a house, it does soon be falling down." Evans adds that a "smoke" in seventeenth-century Irish inventories meant a house. In early New England, the metaphor extended from the fire to the soul to the womb and the promise of fertility; see Taylor, *Poems*, 230, "The Soule's the Womb." Cotton Mather, *Elizabeth in her Holy Retirement: An Essay to Prepare a Pious Woman for her Lying In* (Boston, 1710), 25.

86. Middlesex County Probate Records, docket 2984, Middlesex County Courthouse, East Cambridge, Mass.; Plymouth County Wills and Inventories, 3:368–69, Plymouth County Courthouse, Plymouth, Mass. For an example of lean-to extensions on both ends, see the Zebulon Spaulding house (ca. 1716) in Mrs. Benson Perley Wilkins, "The Century-Old Houses of Carlisle, Massachusetts," *OTNE* 23, no. 2 (October 1932): 54.

87. On the Sowerby lintel, see Christopher Stell, "Pennine Houses: An Introduction," *Folk Life* 3 (1965): 16; a related example from a seventeenth-century house in Halifax, Yorkshire, is illustrated in Mercer, *English Vernacular Houses*, plate 103. See also C. H. Jones, "Curious Doorhead," *Country Life*, November 18, 1949, 1516, and John Hanna, "Folk Architecture of the Pennines," *Country Life*, April 7, 1950, 973. On the Myddle example, see Madge Moran, "Re-erecting Houses in Shropshire in the Late Seventeenth Century," *Archaeological Journal* 146 (1989): 545–46.

88. David Leverenz, *The Language of Puritan Feeling: An Exploration in Literature, Psychology, and Social History* (New Brunswick, N.J.: Rutgers University Press, 1980), 142–44; see also Allan I. Ludwig, *Graven Images: New England Stonecarving and Its Symbols, 1650–1815* (Middletown, Conn.: Wesleyan University Press, 1966), 155–68 ("Erotic Symbolism"), and Richard Godbeer, "'Love Raptures': Marital, Romantic, and Erotic Images of Jesus Christ in Puritan New England, 1670–1730," *NEQ* 68, no. 3 (September 1995): 355–84.

89. Quoted in *The Trelawney Papers*, ed. James Phinney Baxter, Documentary History of the State of Maine, vol. 3 (Portland, Me., 1884), 31–32 (emphasis added).

90. Bradstreet, "A Letter to her Husband, Absent upon Publick Employment," in Miller and Johnson, *The Puritans*, 1:573. William Byrd II to Mrs. Jane Pratt Taylor, April 3, 1729, in *The Correspondence of the Three William Byrds of Westover, Virginia, 1684–1776*, ed. Marion Tinling, 2 vols. (Charlottesville: University Press of Virginia, 1977), 1:391; quoted in Roger Thomson, *Women in Stuart England and America* (Boston: Routledge and Kegan Paul, 1974), 10.

91. "Hadleigh Building Regulations of 1619," in Eric Sandon, *Suffolk Houses: A Study of Domestic Architecture* (Woodbridge, England: Baron Publishers, 1977), 92.

92. John Norden, *The Surveyor's Dialogue* (London, 1607), sig. E2. Petition of William Turner to the

General Court, October 28, 1670, MA, 10:228; see also 1 Cor. 11:3: "the head of every man is Christ; and the head of the woman is the man; and the head of Christ is God." *The Journal of Esther Edwards Burr, 1754–1757*, ed. Carol F. Karlsen and Laurie Crumpacker (New Haven: Yale University Press, 1984), 81.

93. Cecil Hewett, "A Medieval Timber Kitchen at Little Braxted, Essex," *Medieval Archaeology* 17 (1973): 132–34.

94. *Early Records of the Town of Providence*, 23 vols. (Providence: Snow & Farnham, 1892–1915), 6:210–16; SCPR, 9:101 (emphasis added); the 1701 schoolmaster's house contract is reprinted in Abbott Lowell Cummings, "Massachusetts Bay Building Documents," in *Architecture in Colonial Massachusetts*, ed. Abbott Lowell Cummings (Boston: Colonial Society of Massachusetts, 1979), 201. "A book of Allowances From the Major Part of the Justices within the Town of Boston to Persons for Building with Timber in the said Town Beginning April, 1707," in *A Volume of Records Relating to the Early History of Boston, Containing Miscellaneous Papers* (Boston: Municipal Printing Office, 1900), 183. On women in business in colonial Boston, see Mary Beth Norton, *Liberty's Daughters: The Revolutionary Experience of American Women, 1750–1800* (Boston: Little, Brown, and Co., 1980), 143 (Jane Mecom), 147–48 (Elizabeth Murray); and "Accounts of Losses . . . Sustained by the Fire of 1760," in *Volume of Records Relating to the Early History of Boston, Containing Miscellaneous Papers*, 2 (Elizabeth Allcock), 3 (Rebecca Amory), 23 (Sarah Checkley), 37–42 (Sarah McNeal), 45 (Margaret Rogers), 71 (Mary Cross), 77 (Sarah Low).

95. Cotton Mather, *El Shaddai. A Brief Essay . . . Produced by the Death of Mrs. Katharin Willard* (Boston, 1725), 21. On the separation of front and back zones in English houses by the late seventeenth century, see Mercer, *English Vernacular Houses*, 73–75.

96. *Diary of Michael Wigglesworth*, 99.

97. Quoted in Nathaniel Bradstreet Shurtleff, *Thunder and Lightning and Deaths at Marshfield in 1658 and 1666* (Boston: privately printed, 1850), 18. Hull Diary, 231. In 1706 lightning struck the house of Vigilans Fisher in Dedham, and bricks were "beat off the Chimney . . . and one of the Spars of the House split from the chimney down-wards to the Plate, and from thence taking the Post of the fore door" (*Boston Newsletter*, June 10–17, 1706).

98. Mather, *Magnalia*, 2:362–63. See MHS *Proc.*, ser. 1, 12 (1871–73): 249; *Deacon Tudor's Diary, Or Memorandums From 1709, & c. By John Tudor, To 1775 & 1778, 1780 And to '93*, ed. William Tudor (Boston: Wallace Spooner, 1896), 9 (November 18, 1755). For a 1661 earthquake in England "shewing how a Church-steeple, and many gallant houses were thrown down to the ground, and people slain," see "Newes from Hereford. Or, A wonderfull and Terrible Earthquake," in *The Pack of Autolycus or Strange and Terrible News of Ghosts, Apparitions, Monstrous Births, Showers of Wheat, Judgments of God, and other Prodigious and Fearful Happenings as Told in Broadside Ballads of the Years 1624–1693*, ed. Hyder Edward Rollins (Cambridge: Harvard University Press, 1927), 82–83.

99. "The Possession of the Goodwin Children (1688)," in *Witch-Hunting in Seventeenth-Century New England: A Documentary History, 1638–1692*, ed. David D. Hall (Boston: Northeastern University Press, 1991), 269. On witches and property, see Carol Karlsen, *The Devil in the Shape of a Woman: Witchcraft in Colonial New England* (New York: W. W. Norton, 1987), 77–116.

100. ECQCR, 7:355–56, 358. William Morse's original testimony is printed in Abner Morse, *Memorial of the Morses; Containing the History of Seven Puritans of the Name of Morse and Morss* (Boston: Coolidge & Wiley, 1850), unpag. appendix. The Morse case is described in detail in John P. Demos, *Entertaining Satan: Witchcraft and the Culture of Early New England* (New York: Oxford University Press, 1982), 132–52.

101. R[ichard]. C[hamberlain]., *Lithobolia: or, the Stone-Throwing Devil* (London, 1698), reprinted in *Narratives of the Witchcraft Cases, 1648–1706*, ed. George Lincoln Burr (New York: Barnes & Noble, 1914), 62–64; Mather, *Magnalia*, 2:452–53. See also Burr, *Narratives of the Witchcraft Cases*, 23–38.

102. See George Ewart Evans, *The Pattern under the Plough: Aspects of the Folk-Life of East Anglia* (London: Faber and Faber, 1966), 79–80. On the role of the house in providing a shield against witches and demons cross-culturally, see Amos Rapaport, "Sacred Places, Sacred Occasions, and Sacred En-

vironments," *Architectural Design* 9–10 (1982): 75–82; see Stith Thompson, *Motif-Index of Folk Literature* (Bloomington: Indiana University Press, 1955–58), 3:293 (no. G229.8), 296 (nos. G249.3, G.249.7, G249.8). Robert Hunter West, *Invisible World: A Study of Pneumatology in Elizabethan Drama* (Athens: University of Georgia Press, 1939), 28.

103. *The Trial of the Lancashire Witches A.D. MDCXII*, ed. G. B. Harrison (London: Peter Davies, 1929), xxxvi; *New Haven Town Records, 1649–1662*, ed. Franklin B. Dexter (New Haven: Yale University Press, 1917), 1:251; Testimony of Joseph Marsh, in Hoadly, "Some Early Post-Mortem Examinations," 213; John M. Taylor, *The Witchcraft Delusion in Colonial Connecticut, 1647–1697* (Hartford, 1908; reprint, New York: Burt Franklin, 1971), 118–19; *SWP*, 1:97.

104. MA, 135 (Witches, 1656–1750): deposition 1, verso; *SWP*, 2:452, 526.

105. Quoted in Demos, *Entertaining Satan*, 103; Taylor, *Witchcraft Delusion in Colonial Connecticut*, 107; *SWP*, 1:177. See also the account of William Beale of Marblehead, who claimed in August 1692 to have seen the "shade" of mariner Philip English near his chimney: "Where I lay in my bed which was layed low & neire unto the fire towards the norward parte of the roome I beeing broade Awake I then saw up on the south jaame of that Chimny A dark shade w'ch covered the jaam of that chimney aforesayed from the under floore to the upper floore & alsoe a dar[k]ness more then it was beefore in the southerne part of the house & alsoe in the middllee of the darkness in the shade upon the jaame of the chimny aforesayd I beeheld somethinge of the forme or shape of A man" (*SWP*, 1:317).

106. *SWP*, 2:448; 1:225.

107. See Frank Chouteau Brown, "'The Old House' at Cutchogue, New York," *OTNE* 31, no. 1 (July 1940): 11–21. According to Brown, the poppets or "dolls" were "made of twigs bound together and wrapped with home-made linen" (19). *SWP*, 1:101; for compiled references to poppets from the 1692 Salem trials, see Richard Godbeer, *The Devil's Dominion: Magic and Religion in Early New England* (Cambridge: Cambridge University Press, 1992), 38–40. The "magical" power of poppets was linked to their symbolic association with duplicity and vanity; see Richard Baxter to Robert Boyle, June 14, 1664, in *The Works of the Honorable Robert Boyle*, 5 vols. (London, 1744), 5:554: "What a poppet play is the life of sensuality, worldliness, and pride?" Interestingly, the references to "rags" in poppet construction parallels the stereotyping of English people in "rags" as marginal, vagrants, or harlequins.

108. "The Testimony of John Kelley and Bethia his wife," in Hoadly, "Some Early Post-Mortem Examinations," 212.

109. *ECQCR*, 1:265; 7:357; Robert Pike to Jonathan Corwin, August 9, 1692, in *Salem Witchcraft; with an Account of Salem Village, and a History of Opinions on Witchcraft and Kindred Subjects*, ed. Charles W. Upham, 2 vols. (Boston: Wiggin and Lunt, 1867), 2:542. On the relationship and definition of "religion" and "magic," see Godbeer, *Devil's Dominion*, 9–10, 25, 38–39. While Godbeer's thesis is provocative, I disagree with his choice to follow Lawrence Veysey in arguing that early New Englanders "were perfectly able to compartmentalize their thinking" (9) to keep "religion" and "magic" as separate intellectual spheres. I argue here that a syncretic faith that demanded the active creolization of diverse beliefs, not their compartmentalization, was its central dynamic.

110. On the role of church ordinances as a form of family "protection," see the comment in David D. Hall, "Toward a History of Popular Religion in Early New England," *WMQ*, 3d ser., 41, no. 1 (January 1984): 54.

111. Sewall, *Diary*, 1:287, 330, 337, 400: "Our cherubim heads are set up"; see also Hall, *Worlds of Wonder*, 217–18, following Exod. 25:18–22.

112. For works that represent the "collection" approach to house superstitions but that fail to link an assumed need for protection to belief systems or bodily experience, see Albert Sandklef, *Singing Flails: A Study in Threshing-Floor Constructions, Flail-Threshing Traditions, and the Magic Guarding of the House*, Folklore Fellows Communications no. 136 (Helsinki: Suomalainen Tiedeakatemia, 1949), and Ralph Merrifield, *The Archaeology of Ritual and Magic* (New York: New Amsterdam Books, 1987). For the iron artifacts discovered at the Endicott site, I am indebted to Richard B. Trask (letter to author, September 11, 1991).

113. I am indebted to Electa Kane Tritsch for allowing me to examine the Farrington spoon; for comparable examples owned in New England, see Percy E. Raymond, "Latten Spoons of the Pilgrims," *Antiques* 61, no. 3 (March 1952): 242–44. Merrifield, *Archaeology of Ritual and Magic*, 135–36. See the compilations of such discoveries in J. M. Swann, "Shoes Concealed in Buildings," *Northampton Museum and Arts Gallery Journal* 6 (December 1969): 8–21. Two shoes were uncovered during restoration at the Spencer-Pierce-Little house in Newbury (Ann Grady, letter to author, July 1, 1992; Katherine Jones Garmil to June Swann, May 29, 1990; June Swann to Katherine Jones Garmil, June 28, 1990; and P. M. Slocum, letter to author, February 17, 1986). Similar steps were also taken in stables and cow houses to protect animals from evil spirits. Peter Fowler, *Farms in England: Prehistoric to Present* (London: Her Majesty's Stationers Office, 1983), vi, plate 81, shows the use of a "hag-stone" in a stable at Church Farm, Fressingfield, Suffolk. As John Aubrey described its use in the mid-seventeenth century: "To hinder the Night Mare they hang on a String a Flint with a hole in it (naturally) by the manger. . . . It is to prevent the Night Mare *viz.* the Hag riding the Horses who will sometimes sweat at Night. The Flint thus hung does hinder it" (quoted in Evans, *Pattern under the Plough*, 181–96).

114. Evans, *Pattern under the Plough*, 74–78. On London examples, see Catherine Maloney, "A Witch-Bottle from Dukes Place, Aldgate," *Transactions of the London and Middlesex Archaeological Society* 31 (1980): 157–59, and the examples cited in Ralph Merrifield, "The Use of Bellarmines as Witch-Bottles," *Guildhall Miscellany* 3 (1953): 3–15. For examples from Montgomeryshire and Shropshire, see E. S. Thomas, "Short Queries to Readers," *Folk-Lore* 40 (1929): 197. For an example uncovered from the site of the meetinghouse (ca. 1699) that preceded the Brattle Square Church of 1773 in Boston, see "A Greybeard Jug at Fenway Court," in *Fenway Court* (Boston: Isabella Stewart Gardner Museum, 1981), 26–27.

115. Quoted from Joseph Glanvill, *Saducismus Triumphatus; or, Full and Plain Evidence Concerning Witches and Apparitions* (London, 1681), in Evans, *Pattern under the Plough*, 75–77.

116. C[hamberlain]., *Lithobolia*, 74; *Records of Salem Witchcraft, Copied from the Original Documents*, ed. W. Elliot Woodward, 2 vols. (Roxbury: printed for the author, 1864), 2:26–27. For other instances of "urinary experiments," see Godbeer, *Devil's Dominion*, 44–46. On the use of witch bottles, Bellarmines, and bones in East Anglia and nearby Cambridgeshire, see Evans, *Pattern under the Plough*, 32–33, 57–58, 74–82, esp. 77: "In one of the grey-beard jars discovered in Ipswich . . . there was a cloth heart with pins stuck in it among the following objects: sharpened splinters of wood, brass studs, nails, hair, glass chips, and a much-rusted table fork without a handle"; see the contents of a witch bottle now in the Norwich Castle Museum, illustrated in Ivor Nöel Hume, "German Stoneware Bellarmines — An Introduction," *Antiques* 74, no. 5 (November 1958): 441, fig. 6. See Geoffrey Dent, "A Yorkshire Witch Bottle," *Gwerin* 3, no. 4 (April 1962). For a witch bottle recently discovered by archaeologists in Essington, Pennsylvania, dating probably from about 1748, see M. J. Becker, "An American Witch Bottle," *Archaeology* 33, no. 2 (March–April 1980): 19–23 (with illustration of contents, including pins, bird bones, and a pot shard). On witch posts in seventeenth-century English houses, see Mary Nattrass, "Witch Posts," *Gwerin* 3, no. 5 (June 1962): 254–67. For the related practice of tying rows of sprigs to jamb posts, see Evans, *Irish Folk Ways*, 64.

117. Demos, *Entertaining Satan*, 138–39; Lewis Roberts, *The Merchants Mappe of Commerce* (London, 1635), 37–38.

118. See the discussion of Sydenham's approach to diagnosis and Mather's use of inoculation in New England in St. George, "'Set Thine House in Order,'" 2:183–84.

119. Christine Leigh Heyrman, *Commerce and Culture: The Maritime Communities of Colonial Massachusetts* (New York: W. W. Norton, 1984), 320.

120. Mather, *Angel of Bethesda*, 47–48.

121. Samuel Willard, *The Compleat Body of Divinity* (Boston, 1726), quoted in Perry Miller, *The New England Mind: The Seventeenth Century* (Boston: Beacon Press, 1961), 226.

122. *The Essays, Humor, and Poems of Nathaniel Ames, Father and Son, of Dedham, Massachusetts, from their Almanacs, 1726–1775,* ed. Samuel Briggs (Cleveland: Short and Forman, 1891), 199.

123. Quoted in Robert W. Malcolmson, "Workers' Combinations in Eighteenth-Century England," in *Origins of Anglo-American Radicalism,* ed. Margaret Jacob and James Jacob (London: George Allen & Unwin, 1984), 150.

124. See Charles Estienne, *Tres libri de dissectione partium corporis humani* (Paris, 1545), introduction; see the discussion of his relationship with Vesalius, in Gernot Rath, "Charles Estienne: Contemporary of Vesalius," *Medical History* 8 (1964): 354–59. Rath notes that while all three of Estienne's "books" were not published as a single volume until 1545, the first half was printed in 1539, four years before Vesalius's *Fabrica.*

125. Michel Foucault, *The History of Sexuality,* vol. 1, *An Introduction,* trans. Robert Hurley (New York: Pantheon, 1978), 95–96.

126. Ruth Richardson, *Death, Dissection, and the Destitute* (New York: Penguin, 1988), 30–51 ("The Corpse as an Anatomical Object"), 52–72 ("The Corpse as Commodity"); see also Martin Fido, *Body-snatchers: A History of the Resurrectionists, 1742–1832* (London: Weidenfeld and Nicolson, 1988), 1–13.

127. Sewall, *Diary,* 1:22–23. The parodic quality of the Boston dissection is clear when one considers that William Harvey's work on the circulatory system, *Exercitatio anatomica de motu cordis et sanguinis in animalibus,* was published in 1628. See J. R. Macleod, "Harvey's Experiments on Circulation," *Annals of Medical History* 10, no. 4 (December 1928): 138–48.

128. Victor Harris, *All Coherence Gone* (Chicago: University of Chicago Press, 1949), 7; see also Stanley Fish, *Self-Contained Artifacts: The Experience of Seventeenth-Century Literature* (Berkeley and Los Angeles: University of California Press, 1972).

129. Charles Morton, *Compendium physicae,* ed. Samuel Eliot Morison, in CSM *Pub.* 33 (1940): 78.

130. Miller, *New England Mind,* 370; on mystic spiritism, see David D. Hall, "Religion and Society: Problems and Reconsiderations," in *Colonial British America: Essays in the New History of the Early Modern Era,* ed. Jack P. Greene and J. R. Pole (Baltimore: Johns Hopkins University Press, 1984), 328–29. Philip F. Gura, *A Glimpse of Sion's Glory: Puritan Radicalism in New England, 1620–1660* (Middletown, Conn.: Wesleyan University Press, 1984), 134–35, 199, 296; see also James Holstun, *A Rational Millennium: Puritan Utopias of Seventeenth-Century England and America* (New York: Oxford University Press, 1987), 145–50.

131. Quoted in John L. Brooke, *The Refiner's Fire: The Making of Mormon Cosmology, 1644–1844* (New York: Cambridge University Press, 1994), 51.

CHAPTER THREE

1. *Deacon Tudor's Diary, Or Memorandums From 1709, & c. By John Tudor, To 1775 & 1778, 1780 And to '93,* ed. William Tudor (Boston: Wallace Spooner, 1896), 17–18 (entry of August 14, 1765).

2. See Pauline Maier, *From Resistance to Revolution: Colonial Radicals and the Development of American Opposition to Britain, 1765–1776* (New York: Knopf, 1972), 3–76; Gary Nash, *The Urban Crucible: Social Change, Political Consciousness, and the Origins of the American Revolution* (Cambridge: Harvard University Press, 1979), 26–53, 76–101; and Alfred F. Young, "English Plebeian Culture and Eighteenth-Century American Radicalism," in *The Origins of Anglo-American Radicalism,* ed. Margaret Jacob and James Jacob (London: George Allen & Unwin for the Institute for Research in History, 1984), 185–212. Previous studies of Boston crowd actions include Robert S. Longley, "Mobs in Revolutionary Massachusetts," *NEQ* 6, no. 1 (March 1933): 98–130; Arthur M. Schlesinger, "Political Mobs and the American Revolution, 1765–1776," *Proceedings of the American Philosophical Society* 99 (1955): 244–50; Edmund S. Morgan and Helen M. Morgan, *The Stamp Act Crisis: Prologue to Rebellion* (Chapel Hill: University of North Carolina Press for the Institute of Early American History and Culture, 1955), 119–58; and Gordon S. Wood, "A Note on Mobs in the American Revolution," *WMQ,* 3d ser., 23, no. 4 (October 1966): 635–42. For a recent summary essay, see Thomas P. Slaughter, "Crowds in Eighteenth-Century America: Reflections and New Directions," *Pennsylvania Magazine of History and Biography*

115, no. 1 (January 1991): 3–34. My concern in this chapter is to extend analysis to include the cultural significances and aesthetic meanings of symbolic violence and approach them not as "reflective" of social or institutional structure but as constitutive of feeling and symbolic force. For methodological suggestions, see Roger D. Abrahams, "Folk Drama," in *Folklore and Folklife: An Introduction,* ed. Richard M. Dorson (Chicago: University of Chicago Press, 1972), 351–60; Roger D. Abrahams, "An American Vocabulary of Celebrations," in *Time out of Time: Essays on the Festival,* ed. Alessandro Falassi (Albuquerque: University of New Mexico Press, 19), 173–83; and Richard Bauman, "Observations on the Place of Festival in the Worldview of the Seventeenth-Century Quakers," *Western Folklore* 43, no. 2 (April 1984): 133–38. See also J. S. McClelland, *The Crowd and the Mob from Plato to Canetti* (London: Unwin Hyman, 1989), 91–105, 295–334, and J. M. Golby and A. W. Purdue, *The Civilization of the Crowd: Popular Culture in England, 1750–1900* (New York: Schocken, 1985), 30–63, 183–204.

3. For a suggestive overview that discusses attacks and related violence throughout the colonies, see Peter Shaw, *American Patriots and the Rituals of Revolution* (Cambridge: Harvard University Press, 1981), 26–73. See also *Prologue to Revolution: Sources and Documents on the Stamp Act Crisis, 1764–1766,* ed. Edmund S. Morgan (Chapel Hill: University of North Carolina Press for the Institute of Early American History and Culture, 1959), 106–28; Edward Countryman, "The Problem of the Early American Crowd," *Journal of American Studies* 7 (1973): 81–82; and Dirk Hoerder, *Crowd Action in Revolutionary Massachusetts, 1765–1780* (New York: Academic Press, 1977), 85–143. For place-specific treatments, see, for Maine, Alan Taylor, "'A Kind of Warr': The Contest for Land on the Northeastern Frontier, 1750–1820," *WMQ,* 3d ser., 46, no. 1 (January 1989): 17–20, and "2. King v. Stewart, 1773–1774," in *Legal Papers of John Adams,* ed. L. Kinvin Wroth and Hiller B. Zobel, 3 vols. (Cambridge: Harvard University Press, Belknap Press, 1965), 1:106–40; for New York, Paul A. Gilje, *The Road to Mobocracy: Popular Disorder in New York City, 1763–1834* (Chapel Hill: University of North Carolina for the Institute of Early American History and Culture, 1987), 37–68; for North Carolina, Lawrence Lee, "Days of Defiance: Resistance to the Stamp Act in the Lower Cape Fear," *North Carolina Historical Review* 43, no. 2 (Spring 1966): 186–202, and Donna J. Spindel, "Law and Disorder: The North Carolina Stamp Act Crisis," *North Carolina Historical Review* 57 (1980): 1–16; and for the West Indies, Donna J. Spindel, "The Stamp Act Crisis in the British West Indies," *Journal of American Studies* 11, no. 2 (August 1977): 203–22, and Hymie Rubenstein, "Incest, Effigy Hanging, and Biculturation in a West Indian Village," *American Ethnologist* 3, no. 4 (November 1976): 165–81.

4. On the general upheaval of Boston and shifts in property ownership that affected artisans, see Nash, *Urban Crucible,* 16–17, 63–64, 114–23, 419; James Henretta, "Economic Development and Social Structure in Colonial Boston," *WMQ,* 3d ser., 22, no. 1 (January 1965): 81–87, and G. B. Warden, "Inequality and Instability in Eighteenth-Century Boston: A Reappraisal," *Journal of Interdisciplinary History* 6, no. 4 (Spring 1976): 593.

5. *BTR,* 5:99.

6. Clifford K. Shipton, "Immigration to New England, 1680–1740," *Journal of Political Economy* 44 (1936): 233; *BTR,* 2:134, 3:104, 4:207.

7. Quoted in Shipton, "Immigration to New England," 231, 238; Thomas Lechmere to John Winthrop III, August 4, 1718, in MHS *Coll.,* 6th ser., 5 (1892): 387 n.

8. *BSR,* 5:48–49; *BTR,* 6:282.

9. On the scarcity of London-trained woodworkers in New England towns, see Robert Blair St. George, "Fathers, Sons, and Identity: Woodworking Artisans in Southeastern New England, 1620–1700," in *The Craftsman in Early America,* ed. Ian M. G. Quimby (New York: W. W. Norton, 1984), 105–9.

10. *BSR,* 3:2–3, 69, 108, 4:92, 182.

11. The lack of uniformity with which scholars have categorized laboring people and their occupations makes comparative work difficult. I have broken down trades here according to the ecological demands that linked artisans in their reliance on certain materials, tools, and understandings of how these factors influenced workmanship and economic position. For the classification of seventeenth-

and eighteenth-century trades, see also John Patten, "Urban Occupations in Pre-Industrial England," *Transactions of the Institute of British Geographers*, n.s., 2, no. 3 (1977): 296–313. *The Present Melancholy Circumstances of the Province Consider'd* (Boston, 1719), in *Colonial Currency Reprints, 1682–1751*, ed. Andrew McFarland Davis, 4 vols. (Boston, 1910; reprint, New York: Burt Franklin, 1971), 1:360–61. *BSR*, 1:227, 5:212; *BTR*, 2:123.

12. Myrna Kaye, "Appendix A. Eighteenth-Century Boston Furniture Craftsmen," in *Boston Furniture of the Eighteenth Century*, ed. Brock Jobe, Jonathan L. Fairbanks, and Walter Muir Whitehill (Boston: Colonial Society of Massachusetts, 1974), 278, s.v. "Drinker."

13. *BSR*, 3:148.

14. Ibid., 84.

15. Ibid., 1:135.

16. *BTR*, 2:94; *BSR*, 1:64, 238, 2:163, 5:119; *Report of the Record Commissioners of the City of Boston, Containing Miscellaneous Papers* (Boston: Rockwell and Churchill, 1880), 58. On troubles in Boston's sugar-baking industry, see *BSR*, 4:161–62.

17. *BTR*, 2:16–17.

18. *BSR*, 2:96; *BTR*, 4:207. On shingles, see the Hingham offense in *BSR*, 3:229, and the shingle law set by the colony to ensure adequate size and strength of materials in "Trades and Manufactures, 1640–1774," 59:281–84, 366–68, MA. John Colman, *The Distressed State of the Town of Boston, & c. Considered* (Boston, 1720), in Davis, *Colonial Currency Reprints*, 1:398.

19. On the 1726 attempt to split away from Boston, see *BTR*, 3:195. On Chebacco, see Christopher M. Jedrey, *The World of John Cleaveland: Family and Community in Eighteenth-Century New England* (New York: W. W. Norton, 1979), 60–63; John Wise [Amicus Patriae], *A Word of Comfort to a Melancholy Country*, in Davis, *Colonial Currency Reprints*, 2:189.

20. On the general problem of rural transience, see Douglas Lamar Jones, "The Strolling Poor: Transiency in Eighteenth-Century Massachusetts," *Journal of Social History* 8 (1975): 28–54; propertyless-ness and inheritance delays for rural Connecticut are discussed in John J. Waters, "Patrimony, Succession, and Social Stability: Guilford, Connecticut, in the Eighteenth Century," *Perspectives in American History* 10 (1976): 144–59. On social consequences of diversification in southeastern Massachusetts, see St. George, "Fathers, Sons, and Identity," 121–23. See the 1573 Statute of Artificers, as quoted in Joan Thirsk, *Economic Projects and Policy* (Oxford: Oxford University Press, 1978), 108: "a number of apprentices are brought up and taught occupations in husbandmen's houses, which turneth to the superfluous increase of artificers, and to the decay and ruin of such cities as should set forth the honour and strength of the realm." *BSR*, 1:205, 236.

21. On distances traveled by English migrant artisans, see Julian Cornwall, "Evidence of Population Mobility in the Seventeenth Century," *Bulletin of the Institute of Historical Research* 40, no. 2 (November 1969): 143–44; Peter Clark, "The Migrant in Kentish Towns, 1580–1640," in *Crisis and Order in English Towns*, ed. Peter Clark and Paul Slack (London: Routledge and Kegan Paul, 1972), 121, 126–29; and Alan Everitt, "Social Mobility in Early Modern England," *Past and Present* 33 (April 1966): 57–60. *BSR*, 1:41, 2:20, 26, 174.

22. MA, 59:92. On shoemakers' and coopers' successful (for three-year terms) incorporation attempts in 1648, see *MBR*, 3:132–33; on the unsuccessful bid of the hatters in 1672, see *MBR*, 4, pt. 2:526. The fact that wealthy merchants signed the coopers' 1668 petition shows that such documents must be read as divergent texts, that is, as artifacts of groups with different goals that participate for different motives.

23. The Evans inventory is in SCPR, 4:37–40. Richard B. Morris, *Government and Labor in Early America* (New York: Columbia University Press, 1946), 156–58.

24. "Records of the Suffolk County Court, 1671–1680: Part II," in CSM *Pub.* 30 (1933): 82. On the 1675 Langworthy ride and its English precedents, see Young, "English Plebeian Culture and Eighteenth-Century American Radicalism," 185–89.

25. *BTR*, 1:156–57; "The 1677 Petition of the Handycrafts-men of Boston," reprinted in *Bulletin of the*

Public Library of the City of Boston, whole ser., 12, no. 95 (January 1894): 305–306, and unpag. facsimile. "Petition of Boston Inhabitants in 1696, That the Law Relating to Building in Brick Be Repealed," *NEHGR* 16 (1862): 84–87.

26. "Petition of Boston Inhabitants in 1696," 84.

27. Petition of wine drawers is in Records of the Suffolk County Court, docket 2631 (bound volumes), MA, dated September 3, 1691; MA, 119:123. On brewers and distillers in Boston, see "A Liste of the Brewers and Distillers in Said Town," dated November 28, 1702, in MA, 119:206. *BSR*, 1:14, 17; *BTR*, 5:180.

28. Gervase Markham, *The English Husbandman*, ed. John Dixon Hunt (London, 1613; reprint, New York: Garland, 1982), 1; William Henry Drayton, *Letters of a Freeman* (London, 1771), 103–4.

29. Quoted in Robert W. Malcolmson, "Workers' Combinations in Eighteenth-Century England," in Jacob and Jacob, *Origins of Anglo-American Radicalism*, 150.

30. *Severals Relating to the Fund, etc.* (Boston, 1682), in Davis, *Colonial Currency Reprints*, 1:112–14; Davis, *Colonial Currency Reprints*, 1:49 (1719 acct.); [Edward Wigglesworth], *A Letter From One in the Country to his Friend in Boston* (Boston, 1720), in Davis, *Colonial Currency Reprints*, 1:437–38; Colman, *Distressed State of the Town of Boston*, 2:172. Records of the Court of General Sessions of the Peace (1702–12), session of April 6, 1703, MA.

31. *An Addition to the Present Melancholy Circumstances of the Province Considered* (Boston, 1719), in Davis, *Colonial Currency Reprints*, 1:384; *BSR*, 5:170, 6:175.

32. Colman, *Distressed State of the Town of Boston*, 2:75; *BTR*, 4:121 (1735). Quoted in Richard Walsh, *Charleston's Sons of Liberty: A Study of the Artisans, 1763–1789* (Columbia: University of South Carolina Press, 1959), 21–22. On the 1682 almshouse, see *BTR*, 2:157; on almshouse artisan-residents, see *BTR*, 5:260–61. *Some Additional Considerations Addressed unto the Worshipful Elisha Hutchinson, Esq.* (Boston, 1691), in Davis, *Colonial Currency Reprints*, 1:204.

33. [Benjamin Colman], *Some Reasons and Arguments Offered to the Good People of Boston and Adjacent Places, for the Setting Up of Markets in Boston* (Boston, 1719), 2, 4–6, 11–12. See also *Addition To the Present Melancholy Circumstances of the Province Considered*, 1:390. Quoted in Carl Bridenbaugh, *Cities in the Wilderness: The First Century of Urban Life in America, 1625–1742* (New York: Knopf, 1960), 352. According to Thomas Prince, the attack on the market house took place in the middle of the night. "This morn[in]g at 2, ye Town-Dock Market House Pulled down" ("Diary of Thomas Prince," CSM *Pub.* 19 [1916–17]: 342).

34. On counterfeiting artisans, see *The Acts & Resolves, Public and Private, of the Province of Massachusetts Bay*, vol. 8, (Boston: Wright and Potter, 1895), 431–32. On women counterfeiters, see Kenneth Scott, *Counterfeiting in Colonial America* (New York: Oxford University Press, 1957), 46–49. Petitions to the House of Commons Which Lead to the Committee," *House of Commons Journal* 20 (1722–27): 528. See also the 1726 testimony of "Mr. William Pike": "he has seen the Weavers at their Clubs, where none but Weavers are admitted; and that they have their Ensigns and Flags hung out at the Door of their Meetings." (*House of Commons Journal* 20 [1722–27]: 648, session of March 31, 1726). I am indebted to John Rule for this reference.

35. Walter Kendall Watkins, "Subscription List for Building the First Town House," *Bostonian Society Publications* 3 (1906): 105–49.

36. On the increase in number of merchants, their transatlantic regulation, and their consolidation as a network, see Bernard Bailyn, *The New England Merchants in the Seventeenth Century* (Cambridge: Harvard University Press, 1979), 112–42. On early attempts for legal monopolies by artisan groups, see Andrew McFarland Davis, "Corporations in the Day of the Colony," CSM *Pub.* 1 (1874): 183–214.

37. See David D. Hall, *The Faithful Shepherd: A History of the New England Ministry in the Seventeenth Century* (New York: W. W. Norton, 1974), 233–37.

38. James F. Cooper, "The Confession and Trial of Richard Wayte, Boston, 1640," *WMQ*, 3d ser., 44, no. 2 (April 1987): 311–12; *Note-Book Kept by Thomas Lechford, Esq., Lawyer, in Boston, Massachusetts Bay, from June 27, 1638, to July 29, 1641* (Cambridge: John Wilson & Sons, 1885), 188 n. 3, 210 n. 1; Winthrop, *Journal*, 1:284; Richard Frothingham Jr., *The History of Charlestown, Massachusetts* (Boston:

Charles C. Little and James Brown, 1895), 132. On the sermons of John Cotton being a source in the 1630s and 1640s for a subversive strain—which artisans might pick up and isolate for their own ends—of Antinomianism and millennial faith within official discourse, see J. F. Maclear, "New England and the Fifth Monarchy: The Quest for the Millennium in Early Early American Puritanism," *WMQ*, 3d ser., 32, no. 2 (April 1975): 231–34, and George Selement, "John Cotton's Hidden Antinomianism: His Sermon on Revelation 4:1–2," *NEHGR* 129 (July 1975): 278–94. For English background in one location relevant to New England's struggle over Antinomianism in 1637, see Peter Clark, "The Prophesying Movement in Kentish Towns during the 1570s," *Archaeologia Cantiana* 93 (1977): 81–90.

39. Winthrop, *Journal*, 1:177; on Fifth Monarchism's connection with Boston in 1655 (wine cooper Thomas Venner) and again in 1661, see Nash, *Urban Crucible*, 42. Nathaniel Briscoe to Thomas Broughton, October 7, 1652, in MHS *Coll.*, 3d ser., 1 (1846): 34. For 1658 prosecutions against Goold and Turner, see *Records of the First Church in Charlestown, Massachusetts, 1632–1789*, ed. James Frothingham Hunnewell (Boston: David Clapp and Son, 1880), i–v. On the Boston and Charlestown Baptist controversy, see Carla Gardina Pestana, *Quakers and Baptists in Colonial Massachusetts* (New York: Cambridge University Press, 1991), 45–61. *BTR*, 2:125, describes Alexander Callman, a Boston shoemaker, as "a Quaker yt came into ye 3d Meetinge house in a bloody coate," suggesting similar artisan participation in New England Quakerism.

40. Pestana, *Quakers and Baptists in Colonial Massachusetts*, 116.

41. On the connections between early sectarian plays and ecclesiastical rebellion, see Leonard Verduin, "The Chambers of Rhetoric and Anabaptist Origins in the Low Countries," *Mennonite Quarterly Review* 34, no. 3 (July 1960): 192–96, and George Hunston Williams, *The Radical Reformation* (Philadelphia: Westminster Press, 1962), 29, 363–65, 380; I am indebted to John L. Brooke for these references. The actions of the caulkers and tanners are reprinted in Robert Francis Seybolt, ed., "Trade Agreements in Colonial Boston," *NEQ* 2, no. 2 (April 1929): 307–9. See "Boston Carpenters' Rules for Work, 1744," ed. Larry B. Romaine, *OTNE* 46 (1954).

42. On strategies of diversified production, see James Henretta, "Families and Farms: *Mentalité* in Pre-Industrial America," *WMQ*, 3d ser., 35, no. 1 (January 1978): 15–21; on diversification in rural Plymouth and Suffolk Counties between about 1660 and 1720, see St. George, "Father, Sons, and Identity," 120–24. "Records of the Suffolk County Court, 1671–1680: Part I," *CSM Pub.* 29 (1933): 11–12. Annie Haven Thwing files of Boston Inhabitants, Massachusetts Historical Society, Boston, s.v. "Baker." *BSR*, 2:130, 3:3.

43. Thwing files, s.v. "Gilbert"; *BSR*, 3:199; Joyce O. Appleby, "The Social Origins of American Revolutionary Ideology," *Journal of American History* 44 (1978): 954, notes that laboring people exerted "a much greater detachment from the intellectual traditions of the Mother Country than their superiors showed."

44. *BTR*, 4:177, 5:59–60, 260–61.

45. "A book of Allowances from the Major Part of the Justices within the Town of Boston to Persons for Building with Timber in the said Town Beginning April, 1707," in *A Volume of Records Relating to the Early History of Boston, containing Miscellaneous Papers*, Boston Records Commissioners Reports vol. 29 (Boston: Municipal Printing Office, 1900), 187 (hereafter cited as "Timber Building Permits").

46. Suffolk Deeds, 26:113–13, instrument of April 10, 1683 (emphasis added), Suffolk County Courthouse, Boston, Mass.

47. SCPR, 4:261–62.

48. MA, 45:404–405; SCPR, 6:472. Nathaniel Greenwood's inventory, taken September 25, 1684, includes "house[e]s Land & wharfes in Boston . . . £800:00:00" (SCPR, 9:192–93).

49. Suffolk Deeds, 35:141–42; SCPR, 22:640–47, taken May 10, 1722; see also division of estate of Stephen Greenwood, Suffolk Deeds, 56:249–55, instrument of August 29, 1738. The same "3 small Brick Tenements fronting Ship Street North East End Joyning to Land forementioned" were valued at £750 when his son Stephen died in 1742; see SCPR, 36:68–71, esp. schedule for "Real Estate viz." For the Bronsdon bequeathal to the Greenwoods, see Suffolk Deeds, 23:183: "for the said Stephen Greenwood

& Elizabeth his Wife . . . to have use Occupy possess and Enjoy All that Messuage house or Tenement with the Land whereon ye same now stands."

50. "Timber Building Permits," 91, 204. In 1712 John Clark also had "three shops now standing in the Front of his Land on ffish street," and Samuel Wentworth in 1713 had a "Row of Shops," both in Boston's North End. The longest structure for shops was actually built by the town of Boston itself in 1729: "a Row of Low Shops on part of the Town Dock which they Caused to be filled up to Contain 120 feet in length & 20 feet in brea[d]th" ("Timber Building Permits," 207, 225).

51. "Census of 1707," in *Report of the Record Commissioners of the City of Boston, Containing Miscellaneous Papers,* 114–26; *BSR,* 3:209.

52. "Census of 1707"; SCPR, 1:118–42.

53. The Hatch plan accompanied the September 14, 1786, division of the estate; see SCPR, 85:557–61. For his inventory and will, see SCPR, 62:62–65, 111–15. Suffolk Deeds, 41:64 (Cutler to Heaton), 72:261–64 (Loring to Hatch, Wheeler to Hatch), 78:265–66 (Miller to Hatch), 93:167–68 (Loring heirs to Hatch).

54. For Mary Hatch's purchases, see Suffolk Deeds, 104:269–71.

55. *BTR,* 5:12–15, 57. *The Essays, Humor, and Poems of Nathaniel Ames, Father and Son, of Dedham, Massachusetts, from their Almanacs 1726–1775,* ed. Samuel Briggs (Cleveland: Short and Forman, 1891), 183.

56. *BTR,* 5:238, 239.

57. Quoted in Bridenbaugh, *Cities in the Wilderness,* 309.

58. *BTR,* 5:180.

59. Ibid., 5:239. On Hewes, see Alfred F. Young, "George Robert Twelve Hewes (1742–1840): A Boston Shoemaker and the Memory of the American Revolution," *WMQ,* 3d ser., 38, no. 4 (October 1981): 601.

60. Warden, "Inequality and Instability in Eighteenth-Century Boston," 589. See "Accounts of Loss from Original Papers in the Office of the City Registrar: Losses Sustained by the Fire of 1760," in *Report of the Record Commissioners of the City of Boston, Containing Miscellaneous Papers,* 1–88. For a comprehensive study of the fire and what the submitted claims and the records of the Overseers of the Poor suggest about Boston social structure, see William Pencak, "The Social Structure of Revolutionary Boston," *Journal of Interdisciplinary History* 10, no. 2 (Autumn 1979): 267–78, esp. 269, where the author notes that, as in 1707, many working people in 1760 were still renting housing and shops from absentee landlords.

61. See Bernard Bailyn, *The Ideological Origins of the American Revolution* (Cambridge: Harvard University Press, Belknap Press, 1967), 22–93; J. G. A. Pocock, *Virtue, Commerce, and History: Essays on Political Thought and History, Chiefly in the Eighteenth Century* (Cambridge: Cambridge University Press, 1985), 164–65, 107–8, 229–41, 261–62; Gordon S. Wood, *The Creation of the American Republic, 1776–1787* (Chapel Hill: University of North Carolina Press for the Institute of Early American History and Culture, 1969), 3–45.

62. K. J. Lindley, "Riot Prevention and Control in Early Stuart London," *Transactions of the Royal Historical Society,* 5th ser., 33 (1983): 110–12; [Bruno Ryves], *Mercurius Rusticus: Or, the Countries Complaint of the Barbarous Out-rages Committed by the Sectaries of this Late Flourishing Kingdome* (Oxford, 1646), 33–35. I am indebted to David Cressy for this reference.

63. [Ryves], *Mercurius Rusticus,* 4.

64. On Masaniello and the Naples revolt, see Peter Burke, "The Virgin of the Carmine and the Revolt of Masaniello," *Past and Present* 99 (May 1983): 3–21, and Nash, *Urban Crucible,* 48–49. For a 1562 instance of ritual pillaging during Huguenot-Catholic conflicts in Meaux near Paris, see Barbara Diefendorf, "Prologue to a Massacre: Popular Unrest in Paris, 1557–1572," *American Historical Review* 90, no. 5 (December 1985): 1081.

65. Geoffrey Holmes, "The Sacheverell Riots: The Crowd and the Church in Early Eighteenth-Century London," *Past and Present* 72 (August 1976): 56, 64–65. Cotton Mather to Samuel Penhallow, May 22, 1710, in Mather, *Diary,* 2:36.

66. The Rossiter instance is reported in Ezra Stiles, *Extracts from the Itineraries and Other Miscellanies of Ezra Stiles, D.D., and LL.D., 1755–1794*, ed. Franklin Bowditch Dexter (New Haven: Yale University Press, 1916), 152. On Dudley, see Francis S. Drake, "Roxbury in the Provincial Period," in *The Memorial History of Boston, Including Suffolk County, Massachusetts, 1630–1880*, ed. Justin Winsor, 4 vols. (Boston: Ticknor and Company for James Osgood, 1881), 2:332. The incident at Yale is in Records of the Superior Court of the Colony of Connecticut, vol. 15 (New Haven session), August 27, 1765, Connecticut State Archives, Hartford. See also Lawrence H. Gipson, *Jared Ingersoll: A Study of American Loyalism in Relation to British Colonial Government* (New Haven: Yale University Press, 1920), 159–60 n. 4.

67. *The Acts and Resolves, Public and Private, of the Province of Massachusetts Bay*, vol. 2 (Boston: Wright and Potter, 1874), 24–25 (1715), 300–302 (1723); *The Acts and Resolves, Public and Private, of the Province of Massachusetts Bay*, vol. 3 (Boston: Albert S. Wright, 1878): 647–48 (1753).

68. Governor Francis Bernard to the Earl of Halifax, August 31, 1765, Francis Bernard Papers ("Governor Bernard's Official Paper"), Sparks Mss. 4, Letter Books 1765–66, 13 vols., Houghton Library, Harvard University, 4:150–52.

69. Quoted in Howard W. Preston, "The Defenders of Providence during King Philip's War," *Rhode Island Historical Society Collections* 21, no. 2 (April 1928): 60; quoted in J. G. Holland, *History of Western Massachusetts*, 2 vols. (Springfield: S. Bowles and Co., 1855), 1:95–96, 99; MA, 67:282. Increase Mather, *A Brief History of the Warr with the Indians in New-England*, in *So Dreadfull a Judgment: Puritan Responses to King Philip's War, 1676–1677*, ed. Richard Slotkin and James K. Folsom (Middletown, Conn.: Wesleyan University Press, 1978), 124–25; *A New and Further Narrative of the State of New England, Being a Continued Account of the Bloody Indian War* (London, 1676), in *King Philip's War Narratives* (Ann Arbor, Mich.: UMI Press, 1966), 2.

70. Mather, *Brief History of the Warr*, 100–101. *ECQCR*, 6:101. On the destruction and theft of town records, see Preston, "Defenders of Providence during King Philip's War," 61, and Sarah Loring Bailey, *Historical Sketches of Andover* (Boston: Houghton Mifflin, 1880), 182–83. The theft of the Andover pulpit cushion is recorded in Sewall, *Diary*, 1:388.

71. Cotton Mather, "Triparadisus," ca. 1720 ms., octavo vol. no. 49, bk. 3, pp. 1–2, Mather Family Papers 1613–1819, American Antiquarian Society, Worcester, Mass. For earlier examples of fire being interpreted as millennial flame, see Arthur Gurney, *A doleful Discourse and truthful Reports of the great Spoyle and lamentable losse, by fire, in the Town of East Dearham, in the Countie of Norfolke* (London, 1581), and John Dane's memory of his house burning in 1661, in "An Ipswich Tailor," in *Remarkable Providences, 1600–1760*, ed. John P. Demos (New York: John Braziller, 1972), 87–88; Sewall, *Letter-Book*, 1:269.

72. Mather, *Magnalia*, 1:104; Tudor, *Deacon Tudor's Diary*, 10 (entry of March 20, 1760). Attributing an escape from a bad fire to divine intervention is recorded also in John Endicott to John Winthrop Jr., March 18, 1652, in MHS *Coll.*, 4th ser., 6 (1863): 155, concerning the "late great fire at Boston" on March 14: "it was a wonderful favour of God the whole towne was not consumed of the ffire." John Sharpe to Thomas Meekins of Hatfield, March 8, 1678, in "Indian (Philip's) War letter," *NEHGR* 10 (January 1856): 65.

73. *Newport Mercury*, August 26, 1765, 3, reprinting a story from the *Boston Evening Post*.

74. Ibid., September 9, 1765, 2. William Almy to Elisha Story, August 29, 1765, in MHS *Proc.* 55 (October 1921–June 1922): 236.

75. On effigies in western European culture, see Wolfgang Brückner, *Bildnis und Brauch: Studien zur Bildfunktion der Effigies* (Berlin: E. Schmidt Verlag, 1966), 223–27, 283–315. See also these local English studies: W. St. John Hope, "On the Funeral Effigies of the Kings and Queens of England," *Archaeologia* 60 (1907): 517–70; Ida M. Ropes, *The Monumental Effigies of Gloucestershire and Bristol* (Gloucester, 1931); G. Dru Drury, "Early Ecclesiastical Effigies in Dorset," *Proceedings of the Dorset Natural History and Archaeological Society* 53 (1931): 250–64; and R. H. Laurence and T. E. Routh, "Military Effigies in Nottinghamshire before the Black Death," *Transactions of the Thoroton Society* 28 (1924): 114–28. For

the historical context of Hogarth's illustration of the "Burning of ye Rumps," see Tim Harris, *London Crowds in the Reign of Charles II: Propaganda and Politics from the Restoration until the Exclusion Crisis* (New York: Cambridge University Press, 1987), 49, 166, 170, 213–22.

76. The cat-shaving incident is quoted from C. S. L. Davies, *Peace, Print, and Protestantism, 1450–1558* (London: Hart-Davis, MacGibbon, 1976) in Robert Darnton, *The Great Cat Massacre and Other Episodes in French Cultural History* (New York: Basic Books, 1984), 91, 272 n. 28. See Violet Alford, "Rough Music," *Folklore* 70 (1959): 505–18; E. P. Thompson, "Rough Music," in *Customs in Common: Studies in Traditional Popular Culture* (New York: New Press, 1991), 467–533; and Martin Ingram, "Ridings, Rough Music, and the 'Reform of Popular Culture' in Early Modern England," *Past and Present* 105 (November 1984): 79–113.

77. John Brewer, "The Faces of Lord Bute: A Visual Contribution to Anglo-American Political Ideology," *Perspectives in American History* 6 (1972): 95–116. The relationship of effigies to stage dummies in English theatrical tradition is suggested in W. J. Laurence, *Speeding Up Shakespeare: Studies of the Bygone Theater and Drama* (London: Argonaut Press, 1937), 127–43, esp. 129, on the use of stage dummies in mock executions: "Doubtless an equivalent to this was done before the body was brought in again and hung upon a tree: an act which would go to show that the dummy used had a well-joined but removable head and hands." See also John Brewer, *The Common People and Politics, 1750–1790s: The English Satirical Print, 1660–1832* (Teaneck, N.J.: Chadwyck-Healey, 1985), 51–52 (plate 1), and see also 264 (plate 107), "A Poor Man Loaded with Mischief, or John Bull and his Sister Peg." *Newport Mercury*, August 26, 1765, 3. On the association of Bute's boot with the Devil, see the late-fifteenth-century London pilgrim badge linking boots to conjuring—and containing—Satan, in Ralph Merrifield, *The Archaeology of Ritual and Magic* (New York: New Amsterdam Books, 1987), pp. 134–35.

78. *Records of the Colony and Plantation of New Haven, from 1638 to 1649*, ed. Charles J. Hoadly, 2 vols. (Hartford: Case, Tiffany, & Co., 1857), 1:23–24. George Rudé, *Wilkes and Liberty: A Social Study of 1763–1774* (Oxford: Clarendon Press, 1962), 17–36. During the Wilkesite controversy and the ensuing "massacre" in St. George's Fields, London, house attacks were also a common feature of popular symbolic violence; for the 1768 attacks on the London lord mayor's house and Edward Russell's house in Southwark, see Rudé, *Wilkes and Liberty*, 43–44, 199–200; see also Robert B. Shoemaker, "The London 'Mob' in the Early Eighteenth Century," *Journal of British Studies* 26, no. 3 (July 1987): 273–304.

79. *Boston Evening Post*, September 23, 1765.

80. David Humphreys, *An Essay on the Life of the Honorable Major-General Israel Putnam* (Hartford, 1788), 94; see also Gipson, *Jared Ingersoll*, 158–87. "Crimes and Misdemeanors," 2d ser., 4:152a, Connecticut State Archives, Hartford.

81. *Newport Mercury*, September 2, 1765, 2; the Windham effigy hanging represented Connecticut stampman Jared Ingersoll. On Newport, see Thomas Moffatt to Joseph Harrison, in Morgan, *Prologue to Revolution*, 112.

82. Quoted in Maud Lyman Stevens, "The Wanton-Lyman-Hazard House, Newport, Rhode Island," *OTNE* 18, no. 1 (July 1927): 25.

83. Writ of Benjamin Gillam v. Daniel Dimmock et al., April 1768, New Haven Court Records, bk. 7:100, Connecticut State Archives, Hartford. I am indebted to Nina Dayton for this reference.

84. The two reports are in *Newport Mercury*, August 19, 1765, 3, August 26, 1765, 2.

85. Almy to Story, August 29, 1765, 235–36.

86. On the inscriptions attached to the Newport effigies and the "New Song," see ibid. Martin Howard Jr., *A Letter from a Gentleman at Halifax, to his Friend in Rhode Island, Containing Remarks upon a Pamphlet, Entitled, "The Rights of Colonies Examined"* (Newport, 1765), 20. On Howard and his local politics, see Daniel Snydacker Jr., "The Remarkable Career of Martin Howard, Esq.," *Newport History* 61, pt. 1: 208 (Winter 1988): 2–17.

87. *Boston Evening Post*, September 23, 1765.

88. *Newport Mercury*, August 26, 1765, 3.

89. On funerals and public ceremony in early Boston, see the 1687 procession for Lady Andros in Se-

wall, *Diary*, 1:160. Walker also confirmed this street pattern for the funeral procession of Mary Belch-er, the wife of the provincial governor, on October 8, 1736: "she was buried, bro[ugh]tt fro[m] ye Province house thro Cornhill Street went down fro[m] our front into Kingstreet went as far as Colo[ne]l Fitche['s] house turn'd up street on South side off Town house to burying Ground." Diary of Benjamin Walker, Massachusetts Historical Society, Boston, vol. 1 (unpag., entry of August 21, 1727) and vol. 2 (unpag., entries of October 17, 1736, and unspecified date in 1742/43). Sibyl Moholy-Nagy, *Matrix of Man: An Illustrated History of Urban Environment* (New York: Praeger, 1968), 198–240; on early gridded plans and their meaning in Puritan thought, see John Archer, "Puritan Town Planning in New Haven," *Journal of the Society of Architectural Historians* 34, no. 1 (March 1975): 140–49.

90. Almy to Story, August 29, 1765, 235.

91. MA, 44:604–5. On smuggling in Boston and the merchants' reliance on it during the early 1760s, see John W. Tyler, *Smugglers and Patriots: Boston Merchants and the Advent of the American Revolution* (Boston: Northeastern University Press, 1986), 25–108; see also Maier, *From Resistance to Revolution*, 58.

92. For the history of Thomas Hutchinson's house, see Abbott Lowell Cummings, "The Foster-Hutchinson House," *OTNE* 54, no. 3 (January–March 1964): 59–76; Thomas Hutchinson to Robert Wilson, June 15, 1765, quoted in James K. Hosmer, *The Life of Thomas Hutchinson, Royal Governor of the Province of Massachusetts Bay* (Boston: Houghton Mifflin, 1896), 88.

93. Bernard to the earl of Halifax, August 31, 1765, Sparks Mss., Houghton Library, Harvard University. See Christopher Hibbert, *King Mob: The Story of Lord George Gordon and the London Riots of 1780* (Cleveland: World Publishing Co., 1958), and George Gordon, *The Proceedings at Large in the Trial of George Gordon, Esq* (London, 1781).

94. Thomas Hutchinson to Richard Jackson, August 30, 1765, MA, 26:146–47.

95. On Thomas Hutchinson's perspective on economy and politics, see Bernard Bailyn, *The Ordeal of Thomas Hutchinson* (Cambridge: Harvard University Press, Belknap Press, 1974), 70–108; on conse-quences of his "hard-money" stance in the colonial economic debates, see Nash, *Urban Crucible*, 225–26. James H. Bunn, "The Aesthetics of British Mercantilism," *New Literary History* 11 (1980): 303–21.

96. Nash, *Urban Crucible*, 297–99.

97. On millennial republicanism and its links to the radical spiritism of Winstanley, see J. G. A. Pocock, "Post-Puritan England and the Problem of the Enlightenment," in *Culture and Politics from Puritanism to the Enlightenment*, ed. Perez Zagorin (Berkeley and Los Angeles: University of California Press, 1980), 96–97. On the plurality of positions within classical republicanism, see Gordon S. Wood, *The Radicalism of the American Revolution* (New York: Knopf, 1992), 95–145; Charles Chauncy, *Enthu-siasm Described and Cautioned Against* (Boston, 1742), 15. On the line of thought connecting the jere-miad tradition of the 1670s with religious revivals and republican ideology, see Perry Miller, "From the Covenant to the Revival," in *The Shaping of American Religion*, Religion in American Life, vol. 1, ed. James Ward Smith and A. Leland Johnson (Princeton: Princeton University Press, 1961), 335–37. Philip F. Gura, *A Glimpse of Sion's Glory: Puritan Radicalism in New England, 1620–1660* (Middletown, Conn.: Wesleyan University Press, 1984), 327. On the similarity of New Light gatherings to "mob" formations, see Timothy D. Hall, *Contested Boundaries: Itinerancy and the Reshaping of the Colonial American Re-ligious World* (Durham, N.C.: Duke University Press, 1994), 18–19, 47–48.

98. Bernard to Halifax, August 31, 1765. By linking the legacy of radical religion and Harringtonian republicanism, I argue that the artisans in Boston's mobs during the 1760s did more than invert social relations in order to honor the status quo, as argued in Wood, *Radicalism of the American Revolution*, 244. Rather than inverting society, they were seeking to perfect it.

99. In this regard, the appearance during the late seventeenth century of Georgian houses paralleled, interacted with (see fig. 68 above), and ultimately replaced witchcraft, which similarly exposed open spaces in social structure in order to victimize, marginalize, and make resentments clear concerning the distribution of property; see Norman Cohn, "Medieval Millenarianism: Its Bearings on the Com-

parative Study of Millenarian Movements," in *Millennial Dreams in Action*, ed. Sylvia Thrupp (The Hague: Mouton, 1962), 39; see also Richard L. Bushman, "American High-Style and Vernacular Cultures," in *Colonial British America: Essays in the New History of the Early Modern Era*, ed. Jack P. Greene and J. R. Pole (Baltimore: Johns Hopkins University Press, 1984), 377 n. 14.

100. Inventory of William Clark, SCPR, 36:206–9; 37:116–22. For additional descriptions of this structure, see Henry Lee, "Comments on the Clark or Frankland House," MHS *Proc.*, 1st ser., 18 (1880–81): 344–51, and the illustration in Abbott Lowell Cummings, "The Beginnings of Provincial Renaissance Architecture in Boston, 1690–1725," *Journal of the Society of Architectural Historians* 42, no. 1 (March 1983): 48, fig. 8. For other early Georgian structures in Boston, see Walter Kendall Watkins, "The Hancock House and Its Builders," *OTNE* 17, no. 1 (July 1926): 3–19; Thomas Tileston Waterman, "The Thomas Savage House, Dock Square, Boston," and Walter Kendall Watkins, "Notes on the Savage House," both in *OTNE* 17, no. 3 (January 1927): 110–15; and Thomas Tileston Waterman, "Certain Brick Houses in Boston from 1700 to 1776," *OTNE* 23, no. 1 (July 1932): 22–27. On the retention of asymmetrical spaces inside Georgian houses, a characteristic of many colonial structures along the eastern seaboard, see Dell Upton, "Vernacular Domestic Architecture in Eighteenth-Century Virginia," *Winterthur Portfolio* 17, no. 2–3 (Summer–Autumn 1982): 108–14. Dekker and Webster as quoted in Jean-Christophe Agnew, *Worlds Apart: The Theater and the Market in Anglo-American Thought* (New York: Cambridge University Press, 1986), 57. See also A. Arscharir, "False Fronts in Minor Domestic Architecture," *TAMS*, n.s., 4 (1956): 110–22.

101. Quoted from the diary of the Reverend Stephen Williams in *Proceedings at the Centennial Celebration of the Incorporation of Longmeadow, October 17th, 1883, with Numerous Historical Appendices and a Town Genealogy* (Longmeadow, Mass.: Secretary of the Centennial Committee for the Town, 1884), 34. *Diary of Ebenezer Parkman, 1703–1782*, ed. Francis G. Walett (Worcester, Mass.: American Antiquarian Society, 1974), 239, 246.

102. On the Clough and Peirce houses, see Cummings, "Beginnings of Provincial Renaissance Architecture in Boston," 49–50. On the Third Church's house for Pemberton, which was designed in plan in 1705 but not built until 1710, see Hamilton Andrews Hall, *History of the Old South Church (Third Church) Boston, 1669–1884*, 2 vols. (Boston: Houghton Mifflin, 1890), 1:329, 346–47.

103. Andrea Palladio, *The Four Books of Andrea Palladio's Architecture*, trans. Isaac Ware (London, 1738; reprint, New York: Dover, 1965), bk. 1, 1 (emphasis added).

104. For a recent analysis of the house's development, see Arthur L. Finney, "The Royall House in Medford: A Re-Evaluation of the Structural and Documentary Evidence," in *Architecture in Colonial Massachusetts*, ed. Abbott Lowell Cummings (Boston: Colonial Society of Massachusetts, 1979), 23–33. See also William Cushing Wait, "Maps of Medford of Different Periods," *Medford Historical Register* 1, no. 4 (October 1898): 124–26, and John H. Hooper, "The Royall House and Farm," *Medford Historical Register* 3, no. 4 (October 1900): 133–53. See also Sebastian de Grazia, "The Separation of Rulers from the Community," in *The Search for Community in Modern America* (New York: Harper and Row, 1968), 14–21. For the broader context of New England country houses and detailed documentary histories of major extant properties, see Charles Arthur Hammond, "'Where the Arts and the Virtues Unite': Country Life Near Boston, 1637–1864" (Ph.D. diss., Boston University, 1982), 53–68. I am indebted to Chuck Hammond for sharing notes on the original layout of the Royall estate that I have used in preparing figure 94.

105. John Mortimer, *The Whole Art of Husbandry* (London, 1708), 33–37. Isaac Royall's room-by-room inventory, with a section marked "a Cattalogue of Books," is reprinted in Finney, "Royall House in Medford," 34–41. For the influence of classical Latin agrarian writers on the georgic revival in early-eighteenth-century England, see Robert Castell, *The Villas of the Ancients Illustrated* (London, 1728).

106. On cleanliness as part of the neoclassical aesthetic, see John Martin Robertson, *Georgian Model Farms: A Study of Decorative and Model Farm Buildings in the Age of Improvement, 1700–1846* (Oxford: Clarendon Press, 1983), 93–98. John Prentice's farmstead, representing its development until his death in May 1748, was drawn for a division of estate that was executed the following December; see Worces-

ter County Probate Records, 3:125–31, Worcester County Courthouse, Worcester, Mass. On the John Cogswell property, see Nina Fletcher Little, "John Cogswell's Grant and Some of the Houses Thereon, 1636–1839," *EIHC* 76, no. 2 (April 1940): 151–72.

107. "Accounts of Losses . . . Sustained by the Fire of 1760," in *Report of the Record Commissioners of the City of Boston, Containing Miscellaneous Papers*, 23, 45, 69–71.

108. Ibid., 104–8.

109. Quoted in Tyler, *Smugglers and Patriots*, 62. Charles Paxton to Lord Townsend, November 6, 1768, in "Letters of Charles Paxton," ed. George G. Wolkins, MHS *Proc.* 56 (1923): 350.

110. Bernard to Halifax, August 31, 1765. *BTR*, 7:100–101. SCPR, 34:521–25. *Diary of Joshua Hempstead of New London, Connecticut Covering a Period of Forty-seven Years from September, 1711, to November, 1758* (New London: New London County Historical Society, 1901), 234 (entry of May 7, 1731); "Madam Winthrop" refers to the widowed daughter-in-law of Fitz-John and Elizabeth Winthrop, who had inherited their sizable landholdings in New London County from John Winthrop Jr. John Adams wrote to Mercy Otis Warren in July 1807 that "as early as 1760, orders came to Paxton and Cockle to demand Writs of Assistance to break open houses, cellars, shops, and ships, to search for uncustomed goods" ("Correspondence between John Adams and Mercy Otis Warren," MHS *Coll.*, 5th ser., 4 [1877]: 340).

111. *The Book of the General Lawes and Libertyes Concerning the Inhabitants of the Massachusets* (Cambridge: Harvard University Press, 1929), 4–5.

112. Hoadly, *Records of the Colony and Plantation of New Haven*, 1:77, 149. On routine, dispersed theft, see Laurel Thatcher Ulrich, "It 'went away shee knew not how': Food Theft and Domestic Conflict in Seventeenth-Century Essex County," in *Foodways in the Northeast*, ed. Peter Benes (Boston: Boston University Press for the Dublin Seminar for New England Folklife, 1984), 94–104, and Barbara Ritter Dailey, " 'Where Thieves Break Through and Steal': John Hale versus Dorcas Hoar, 1672–1692," *EIHC* 128, no. 4 (October 1992): 255–69. *Boston Evening Post*, July 24, 1738. Abstracts of Inferior Court of Pleas of Suffolk County, 41, 42; meeting of the Superior Court of Judicature, Springfield session, September 24, 1754, MA, 44 (Judicial 1754–74): 10.

113. Quoted in David Grayson Allen, "*Vacuum Domicilium*: The Social and Cultural Landscape of Seventeenth-Century New England," in *NEB*, 1:1. On the one-night house tradition, recorded as early as the mid-seventeenth century, see R. U. Sayce, "The One-Night House, and Its Distribution," *Folk-Lore* 53, no. 3 (September 1942): 161–63; Gilbert Slater, *The English Peasantry and the Enclosure of Common Fields* (London: Archibald Constable, 1907), 113–14; "Popular Enclosures and the One-Night House," *Montgomeryshire Collections* 47, pt. 2 (1947): 109–20; and Ann R. Everton, "Built in a Night," *Conveyancer and Property Lawyer* 35, no. 4 (July–August 1971): 249–54 and esp. 251 for this description from Ottery St. Mary, Devon, quoted from *Devon and Cornwall Notes and Queries* 14 (April 1926): "It appears that a custom obtained in . . . the West Hill district of Ottery St. Mary . . . until recent years, that if a man started to build a cottage on waste ground which others claimed (i.e., common land), the objectors were free to pull down during the night what the builder had put up during the day. Once the roof was on, and rain had fallen on it, this privilege lapsed. In consequence, the building was often done at night, and a bit of thatch was put out as soon as possible, and water poured over it. This was held to protect the building against interference" (2). For a claim from a Newport victim, see "Account of Property Lost by Martin Howard Jr., August 28, 1765," in Stevens, "Wanton-Lyman-Hazard House," 26.

114. Richard Neve, *The City and Countrey Purchaser and Builder's Dictionary* (London, 1703), 84.

115. Anne Bradstreet, "As Weary Pilgrim Now at Rest," in *The Puritans*, ed. Perry Miller and Thomas H. Johnson, 2 vols. (New York: Harper and Row, 1963), 2:579; Cotton Mather, *Ornaments for the Daughters of Zion, Or, the Character and Happiness of a Vertuous Woman* (Boston, 1691), 110; Taylor, *Poems*, 46, 218–19.

116. *Essays, Humor, and Poems of Nathaniel Ames*, 99. See *The Confession and Dying Warning of Hugh Henderson, Who Was Executed at Worcester, in the County of Worcester, Nov. 26. 1737* (Boston, 1737).

117. Ronald Paulson, *Hogarth's Graphic Works*, 3d ed. (London: Print Room, 1989), 119–20, 376–77 (no. 190). On local bitterness against Hutchinson, see Nash, *Urban Crucible*, 293–95.

118. Thomas Hooker, *A Survey of the Summe of Church-Discipline* (London, 1648), 188.

119. Writ of Benjamin Gillam v. Daniel Dimmock et al. (April 1768), New Haven County Court Records, bk. 7:100. *Newport Mercury*, August 26, 1765, 3.

120. *Newport Mercury*, September 9, 1765, 3. Bernard to Halifax, August 31, 1765. Thomas Hutchinson to Richard Jackson, August 30, 1765, in MA, 26:146–47. In Newport Thomas Moffatt, after weathering a steady stream of rumors that his house might be mobbed, actually confronted a ringleader responsible for the job, merchant Samuel Vernon, in the street, and asked "how [you] or any other Person could think of using me in that contemptuous shocking manner?" Vernon responded by cataloging Moffatt's social and political infractions in detail, including his agreement with the economic policies of Martin Howard, whose house they would also demolish two days later (Thomas Moffatt to Joseph Harrison, October 16, 1765, Chalmers Paper, New York Public Library).

121. On the background and passage of the Riot Act in England, see W. S. Holdsworth, *A History of English Law*, 12 vols. (London: Methuen, 1922–38), 10:62–67.

122. Copy of a letter from the collector and comptroller of New London to the commissioners of the customs at Boston, July 1769, CO 5/1282, p. 201, Public Record Office, London. Ashis Nandy, *The Intimate Enemy: Loss and Recovery of Self under Colonialism* (New York: Oxford University Press, 1983), 8.

123. George Withers, *An Improvement of Imprisonment, Disgrace, Poverty, into Real Freedom; Honest Reputation; Perdurable Riches; Evidenced in a Few Crumbs and Scraps Lately Found in a Prisoners-Basket at Newgate* (London, 1661), 56; on effeminization of merchants experiencing loss, see Toby Ditz, "Shipwrecked; or, Masculinity Imperiled: Mercantile Representations of Failure and the Gendered Self in Eighteenth-Century Philadelphia," *Journal of American History* 81, no. 3 (June 1994): 51–80. I am indebted to Toby Ditz for suggesting the connection between the Hutchinson narrative of flight and the captivity narrative tradition that I explore here.

124. For Hutchinson's awareness of the Rowlandson narrative, see Thomas Hutchinson, *The History of the Colony of Massachusetts Bay*, 3 vols. (Boston, 1764; reprint, New York: Arno Press, 1972), 1:301–2. Mary White Rowlandson, *The Sovereignty and Goodness of God, Together with the Faithfulness of His Promises Displayed; Being a Narrative of the Captivity and Restoration of Mrs. Mary Rowlandson* (Cambridge, Mass., 1682), reprinted in *Puritans among the Indians: Accounts of Captivity and Redemption*, ed. Alden T. Vaughan and Edward W. Clark (Cambridge: Harvard University Press, Belknap Press, 1981), 33–34. See also Gary L. Ebersole, *Captured by Texts: Puritan to Postmodern Images of Indian Captivity* (Charlottesville: University Press of Virginia, 1995), 15–60; Mitchell Robert Breitwieser, *American Puritanism and the Defense of Mourning: Religion, Grief, and Ethnology in Mary White Rowlandson's Captivity Narrative* (Madison: University of Wisconsin Press, 1990); and Michelle Burnham, "The Journey Between: Liminality and Dialogism in Mary White Rowlandson's Captivity Narrative," *Early American Literature* 28, no. 1 (1993): 60–75.

125. Hutchinson to Jackson, August 30, 1765. *OED*, s.v. "camlet," "surtout"; Samuel Johnson, *A Dictionary of the English Language*, 2 vols. (London, 1756), vol. 2, s.v. "surtout." Florence M. Montgomery, *Textiles in America, 1650–1870* (New York: W. W. Norton, 1984), 188, and plate D-9 for the sample of camlet used by Mary Alexander to order garter material in 1736 in New York. See the description of men's costume in Barbara Neville Parker and Anne Bolling Wheeler, *John Singleton Copley: American Portraits in Oil, Pastel, and Miniature with Biographical Sketches* (Boston: Museum of Fine Arts, 1938), p. 43, for Nicholas Boylston's 1767 portrait, "His loose blue-green banyan of flowered silk is worn over a yellow & cream waistcoat. His shirt and hose are white. On his shaved head he wears a crimson turban"; p. 44, for his 1773 portrait, "He wears a blue banyan, buff waistcoat, and crimson turban. His slippers are red and his hose are grey."

126. Thomas Hutchinson to Peter Lietch, July 13, 1764, Thomas Hutchinson Letterbooks, Massachusetts, MA, 26:89–90; I am indebted to John W. Tyler for this reference. Johan Huizinga, *Homo Ludens: A Study of the Play Element in Culture* (Boston: Beacon Press, 1955), 77.

127. Quoted in George P. Anderson, "Ebenezer Mackintosh, Stamp Act Rioter and Patriot," CSM *Pub.* 26 (1924–26): 32.

128. Rowlandson, *Sovereignty and Goodness of God*, 37. On the implication of political rape, recall that Bostonians claimed that household searches by Crown customs officers constituted, even in "our bed chambers," being "broke open" and "ravaged."

129. Thomas Hutchinson to Richard Jackson, August 30, 1765, in MA, 26:146–47. On Hutchinson's refined and elite, restrained taste in fashion that almost bordered paradoxically on a republican leveling of emblems of distinction, see the comments in Bailyn, *Ordeal of Thomas Hutchinson*, 20. Bernard to Halifax, August 31, 1765. See the complete listing of objects destroyed or stolen and their value in Hutchinson, "Furniture Destroyed or Carried from My House and Lost the Night of the 26th of August, 1765," in MA, 6 (Colonial, 1724–76): 301–20, reprinted in James K. Hosmer, *The Life of Thomas Hutchinson, Royal Governor of the Province of Massachusetts Bay* (Boston: Houghton Mifflin, 1896), 352–62.

130. Hutchinson to Jackson, August 30, 1765. On the subject of cultural memory, the mob made off with, among other manuscripts, the journal kept by regicide Thomas Goffe when he was in New England between 1660 and 1667 eluding capture by Crown forces for assisting in the execution of Charles I; see Stiles, *A History of Three of the Judges of King Charles I* (Hartford, 1794), 21–24, 29: "the Governor obtained Goffe's manuscript, and himself shewd me, in 1766, one of these little manuscript books . . . with Goffe's other papers, in the Governor's hands, were irrevocably lost when the Governor's house was demolished in the tumults of the Stamp Act, 1765."

131. Bernard to Halifax, August 31, 1765.

132. Ibid.

133. See [Edward Wigglesworth], *A Letter from One in the Country to his Friend in Boston* (Boston, 1720), reprinted in Davis, *Colonial Currency Reprints*, 1:422; *Boston Gazette and Country Journal*, April 26, 1756, quoted in Bailyn, *Ideological Origins of the American Revolution*, 104; and *Peter Oliver's Origin and Progress of the American Revolution: A Tory View*, ed. Douglass Adair and John A. Schultz (Stanford: Stanford University Press, 1967), 65. Even John Adams (*The Works of John Adams*, ed. Charles Francis Adams, 10 vols. [Boston: Little, Brown, 1856], 2:219), uses the phrase "political engine." Bailyn, *Ideological Origins of the American Revolution*, 126, quotes Philadelphia prewar handbills proclaiming that "a corrupt and prostituted ministry are pitting their destructive *machines* against the sacred liberty of the Americans."

134. Quoted in Bailyn, *Ideological Origins of the American Revolution*, 176, from William Hicks, *Considerations upon the Rights of the Colonists to the Privileges of British Subjects* (1766), 1.

135. Quoted in Fernard Braudel, *Capitalism and Material Life, 1400–1800*, trans. Miriam Kochan (New York: Harper and Row, 1975), 327.

136. On the Boston bawdy-house riots, see *Boston Weekly Newsletter*, March 10, 1737, and John Kern, "The Politics of Violence: Colonial American Rebellions, Protests, and Riots, 1676–1747" (Ph.D. diss., University of Wisconsin–Madison, 1976), 207, 222 n. 26.

137. Bernard to Halifax, August 31, 1765.

138. On playful rebellion and wrongfooting, see Anthony D. Buckley, "Playful Rebellion: Social Control and the Framing of Experience in an Ulster Community," *Man*, n.s., 18, no. 2 (June 1983): 383–95; for cruel laughter, see C. J. Sisson, *Lost Plays of Shakespeare's Age* (Cambridge: Cambridge University Press, 1936), 188; dark play is discussed in Richard Schechner, "Playing," *Play and Culture* 1, no. 1 (February 1988): 12–13. On breakthrough and breakout in performance, see Dell Hymes, "Breakthrough into Performance," in *"In Vain I Tried to Tell You": Essays in Native American Ethnopoetics* (Philadelphia: University of Pennsylvania Press, 1981), 81–86, 139.

139. John Cotton, "Purchasing Christ," in Miller and Johnson, *The Puritans*, 1: 327–34; BTR, 7:101 (1772). See E. P. Thompson, "The Moral Economy Reinvented," in *Customs in Common*, 264: "Riots may even be a signal that the *ancien regime* is ending."

CHAPTER FOUR

1. Elizabeth Mankin Kornhauser, "Ralph Earl: The Face of the Young Republic," in *Ralph Earl: The Face of the Young Republic,* ed. Elizabeth Mankin Kornhauser (New Haven: Yale University Press for the Wadsworth Atheneum, 1991), 34–35. All subsequent references to paintings by Earl may be consulted in this catalog.

2. Kornhauser, "Ralph Earl," 39–42. The term "anatomy" here was confirmed when one early-nineteenth-century painter reported that once his sitter posed, "I operated on her at once." Quoted in John Michael Vlach, *Plain Painters: Making Sense of American Folk Art* (Washington, D.C.: Smithsonian Institution Press, 1988), 67.

3. John Barrell, *The Political Theory of Painting from Reynolds to Hazlitt: "The Body of the Public"* (New Haven: Yale University Press, 1986), 69–99; a compressed statement is available in John Barrell, "Sir Joshua Reynolds and the Political Theory of Painting," *Oxford Art Journal* 9, no. 2 (1986): 36–41. See also John Barrell, "Sir Joshua Reynolds and the Englishness of English Art," in *Nation and Narration,* ed. Homi K. Bhabha (New York: Routledge, 1990), 154–76. Contrast this view of painting and republican political theory with that of John Singleton Copley; Paul Staiti, "Character and Class," in *John Singleton Copley in America* (New York: Metropolitan Museum of Art, 1995), 53, terms Copley's portraits of New England merchants "persuasive fictions."

4. George Berkeley, *The Querist* (Dublin, 1735), in *The Works of George Berkeley, Bishop of Cloyne,* ed. A. A. Luce and T. E. Jessup, 9 vols. (London: Thomas Nelson and Sons, 1948–57), 6:119, no. 176. Margaretta M. Lovell, "Reading Portraits: Social Images and Self-Images in Eighteenth-Century American Family Portraits," *Winterthur Portfolio* 22, no. 4 (Winter 1987): 53, 57. See also Roger B. Stein, "Thomas Smith's Self-Portrait: Image/Text as Artifact," *Art Journal* 44 (Winter 1984): 316–27, and John Peacock, "The Politics of Portraiture," in *Culture and Politics in Early Stuart England,* ed. Kevin Sharpe and Peter Lake (Stanford: Stanford University Press, 1993), 199–228.

5. Timothy H. Breen, "The Meaning of 'Likeness': American Portrait Painting in an Eighteenth-Century Consumer Society," *Word and Image* 6, no. 4 (October–December 1990): 338, 327. Breen's approach to portraits is linked to a larger argument concerning the formative impact of commerce and the circulation of imported commodities on American national "imagining" during the eighteenth century; see Timothy H. Breen, "The Empire of Goods: The Anglicization of Colonial America, 1690–1776," *Journal of British Studies* 25, no. 4 (October 1986): 467–99, and Timothy H. Breen, "'Baubles of Britain': The American and Consumer Revolutions of the Eighteenth Century," *Past and Present* 119 (May 1988): 73–104; see also Timothy H. Breen, "The Meaning of Things: Interpreting the Consumer Economy in the Eighteenth Century," in *Consumption and the World of Goods,* ed. John Brewer and Roy Porter (New York: Routledge, 1993), 249–60. Benedict Anderson, *Imagined Communities: Reflections on the Origin and Spread of Nationalism* (London: Verso, 1991), 26–46.

6. J. G. A. Pocock, "Modes of Political and Historical Time in Eighteenth-Century England," in *Studies in Eighteenth-Century Culture,* vol. 5, ed. Ronald C. Rosbottom (Madison: University of Wisconsin Press, 1976), 88, 89; see also J. G. A. Pocock, "Time, Institutions, and Actions: An Essay on Traditions and Their Understanding," in *Politics and Experience: Essays Presented to Professor Michael Oakeshott on the Occasion of His Retirement,* ed. Preston King and B. C. Parekh (Cambridge: Cambridge University Press, 1968), 209–38. On the function of portraits in marking absence, see Bushrod Washington to Hannah Bushrod Washington, April 12, 1783: "the principal End [of a portrait], is to give an absent friend, or posterity, an idea of a face whi[ch] they had never seen" (in Stephen E. Patrick, "'I have at Length Determined to Have my Picture Taken': An Eighteenth-Century Young Man's Thoughts about his Portrait by Henry Benbridge," *American Art Journal* 22, no. 4 (Winter 1990): 79).

7. Homi K. Bhabha, "Introduction: Narrating the Nation," in *Nation and Narration,* 4. In stressing what he terms "the nation's ambivalent emergence" from transient historical circumstances and its narration in the "from time immemorial" mythology of claimed legitimacy, Bhabha could be read

alongside Eric Hobsbawm, "Introduction: Inventing Traditions," in *The Invention of Tradition*, ed. Eric Hobsbawm and Terence Ranger (New York: Cambridge University Press, 1983), 10–14. On images as visual texts, see Raphael Samuel, "Art, Politics, and Ideology: Editorial Introduction," *History Workshop* 6 (Autumn 1978): 101–6.

8. On the Chapin chairs, see Kornhauser, "Catalog," in Kornhauser, *Ralph Earl*, 181. On Eliphalet Chapin (1741–1807), see also Nancy E. Richards, "Furniture of the Lower Connecticut River Valley: The Hartford Area, 1785–1810," *Winterthur Portfolio* 4 (1968): 1–26; Philip Zea, "Furniture," in *The Great River: Art and Society of the Connecticut Valley, 1635–1820*, ed. William N. Hosley Jr. and Gerald W. R. Ward (Hartford: Wadsworth Atheneum, 1985), 188–89, 228–30, nos. 109, 110; and Robert F. Trent and Joseph Leonetti, "New Information about Chapin Chairs," *Antiques* 127, no. 5 (May 1986): 1082–95. Aileen Ribeiro, "Notes on Costume," in Kornhauser, "Catalog," 181.

9. William Strickland, *Journal of a Tour in the United States of America, 1794–1795*, ed. J. E. Strickland (New York: New-York Historical Society, 1971), 77–78 (entry of October 28, 1794). On the early advance of consumer consciousness and imported objects into the Connecticut River valley, see Kevin M. Sweeney, "Furniture and the Domestic Environment in Wethersfield, Connecticut, 1636–1800," in *Material Life in America, 1600–1860*, ed. Robert Blair St. George (Boston: Northeastern University Press, 1988), 261–90.

10. Samuel Cooper to Thomas Pownall, October 12, 1770, in "Letters of Samuel Cooper to Thomas Pownall, 1769–1777," ed. Frederick Tuckerman, *American Historical Review* 8, no. 2 (January 1903): 321.

11. Hannah Arendt, *The Human Condition* (Chicago: University of Chicago Press, 1958), 33, 35. See also Nathan Gardels, "Two Concepts of Nationalism: An Interview with Isaiah Berlin," *New York Review of Books*, November 21, 1991, 19–23, esp. 19, where Berlin observes that for many cultures nationalism involves "the process of recovering their submerged pasts stifled by imperialism."

12. J. G. A. Pocock, *Virtue, Commerce, and History: Essays on Political Thought and History, Chiefly in the Eighteenth Century* (New York: Cambridge University Press, 1985), 41–42.

13. Gordon S. Wood, *Creation of the American Republic, 1776–1787* (Chapel Hill: University of North Carolina Press, 1969), 8, 65 ("fragile beauty"). On republicanism as an ideology with its own language and forms of symbolic action (among which I would include portraits) that assume moral dimensions, see Robert E. Shalhope, "Toward a Republican Synthesis: The Emergence of an Understanding of Republicanism in American Historiography," *WMQ*, 3d ser., 21, no. 1 (January 1972): 51, 78, 91.

14. Quoted in Wood, *Creation of the American Republic*, 67.

15. Michael Zuckerman, "A Different Thermidor: The Revolution beyond the American Revolution," in *The Transformation of Early American History: Society, Authority, and Ideology*, ed. James A. Henretta, Michael Kammen, and Stanley N. Katz (New York: Knopf, 1991), 181.

16. Peter K. Kafer, "The Making of Timothy Dwight: A Connecticut Morality Tale," *WMQ*, 3d ser., 47, no. 2 (April 1990): 189–209. Although Kafer focuses on Dwight's early career in the 1770s, he admits that Dwight later became a "mercantile capitalist."

17. Dwight, *Travels*, 1:138–39, 223. On Dwight, see the comments of Solomon, introduction to ibid., 1:xxii: "A first-generation Federalist, he believed in the efficacy of the republican form of government with the people participating under the leadership of the wise and well-to-do men of property."

18. Joyce O. Appleby, "Republicanism in Old and New Contexts," in *Liberalism and Republicanism in the Historical Imagination* (Cambridge: Harvard University Press, 1992), 323. Paine is quoted in Wood, *Creation of the American Republic*, 69–70.

19. Pocock, *Virtue, Commerce, and History*, 48–49, 95.

20. Quoted from Edmund Burke, *Letters on a Regicide Peace* (London, 1796), in Pocock, *Virtue, Commerce, and History*, 49.

21. Dwight, *Travels*, 1:220–21.

22. John Adams, "Review of the Propositions for Amending the Constitution submitted by Mr. Hillhouse to the Senate of the United States, in 1808," in *The Works of John Adams*, ed. Charles Francis Adams, 10 vols. (Boston: Little, Brown, 1856), 6:530. On Dwight's almost inscrutable subtlety in repre-

senting the patrician class's ambiguous role in republican Connecticut, see Richard L. Bushman, "Portraiture and Society in Late Eighteenth-Century Connecticut," in Kornhauser, *Ralph Earl*, 81–83.

23. Stephen P. McGrath, "Connecticut's Tory Towns: The Loyalty Struggle in Newtown, Redding, and Ridgefield, 1774–1783," *Connecticut Historical Society Bulletin* 44, no. 3 (July 1977): 88. On the heterogeneity of political life in postrevolutionary Massachusetts that I see as symptomatic for New England in general, see John L. Brooke, "To the Quiet of the People: Revolutionary Settlements and Civil Unrest in Western Massachusetts, 1774–1789," *WMQ*, 3d ser., 46, no. 3 (July 1989): 450–62.

24. On Wethersfield houses, I am indebted to Dionne Longley, "'Mansions of Comfort and Independence': Wethersfield's Role in Architecture, 1750–1800," internship paper for the Webb-Deane-Stevens Museum, 1981, 14–20, and to Kevin M. Sweeney for sending me a copy. See also Kevin M. Sweeney, "Mansion People: Kinship, Class, and Architecture in Western Massachusetts in the Mid-Eighteenth Century," *Winterthur Portfolio* 19, no. 4 (Winter 1984): 231–56. Sweeney's work is particularly valuable for its correlation of real property, tax lists, and social position (occupation) to the occurrence of Georgian houses.

25. Thomas Anburey, *Travels through the Interior Parts of America*, ed. William Harding Carter, 2 vols. (Boston: Houghton Mifflin, 1923), 2:152–53; *Diary and Autobiography of John Adams*, ed. Lyman H. Butterfield, 4 vols. (Cambridge: Harvard University Press, 1961), 2:31. For an expanded discussion of the Georgian house in the theater of dominance and resistance in eighteenth-century Connecticut, see Robert Blair St. George, "Artifacts of Regional Consciousness in the Connecticut River Valley, 1700–1780," in St. George, *Material Life in America*, 335–56.

26. Anburey, *Travels through the Interior Parts of America*, 2:152; the tailor: Capt. Nathaniel Talcott of Glastonbury; the joiner: Judah Woodruff of Farmington. Woodruff built his house in 1762; see Amelia F. Miller, *Connecticut River Valley Doorways: An Eighteenth-Century Flowering* (Boston: Boston University Press for the Dublin Seminar for New England Folklife, 1983), 24 (no. 7), 129–30. For comparisons of multifamily residences and the English use of unit-system houses for the purpose of guaranteeing persistence in systems of partible inheritance (or gavelkind), see Robert Machin, "The Unit System: Some Historical Explanations," *Archaeological Journal* 132 (1975): 187–94.

27. Bruce C. Daniels, *The Connecticut Town: Growth and Development, 1635–1790* (Middletown, Conn.: Wesleyan University Press, 1979), 34, 144–79, 190–92.

28. Zephaniah Swift, *A System of the Laws of the State of Connecticut*, 2 vols. (Windham, Conn., 1795), 1:55–56. On anti-Federalists and the Connecticut context of critique, see Jackson Turner Main, *The Anti-Federalists: Critics of the Constitution, 1781–1788* (Chapel Hill: University of North Carolina Press for the Institute of Early American History and Culture, 1961), 5, 51–54; see also Chilton Williamson, "The Connecticut Property Test and the East Guilford Votes: 1800," *Connecticut Historical Society Bulletin* 19 (1954): 101–4.

29. Jared Eliot, *Essays upon Field Husbandry in New England and Other Papers, 1748–1762*, ed. Harry J. Carman and Rexford G. Tugwell (New York: AMS Press, 1967), 17; *Litchfield Monitor* and John Deland, as quoted in Richard S. Purcell, *Connecticut in Transition, 1775–1818* (Middletown, Conn.: Wesleyan University Press, 1963), 116, 156. Leland's own critique of the mythology of "charter-constitution continuity" maintained that such a mythology lived at the expense of the disenfranchisement of the citizenry: "The people of Connecticut have never been asked, by those in authority, what form of government they would choose; nor in fact, whether they would have any form at all. For want of a specific constitution, the rulers run without bridle or bit, or anything to draw them up to the ring-bolt. Should the legislature make a law, to perpetuate themselves in office for life; this law would immediately become part of their constitution; and who would call them to account for it?" (Quoted in Purcell, *Connecticut in Transition*, 157). Fisher Ames to Thomas Dwight, January 25, 1804, in *Works of Fisher Ames, With a Selection from his Speeches and Correspondence*, ed. Seth Ames, 2 vols. (Boston: Little, Brown, 1854), 1:337. During the election of 1800 Federalist antipathy ran so high among Connecticut's standing order that they insisted on linking Jeffersonian republicanism with the Jacobin party during the French Revolution; Hartford's Thomas Robbins confided his anti-Jeffersonianism to his diary,

writing, "Blessed be God that all things are in his hands, and may he avert such an evil from this country, for his Name's sake. I do not believe that the Most High will permit a howling atheist to sit at the head of this nation" (quoted in Purcell, *Connecticut in Transition*, 198).

30. Appleby, "Republicanism in Old and New Contexts," 336–337, 323.

31. Purcell, *Connecticut in Transition*, 68 n. 32. See also *Connecticut Gazette*, September 6, 1792: "The trade and manufactures of this state, (says a correspondent,) have long struggled under the want of a capital proportioned to the industry and enterprise of its citizens;—that want may now be supplied by means of the banks established at New London and Hartford. Every useful occupation and every industrious citizen may be assisted with money, as circumstances may require and justify: but in order to carry the means of the bank into the fullest effect, their bills must circulate among all ranks of people as freely as money: it behooves, therefore, every well wisher to the prosperity of the community, to give credit to the notes of the bank. Although trade more immediately, and in a more considerable degree, be benefited by these institutions, yet every other branch of business will come in for a proportionable share; a flourishing commerce dispenses blessings to all within the sphere of its operations, and adds to the value of the landed interests, as well as the articles in which it principally deals. The notes of the banks will be found more convenient for a circulating medium, and may be kept by the owners in greater safety, than hard money, and none need be apprehensive of any deception in them, as the promise on the face of them will be carefully and punctually filled" (Fisher Ames to Thomas Dwight, January 15, 1804, in *Works of Fisher Ames*, 1:337).

32. Purcell, *Connecticut in Transition*, 31–32, 45, 196–97. An important locus of middle-class entrenchment against the standing order remained Freemasonry, a lodge that was established in Connecticut in 1789. See the convincing argument relating antiorthodox religious persuasion and Masonic membership in Dorothy Anne Lipson, *Freemasonry in Federalist Connecticut* (Princeton: Princeton University Press, 1977), 62–85. On New Haven's early tolerationist cell, see James H. Trumbull, "Sons of Liberty in 1755," *New Englander* 35 (1876): 299–313. On critiques of Dwight, see Alan V. Briceland, "The Philadelphia Aurora, the New England Illuminati, and the Election of 1800," *Pennsylvania Magazine of History and Biography* 100, no. 1 (January 1976): 12–13.

33. Dwight, *Travels*, 1:139. Probate inventories are from the following sources: Danbury Probate District, docket no. 866 (Booth), taken January 12, 1794, total estate valued of £386.1.7; New Haven Probate District, docket no. 10755 (Trowbridge), taken October 6, 1806, total estate value of $6,527.05; and New Haven Probate District, docket no. 4737 (Houghton), proven in court March 1, 1813, total estate value of $7,693.77; all in Connecticut State Archives, Hartford.

34. James P. Walsh, "'Mechanics and Citizens': The Connecticut Artisan Protest of 1792," *WMQ*, 3d ser., 42, no. 1 (January 1985): 69.

35. Walter Brewster, "Common Reason," *Norwich Packet*, September 27, 1792, and "A Mechanic, not yet a Freeman," *Norwich Packet*, September 8, 1792.

36. *BTR*, 5:239.

37. Kevin M. Sweeney, "Furniture and Furniture Making in Mid-Eighteenth-Century Wethersfield, Connecticut," *Antiques* 125, no. 5 (May 1984): 1156–57. For references to a Boston goldsmith named Theophilus Barrell working in New London (1739), and Boston ship carpenter Jonathan Maxwell working at Groton ferry (1743), see *Diary of Joshua Hempstead of New London, Connecticut, Covering a Period of Forty-seven Years from September, 1711, to November, 1758* (New London: New London County Historical Society, 1901), 422 (entry of April 26, 1743).

38. Justin Hobart Jr. to Mary Hobart, April 21, 1800, quoted in Edward S. Cooke Jr., *Fiddlebacks and Crooked-backs: Elijah Booth and Other Joiners in Newtown and Woodbury, 1750–1820* (Waterbury, Conn.: Mattatuck Historical Society, 1982), 22 (emphasis added).

39. Quoted in Robert A. Gross, *The Minutemen and Their World* (New York: Hill and Wang, 1976), 27; see also Richard H. Randall Jr. and Martha McElman, "Ebenezer Hartshorne, Cabinetmaker," *Antiques* 87, no. 1 (January 1965): 79.

40. Jonathan Prude, *The Coming of Industrial Order: Town and Factory Life in Rural Massachusetts*

(New York: Cambridge University Press, 1983), 69. On artisan communities in Lynn and Newark from about 1790 to 1820, see Alan Dawley, *Class and Community: The Industrial Revolution in Lynn* (Cambridge: Harvard University Press, 1976), 42–72, and Susan E. Hirsch, *Roots of the American Working Class: The Industrialization of Crafts in Newark, 1800–1860* (Philadelphia: University of Pennsylvania Press, 1978).

41. On urban entrepreneurs and merchants exploiting rural labor, see (for France) William M. Reddy, "The Textile Trade and the Language of the Crowd at Rouen, 1752–1871," *Past and Present* 74 (1977): 67, and (for England) J. H. Marshall, "Capitalism and the Decline of the English Guilds," *Cambridge Historical Journal* 3 (1929): 29. Dawley, *Class and Community*, 20–22. On pieceworking in the late-eighteenth-century woodworking trades, see Margaret Burke Clunie, "Joseph True and the Piecework System in Salem," *Antiques* 111, no. 5 (May 1977): 1006–13. On the irregular persistence of outwork and the household mode of production well into the nineteenth century, see Christopher Clark, "Household Economy, Market Exchange, and the Rise of Capitalism in the Connecticut River Valley, 1800–1860," *Journal of Social History* 13, no. 2 (Winter 1979): 169–90.

42. The text of the Blacksmiths' Convention in Worcester is reprinted in William Lincoln, *History of Worcester, Massachusetts, From Its Earliest Settlement to September, 1836* (Worcester: Moses D. Phillips and Co., 1837), 102–3.

43. "The May Manuscript Petition," quoted in Walsh, "'Mechanics and Citizens,'" 88.

44. Quoted in Edward S. Cooke, *Making Furniture in Preindustrial America: The Social Economy of Newtown and Woodbury, Connecticut* (Baltimore: Johns Hopkins University Press, 1996), 25.

45. Quoted in Irving W. Lyon, *Colonial Furniture of New England: A Study of the Domestic Furniture in Use in the Seventeenth and Eighteenth Centuries* (Boston: Houghton Mifflin, 1925), 267.

46. On the Timothy Loomis III (1724–86) ledger and his price lists for 1759 and 1760, see William N. Hosley Jr., "Timothy Loomis and the Economy of Joinery in Windsor, Connecticut, 1740–1786," in *Perspectives on American Furniture*, ed. Gerald W. R. Ward (New York: W. W. Norton, 1988), 134, 150 (app. 1).

47. The Hartshorne memorial is cited in John Warner Barber, *Historical Collections of Connecticut* (New Haven: printed by the author, 1836), 505.

48. Daniel Foster, *Consolation in Adversity and Hope in Death. A Sermon Preached on the Death of Jedutha Baldwin* (Worcester, Mass., 1789), 12. Dwight, *Travels*, 1:195.

49. On allegory, see Walter J. Ong, "From Allegory to Diagram in the Renaissance Mind: A Study in the Significance of the Allegorical Tradition," *Journal of Aesthetics and Art Criticism* 17 (1959): 423–40. For approaches to nostalgia, see Lawrence Larner, *The Uses of Nostalgia: Studies in Pastoral Poetry* (London: Chatto & Windus, 1972), 41–62 ("On Nostalgia"), 197–212 ("The Loss of Paradise"), 228–44 ("The Proper Place of Nostalgia"); and Isaac Cramnick, *Bolingbroke and His Circle: The Politics of Nostalgia in the Age of Walpole* (Cambridge: Harvard University Press, 1968).

50. Homi K. Bhabha, "DissemiNation: Time, Narrative, and the Margins of the Modern World," in Bhabha, *Nation and Narration*, 298. See also Sigmund Freud, "The Uncanny" (1919), in Freud, *Studies in Parapsychology* (New York: Macmillan, 1963), 19–60. Ernest Renan, "What Is a Nation?" trans. Martin Thom, in Bhabha, *Nation and Narration*, 11.

51. On the seventeenth-century origins of the New Haven gridded plan, see John Archer, "Puritan Town Planning in New Haven," *Journal of the Society of Architectural Historians* 34, no. 1 (March 1975): 140–49. It was no accident that the image of urban order and deference was linked to the treatment of landscape as political allegory; perhaps the earliest essay to appear in the new nation on landscape painting, "Thoughts on American Genius," appeared in the *New Haven Gazette* and *Connecticut Magazine* in February 1787. See William G. Gerdts, "American Landscape Painting: Critical Judgments, 1730–1845," *American Art Journal* 17, no. 1 (Winter 1985): 29–31.

52. Strickland, *Journal of a Tour in the United States,* 197 (entry of November 2, 1794). Strickland was, of course, searching for the "authentic" New England, probably in an effort to find an uncorrupted English countryside and social milieu. On November 3 (the next day) he wrote upon leaving Hart-

ford and choosing not to take the normal post road, "Wishing to see as much of the country and manners of the people as possible, where the least affected by the intercourse of travellers" (204). On Friday, October 31, 1794, traveling along the Connecticut River between Northampton and Springfield, Strickland wrote, "The country here and every thing in it puts on the most perfect resemblance of the finest parts of England; the fields are dotted over with trees, and the rows of apple trees in them, many of which are grown to an unusual size, and under all of which is the finest meadow, add variety and beauty to the scene. The Houses have the appearance of those in England, the modern ones resembling those of later date, while some of an earlier period interspersed among them, resembling those of the last century, and have generally a few large trees growing before or near them. . . . The people in the plainness of their manners resemble those at home of a similar rank. . . . You every where discern the blessed effects of order, good government, comfort, plenty, content and a happy state of society."

53. Edward Shils, "Deference," in his *The Constitution of Society* (Chicago: University of Chicago Press, 1982), 169.

54. Strickland, *Journal of a Tour in the United States*, 197 (entry of November 2, 1794). For another example of the retention of the high symbolic center, see de Chastellux's description of Litchfield: "Litchfield, or the *Meetinghouse* of Litchfield, is situated on a large plain more elevated than the surrounding heights; about fifty houses pretty near each other, with a large square, or rather area, in the middle, announces the progress of this town, which is already the county town" (Marquis de Chastellux, *Travels in North America, in the Years 1780–81–82* [New York, 1827; reprint, New York: Augustus M. Kelley, 1970], 35–36). The "elevated" center of these Connecticut towns suggests an important connection between the panopticon and nationalism, and through the panopticon the collection, which affords the illusion of omniscient political sovereignty as well. Henry Wansey, for example, recorded his visit to Yale in 1794, where, among other sites, he records viewing a "cabinet of curiosities, with which I was much entertained; viz. Indian helmets, curiously woven with feathers; warlike dresses and belts of Wampum. Two large teeth of the Mammoth, found on the banks of the Ohio, in the shape of human cheek teeth; I measured them with my handkerchief, and applied it to a foot rule, and found their dimensions to be twenty-two inches round horizontally, and twenty inches long when I measured longitudinally, over the top and between the roots. The skins of two beautifully spotted snakes, eighteen feet long, from South America; an Indian calumet or pipe of peace; a young alligator preserved in spirits; instruments of war and of fishing, from Nootka Sound. Cloth made of a Otaheite. A curious frog, with a long tail like a lizard. Several pieces of asbestos found in that neighbourhood. But what particularly struck me, was a snake with two distinct heads" (*Henry Wansey and his American Journal, 1794*, ed. David John Jeremy, Memoirs of the American Philosophical Society no. 82 [Philadelphia: American Philosophical Society, 1970], 74).

55. Anderson, *Imagined Communities*, 19.

56. Nathaniel Hawthorne, "Sights from a Steeple," in *Twice-Told Tales* (London: J. M. Dent, 1961), 138–39. The aesthetic of distant observation has origins in early-eighteenth-century England; see Daniel Defoe, *A Tour thro' the Whole Island of Great Britain*, 4 vols. (London, 1724–26), 1:24. Referring to buildings, Defoe wrote: "There is a beauty of these things at a distance, taking them en passant, and in perspective which few people value, and fewer understand."

57. Dwight, *Travels*, 1:162, 222. See the observation of Henry Wansey, on the road to Connecticut: "The houses which we passed in the woods are generally built after the following manner: a framed work of timber, weather boarded and roofed with shingles, two story high, besides the attick; a good cellar beneath with three steps up into the house, two windows on each side the door, five in the next story, all sashed, and the whole neatly painted; some of a free stone colour, others white with green doors and window shutters" (from Jeremy, *Henry Wansey and His American Journal*, 74).

58. Quoted in Barber, *Historical Collections of Connecticut*, 498.

59. *Hartford Courant*, June 12, 1797, quoted in Barber, *Historical Collections of Connecticut*, 58.

60. Karen Halttunen, "Early American Murder Narratives," in *The Power of Culture*, ed. T. J. Jackson Lears and Richard W. Fox (Chicago: University of Chicago Press, 1993), 82–83; Halttunen quotes from

A Narrative of the Life of William Beadle (Hartford, 1783), 14. On portrait painting as a related form of mimetic violence, see Oliver Wendell Holmes, "Sun-Painting and Sun-Sculpture," *Atlantic Monthly* 8 (July 1861): 14; he could "remember how few painted portraits really give their subjects. Recollect those wandering Thugs of Art whose murderous doings with the brush used frequently to involve whole families."

61. Dwight, *Travels,* 1:272–73. See also his comment on order in Wethersfield: "At the same time, they are ordinarily fashioned with a degree of neatness and elegance which is unrivaled" (1:163).

62. Jedidiah Morse, *The American Geography* (Elizabethtown, N.J., 1789; reprint, New York: Arno Press, 1970), v. On Morse and cartographic nationalism, I am indebted to Jochen Weirich, "Mapping Private and Global Spaces: Images of the Standing Order in the Early Republic," paper for American Studies 502 "American Vernacular Architecture" seminar, College of William and Mary, fall 1993.

63. Cotton Mather, "Triparadisus," ca. 1720 mss., octavo vol. 49, f. 1, Mather Family Papers, 1613–1819, American Antiquarian Society, Worcester, Mass. *The Literary Diary of Ezra Stiles,* ed. Franklin Bowditch Dexter (New York: Charles Scribner's Sons, 1901), 85 (entry of January 21, 1771). See also J. B. Harley, "Maps, Knowledge, and Power," in *The Iconography of Landscape,* ed. Denis Cosgrove and Stephen Daniels (Cambridge: Cambridge University Press, 1988), 277–79; Roy Porter, "The Terraqueous Globe," in *The Ferment of Knowledge,* ed. G. S. Rousseau and Roy Porter (Cambridge: Cambridge University Press, 1989), 9–10; and Everett C. Wilkie Jr., "Jonathan Carver, Oliver Wolcott, and Jedidiah Morse's *American Geography.*" *Connecticut Historical Society Bulletin* 54, nos. 3–4 (Summer–Fall 1989): 249–55.

64. On poverty in eighteenth-century Natick, see Daniel Mandell, "'To Live More Like My Christian English Neighbors': Natick Indians in the Eighteenth Century," *WMQ,* 3d ser., 46, no. 4 (October 1991): 552–59. Eleazer Wheelock to George Whitefield, July 4, 1761, quoted in Laura J. Murray, "What Did Christianity Do for Joseph Johnson?" in *Possible Pasts: Becoming Colonial in Early America,* ed. Robert Blair St. George (Ithaca, N.Y.: Cornell University Press, forthcoming). Barber, *Historical Collections of Connecticut,* 546.

65. On Separate Baptist and New Light itinerants' impact on the Pequot, see William S. Simmons and Cheryl L. Simmons, "Joseph Fish and the Narragansett," in *Old Light on Separate Ways: The Narragansett Diary of Joseph Fish, 1765–1776* (Hanover, N.H.: University Press of New England, 1982), xxiii–xxiv. See also William S. Simmons, "The Great Awakening and Indian Conversion in Southern New England," in *Papers of the Tenth Algonquian Conference,* ed. William Cowan (Ottawa: Carlton University Press, 1979), 25–36.

66. Murray, "What Did Christianity Do for Joseph Johnson?" See also Laura J. Murray, "'Pray Sir, Consider a Litle': Rituals of Subordination and Strategies of Resistance in the Letters of Hezekiah Calvin and David Fowler to Eleazar Wheelock, 1764–1768," *Studies in American Indian Literature* 4, nos. 2–3 (Summer–Fall 1992): 48–74. Compare the subversive and resistant styles of self-abasement with those in Keith Basso, *Portraits of the Whiteman: Linguistic Play and Cultural Humor among the Western Apache* (New York: Cambridge University Press, 1979).

67. On carding machines and Denny's involvement in local textile production, see John L. Brooke, *The Heart of the Commonwealth: Society and Political Culture in Worcester County, Massachusetts, 1713–1861* (New York: Cambridge University Press, 1989), 305. Anna Henshaw (1778–1854), manuscript collection, Worcester Art Museum, quoted in Kornhauser, "Catalog," 236.

68. *Massachusetts Yeoman and Worcester Saturday Journal and Advertiser,* October 25, 1825. I am indebted to Nora Pat Small for this reference.

69. Dwight, *Travels,* 1:238–39.

70. See Joseph S. Wood, "Village and Community in Colonial New England," in St. George, *Material Life in America,* 159–70. Chastellux, *Travels in North America,* 24–25. Barber, *Historical Collections of Connecticut,* 343 (emphasis added).

71. Dwight, *Travels,* 1:236–37.

72. Ibid., 1:236; 1:158.

73. Barber, *Historical Collections of Connecticut*, 92.

74. Isaiah Berlin, quoted in Gardels, "Two Concepts of Nationalism," 22: "Variety is a new virtue, brought to us by the Romantic movement, of which Herder and Vico, whom I regard as the *prophets of variety*, were an important part" (emphasis added). On its use as an aesthetic category, see Nina Fletcher Little, *American Decorative Wall Painting, 1700–1850* (New York: E. P. Dutton, 1989), 28, quoting *Art's Treasury of Rarities: and Curious Inventions* (owned by 1815 in New England); under heading "How to Colour Buildings" was advice to landscape artists: "In colouring Buildings, you must use much Variety, the better to set them off; yet not so as they may appear extravagantly adorned, or contrary to the like of this kind." On temporality, see David Carroll, *The Subject in Question: The Languages of Theory and the Strategies of Fiction* (Chicago: University of Chicago Press, 1982), 119–26, especially building on Braudel and Foucault, and 132–36 on novels; Johannes Fabian, *Time and the Other: How Anthropology Makes Its Object* (New York: Columbia University Press, 1983); and the essays gathered in *Chronotopes: The Construction of Time*, ed. John Bender and David E. Wellbery (Stanford: Stanford University Press, 1991).

75. Anderson, *Imagined Communities*, 24. On Morse's family background, see Joseph Phillips, *Jedidiah Morse and New England Congregationalism* (New Brunswick, N.J.: Rutgers University Press, 1983), 10–23 and passim. For historically grounded critical treatments of time, space, and society, see Louis T. Milic, "The Metaphor of Time as Space," in *Probability, Time, and Space in Eighteenth-Century Literature*, ed. Paula R. Backscheider (New York: AMS Press, 1979), 249–58, and Alun Howkins and C. Ian Dyck, "'The Time's Alteration': Popular Ballads, Rural Radicalism, and William Cobbett," *History Workshop* 23 (Spring 1987): 21–38. For other approaches, see Nancy D. Munn, "The Cultural Anthropology of Time: A Critical Essay," *Annual Review of Anthropology* 21 (1992): 93–123, and Gilles Provonost, *The Sociology of Time*, special issue of *Current Sociology* 37, no. 3 (Winter 1989), esp. "Time and Social Class," 63–73.

76. On Sterne's use of the "time-shift" technique, see Adam A. Mendilow, *Time and the Novel* (New York: Humanities Press, 1952), 189–99; see also Viktor Shklovsky, "A Parodying Novel: Sterne's *Tristram Shandy*," in *Laurence Sterne: A Collection of Critical Essays*, ed. John Traugott (Englewood Cliffs, N.J.: Prentice-Hall, 1968), 66–89, and Carroll, *Subject in Question*, 119–21. On Trumbull's *M'Fingal* and Sterne, see Victor E. Gimmestad, *John Trumbull* (New York: Twayne, 1974), 17–18, 129–33. On *The Anarchiad*, Dr. Hopkins wrote (quoting from Barber, *Historical Collections of Connecticut*, 50): "It was a mock critical account of a pretended ancient epic poem, interspersed with a number of extracts from the supposed work. By a fable contrived with some ingenuity, this poem is represented as known to the ancients, and read and imitated by some of the most popular modern poets. By this supposition, the utmost license of parody and imitation is obtained, and by the usual poetical machinery of episodes, visions and prophecies, the scene is shifted backwards and forwards, from one country to another, from earth to heaven, and from ancient to modern times. This plan is filled up with great spirit; the humorous is indeed much better than the serious part, but both have merit, and some of the parodies are extremely happy. The political views of the authors were to support those designs which were then forming for an efficient federal Constitution." See also Leon Howard, *The Connecticut Wits* (Chicago: University of Chicago Press, 1943), and Emory Elliott, *Revolutionary Writers: Literature and Authority in the New Republic, 1725–1810* (New York, 1982). The literati in Connecticut included many of Earl's sitters; in New Milford in 1796, for example, all of his sitters were on a list of fifty-eight members of the Union Library; see Samuel Orcutt, *History of the Towns of New Milford and Bridgewater, Connecticut, 1703–1882* (Hartford: Case, Lockwood and Brainard, 1882), 188.

77. Quoted in Barber, *Connecticut Historical Collections*, 63 n.

78. Strickland, *Journal of a Tour in the United States*, 205.

79. Dwight, *Travels*, 1:193; Treadwell quoted in George S. Roberts, *River Towns of the Connecticut River Valley* (Schenectady, N.Y.: Robson and Ades, 1906), 185.

80. *The Diary of Julia Cowles: A Connecticut Record, 1797–1803*, ed. Laura Hadley Moseley (New Haven: Yale University Press, 1931), 25 (entry of June 12, 1799).

81. Strickland, *Journal of a Tour through the United States*, 203 (emphasis added). Note: Jeremiah Wadsworth was at this point a representative to Congress.

82. Bhabha, "DissemiNation," 295.

83. Dwight, "Greenfield Hill," in *The Major Poems of Timothy Dwight (1752–1817)*, ed. William J. Mc-Taggart and William K. Bottorf (Gainesville: University of Florida Press, 1969), 300–302.

84. Smith and criticism of Paine (from James Chalmers, *Plain Truth*) are quoted in Wood, *Creation of the Republic*, 95, 120 n.

85. On Malbone and Trinity Church, Brooklyn, Connecticut, see Donald R. Friary, "The Architecture of the Anglican Church in the Northern American Colonies: A Study of Religious, Social, and Cultural Expression," 4 vols. (Ph.D. diss., University of Pennsylvania, 1971), 2:632.

86. Dwight, *Travels*, 1:169. On Bulfinch and his Connecticut buildings, see Harold Kirker, *The Architecture of Charles Bulfinch* (Cambridge: Harvard University Press, 1969), 54–65. On the availability and circulation of architectural pattern books in early national Connecticut, see William M. Hosley Jr., "Architecture," in Hosley and Ward, *The Great River*, 67–68. On the Litchfield courthouse, see William Lamson Warren, "William Sprats and His Civil and Ecclesiastical Architecture in New England," *OTNE* 44, no. 3 (January–March 1954): 66–70.

87. On Hayden's architectural books and their probable authors, see Hosley, "Architecture," 70–71 n. 34.

88. Rodney C. Loehr, "Self-Sufficiency on the Farm," *Agricultural History* 26 (1952): 39.

89. On this structure and an additional "two-thirds" example (a house with one wing and dependency), see Little, *American Decorative Wall Painting*, plate IV, fig. 112.

90. *Massachusetts Magazine* 4 (November 1792); for other gardens similar to Gill's, see Abbott Lowell Cummings, "Eighteenth-Century New England Garden Designs: The Pictorial Evidence," in *British and American Gardens in the Eighteenth Century*, ed. Robert P. Maccubbin and Peter Martin (Williamsburg: Colonial Williamsburg Foundation, 1984), 130–35. Dwight, *Travels*, 1:273.

91. Anburey, *Travels through the Interior Parts of America*, 2:520.

92. Jeremy, *Henry Wansey and His American Journal*, 66. The prevalence of log dwellings in Connecticut at the time of the 1798 Direct Tax is suggested in Bushman, "Portraiture and Society," 71; a specific example is described in J. Frederick Kelly, "A Seventeenth-Century Connecticut Log House," *OTNE* 31, no. 2 (October 1940): 29–46. On the "Oyster Huts on Milford Point," see Barber, *Historical Collections of Connecticut*, 238; for an earlier description of a "hovel" with log walls and a roof thatched with hay, sedge, and "rushes," see *Diary of Joshua Hempstead*, 355, 357, 360.

93. Chastellux, *Travels in North America*, 35.

94. *Journal of Madam Knight* (Boston: David Godine, 1972), 13; *The Massachusetts Tax Valuation List of 1771*, ed. Bettye Hobbs Pruitt (Boston: G. K. Hall, 1978), 796–97.

95. Elias Canetti, "The Regulation of Time," in his *Crowds and Power*, trans. Carol Stewart (New York: Viking Press, 1962), 397. John Berger, "Painting and Time" (1979), in *The Sense of Sight: Writings by John Berger*, ed. Lloyd Spencer (New York: Pantheon, 1985), 209–10; see also George Kubler, "Time's Perfection and Colonial Art," in *Spanish, French, and English Traditions in the Colonial Silver of North America* (Charlottesville: University Press of Virginia, 1969), 7–12.

96. John Vanderlyn to John Vanderlyn Jr., September 9, 1825, in Barbara C. Holdridge and Lawrence B. Holdridge, *Ammi Phillips: Portrait Painter, 1788–1865* (New York: Museum of American Folk Art, 1968), 14; *Litchfield Weekly Monitor*, May 18, 1796, quoted in "The Artist in the Eighteenth Century: Four Notices," in *American Art: Readings from the Colonial Era to the Present*, ed. Harold Spencer (New York: Charles Scribner's Sons, 1980), 22. On indictments of itinerant painters as able entrepreneurs at best and outright frauds at worst, see Vlach, *Plain Painters*, 55–69. Stephen H. Kornhauser, "Ralph Earl's Working Methods and Materials," in Kornhauser, *Ralph Earl*, 90. *The Diary of a Country Parson: The Reverend John Woodforde*, ed. John Beresford, 4 vols. (London: Humphrey Milford, Oxford University Press, 1924–31), 1 (1758–1781): 163 (entry of June 13, 1775). For two studies that explore the connections between portrait painters, the growth of rural capitalism, and the stylistic problem of "plain

painting," see David Jaffee, "One of the Primitive Sort: Portrait Makers of the Rural North, 1760–1860," in *The Countryside in the Age of Capitalist Transformation,* ed. Steven Hahn and Jonathan Prude (Chapel Hill: University of North Carolina Press, 1985), 103–40, and Charles Bergengren, "'Finished to the Utmost Nicety': Plain Portraits in America, 1760–1860," in *Folk Art and Art Worlds,* ed. John Michael Vlach and Simon J. Bronner (Ann Arbor: UMI Research Press, 1986), 85–122.

97. Mary Breed to Mason Fitch Cogswell, February 18, 1795, Mason Fitch Cogswell Papers, Connecticut Historical Society, Hartford. *The Journal of Esther Edwards Burr, 1754–1757,* ed. Carol F. Karlsen and Laurie Crumpacker (New Haven: Yale University Press, 1984), 79, 81.

98. John Singleton Copley to Henry Pelham, September 2, 1774, in *Letters and Papers of John Singleton Copley and Henry Pelham, 1739–1776* (Boston: Massachusetts Historical Society, 1914), 246. Gerard de Lairesses, *The Art of Painting in All Its Branches,* trans. J. F. Fritsch (London, 1738), 31; quoted in James Northcote, *The Life of Sir Joshua Reynolds,* 2 vols. (London, 1819), 1:55. Steward quoted in Kornhauser, "Catalog," 237: "I saw that portrait painted at Hampton, Conn., when I was sitting for college with Parson Ludovicus Weld who sat for the lower half of the picture."

99. *Literary Diary of Ezra Stiles,* 131–32.

100. Ibid., 131–32.

101. On Copley's attention to individualizing detail, see Staiti, "Character and Class," 54–56; compare with Joshua Reynolds, *Discourses on Art,* ed. Robert R. Wark (New Haven: Yale University Press, 1975), 72 (Discourse IV); if a painter "is desirous to raise and improve his subject," he should exclude "all the minute breaks and peculiarities in the face." On the restoration of the body to perfection in resurrection, see chapter 2.

102. Samuel Mather, *A Testimony from the Scripture against Idolatry and Superstition* (Cambridge, Mass., 1672; 1725 ed.), quoted in Dickran Tashjian and Ann Tashjian, *Memorials for Children of Change: The Art of New England Stonecarving* (Middletown, Conn.: Wesleyan University Press, 1974), 8–9. Anburey, *Travels through the Interior Parts of America,* 2:68. See also Harriette Merrifield Forbes, "Early Portrait Stones in New England," *OTNE* 19, 4 (April 1929): 159–61. On the inclusion of pragmatic qualities as a way to reference the similarity of Sherman to the "binding durability of . . . old-Roman virtues of *gravitas, dignitas, fides,* which were the pride of the conservative aristocracy," see Sheldon Nodelman, "How to Read a Roman Head," *Art in America* 63, no. 1 (January–February 1995): 28.

103. On Elijah Boardman and speculation, see Kornhauser, "Catalog," 154–56. For Dwight's key passage condemning speculation, written about 1800, looking back on the impact of the so-called Funding Scheme to pay for the Revolution, see Dwight, *Travels,* 1:159. For a detailed look at one town's lotteries of Pennsylvania lands, see Charles Grant, *Democracy in the Connecticut Frontier Town of Kent* (New York: Columbia University Press, 1961), 18–22.

104. Dwight, *Travels,* 1:158, 159; Barber, *Historical Collections of Connecticut,* 111.

105. Dwight, *Travels,* 1:158.

106. George Kubler, "Style and the Representation of Historical Time" (1967), in *Studies in Ancient American and European Art: The Collected Essays of George Kubler,* ed. Thomas F. Reese (New Haven: Yale University Press, 1985), 386; William Dunlap, *A History of the Rise and Progress of the Arts of Design in the United States,* 3 vols. (New York, 1834; reprint, Boston: C. E. Goodspeed, 1918), 2:151. Pamela Sedgwick, writing to her husband, says of Steward that he thought "the children's [portraits] taken together with mine would make an odd appearance," suggesting, perhaps, the need to capture the individual soul in a New England "likeness." After the completion of her portrait, Sedgwick opined that although her likeness is "said to be a very good one, I think its not, but handsomer than it should be." Sedgwick to Sedgwick, December 1794 or January 1795, in Sedgwick Papers, Massachusetts Historical Society, Boston.

107. William Hubbard, *The Happiness of a People in the Wisdom of their Rulers Directing and the Obedience of their Brethren Attending Unto What Israel Ought* (Boston, 1676), 9–10.

108. Bhabha, "DissemiNation," 295; Pocock, "Modes of Political and Historical Time in Eighteenth-Century England," 89.

1. For examples of declensionist histories that stress the challenge that eighteenth-century commerce and "covetousness" presented to seventeenth-century asceticism, see Richard L. Bushman, *From Puritan to Yankee: Character and the Social Order in Connecticut, 1690–1765* (New York: W. W. Norton, 1970), esp. 135–46, 267–90, and John E. Crowley, *This Sheba, Self: The Conceptualization of Economic Life in Eighteenth-Century America* (Baltimore: Johns Hopkins University Press, 1974). For Bernard Bailyn, *The New England Merchants in the Seventeenth Century* (Cambridge: Harvard University Press, 1979), the conflict between Puritan piety and commercial pursuits was already under way in the 1660s. Important exceptions to the linear pattern of course exist that have sparked my interest here in the dialectical interrelationship of metaphysics and markets; see Joyce Oldham Appleby, *Economic Thought and Ideology in Seventeenth-Century England* (Princeton: Princeton University Press, 1978); Stephen Innes, *Labor in a New Land: Economy and Society in Seventeenth-Century Springfield* (Princeton: Princeton University Press, 1974); and David D. Hall, "Religion and Society: Problems and Reconsiderations," in *Colonial British America: Essays in the New History of the Early Modern Era*, ed. Jack P. Greene and J. R. Pole (Baltimore: Johns Hopkins University Press, 1984), 334–38. Another way of conceiving the persistence of religion in emergent capitalism is suggested by the "shadow" argument; see Herbert Leventhal, *In the Shadow of the Enlightenment: Occultism and Renaissance Science in Eighteenth-Century America* (New York: New York University Press, 1976).

2. Quoted in Bailyn, *New England Merchants in the Seventeenth Century*, 110.

3. For a critique of the "declension" model of community study, see Christine Leigh Heyrman, *Commerce and Culture: The Maritime Communities of Colonial Massachusetts, 1690–1750* (New York: W. W Norton, 1984), 15–18, 19, 52–95, 366–405.

4. Otto von Simpson, *The Gothic Cathedral: Origins of Gothic Architecture and the Medieval Concept of Order* (Princeton: Princeton University Press, 1982), 78–79.

5. Ibid., 164–67.

6. Robert Tittler, *Architecture and Power: The Town Hall and English Urban Community, c. 1500–1640* (New York: Oxford University Press, 1991), 26–30, 13–35, plate 2; on Thaxted town hall/market house, see M. Arman and James Boutwood, "Thaxted Guildhall, the Story of a Building in Use for Almost Six Centuries," Essex County Council Research Report no. TL611310, n.d., Essex County Record Office, Chelmsford, England. See also Frederick W. Emmison, "A Survey of Chelmsford, 1591," *Transactions of the Essex Archaeological Society*, n.s., 23 (1942–45): 133–40.

7. Von Simpson, *Gothic Cathedral*, 165 (emphasis added).

8. Heyrman, *Commerce and Culture*, 19.

9. Arjun Appadurai, "Introduction: Commodities and the Politics of Value," in *The Social Life of Things: Commodities in Cultural Perspective*, ed. Arjun Appadurai (New York: Cambridge University Press, 1986), 16–17, 22–23 (emphasis added).

10. Quoted in Perry Miller, *The New England Mind: The Seventeenth Century* (Boston: Beacon Press, 1961), 213.

11. Richard Baxter, *The Saints Everlasting Rest: or, a Treatise of the Blessed State of the Saints in their Enjoyment of God in Glory* (London, 1650), pt. 4, 242; Taylor, *Poems*, 6, 16.

12. Taylor, *Poems*, 36, 234, 250.

13. Sewall, *Diary*, 1:12, 367, 413. On another occasion "Cousin Quinsey" was dining with the Sewall family in their new house, and he "was much pleas'd with our painted shutters; in pleasancy [he] said he thought he had been got into Paradise." George Herbert held the same belief: "I looked on thy Furniture so fine, / And made it fine to me; / Thy glorious houshold-stuffe did me entwine, / And 'tice me unto thee." *The Complete Works of George Herbert*, ed. Alexander B. Grosart, 3 vols. (New York: AMS Press, 1981), 1:51–52.

14. William Perkins, "A Faithful and Plain Exposition upon Zephaniah 2.1–2," in *The Work of William Perkins*, ed. Ian Breward (Abingdon, England: Sutton Courtenay Press, 1970), 300.

15. John Cotton, "Purchasing Christ," in *The Puritans,* ed. Perry Miller and Thomas H. Johnson, 2 vols. (New York: Harper and Row, 1963), 1:328, 329.

16. Christine Leigh Heyrman, "The Fashion among More Superior People: Charity and Social Change in Provincial New England, 1700–1740," *AQ* 34, no. 2 (Summer 1982): 109.

17. Quoted in ibid., 112, 113.

18. Taylor, *Poems,* 259; Samuel Willard, *A Compleat Body of Divinity* (Boston, 1726), 233.

19. Karl Marx, *Capital: A Critique of Political Economy,* trans. Ben Fowkes, 3 vols. (New York: Vintage, 1976), 1:163–64, 167.

20. *ECQCR,* 32:130–33.

21. Elaine Scarry, *The Body in Pain: The Making and Unmaking of the World* (New York: Oxford University Press, 1985), 243–67.

22. Don De Lillo, *White Noise* (New York: Viking, 1985), 37.

23. Ibid., 37–38.

24. Thomas L. Dumm, *United States* (Ithaca, N.Y.: Cornell University Press, 1994), 144, 146, 147. Marx, *Capital,* 1:169.

25. William Goodwin to John Winthrop Jr., January 10, 1653, in MHS *Coll.,* 4th ser., 7 (1965): 49.

26. Edward Howes to John Winthrop Jr., April 14, 1639, in MHS *Coll.,* 4th ser., 6 (1863): 505–6. On protoindustrialization, see Franklin F. Mendels, "Proto-industrialization: The First Phase of the Industrialization Process," *Journal of Economic History* 32, no. 1 (March 1972): 241–61, and Peter Kriedte, "The Origins, the Agrarian Context, and the Conditions in the World Market," and Hans Medick, "The Proto-Industrial Family Economy," both in Peter Kriedte, Hans Medick, and Jürgen Schlumbohm, *Industrialization before Industrialization: Rural Industry and Genesis of Capitalism,* trans. Beate Schempp (New York: Cambridge University Press, 1981), 23–37, 38–73. For critical comments on how these two works should be situated in the rural economy of late-eighteenth- and early-nineteenth-century Massachusetts, see Christopher Clark, *The Roots of Western Capitalism: Massachusetts, 1780–1860* (Ithaca, N.Y.: Cornell University Press, 1990), 179–89.

27. Rosemary Freeman, *English Emblem Books* (New York: Octagon Books, 1970), 20; Ralph Waldo Emerson, "The Poet," in *The Collected Works of Ralph Waldo Emerson,* vol. 3, *Essays: Second Series,* ed. Joseph Slater, Albert R. Ferguson, and Jean Ferguson Carr (Cambridge: Harvard University Press, Belknap Press, 1983), 12. The continuing impact of the seventeenth-century house-body metaphor on the New England transcendentalists emerges further in the same essay, when Emerson said the task of the poet was to "put eyes, and a tongue, into every dumb and inanimate object" (12).

Earl, Ralph, 11, 298, 299, 301, 302, 303, 305, 306, 309, 310, 313, 318, 321, 322, 324, 328, 329, 332, 337, 342, 347, 348, 352, 354, 356, 359, 364, 365, 366, 368, 369, 371, 372, 376

Eaton, Theophilus, 82, 83, 87, 90; house of, in New Haven, 22, 85, 86

Economy, 26, 33, 45, 46, 57, 98, 108, 119, 122, 160, 162. *See also* Capitalism; Markets; Trades

Eden, Peter, 55, 66, 67

Eden, Richard, 172

Effigies, 207, 250–51, 252–54, 258–59, 261, 263, 283–85, 292, 294; soul, 11, 371, 395. *See also* Executions; Funerals; Magic

Elias, Norbert, 155

Eliot, Jared, 16, 17, 18, 19, 25, 26, 40, 86, 104, 107, 108, 112, 203, 273, 314

Eliot, John, 37, 147, 158, 163, 203

Eliot, Joseph, 40, 86

Ellsworth, Oliver and Abigail, 302, 303, 305, 309–10, 317, 371, 349–50

Emblems, 303, 304, 385

Emerson, Ralph Waldo, 284, 397

Enclosure, 34, 41, 46, 88, 93, 336–37

Endicott, John, 20, 82

Endicott, Zerubbabel, 190–91

England, 3, 10, 12, 24, 40, 44, 45, 59, 66, 84, 101, 117, 127, 130, 156, 159, 161, 179, 192, 201, 203, 214, 218, 228, 232, 249, 269, 343; Bedfordshire, Berkshire, and Buckinghamshire, 45; Cornwall and Coventry, 54; Derbyshire, 45, 185; Dorset, 44, 55, 66, 94; East Anglia, 70, 192; Hertfordshire, 45, 55, 63, 67, 71; Lancashire, 45, 101; Leicestershire, 55; Lincolnshire, 55, 72, 192, 387; Newcastle, 54; Nottinghamshire, 55; Rutland, 45; Shropshire, 176; Southampton, 63; West Country, 18, 45, 59, 60, 66, 74, 95, 200, 346; Westmoreland, 43; Wiltshire, 45, 200; Yorkshire, 45, 57, 112, 176. *See also* Cambridgeshire, West; Devon; Essex; Highland zone; Huntingdonshire; Kent; London; Lowland zone; Norfolk; Northamptonshire; Northumberland; Oxfordshire; Somerset; Suffolk; Surrey; Sussex

Entries: cross-passage, 44, 47, 49, 51, 53, 59, 66, 70, 74, 92, 93; direct, 59, 73, 75; lobby, 49, 55, 75, 178, 270. *See also* Doors; Houses

Essex, 45, 54, 55, 63; Chelmsford, 63, 88, 243, 382; Little Braxted, 180; White Roding, 59

Estienne, Charles, 90, 91, 92, 98, 100, 107, 108, 118, 128, 129, 200

Everyday life, 161, 302, 345, 376

Exchange, 20, 201, 375, 385; "great," 125, 366, 384, 395, 396; Royal, 61. *See also* Marketplaces; Soul; Value

Executions, 150, 166, 258, 336, 437 (n. 77)

Facades, 59, 61, 269, 290, 294, 349; Georgian, 276, 293; of house-body, 133, 135, 137; as masks, 273, 281, 286

Fairs, 384–85, 386

Family, 16, 34, 47, 179, 180. *See also* Inheritance

Farmsteads, 10, 18, 21, 27, 88, 91, 93–95, 98, 103–4, 108, 273, 276, 277. *See also* Barns; Bull, Jireh; Desborough, Samuel

Farnum, John, 229

Fashion, 85, 304, 347

Feasts, 34, 146

Federalists, 11, 313, 316, 317, 318, 326, 344, 345, 348, 360, 377

Fenwick, George, 41

Fields: anthropomorphic markers, 174; common or open, 45, 71; in Guilford, 17

Fifth Monarchism, 203, 228

Fire, 188, 247–50, 261, 280. *See also* Apocalypse; Bonfires; Revelation

Fish, Joseph, 341

Fishermen, 197, 198, 203

Fitch, Thomas, 213, 236

Floyd, William, 359

Folk healers, 196

Folk justice, 285

Folklore, 2, 207, 302

Folktales, 149, 184

Foster, John (astrologer), 139, 140

Foster, John (merchant), 264, 270, 271

Foucault, Michel, 201

Fowler, David, 340

Fox, Cyril, 45, 57

France, 63, 93, 103, 116, 210

Freeman, Rosemary, 397

Freemasonry, 203, 317

Freud, Sigmund, 328

Funerals, mock, 207, 257, 261–62, 438 (n. 89). *See also* Effigies

Furniture, household, 206, 243, 263, 264; beds and bedding, 85, 207; boxes, 282; cabinets, 385–86, 387; chairs, 85, 303, 325; chests, 85, 202, 389; cupboards, 86; mirrors, 207, 263, 389; trunks, 282

Huizinga, Johann, 290
Hull, John, 172, 181
Human body. *See* Body, human
Hume, Ivor Nöel, 28
Huntingdonshire, England, 54; Desborough, 71; Elton, 67; Keyston, 23, 71, 72
Hutchinson, Anne, 169, 171–72, 228
Hutchinson, Edward, 83
Hutchinson, Richard, 65
Hutchinson, Samuel, 65
Hutchinson, Thomas, 207, 242, 246, 264, 265, 266, 280, 281, 285, 287, 288–89, 290, 291–92, 323. *See also* House attacks; Houses
Hutchinson, William, 65, 82
Hutton, Barbara, 46, 57
Hybridity, architectural, 7, 66, 67, 71, 72, 74, 75, 127. *See* Highland zone; Lowland zone

Ideology, 47, 267, 268, 299, 307
Imagination, 37, 120, 148, 156, 302
Implication, 3, 9, 10, 13, 19, 103, 144, 251, 305, 320, 348, 396. *See also* Places
Improvement, 17, 46, 103, 107, 158
Industries, 33, 200, 240. *See also* Occupations; Trades
Ingersoll, Jared, 254, 258, 261
Inheritance, 54, 76, 215
Inoculation, 196, 197, 198, 200
Ireland, 11, 27, 28, 29, 35, 43, 44, 214, 218, 300; Dublin, 30, 95; Kinsale, 34; Munster, 30; Tiperary, 63. *See also* Northern Ireland; Tenants; Trade companies; Ulster
Isham, Norman M., 21, 22, 26, 85, 108
Italy, 8; Naples, 244; Venice, 137

James I (king of England), 33, 34, 40, 134, 154
John of Salisbury, 150
Johnson, Augustus, 258, 259
Johnson, Joseph, 338, 340, 341, 342
Jones, Howard Mumford, 28
Jones, Inigo, 61, 63, 281
Jones, Sydney E., 45, 57
Jope, E. M., 98
Jordan, Winthrop, 155
Josselyn, John, 36, 149, 161, 162, 172
Journeymen, 224, 319, 320, 321

Kantorowicz, Ernst, 150
Keayne, Robert, 65, 405 (n. 20)
Kelley, Elizabeth, 116–18, 185, 198, 200–201

Kelly, J. Frederick, 29
Kent, 45, 49, 54, 55, 72; Canterbury, 65; Fosten Green, 94; North Cray, 59
King, Samuel, 366, 367
King Philip's War, 201, 220, 247–50, 348
Kornhauser, Stephen, 365
Knapp, Elizabeth, 186
Kubler, George, 376

Labor, 5, 12, 40, 79, 88, 90, 92, 173, 322; as commodity, 200, 223; consciousness, 207, 219, 230, 319, 322; disputes, 342; division of, 222; organized, 318; radical politics of, 319; value of, 200, 202, 389. *See also* Artisans; Journeymen; Piecework; Trades
Laborers, 47, 48, 49, 94, 215, 217, 231, 236, 283
Lambert, Edward R., 85
Land: as basis of citizenship, 156; common, 283; enclosure of, 34; reclamation of, 90; shortage, 17, 215; speculation and, 46; tenure, 34, 57; wealth and, 23
Landscape: agrarian, 17, 98; colonized, 149; early national, 333; English, 59, 66; ideal, 122; intimate, 65; of memory, 371; metaphysical, 37–39, 104; neo-Augustan country, 12; New World, 93; popular, 348; providential, 121; Rhode Island, 74; sacred, 145; secular, 262; of theater, 160; urban, 65
Language: of artisans' combinations, 281; borrowed, 387; of Canaan, 120; of captivity narratives, 290; of communion, 145; of embodiment, 150; of imperial critique, 242; Manx, 59; of market advocates, 225; of market and theater, 150; of marketplace, 385, 386; of mercantile theory, 198; Narraganset, 160, 161; of rational calculation, 388; of republican ideology, 299; of self-abasement, 341; of sublime, 337; of witchcraft, 288, 290. *See also* Discourse; Narratives
Layman, 366
Leete, William, 23, 24, 71, 81, 83
Leffingwell, Christopher, 323, 324
Levelers, 202
Leverenz, David, 176
Liebault, Jean [John], 90, 91, 92, 93, 98, 100, 107, 108, 128, 129
Likeness, 11, 298, 300, 301, 365, 376
Lillie, Theophilus, 253–54
Locke, John, 195
Loehr, Rodney C., 352

London, 23, 54, 59, 60, 63, 64, 65, 70, 82, 83, 86, 88, 90, 94, 117, 171, 173, 192, 195, 208, 210, 211, 216, 223, 236, 242, 244–45, 251, 266, 290, 298, 299. *See also* Migration

Loomis, Timothy, 326

Lovell, Margaretta M., 300

Lowland zone, 45, 46, 47, 48, 57, 59, 72, 74, 76, 127

Machin, Robert, 46, 57

Macintosh, Ebenezer, 208

Magic: book of, 188; of commodities, 104; image-, 186, 190; sympathetic, 258. *See also* Countermagic; Effigies; Poppets

Magistrates, 65, 84, 86, 190

Maine, 37, 215, 273; Arrowsic, 44; Kittery, 273; Richmond Island, 178; Scarborough, 207, 273

Malbone, Godfrey, 348

Malbone, Richard, 83, 84

Mandeville, Bernard, 166

Man of Signs, 198

Marblehead, Mass., 149, 196, 197, 198, 199, 203, 247, 269, 321

Marketplaces, 61, 214, 337, 352, 382, 386; destruction of, 225–26; language of, 385; metaphysics of, 301, 390; as theater of moral action, 308

Markets: in dead bodies, 201; food, 88; and hawkers, 225; labor, 208, 216, 218, 230; land, 93; London, 88; metaphysical implications of, 396; in New Haven, 307; open, 46, 295; public, 308; regulated, 225; subscriptions for, 226. *See also* Capitalism; Economy

Markham, Gervase, 88, 89, 90, 93, 98, 107, 222

Marx, Karl, 389, 393, 394, 395, 398

Mascall, Leonard, 90, 100, 107

Massachusetts, 6, 35, 49, 73, 75, 215, 247, 302, 304, 320, 322, 323, 325, 326, 337, 342, 345, 358, 387; Cambridge, 216, 262, 273; Charlestown, 65, 148, 216, 269, 320, 326; Dedham, 57, 75, 192; Deerfield, 75, 273, 320; Dorchester, 9, 82, 83, 216; Duxbury, 100, 108, 161, 207; Ipswich, 53, 100, 166, 181, 215; Lynn, 188, 216, 240, 321, 322; Malden, 181, 247, 321; Newbury, 174, 183, 195, 239; Roxbury, 110, 216, 245; Springfield, 110, 148, 247, 273. *See also* Boston; Marblehead; Plymouth; Salem

Massachusetts Bay Colony, 121, 159, 203; General Court of, 147

Massachusetts Bay Company, 82, 85; library of, 90

Material culture, 2; of American Indians, 36, 37, 134, 159, 161–62. *See also* Architecture; Furniture; Houses; Wigwams

Mather, Cotton, 8, 12, 120, 121, 123, 125, 135, 144, 145, 147, 162, 163, 175, 180, 182, 183, 190, 195, 196, 197, 198, 244, 245, 249, 250, 284, 338, 388

Mather, Increase, 121, 229, 247

Mather, Samuel, 371

Medicine, 83, 158, 195, 202

Meetinghouses, 37, 39, 120, 185; Andover, 249; Boston Baptist, 229; Boston Third Church (Old South), 9, 262; proximity of to monstrous births, 169; as targets of London mobs, 244–45; Westfield, 120. *See also* Churches

Melville, Henry, 284

Memory: cultural, 36, 292, 294, 328, 371

Mendilow, Adam, 345

Mercantilism, 224, 226, 266, 307, 380

Mercer, Eric, 48

Merchants: Boston, 35, 61, 144, 264, 269, 303; control of property by, 208; English, 31, 54, 61, 63, 82, 171, 195, 381; houses of, 236–38; New England, 59, 84, 85, 86, 108, 197, 198, 220, 221, 231, 236, 237, 260, 270, 273, 388; premises of, 10, 20, 66, 95; smuggling by, 263, 266, 281; Whig, 267, 268, 293

Metaphor, 3, 208; bodily, 126, 132, 150; compression of, 5, 10, 303, 380; corporate, 183; of English nation, 150; house-body, 121, 189; mechanical, 197–98, 293; performance of, 207

Midwives, 166

Migration, 59, 72, 83; of artisans, 210–18, 279, 319, 323; into Boston, 209; long-distance in England, 54. *See also* Population

Millennialism, 107, 119, 203, 294. *See also* Covenant: of grace; Spiritism

Miller, Perry, 202

Mimicry, colonial, 269

Ministers, 59, 86, 176, 183, 188, 308; "hireling," 203, 341; houses of, 182, 190, 270

Missionaries, 154, 340

Mobs, 197, 244, 245, 252, 267, 281, 285, 286, 287, 288, 289, 290, 292, 293, 294

Moffatt, Thomas, 258, 259

Money, 63, 148, 264, 388; generative power of, 372; hard, 223, 225, 238, 266; paper, 224, 347

Morse, Jedediah, 337, 338, 345

Morse, William, 184, 193, 195, 393

Mortimer, John, 273, 274

Morton, Charles, 202, 396

Taxes, 215, 244, 253, 268, 362

Taylor, Edward, 120, 121, 124, 126, 135, 139, 145, 174, 178, 202, 250, 284, 385–86, 389, 397

Temporality, 345–47; of custom and ancestry, 358–60; of emblematic self, 364; overlapping, 385; transcendent, 371. *See also* Time

Tenants, 30, 33, 40, 47, 71, 92, 127. *See also* Labor

Theater, 65, 66, 283; of affliction and judgment, 161, 190; anatomy, 117, 201, 202; of colonial masculinity, 288; of dominance, 86; of hospitality, 127; memory, 8; street, 261; of virtue, 348

Time: allegorical, 364; customary, 359–60; lineal concept of, 8; messianic, 345; split representations of, 301

Todorov, Tzvetan, 156

Toleration Act (Conn., 1784), 317, 368

Tools, 184, 200, 321

Toothaker, Roger, 193

Topography, 333, 334, 338

Tourist attraction: Hutchinson house as, 265

Tourist route, Federalist, 360

Town plans: of American Indians and native Irish, 37; concentricity in, 328, 329, 334, 335, 342, 343, 344; grids in, 37, 262, 328, 329, 343; nucleated villages, 45, 333, 334. *See also* Landscape

Trade companies, 219–20; of London, 28, 30, 33, 95

Trade guilds, 382

Trades: building/woodworking, 210, 214, 218, 220, 221; butchering, 238, 240; carpentry, 326; cloth, 210, 217, 218, 221, 242; competition among, 208, 218; coopering, 324; diversification in, 219, 230–31; food and drink, 221; leather, 210, 216, 217, 218, 221; maritime, 208; metal, 210, 217, 218, 221, 242; overcrowding of, 211, 229; retail, 218, 221; service, 218, 221; shipbuilding, 238; wheelwrighting, 324. *See also* Artisans; Labor; Occupations

Tradition: Atlantic republican, 65; folk dramatic, 258, 258; utopian, 107

Transubstantiation, 148. *See also* Communion

Transvestism, 150, 252

Treaty of Utrecht, 208

Tudor, John, 206, 207, 250

Turkey, 196, 290

Turner, William, 179, 228, 229

Turrell, Jane Colman, 146

Ulster, 28, 30, 33, 34, 37, 61, 97, 103. *See also* Bawns

Underwood, Robert, 126, 127, 129–32, 134–35, 137, 139, 154, 175, 250, 284

Unemployment, 210

Value: alienated, 394; iconic, 397; inflated land, 215; of labor, 200, 202, 389; of soul, 395; surplus, 103

Vanderlyn, John, 365

Vermont, 302; Bennington, 332, 338

Vesalius, Andreas, 118, 195, 198, 200

Violence, 12, 40, 207, 243, 288, 289, 293, 294. *See also* House attacks

Virginia, 27, 29, 30, 61, 178, 214, 273; American Indian from, 162

Virtue, 10, 93, 154, 214, 269, 285, 299, 302, 306, 307, 309, 310, 316, 326, 342, 347, 352, 359, 376

Wadsworth, Jeremiah, 317, 347

Wage labor, 321, 396

Wales, 55, 101, 283

Walker, Benjamin, 262, 438 (n. 89)

Walpole, Robert, 263

Walsh, James P., 319

Walton, George, 184

Walton, James, 112

Wansey, Henry, 361, 448 (n. 54)

Ward, Nathaniel, 149

Water, indoor running, 70, 412 (n. 76)

Waterhouse, 18, 70

Waters, John J., 76, 81, 83

Wealth, 2, 11, 23, 83, 282, 307

Webb, John, 281

Webster, John, 270

West, Benjamin, 298, 371

West, Robert, 185

West Indies, British, 207, 211, 273

Wheelock, Eleazar, 338, 339, 366

Wheelwright, John, 171

Whitefield, George, 268

Whitfield, Henry, 22, 23, 24, 28, 48, 61, 65, 79, 80, 81, 86. *See also* Houses; Isham, Norman M.; Kelly, J. Frederick

Whitfield, Nathaniel, 65

Wickham, Benjamin, 287

Widows, 221, 222, 284. *See also* Women

Wigglesworth, Edward, 224

Wigglesworth, Michael, 121, 181